Cultural Anthropology

A Global Perspective

SIXTH EDITION

Raymond Scupin

Lindenwood University

PEARSON

Prentice
Hall

Upper Saddle River, New Jersey 07458

Library of Congress Cataloging-in-Publication Data

Scupin, Raymond.
    Cultural anthropology : a global perspective / Raymond Scupin.—6th ed.
      p. cm.
    Includes bibliographical references and index.
    ISBN 0-13-192884-8 (pbk.)
    1. Ethnology. I. Title.

GN316.S39 2005
306—dc22

                                            2004060213

Editorial Director: Leah Jewell
Publisher: Nancy Roberts
Editorial Assistant: Lee Peterson
Media Project Manager: Kate Ramunda
Senior Marketing Manager: Marissa Feliberty
Full-Service Liaison: Fran Russello
Permissions Coordinator: Kathleen Karcher
Manufacturing Buyer: Benjamin Smith
Cover Design: Michelle Wiggins
Cover Illustration/Photo: Gavriel Jecan/Corbis
Photo Researcher: Emily Tietz
Image Permission Coordinator: Carolyn Gauntt
Composition/Full-Service Project Management: GGS Book Services,
Atlantic Highlands
Printer/Binder: Courier Companies, Inc.
Cover Printer: Phoenix Color Corp.

Credits and acknowledgments borrowed from other sources and reproduced,
with permission, in this textbook appear on appropriate page within text
(or on page 524).

Pearson Education LTD., London
Pearson Education Singapore, Pte. Ltd
Pearson Education, Canada, Ltd
Pearson Education–Japan
Pearson Education Australia PTY,
   Limited
Pearson Education North Asia Ltd
Pearson Educación de Mexico, S.A. de C.V.
Pearson Education Malaysia, Pte. Ltd
Pearson Education, Upper Saddle River,
   New Jersey

10 9 8 7 6 5 4 3 2 1

ISBN 0-13-192884-8

Contents

vi Contents

viii   Contents

x Contents

Boxes

Anthropologists at Work

Critical Perspectives

Applying Anthropology

Preface

EDUCATIONAL GOALS AND ORIENTATION OF THIS TEXT

We all recognize that the world is getting smaller. Instantaneous global communications, trade among far-flung nations, geopolitical events affecting countries and hemispheres, and the ease of international travel are bringing people and cultures into more intimate contact with one another than ever before, forcing this generation of students to become more knowledgeable about societies other than their own. With that in mind, this textbook is grounded in the belief that an enhanced global awareness is essential for people preparing to take their place in the fast-paced, increasingly interconnected world of the twenty-first century. Anthropology is ideally suited to introduce students to a global perspective. Each of the subfields of anthropology has a broad focus on humanity; this helps liberate students from a narrow, parochial view and enables them to see and understand the full sweep of the human condition.

The anthropological perspective, which stresses critical-thinking processes, the evaluation of competing hypotheses, and the skills to generalize from specific data and assumptions, contributes significantly to a well-rounded education. This text engages readers in the varied intellectual activities underlying the anthropological approach by delving into both classic and recent research in the fields that make up anthropology.

This text reflects a strong commitment to anthropology's traditional holistic and integrative approach. It spells out how the four basic subfields of anthropology—physical anthropology, archaeology, linguistics, and ethnology—together yield a comprehensive understanding of humanity. Because the subfields tend to overlap, insights from all of them are woven together to reveal the holistic fabric of a particular society or the threads uniting all of humanity.

An interdisciplinary outlook resonates throughout this book. All contemporary anthropologists draw on the findings of biologists, paleontologists, geologists, economists, historians, psychologists, sociologists, political scientists, religious studies specialists, philosophers, and researchers in other fields whose work sheds light on anthropological inquiry. In probing various anthropological topics, this text often refers to research conducted in these other fields. In addition to enlarging the scope and reach of the text, exploring interactions between anthropology and other fields sparks the critical imagination that brings the learning process to life.

The comparative approach, another traditional cornerstone of the anthropological perspective, is spotlighted in this text as well. When anthropologists assess fossil evidence, artifacts, languages, or cultural beliefs and values, they weigh comparative evidence while acknowledging the unique elements of each society and culture. This text casts an inquiring eye on materials from numerous geographical regions and historical eras to enrich student understanding.

A diachronic approach also characterizes this book. In evaluating human evolution, prehistoric events, language divergence, or developments in social structure, anthropologists must rely on models that reflect changes through time, so this diachronic orientation suffuses the text.

THREE UNIFYING THEMES OF THIS TEXT

In the last edition of this textbook, we emphasized three unifying themes that structured the material in the text. We wanted to introduce students to the *diversity of human societies* and cultural patterns the world over and to the *similarities that make all humans fundamentally alike*. To achieve these two parallel goals, we paid as much attention to universal human characteristics as we did to particular cultural characteristics of local regions. We emphasized the growing interconnectedness of humans throughout the world and the positive and negative consequences of this reality. Contacts and interactions among people in different societies have occurred throughout history. However, modern advances in communication and transportation have accelerated the process of globalization in recent decades. One goal of this text is to call on anthropological studies of various societies to discover how people are responding to the process of globalization. We continue this approach with this sixth edition of this textbook.

The third theme we emphasize more prominently in this edition focuses on the fundamental bridge between the sciences and humanities within anthropology. We call this the *synthetic-complementary approach*, which views the scientific method and the methods in the humanities as complementary and suggests that one is incomplete without the other. This theme had been mentioned in previous editions of this textbook, but we make it much more of a centerpiece in this sixth edition.

In another, earlier anthropology textbook published by Prentice Hall (1964), the late Eric Wolf emphasized that anthropology has always had one foot in the sciences and one foot in the humanities. Wolf said, "Anthropology is both the most scientific of the humanities and the most humanistic of the sciences" (1964, 88). Eric was kind enough to give us suggestions for this globally focused textbook in anthropology. We would like to carry on the tradition that Eric Wolf accentuated in his book. One of the important goals in the revision of this textbook is to highlight the fundamental importance of the synthetic-complementary approach to science and the humanities in anthropology.

Some anthropologists have concluded that the scientific approach is not suitable for assessing and interpreting human behavior and culture, whereas others believe that the humanistic approach is not appropriate for developing general cross-cultural and causal explanations about human behavior and culture. This has led to textbooks that focus either on one or the other approach. In this textbook, we highlight how the interpretive-humanistic perspective is complementary to the scientific method, which seeks general cross-cultural and causal explanations for human behavior and culture. This third important theme will dovetail with the two other themes, demonstrating how human behavior is both culturally unique and particular to a specific culture, and how it is also universal. The interpretive-humanistic perspective provides insight into the specifics of human behavior within different cultures, whereas the scientific approach offers a method to test causal explanations that allow for insight into universal aspects of human behavior.

The arrangement and treatment of topics in this text differ from that of other textbooks in anthropology. In Part 1, we introduce the basic concepts of the four fields of anthropology and the understanding of culture, language, and globalization that anthropologists study. Chapter 1 introduces the field of anthropology and explains how it relates to both the sciences and humanities. This lead-in chapter also examines how anthropologists use the scientific method as well as the humanistic-hermeneutic-interpretive approach to understand culture and society. Chapter 2 examines the field of human evolution and the studies of paleoanthropologists, archaeologists, and other scientists who study evolutionary processes, fossil and artifactual evidence, and heredity and genetics to determine what these fields contribute to our understanding of humanity.

Chapters 3–7 reinforce one another. Chapter 3 examines the concept of culture as it is understood in anthropology. Beginning with the notions of material and nonmaterial culture, this chapter goes on to cite examples of cultural diversity found throughout the world. However, we emphasize how anthropologists have refined their understanding of the term "culture" today so as not to think in stereotypical or monolithic images of other societies. In this chapter we also stress cultural universals and similarities that unify all of humanity. We also integrate the discussion of the concept of culture with the process of enculturation in order to bridge Chapters 3 on culture with Chapter 4 on the enculturation process. To refine our discussion of culture and enculturation, we develop some new materials on recent research in cognitive anthropology.

In Chapter 4, we emphasize how anthropologists bridge the gap between biology and culture as they gain a greater understanding of enculturation and personality development in unfamiliar societies. To explore this topic, we turn to the classic studies conducted by Ruth Benedict and Margaret Mead, as well as the most recent research in psychoanalytic anthropology, childhood training in societies around the world, incest, sexuality, cognition, emotions, and the cross-cultural research on personality disorders. In addition, we also discuss the fields of cognitive anthropology and the recent field of evolutionary psychology. Many psychological anthropologists have been attempting to incorporate the findings from this new field into their hypotheses.

Chapter 5, on language, dovetails with the previous chapter in several key ways. We have refined our discussion of the differences between ape communication and human language. New conclusions have been reached recently in laboratory research and primatological fieldwork comparing ape communication with human languages. Following up on these studies, we have revised our section on Chomsky's transformational model and other related anthropological findings that suggest interactive relationships between biology and culture. We have expanded our discussion of the Sapir–Whorf hypothesis. Other research findings in linguistic anthropology, including historical linguistics, complement material in the emerging field of sociolinguistics and introduce students to the most recent developments in the field.

In order to illustrate the global focus of this textbook, we have developed a new chapter on globalization and culture, Chapter 6, that sets the stage for contemporary undergraduate students in assessing this important and significant factor in its impact on their own lives and other people throughout the world. We discuss how anthropologists are refining their concepts of globalization and how it has an impact on the societies presently. After providing the undergraduate with some basic hands-on understandings of how globalization is influencing popular culture, sports, or the outsourcing of jobs to other countries that has an influence on their lives, we move on to show how anthropologists are studying this process of globalization all over the world. We provide a critique of the terminology of First, Second, and Third Worlds as being too simplistic to apply to what anthropological data demonstrate. This Cold War terminology is outdated from today's standpoint, especially based on ethnographic data regarding the complex levels of development and diversity found in the so-called Third World— and the formerly industrial socialist societies of the Second World that have mostly dissipated.

In this globalization chapter, we delve into the theoretical paradigms that anthropologists have modified to understand the interrelationships among various societies of the world. Modernization, dependency, and world-systems theories (and criticisms of them) are introduced to develop the global perspective. We emphasize that societies cannot be understood as independent, isolated units. This global perspective informs all the subsequent chapters, reinforcing a sense of global awareness among students.

In this chapter, we indicate how anthropologists are assessing both the negative and positive aspects of globalization in different communities throughout the world. We try to provide a balanced assessment of some aspects of globalization that may result in positive developments representing improvements in people's lives in various areas of the world. However, we emphasize that this process of globalization can result in some very negative consequences and problems that must be assessed and evaluated for a comprehensive understanding and possible solutions for humanity today.

Chapter 7 continues the global focus as we assess the important topic of race and ethnicity and how contemporary trends influence these areas. This chapter reviews the extensive research that anthropologists have been doing since the beginning of the twentieth century. We cover the material related to the development of racism in Western society, with an anthropological critique of racism based on scientific evidence. We also provide perspectives on ethnicity that anthropologists have developed for understanding race and ethnic relations. Examples of this research are provided by a review of race and ethnic relations in U.S. society from an anthropological perspective. We believe that the placement of this chapter within the globalization section reinforces how the process of globalization has had broad consequences for race and ethnicity issues worldwide.

THE GLOBAL FOCUS REALIZED

Part 2 of this text presents a much different organizational scheme compared with that of other texts. Instead of structuring the book according to specific topics in anthropology such as subsistence, economy, family, kinship, political organization, and religion, this text organizes the material based on levels of societal organization and regional topics.

As in previous editions of this textbook, in this sixth edition of *Cultural Anthropology: A Global Perspective*, Chapter 8 walks students through the methods, research strategies, and ethical dilemmas that confront cultural anthropologists. Then readers learn about the major variables cultural anthropologists analyze to gain insight into different types of societies: environment and subsistence, demography, technology, economy, social structure, family, kinship, gender, age, political systems, law, and religion. With this background, students are ready to understand subsequent chapters.

Chapter 8 also presents the multidimensional approach, which most contemporary anthropologists use to analyze the elements of society and culture.

Rather than grounding an understanding of society and culture in a single factor, this orientation taps into both material and nonmaterial aspects of culture to view the full spectrum of society holistically and to produce a balanced treatment of key issues that are aspects of anthropological analysis. Again, we integrate the scientific and humanistic approaches in this chapter.

Unlike the previous edition of this textbook, in Part 3 of this sixth edition we integrate the globalization focus into the rest of the chapters in the textbook. In Chapters 9, 10, and 11, the textbook reports and critically evaluates the major anthropological findings related to what have been bands, tribes, and chiefdoms. Because these classifications have been open to interpretation among anthropologists, these labels and questionable categories are used with extreme caution. Even though many anthropologists either shun these terms or seriously question their utility in describing complex, changing societies, we believe that these classifications give students who are first exposed to the discipline a good grasp of the fundamentals of prestate societies. However, what makes this edition different is that we conclude each of these chapters with a discussion of how globalization is influencing all these societies as they are incorporated into the world economy and nation states. The chapter considers the problems generated by contact between the industrial states and prestate aboriginal societies. It goes on to address a number of salient questions raised by these contacts: How are these indigenous societies becoming absorbed into global economic and political networks? How are these indigenous peoples responding to this situation? And what are anthropologists doing to enhance the coping strategies of these indigenous peoples?

Chapters 12 and 13 move on to agricultural and industrial state societies, whose key characteristics emerge in the interconnections among variables such as political economy and social stratification. Chapter 12 features the basic elements of agricultural societies as revealed by archaeologists, historians, and anthropologists. Chapter 13 opens with a historical and anthropological perspective on the Industrial Revolution and the process of modernization, segueing into comparative research conducted in England, Western Europe, the United States, the former Soviet Union, and Japan to illustrate the dynamics of industrial states. In doing so, we hope to correct the racist and ethnocentric beliefs of many undergraduates regarding the evolution of industrial and postindustrial societies.

Sound pedagogical logic underlies this approach. Instead of presenting important anthropological research on demography, gender, economy, kinship, ethnicity, political systems, and religion as single chapters (usually corresponding to single lectures), this organizational scheme spotlights how these variables permeate the entire spectrum of human experience in different types of societies. Whereas the single-chapter format tends to marginalize these topics, this text's approach—based on different levels of societal organization—allows students to focus on the interconnections between the political economy and gender, age, family, kinship, religion, demography, technology, environment, and how these factors are influenced by globalization. As a result, students gain a holistic and global understanding of human societies.

Organizing material according to levels of societal organization in no way implies or endorses a simplistic, unilineal view of sociocultural evolution. In fact, the ladderlike evolutionary perspective on society comes in for criticism throughout the text. While recognizing the inherent weaknesses of using such classifications as "tribes" and "chiefdoms"—including the parallel tendencies to lump diverse societies into narrow categories and create artificial boundaries among societies—we believe that these groupings nonetheless serve the valuable purpose of introducing beginning students to the sweeping concepts that make anthropology distinctive. Generalizations about tribes and chiefdoms help students unfamiliar with anthropology's underpinnings to absorb basic concepts and data; the complexities and theoretical controversies within the discipline can always be addressed in more specialized advanced courses.

Part 3, "Globalization," begins with Chapters 14 and 15, in which we continue the globalization focus and evaluate the current research findings by cultural anthropologists in Latin America, the Caribbean, Africa, the Middle East, and Asia. These two chapters emphasize the globalization process in these regions and reveal what anthropologists are finding in their local studies related to the overall trend of globalization. We emphasize how all these cultural regions are becoming more interconnected within the global political economy. In addition to probing classic ethnographic research, contemporary issues in each region are placed within a broad historical context, offering readers finely honed diachronic insights into social and political developments in each of these different regions.

Chapter 16 highlights contemporary global trends that are changing the entire world. Anthropological research is brought to bear on the environmental, demographic, economic, political, ethnic, and religious trends that are shaking the foundations of many societies. Among the topics addressed in this context are global warming, the Green Revolution, the increasing consumption of nonrenewable energy by industrial societies, the impact of multinational corporations, the demise of socialist regimes, and the rise of new ethnic and religious movements.

Chapter 17 sheds light on the fifth subfield of anthropology: applied anthropology. Here we consider key issues in applied anthropology, including medical anthropology, cultural resource management, and recent research aimed at solving practical problems in societies the world over. However, the most important goal of this chapter is to highlight how anthropologists are conducting research on global problems and how they may be able to aid in solving some of those problems. We conclude the textbook with a discussion of the human rights issues on which anthropologists focus in their research to help provide a better means of attaining improvements in human rights issues throughout the world.

FEATURES OF THIS TEXT

BOXES

In *Critical Perspectives* boxes, designed to stimulate independent reasoning and judgment, students take the role of anthropologist by engaging in the critical analysis of specific problems and issues that arise in anthropological research. A successful holdover from the first edition, these Critical Perspectives boxes encourage students to use rigorous standards of evidence when evaluating assumptions and hypotheses regarding scientific and philosophical issues that have no easy answers. We have added several new Critical Perspective boxes for this sixth edition. By probing beneath the surface of various assumptions and hypotheses in these exercises, students stand to discover the excitement and challenge of anthropological investigation.

Anthropologists at Work boxes, profiling prominent anthropologists, humanize many of the issues covered in the chapters. These boxes—another carryover from the first edition—go behind the scenes to trace the personal and professional development of some of today's leading anthropologists.

Finally, *Applying Anthropology* boxes—new to previous editions—show students how research in anthropology can help solve practical problems confronting contemporary societies. Students often ask: What relevance does anthropology have to the problems we face in our generation? These Applying Anthropology boxes answer the relevance question head on. For example, one box notes that anthropologists unearth research data to help ease tensions in multicultural relations in U.S. society. Another box describes how linguistic anthropologists work with indigenous peoples to preserve their languages as the indigenous peoples adjust to the modern world. The concluding chapter of the text ties together many of these Applying Anthropology boxes by placing in perspective the full panoply of issues addressed in applied anthropology.

PEDAGOGICAL AIDS

For sound pedagogical reasons, we have retained some features in this sixth edition of *Anthropology: A Global Perspective*. Each chapter opens with a Chapter Outline and Chapter Questions that will help guide students to the most important issues addressed in the chapter. And each chapter ends with Questions to Think About, which address issues covered in the chapter that students can use to help comprehend the material in the chapter. In addition, each chapter ends with a Summary and a list of Key Terms that will help students focus on important concepts introduced in the chapter. Finally, Internet Exercises help students use the World Wide Web to explore various topics and issues addressed in the chapters.

SUPPLEMENTS

This carefully prepared supplements package is intended to give the instructor the resources needed to teach the course and the student the tools needed to successfully complete the course.

FOR THE INSTRUCTOR

Instructor's Resource and Testing Manual This essential instructor's tool includes chapter overviews, chapter objectives, lecture and discussion topics, classroom activities, research and writing topics, print and nonprint resources, and more than 1,600 questions in multiple-choice, true/false, and essay formats. All test questions are page-referenced to the text.

TestGEN This computerized software allows instructors to create their own personalized exams, to edit any or all test questions, and to add new questions. Other special features of this program, which is available for Windows and Macintosh, include random generation of an item set, creation of alternate versions of the same test, scrambling question sequence, and test preview before printing.

Videos Prentice Hall is pleased to offer two video series: *The Changing American Indian in a Changing America: Videocases of American Indian Peoples*, and *Rites of Passage: Videocases of Traditional African Peoples*. In addition, a selection of high quality, award-winning videos from the Filmmakers Library collection is available upon adoption. Please see your Prentice Hall sales representative for more information.

Anthropology Transparencies, Series IV Taken from graphs, diagrams, and tables in this text and other sources, more than 50 full-color transparencies offer an effective means of amplifying lecture topics.

Instructor Resource CD-ROM Pulling together all of the print and media assets available to instructors, this interactive CD allows instructors to have all of the ancillaries in one place. In addition, they can insert media—PowerPoint® slides, graphs, charts, maps—into their interactive classroom presentations.

FOR THE STUDENT

Anthropology Notes Plus A useful and exciting study guide, *Anthropology Notes Plus* is Prentice Hall's one-stop resource for students studying cultural anthropology. Designed around the chapters in *Cultural Anthropology, Sixth Edition*, it helps students keep their course notes and lecture information in order. *Anthropology Notes Plus* includes chapter outline, key terms, a note-taking section, and two chapter review tests. *Anthropology Notes Plus* is FREE when packaged with new copies of this text. Please see your local Prentice Hall representative for more details.

Companion Website™ This online study guide provides unique support to help students with their studies in cultural anthropology. Featuring a variety of interactive learning tools, including online quizzes with immediate feedback, this site is a comprehensive resource organized according to the chapters in *Cultural Anthropology, Sixth Edition*. It can be found at **www.prenhall.com/scupin**

One Search with Research Navigator™: Anthropology This guide focuses on using *Research Navigator™—Prentice Hall's own gateway to databases*—including *The New York Times* Search-by-Subject Archive, *ContentSelect™* Academic Journal Database powered by EBSCO, *The Financial Times*, and the *Best of the Web* Link Library. It also includes extensive appendices on documenting online sources and on avoiding plagiarism. This guide, along with the Research Navigator access code, is free to students when packaged with *Cultural Anthropology, Sixth Edition*.

The New York Times/Prentice Hall *Themes of the Times* *The New York Times* and Prentice Hall are sponsoring *Themes of the Times*, a program designed to enhance student access to current information relevant to the classroom. Through this program, the core subject matter provided in the text is supplemented by a collection of timely articles from one of the world's most distinguished newspapers, *The New York Times*. These articles demonstrate the vital, ongoing connection between what is learned in the classroom and what is happening in the world around us. Access is available on the *Cultural Anthropology, Sixth Edition* Companion Website.

ACKNOWLEDGMENTS

A textbook like this one requires the enormous effort of many people. I would like to thank the following reviewers for their valuable comments on the various editions of this textbook:

Harumi Befu, Stanford University; Donald E. Brown, University of California—Santa Barbara; Robert Carmack, SUNY—Albany; A. H. Peter Castro, Syracuse University; Miriam S. Chaiken, Indiana University of Pennsylvania; Tom Connelly, Indiana University of Pennsylvania; Dale Eickelman, Dartmouth College; Raymond Hames, University of Nebraska; Robert W. Hefner, Boston University; Ronald Kephart, University of North Florida; Rita S. Kipp, Kenyon College; Robert Lawless, Witchita State University; James Lett, Indian River Community College; Ronald Lukens-Bull, University of North Florida; Henry Munson, University of Maine; Tim

O'Meara, Asian and Pacific Bank Development; Paul (Jim) Roscoe, University of Maine, Susan D. Russell, Northern Illinois University; Michael Salovesh, Northern Illinois University; Paul Shankman, University of Colorado at Boulder; Stephen A. Tyler, Rice University. I also extend thanks to all colleagues who sent photos and information for use in the biography boxes.

In particular, I would like to thank Mark Spencer of the Institute of Human Origins at Arizona State University for his evaluation of the human evolution chapter. His expertise in the most current hypotheses within paleoanthropology and genetics were extremely helpful. Susan Brownell carefully evaluated the chapters on globalization and race and ethnicity for this textbook also. I appreciate her devotion to an understanding of the undergraduate audience and what anthropologists ought to be teaching in their courses. Robert Hitchcock at the University of Nebraska at Lincoln was extremely helpful in providing extensive comments on the chapter on band or foraging societies. Robert helped organize and evaluate the ethnographic research on bands and assess the human rights dilemmas and global problems that these societies are facing today. Dustin Wax of the New School University assessed the final discussion of human rights and cultural and ethical relativism with a deep philosophical appreciation of the nuances of these discussions. Hoyt Alverson of Dartmouth College and Steven Pinker of Harvard University reviewed some of the basic content of the language chapter with their different approaches to this topic.

I am grateful for the unwavering support given to this project by Prentice Hall. Without the moral support and encouragement of publisher Nancy Roberts and freelance editor Sharon Chambliss, I never would have been able to complete it.

My warmest appreciation goes to my wife Susan, whose emotional support, patience, love, and endurance made possible the publication of the sixth edition of this project.

Anyone with comments, suggestions, or recommendations regarding this text is welcome to send e-mail (Internet) messages to the following address: **Rscupin@lindenwood.edu**

Raymond Scupin

About the Author

Raymond Scupin is Professor of Anthropology and International Studies at Lindenwood University. He received his B.A. degree in history and Asian studies, with a minor in anthropology, from the University of California—Los Angeles. He completed his M.A. and Ph.D. degrees in anthropology at the University of California—Santa Barbara. Dr. Scupin is truly a four-field anthropologist. During graduate school, Dr. Scupin did archaeological and ethnohistorical research on Native Americans in the Santa Barbara region. He did extensive ethnographic fieldwork in Thailand with a focus on understanding the ethnic and religious movements among the Muslim minority. In addition, he taught linguistics and conducted linguistic research while based at a Thai university.

Dr. Scupin has been teaching undergraduate courses in anthropology for more than 30 years at a variety of academic institutions, including community colleges, research universities, and a four-year liberal arts university. Thus, he has taught a very broad spectrum of undergraduate students. Through his teaching experience, Dr. Scupin was prompted to write this textbook, which would allow a wide range of undergraduate students to understand the holistic and global perspectives of the four-field approach in anthropology. In 1999 Dr. Scupin received the Missouri Governor's Award for Teaching Excellence.

Dr. Scupin has published many studies based on his ethnographic research in Thailand. He recently returned to Thailand and other countries of Southeast Asia to update his ethnographic data on Islamic trends in that area, an increasingly important topic in the post 9/11 world. He is a member of many professional associations, including the American Anthropological Association, the Asian Studies Association, and the Council of Thai Studies. Dr. Scupin has recently authored *Religion and Culture: An Anthropological Focus* and *Race and Ethnicity: An Anthropological Focus on the U.S. and the World*, both published by Prentice Hall. Another recent textbook, *Peoples and Cultures of Asia,* is the newest forthcoming publication by Prentice Hall and Dr. Scupin.

Chapter 1

Introduction to Anthropology

CHAPTER OUTLINE

ANTHROPOLOGY: THE FOUR SUBFIELDS

Physical Anthropology / Archaeology / Linguistic Anthropology / Cultural Anthropology and Ethnology

HOLISTIC ANTHROPOLOGY, INTERDISCIPLINARY RESEARCH, AND THE GLOBAL PERSPECTIVE

APPLIED ANTHROPOLOGY

ANTHROPOLOGICAL EXPLANATIONS

The Scientific Method

ANTHROPOLOGY AND THE HUMANITIES

WHY STUDY ANTHROPOLOGY?

Critical Thinking and Global Awareness

 CHAPTER QUESTIONS

- What is unique about the field of anthropology as compared with other disciplines?

- How does the field of anthropology bridge both the sciences and the humanities?

- Why should any student study anthropology?

Anthropologist Morton Fried once pointed out the similarities among space travel, science fiction, and the field of anthropology (1977). He noted that when Neil Armstrong became the first human to set foot on the moon in July 1969, his step constituted first contact. To space travelers and science fiction writers, *first contact* refers to the first meeting between humans and extraterrestrial beings. To anthropologists, the phrase refers to initial encounters between peoples of different societies. For thousands of years, peoples throughout the world have had first contacts with each other. Perhaps in the future, through further exploration in space, there may be initial encounters between humans and creatures from other worlds.

Imagine the year 2100, when space travelers from Earth have these first contacts with extraterrestrials in far-off galaxies. Undoubtedly, the travelers from Earth will want to grasp the nature of these beings. Because the extraterrestrial beings will certainly differ physically from humans, the space travelers will attempt to investigate their physical characteristics. For this investigation, they will examine the environmental conditions of the distant planet to determine how these creatures originated and why they developed specific physical traits. They will also look closely at physical variations within the extraterrestrial population.

Beyond individual physical characteristics of the extraterrestrial beings, the space explorers will wonder how the extraterrestrial society developed, so they will try to study the technology and other aspects of the alien society that would indicate patterns of change over time. In the year 2100, space scientists may be able to conduct this analysis with sophisticated equipment and methods that allow them to examine the layers of the newly discovered planet's crust to locate different inventions, buildings, or art forms that have emerged in specific time periods.

One of the first problems the space travelers will almost surely encounter is communicating with the extraterrestrials. They will need to determine the form of communication used by these creatures and attempt to distinguish patterns of sounds or other methods used to transmit information. The space travelers may discover that different forms of communication are used in different places on the planet, prompting the human visitors to compare these disparate communication patterns to understand the different language groupings found on the planet.

Edwin "Buzz" Aldrin on the moon.

The space scientists could also gain an understanding of the extraterrestrials by living in their communities and observing their behavior. In addition to recording these behaviors as accurately as possible, the space travelers might have to participate in the extraterrestrials' rituals and daily activities to gain an insider's perspective.

The space travelers would strive to determine in what ways these extraterrestrials resemble and differ from human beings on Earth. Drawing on all their findings, they would compare the extraterrestrials' physical characteristics, the development of their society over time, their forms of communication, and their overall behavior and thought with that of humans.

As we shall see in this chapter, the field of anthropology seeks to understand humanity in much the same way that future space travelers would investigate the lifestyles of extraterrestrials. Anthropologists have developed specialized procedures over the past hundred years to conduct their investigations. There are two major goals of anthropology: to understand the *uniqueness and diversity* of human behavior and human societies around the world and to discover the *fundamental similarities* that link human beings the world over both in the past and the present. To accomplish these goals, anthropologists undertake systematic case studies of people living in particular locations, in the past and present, and use comparative techniques to assess the similarities and differences among societies.

Using these goals as a springboard, anthropology has forged distinctive objectives and propelled research that has broadened our understanding of humanity, from the beginnings of human societies to the present. This chapter introduces the distinctive approaches used in anthropology to achieve these goals.

Anthropology: The Four Subfields

The word *anthropology* stems from the Greek words *anthropo*, meaning human beings or humankind, and *logia*, translated as knowledge of or the study of. Thus, we can define **anthropology** as the systematic study of humankind. This definition in itself, however, does not distinguish anthropology from other disciplines. After all, historians, psychologists, economists, sociologists, and scholars in many other fields systematically study humankind in one way or another. Anthropology stands apart because it combines four subdisciplines, or subfields, that bridge the natural sciences, the social sciences, and the humanities. These four subdisciplines—physical anthropology, archaeology, linguistic anthropology, and ethnology or cultural anthropology—give anthropologists a broad approach to the study of humanity the world over, both past and present. Figure 1.1 shows these subfields and the various specializations that make up each one. A discussion of these subdisciplines and some of the key specializations in each follows.

These subfields of anthropology emerged in Western society in an attempt to understand non-Western peoples. Europeans, including Christopher Columbus, had been exploring and colonizing the world since the fifteenth century. These Western peoples had encounters with non-Western native peoples in the Americas, Africa, the Middle East, and Asia. Various European travelers, missionaries, and

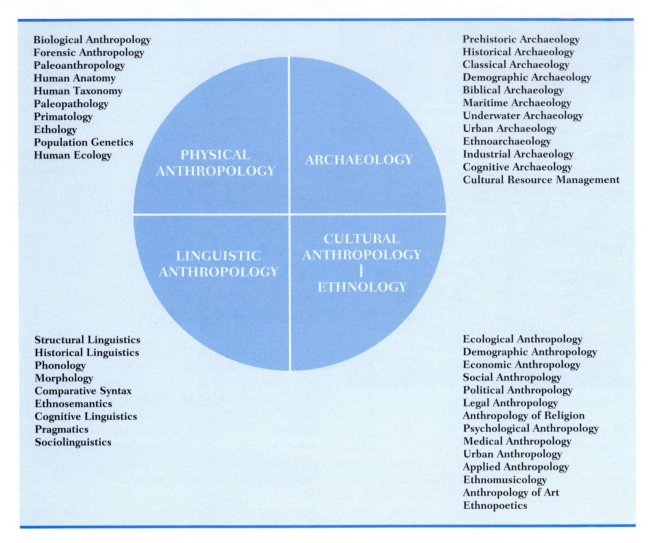

Biological Anthropology
Forensic Anthropology
Paleoanthropology
Human Anatomy
Human Taxonomy
Paleopathology
Primatology
Ethology
Population Genetics
Human Ecology

Prehistoric Archaeology
Historical Archaeology
Classical Archaeology
Demographic Archaeology
Biblical Archaeology
Maritime Archaeology
Underwater Archaeology
Urban Archaeology
Ethnoarchaeology
Industrial Archaeology
Cognitive Archaeology
Cultural Resource Management

PHYSICAL ANTHROPOLOGY

ARCHAEOLOGY

LINGUISTIC ANTHROPOLOGY

CULTURAL ANTHROPOLOGY
|
ETHNOLOGY

Structural Linguistics
Historical Linguistics
Phonology
Morphology
Comparative Syntax
Ethnosemantics
Cognitive Linguistics
Pragmatics
Sociolinguistics

Ecological Anthropology
Demographic Anthropology
Economic Anthropology
Social Anthropology
Political Anthropology
Legal Anthropology
Anthropology of Religion
Psychological Anthropology
Medical Anthropology
Urban Anthropology
Applied Anthropology
Ethnomusicology
Anthropology of Art
Ethnopoetics

FIGURE 1.1 This figure shows the four core subfields of anthropology. It also includes some of the various specializations that have developed within each of the subfields, which will be introduced in this text. Many of these specializations overlap with one another in the actual studies carried out by anthropologists.

government officials had described some of these non-Western societies, cultures, and races. By the nineteenth century, anthropology had developed into the primary discipline and science for understanding these non-Western societies and cultures. The major questions that these early nineteenth-century anthropologists grappled with had to do with the basic differences and similarities of human societies, cultures, and the physical variations of people throughout the world. Anthropologists have continued to answer these basic questions through systematic research efforts within the four fields described below.

Physical Anthropology

Physical anthropology is the branch of anthropology concerned with humans as a biological species. As such, it is the subdiscipline most closely related to the natural sciences. Physical anthropologists conduct research in two major areas: human evolution and modern human variation. The investigation of human evolution presents one of the most tantalizing areas of anthropological study. Research has now traced the African origins of humanity back over six million years. Fieldwork in

Although anthropologists study the distinctive features of different cultures, they also recognize the fundamental similarities among people throughout the world.

other world areas has traced the expansion of early human ancestors throughout the world. Much of the evidence for human origins consists of **fossils,** the fragmentary remains of bones and living materials preserved from earlier periods. The study of human evolution through analysis of fossils is called **paleoanthropology** (the prefix *paleo* means "old" or "prehistoric"). Paleoanthropologists use a variety of sophisticated scientific techniques to date, classify, and compare fossil bones to determine the links between modern humans and their

biological ancestors. They may work closely with archaeologists when studying ancient tools and activity areas to learn about the behavior of early human ancestors.

Other physical anthropologists explore human evolution through **primatology,** the study of primates. **Primates** are mammals that belong to the same overall biological classification as humans and therefore share similar physical characteristics and a close evolutionary relationship with us. Many primatologists observe primates such as

Anthropologists at Work

Mark Spencer: Physical Anthropologist (Biological Anthropology)

Mark Spencer was first attracted to physical or biological anthropology as an undergraduate student at Indiana University, when he took an introductory course. He had always been generally interested in science and technology and had briefly considered majoring in astronomy or computer programming. These interests followed from previous hobbies, but he didn't like the introductory courses in these fields, which started with the electromagnetic spectrum and sorting algorithms, respectively. He had already been photographing galaxies with his amateur telescope and writing his own computer games, so the foundations of these fields seemed dull to his young mind. He had never really considered going into biology. Although he had a good biology teacher in high school, Mark had not been exposed to evolutionary theory, which is not really surprising given his education in Kentucky, which tends to be a part of the country where the teaching of evolution is frowned upon (see the

box "Creationism and Evolution" in Chapter 2). However, Mark does remember watching fascinating public television shows when he was young that discussed some amazing anatomical adaptations of living things—the mechanism by which some beetles adhere to surfaces stood out in his mind. Also, Mark's father was a physician, and he was raised to have a strong interest in how things work, especially living things. Particularly vivid in Mark's memory was watching his father, who was a hunter, cleaning a squirrel and showing him the various organs (his father even dissected out the lungs and inflated them using the barrel of a disassembled ballpoint pen inserted into the trachea).

The introductory course in physical anthropology that Mark took as an undergraduate seemed to bring all these interests together for him, and he remembers especially being very curious about the strange faces of some of the early hominid fossils such as the *Paranthropines* (see Chapter 2). Ultimately

Mark received a bachelor's degree with a double major in anthropology and biology. However, Mark was interested in organismic biology and anatomy, and these were not the popular subjects in the mid-1980s in biology departments moving toward molecular biological approaches. Physical anthropology seemed to be a place where Mark could learn more about whole animals.

Mark had the good fortune to attend graduate school at the State University of New York at Stony Brook. There he learned about the fields of functional morphology and biomechanics of living organisms and learned a great deal about evolutionary theory and how adaptation is studied. Mark took courses in quantitative and comparative approach, where measurements of living species are taken to test hypotheses about the interplay of anatomy and behavior. He also learned the importance of experimental work, in which function is measured in living organisms (e.g., electromyography is used to

chimpanzees, gorillas, gibbons, and orangutans in their natural habitats to ascertain the similarities and differences between these other primates and humans. These observations of living primates may provide insight into the behaviors of early human ancestors.

Another group of physical anthropologists focuses their research on the range of physical variation within and among different "modern" human populations. These anthropologists study human variation by measuring physical characteristics, such

as body size, variation in blood types, differences in skin color, or various genetic traits. Human *osteology* is the particular area of specialization within physical anthropology dealing with the study of the human skeleton. Such studies have wide-ranging applications, including the identification of murder victims from fragmentary skeletal remains to the design of ergonomic airplane cockpits. Physical anthropologists are also interested in evaluating how disparate physical characteristics reflect evolutionary adaptations to different environmental monitor muscle activity and is crucial to understanding how muscles are used during particular behaviors such as in walking for chimpanzees and other primates).

Throughout his graduate training, Mark retained an interest in the mechanics and evolution of the face and ultimately did his Ph.D. dissertation on this subject. He had become aware that the demands associated with feeding are substantial and that most interpretations of facial evolution depended on mechanical models of how the jaws work. He came to wonder whether the differences in facial form among various primates, including early human ancestors, might relate to differences in the food these animals eat and might therefore serve as a guide to past diets. This was not a new idea among physical anthropologists who study fossil evidence, and attempts to evaluate it previously had relied on fairly simple mechanical models. So, for Mark's Ph.D. research, he tested these models and identified some hypotheses that really didn't work, as well as others that did offer more valid explanations with careful observations.

After graduate school Mark was hired as a research assistant professor in the Department of Biological Anthropology and Anatomy at Duke University, one of the leading centers of primate studies and evolution. Mark continued to work on facial form and function, and it was also here that he began to develop a more mature understanding of evolutionary theory and the history of science, topics that stimulated his growing interests.

Following this, Mark was hired as an assistant professor in the Department of Anthropology at the University of Colorado at Denver. Most recently he has taken a new position with Arizona State University, where he holds a joint position with the Anthropology Department and the Institute of Human Origins, with a team of prominent physical anthropologists who do studies of fossil evidence of ancestors of humans dating back millions of years. In Mark's recent research he has continued to explore issues related to the function and evolution of the face in humans and nonhuman primates. He has explored a range of topics: facial diversity in

Mark Spencer.

contemporary Inuit (Eskimo people) and ancient Neandertals, and the nature of chewing muscle activity, and the function and evolution of teeth and diet. In addition, Mark is developing realistic computer models of the primate face during feeding, using sophisticated engineering software. These models can be used to generate predictions and should strengthen our ability to understand the function and evolution of the skull in hominid fossil species. His research brings together some of the most sophisticated new technologies of the twenty-first century to study our ancient human past.

conditions, thus shedding light on why human populations vary.

An increasingly important area of research for some physical anthropologists is *genetics*, the study of the biological "blueprints" that dictate the inheritance of physical characteristics. Research on genetics examines a wide variety of questions. It has, for example, been important in identifying the genetic sources of some diseases, such as sickle cell anemia, cystic fibrosis, and Tay-Sachs disease. A new example of genetics research on a modern population

has been conducted by physical anthropologist Cynthia Beall in the Himalayan mountains of Tibet. Beall and her team did detailed genealogical and historical interviews with thousands of women between 20 to 60 years of age who had moved and were adapting to new environmental conditions at the altitude of 4,000 meters at low oxygen levels. Ruling out such factors as age, illness, or smoking, the team found that one group of these women had blood oxygen levels that were 10 percent higher than normal. Beall and her team found that the children of these women were much more likely to survive to the age of 15 or older. In contrast, the children of the low-oxygen group of women had an average of 2.5 children that died during childhood. The high-oxygen group's average for childhood death was .04. Thus, Beall and her team found that the gene or genes that determine high-oxygen blood count for women gave survival and adaptive capacities in this high mountain altitude (Beall, Song, Elston, and Goldstein 2004).

Genetics has also become an increasingly important complement to paleoanthropological research. Through the study of the genetic makeup of modern humans, physical anthropologists have been working on calculating the genetic distance among modern humans, thus providing a means of inferring rates of evolution and the evolutionary relationships within the species. These data have helped provide independent evidence for the African origins of the modern human species and human ancestors. These genetic studies have also been used to determine the physical and evolutionary connections between Native Americans and Asiatic peoples (Cavilla-Sforza 1994).

Archaeology

Through **archaeology,** the branch of anthropology that seeks out and examines the artifacts of past societies, we learn about the culture of those societies—the shared way of life of a group of people that includes their values, beliefs, and norms. **Artifacts,** the material products of former societies, provide clues to the past. Some archaeological sites reveal spectacular jewelry like that found by the movie character Indiana Jones or the treasures of a pharaoh's tomb. Most artifacts are not so glamorous, however. Despite the popular image of archaeology as an adventurous, even romantic pursuit, it usually consists of methodical, rigorous scientific research (see the box "Patty Jo Watson: Archaeologist"). Archaeologists often spend hours sorting through ancient trash piles, or **middens,** to discover how members of past societies ate their meals, what tools they used in their household and in their work, and what beliefs gave meaning to their lives. The broken fragments of pottery, stone, glass, and other materials are collected and carefully analyzed in a laboratory setting. It may take months or even

years to fully complete the study of an excavation. Unlike the glorified adventures of fictional archaeologists, the real-world field of archaeology thrives on the intellectually challenging adventure of systematic, scientific research that enlarges our understanding of the past.

Archaeologists have examined sites the world over, from campsites of the earliest humans to modern landfills. Some archaeologists investigate past societies whose history is primarily told by the archaeological record. Known as *prehistoric archaeologists*, they study the artifacts of groups such as the ancient inhabitants of Europe or the first humans to arrive in the Americas. Because these researchers have no written documents or oral traditions to help interpret the sites and artifacts that they recover, the archaeological record provides the primary source of information for their interpretations about the past. *Historical archaeologists*, on the other hand, work with historians in investigating the artifacts of societies of the more recent past. For example, some historical archaeologists have probed the remains of plantations in the southern United States to gain an understanding of the lifestyles of enslaved Africans and slave owners during the nineteenth century. Other archaeologists, called *classical archaeologists*, conduct research on ancient civilizations such as in Egypt, Greece, and Rome.

There are many more areas of specialization within archaeology that reflect area or topical specializations, or the time period on which the archaeologist works (see Figure 1.1). There are, for example, industrial archaeologists, biblical archaeologists, medieval and postmedieval archaeologists, and Islamic archaeologists. Underwater archaeologists work in a variety of places and time periods the world over; they are distinguished from other archaeologists by the distinctive equipment, methods, and procedures needed to excavate under water.

In a novel approach, still other archaeologists have turned their attention to the very recent past. For example, in 1972 William L. Rathje began a study of modern garbage as an assignment for the students in his introductory anthropology class. Even he was surprised at the number of people who took an interest in the findings. A careful study of garbage reveals insights about modern society that cannot be ferreted out in any other way. Whereas questionnaires and interviews depend on the cooperation and interpretation of respondents, garbage provides

Anthropologists at Work

Patty Jo Watson: Archaeologist

After two years of studies in zoology at Iowa State College, Patty Jo Watson changed course and decided to pursue graduate study in archaeology at the University of Chicago. Working with Robert Braidwood, Watson became adept at using systematic scientific methods to assess artifacts and other remains left behind by past societies. Early in her career, Watson participated in excavations of prehistoric communities in the Middle East. Later, after marrying philosopher and geologist Richard (Red) Watson, professor of philosophy at Washington University in St. Louis, who introduced her to cave exploration, she focused her energies on cave archaeology. Watson took an especially keen interest in Native American Indian cave explorers in Kentucky, especially their activities in the Mammoth Cave system, which is the longest network of caves in the

world, with approximately three hundred sixty miles of interconnected passageways. The system includes Salts Cave, Colossal Cave, Unknown Cave, Crystal Cave, and many others. For more than thirty years, Watson and her colleagues surveyed, mapped, and explored materials left in portions of the Mammoth Cave system by ancient cavers. They documented evidence that these people were not only the best cavers in the world 3,000 years ago, but also that they were among the first farmers north of Mexico. This discovery has yielded major insights concerning the development of agriculture in Native North America. Watson, the Edward Mallinckrodt Distinguished University Professor of Anthropology at Washington University, and two of her colleagues have written two major books on the philosophy of archaeology: *Explanation in Archaeology: An*

Patty Jo Watson.

Explicitly Scientific Approach (1971) and *Archaeological Explanation: The Scientific Method in Archaeology* (1984). As a result of her contributions to archaeology and the prehistory of Native American culture made over a thirty-five-year career, Watson was inducted into the National Academy of Sciences, an honor *The New York Times* described as "second only to the Nobel Prize." She is one of a small number of American women selected for membership in this prestigious organization.

an unbiased physical record of human activity. Rathje's "garbology project" is still in progress and, combined with information from respondents, offers a unique look at patterns of waste management, consumption, and alcohol use in contemporary U.S. society (Rathje and Ritenbaugh 1984).

Linguistic Anthropology

Linguistics, the study of language, has a long history that dovetails with the discipline of philosophy but is also one of the integral subfields of anthropology. **Linguistic anthropology** focuses on the relationship between language and culture, how

language is used within society, and how the human brain acquires and uses language. As do other types of anthropologists, linguistic anthropologists seek to discover the ways in which languages are different from one another as well as how they are similar to one another. Two wide-ranging areas of research in linguistic anthropology are structural linguistics and historical linguistics.

Structural linguistics explores how language works. Structural linguists compare grammatical patterns or other linguistic elements to learn how contemporary languages mirror and differ from one another. Structural linguistics has also uncovered some intriguing relationships between language

Anthropologists at Work

Bambi B. Schieffelin: Linguistic Anthropologist

Bambi Schieffelin.

As an undergraduate at Columbia University, Bambi Schieffelin was drawn to two fields: anthropology and comparative literature. After spending a summer on a field trip to rural Bolivia and a year in the southern highlands of Papua New Guinea, Schieffelin decided to pursue a doctorate in anthropology, with a specialty in linguistic anthropology. She combined the fields of developmental psychology, linguistics, and anthropology, which prepared her for fieldwork among the Kaluli people in Papua New Guinea. After completing her Ph.D., Schieffelin spent a year teaching at the University of California at Berkeley and also teaching linguistics at Stanford University. Since 1986 she has been teaching at New York University in the department of anthropology.

Schieffelin's work focuses on language use and socialization. She studies how language is learned and acquired by children and how it is used in various social contexts. She has collaborated with Elinor Ochs to develop innovative approaches to understanding how language use is influenced by socialization. Together they have edited several volumes, including *Language Socialization across Cultures* (1987). In addition, Schieffelin has developed these topics in her own book, *The Give and Take of Everyday Life: Language Socialization of Kaluli Children* (1990).

Through their research on children's language socialization, Schieffelin and Ochs contributed to a cross-cultural understanding of this process. Until the early 1970s, most of the theories on language and socialization had been drawn from psychological research on middle-class Americans. Schieffelin and Ochs focused instead on language and socialization among many different societies. They emphasized the importance of cultural practices in shaping verbal activities. For example, prior to their research, it was assumed that "baby talk" was the same all over the world. They found, however, that "baby talk" is not universal and is linked to ideas that people have about children.

In her ethnographic research, Schieffelin tape-records and transcribes everyday social interactions in different speech communities. She has carried out research in Papua New Guinea since 1967, focusing not only on language socialization, but on language change and the introduction of literacy into a nonliterate society. In addition to this work in a relatively traditional society, Schieffelin has worked in a number of urban speech communities in the United States, where linguistic diversity is apparent on every street corner. Her research in Philadelphia among Sino-Vietnamese people focused on language socialization and literacy, and her studies of Haitians in New York analyzed language socialization and code-switching practices.

As a linguistic anthropologist, Schieffelin tries to integrate two perspectives. First, she focuses on how the study of language use can lead to insights into how culture is transmitted from generation to generation in everyday social interactions. Second, she analyzes the ways in which language expresses social relationships and cultural meanings across different social and political contexts. Her work represents the most current developments in linguistic anthropology today.

Linguistic anthropologists have broadened their vision of places in which to investigate language use—including legal, medical, scientific, educational, and political arenas—as these contexts are critical to understanding how power is acquired and distributed. They are also studying all varieties of literacy, including television and radio, providing new perspectives on these new forms of global communication.

and thought patterns among different groups of people. Do people who speak different languages with different grammatical structures think and perceive the world differently from each other? Do native Chinese speakers think or view the world and life experiences differently from native English speakers? These are some of the questions that structural linguists attempt to answer. We will address these issues in Chapter 5, "Language."

Linguistic anthropologists also examine the connections between language and social behavior in different cultures. This specialty is called **sociolinguistics**. Sociolinguists are interested both in how language is used to define social groups and how belonging to particular groups leads to specialized kinds of language use. In Thailand, for example, there are thirteen forms of the pronoun *I*. One form is used with equals, other forms come into play with people of higher status, and some forms are used when males address females (Scupin 1988).

Another area of research that has interested linguistic anthropologists is historical linguistics. **Historical linguistics** concentrates on the comparison and classification of different languages to discern the historical links among languages. By examining and analyzing grammatical structures and sounds of languages, researchers are able to discover rules for how languages change over time, as well as which languages are related to one another historically. This type of historical linguistic research is particularly useful in tracing the migration routes of various societies through time, confirming archaeological and paleoanthropological data gathered independently. For example, through historical linguistic research, anthropologists have corroborated the Asian origins of many Native American populations.

Cultural Anthropology and Ethnology

Cultural anthropology, sometimes also known as **ethnology,** is the subfield of anthropology that examines various contemporary societies and cultures throughout the world. Cultural anthropologists do research in all parts of the world, from the tropical rainforests of the Democratic Republic of the Congo and Brazil to the arctic regions of Canada, from the deserts of the Middle East to the urban areas of China. Until recently, most cultural anthropologists conducted research on non-Western or remote cultures in Africa, Asia, the Middle East, Latin America, the Pacific Islands, and on the Native American populations in the United States. Today, however, many cultural anthropologists have turned to research on their own cultures to gain a better understanding of its institutions and cultural values.

Cultural anthropologists or ethnologists (sometimes the terms *sociocultural anthropologist* or *ethnographer* are used interchangeably with *cultural anthropologist* or *ethnologist*) use a unique research strategy in conducting their fieldwork in different settings. This research strategy is referred to as **participant observation,** which involves learning the language and culture of the group being studied by participating in the group's daily activities. Through this intensive participation, the cultural anthropologist becomes deeply familiar with the group and can understand and explain the society and culture of the group as an insider. We discuss the methods and techniques of cultural anthropologists at greater length in Chapter 8.

The results of the fieldwork of the cultural anthropologist are written up as an **ethnography,** a description of a society. A typical ethnography reports on the environmental setting, economic patterns, social organization, political system, and religious rituals and beliefs of the society under study. This description of a society is based on what anthropologists call *ethnographic data*. The gathering of ethnographic data in a systematic manner is the specific research goal of the cultural anthropologist. Technically, the term *ethnologist* refers to anthropologists who focus on the cross-cultural aspects of the various ethnographic studies done by the cultural anthropologists. Ethnologists take the data that are produced by the individual ethnographic studies and analyze this data to produce cross-cultural generalizations about humanity and cultures everywhere.

Holistic Anthropology, Interdisciplinary Research, and the Global Perspective

Most anthropologists are trained in all four subfields of anthropology. Because of all the research being done in these different fields (more than three hundred journals and hundreds of books are published

Anthropologists at Work

Bruce Knauft: Cultural Anthropologist

Though he planned to major in philosophy as an undergraduate at Yale University, Bruce Knauft took an anthropology course and became fascinated by the idea of living and working in a different cultural environment. He explored this idea by living in an inner-city ghetto in New Haven, Connecticut, and then by working and traveling in southern France. Following graduate work at the University of Michigan, Knauft and his wife, Eileen Cantrell, conducted two years of field research among the Gebusi people of Papua New Guinea—just north of Australia— from 1980 to 1982. Gebusi lived in a remote lowland rainforest and continued to practice customs such as male initiation, spirit mediumship, sorcery divination, festive dancing in elaborate costume, and ritual homosexuality. Because Gebusi did not speak an outside language, Knauft had to learn the vernacular without the aid of translators. His work focused on matters of symbolism, religion, and politics. While collecting genealogies and analyzing kinship, Knauft found

that a large number of Gebusi had been executed by other Gebusi as sorcerers. Elaborate beliefs in sorcery alternately masked and revealed important causes of violence in Gebusi society. Knauft documented that Gebusi had one of the highest rates of homicide documented in the cross-cultural record. His first book, *Good Company and Violence*, explored the tension between spiritual beliefs, social organization, and violence among Gebusi. His second book, *South Coast New Guinea Cultures*, considered the relation between religious beliefs and political systems comparatively across a wide range of so-called flamboyant cultures in southern New Guinea.

More generally, Knauft's work combines the interpretive study of symbols and meanings with political patterns of coercion, inequality, or domination by some groups or types of people over others. He has explored this issue in a number of different contexts—including with respect to gender, sexuality, ethnicity, state organization, and, at the other end of the spectrum, the

origin of language and the development of social organization in early human evolution. On one hand, cultural anthropologists such as Knauft try to appreciate cultures by "getting inside" their world view and empathizing with it as much as possible. On the other hand, they use a broader explanatory framework to understand how local culture interacts with political and economic forces to produce social inequalities and to maintain or change them over time.

These issues have deepened in cultural anthropology in recent years. Critics have questioned how anthropologists represent the people they study: What biases and political effects do anthropologists themselves produce or perpetuate? Are anthropologists effectively representing the concerns of local people in a contemporary world? These questions were taken up by Knauft in his third book, *Genealogies for the Present in Cultural Anthropology*. In this work, Knauft addressed a wide range of critical issues that had intensified since he had himself

every year dealing with anthropological research), no one individual can keep abreast of all the developments across the discipline's full spectrum. Consequently, anthropologists usually specialize in one of the four subfields. Nevertheless, most anthropologists are firmly committed to a **holistic** approach to understanding humankind—a broad, comprehensive account that draws on all four subfields under the umbrella of anthropology. This holistic approach

involves the analysis of biological, environmental, psychological, economic, historical, social, and cultural conditions of humanity. In other words, anthropologists study the physical characteristics of humans, including their genetic endowment, as well as their prehistoric, historical, and social and cultural environments. Through collaborative studies among the various specialists in the four subfields, anthropologists can ask broadly framed questions about humanity.

been a graduate student during the late 1970s. As he consulted a range of recent ethnographies and theories, he developed a new concept of "critical humanism." This notion retains anthropology's long-standing commitment to appreciating cultural diversity but combines it with deeper understanding of social and cultural inequalities—including their relation to anthropologists' own research and writing. Relatedly, Knauft suggests that anthropology needs stronger representation from different vantage points and especially from larger numbers of minority scholars, women, and researchers born or raised in different countries or world areas. His perspective emphasizes the importance of social and cultural change in a contemporary world. The is especially true in regions such as New Guinea, which were the focus of classic anthropological fieldwork but have since undergone major changes. These themes are considered in Knauft's fourth book, a regional study entitled *From Primitive to Post-colonial in Melanesia and Anthropology*.

Applying these themes in his own fieldwork, Knauft went back for a six-month restudy of the

Gebusi in 1998. He found that the Gebusi with whom he had previously lived had relocated next to the government station and had transformed their way of life. Gebusi are now converts to Christianity; they go to church and market, their children go to school, and they even have their own community soccer and rugby teams, who play in a local sports league against their erstwhile tribal enemies. Having documented these changes, Knauft is presently finishing his latest monograph, *Exchanging the Past*, as well as an edited volume, *Critically Modern*. These works document and put in broader perspective aspects of culture change in relation to inequality in a contemporary world. Along with most cultural anthropologists, Knauft wants to keep cultural anthropology in tune with the changes of a modern world while appreciating how current developments are influenced by longstanding local beliefs and practices. He remains highly committed to cultural anthropology as a process of rich personal engagement, interpretive understanding,

Bruce Knauft.

and critical analysis based on empirical documentation.

Since 1985, Knauft has been a faculty member of Emory University in Atlanta, where he is presently Samuel C. Dobbs Professor of Anthropology. Emory's Department of Anthropology maintains an active dialogue between the humanistic and the scientific sides of the field. Likewise, Knauft pursues an interdisciplinary approach to anthropology that encourages ongoing conversation between interpretive and explanatory points of view. He enjoys teaching and has mentored undergraduate and graduate students who have gone on to conduct their own ethnographic research in a number of world areas, including Melanesia, Australia, South Asia, the Mideast, Africa, South America, Eastern Europe, and the United States.

Anthropology does not limit itself to its own four subfields to realize its research agenda. Although it stands as a distinct discipline, anthropology has strong links to other social sciences. Cultural anthropology or ethnology, for instance, is closely related to sociology. In the past, cultural anthropologists examined the traditional societies of the world, whereas sociologists focused on modern societies. Today cultural anthropologists and sociologists

explore many of the same societies using similar research approaches. For example, both rely on statistical and nonstatistical data whenever appropriate in their studies of different types of societies.

As we shall discover in later chapters, cultural anthropology also overlaps the fields of psychology, economics, and political science. Cultural anthropologists draw on psychology when they assess the behavior of people in other societies. Psychological questions bearing on perception, learning, and motivation all figure in ethnographic fieldwork. Additionally, cultural anthropologists or ethnologists probe the economic and political behavior and thought of people in various societies, using these data for comparative purposes.

Finally, anthropology dovetails considerably with the field of history, which, like anthropology, encompasses a broad range of events. Every human event that has ever taken place in the world is a potential topic for both historians and anthropologists. Historians describe and explain human events that have occurred throughout the world; anthropologists place their biological, archaeological, linguistic, and ethnographic data in the context of these historical developments.

Through the four subfields and the interdisciplinary approach, anthropologists have emphasized a global perspective. The global perspective enables anthropologists to consider the biological, environmental, psychological, economic, historical, social, and cultural conditions of humans at all times and in all places. Anthropologists do not limit themselves to understanding a particular society or set of societies but rather attempt to go beyond specific or local conditions and demonstrate the interconnections among societies throughout the world. This global perspective is used throughout this text to show how anthropologists place their findings in the interconnecting worldwide community of humanity. As anthropologists we have done an excellent job of working with other disciplines, we have often been warmly welcomed and accepted as collaborators. We are willing to learn other disciplines of knowledge to help provide insights into humans in the past and present.

Applied Anthropology

Although the four major subfields of anthropology (physical anthropology, archaeology, linguistic anthropology, and cultural anthropology) are well established, a fifth major subfield has in recent years come to be recognized. **Applied anthropology** is the use of data gathered from the other subfields of anthropology in an effort to offer practical solutions to problems within modern societies. These problems may be environmental, technological, economic, social, political, or cultural. Many anthropologists are at work attempting to solve different types of problems through the use of anthropological data, as is discussed more thoroughly in Chapter 17.

Anthropological Explanations

In his conclusion in an excellent book entitled *Culture, Self, and Meaning* (2000), anthropologist Victor de Munck writes about how anthropology needs to engage itself in an interdisciplinary effort to understand human behavior and culture as mentioned above. He refers to the ancient Hindu–Buddhist story regarding the blind men and the elephant. This story was popularized by the nineteenth-century poet John Godfrey Saxe in 1900 and begins:

It was six men of Indostan
To learning much inclined
Who went to see the Elephant
(Though all of them were blind),
That each by observation
Might satisfy his mind.
The First approached the Elephant,
And happening to fall
Against his broad and sturdy side,
At once began to bawl:
"God bless me! but the Elephant
Is very like a wall!"

In the poem each of the blind men steps forward to examine the elephant. One feels the tusk and says the elephant is like a spear. Another grabs the trunk and likens the elephant to a snake. The poet concludes:

And so these men of Indostan
Disputed loud and long,
Each in his own opinion
Exceeding stiff and strong,
Though each was partly in the right
And all were in the wrong!

Thus, each of the blind men was mistaking his own limited understanding of the part of the elephant for the fuller reality of the whole. When thinking about the field of anthropology we need to keep this legendary fable in mind. Anthropologists in every age have been attempting to understand humanity as a whole, but in reality they had only partial understandings. Yet each of these types of explanations has provided some limited perspectives on human behavior and culture. And, eventually, the knowledge accumulated from these partial perspectives has been probed and evaluated

This photo of a Japanese woodblock print illustrates the story of the "Blind Men and the Elephant."

by anthropologists to offer a far more comprehensive picture of humanity in the twenty-first century than what we had in earlier centuries.

Another thing we need to keep in mind is how anthropology comprises both the scientific and humanistic orientations. Although anthropology relies on the scientific method, its major objective is to provide explanations of human society and behavior. Human behavior is extremely complicated. The product of many different, interacting variables, it can seldom, if ever, be predicted. Anthropologists cannot predict the outcome of interactions between two individuals or among small groups, let alone among large groups at the societal level. Consequently, anthropology as a discipline does not have any specific theories and laws that can be used to predict human action or thought. For the most part, anthropologists restrict their efforts to testing hypotheses and improving their explanations of human society and behavior.

We need to remember that anthropology also employs methods in the humanities to interpret human endeavors such as religious, artistic, folklore, oral and written poetry, and other complex symbolic activities.

A fundamental question faced by all anthropologists is how to evaluate the data that they gather from the particular social, cultural, or biological phenomena they study. Human knowledge is rooted in personal experience, as well as in the beliefs, traditions, and norms maintained by the society people live in. This includes such knowledge as assumptions about putting on warm clothing in cold weather and bringing an umbrella if it is going to rain, for example. Yet it also includes notions about how food should be prepared, what constitutes "appropriate" behavior, and perceptions about the social and cultural roles of men and women.

Religion constitutes another source of human knowledge. Religious beliefs and faith are most often derived from sacred texts, such as the Bible, Qu'ran (Koran), and Talmud, but they are also based on intuitions, dreams, visions, and extrasensory perceptions. Most religious beliefs are cast in highly personal terms and, like personal knowledge, span a wide and diverse range. People who do not accept these culturally coded assumptions may be perceived as different, abnormal, or nonconformist by other members of their society. Yet ethnographic and cross-cultural research in anthropology demonstrates that such culturally constituted knowledge is not as general as we might think. This research indicates that as humans, we are not born with this knowledge. Such knowledge tends to vary both among different societies and among different groups within the same society.

Popular perceptions about other cultures have often been based on ethnocentric attitudes.

Ethnocentrism is the practice of judging another society by the values and standards of one's own society. To some degree, ethnocentrism is a universal phenomenon. As humans learn the basic values, beliefs, and norms of their society, they tend to think of their own culture as preferable, ranking other cultures as less desirable. Members of a society may be so committed to their own cultural traditions that they cannot conceive of any other way of life. They often view other cultural traditions as strange or alien, perhaps even inferior, crazy, or immoral.

Such deeply ingrained perceptions are difficult to escape, even for anthropologists. Nineteenth-century anthropologists, for example, often reinforced ethnocentric beliefs about other societies. The twentieth century saw the co-opting of anthropological data to serve specific political and social ends. In the twentieth century, however, anthropologists also increasingly began to recognize the biases that prevented the interpretation of other cultures in more valid, systematic ways.

The Scientific Method

Given the preceding concerns, it is critical to understand how anthropological interpretations are evaluated. In contrast to personal knowledge and religious faith, anthropological knowledge is not based on traditional wisdom or revelations. Rather, anthropologists employ the **scientific method,** a logical system used to evaluate data derived from systematic observation. Researchers rely on the scientific method to investigate both the natural and the social worlds because the approach allows them to make claims about knowledge and to verify those claims with systematic, logical reasoning. Through critical thinking and skeptical thought, scientists strive to suspend judgment about any claim for knowledge until it has been verified.

Testability and *verifiability* lie at the core of the scientific method. There are two ways of developing testable propositions: the inductive method and the deductive method. In the **inductive method,** the scientist first makes observations and collects data (see Figure 1.2). Many of the data collected are referred to as variables. A **variable** is any piece of data that changes from case to case. For example, a person's height, weight, age, and sex all constitute variables. Researchers use the observations about different variables to develop hypotheses

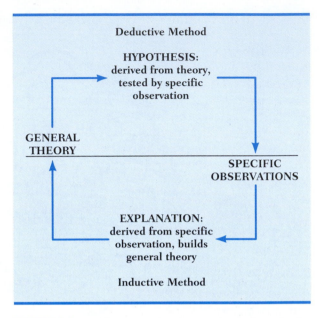

FIGURE 1.2   Deductive and inductive research methods.

about the data. A **hypothesis** is a testable proposition concerning the relationship between particular sets of variables in the collected data. The practice of testing hypotheses is the major focus of the scientific method, as scientists test one another's hypotheses to confirm or refute them. If a hypothesis is found to be valid, it may be woven together with other hypotheses into a more general theory. **Theories** are statements that explain hypotheses and observations about natural or social phenomena. Because of their explanatory nature, theories often encompass a variety of hypotheses and observations. One of the most comprehensive theories in anthropology is the theory of evolution (see Chapter 2). This theory helps explain a diversity of hypotheses about biological and natural phenomena, as well as discoveries by paleoanthropologists and geneticists.

In contrast to the inductive method, the **deductive method** of scientific research begins with a general theory from which scientists develop testable hypotheses. Data are then collected to evaluate these hypotheses. Initial hypotheses are sometimes referred to as "guesstimates" because they may be based on guesswork by the scientist. These hypotheses are tested through experimentation and replication. As with the inductive method, the testing and retesting of hypotheses and theories is used to ensure the reliability of observations made.

Through these methods researchers do not arrive at absolute truths. Theories may be invalidated or falsified by contradictory observations. Yet even if numerous observations and hypotheses suggest a particular theory is true, the theory always remains open to further testing and evaluation. The systematic evaluation of hypotheses and theories enables scientists to state their conclusions with a certainty that cannot be applied to personal and culturally construed knowledge.

Despite the thoroughness and verification that characterize the research, anthropological explanations have limitations. Unlike conclusions drawn in the natural sciences, anthropological knowledge is frequently presented as tentative and hypothetical because the conclusions are based on assumptions and presuppositions about the myriad variables that affect human thought and behavior. The complexities of the phenomena being studied make it difficult to assess all of the potential variables, and disagreements about interpretations are common. The point here, however, is not that progress is impossible. Anthropological evidence can be verified or discarded by making assumptions explicit and weeding out contradictory, subjective knowledge. Poor hypotheses are rejected and replaced by better explanations. Explanations can be made stronger by drawing on independent lines of evidence to support and evaluate theories. This process makes the scientific method much more effective than other means of acquiring knowledge.

Anthropology and the Humanities

As we mentioned before, the scientific method is not the only means used by anthropologists to study different societies and cultures. Anthropologists also employ a more humanistic-interpretive approach as they study specific cultures in different regions of the world. Think of this analogy. When botanists examine a flower, they attempt to understand the different components of the plant within a scientific framework; they analyze the biochemistry and physical aspects of the flower. However, when painters, poets, or novelists perceive a flower, they understand the plant from an aesthetic standpoint. They might interpret the flower as a symbolic phenomenon that represents nature. The scientist and the humanist use different approaches and perspectives when examining the natural world. Anthropologists employ a humanistic-interpretive approach in many circumstances.

James Peacock uses another type of analogy to discuss the difference between the scientific and humanistic-interpretive approach in anthropology (1986). Peacock draws from the field of photography to construct his analogy. He discusses the "harsh light" of the rigor of scientific analysis, including the study of biological and material conditions of a society, versus the "soft focus" used when interpreting the symbols, art, literature, religion, or music of different societies. Peacock concludes that both the "harsh light" and "soft focus" are vital ingredients of the anthropological perspective.

Cultural anthropologists utilize the humanistic-interpretive method as they conduct ethnographic research. However, archaeologists also try to employ these same methods when examining artifacts from ancient societies. When cultural anthropologists or archaeologists examine various practices and institutions in different societies, they often find that an outsider cannot easily comprehend these phenomena. In order to comprehend these different practices and institutions, the cultural anthropologist or archaeologist often has to interpret these phenomena, just as one might interpret a literary, poetic, or religious text. Cultural beliefs and practices may not be easily translatable from one society to another. Cultural anthropologists or archaeologists frequently find practices and institutions that have meaning and significance only within a specific language and culture. The cultural anthropologist or archaeologist endeavors to understand a cultural practice or institution that may have a rich, deep, localized meaning within the society being examined but is not easily converted into a transcultural or cross-cultural meaning.

Thus, in addition to its interconnections with the natural and social sciences, the discipline of anthropology is also aligned with the humanistic fields of inquiry. This is particularly true with respect to the field of cultural anthropology, as these researchers are involved in the study of different contemporary cultures. When participating in the life and experience of people in various societies, ethnologists must confront a multitude of different behaviors and values that may have to be translated and interpreted. As mentioned above, the archaeologist also confronts this type of problem when studying past cultures and civilizations from different regions of the world. Similar issues confront linguistic anthropologists as they translate and understand various languages.

Many anthropologists explore the creative cultural dimensions of humanity, such as myth, folklore, poetry, art, music, and mythology. **Ethnopoetics** is the study of poetry and how it relates to the experiences of people in different societies; for example, a provocative study of the poetry of a nomadic tribe of Bedouins in the Middle East has yielded new insights into the concepts of honor and shame in these societies (Abu-Lughod 1987; Caton 1990). Another related field, **ethnomusicology,** is devoted to the study of musical traditions in various societies throughout the world. Ethnomusicologists record and analyze music and the traditions that give rise to musical expressions, exploring similarities and differences in musical performance and composition. Other anthropologists study the art of particular societies, such as pottery styles among Native American Indian groups.

Studies of fine art conducted by anthropologists have contributed to a more richly hued, global portrait of humankind. Artistic traditions spring up in all societies, and anthropologists have shed light on the music, myths, poetry, literature, and art of non-Western and other remote peoples. As a result, we now have a keener appreciation of the diverse creative abilities exhibited by humans throughout the world. As anthropologists analyze these humanistic and artistic traditions, they broaden our understanding of the economic, social, political, and religious conditions that prevail within these societies.

One fundamental difference exists between the scientific aspect of anthropology and the humanistic-interpretive side. This difference pertains to the amount of progress one can achieve within these two different but complementary enterprises. Science has produced a cumulative increase in its knowledge base through its methodology. Thus, in the fields of astronomy, physics, chemistry, biology, and anthropology there has been significant progress in the accumulation of knowledge. We know much more about these fields of science than our ancestors knew in the fifteenth or nineteenth centuries. As we shall see in many chapters in this textbook, anthropologists today have a much better understanding of human behavior, language, culture, race, and ethnicity than did anthropologists in the nineteenth century. Through the use of the scientific method, anthropology has been able to make strides in assessing human behavior and cultural developments.

Ethnomusicologists study the musical traditions of different societies. This photo shows Tibetan Buddhist monks playing religious musical instruments.

In contrast, one cannot discuss the progress in the humanities in the same manner. Myth, literature, music, and poetry have not progressed in the way that scientific explanations have. One certainly cannot say that the literature or music of the twenty-first century has progressed beyond that of Sophocles', Shakespeare's, Dante's, Bach's, or Beethoven's time period. As we shall see, the various humanistic endeavors involving beliefs, myths, and artistic expression in small-scale and ancient civilizations are extremely sophisticated and symbolically complex, and one cannot assess modern societies as "superior" or more "progressive" in those domains. The same thing, however, cannot be said for the scientific discoveries and developments in such areas as astronomy, physics, chemistry, biology, geology, or anthropology. The scientific knowledge in these areas has definitely become more effective in offering explanations regarding the natural and social world.

The essence of anthropology consists of understanding and explaining human behavior and culture with endeavors monopolized by no single approach. Such an enlarged perspective within anthropology requires peaceful coexistence between scientism and humanism, despite their differences. In a recent discussion of this issue within anthropology, Anne Campbell and Patricia Rice suggest that many anthropologists do not agree with one another's assumptions from either a humanistic or scientific perspective because of their philosophical commitments to one or the other area (Campbell and Rice 2003). However, anthropologists recognize these differences among themselves and to a great degree it is helpful to making progress in our field because we continue to criticize and challenge one another's assumptions and orientations which culminates in better understanding of both the scientific explanations and humanistic understandings within our field.

What we are going to find in this textbook is that the many great syntheses of anthropological knowledge require the fusion of both the scientific and humanistic perspectives. When the archaeologist studies the precision and beauty embodied in the 4,500-year-old pyramids of Egyptian civilization, he finds that their inspiration came partly from the mathematics of numbers considered sacred and divine and partly from emulating nature. Both science and humanistic approaches enable anthropologists to study the sacred and mundane aspects of nature and culture.

Why Study Anthropology?

Many students today question the practical benefits of their educational experience. Hence, you might ask, "Why study anthropology?" First, anthropology contributes to a general liberal arts education, which helps students develop intellectually and personally, as well as professionally. Numerous studies indicate that a well-rounded education contributes to a person's success in any chosen career, and because of its broad interdisciplinary nature, anthropology is especially well suited to this purpose.

Critical Thinking and Global Awareness

In the context of a liberal arts education, anthropology and anthropological research cultivate critical thinking skills. As we noted earlier, the scientific method relies on constant evaluation of, and critical thinking about, data collected in the field. By being exposed to the cultures and lifestyles of unfamiliar societies, students may adopt a more critical and analytical stance toward conditions in their own society. Critical thinking skills enhance the reasoning abilities of students wherever life takes them.

Anthropology also creates an expanding global awareness and an appreciation for cultures other than our own. In this age of rapid communication, worldwide travel, and increasing economic interconnections, young people preparing for careers in the twenty-first century must recognize and show sensitivity toward the cultural differences among peoples, while understanding the fundamental similarities that make us all distinctly human. In this age of cultural diversity and increasing internationalization, sustaining this dual perception of underlying similar human characteristics and outward cultural differences has both practical and moral benefits. Nationalistic, ethnic, and racial bigotry are rife today in many parts of the world, yet our continuing survival and happiness depend on greater mutual understanding. Anthropology promotes a cross-cultural perspective that allows us to see ourselves as part of one human family in the midst of tremendous diversity. Our society needs citizens not just of some local region or group but also, and more importantly, we need world citizens who can work cooperatively in an inescapably multicultural and multinational world to solve our most pressing problems of bigotry, poverty, and violence.

In addition, an anthropology course gives students a chance to delve into a discipline whose roots lie in both science and the humanities. As we have seen, anthropology brings to bear rigorous scientific methods and models in examining the causes of human evolution, behavior, and social relationships. But anthropologists also try to achieve a humanistic understanding of other societies in all their rich cultural complexity. Anthropology casts a wide net, seeking an understanding of ancient and contemporary peoples, biological and societal developments, and human diversity and similarities throughout the world.

Viewing life from the anthropological perspective, students will also gain a greater understanding of their personal lives in the context of the long period of human evolution and development. In learning about behavior patterns and cultural values in distant societies, students question and acquire new insights into their own behavior. Thus, anthropology nurtures personal enlightenment and self-awareness, which are fundamental goals of education.

While these general goals are laudable, the study of anthropology also offers more pragmatic applications (Omohundro 1998). As seen in the discussion of applied anthropology, all the traditional subfields of anthropology have areas of study with direct relevance to modern life. Many students have found it useful to combine an anthropology minor or major with another degree. For example, given the increasingly multicultural and international focus of today's world, students preparing for careers in business, management, marketing, or public service may find it advantageous to have some anthropology courses on their résumés. The concepts and knowledge gleaned from anthropology may enable students to find practical applications in dealing with issues of cultural and ethnic diversity and multiculturalism on a daily basis. Similarly, policy makers in federal, state, and local governments may find it useful to have an understanding of historic preservation issues and cultural resource management concerns. In education, various aspects of anthropology—including evolution, study of the human past, non-European cultures, and the interpretation of cultural and social phenomena—are increasingly being integrated into elementary and secondary school curricula. Education majors preparing for the classroom can draw on their background in anthropology to provide a more insightful context for some of these issues.

SUMMARY

Anthropology consists of four subfields: physical anthropology, archaeology, linguistic anthropology, and cultural anthropology or ethnology. Each of these subfields uses distinctive methods for examining humanity in the past and in all areas of the world today. Physical anthropologists investigate human evolution and the physical variation of human populations across many geographical regions. Archaeologists study the past by analyzing artifacts (material remains) of past societies. Linguistic anthropologists focus their studies on languages, seeking out historical relationships among languages, pursuing clues to the evolution of particular languages and comparing one language with another to determine differences and similarities.

Cultural anthropologists conduct fieldwork in various societies to examine people's lifestyles. They describe these societies in written studies, called ethnographies, which highlight behavior and thought patterns characteristic of the people studied. In examining societies, cultural anthropologists use systematic research methods and strategies, primarily participant observation, which involves participating in the daily activities of the people they are studying.

Anthropologists draw on the scientific method to investigate humanity, while recognizing the limitations of science in grasping the subtleties of human affairs. Yet anthropology is also a humanistic discipline that focuses on such cultural elements as art, music, and religion. By bridging science and the humanities, anthropology enables us to look at humanity's biological and cultural heritage with a broad perspective.

For students, anthropology creates a global awareness and a deep appreciation of humanity past and present. By evaluating anthropological data, students develop critical thinking skills. And the process of anthropological inquiry—exploring other cultures and comparing them to one's own—sheds light on one's personal situation as a human being in a particular time and place.

QUESTIONS TO THINK ABOUT

1. As an anthropologist on a starship in the twenty-first century, you are a specialist in "first contact" situations. Briefly describe your goals and methods.

2. As an anthropologist, you find out about the existence of a group of humans in the Amazon rainforest that has never been contacted. How would you use the four subfields of anthropology to investigate this human community?

3. How do anthropologists utilize the scientific method in their studies? What are the limitations of the scientific method in anthropological studies?

4. You are talking with a friend who asks, "Why would anyone want to study anthropology? What practical benefits may be gained from taking a course in anthropology?" How would you answer your friend?

5. What is the holistic approach, and how is it related to anthropology, the four subfields, and other disciplines?

KEY TERMS

anthropology
applied anthropology
archaeology
artifacts
cultural anthropology
deductive method
ethnocentrism
ethnography
ethnology
ethnomusicology

ethnopoetics
fossils
historical linguistics
holistic
hypothesis
inductive method
linguistic anthropology
linguistics
middens
paleoanthropology

participant observation
primates
primatology
scientific method
sociolinguistics
structural linguistics
theories
variable

INTERNET EXERCISES

1. Peruse **http://www.wsu.edu:8001/vcwsu/commons/topics/culture/culture-index.html**. How do the twelve definitions of culture presented by Clyde Kluckhohn compare to the field of anthropology explained in this chapter?

2. After reading the section about archaeology in Chapter 1, look at the following website: **http://www.pbs.org/wgbh/nova/ubar/tools/**. How does modern high technology help archaeologists do their jobs? Why is remote sensing so valuable a tool?

Chapter 2

Human Evolution

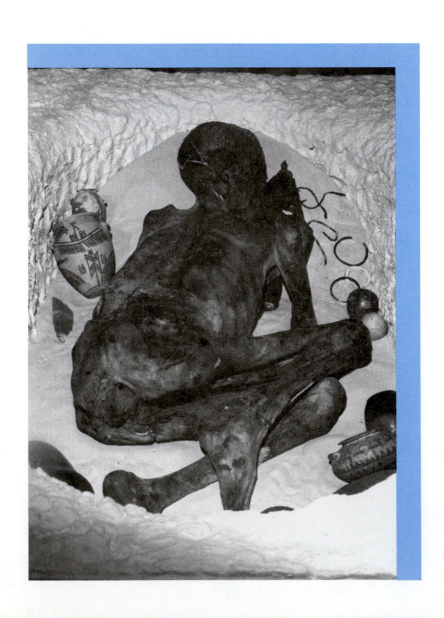

CHAPTER QUESTIONS

- How does evolutionary theory differ from origin myths?

- What is natural selection?

- What are the earliest forms of hominids, and what makes them different from other primates?

- How does *Homo habilis* differ from the Australopithecines?

- How do anthropologists explain the migration of *Homo erectus* out of Africa?

- What are the cultural characteristics of *Homo erectus*?

- What are the physical and cultural characteristics of the Neandertals of Europe?

- What are the two different models of evolutionary development of modern humans?

- What are the cultural features of the Upper Paleolithic?

- What factors of natural selection are thought to have been responsible for differences of skin color in modern humans?

Theories of Evolution

The most profound human questions are the ones that perplex us the most. Who are we? Why are we here? Where did we come from? What is our place in the universe? What is the purpose of our lives? Is there a purpose to our lives? What happens after death? Universally, all peoples have posed these questions throughout time. Most cultures have developed sophisticated beliefs and myths to provide answers to these fundamentally important questions. **Cosmologies** are conceptual frameworks that present the universe (the cosmos) as an orderly system and include answers to those basic questions about the place of humankind in the universe.

Origin Myths

Traditionally, these questions have been the basis for origin myths, usually considered the most sacred of all cosmological conceptions. Origin myths account for the ways in which supernatural beings or forces formed the earth and people. They are transmitted from generation to generation through ritual, education, laws, art, and cultural performances such as dance and music. They are highly symbolic and are expressed in a language rich with various levels of meaning. These supernatural explanations are taken on the basis of faith and provided partially satisfying answers to these profound questions.

Many origin myths deal with the origin of humans in the context of the origin of the universe.

For example, the Navajo Indians traditionally believed that Holy People, supernatural and sacred, lived below ground in twelve lower worlds. A massive underground flood forced the Holy People to crawl through a hollow reed to the surface of the earth, where they created the universe. A deity named Changing Woman gave birth to the Hero Twins, called Monster Slayer and Child of the Waters. Mortals, called Earth Surface People, emerged, and First Man and First Woman were formed from the ears of white and yellow corn.

Another cosmological tradition, found in India, teaches that life resulted from the opening of a cosmic egg, which is the source of all life. In China, in the religious tradition of Taoism, male and female principles known as yin and yang are the spiritual and material sources for the origins of humans and other living forms. Yin is considered the passive, negative, feminine force or principle in the universe, the source of cold and darkness; yang is the active, positive, masculine force or principle, the source of heat and light. Taoists believe that the interaction of these two opposite yet complementary principles brought forth the universe and all living forms out of chaos.

Western Origin Myths In the Western tradition, the ancient Greeks had various mythological explanations for the origin of humans. One early view was that Prometheus fashioned humans out of water and earth. Another had Zeus ordering Pyrrha to throw stones behind his back; these stones became men and women. Later Greek cosmological views were more scientifically based. Thales of Miletus (c. 636–546 BC) argued that life originated in the sea and that humans initially were fishlike, eventually moving onto dry land and evolving into mammals. few hundred years later, Aristotle (384–322 BC) suggested an early theory of creation through evolution. Based on comparative physiology and anatomy, his argument stated that life had evolved from simple lower forms such as single-celled amoebas, to complex higher forms such as humans.

The most important cosmological tradition that influenced Western views of creation is found in the book of Genesis in the Bible. This Judaic tradition describes how God created the cosmos. It begins with "In the beginning God created the heaven and the earth," emphasizing that the Creation took six days, during which light, heaven, earth, vegetation, sun, moon, stars, birds, fish, animals, and humans originated. In Genesis the creator is given a name, Yahweh, and is responsible for creating man, Adam, from "dust" and placing him in the Garden of Eden. Adam names the animals and birds. Woman, Eve, is created from Adam's rib. Eventually, according to this ancient Hebrew tradition, Yahweh discovers that his two human creations have disobeyed his laws and eaten fruit from the forbidden tree of knowledge of good and evil. Yahweh expels Adam and Eve from the Garden of Eden.

As generations pass, humans continue to disobey God's laws. As punishment, God produces a catastrophic flood that destroys all of his creations except Noah and his family, the descendants of Adam and Eve. Noah and his family take two of every animal on an ark built according to God's directions. Noah, his family, and the different species of animals are saved from the flood on the ark. Eventually, Noah and his family give birth to all the peoples throughout the earth. Later, as the Judeo-Christian tradition spread throughout Europe, the biblical cosmology became the dominant origin myth in the Western world.

The Darwinian Revolution

In the Western world following the medieval period (c. AD 1450), scientific discoveries began to influence conceptions about humanity's relationship to the rest of the universe. Copernicus and Galileo presented the novel idea that Earth is just one of many planets revolving around the sun, rather than the center of the universe, as had traditionally been believed. As this idea became accepted, humans could no longer view themselves and their planet as the center of the universe. This shift in cosmological thinking set the stage for entirely new views of humanity's links to the rest of the natural world.

New developments in the geological sciences began to expand radically the scientific estimates of the age of the earth. These and other scientific discoveries in astronomy, biology, chemistry, mathematics, and other disciplines dramatically transformed Western thought.

Darwin, Wallace, and Natural Selection Two individuals affected strongly by this scientific revolution were Charles Darwin and Alfred Wallace, nineteenth-century British naturalists (a term used at that time to

Charles Darwin (1809–1882).

refer to biologists). These biologists contributed significantly to the growth of scientific knowledge through their ideas on evolution. **Evolution** refers to the process of change within species over time. Evolutionary theory holds that existing species of plants and animals have emerged over millions of years from simple organisms. Before the mid-1800s, a few thinkers had suggested evolutionary theories, but because of a lack of understanding of how old the earth really was and the absence of a reasonable explanation for the evolutionary process, most people could not accept them.

Working independently, Darwin and Wallace made observations of living species around the world. Impressed by the diversity of living species, they developed an explanation of the central mechanism of evolution. This mechanism is known as natural selection.

In 1831, Darwin began a five-year voyage around the world on a British ship, the HMS *Beagle*. During this journey he collected numerous species of plants and animals from many different environments. Meanwhile, Wallace was observing different species of plants and animals on the islands off Malaysia. Although both Darwin and Wallace arrived at the

theory of natural selection independently, Darwin went on to present a thorough and completely documented statement of the theory in his book *On the Origin of Species by Means of Natural Selection*, published in 1859.

In their theory of natural selection, Darwin and Wallace emphasized the enormous variation that exists in all plant and animal species. They also noted that individuals in a species reproduce at a rate that cannot be supported by the environment; thus, their offspring must compete for food to survive. Offspring born with variations or traits that make them better able to compete are the ones that survive and pass on their traits to their offspring. Darwin and Wallace called this process natural selection because nature, or the demands of the environment, influences which individuals (with certain traits) survive. This process, repeated countless times over millions of years, leads to evolution and is the means by which species adapted to their environments.

Examples of Natural Selection   One problem Darwin faced in writing *On the Origin of Species* was a lack of well-documented examples of natural selection at work. Most major changes in nature take place over a period of thousands or millions of years.

A classic case of natural selection, known as industrial melanism, was occurring in the industrial areas of England during Darwin's lifetime, although he was unaware of it. During the 1850s, populations of English moths showed variations in color—some were light, others were dark. The lighter-colored moths were more common. After this period, however, the darker-colored variety became more common. The reason for this was a change in the environment, as black soot from industrial pollution gradually covered the trees. The light-colored moths, being highly visible against the blackened trees, were eaten as prey by birds. In contrast, the dark-colored moths had an adaptive advantage because they were concealed against the background of the dark-colored trees; hence, this population survived and reproduced in greater numbers. This process of natural selection has been confirmed experimentally with the release of light-colored and dark-colored moths in urban areas (Bishop, Cook, and Muggleton 1978; Majerus 1998, Gishlick 2004).

Natural selection is currently viewed as a major guiding force in the evolution of living species. It enabled Darwin to explain the mechanisms of biological evolution, and it remains a powerful explanation for the development of living species of plants and animals today.

Principles of Inheritance

Darwin contributed to the modern understanding of biological evolution by thoroughly documenting the variation of living forms and by identifying the process of natural selection. But Darwin did not understand how individuals pass on traits to their offspring. This discovery, and the study of heredity, was left to the experiments of an Austrian monk, Gregor Mendel (1822–1884). During the 1860s Mendel began a series of breeding experiments with pea plants. The results of these experiments revolutionized biological thought. Although his findings were not recognized until the twentieth century, they have shaped our basic understanding of inheritance. Through his experiments Mendel established the new science of **genetics**, a field of biology that deals with the inheritance of different characteristics.

Gregor Mendel (1822–1884).

From the work of Mendel and other biologists, we now know that physical traits are designed and produced by genes. A **gene** is a discrete unit of hereditary information that determines specific characteristics of organisms. It is estimated that a human being inherits less than 30,000 genes that specify various characteristics. Most sexually reproducing plants and animals have two genes for every trait, one inherited from each parent.

The Evolution of Life

Modern scientific findings indicate that the universe as we know it began to develop between 10 billion and 20 billion years ago. Approximately 4.6 billion years ago, the sun and the earth developed, and about a billion years later the first forms of life appeared in the sea. Through the process of natural selection, living forms that developed adaptive characteristics survived and reproduced. Geological forces and environmental alterations bringing about both gradual and rapid changes led to the evolution of new forms of life. Plants, fish, amphibians, reptiles, and eventually mammals evolved over millions of years of environmental change.

About 67 million years ago, groups of mammals known as primates—a diverse group of mammals that share similarities began to develop. Primates include *prosimians*, such as lemurs, tarsiers, and lorises; and anthropoids, such as monkeys, apes, and humans. Compared to other mammals **primates** are characterized by traits such as increased brain size compared with body size, improved vision, grasping hands and feet, longer periods of offspring dependence on their mothers, a complex social life, and enhanced learning abilities. The most successful primates have been humans, who today exist in most environments. The human primate, with its upright posture, large brain, and increased learning capacities, has been able to adapt to many types of environments through culture, as we discuss in Chapter 3.

Recently, paleontologists discovered significant fossils in Spain of a primate that has been classified as the "missing link" between the various ape species of gorillas, chimpanzees, orangutan, and humans. This creature, named *Pierolapithecus catalaunicus*, has physical traits that connect it with early apes and early hominids or ancestors of the human lineage. *P. catalaunicus* had a very flat face with

Critical Perspectives

CREATIONISM AND EVOLUTION

As introduced in the opening of this chapter, all peoples throughout the world have attempted to explain the evolution or creation of the universe, plants, animals, and humans. Native American Indians, Taoists, Buddhists, Hindus, Jews, Christians and people of other traditions have offered various creationist cosmologies to answer these basic existential questions about the universe and life. Despite the acceptance of scientific explanations by many people, not all segments of American and Western society have accepted the lines of evidence from geological, genetic, or fossil data that is used for understanding evolution. Survey polls indicate that many Americans assume that the creation-evolution controversy is based on a dichotomy between believers in God and secular atheists who are antireligious. This is a fundamental misunderstanding of both science and religious faith on this issue. There are many different faces or varieties of both creationism and evolutionary explanations. Scientists and others who accept evolution and its evidence are not necessarily atheists (Scott 2004; Pennock 2003).

Numerous versions of creationism are taught within various American Christian, Jewish, and other religious denominations and schools. For example, many members of the Old Order Amish (discussed in Chapter 3) accept an extreme literal reading of the biblical passage that refers to "four

corners of the Earth held up by angels" and believe that the Earth is a two-dimensional flat plane. Members of the International Flat Earth Society have similar beliefs about a flat earth (R. J. Schadewald 1980). Other creationists accept that the Earth is a sphere but refer to themselves as "geocentrists," reject the findings of modern science since Copernicus and Galileo, and believe that Earth rather than the Sun is the center of the solar system. Both these views reflect the ancient Hebrew description in the biblical passages referring to Earth as a flat disk floating on water with the heavens held up by a dome (or firmament) with the Sun, Moon, and stars attached to it.

Another group of creationists active in campaigns against the teaching of evolution call themselves "Scientific Creationists." They founded the Institute for Creation Research (ICR). The ICR propose a biblically based explanation for the origins of the universe and of life. They reject modern physics, chemistry, and geology concerning the age of the Earth. They argue that the entire universe was created within a period of six days, based on the account in Genesis 1:2. They believe that the universe was spontaneously created by divine fiat about 6,000 to 10,000 years ago, challenging modern scientific theories that propose billions of years of evolution. These creationists explain the existence of fossilized remains of ancient and prehistoric life by

referring to a universal flood that covered the entire Earth for 40 days. Surviving creatures were saved by being taken aboard Noah's ark. Creatures that did not survive this flood, such as dinosaurs, became extinct. This creationist view is taught in some of the more fundamentalist denominations of Protestantism, Judaism, and Islam in America and elsewhere.

Scientific creationists read the texts and theories presented by biologists, geologists, and paleontologists and then present their arguments against the evolutionary views. They do very little, if any, direct biological or geological research to refute evolutionary hypotheses. Consequently, their views are based on arguments derived from biblical sources, mixed with misunderstandings of science and evolutionary hypotheses (Kitcher 1982). The cosmological framework espoused by the scientific creationists is not buttressed by the precise testing of hypotheses that is required by the scientific method. Creationist ideas regarding physical laws, geological findings, and biological processes are not based on empirical findings. For example, scientists around the world find no physical evidence of a universal flood. Local floods did occur in the Near East and may be related to the story of Noah that appears in the Bible (and in earlier Babylonian texts). But to date, no evidence exists for a universal flood that had the potential to wipe out creatures such as dinosaurs (Steibing 1984).

Another group of creationists attempted to coordinate the account in Genesis 1:2 about the six days of creation with geological discoveries beginning in the nineteenth century by rendering the Hebrew term *day* as referring to long periods of time from thousands to millions of years, rather than 24 hours. Some contemporary creationists' teachings reflect these views today, and they are sometimes referred to as "Day-Age" creationists. However, the vast majority of activists in the campaign against teaching evolution call themselves "Progressive Creationists." The Progressive Creationists do accept the modern scientific view of the Big Bang and that the Earth is billions of years old but do not accept the evolution of life, plants, and animals. They believe that God not only created the Big Bang, but also created separate "kinds" of plants and animals with genetic variation that resulted in the development of contemporary species of living organisms.

Another more recent form of creationism has been referred to as "Intelligent Design Creationism" (IDC). The historical roots of IDC go back to an argument made by British theologian William Paley (1803). Reverend Paley argued that one could see God's existence by examining the Earth and the remarkable adaptations of living organisms to their environments on Earth. He used a famous analogy that is referred to

today about how one had to have a watchmaker in order to make a "watch," which has influenced the contemporary IDC theorists. Two of the major scientists who maintain this IDC position presently are LeHigh University's biochemist Michael Behe, author of a book called *Darwin's Black Box* (1996), and Baylor University's philosopher and mathematician William Dembski, who authored the major book *Intelligent Design* (1999). Although both these scientists and their followers agree that microevolution and macroevolution has occurred, they contend that some biological phenomena and the complexity of life cannot be explained by modern science and that this complexity itself is proof that there must be an intelligent supernatural designer.

Just as there are different versions of creationism, there are a variety of positions regarding evolution. One major view of evolution is known as *theistic evolution*, which promotes the view that God creates through the evolutionary process. They accept the modern scientific findings in astronomy, biology, genetics, fossil and geological evidence but see God as intervening in the process of evolution. Theistic evolution is the official view accepted by the Roman Catholic Church and it was recently reiterated by Pope John Paul II in 1996. In this statement by John Paul II, he emphasized that evolution was not just "theory" but was based on an enormous amount of empirical evidence, or "facts." However, the Roman Catholic theological

position is that although humans may indeed be descended from earlier forms of life, God created the human soul (1996). Some other contemporary mainstream Protestant, Jewish, Muslim, Hindu, and Buddhist scientists also accept the theistic evolution position. This theistic evolutionary position holds that there is no conflict between religion and science and the view reflects a continuum between the creationist and evolutionary views.

The other major view of evolution, sometimes referred to as *materialist evolutionism* or *philosophical materialism*, is a version associated with zoologist Richard Dawkins, philosopher Daniel Dennett, and physicist Steven Weinberg. These scientists and philosophers believe that the evidence from modern science and evolution had resulted in a proof of atheism or the nonexistence of a creator being, intelligent designer, or God. During Darwin's life he recorded in his memoirs how he vacillated between a confusion of muddled religious faith, atheism, and what he later accepted as agnosticism (the belief that one cannot know as humans whether God exists or not) (Desmond and Moore 1991).

Survey polls demonstrate that most Americans believe this materialist evolutionism is the dominant view among biologists, geologists, and anthropologists, and other scientists. This is one of the primary reasons why religious-based groups oppose the teaching of evolution in the public schools in the United States. In actuality, there are many scientists who accept the theistic view or other spiritual views along with their acceptance of modern empirical evidence in science. For example, one of the leading critics of intelligent design creationism is the practicing Roman Catholic biologist at Williams College, Kenneth Miller. Miller has authored a book called *Finding Darwin's God: A Scientist's Search for Common Ground Between God and Evolution* (2000). In this book Miller uses his extensive background in biology, genetics, and evolutionary data to examine the views of IDC and finds empirical weaknesses in their claims about how the complexity of life demonstrates an intelligent designer. Paul Weiss, a Protestant theologian and philosopher who authored the book *The Fifth Miracle* about faith and the evolution of life is also critical of the intelligent design creationist model and relies on the empirical findings in science and evolution to refute their claims.

Both of these individuals and many other scientists accept theistic views of evolution but emphasize that scientific understanding of the universe and life must be based on the methods of *naturalism*. This *methodological naturalism* requires the scientist to rely on "natural" or "materialist" (biological and physical) explanations rather than spiritual or theological explanations for examining the universe and evolution, *but it does not compel one to accept atheism.* In fact, many major philosophers and scientists such as Michael Shermer (editor of *Skeptic*

magazine), Eugenie Scott (Director of the National Center for Science Education), and the famed Albert Einstein have argued that one cannot prove or disprove the existence of God or other spirits through the use of science. This methodological naturalism does not result in a conflict between faith and science. Faith and science are viewed as two separate spheres and modes of understanding the world. This method of naturalism coincides with the teachings of the Roman Catholic position and many of the mainstream Protestant, Jewish, Muslim, Hindu, and Buddhist teachings. In the Christian New Testament a passage states "Now faith is the assurance of things hoped for, the conviction of things not seen. By faith we understand that the worlds were prepared by the word of God, so that what is seen was made from things that are not visible" (Hebrews 11:1).

Yet, there are the multiple creationist teachings that *do* obviously conflict with scientific and evolutionary evidence. Can these religious views be falsified by science or logic? For example, anthropologists find that many Native American Indians do not accept scientific views of their past and evolution. Can the creationist views of the Navajo, Hopi, Cherokee, or any other spiritual views be falsified by science? Most scientists, philosophers, and theologians agree that science or logic cannot be used to falsify anyone's religious or spiritual views. This is one of the reasons that scientists oppose the teaching

of spiritual or creationist views in biology courses in the public schools. Whose spiritual or creationist view is the biologist going to teach without imposing one over the other spiritual view learned in a child's religious tradition?

The empirical findings in modern physics discussed in such books as Brian Green's *The Elegant Universe* or *The Fabric of the Cosmos* refer to parallel universes, twelve dimensions (rather than the three that we perceive in our everyday life), and other very strange and counterintuitive phenomena such as curved space. Scientific explanations do not usually answer or satisfy our cognitive intuitions or our deep spiritual questions and moral concerns. Most scientists, philosophers, and theologians agree that science can give us some basic answers about the universe and life, but given our limited cognitive capacities, the scientific method cannot reveal invisible factors or spiritual insights. And yet, a scientific perspective does tend to leave us in a state of "spiritual awe" as described by Darwin in the famous closing passage of the *Origin of Species*, "There is grandeur in this view of life."

POINTS TO PONDER

1. Have any of the scientific creationist claims convinced you of the falsity of evolution?

2. Do you think that faith and science are compatible when assessing the scientific record regarding evolution?

Michelangelo's painting in the Sistine Chapel shows the biblical tradition of human creation.

nostrils that are in almost the same plane as its eye sockets. Its face would resemble that of a modern gorilla today. Paleoanthropologists believe that this creature existed in Africa and Europe during the Miocene Epoch at about 13 million years ago (Moyá-Solá 2004).

Hominid Evolution

Anthropologists have been evaluating hypotheses regarding hominid evolution for the past 150 years (see Figure 2.1). **Hominids**, a family of primates that includes the direct ancestors of humans, share certain subtle features in their teeth, jaws, and brain. However, by far the major characteristic that identifies them as a distinct group is the structural anatomy needed for **bipedalism**, the ability to walk erect on two legs. Bipedalism is not a characteristic of modern apes, such as chimpanzees and gorillas, who can stand upright but do most of their walking on four limbs. Fossil evidence of the early evolution of the hominids remains very incomplete.

Recent fossil evidence discovered in 2001 and 2002 of hominids predating 4 million years ago in Kenya, Ethiopia, and Chad is fragmentary, but intriguing for understanding early evolution. The earliest dated fossil evidence for hominids was discovered in the country of Chad in Central Africa (Brunet, Guy, and Pilbeam 2002). The Chad find is especially notable, because it was recovered some 1,500 miles farther west than any other early hominid find. This hominid specimen is named *Sahelanthropus tchadensis.* The specimen is a complete, though distorted, cranium and is dated to approximately 7 mya (million years ago). It is, therefore, the oldest hominid fossils found so far, and the dental and cranial evidence does not link this hominid to any "missing link" between later hominids and ancestors of ancient chimpanzees. This fossil discovery in Chad challenges earlier hypotheses regarding the evolution of the early hominids and bipedalism because it was discovered east of the Rift Valley in East Africa, which was primarily tropical rain forest and not a savannah area. Earlier hypotheses connected the evolution of bipedalism and hominids as an adaptation to the savannah area coinciding with the climactic changes in the Rift Valley area of East Africa. Another collection of some of 110 fossils for a hominid discovered by paleoanthropologist Tim White and colleagues in Ethiopia and dated at 4.4 mya also present new

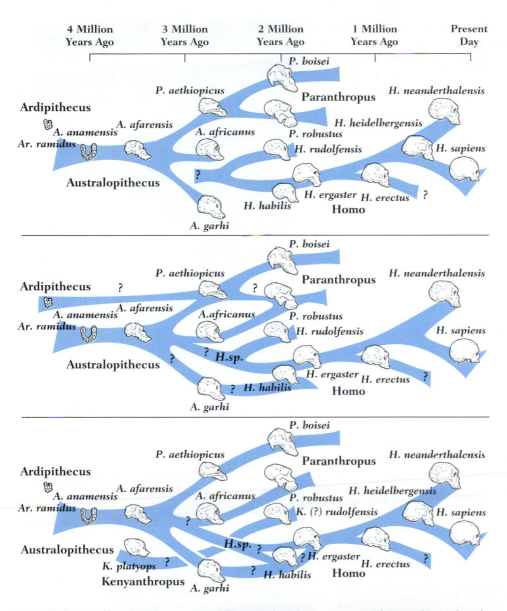

FIGURE 2.1 Different interpretations of hominid evolution. Various theories have placed *Australopithecus africanus* in a position ancestral to *Homo*, or to both *Homo* and later australopithecines. The robust australopithecines are placed on their own side branch. In 1979 Johanson and White named a new species, *A. afarensis*, which they placed at the base of the hominid family tree leading to both the australopithecines and *Homo*. *A. africanus* was then moved to a side branch leading to the robust australopithecines. Meave Leakey discovered *Kenyanthropus platyops* dated at 3.5 million.

models for early hominid evolution (White, Suwa, and Asfaw 1995). These fossils are so different from early australopithecines (described below) that they have been classified as a new genus *Ardipethecus ramidus*. *A. ramidus* fossils combine

apelike dentition with bipedal-like postcranial and cranial traits that suggest bipedalism.

Two other intriguing new fossil discoveries of early hominids were described in 2001, both from Kenya. The first is *Orrorin tugenensis*, a collection of postcranial and dental material dated at about 6 mya. Another early hominid fossil discovery in 2001, *Kenyanthropus platyops*, was found at Lake Turkana and dated at 3.5 mya by Meave Leakey and her team of paleoanthropologists (Leakey et al. 2001). These early hominid finds are fascinating because they suggest a common ancestry with the later evolution of our genus *Homo* rather than - *Australopithecus* described below. Thus, the field of paleoanthropology has been faced with new challenges in hypothesis testing, explaining, and interpreting these new fossil discoveries of early hominids.

Australopithecus

An enormous amount of fossil evidence for at least six different species of australopithecines has been discovered in Africa. The most complete early known form of this genus, found in the Afar region of Ethiopia, is known as *Australopithecus afarensis*. It was discovered in 1974 by a joint American–French team of paleoanthropologists led by Donald Johanson. The best-known *A. afarensis* individual is popularly known as "Lucy" (named after the Beatles' song "Lucy in the Sky with Diamonds"). Forty percent of the skeleton of this individual was preserved, allowing paleoanthropologists to determine its precise physical characteristics. Lucy is a female Australopithecus with features such as a small cranium, or skull—440 cubic centimeters (cc), compared with a capacity of 1,000 to 1,800 cc for modern humans—indicating a small brain and large teeth. Fragments of Lucy's skull resemble that of a modern chimpanzee; however, below the neck, the anatomy of the spine, pelvis, hips, thigh bones, and feet has characteristics of a bipedal creature, though one that did a lot of climbing also. Lucy was fairly small, weighing approximately 75 pounds, and was about 3.5 to 4 feet tall. Lucy is dated at 2.9 mya.

There are many other *A. afarensis* fossils, including skulls that have been discovered. For example, other important discoveries at Hadar came in 1975 at a fossil locality known as site 333. Johanson and his crew found many hominid bones scattered along a hillside. Painstakingly piecing them together, the researchers reconstructed thirteen individuals, including both adults and infants, with anatomical characteristics similar to those of Lucy. Experts hypothesize that these finds may represent

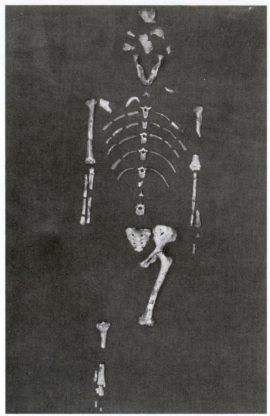

The skeletal remains of "Lucy" Australopithecus afarensis.

one social group that died at the same time, perhaps during a flash flood (Johanson and Edey 1981). The *Australopithecus afarensis* fossils discovered at Hadar have been dated between 3 million and 4 million years ago, making these some of the earliest well-described hominid remains.

Another species of *Australopithecus* was found in the mid-1990s by Meave Leakey, also near Lake Turkana in Kenya (Leakey et al. 1995). It is called *Australopithecus anamensis* and is older than *A. afarensis* at 3.9–4.2 mya. It fits pretty well with what we have expected for a species that predates *afarensis*—generally very similar but with more apelike dental features.

Other early hominid fossils further complicate the evolution of these australopithecines, including *A. africanus, A. aethiopicus, A. boisei,* and *A. garhi.* Another group of fossils used to be identified as *A. robustus,* but further studies indicate that this "robust" form of hominid is much different than other australopithecines and has now been reclassified as *Paranthropus*, including three different species, *P. robustus*, *P. boisei*, and *P. aethiopicus* dated between 1.8 and 1 mya. All these new discoveries of early hominids have resulted in a very complex picture of hominid evolution that emphasizes a lot of diversity expected within these different hominids and what paleoanthropologists emphasize as "bushiness." Instead of a ladderlike, unidirectional evolution of bipedal hominids from simple to complex or progressive forms, there were multiple species of these creatures between 7 and 1 mya roaming East and South Africa. This same pattern of bushiness prevails when paleoanthropologists investigate the later evolution of hominids also.

Homo

As mentioned before, a major challenge for paleoanthropologists is to determine which of these branches of hominids led to the major branch of the genus Homo, which includes two different species, *H. rudolfensis* and *H. habilis* (though contemporary paleoanthropologists differ on whether these hominids are one or two species). The fossil evidence for both species is located throughout South and East Africa. The average size of the skull of *H. habilis* is 640 cc, indicating a much larger brain than that of the australopithecines. *H. habilis* dates from between 2.2 million and 1.6 million years ago; it therefore also coexisted with later species of australopithecines. This is what would be expected in an evolutionary perspective.

Oldowan Technology   At several sites in eastern and southern Africa, archaeologists have discovered early stone tools known as *chopper tools* or *hammer stones*. Hammer stone tools were used to knock off "flakes" to form "cores" (or choppers), which then could be used for making more tools. This technique is referred to by archaeologists as *percussion flaking*. Called Oldowan tools (because they were first discovered at Olduvai Gorge in Tanzania), these tools could be used for cutting the hides of animals and perhaps whittling wood for making wooden spears or digging sticks (though no evidence of wood remains).

Archaeologists are not definitely sure whether the Oldowan tools are associated with australopithecines or *H. habilis*. The importance of the

discovery of the Oldowan tools is that the tools suggest early hominids had the intellectual capacity to fashion stone tools to develop a more effective means of subsistence. This innovation indicates an increased brain size, which led, in turn, to new forms of complex learning. The Oldowan technology marks the beginnings of what is known as the Lower Paleolithic period of hominid evolution, or the earliest period of the Old Stone Age. The oldest Paleolithic stone tools (some 300 in all) come from a site in Gona in Ethiopia and are dated to 2.5 mya (Semaw et al. 1997; de la Torre 2004).

Homo erectus

Other early fossil findings of hominid evolution have been discovered both inside and outside of Africa. In China, Java (a major island in Indonesia), the Middle East, Europe, and Africa, paleoanthropologists have investigated fossil remains of a hominid population known as *Homo erectus*. These finds date to between 1.8 million and 250,000 years ago. In early periods in Africa, *H. erectus* coexisted with other species of earlier hominids such as *Paranthropus boisei*. Currently, paleoanthropologists are in disagreement about the fossils of *H. erectus* discovered in Germany in 1907 as to whether it should be considered a separate species called *H. heidelbergensis* (discovered in Heidelberg, Germany).

Anatomically, *H. erectus* fossils represent a major new stage of hominid evolution, especially with respect to brain size. The cranial capacity of *H. erectus* ranges between 895 and 1,040 cc, making the skull size of some of these individuals smaller than that of modern humans (Kramer 2002). This evidence indicates that most of the growth in brain size occurred in the frontal lobes, an area associated with intellectual skills (Wolpoff and Caspari 1997). The populations of *H. erectus* differed from modern humans in that they had a low, sloping forehead and thick, massive jaws with large teeth. From the neck down, their skeletal features are similar to those of modern humans, but their bones are much heavier, indicating a very powerful musculature. During this period of hominid evolution there appears to be very little anatomical change among the *H. erectus*.

Migration of *Homo erectus*   Given that the early hominids lived in Africa, the question arises of how *H. erectus* became so widely dispersed throughout the world. The major hypothesis is that as populations increased, a certain percentage migrated into new territories by a process known as budding (Anton and Swisher 2004). Through this process, a few individuals would split from an original group and form a new, autonomous group in a more favorable territory. If each budding group moved 15 miles in each generation (25 years), then *H. erectus* could have migrated from Africa to Europe in 5,000 years and to China in 15,000 years.

As these populations migrated across continents, they encountered different climates and environments. This movement occurred during a period known as the Pleistocene epoc, which marked the later stages of what we popularly call the Ice Ages. At intervals during this time, huge masses of ice, called glaciers, spread over the northern continents, producing colder climates in the temperate zones such as Europe and northern Asia and increases in rainfall in the tropical areas, creating grasslands and new lakes. *H. erectus* populations had to adapt to a wide variety of climatic and environmental conditions whether they remained in the tropics, as many did, or migrated to new areas of the world.

Fire *Homo erectus* probably could not have survived in the colder climates without the use of fire. The earliest use of fire, however, appears to be in Africa (Sillen and Brain 1990). Later, fire was also associated with *H. erectus* sites in both Europe and in Asia. The use of fire to cook food added an important element to the diet. Cooking food made it more digestible and safer to consume. In addition, fires could be used to keep predators away, enabling *H. erectus* to survive more effectively. It is unclear whether *H. erectus* knew how to make fire (fire begun by lightning or forest fires could have been kept lit), but there is no question that fire was controlled.

Acheulian Technology An abundance of stone tools associated with *H. erectus* indicates a remarkable evolution in technology. This new technology is known as the Acheulian. The Acheulian is named after the town of St. Acheul, France, where some of the first finds were made. Like the Oldowan choppers, Acheulian tools were produced by percussion flaking, but they exhibit more complexity. Most characteristic of the Acheulian is the hand ax, a sharp, bifacially flaked stone tool shaped like a large almond,

which would have been effective for a variety of chopping and cutting tasks. Unlike Oldowan choppers, which consisted of natural cobbles with a few flakes removed, the hand ax was fashioned by removing many flakes to produce a specific form. In other words, the toolmaker had to be able to picture a specific shape in a stone. Late Acheulian tools were produced through a more refined brand of percussion flaking, the *baton method*. In this technique a hammer, or baton, of bone or antler was used to strike off flakes. The baton allowed for more accurate flaking and produced shallower, more delicate flakes than a hammer stone. This Acheulian technology is found throughout areas of Africa and Europe, with scattered remains as far east as China.

The tools produced through this technology made *H. erectus* efficient hunters, able to kill large game animals such as bear, deer, and elephant, as well as smaller game. Major *H. erectus* sites in Spain and East Africa have evidence of hunters butchering various types of animals that are killed (Fagan and DeCorse 2005). Thus, the Acheulian technology made possible a more effective means of subsistence, which required both cooperative and intellectual efforts. Most paleoanthropologists suggest that improvements in language and modes of communication probably began to evolve with the *H. erectus* lifestyle. Undoubtedly, the increase in brain size, especially in the frontal lobes, indicates a capacity for more complex learning and possibly linguistic abilities. The capacity for communication would have aided cooperation in activities such as hunting and improvements in technological development. The *H. erectus* period of hominid evolution represents a very complex adaptation to the conditions of the Pleistocene epoch.

An Ancient Hobbit?

A recent amazing and astonishing discovery of fossil evidence in the small island of Flores in Indonesia appears to have dramatically changed the traditional paleoanthropological view of hominid evolution and *Homo erectus*. As suggested previously, *Homo erectus* spread out of Africa some 2 million years ago and paleoanthropologists found evidence of this hominid in Europe, China, and the Indonesian island of Java. However, in a small cave called Liang Bua on the island of Flores in Indonesia, a new species of hominid was found by

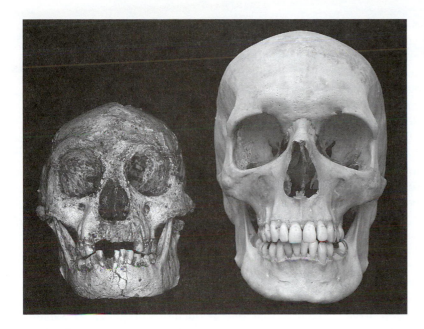

This photo shows the differences between Homo floresiensis *(left) and modern* Homo sapiens *(right) skulls.*

Australian paleoanthropologist Peter Brown and a team of Indonesian paleoanthropologists (2004). This hominid was only about 3 feet tall and had a small cranium of only 380 cc, less than one-half of the size of *Homo erectus.* This creature has a mixture of primitive and advanced physical traits. The brain is about the size of a chimpanzee or an *Australopithecus afarensis* like Lucy, but the facial characteristics are much more delicate and similar to a modern human. The teeth are also very similar to modern human teeth. Because of the small size of this creature, it has been referred to popularly as a "hobbit," in reference to the small creatures of the British author J. R. R. Tolkien's *Lord of the Rings.* The scientific name of this creature is *Homo floresiensis* (or man of Flores, although the skeletal material actually seems more female).

Two different sophisticated dating methods were used and both resulted in a date of about 18,000 years ago. The implication of this date for this small "hobbit" creature means that modern *Homo sapiens* (discussion to follow) may have coexisted with these creatures at some point. The leading hypothesis at this time is that *Homo erectus* could have reached the island some one million years ago to hunt small dwarf elephants, or *stegodon,* and Komodo dragons (fossil evidence of these extinct creatures are abundant in Flores). However, through isolation and perhaps inbreeding, a whole new species of dwarf "hobbit" creatures emerged on this small island. This process has been found for other small isolated animals too. After 100,000 years, as more modern *Homo sapiens* began to populate the islands of Indonesia, these creatures eventually became extinct. Yet, the origins of these creatures may extend back as far as 800,000 years ago, as some stone tools have been dated from Flores at that time. These new startling fossil finds have paleoanthropologists continuing their investigations into this region of Indonesia for new evidence to gain a more comprehensive picture of what may have occurred in early hominid evolution. They are also trying to find DNA in the fossil bones to extract it to help clarify the links between these small creatures and other hominids. Paleoanthropologists also discovered some preserved hair that may have DNA that could be used to determine how close to modern *Homo sapiens* this "hobbit" creature is.

"Premodern" or Archaic *Homo sapiens*

The fossil evidence for the next major period of hominid evolution—archaic *Homo sapiens*—is dated from about 300,000 to 35,000 years ago, although a recent discovery in Spain called *Homo antecessor* is dated at around 800,000 years ago and may be an ancestor of *Homo neanderthalensis* and modern humans (Castro et al. 1997). The "premodern" or archaic *Homo sapiens* were widespread in over 60 sites throughout Europe (including England), Africa, Asia, and the Middle East and represent challenges in understanding our genealogical connections with these early hominids. The best-known example is the Neandertal, or *H. neanderthalensis*, the hominid population that lived in Europe about 300,000 to 30,000 years ago. Because of inconclusive evidence, some paleoanthropologists include this species within our own as *H. sapiens neanderthalensis* (Trinkaus and Shipman 1993; Tattersall 1999; Mellars 1998).

Physically, all archaic *H. sapiens* populations shared some general characteristics, although distinctive variations existed from region to region. The skeletal evidence suggests that they were short, about five feet tall, but powerfully built. The hands and feet were wider and thicker than those of modern humans. The skull and face were broad, with a larger jaw, larger teeth, and extremely prominent brow ridges. The Neandertal physique, which is very distinct from other archaic *H. sapiens*, has become the model for the stereotype of "cavemen" frequently portrayed in cartoons and other popular entertainment.

This image of a brutish prehistoric creature is misleading. The skull of the Neandertal was large, ranging from 1,200 cc to 2,000 cc, and could accommodate a brain as large as, or even larger than, that of a modern human. Moreover, recent studies of the Neandertal skull indicate that the structure of the brain was essentially the same as that of modern humans, suggesting similar intellectual capacities. Recently, a portion of DNA was extracted from a Neandertal discovered in Germany and was compared with the DNA from modern human populations. The comparison of DNA showed that the Neandertal was genetically distinct from modern humans (Kring et al. 1997). This finding conforms to the differences found in the skeletal anatomy between Neandertals and modern humans.

Neandertal Technology The stone tool industry associated with Neandertal populations is called the **Mousterian tradition**, named after a rock shelter at Le Moustier, France, where it was first described. It shows a remarkable variability compared with earlier technologies. Mousterian implements could have been used for cutting, leather working, piercing, food processing, woodworking, hunting, and producing weapons (Binford and Binford 1966; Bordes 1972; Hayden 1993). Neandertals also must have been capable of making some type of clothing, or else they would not have been able to survive the cold European climate. In addition, archaeologists have discovered evidence of the extensive occupation of caves and rock shelters, as well as open-air sites that may have been temporary camps occupied during the summer months. Archaeological evidence includes the remains of charcoal deposits and charred bones, indicating that, like earlier *H. erectus*, Neandertals used fire not only for warmth but also for cooking and perhaps for protection against dangerous animals.

The remains discovered at the Neandertal sites suggest that, like populations of archaic *H. sapiens* in other areas, Neandertals were efficient hunters. They hunted both small and large game, including such extinct creatures as European elephants, giant elk, bison, and huge bears weighing up to 1,500 pounds and standing over 12 feet high. These bears, related to the Alaskan brown bear, are known as "cave bears" and were formidable prey for Neandertal hunters.

Neandertal Ritual and Beliefs? Study of Neandertal sites has also given archaeologists the first hints of activities beyond hunting-gathering and the struggle for subsistence—possible evidence that Neandertals practiced rituals. Regrettably, much of this evidence, portrayed in countless movies, novels, and caricatures, is far more circumstantial than archaeologists would like. Finds that have been examined include both bear bones and Neandertal artifacts. From Drachenlock Cave in Switzerland, it was even reported that twenty bear skulls had been found in an arrangement of stone slabs— a discovery interpreted as a crude shrine. Some writers have used these discoveries to paint a complex picture of Neandertal ritual.

Despite the romantic appeal of a Neandertal "cave bear cult," however, these interpretations lack the most important thing archaeologists need to glean insights into such complex issues as prehistoric ritual beliefs: clearly documented archaeological context (Chase and Dibble 1987; Trinkaus and Shipman 1994). In the absence of clear associations

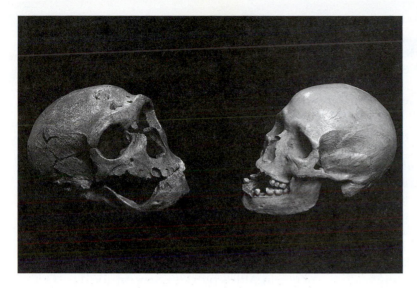

This photo shows the difference between Neandertal (left) and the modern Homo sapiens (right) skulls. There are demonstrable differences in morphology.

between the bear bones and the tools, this evidence suggests only that Neandertals visited a cave in which bears may have hibernated and occasionally died. The Drachenlock Cave finds were not excavated by trained archaeologists, and no plans or photographs of the discovery were made at the time of excavation (Rowley-Conwy 1993). Without this information, interpretation of a Neandertal shrine remains entirely speculative.

More convincing than the evidence for a bear cult are discoveries suggesting that Neandertals were the first hominids to intentionally bury their dead. Finds at a number of sites—including Shanidar, Iraq; Teshik-Tash, Uzbekistan; La Chapelle-aux-Saints, France; and Kebara, Israel (Rowley-Conwy 1993; Trinkaus 1999)—have been interpreted as burials. Of these finds, the evidence for intentional burial is most compelling at the French and Israeli sites. In both instances, the skeleton of a Neandertal man was found in a pit that seems to be too regular in shape to have been formed naturally. However, currently archaeologists and paleoanthropologists are divided on whether these are actually intentional burials. More evidence is needed to completely understand these Neandertal burial sites.

Other skeletal evidence indicates that Neandertals cared for individuals with disabilities. At the Shanidar site, for example, archaeologists identified the remains of one individual who had the use of only one arm—the result of an accident or a birth defect. Despite that disability, this individual lived a relatively long life. Although no set of ritual beliefs can be inferred on the basis of these finds, they clearly do indicate the growing group communication, social complexity, and awareness that distinguish humans.

Modern *Homo sapiens*

The first anatomically "modern" *H. sapiens* began to appear about 100,000 years ago in Africa and the Middle East. Between 60,000 and 10,000 years ago, these populations migrated to places all over the globe, adapting both physically and culturally to conditions in different regions. Physically, these modern *Homo sapiens* populations were much the same as modern humans. These fossilized skeletons do not have the heavy, thick bones, large teeth, and prominent brow ridges associated with the Neandertals and other archaic forms. The high, vaulted shape of the skull is modern, and the dimensions are similar to those of modern-day humans. From the cold climates of northern Asia to the deserts of Africa, groups of *H. sapiens* shared similar characteristics as part of one species. However, like populations today, these early groups developed different physical traits, such as body size and facial features, as a result of local environmental conditions and selective pressures.

The Evolution of Modern *Homo sapiens*   Although paleoanthropologists generally agree that *H. erectus* evolved into *H. sapiens*, they disagree about how, where, and when this transition took place. Early interpretations were based on limited information and often emphasized the uniqueness of individual finds. More recent researchers have offered a number of different theories (Howell 1976; Stringer and Andrews 1988; Mellars 1989). Two general models representing opposing perspectives have been developed as hypotheses to be tested: the *multiregional evolutionary model* and the *replacement model* (see Figure 2.2).

The multiregional evolutionary model suggests that the gradual evolution of *H. erectus* into modern *H. sapiens* took place in different regions of the Old World. Evolutionary processes affected genetic variation in local *H. erectus* populations, creating regional variation. In this context, *H. sapiens* traits first appeared in certain areas, but widespread sharing of genes between populations prevented the evolution of distinct species. The emergence of modern *H. sapiens* was, therefore, a widespread phenomenon, though different regional populations continued to exhibit distinctive features. Some fossil evidence from Southeast Asia and China support this particular hypothesis.

The *replacement model* suggests that modern *H. sapiens* evolved in one area of the world (Africa) and migrated to other regions, where the species replaced earlier *H. sapiens* such as the Neandertal. Thus, this hypothesis proposes that *modern H. sapiens* populations are all descended from a common ancestral group; consequently, the diversity among modern humans is marginally small (Stringer 1993).

This replacement hypothesis has sometimes been referred to as the "Eve hypothesis" in the media, because it suggests that there is a direct genetic link between a woman or a group of women in Africa about 200,000 years ago and modern *H. sapiens*. This model was based on primarily genetic evidence, (MtDNA molecular samples from populations of women throughout the world) (Cann et al. 1987). In addition, some fossil evidence in Africa provides support for this "Out of Africa" hypothesis. However, since that time other geneticists and paleoanthropologists have discovered complexities in both the fossil and genetic evidence that suggests more intermediate models that refine the replacement model. Thus, we need much more evidence and evaluation to provide a more comprehensive understanding of the emergence of modern humans.

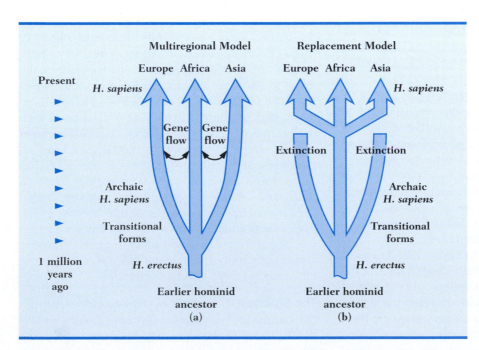

FIGURE 2.2 Two different interpretations of the emergence of *H. sapiens*. The multiregional evolutionary model (a) suggests regional continuity and the gradual evolution of all *H. erectus* and archaic *H. sapiens* populations into modern humans. In contrast, supporters of the replacement model (b) see modern humans as evolving in one world area and spreading out, replacing earlier hominid populations.

Modern *Homo sapiens* Culture: The Upper Paleolithic

In general, the material artifacts associated with modern *H. sapiens* populations become increasingly complex. Throughout Africa, the Middle East, Asia, the Americas, and Australia, complicated and elaborate technologies and other culturally decorative artifacts are found in abundance. This period is called the **Upper Paleolithic**; the term Paleolithic refers to "Old Stone Age," whereas Upper indicates the later period of this era. The Upper Paleolithic dates between the time period of 40,000 and 10,000 years ago, approximately.

The technological and social innovations of the Upper Paleolithic represent a creative explosion in technology. Innovation of this magnitude required a highly developed capacity for the accumulation and transmission of knowledge, likely indicating that the inhabitants had developed efficient subsistence strategies that allowed free time for experimentation and innovation.

Tools

These different Upper Paleolithic traditions encompass a tremendous amount of variation in stone tool types. The most important technological shift in stone tool production involved the making of blades: long, narrow flakes that could be used to produce many types of knives, harpoons, and spear points. Among the most striking examples of Upper Paleolithic percussion flaking are Solutrean projectiles, dated to 20,000 years ago. These implements, often several inches long, probably functioned as spear points. Yet the flaking is so delicate and the points so sharp that it is difficult to imagine them fastened to the end of a spear. It has, in fact, been suggested that they were made as works of art, not tools for everyday use.

In addition, specialized stone tools, including borers, or drills, and burins, chisel-like tools for working bone or ivory, were produced. Tools such as these would have aided in the manufacture of the bone, antler, and ivory artifacts that become increasingly common during the Upper Paleolithic. A particularly important piece of equipment that appeared during this time period is the spear-thrower (or *atlatl*, the Aztec word for this tool), a piece of wood or ivory that increased the power of the hunter's arm. The increased leverage provided by the spear-thrower enabled Upper Paleolithic hunters to hurl projectiles much faster than they could otherwise.

Another category of artifact that became common is the **composite tool**, an implement fashioned from several different materials. An example of a composite tool is the harpoon, which might consist of a wooden shaft that is slotted for the insertion of sharp stone flakes. Also discovered at Upper Paleolithic sites were needles for sewing clothing, and fibers for making rope, nets, trapping equipment, and many other artifacts.

Shelters Upper Paleolithic sites have also produced numerous indications of shelters, some of which were quite elaborate, in many parts of the world. Some of the more spectacular were found at a 15,000-year-old site at Mezhirich in the Ukraine. This site contained five shelters constructed of bones from mammoths, an extinct species of elephant (Gladkih et al. 1984). The mammoth's jaws were used as the base, and the ribs, tusks, and other bones were used for the sides. The interiors contained work areas, hearths, and accumulations of artifacts, suggesting that they were inhabited for long periods. Storage pits were located in areas between the structures. This settlement may have been occupied by as many as fifty people.

Variation in Upper Paleolithic Technologies

Variations in tools found in different regions suggest that early humans had developed specialized technologies suited to particular environments. These variations also reflect the fact that different regions contained different forms of stone from which tools could be manufactured. In addition, regional differences may also reflect variations in culture, ethnicity, and individual expression. Archaeologist James Sackett, who has studied the classic Middle and Upper Paleolithic finds of France, notes that even tools that may have served the same function exhibit a great deal of variation (1982). Many Upper Paleolithic artisans made their

Reconstruction of an Upper Paleolithic dwelling constructed with mammoth bones.

stone tools in distinctive styles that varied from region to region. Today we often associate distinctive dress, decoration, and housing with different ethnic groups. To archaeologists, expressions of ethnic identity preserved in material remains are extremely important. Frequently we refer to archaeological cultures, which are defined on the basis of the distinctive artifacts they left behind. Stone tools may provide the first indications of ethnic and cultural divisions in human populations.

Expressive elements are also seen in other Upper Paleolithic artifacts. In comparison with the Middle Paleolithic, there are more nonutilitarian objects, including items for personal adornment (White 1982). Some of these artifacts were obtained from distant sources, providing evidence of the development of trade networks.

Upper Paleolithic Subsistence and Social Organization

Middle and Upper Paleolithic societies employed many of the same subsistence strategies as had Lower Paleolithic groups. The Upper Paleolithic technology indicates that early modern *H. sapiens* were efficient hunters. Many sites contain large heaps of bones of mammoths and other animals. In addition, piles of animal bones have been found at the bottoms of high cliffs, which suggests that *H. sapiens* hunters had stampeded the animals off cliffs to be killed and butchered by hunters waiting below. Archaeologists have also found remains of

traps used by Upper Paleolithic hunters to snare animals.

Upper Paleolithic people also gathered plants to supplement their food resources. Plants were probably used for both nutritional and medicinal purposes. However, the generally small size of Upper Paleolithic living areas and the limited amount of plant remains recovered from archaeological sites provide only an incomplete view of diet during that period.

Social Organization One way to develop hypotheses about the lifestyle and social organization of prehistoric people is to study the social organization of contemporary groups with similar subsistence strategies (Price and Brown 1985). Anthropologists recognize, however, the limitations of this approach. Present-day hunters and gatherers occupy marginal areas such as the dry desert regions of southern Africa. In contrast, Paleolithic foraging populations resided in all types of environments, many of which were rich in food resources. Most likely, these abundant food resources enabled Paleolithic foragers to gather adequate food supplies without expending excessive amounts of energy.

Contemporary foraging societies, with their relatively small groups, low population density, highly nomadic subsistence strategies, and loosely defined territorial boundaries, have social organizations that serve to tie kin (related individuals) together and foster unity within and among groups. In the past, these flexible social relationships may have enabled foragers to overcome ecological and organizational problems.

Whether ethnographic data on the social organization of "modern" foragers can instruct us on the type of social systems Paleolithic foragers had is as yet an open question. Some archaeological studies suggest that the size of domestic groups of Paleolithic societies corresponds to that of contemporary foragers (Pfeiffer 1985; Campbell 1987), but other anthropologists suggest that ethnographic models underestimate the diversity of prehistoric hunting and gathering adaptations. They also point out that modern hunter-gatherer societies may have been greatly modified through recent encounters with the outside world. We return to this topic in Chapter 7.

The Upper Paleolithic in Africa and Europe

Changes seen in the Upper Paleolithic period in both Africa and Europe are indicative of developments in much of the world. The best-known people of the Upper Paleolithic in Europe are the Cro-Magnon. The name Cro-Magnon comes from a site in Dordogne, France, dated at about 25,000 years ago. The fragmentary remains of five or six individuals recovered from a rock shelter in 1868 provided the first evidence for what was initially identified as the Cro-Magnon. The Cro-Magnon remains are typified by the skull of the so-called Old Man, which belonged to an adult male less than 50 years of age. The skull is high and vaulted, with a cranial capacity of approximately 1,600 cc. Other skulls in the collection display a combination of archaic and modern traits. Some have heavy bones and developed brow ridges, suggesting similarities with Neandertals.

The finds at Cro-Magnon are not associated with any particular group sharing physical characteristics. Skeletal remains bearing many similar features have been found in other parts of western Europe and North Africa, as have tool remains comparable to those found at Cro-Magnon. The different Cro-Magnon sites contain artifacts that demonstrate an elaborate technology, far superior to that of previous societies.

Cro-Magnon Culture In Europe about 17,000 years ago, some Cro-Magnon groups became specialists in procuring game from migrating herds of reindeer. These groups established summer camps, perhaps with lightweight tents built on rises that provided a good view of the herds. In the winter the groups would relocate in smaller groupings back in the warmth and shelter of the caves.

Another critical element of Cro-Magnon technology was the ability to start a fire whenever one was needed. Cro-Magnons used materials such as iron pyrite to make sparks to ignite dry tinder. Archaeological evidence for this mastery of fire is widespread, ranging from Belgium to the heartland of Russia. Hearths are found in caves and sometimes in open-air sites with remnants of shelters. Many of these sites contained charred wood and large quantities of bone ash, indicating that Cro-Magnons used fire for cooking as well as for heat.

In addition to their other technological accomplishments, the Upper Paleolithic peoples of both Africa and Europe (and elsewhere, as seen later) produced an impressive array of artistic creations. In Africa, large naturalistic paintings have been dated at 28,000 years ago (Philipson 1993). Thousands of bone, ivory, and stone sculptures of anatomically elaborate figures, including some known as the

Upper Paleolithic Venus figurine statue.

Venus fertility goddesses, (female figurines with large hips, large breasts, and abdomens indicating fertility) are found throughout Europe. As in Africa, mural paintings found in the caves of Spain and France, such as those of the Lascaux Caves, are magnificent abstract and naturalistic paintings of animals and sometimes of humans dressed in the hides of animals. These murals might have been intended to celebrate a successful hunt or to ensure a better future. That some murals are located deep within underground caves may indicate that this art held profound spiritual and religious significance for its creators. What could be a more awe-inspiring site for a religious celebration or initiation ceremony than a dark underground chamber with beautiful paintings? On the other hand, some art may in essence be "art for art's sake," painted solely for enjoyment (Halverson 1987).

Migration of Upper Paleolithic Humans

Upper Paleolithic hunters and gatherers developed specialized technologies that helped them to adapt to different environments in ways their precursors could not have. The remarkable abilities of modern *H. sapiens* to exploit such a wide variety of environments enabled these peoples to increase their populations, leading to modern human habitation of all parts of the globe. During the Upper Paleolithic, modern *H. sapiens* migrated throughout the world, including North and South America and Australia, continents that had previously been unoccupied by hominids.

The movement of modern *H. sapiens* populations into new areas was aided by changes in world climatic conditions during the past 100,000 years. This period encompasses the latter part of the Pleistocene, or Ice Age, when climatic conditions were much cooler and moister than they are now. Northern Europe, Asia, and North America were covered by glaciers, which were extensions of the polar ice caps. The vast amount of water frozen in these glaciers lowered world sea levels by hundreds of feet, exposing vast tracks of land, known as continental shelves, that were previously (and are currently) beneath the sea. Many world areas that are today surrounded by water were at that time connected to other areas.

Upper Paleolithic Hunters in America Archaeologists believe that the first humans came to the Western Hemisphere from Siberia over what is now the Bering Strait into the area of modern Alaska. Following herds of large game animals, these people migrated southward into North and South America. Today, the Bering Strait is a frigid body of water connecting the Pacific and Arctic oceans. Between 75,000 and 11,500 years ago, however, the glaciers and lower sea levels transformed this region on several occasions into a land mass more than 1,000 miles wide known as Beringia (Hopkins 1982). Beringia served as a natural land bridge connecting Asia with North America. However, some archaeologists think that some of these early migrants may have sailed down the coast of the Americas along the ice formations located along the Pacific Ocean.

The Asian origin of Native Americans is supported by several lines of evidence, including physical similarities such as blood type and tooth shape and DNA comparisons between Asian and Native American populations. In addition, studies of the languages spoken and artifacts discovered in both areas indicate a common origin.

Although most anthropologists agree that Native Americans migrated from Asia, they do not agree on when this migration occurred; the estimates run from 30,000 to 12,000 years ago. The most recent archaeological research from a site in Chile and sites in Pennsylvania, South Carolina, and Virginia indicate that the date of 30,000 years ago for settlement of the Americas is more likely (Dillehay 1997a, 1997b; Carr et al. 1996; Goodyear 1999). Eventually, these early Native American peoples, known as *Paleo-Indians*, populated most of the areas of what is known today as the United States, Canada, and Mexico. They produced a complex set of tools and subsistence hunting-gathering strategies that enabled them to adapt to the environment of the last period of the Ice Ages in Pleistocene America.

Human Variation

As we have seen, modern *H. sapiens* populations migrated throughout the world, adjusting to different environmental conditions. As different populations settled in different environments, they developed certain variations in physical characteristics as a result of natural selection and other evolutionary processes. Although *H. sapiens* is one species, some physical differences exist among groups. Variations occur with respect to body size, eye color, hair texture and color, shape of lips and nose, blood type, and eyelid form. In certain cases, these characteristics are related to the types of selective pressures that existed in a particular environment; in other cases, they are simply the result of physical isolation in certain areas during past eras.

Skin Color

An obvious physical trait that varies in humans is skin pigmentation. Skin pigmentation became the primary basis for classifying different populations into different races for many people throughout the world (see Chapter 7). In general usage, the term *race* refers to the physical characteristics of a population that are based on common descent. As we see in Chapter 7, anthropologists have been attempting to classify and measure physical characteristics of differing populations for more than two centuries. One eighteenth-century approach placed all peoples in one of four racial categories: Europeans (white), Americans (red), Asiatics (yellow), and Africans (black). These early attempts to classify humans by skin color led to stereotypes among Europeans regarding different human populations.

Modern classifications, which are based on more scientific knowledge of genetics, evolution, and geography, sometimes include hundreds of racial categories (Garn 1971). However, modern physical anthropologists have concluded that any system of racial classification is too rigid and inflexible to deal with the actual dynamics of population movement, genetic change, intermarriage, and other conditions affecting the physical characteristics of a population (Templeton 1998; MacEachern 2003; Scupin 2003).

In general, however, it does appear that a dark pigmentation provides protection from ultraviolet radiation, which can cause sunburn, sunstroke, and skin cancers such as melanoma. In addition, large amounts of melanin, which protects the skin, also aid in preserving the amount of Vitamin B complex needed for successful reproduction of healthy infants (Jablonski and Chaplin 2000). Originally, as *H. sapiens* evolved in the tropical zones near the equator, a darker skin pigmentation most likely proved adaptive. But later, as populations moved into more temperate regions with less sunlight, other selective pressures produced lighter skin pigmentations. For example, the human need for Vitamin D may have played an important role. Vitamin D helps the body absorb calcium and deposit it in bones, an important function, especially in fast-growing embryos. Insufficiency of Vitamin D can result in the disease known as rickets, a disease that causes abnormal growth of bones. People living in equatorial regions with ample exposure to direct ultraviolet radiation from the sun that stimulates the production of Vitamin D would be able to have dark skin coloration. In contrast, people who had migrated to northern climates and wore heavy clothing would have been disadvantaged in obtaining enough direct ultraviolet radiation to get enough Vitamin D. The fossil record indicates that some Neandertals in northern Europe had rickets (Boaz and Almquist 1997). Thus, over time natural selection would have favored the development of a lighter-skinned population among *H. sapiens* groups in these northern regions.

Physical anthropologists have found that within the indigenous native populations of the world, the weaker the ultraviolet light, the fairer the skin, and the stronger the ultraviolet light, the darker the skin (Jablonski and Chaplin 2000; Jablonski 2004; Holden 2000). These observations, along with other data from a variety of studies, indicate that environmental conditions were important in selecting for adaptations in skin coloration in different regions of the world (Relethford 1997).

It must be emphasized that these physical variations among modern *H. sapiens* populations are only "skin deep." In fact, geneticists believe that only a few genes out of less than 30,000 code for skin color. Racial theories claiming the supposed superiority of certain groups over others have no scientific basis. Except for general similarities in color and body size, individuals in any given population differ widely from one another in respect to longevity, vitality, athletic ability, intelligence, and other personal characteristics. All populations throughout the world produce individuals who differ widely in their physical and mental abilities. Racism or ethnic prejudice based on the belief in the superiority or inferiority of a particular group is unjustifiable, not only morally but also scientifically.

Variation in skin pigmentation among humans reflect adaptations to Paleolithic environments with different amounts and intensities of sunlight.

SUMMARY

All peoples have explanations for the origins of the universe and humankind. Following the scientific revolution in the West, various developments in the natural sciences led to what is known as the Darwinian revolution. Charles Darwin and Alfred Wallace developed separately the model of natural selection to explain the origins and development of life. Later scientific developments in the field of genetics, along with the ideas of natural selection, are used by modern scientists to explain the evolution of life.

Paleoanthropologists have been investigating hominid evolution for more than 150 years. Many different early species of hominid fossils have been discovered in East and South Africa. A number of early species known as Australopithecines existed in Africa at least 4 million years ago. These creatures were fully bipedal. Other later hominids, referred to as *Homo habilis*, were discovered in Africa and are associated with toolmaking.

Later hominids, known as *Homo erectus*, were dispersed across several continents, including Africa, Europe, and Asia. *H. erectus* had a large brain and is associated with a sophisticated technology that includes the use of fire. The fossil record indicates that by 200,000 years ago, populations of hominids known as archaic *Homo sapiens* inhabited different regions of the world. One example of archaic *Homo sapiens* is referred to as Neandertal. Neandertal is associated with a refined material culture that includes various types of stone tools, fire, clothing, and perhaps religious rituals and beliefs.

Anatomically modern *H. sapiens* date to as early as 90,000 years ago. The technology of modern *H. sapiens* is referred to as the Upper Paleolithic. Many different types of specialized tools were developed in different environments in the Upper Paleolithic. In addition, cave paintings, sculpture, and engravings are associated with this period.

Paleoanthropologists and geneticists are trying to determine the evolutionary relationships of archaic and anatomically modern *H. sapiens*. One of the most recent hypotheses is based on genetic data from modern females that indicates an ancestral line in Africa dating to about 200,000 years ago. Many leading scientists have questioned the basic tenets of this genetic model. Much more research needs to be done on this important question.

As modern humans adjusted to different environments, natural selection continued to play a role in determining physical characteristics. For example, variations in skin pigmentation reflect adaptations to environments with different amounts and intensities of sunlight. However, modern scientific evidence demonstrates that skin color does not correspond to any difference in the mental capacities of any population.

QUESTIONS TO THINK ABOUT

1. Your parents have phoned you to find out how things are going at college (translation: Do you need money?) and what you are studying. You tell them that you are learning about early hominids, the Australopithecines, *Homo habilis*, and *Homo erectus*. Your mother and father say, "I just can't believe that we came from chimpanzees!" How do you answer them?

2. What is natural selection, and how does it work? Give an example of natural selection in action.

3. Where were the earliest hominids found? Describe the hominid "Lucy."

4. Discuss the emergence of the species *Homo erectus*. Where are these fossils found? How old are they?

5. Discuss the differences between the Neandertals and modern *Homo sapiens*.

6. Describe the specific changes that characterized the evolution of technology from the Oldowan through the Acheulian, Mousterian, and Upper Paleolithic periods.

7. Contrast the multiregional evolutionary model with the replacement model.

8. Is skin color related to any environmental factors? Discuss whether different skin colors are more adaptive in different environments.

9. Should contemporary models of human evolution be classified as origin myths? Why or why not?

KEY TERMS

bipedalism	gene	natural selection
composite tool	genetics	primates
cosmologies	hominids	Upper Paleolithic
evolution	Mousterian tradition	

INTERNET EXERCISES

1. After reading Chapter 2 on human evolution, look at the Skull Module Website at the California State University—Chico anthropology department: **http://www.csuchico.edu/anth/Module/skull. html**. Explore the site. How can anthropology students use this site? How does this site relate to the chapter? Does it help in understanding the anatomy of the skull as described in the chapter? Why or why not?

2. Read the section of Chapter 2 titled "Hominid Evolution." Explore **http://www.cruzio.com/ ~cscp/index.htm.** How does the fossil skull on the first page compare with a modern human skull (compare this to the skull used in the first Internet exercise of this chapter)? What type of skull is it? What is the evidence for human evolution in China?

Culture

CHAPTER QUESTIONS

- What are the basic characteristics of the term culture as discussed by anthropologists?

- What are the basic components of culture?

- How have anthropologists refined their understanding of culture today?

- How does culture lead to both differences and similarities among people in widely separated societies?

The Characteristics of Culture

As is obvious from the title of this textbook, culture is a fundamental element within the discipline of anthropology. We noted that, in everyday use, most people in this country use the word culture to refer to "high culture," Shakespeare's works, Beethoven's symphonies, Michelangelo's sculptures, gourmet cooking, imported wines, and so on. E. B. Tylor, the first professional anthropologist, proposed a definition of culture that includes all of human experience:

Culture . . . is that complex whole which includes knowledge, belief, arts, morals, law, custom, and any other capabilities and habits acquired by man as a member of society. (1871)

This view suggests that culture includes tools, weapons, fire, agriculture, animal domestication, metallurgy, writing, the steam engine, glasses, airplanes, computers, penicillin, nuclear power, rock and roll, video games, designer jeans, religion, political systems, subsistence patterns, science, sports, and social organizations. In Tylor's view, culture includes all aspects of human activity, from the fine arts to popular entertainment, from everyday behavior to the development of sophisticated technology. It contains the plans, rules, techniques, designs, and policies for living.

This nineteenth-century definition of culture has some terminology that would not be acceptable to modern anthropologists. For example, it relies on the word *man* to refer to what we currently would refer to as *humanity*. In the past, most anthropologists would accept a broad conception of culture as a shared way of life that includes values, beliefs, and norms transmitted within a particular society from generation to generation; however, as we discuss later in this chapter, contemporary anthropologists have a much more refined view of the concept of culture.

Notice that this definition includes the term *society*. In general terms, *society* refers to a particular group of animals within a specific territory. In particular, it refers to the patterns of relationships among the animals within this definite territory. Biologists often refer to certain types of insects, herd animals, and social animals such as monkeys and apes as living in societies.

In the past, anthropologists attempted to make a simple distinction between culture and society.

Society was said to consist of the patterns of relationships among people within a specified territory, and **culture** was viewed as the by-products of those relationships. This view of society as distinguishable from culture was derived from ethnographic studies of small-scale societies. In such societies, people within a specific territory were believed to share a common culture. However, contemporary anthropologists have found this notion of shared culture to be too simplistic and crude. For example, in most countries where modern anthropologists conduct ethnographic research, the societies are extremely complex and consist of distinctive groups that maintain different cultural traditions. Thus, this simple distinction between society and culture is too artificial for modern anthropologists. And, even in small-scale societies, the conception that all these people share a collective "culture" is also too crude and simplistic. As we shall see in this chapter, this crude conception of a collectively shared culture often resulted in gross stereotypes and vulgar generalizations of groups of people and their behavior.

Many anthropologists have adopted the hybrid term *sociocultural system*—a combination of the terms society (or social) and culture—to refer to what used to be called "society" or "culture." As we shall see in later chapters, many anthropologists use the term sociocultural system as the basic conceptual framework for analyzing ethnographic research.

Culture Is Learned

The unique capacity for culture in the human species depends on learning. We do not inherit our culture through our genes in the way we inherit our physical characteristics, as we discussed in Chapter 2. Instead, we obtain our culture through the process of enculturation. **Enculturation** is the process of social interaction through which people learn and acquire their culture. We will study this process in more detail in the next chapter. Humans acquire their culture both consciously, through formal learning, and unconsciously, through informal interaction. Anthropologists distinguish among several types of learning. One type is known as **situational learning**, or trial-and-error learning, in which an organism adjusts its behavior on the basis of direct experience. In other words, a stimulus is presented in the environment, and the animal responds and receives reinforcement

A pigeon being conditioned to behave in a specific manner. This is an example of situational learning.

or feedback from the response, either in the form of a reward (pleasure) or punishment (pain). Psychologists refer to this type of learning as conditioning.

Humans and many other animals, even single-celled organisms, learn situationally and modify their behavior in different situations. For example, dogs can learn a variety of tricks through rewards such as treats given after the completion of the trick. In some cases, human behavior can be modified through conditioning. Overeating, gambling, and smoking can sometimes be reduced through psychological techniques involving rewarding new forms of behavior.

Another form of learning, called **social learning**, occurs when one organism observes another organism respond to a stimulus and then adds that response to its own collection of behaviors. Thus, the organism need not have the direct experience; it can observe how others behave and then imitate or avoid these behaviors. Obviously, humans learn by observing classmates, teachers, parents, friends, and the media. Other social animals also learn in this manner. For example, wolves learn hunting strategies by observing pack members. Similarly, chimpanzees observe other chimps fashioning twigs with which to hunt termites and then imitate these behaviors.

Symbols and Symbolic Learning

The form of learning that is uniquely human and that provides the basis for the capacity for culture is known as symbolic learning. **Symbolic learning** is

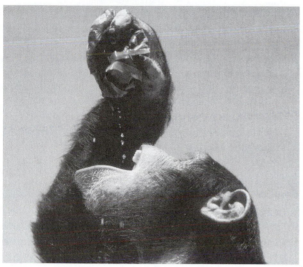

This photo shows a chimpanzee using a tool, a crumpled leaf as a sponge for drinking water. The chimp learned this behavior by observing other chimps—an example of social learning.

based on our linguistic capacity and ability to use and understand **symbols**, arbitrary meaningful units or models we use to represent reality. An example of the arbitrary aspects of symbolism would be the colors red, yellow, and green for traffic lights in the United States (Sahlins 1976; Pierce 1960). Traffic lights could have other colors in different societies, but in the United States they take this arbitrary form.

Sounds such as "cat," "dog," "tree," "one," "two," and "three" in English are symbolic and arbitrary, because as we know these sounds can be completely different to symbolize those words in languages such as Chinese, Navajo, or Russian. However, linguistic anthropologists know that symbols do not just refer to items such as animals or numbers. Symbolic communication and language can be used to represent emotions, or abstract ideas and values. Symbols are the conceptual devices that we use to communicate abstract ideas to one another. We communicate these symbols to one another through language. For example, children can learn to distinguish and name coins such as pennies, nickels, and quarters and use this money as a symbolic medium of exchange. The symbols of money in the United States or other societies are embedded within a host of many other symbols. Symbols are not standing in isolation from one another; instead, they are interconnected within linguistic symbol systems that enable us to provide rules and meanings for objects, actions, and abstract thought processes. The linguistic capacity that we are born with gives us the unique ability to make and use symbolic distinctions.

Humans learn most of their behaviors and concepts through symbolic learning. We do not have to depend on situational learning or observations of others to perceive and understand the world and one another. We have the uniquely human ability to abstract the essence of complex events

A teacher is communicating ideas to a child—an example of symbolic learning.

and patterns, creating images through symbols and bestowing meaning on them.

Through the ability to symbolize, humans can learn and create meanings and transmit these meanings to one another effectively. Parents do not have to depend on direct experience to teach children. As children mature, they can learn abstract rules and concepts involving symbolic communication. When we study mathematics, we learn to manipulate abstract symbols. As you read this textbook, you are learning new ideas based on symbols transmitted to you through English words in ink on a page. Symbolic learning has almost infinite possibilities in terms of absorbing and using information in creative ways. Most of our learning as humans is based on this symbolic-learning process.

Symbols and Signs   Symbols are arbitrary units of meaning, in contrast to **signs**, which are directly associated with concrete physical items or activities. Many nonhuman animals can learn signs. For example, a dog can learn to associate the ringing of a bell (a physical activity) with drinking water. Hence, both humans and other animals can learn signs and apply them to different sorts of activities or to concrete items.

Symbols are different from signs in that they are not associated with any direct, concrete item or physical activity; they are much more abstract. A symbol's meaning is not always obvious. (See the Critical Perspectives box "Key National Symbols.") However, many symbols are powerful and often trigger unconscious stimuli of behaviors or emotional states. For example, the designs and colors of the flags of different countries represent symbolic associations with abstract ideas and concepts. In some flags the color red may refer to blood, whereas in others it may symbolize revolution. In many countries, the desecration of the national flag, itself a symbol, is considered a crime. When the symbols associated with particular abstract ideas and concepts that are related to the national destiny of a society are violated, powerful emotions may be aroused.

The ability of symbolization, creating symbols and bestowing meaning on them, enhances our learning capacities as humans in comparison with other types of animals. Anthropologist Leslie White

maintained that the most distinctive feature of being human is the ability to create symbols:

> *It is impossible for a dog, horse, or even an ape, to have any understanding of the meaning of the sign of the cross to a Christian, or of the fact that black (white among the Chinese) is the color of mourning. No chimpanzee or laboratory rat can appreciate the difference between Holy water and distilled water, or grasp the meaning of Tuesday, 3, or sin. (1971; 23–24)*

Symbols and Culture   The human capacity for culture is based on our linguistic and cognitive ability to symbolize. Culture is transmitted from generation to generation through symbolic learning and language. (In Chapter 5 we discuss the relationship between language and culture.) Through the transmission of culture, we learn how to subsist, how to socialize, how to govern our society, and what gods to worship. Culture is the historical accumulation of symbolic knowledge that is shared by a society. This symbolic knowledge is transmitted through learning, and it can change rapidly from parents to children and from one generation to the next. Generally, however, people in societies go to great lengths to conserve their culture and symbolic traditions. The persistence of cultural and symbolic traditions is as widespread as cultural change.

Culture Is Shared

Culture consists of the shared practices and understandings within a society. To some degree, culture is based on shared meanings that are to some extent "public" and thus beyond the mind of any individual (Geertz 1973). Some of this culture exists before the birth of an individual into the society, and it may continue (in some form) beyond the death of any particular individual. These publicly shared meanings provide designs or recipes for surviving and contributing to the society. On the other hand, culture is also within the mind of individuals. For example, we mentioned that children learn the symbolic meanings of money in coins of different denominations and bills. The children figure out the meanings of money by observing practices and learning the various symbols that are public. However, the child is not just a passive assimilator of that cultural knowledge. Cognitive anthropologists such as Roy D'Andrade and Naomi Quinn emphasize **schemas**, or cultural models that are internalized by individuals and have an influence on decision making and behavior. They emphasize how culture is acquired by and modeled as schemas within individual minds and can motivate, shape, and transform the symbols and meanings (Quinn and Holland 1987; D'Andrade 1989, 1995).

Contemporary anthropologists recognize that cultural understandings are not shared equally by all members of a society (Fox and King 2002; Barth 2002; Trouillot 2002; Kuper 1999; Durham 2002; Boyd and Richerson 2004; Ortner 1999; DeMunck 2000). Even in small-scale societies, culture is shared differently by males and females or by young and old. Some individuals in these societies have a great deal of knowledge regarding agriculture, medical practices, or religious beliefs; those beliefs and that knowledge are not equally distributed. In our complex industrialized society, culture consists of a tremendous amount of information and knowledge regarding technology and other aspects of society. Different people learn different aspects of culture, such as repairing cars or television sets, understanding nuclear physics or federal tax regulations, or composing music. Hence, to some extent culture varies from person to person, from subgroup to subgroup, from region to region, from age group to age group, and from gender to gender. Contemporary anthropologists also note how culture is "contested," referring to how people question and may fundamentally disagree and struggle over the specifics of culture. Yet despite this variation, some common cultural understandings allow members of society to adapt, to communicate, and to interact with one another (Barth 2000). Without some of these common understandings, a society could not exist.

The Components of Culture

Within a broad and refined understanding, contemporary anthropologists have tried to isolate the key elements that constitute culture. Two of the most basic components are material and nonmaterial culture.

Material culture consists of the physical products of human society (ranging from weapons to clothing styles), whereas **nonmaterial culture** refers to the intangible products of human society (values, beliefs, and norms). As we discussed in Chapter 2, the earliest traces of material culture are stone tools associated with early hominids. They consist of a collection of very simple choppers, scrapers, and flakes. Modern material culture consists of all the physical objects that a contemporary society produces or retains from the past, such as tools, streets, buildings, homes, toys, medicines, and automobiles. Cultural anthropologists investigate the material culture of the societies they study, and they also examine the relationship between the material culture and the nonmaterial culture: the values, beliefs, and norms that represent the patterned ways of thinking and acting within a society. Archaeologists, meanwhile, are primarily concerned with interpreting past societies by studying their material remains.

Values

Values are the standards by which members of a society define what is good or bad, holy or unholy, beautiful or ugly. They are assumptions that are widely shared within the society. Values are a central aspect of the nonmaterial culture of a society and are important because they influence the behavior of the members of a society. The predominant values in the United States include individual achievement and success, efficiency, progress, material comfort, equality, freedom, science, rationality, nationalism, and democracy, along with many other assumptions (Williams 1970; Bellah et al. 1985, 2000). Although these values might seem normal to Americans, they are not accepted values in all societies. For instance, just as American society tends to emphasize individualism and self-reliance; other societies, such as Japan or the Old Order Amish in the Unites States, stress cooperation and community interest instead.

Beliefs

Beliefs held by the members of a society are another aspect of nonmaterial culture. Beliefs are cultural conventions that concern true or false

Critical Perspectives

KEY NATIONAL SYMBOLS

Societies throughout the world have drawn upon important cultural symbols as a means of distinguishing their community from others. Some of these cultural symbols are secular or nonreligious in meaning, whereas others have religious connotations. Anthropologist Victor Turner (1967) described symbols as "multivocal," suggesting that they have multiple meanings for people within a society. He also said that symbols have the characteristic of "condensation," having the ability to unify many things and actions into a single formation.

National symbols such as flags have the potential for expressing deep-felt emotions in condensed forms. Flags, with their great public visibility, have been an extremely important symbolic medium of political communication throughout the centuries. In U.S. society, the flag is a key secular symbol reflecting deeply felt community ties. A number of legal battles have been waged over the so-called desecration of the U.S. flag. For example, members of the Jehovah's Witnesses religious sect refuse on principle to salute the flag, for which they have been prosecuted. Political protesters, such as those opposed to the Vietnam War in the 1960s, tried to dramatize their cause by burning the flag or otherwise defacing it. In the late 1980s, the issue found its way to the Supreme Court, which ruled that a protester who had burned the flag at the

1988 Republican National Convention was merely expressing free speech. The Court later ruled that a law protecting the flag from desecration was unconstitutional. This issue remains controversial for many U.S. citizens. There is a political movement to amend the Constitution to protect the flag.

The recent controversy over the flying of the Confederate flag over the South Carolina state house also demonstrates the potency of symbols and the different meanings evoked by symbols for different peoples. Some white southerners view the Confederate flag as part of their cultural heritage, whereas many African Americans understand the flag as a symbol of slavery.

Various religious symbols have produced fundamental meanings and metaphors for many countries throughout the world. For example, the symbols associated with the Virgin Mary in Roman Catholicism have developed into national symbols of unity for some countries.

In Mexico, the symbolism associated with the Virgin of Guadalupe has served to unify different ethnic communities (Wolf 1958; Kurtz 1982; Ingham 1986). After Spain had colonized the indigenous Indian communities of Mexico beginning in the sixteenth century, many of the Indians, such as the Aztecs, were converted to Roman Catholicism. According to Mexican tradition, the Virgin Mary appeared before a Christianized Indian, Juan Diego, in 1531, in the

form of a brown-skinned Indian woman.

Tepeyac, the place where the apparition occurred, was the sacred site of an Aztec fertility goddess, Tonantzin, known as Our Lady Mother. Aztec cosmology contained many notions regarding the virgin births of deities. For example, Huitzilopochtli, the deity believed to have led the Aztecs to their home in Tenochtitlán, had been miraculously conceived by the Aztec mother goddess. Thus, Aztec religious beliefs regarding Tonantzin somewhat paralleled Catholic teachings about Mary.

During the Virgin's appearance, she commanded Juan Diego to inform the bishop of Mexico that a shrine should be built at the spot. The Shrine of the Virgin of Guadalupe is today a huge church, or basilica. Over the altar, Juan Diego's cloak hangs, embossed with the image of a young, dark-skinned woman wearing an open crown and flowing gown, standing on a half-moon that symbolizes the Immaculate Conception.

The Virgin of Guadalupe became a potent symbol that has endured throughout generations, assuming different meanings for different social groups. To the Indians of Mexico, the Virgin embodies both Tonantzin and the newer Catholic beliefs and aspirations concerning eternal salvation. To the mestizos, people with mixed Spanish and Indian ancestry, she represents the supernatural mother who gave them a place in both the indigenous and colonial worlds. To Mexicans in general, the Virgin represents the symbolic resolution of the many conflicts and problems that resulted from violent encounters between the Europeans and the local population (Kurtz 1982). The Guadalupe shrine has become one of the most important pilgrimage sites in Mexico.

The Virgin Mary has also played an important symbolic role in a European country that has undergone major political and social transformations. Until recently Poland was a socialist country under the indirect control of the former Soviet Union. Beginning in the 1980s, however, the Polish people, who were organized through a union-based political party known as Solidarity, began to challenge the Communist Party that ruled Poland. During Communist Party rule in Poland, religious symbolism and Roman Catholicism, deeply rooted in Polish history, were to some degree repressed by the government. One of the most important symbols of Polish Catholicism is a famous picture of the Virgin Mary in a Paulite monastery. According to Polish tradition, the picture, known as the Black Madonna of Czestochowa, was painted by St. Luke the Evangelist, one of the authors of the Christian New Testament, on a piece of cypress wood from the table used by Mary. After the picture was placed in the monastery, where it was revered by many Polish Catholics, a party of robbers raided the monastery for treasures in 1430 and slashed the image of the Madonna with a sword. Although painstakingly restored, the picture still bears the scars of that destruction, with sword slashes on the cheek of the Black Madonna.

As Poland was divided among different countries such as Sweden, Germany, Turkey, and Russia during various periods, the image of the Black Madonna served as a symbol of Polish religious and national unity. It became one of the most important pilgrimage sites for Polish Catholicism. Millions of pilgrims from Poland and other European countries made their way to the Czestochowa shrine every year to take part in various religious rites. When the Solidarity movement in Poland challenged the Communist Party during the 1980s, leaders such as Lech Walesa wore an image of the Black Madonna on their suit lapels. Pope John Paul II visited the Black Madonna shrine and placed a golden rose there to help resuscitate religiosity in Poland. Thus, the Black Madonna image served to unify Polish Catholics in their struggle against the antireligious stance of the communist authorities. Other Madonna shrines in Spain and France provided symbols of nationalism and political-religious identity for Catholics in Europe (Bowen 2005).

National symbols, whether religious or secular, have played extremely important roles in mobilizing people and countries in times of transition and struggle. These national symbols reflect the deep feelings that tie peoples together in what some scholars have referred to as "imagined communities"

A portrait of the Madonna. Murillo, Bartolomeo Esteban. "The Immaculate Conception of Excorial." Museo del Prado, Madrid, Spain. Scala/Art Resource. N.Y.

(Anderson 1983). Regardless of whether these communities are imagined or not, such symbols are key aspects of culture that are likely to be retained by societies worldwide in the twenty-first century.

POINTS TO PONDER

1. What kinds of feelings and emotions do you have when you hear your national anthem played as you watch your flag?

2. Can you think of any other examples of national symbols that have played a role in world history or politics?

3. Are there any disadvantages of national symbols that have influenced various societies?

4. Could international symbols be developed that would draw all of humanity together?

assumptions, specific descriptions of the nature of the universe and humanity's place in it. Values are generalized notions of what is good and bad; beliefs are more specific and, in form at least, have more content. "Education is good" is a fundamental value in American society, whereas "Grading is the best way to evaluate students" is a belief that reflects assumptions about the most appropriate way to determine educational achievement.

Most people in a given society assume that their beliefs are rational and firmly grounded in common sense. As we saw in Chapter 2, however, some beliefs may not necessarily be scientifically accepted. For example, our intuitive and commonsense understandings may lead us to conclude that the earth is flat and stationary. When we look around us, the plane of the earth looks flat, and we don't feel as if the earth is rotating around the sun. Yet our cognitive intuitions and commonsense beliefs about these notions are contradicted by the knowledge gained by the scientific method.

Some anthropologists in the past have referred to the worldview of a particular society. A *worldview* was believed to consist of various beliefs about the nature of reality that provided a people with a more or less consistent orientation toward the world. Worldviews were viewed as guides to help people interpret and understand the reality surrounding them. Early anthropologists believed that the worldviews were carried as meaningful beliefs about witches among the traditional Azande of East Africa or the traditional Navajos of the southwest region of the United States (Evans-Pritchard 1937; Kluckhohn 1944, 1967). In these societies, witchcraft is believed to cause illnesses in some unfortunate individuals. In other societies, such as that of Canada, medical doctors diagnose illness by using the scientific method, and the causes of illness are attributed to viruses, bacteria, or other material forces. In the past, these anthropologists maintained that this reflected different worldviews among these societies. However, modern anthropologists remain very skeptical about these notions of worldviews shared by an entire culture. Presently, anthropologists concur that the concept of a people sharing a worldview together is highly questionable. Instead, anthropologists discover a great deal of variation in cultural beliefs held within any society.

In particular circumstances within a society, some beliefs may be combined into an ideology.

An **ideology** consists of cultural symbols and beliefs that reflect and support the interests of specific groups within society (Yengoyan 1986). Particular groups promote ideologies for their own ends as a means of maintaining and justifying economic and political authority. Different economic and political systems—capitalism, socialism, communism, democratic institutions, and totalitarian governments—are based on differing ideologies. For example, many political leaders in capitalist societies maintain the ideology that individuals should be rewarded monetarily based on their own self-interest. In contrast, leaders in socialist societies use the ideology that emphasizes the well-being of the community or society over individual self-interest.

In some societies, especially complex societies with many different groups, an ideology may produce **cultural hegemony**, the ideological control by one dominant group over beliefs and values. For example, one dominant ethnic group may impose its cultural beliefs on subordinate groups. In the United States, the dominant ethnic group in the eighteenth and nineteenth centuries, white Anglo-Saxon Protestants, was able to impose its language, cultural beliefs, and practices on the Native American Indians in U.S. society. In many areas of the world, minority groups are often forced to accept the ideologies of the economically and politically dominant groups through the process of cultural hegemony.

Norms

Norms—a society's rules of right and wrong behavior—are another aspect of nonmaterial culture. Norms are shared rules or guidelines that define how people "ought" to behave under certain circumstances. Norms are generally connected to the values, beliefs, worldviews, and ideologies of a society. For example, we have seen that in American culture individualism is a basic value that is reflected in the prevailing worldview. Not surprisingly, then, American society has many norms based on the notion of individual initiative and responsibility. Individuals are admonished to work for their own self-interest and not to become a burden to their families or community. Older Americans, if self-sufficient, are not supposed to live with their children. Likewise, self-sufficient young adults beyond a certain age are not supposed to live with

Saudi Arabian women and families in Islamic dress.

their parents. These individualistic norms reflect the values of U.S. society and contrast with norms existing in many other societies. In many agricultural societies, it would be considered immoral to allow aging parents to live outside the family. In these societies, the family is a moral community that should not be separated. Rather than individualism, these norms emphasize communal responsibility within the family unit.

Folkways Norms guiding ordinary usages and conventions of everyday life are known as **folkways**. Members of a society frequently conform to folkways so readily that they are hardly aware these norms exist. For example, if a Chinese anthropologist were to ask an American why Americans eat with knives and forks, why Americans allow dating between single men and women without chaperones, or why American schoolchildren are not allowed to help one another on exams, he or she might get vague and uninformative answers, such as "Because that's the way it is done," or "It's the custom," or even "I don't know." Cultural anthropologists are accustomed to receiving these kinds of answers from the members of the society they are studying. These folkway norms or standards of etiquette are so embedded in the society that they are not noticeable unless they are openly violated.

Folkways help ensure that social life proceeds smoothly by providing guidelines for an individual's behavior and expectations of other people's behavior. At the same time, folkways allow for some flexibility. Although most people conform to folkways most of the time, folkways are sometimes violated, but these violations are not severely punished. Thus, in American society people who eat with chopsticks rather than with a knife and fork or who do not keep their lawns neatly mowed are not considered immoral or depraved, nor are they treated as criminals.

Mores **Mores** (pronounced MOR-ays) are much stronger norms than are folkways. Members of society believe that their mores are crucial for the maintenance of a decent and orderly way of life. People who violate mores are usually severely punished, although punishment for the violation of mores varies from society to society. It may take the form of ostracism, vicious gossip, public ridicule, exile, losing one's job, physical beating, imprisonment, commitment to a mental asylum, or even execution.

For example, in some Islamic societies such as Iran and Saudi Arabia, the manner in which a woman dresses in public is considered morally significant. If a woman violates the dress code in these societies, she may be arrested and imprisoned. As we shall see later in the text, in hunting-and-gathering societies, individuals who do not share goods or resources with others are often punished by gossip, ridicule, and occasionally ostracism.

Not all norms can be neatly categorized as either folkways or mores. Distinguishing between the two is especially difficult when dealing with societies other than our own. In reality, norms fall at various points on a continuum, depending on the particular circumstances and the society under consideration. The prohibition of public nudity may be a strong norm in some societies, but it may be only a folkway or pattern of etiquette in another society. Even within a society, rules of etiquette may come to have moral significance. For example, as already discussed, the proper form of dress for women in some societies is not just a matter of etiquette but has moral or religious connotations.

Values, beliefs, norms, and worldviews are used by many social scientists when referring to nonmaterial culture. However, not all anthropologists agree with concise, clear-cut distinctions among these terms. The terms are used only to help us understand the complex symbolic aspects of nonmaterial culture.

Ideal versus Real Culture

When discussing values, beliefs, and norms, cultural anthropologists often distinguish between ideal culture and real culture. **Ideal culture** consists of what people say they do or should do, whereas **real culture** refers to their actual behaviors. Cultural anthropologists have discovered that the ideal culture frequently contrasts with people's actual behavior. For instance, a foreign anthropologist may learn that Americans cherish the value of equal opportunity, yet in observing Americans, the anthropologist might encounter many cases in which people from different economic, class, racial, ethnic, and religious backgrounds are treated in a highly unequal manner. In later chapters, we discuss how some societies are structured around kinship ties and principles of lineage such as patrilineal and matrilineal descent. Anthropologists often discover, however, that these kinship and descent principles are violated by the actual practices of people (Kuper 1988). Thus, in all societies anthropologists find that there are differences between the ideal and real cultural practices of individuals.

Cultural Diversity

Throughout history, humans have expressed an interest in cultural diversity. People have recognized differences in values, norms, beliefs, and practices everywhere. Whenever different groups have come into contact with one another, people have compared and contrasted their respective cultural traditions. Societies often differentiated themselves from one another based on these variant cultural patterns. For example, one of the first Western historians, Herodotus, a Greek scholar of the fifth century B.C., wrote about the different forms of behavior and belief in societies such as Egypt. He described how the Egyptians behaved and thought differently from the Greeks.

Writings on the diversity of cultures have often been based on ethnocentric attitudes. As we saw in Chapter 1, *ethnocentrism* is the practice of judging another society by the values and standards of one's own society. It appears that ethnocentrism is a universal phenomenon (Brown 2003). As humans learn the basic values, beliefs, and norms of their society, they tend to think of their own group and culture as preferable, ranking other cultures as less desirable. In fact, members of a society become so committed to particular cultural traditions that they cannot conceive of any other way of life. They often view other cultural traditions as strange, alien, inferior, crazy, or immoral.

The study of cultural diversity became one of the principal objectives of anthropology as it developed as a profession in the nineteenth century. But like earlier writers, nineteenth-century anthropologists often reinforced ethnocentric beliefs about other societies (see Chapter 7). In the twentieth century, however, anthropologists began to recognize that ethnocentrism prevents them from viewing other cultures in a scientific manner.

To combat the problem of ethnocentrism, twentieth-century anthropologists developed the concept of cultural relativism. **Cultural relativism** is the view that cultural traditions must be understood within the context of a particular society's solutions to problems and opportunities. Cultural relativism is a method or procedure for explaining and interpreting other people's cultures. Because cultural traditions represent unique adaptations and symbolic systems for different societies, these traditions must be understood by anthropologists as objectively as possible. In order to do an ethnographic study, anthropologists must suspend their own judgments to examine another society in terms of its history and culture. Cultural relativism offers anthropologists a means of investigating other societies without imposing ethnocentric assumptions. The cultural anthropologist attempts to understand the logic of the people she or he is studying. Perhaps that logic does not make sense from the anthropologist's perspective, but the task is to understand and explain the reasoning of the people studied.

Although cultural relativism provides a sound methodological basis for ethnographic research, it may involve some serious ethical problems. For example, many cultural anthropologists have found themselves in societies in which cultural practices may produce physical harm for people. How does the cultural anthropologist refrain from making a value judgment about such cultural practices as infanticide or child or spousal abuse, torture, murder, or other harmful practices? This issue is an ever-present problem for anthropologists and deserves careful thought. Anthropologists don't argue that any practice or culture is as good or worthy as another. In fact, one of the major goals in anthropology is to improve conditions and enhance human rights for all people. After learning about different practices and traditions in other societies throughout this text, the moral problems raised by cultural relativism are discussed in Chapter 17.

Food and Diversity

To understand the difference between human biological and cultural behaviors, we may simply observe the variety of ways in which different societies satisfy a basic biological drive such as hunger. Although humans are omnivorous animals with the ability to digest many types of plants and animals for nutrition, there are many differences in eating behaviors and food preferences throughout the world.

In general, American culture labels animals as either edible or inedible. Most Americans would be repulsed by the thought of eating insects and insect larvae, but many societies consider them to be delicacies. American culture also distinguishes between pets, which are not eaten, and farm animals, such as chickens, cows, and pigs, which can be eaten. In the United States, horses are considered pets, and there are no industries for raising them for human consumption. Yet horsemeat is a regular part of the continental European diet. The French, Belgians, Dutch, Germans, Italians, Poles, and other Europeans consume significant quantities of horsemeat each year (Harris 1985).

In a new, fascinating ethnographic study, anthropologist Steve Striffler went to work undercover in the Tyson Food's poultry plant in Arkansas (2002, 2005). First he found that practically no white Americans were employed at the plant except in management and secretarial roles. When Steve applied for the job he was asked by the white American women why he would want to work in a chicken plant as an assembly worker. Following a drug test and quick reference check, Steve was hired. He found that the workers were primarily from Mexico and other Latin American countries and included some Laotian and Pacific island peoples. These refugees are willing to work in very difficult working conditions to gain economic opportunities for their families in the United States. The average worker makes $8 an hour and the supervisors are paid about $30,000 a year. Tyson plant processes 80 chickens per minute, or 40,000 pounds per day. Steve describes the process of "live hanging," when the live chickens flood into the slaughter plant at 200 hundred a minute and are grabbed by the workers, who hang them by their feet as blood, feathers, and feces fly across the room. Most white Americans are not employed in any animal-slaughter houses in the United States. Other nonwhite American immigrants are employed in these plants to serve Americans who go to fast food restaurants and supermarkets to buy their meat products without any understanding of factory farming and the deplorable conditions that these workers have to endure to satisfy their American dreams for their families. Part of the reason that most Americans do not work in animal-slaughter houses is due to how they think of and treat animals that are classified as food.

Anthropologists explain differences in dietary preferences in different ways. For example, Mary Douglas offers an explanation of why the Jewish people have prohibitions about eating pork. She describes this prohibition in her book *Purity and Danger: An Analysis of the Concepts of Pollution and Taboo* (1966) by suggesting that all societies

Critical Perspectives

NINETEENTH-CENTURY EVOLUTIONISM AND THE CONCEPT OF CULTURE

Although many philosophers and historians in Western society, such as Aristotle and Herodotus in Greek society and later Europeans such as John Locke, Immanuel Kant, and Johann Gottfried Herder, who reflected on the concept of culture, it was nineteenth-century anthropologists who began to investigate the concept of "culture" as used today. Modern anthropology emerged from the intellectual atmosphere of the Enlightenment, an eighteenth-century philosophical movement that stressed social progress based on human reason, and Darwin's theory of evolution. The first professional anthropologist—that is, an individual appointed to an academic position of anthropology—was a nineteenth-century British scholar, Edward B. Tylor. In 1871 Tylor published a major work titled *Primitive Culture*. At that time, Great Britain was involved in imperialistic expansion all over the world. Tylor thus had access to descriptions of non-Western societies through his contacts with travelers, explorers, missionaries, traders, and government officials. He combined these descriptions with nineteenth-century philosophy and Charles Darwin's ideas to develop a theory of societal evolution.

UNILINEAL EVOLUTION OF CULTURE

The major question addressed by early anthropologists was: Why are societies at similar or different levels of evolution and development?

Many people ask the same kinds of questions today. Tylor tried to answer that question through an explanation known as unilineal evolution. Unilineal evolution is the view that societies evolve in a single direction toward complexity, progress, and civilization. Tylor's basic argument was that because all humans are bestowed with innate rational faculties, they are continuously improving their societies. Through this process of evolution, societies move toward "progress" and "civilization."

In arriving at this conclusion, Tylor used accounts from Western observers to compare certain cultural elements from different societies, including technology, family, economy, political organization, art, religion, and philosophy. He then organized this evidence into categories or stages, ranging from what he termed "savagery" to "barbarism" to "civilization." Theorists like Tylor assumed that hunter-gatherers and other non-Western societies were living at a lower level of existence than were the "civilized" societies of Europe. This was an ethnocentric view of societal development based on the belief that Western society is the center of the civilized world and that non-Western societies are inherently inferior both in culture, race, and society. We have to remember that this was a very general view of humans and different races during the period of U.S. slavery and European colonialism throughout the world.

Tylor and other nineteenth-century thinkers also claimed that "primitives" would eventually evolve through the stages of barbarism to become civilized like British gentlemen and ladies. However, Tylor believed that these societies would need some assistance from the civilized world to reach this stage.

UNILINEAL EVOLUTION: MORGAN

Another nineteenth-century anthropologist who developed a unilineal scheme of evolution was an American, Lewis Henry Morgan (1818–1881). Morgan was a lawyer and banker who became fascinated with Native American Indian societies. He gathered information on the customs, language, and other aspects of the culture of the Iroquois-speaking peoples of upstate New York. His major informant was a Seneca Iroquois Indian by the name of Ely Parker, who also spoke English and later became an important government official under President Ulysses Grant. Morgan later extended his research beyond American Indians, and under the auspices of the Smithsonian Institution, he distributed questionnaires to missionaries and travelers to collect information about many other non-Western societies.

Morgan was particularly interested in kinship terms used in different parts of the world. He observed that the Iroquois kinship

Ely Parker, Seneca Indian and informant to Lewis Morgan.

terms were very different from those of English, Latin, Greek, and other European societies. He also noticed that these kinship terms were similar to those of the Ojibwa Indians, a group living in the midwestern United States. This led him to explore the relationship between the Iroquois and other peoples. Using the aforementioned questionnaires, he requested specific information on kinship terms from people all over the world.

From these data, Morgan began to conceive of the evolution of the family in a worldwide sense. He speculated that humans originally lived in "primitive hordes," in which sexual behavior was not regulated and individuals didn't know who their fathers were. He based this assumption on the discovery that certain peoples, such as Hawaiians, use one general term to classify their father and all male relatives in their father's generation (see Chapter 5). He postulated that brother-sister marriage then developed, followed by group marriage, and eventually a matriarchal family structure in which women held economic and political power.

Morgan believed that the final stage of the evolution of the family began when males took control of the economy and politics, instituting a patriarchal system.

In addition to exploring the evolution of the family, Morgan, like Tylor, surveyed technological, economic, political, and religious conditions throughout the world. He compiled this evidence in his book *Ancient Society* ([1877] 1964), which presented his overall scheme of the evolution of society. Paralleling Tylor's views, Morgan believed in a hierarchy of evolutionary development from "savagery" to "civilization."

According to Morgan, one crucial distinction between civilized society and earlier societies is private property. He described the "savage" societies as "communistic," in contrast to "civilized" societies, whose institutions are based on private property. Interestingly, this view was adopted by the famous Karl Marx and his colleague Frederick Engels in their attempt to develop a model of how societies had evolved from earlier stages through the period of capitalism; they then hoped for further evolution to socialism and then on to communism. This unilineal model of cultural evolution remained the dominant anthropological approach to understanding history and the development of human societies in the former Soviet Union up until recently.

Although these nineteenth-century thinkers shared the view that humanity was progressing through various stages of development, their views were ethnocentric, contradictory, and speculative, and their evidence was secondhand, based on the accounts of biased Europeans. The unilineal scheme of evolution was much too simplistic to account for the development of different societies.

In general, the unilineal evolutionists relied on nineteenth-century racist views of human development and misunderstandings of biological evolution to explain societal differences. For example, both Morgan and Tylor believed that people in various societies have different levels of intelligence. They believed that the people in so-called savage societies have less intelligence than those in "civilized societies." As discussed in Chapter 7, this view of different levels of intelligence among different groups is no longer accepted by the scientific community or modern anthropologists. Nevertheless, despite their inadequate theories and speculations regarding the evolution of society, these early anthropologists provided the first systematic methods for thinking about and explaining the similarities and diversity of human societies.

UNILINEAL EVOLUTION OF CULTURE: AN ANTHROPOLOGICAL CRITIQUE

An early-twentieth-century movement that developed in response to the unilineal evolutionary theory of society and culture was led by the U.S. anthropologist Franz Boas, whom we discuss further in Chapter 7. This movement proposed an alternative answer to why societal similarities and differences exist. Boas was educated in Germany as a natural scientist. Eventually he conducted fieldwork among the Eskimo (Inuit) in northern Canada and a Native American Indian people known as the Kwakiutl, who lived on the northwest coast. He later solidified his position as the nation's foremost leader in anthropology at Columbia University in New York, where he trained many pioneers in the field until his retirement in 1937. Boas had a tremendous impact on the development of anthropology in the United States and internationally.

BOAS AND HISTORICAL PARTICULARISM

Boas became a vigorous opponent of the unilineal evolutionists. He criticized their attempts to propose stages of evolution through which all societies evolve. He also criticized their use of the comparative method and the haphazard manner in which they organized the data to fit their theories of evolutionary stages. He maintained that these nineteenth-century schemes of evolution were based on insufficient empirical evidence. Boas called for an end to "armchair anthropology," in which scholars took data from travelers, traders, and missionaries and plugged these data into a speculative model of evolution. He proposed that all anthropologists do rigorous, scientifically based fieldwork to collect basic ethnographic data.

Boas's fieldwork experience and his intellectual training in Germany led him to conclude that each society has its own unique historical development. This theory, known as *historical particularism*, maintains that each society must be understood as a product of its own history. This view led Boas to adopt the notion of cultural relativism, the belief that each society should be understood in terms of its own cultural practices and values. One aspect of this view is that no society

have symbolic classifications of certain objects or foods that are unclean, tabooed, polluted, or dirty, as well as what is clean, pure, or undefiled. To illustrate her ideas regarding the classification of matter or foods, Douglas examined the ancient Israelite's classification of animals and taboos against eating certain animals such as pigs and shellfish, as described in Leviticus in the Bible. Douglas argues that, like other humans, the ancient Israelites classify reality by placing things into distinguishable "mental boxes." However, some things don't fit neatly into distinguishable mental boxes. Some items are anomalous and ambiguous and fall between the basic categories that are used to define cultural reality. These anomalous items are usually treated as unclean, impure, unholy, polluting, or defiling.

Douglas refers to how these processes influenced the classification of animals among the ancient Israelites. She alludes to the descriptions in the first chapter of the Bible, Genesis, where God evolved higher or lower than an- other. Thus, we cannot rank any particular society above another in terms of degree of savagery, bar- barity, or civility. Boas called for an end to the use of these deroga- tory, ethnocentric terms.

The Boasian view became the dominant theoretical trend in an- thropology during the first half of the twentieth century. Anthropol- ogists began to do rigorous ethnographic fieldwork in differ- ent societies to gather sound em- pirical evidence. Boas instituted the participant-observer method as a basic research strategy of ethnographic fieldwork (see Chapter 1). This strategy enabled ethnographers to gather valid em- pirical data to explain human be- havior. Boas also encouraged his students to develop their linguistic skills so that they could learn the languages of the peoples they studied.

Boas worked in all four sub- fields of anthropology: physical anthropology, archaeology, cul- tural anthropology, and linguis- tics. As we will see in Chapter 7, some of his most important work involved taking precise assess- ments of the physical characteris- tics, including brain size and

cranial capacity, of people in dif- ferent societies. Boas was one of the first scientists in the United States to demonstrate that brain size and cranial capacities of mod- ern humans are not linked directly to intelligence. His research indi- cated that brain size and cranial capacity differ widely within all races. Boas's findings challenged the racist assumptions put forward by the unilineal evolutionists. They also repudiated the type of racism that characterized black-white relations in the United States, as well as Nazi theories of racial superiority.

A direct outgrowth of the Boasian approach was the emer- gence of culture-and-personality theory in American anthropology. Boas trained two particularly note- worthy students, Ruth Benedict and Margaret Mead, pioneering anthropologists whose research is described in the next chapter. The anthropological research and fieldwork represented by Benedict and Mead resulted eventually in the development of more care- ful research regarding personality and culture. The methods used in this field have been refined and tested by many anthropologists. As a result, we now have a better

understanding of enculturation and personality formation in dif- ferent societies. Boas's efforts set the stage for a sound scientific ap- proach in anthropology that led to definite progress in our com- prehension of race and other is- sues in explaining human behav- ior and culture. Additionally, Boas pioneered the study of art, religion, folklore, music, dance, and oral literature, pro- viding the humanistic aspect of anthropology and merging both science and humanistic approaches.

POINTS TO PONDER

1. Why did nineteenth-century anthropologists believe that societies were evolving in one single direction in a unilineal manner?

2. Do you believe that cultures are progressing in evolution and improving conditions for humanity?

3. How did the Franz Boaz his- torical particularist perspec- tive compare with the early unilineal evolutionary views?

creates the animals with specific characteristics: birds with feathers are soaring in the sky; fish with scales and fins are swimming in the water; and creatures with four feet are walking, hopping, or jumping on the land. However, some animals did not easily fit into the cultural categories used for the classifica- tion of animals. Animals that combined elements of different realms were considered ambiguous, and therefore unclean or unholy. For example, terres- trial animals that moved by "swarming upon the earth" were declared unclean and were prohibited

from being eaten. Pigs were also unclean and prohibited in the ancient Israelite diet. Clean edible animals such as sheep, goats, and cattle had cloven hoofs and chewed cud. These animals were con- sidered clean and could be eaten. However, pigs had cloven hoofs but did not chew cud. Con- sequently, the pig was unclean, polluting, and tabooed because it failed to fit into the cultural classification of reality accepted by the ancient Israelites. Shellfish and eels are also unclean ani- mals because they swim in the water but lack fins

Chinese farmer with a pig.

and scales. These anomalous creatures fall outside of the systematic classification of animals. Douglas maintains that the dietary laws of Leviticus represented an ideal construction of reality that represented God's plan of creation, which was based on perfection, order, and holiness. This became integral to the worldview of the ancient Israelites and affected their dietary preferences.

The late anthropologist Marvin Harris hypothesized that cultural dietary preferences frequently have an adaptive significance (1977, 1985). For example, he explained the origins of the pig taboo in Judaism (and later Islam) by analyzing the ecological conditions of the ancient Middle East. Like Douglas, he emphasizes that among the ancient Israelites, pigs were viewed as abominable animals not suited for human consumption. Yet pigs have been a primary source of protein and fat throughout China and Europe. In some societies in the Pacific Islands, pigs are so highly regarded they are treated as members of the family (but they are also eaten). Because so many societies show no aversion to the

consumption of pork, Harris has tried to explain the prohibitions in Judaism and Islam. One medical explanation is that the pig is an unclean animal and that it carries diseases such as trichinosis, which is caused by a type of tapeworm. Harris, however, considered these explanations to be unsatisfactory. Regarding cleanliness, Harris acknowledged that because pigs cannot sweat, in hot, dry climates such as the Middle East they wallow in their excrement to keep cool. He noted, however, that other animals, such as goats and chickens, can also be dirty, but they are eaten. Similarly with disease, Harris emphasized that many other animals, such as cows, which are widely consumed, also carry diseases.

Harris explained the pig taboo with reference to the ecological conditions of the Middle East. He maintained that the restrictions represented a cultural innovation that helped the societies of this region to adapt. About 1200 B.C., the ancient Israelites had settled in a woodland area that had not been cultivated. As they rapidly cut down trees to convert areas to irrigated agricultural land, they also severely restricted areas suitable for raising pigs on natural forage. Eventually, pigs had to be fed grains as supplements, which made them extremely costly and direct competitors with humans. Moreover, they required artificial shade and moisture to keep cool. In addition, pigs were not useful for pulling plows or producing milk, hides, or wool for clothing.

According to Harris, despite the increasing costs associated with pig raising, people were still tempted to raise them for nutritional reasons. He hypothesized that the pig taboo was established through religious authorities and texts to inhibit this practice. Therefore, the pig was redefined as an unclean animal. Neighbors of the ancient Israelites, such as the Egyptians, began to share the abhorrence of the pig. The pig taboo was later incorporated into the Islamic religious text, the Qur'an, so that today both Muslims and Jews are forbidden to eat pork.

Thus, in Harris's hypothesis, in the hot, dry regions of the world where pigs were poorly adapted and extremely costly to raise, the meat of the pig came to be forbidden. He emphasized the practical considerations of pig raising, including the fact that they are hard to herd and are not grazing animals like goats, sheep, or cattle. In contrast, in the cooler, wetter areas of the world that are more appropriate for pig raising, such as China or

New Guinea, pig taboos were unknown, and pigs are the prized foods in these regions.

Both Douglas and Harris offer insights into the development of dietary preferences of Jews and Christians. While Douglas explores the important symbolic significance of these preferences, Harris examines the cost effectiveness and practical aspects of these food taboos. Anthropologists such as Harris and others have been studying dietary diversity, such as why some people prohibit the eating of beef, whereas other people have adopted it as an integral aspect of their diet. Food preferences illustrate how humans the world over have universal needs for protein, carbohydrates, minerals, and vitamins but obtain these nutrients in different ways, depending on the dietary preferences established within their culture.

Dress Codes and Symbolism

Although some cultural differences may relate to the environmental adaptations of societies emphasized by anthropologists such as Harris, much more of our cultural diversity is a consequence of symbolic creations. Symbols provide the basis of meaningful shared beliefs within a society. Because of our inherent cultural capacity, we tend to be meaning-seeking creatures. In addition to the satisfaction of biological needs, we have needs for meaning and significance in our personal and social lives.

The importance of symbols as a source of cultural diversity can be seen in the dress codes and hairstyles of different societies. In most situations, the symbolism of clothing and hairstyles communicates different messages, ranging from political beliefs to identification with specific ethnic or religious groups. The tartan of a Scottish clan, the Mao jacket of a Chinese revolutionary, the black leather jacket and long hair of a motorcycle gang member in the United States, and the veil of an Islamic woman in Saudi Arabia provide a symbolic vocabulary that creates cultural diversity.

Many examples of clothing styles could be used to illustrate how symbols contribute to cultural diversity. Consider, for instance, changing dress codes in the United States. During the 1960s, many young people wore jeans, sandals, and beads to symbolize their rebellion against what they conceived as the conformist inclinations of American society. By the 1980s, many of the same people were wearing three-piece "power suits" as they sought to advance up the corporate ladder.

An example of how hairstyles can create meaningful symbolic codes can be seen in a group known as the Rastafarians (sometimes known as Rastas or Rastaman) of Jamaica. The majority of the people of Jamaica are of African descent. During the eighteenth and nineteenth centuries, they were brought to Jamaica by European slave traders to work on plantations. The Rastafarians are a specific religious group within Jamaica who believe that Haile Selassie (1892–1975), the former emperor of Ethiopia whose original name was Ras Tafari, was the black Messiah who appeared in the flesh for the redemption of all blacks exiled in the world of white oppression. Rastafarian religion fuses Old Testament teachings, Christian mysticism, and Afro-Jamaican religious beliefs. The Rastafarian movement originated as a consequence of harsh economic, political, and living conditions in the slums of Jamaica.

In the 1950s, during the early phase of the Rastafarian movement, some male members began to grow their hair in "locks" or "dreadlocks" to symbolize their religious and political commitments. This

The late Bob Marley, a Rastafarian musician.

hairstyle became well known in Western society through reggae music and Rasta musicians such as the late Bob Marley. Rastafarians derive the symbolism of their dreadlock hairstyle from the Bible. They view the unshaven man as the natural man and invoke Samson as one of the most important figures in the Bible. Dreadlocks also reflect a dominant symbol within the Rastafarian movement—the lion—which is associated with Haile Selassie, one of whose titles was the "Conquering Lion of Judah." To simulate the spirit of the lion, some Rastas do not cut their hair, sometimes growing their locks 20 inches or more.

In addition, the dreadlock hairstyle has a deeper symbolic significance in Jamaican society, where hair was often referred to as an index of racial and social inequality. Fine, silky hair was considered "good," whereas woolly, kinky hair was frowned on (Barrett 1977). The white person with fine, silky hair was considered higher on the social ladder than was the typical African descendant in Jamaica. Thus, the Rastafarian hairstyle was a defiant symbol of resistance to the cultural values and norms of Jamaican society.

The cultural symbolism of the Rastafarian dreadlocks and long beards represents savagery, wildness, danger, disorder, and degeneration. It sends the message that Rastafarians are outside of Jamaican society. Many Jamaicans view the dreadlocks as unkempt, dangerous, and dirty, yet to the Rastafarians, dreadlocks symbolize power, liberation, and

defiance. Through their hairstyle, they announce to society that they do not accept the values, beliefs, and norms of the majority of the people.

Thus, to a great extent, culture consists of a network of symbolic codes that enhance values, beliefs, worldviews, and ideologies within a society. Humans go to great lengths to create symbols that provide meaning for individuals and groups. These symbolic meanings are a powerful source of cultural diversity. When anthropologists study these symbolic codes and meanings, they often draw on the humanistic-interpretive approach to comprehend these phenomena.

Ethnicity

One important aspect of culture is the recognition of one's own group as distinct from another based on different values, beliefs, norms, and other characteristics. When referring to these differences, anthropologists use the terms *ethnic group* and *ethnicity*. **Ethnicity** is based on perceived differences in ancestral origins or descent and shared historical and cultural heritage. An **ethnic group** is a collectivity of people who believe they share a common history, culture, or ancestry. For example, a small ethnic group known as the Old Order Amish maintain very strong ethnic boundary markers in U.S. society (Hostetler 1980; Kephart and Zellner 1994). Amish ethnicity originated in Switzerland during

Amish family.

the sixteenth century. The Amish descended from a group of Anabaptists who split off with their own leadership during the Protestant Reformation. After this split, the Amish began to define themselves as different from other Anabaptists, Protestants, and Catholics, and they faced a great deal of persecution from the religious authorities (Kephart and Zellner 1994). Eventually, the Amish fled to the United States in the 1700s, settling first in Lancaster, Pennsylvania. From there, they have grown in size and live in twenty different states in the United States. The Amish population is about 100,000. There are no longer any Amish in Europe.

The Amish in the United States emphasize their ethnic difference through language by speaking a German dialect within their communities. The Amish dress in a traditional manner similar to the cultural codes of the 1600s. Men wear hats and long beards; women wear long hair, which is always covered by a hat in public. Based on their interpretation of the Bible, the Amish strive to maintain a conservative, traditional way of life that does not allow the adoption of modern technology such as electricity, automobiles, or television. They do not allow their children to be educated beyond the eighth grade so that they are not exposed to modern U.S. culture. The Amish have a deeply emotional attachment to their ethnicity and culture. These sentiments are deeply rooted within Amish culture and are evident in their language, dress, and a traditional style of life, which distinguish them from other North Americans.

We will discuss many different ethnic groups throughout the various chapters in this text, and in Chapter 7, we elaborate on how anthropologists have developed methods to investigate the complexities of ethnicity, ethnic groups, and ethnic movements around the world.

Cultural Universals

As previously discussed, early anthropologists emphasized the realities of cultural diversity in their research and writings. Some anthropologists, however, began to recognize that humans throughout the world share some fundamental behavioral characteristics. George Murdock, an anthropologist who devoted himself to cross-cultural analysis, compiled a lengthy list of cultural universals from hundreds of societies. **Cultural universals** are essential behavioral characteristics of societies, and they are found all over the world. Murdock's list of cultural universals can be seen in Table 3.1; it

Table 3.1	A List of Some Cultural Universals Described by Murdock		
age grading	faith healing	joking	pregnancy usages
athletics	family	kin groups	property rights
bodily adornments	feasting	kin terminology	propitiation of supernatural
calendar	fire making	language	beings
community organization	folklore	magic	puberty customs
cooking	food taboos	marriage	religious rituals
cooperative labor	funeral rites	mealtimes	residence rules
cosmology	games	medicine	sexual restrictions
courtship	gestures	modesty	soul concepts
dancing	gift giving	mourning	status differentiation
decorative art	greetings	music	tool making
division of labor	hair styles	mythology	trade
dream interpretation	hospitality	numerals	visiting
education	housing	obstetrics	weaning
ethics	hygiene	personal names	weather control
ethnobotany	incest taboos	population policy	
etiquette	inheritance	postnatal care	

Source: Adapted from George Peter Murdock, "The Common Denominator of Cultures." In *The Science of Man in the World Crisis* by Ralph Linten. Copyright © 1945 by Columbia University Press. Reproduced with permission of Columbia University Press in the format textbook via Copyright Clearance Center.

includes such basics as language, cooking, family, folklore, games, community organizations, decorative art, education, ethics, myths, food taboos, numbers, personal names, magic, religion, puberty customs, toolmaking, and sexual restrictions. Although the specific content and practices of these universals may vary from society to society, the fact that these cultural universals exist underlies the essential reality that modern humans are of one biological family and one species.

In an influential book entitled *Human Universals* (1991), anthropologist Donald E. Brown suggests that in their quest for describing cultural diversity, many anthropologists have overlooked basic similarities in human behavior and culture. This led to stereotypes and distortions about people in other societies, who were viewed as "exotic," "inscrutable," and "alien."

Following in Murdock's footsteps, Brown describes many human universals. In one imaginative chapter, Brown creates a group of people he refers to as the "Universal People," who have all the traits of any people in any society throughout the world. The Universal People have language with a complex grammar to communicate and think abstractly; kinship terms and categories for distinguishing relatives and age groupings; gender terms for male and female; facial expressions to show basic emotions; a concept of the self as subject and object; tools, shelter, and fire; patterns for childbirth and training; families and political groupings; conflict; etiquette; morality, religious beliefs, and worldviews; and dance, music, art, and other aesthetic standards.

Donald E. Brown.

Brown's depiction of the Universal People clearly suggests that many behaviors and other aspects of human behavior result from certain problems that all societies face to maintain their physical and social survival. For a society to survive, it must have mechanisms to care for children, adapt to the physical environment, produce and distribute goods and services, maintain order, and provide explanations of the natural and social environment. In addition, many universal behaviors result from fundamental biological characteristics common to all people.

Anthropologists have discovered that culture can be both diverse and universal. The challenge for anthropology is to understand the basis of both this diversity and this universality. To paraphrase a saying of the late anthropologist Clyde Kluckhohn: Every human is like all other humans, some other humans, and no other human. The major objective of cultural anthropology is to investigate the validity of this statement.

SUMMARY

Culture is a key concept in anthropology. Culture is learned and is transmitted from generation to generation in a society. Humans learn through direct experience (situational learning), observation (social learning), and symbols (symbolic learning). Symbols are arbitrary meanings that vary from society to society. Many anthropologists view symbolic learning as the major distinction between human and nonhuman animals.

Culture includes material and nonmaterial components. The material aspect of culture consists of tools, clothing, shelter, armaments, and other

innovations that enable humans to adapt to their environments. The nonmaterial components of culture are values, beliefs, norms, worldviews, and ideologies.

Different societies maintain different cultural and symbolic structures, creating the great variety and diversity of norms, values, worldviews, and behaviors. Cultural anthropologists have discovered that cultural items—ranging from dress to technology to sexual practices to dietary habits— are enormously diverse. Anthropologists also recognize that many patterns of human behavior are universal. The universal distribution of certain cultural traits suggests that humans everywhere have similar biological requirements and tendencies that influence behavior. Thus, anthropologists have been engaged in exploring both the diversity and the similarity of human cultures throughout the world.

QUESTIONS TO THINK ABOUT

1. How do anthropologists differentiate culture from nonhuman animal behavior?

2. As a college student, you have probably heard quite a bit about "cultural diversity" or "multiculturalism" and the changing demographics in the United States. What is multiculturalism? Why is it important to understand this concept? Are there any dangers in implementing multicultural education programs?

3. Using an anthropological perspective, explain the statement, "You are what you eat."

4. After reading the section on dress codes and symbolism, pick another example of dress codes and hairstyles and explain what they symbolize to the individuals involved.

5. Can you distinguish ethnic groups from each other in your own society? How do you make that distinction?

6. If you were to create the "Universal People" (see page 66), how would they behave and organize themselves? What would they believe? And how might they act? After you have constructed these imaginary people, read the summary of Donald E. Brown's chapter on "Universal People" in *Human Universals* (1991) for comparison.

7. Interpret the statement, "Every human is like all other humans, some other humans, and no other human."

KEY TERMS

beliefs	folkways	schemas
cultural hegemony	ideal culture	signs
cultural relativism	ideology	situational learning
cultural universals	material culture	social learning
culture	mores	society
enculturation	nonmaterial culture	symbolic learning
ethnic group	norms	symbols
ethnicity	real culture	values

Chapter **4**

The Process of Enculturation: Psychological Anthropology

 CHAPTER QUESTIONS

- What is the relationship between individuals and culture as studied by psychological anthropologists?

- How does nonhuman animal behavior differ from human behavior?

- How have anthropologists studied enculturation and its relationship to personality formation, sexual behavior, cognition, emotions, and mental disorders?

- In what way are the studies of enculturation limited?

In the previous chapter, we explored the concept of culture as it reflects the differences and similarities in human behavior and thought around the world. This chapter focuses on how anthropologists study the relationship between the individual and culture, or the process of enculturation. Anthropologists who focus on the process of enculturation are known as **psychological anthropologists**. Recall from Chapter 3 that enculturation is the process of social interaction through which people learn their culture. Unlike psychologists, who tend to study people within the psychologists' own societies, psychological anthropologists observe people and the process of enculturation in many different types of societies. Their research findings are then used as the basis of cross-cultural studies to determine how and why behavior, thoughts, and feelings differ and are similar from society to society.

Psychological anthropologists study the development of personality characteristics and individual behaviors in a given society and how they are influenced by enculturation. In their studies, anthropologists need to question basic assumptions regarding human nature. Is human nature primarily a matter of biological influences or of cultural factors? In order to study this question, psychological anthropologists focus on the enculturation process and precisely how this process influences personality characteristics, sexual behavior, thinking and cognition, emotional development, and particular abnormal behaviors in different societies. This chapter considers some of the major research by psychological anthropologists on the process of enculturation.

Biology versus Culture

Before we explore the specific aspects of psychological anthropology, we need to consider some questions. One fundamental concept that anthropologists reflect on is what is frequently referred to as "human nature." Two questions immediately arise when discussing this concept. If there are basic similarities or universal patterns of human behavior, does that mean that human nature is biologically transmitted through heredity? If this is the case, to what extent can culture or learning change human nature to produce variation in behavior within different societies? These questions have led to a controversy in anthropology, with some anthropologists emphasizing biological influences on human behavior and others emphasizing the social or cultural influences that affect behavior.

Today, however, most anthropologists realize that neither of these influences exists in absolute, pure form. Modern anthropologists are, therefore, adopting an interactionist perspective, which combines the effects of biology and culture to explain human behavior. Anthropologists recognize that human behavior depends on both our biological endowment and what we learn from our society or culture. What interactionists care about is the interrelationship between the biologically based and learned factors in any behavior.

Instincts and Human Nature

Another fundamental question addressed by anthropologists is to what extent human nature is similar to that of other animals. For example, according to the traditional view of humans, the human body is "animal-like" or "machinelike," and the human mind is separate from the body. For many Westerners, this image of humans was used to distinguish humans from other types of animals.

Human Beings as Animals

What do we mean when we say that humans are animal-like? This statement can create misunderstandings because of the different meanings we give to the word *animal*. On the one hand, we distinguish animals scientifically from plants and minerals. This system of classification places humans in the animal category. On the other hand, animal is sometimes used in a derogatory or pejorative sense. For example, in one of the earliest uses of the word in written English, Shakespeare wrote:

> *His intellect is not replenished, bee is only an animal, only sensible in the duller parts.* (Love's Labour's Lost, *IV. ii*)

This is the negative meaning of the term that we associate with films such as Animal House, referring to "uncivilized," "irrational," "unthinking," and "brutish" behaviors. In attempting to understand humans fully, anthropologists emphasize only the scientific meaning of the word animal. Anthropologists maintain that humans are partly like all animals, partly like certain types of animals and partly like no other animal.

Because we are part of the animal kingdom, humans share certain characteristics with all animals. We have to consume certain amounts of carbohydrates, proteins, and minerals to survive, just as other animals do. We cannot photosynthesize and process our own foods from within, as plants do. In addition, we share certain characteristics with particular types of animals. For example, like other mammals, we have body hair, and human mothers have the capacity to suckle their offspring with milk produced after birth. Similarly, like other primates such as chimpanzees and gorillas, we have stereoscopic, color vision; we have nails instead of claws; we are extremely sociable; and our infants experience a long period of dependence on adults.

Despite these similarities with other animals, humans are unquestionably the most complex, intelligent, and resourceful creatures on the planet. Humans have spread and adapted to every continent, becoming the most widely dispersed animal on the earth. We have been the most creative species in respect to our abilities to adjust to different conditions, ranging from tropical rainforests to deserts to rural agricultural areas to urban environments.

Instincts in Animals

Anthropologists have asked the question: What gives the human species its tremendous flexibility in adjusting to these different environments? One way of answering this question is to compare the fundamental behaviors of human and nonhuman animals. Many animals inherit instincts that allow them to take advantage of the specific conditions of their environment. Instinctive behaviors occur widely within the animal kingdom. For example, certain species of birds migrate during the winter season. Temperature changes or differences in ultraviolet radiation from the sun trigger biochemically based, inborn hormonal reactions that act on neurological mechanisms, stimulating all normal individuals within a particular species of bird to fly in a certain direction. This behavior enables the birds to find sufficient feeding grounds for survival during the winter season. But notice that these birds are also influenced by external factors such as temperature conditions and environmental factors that contribute to their behavior. Their "instincts" alone do not "determine" their behavior.

Another example of these species-specific instincts is the nest-building behavior of certain bird populations. In an experiment, scientists isolated as many as five generations of weaver finches and did not supply them with nest-building materials. (Weaver finches are small, brightly colored, seed-eating birds that construct complicated nests with side entrances.) When the scientists released the sixth generation of birds, however, these birds automatically built nests identical to those of their ancestors.

Bears hibernating, salmon swimming upstream to lay eggs during a specific season, spiders spinning perfect webs, and infant turtles and alligators walking unaided toward the water after hatching from eggs are other examples of instinctive behaviors. These behaviors can be thought of as a kind of innate knowledge with which these animals are born and enable them to adapt, survive, and perpetuate

A weaver finch building a nest—an example of instinctive behavior.

their offspring. However, these instincts alone do not influence the behavior of these animals. This will be emphasized in this next section.

Instincts and Learned Behaviors

As emphasized before, the fact that some animal behaviors are instinctive does not mean that environment has nothing to do with these behaviors. Although some animal behavior is near-perfect when it first appears, typically the development of most animal behavior involves a continuous interaction between the organism and the environment.

This does not mean that nonhuman animals do not learn their complex behaviors, however. For example, most birds have to learn their particular song that they sing for various purposes after being exposed to the song of their particular species. However, when bird song is studied by biologists they find that there is a very complex process that involves both nature and nurture in learning these songs that help them communicate with one another. For example, song learning by birds varies from species to species. Some species do not need to be exposed to the specific vocalizations to reproduce them in near-perfect form. A particular species of dove sings a species-specific type of "coo" in perfect form even when reared with other species of doves. In contrast, parrots can learn to imitate any song they hear. But generally, many other birds, such as chaffinches, need to be exposed to the adult song during their early months to acquire the specific vocalization for their particular species (Catchpole and Slater 1995; Hinde and Stevenson-Hinde 1987). In fact, much of animal behavior is a result of both their genetically based neurological capacities as well as how "nurture" or learning provides them with experience so that they can adapt and survive within the world.

Most ethologists (scientists who study animal behavior) agree that complex instincts in different types of animals can be classified as exhibiting a closed or more open type of genetic program. Closed types of instincts remain fairly stable, even when environmental conditions change, whereas open types respond more sensitively to changing circumstances. For example, many species of birds that migrate, such as geese, have changed their migratory behavior in response to environmental changes. Thus, even behaviors that are genetically based can be modified to some degree by experience and by specific environmental conditions.

Do Humans Possess Instincts?

Because humans are part of the animal kingdom, the question arises: Do we have any instinctive behaviors? This question is difficult to answer because we use the word *instinct* in different contexts. Sometimes we refer to athletes as having the right kind of instincts in going toward the basket or goal line. Upon further reflection, however, it is obvious that basketball or football players who respond in an automatic way to a play situation do so only after practicing for long hours and developing the coordination and skillful moves necessary for competitive sports. Because athletic skills are learned, they are not comparable to the instinctive behaviors of animals. We also use the term to refer to some intuitive processes. For example, we have all heard about relying on our instincts in making difficult decisions. Usually, when we refer to our "gut instincts," what we really mean are our "intuitions." Some "cognitive intuitions" may very

well be based on "innate predispositions" that develop as a result of our brain and neurological developments as well as early learning in infancy. However, as mentioned before, closed instincts are genetically prescribed behaviors that rigidly determine behavior, whereas our intuitions are internal feelings and cognitive states that tend to motivate us in certain directions. It appears that some of our intuitions are more like open instincts, which involve a great deal of learning from the environment. As Matt Ridley, a well-known biologist who emphasizes an interactionist understanding of human behavior states, "Instincts, in a species like the human one, are not immutable genetic programmers; they are predispositions to learn" (1996).

Thus, we can ask: Do humans, then, have any closed instincts like those of other nonhuman animals? Do we have any automatic, biologically controlled behaviors? Because of the wide range of behaviors shown by humans, most anthropologists, psychologists, and other social scientists concur that humans do not have any instincts that automatically motivate and drive our behavior.

We do have some genetically determined behaviors called simple reflexes, or involuntary responses, such as being startled by a loud noise, blinking our eyes, breathing, or throwing out our arms when we lose our balance. These reflexive behaviors are automatic responses to environmental conditions, and we do them unconsciously. But these are not comparable to the complex behaviors related to the closed instincts of some other species. Some anthropologists, however, influenced by evolutionary psychology, hypothesize that humans also have some genetically prepared behaviors that have enabled us to adapt to varying conditions in our evolutionary history. As mentioned above, evolutionary psychologists do think that humans have built-in "cognitive intuitions" that predispose certain "forms of thinking and perhaps action." Yet they do not view these cognitive intuitions as automatically motivating and driving human behavior; instead these cognitive intuitions are definitely shaped by experience and learning as well as brain and neurological developments while we are infants. Psychologist David Myers has followed the research on "intuitions" for many years and concludes that although we as humans rely on our intuitions for many decisions and actions we take, our intuitions can be very faulty guides for understanding the reality around us (2002). Psychologists and anthropologists have been doing experimental studies on intuitions in the United States and around the world and find that they often result in misleading our thinking and perceptions of the world.

Drives

We humans also have basic, inborn **drives**—biological urges such as hunger, thirst, and sex—that need satisfaction. These drives are important for the survival of the species. Yet, again, these drives are not comparable to the closed instincts of nonhuman animals. We are not programmed to satisfy them in a rigid, mechanical manner. Rather, the ways in which we satisfy such drives are learned through experience. We do not automatically build a spider's web to capture our food; we have to learn to find food in ways that vary widely in many different types of environments. And, unlike some other animals, we may choose to override rather than to satisfy these drives. For example, people can ignore the hunger drive by going on hunger strikes as a political protest.

If we do not have closed instincts that rigidly prescribe our behavior, what do we have that makes us so successful and creative? The answer is that we have the capacity for flexibility in creating conditions and providing solutions for human survival. Some animals have a closed biogram, a genetically closed behavioral complex that is related to their adaptations to their specific environment niche. In contrast, humans have an open biogram, an extremely flexible genetic program that is shaped by learning experiences.

Culture versus Instinct

In addition to open biograms, our unprecedented success in adapting to different conditions reflects the influence of human culture. Our capacity for culture, an inherent aspect of the human mind, has enabled us to modify our behaviors and to shape and adjust to our natural environment. The capacity for culture is genetically programmed through the human brain and nervous system. But as we emphasized in Chapter 3, culture is not transmitted biologically through genetic programming. Instead, it is learned through the enculturation process and is passed on from generation to generation. Culture frees us from relying on the slow process of natural selection to adapt to specific environments.

Most genes do not specifically encode for narrowly defined types of human behavior. We are not genetically programmed to build shelters in a certain manner, to devise patterns of economic distribution, to get married, to vote for a president, to carry out a revolution, or to believe in a particular religion. These are learned behaviors based on the enculturation processes that make up the economic, social, political, and religious practices and concepts of a particular society. Without culture, we would not be able to adjust to the tremendous range of environments throughout the world. We would not be able to adapt to Arctic conditions, hunt animals and collect plants, herd cattle, plant crops, or drive a car. The development of the human mind, with the capacity for culture, represents the greatest revolutionary breakthrough in the evolution of life.

Enculturation: Culture and Personality

Enculturation is a lifelong process, and it links individuals with the specific culture to which they are exposed. Immediately after they are born, infants begin to absorb their language and culture through both unconscious and conscious learning—situational, social, and symbolic—the etiquette, mores, values, beliefs, and practices of their society. Anthropologist Meredith Small in her recent book *Kids: How Biology and Culture Shape the Way We Raise Our Children* (2001) explores how both biological factors interact with learning in enculturation processes in many different societies throughout the world.

Enculturation is a vital foundation of our humanity. Virtually helpless at birth, an infant needs care and is completely dependent on others for survival. Through the interaction of enculturation with biologically based predispositions, a person acquires his or her **personality**, the fairly stable patterns of thought, feeling, and action associated with a specific person. Personality includes several components: the cognitive, emotional, and behavioral.

The cognitive component of personality consists of thought patterns, memory, belief, perception, and other intellectual capacities. The emotional component includes emotions such as love, hate, envy, jealousy, sympathy, anger, and pride. The behavioral component consists of the skills, aptitudes, competence, and other abilities or potentials that are developed throughout the course of a person's life.

Early Studies of Enculturation

During the 1930s and 1940s, a number of anthropologists began to research enculturation to learn about the influence of culture on personality development. At this time, some social scientists suggested that biology and race are the most influential determinants of human behavior (see Chapter 7). In Germany, for example, social scientists who were members of the Nazi Party promoted the idea that because of biological characteristics, some races are superior to others in respect to behavior and thought. Cultural anthropologists in the United States began to challenge this view of biological or racial determinism through research on enculturation (Degler 1991; Konner 2002). In particular, two women anthropologists, Ruth Benedict and Margaret Mead, became pioneers in early psychological anthropology. They published extensively and became prominent in this area of research. Both of these anthropologists maintained that each society and culture has a unique history. After studying processes such as child rearing and enculturation, they proposed that every culture is characterized by a dominant personality type. Culture, they argued, is essentially "personality writ large." The field studies they did became the basis of what was then called culture-and-personality theory.

Benedict and Culture Types One classic example of the application of culture-and-personality theory is Benedict's analysis of the Plains and Pueblo Native American societies. In an essay titled "Psychological Types in the Cultures of the Southwest" (1928) and in a classic book, *Patterns of Culture* (1934), Benedict classified Pueblo societies as having an Apollonian (named for the Greek god Apollo) culture. The Pueblo cultural ethos stressed gentleness, cooperation, harmony, tranquility, and peacefulness. According to Benedict, these values explain why members of Pueblo societies were

Ruth Benedict portrayed the Plains Indians, such as those with her in this photo, as "Dionysian," or excessive in their behavior.

"moderate." The Pueblo rarely indulged in violence, and they avoided the use of drugs and alcohol to transcend their senses.

In contrast, Benedict characterized the Plains societies as Dionysian (after the Greek god Dionysius). She described how the values and ethos of the Plains groups were almost the direct opposite of those of the Pueblo. The Plains Indians were involved in warfare and violence, and their ritual behavior included the use of drugs, alcohol, fasting, and bodily self-torture and mutilation to induce religious ecstasy. Benedict extended her analysis to such groups as the Kwakiutl Native American peoples and the Dobu of Melanesia. She referred to the Kwakiutl as "megalomaniacs" and the Dobuans as "paranoid," fearing and hating one another. In each case, she claimed that the group's values and ethos had created a distinctive cultural personality. In Benedict's analysis, the culture of a particular society can be studied by studying the personality of its bearers. The patterning or configuration of a particular culture is simply reflected in an individual's personality.

Mead in Samoa Margaret Mead was one of the most influential contributors to the field of culture and personality. Although most of her ethnographic reports focused on fairly isolated, small-scale societies located in the Pacific islands, she addressed issues that concerned U.S. society, particularly adolescence, child care, and relationships between males and females. At the age of 23, Mead went to the islands of American Samoa to study adolescent development. In the United States and other societies, adolescence was usually identified with emotional conflict and rebellion against parental authority. Her mentor, Franz Boas (see Chapter 7), wanted her to investigate this aspect of life in Samoa to determine whether this pattern of adolescent development was universal. The central research question that Mead was to investigate was to what extent adolescent problems are the products of physiological changes occurring at puberty or the result of cultural factors.

Mead resided in Samoa for nine months and interviewed sixty-eight Samoan girls in three villages, interviewing twenty-five in depth. She concluded that, in contrast to U.S. society, adolescence in Samoa was not characterized by problems between the young and the old. She attributed the difference between the two societies to different sets of values, which produced different cultural personalities. In her book *Coming of Age in Samoa* (1928), she argued that Samoan society emphasized group harmony and cooperation. These values arose, according to Mead, from Samoan child-rearing practices. Samoan children were raised in family units that included many adults. Therefore, youngsters did not develop strong emotional ties to any one adult. Consequently, she argued, emotional bonds were relatively shallow.

For this reason, Mead continued, Samoan society was more permissive than U.S. society. Children learned privately and often secretly about sexuality and adolescents learned freely, but had hidden, clandestine premarital sex. In addition, Mead contended that Samoan society shared a common set of values and standards. Therefore, Samoan children were not exposed to conflicting values and differing political and religious beliefs, as were U.S. adolescents. For these reasons, Mead

concluded, Samoan children experienced a much easier transition from adolescence into adulthood than did their counterparts in the United States.

The Culture-and-Personality School: An Evaluation

The anthropological tradition represented by Mead and Benedict stimulated more careful research regarding personality and culture. Much of the data provided by these early psychological anthropologists were important in understanding the enculturation process. As a result of these early studies, we now have a better understanding of personality formation, thought, behavior, and emotional development within different human societies.

Despite these accomplishments, the culture-and-personality school has been criticized on many fronts. One major shortcoming cited is the practice of characterizing an entire society in terms of one dominant personality. Culture-and-personality theorists assume that all members of a given society share the same cultural knowledge. This assumption produced highly stereotyped presentations of various cultures and peoples. In fact, culture and knowledge are distributed differently and unequally within society. Some people have a cultural knowledge of values, beliefs, and ideologies that others do not have. As discussed in Chapter 3, people do not all share the same culture. Culture is variously distributed among different individuals. Thus, defining an entire society as a single personality creates cultural stereotypes rather than a realistic portrait of a people. Benedict, for example, neglected many data that suggested that both the Plains and Pueblo societies exhibited Apollonian and Dionysian behaviors.

The culture-and-personality school has also been criticized for focusing entirely on the nonmaterial aspects of culture. Theorists such as Benedict went so far as to argue that cultural values are completely autonomous from material conditions (Hatch 1973). Therefore, they did not include such factors as technology or the physical environment in their explanations of human behavior. Again using Benedict as an example, the fact that traditional Plains Indians were primarily bison-hunting groups, whereas the Pueblo peoples were agriculturalists in a semiarid desert, was not included in her analysis, yet this fact was obviously important in their societies.

A final criticism of the culture-and-personality theorists is their perceived tendency to attribute human behavior entirely to cultural factors. Of course, their emphasis on cultural determinants rather than biological determinants reflects the attempt to criticize the biological and racist determinism prevalent during that period. However, in their descriptions they tended to dismiss any biological basis of behavior. This extreme culturalist perspective has since come under attack by a number of critics, first by the late Australian anthropologist Derek Freeman.

The Freeman-Mead Controversy In 1983 Freeman attracted a great deal of attention when he published a controversial book titled *Margaret Mead and Samoa: The Making and Unmaking of an Anthropological Myth.* Having conducted fieldwork in Samoa intermittently since 1940, Freeman concluded that Mead's findings were largely erroneous. Whereas Mead had portrayed the Samoan people as lacking strong passions, aggression, warfare (warfare had been suppressed by the government, but it did exist well into the colonial period in which Mead was there), a sense of sin or guilt, rape, suicide, and other behaviors associated with intense emotions, Freeman claimed to find all of these behaviors.

Freeman challenged Mead by asserting that strong emotional ties did exist between parents and children in Samoan society. He also challenged Mead's conclusions concerning casual attitudes toward sexuality. Pointing out that Samoa had converted to Christianity during the 1830s, Freeman asserted that most Samoans had puritanical views toward sexuality. He found that virginity for girls was highly valued, casual sexual liaisons were prohibited, and adultery was severely punished. Government records indicated that the incidence of rape in Samoa (proportionate to population size) was twice as high as that in the United States.

Freeman also rejected Mead's claims for an easy transition from adolescence to adulthood. He noted that adolescents were severely punished by their parents for any transgressions. He presented charts illustrating that offenses and delinquent behaviors among Samoans peaked at the age of 16, especially for males. Thus, Freeman concluded that adolescents in Samoa go through a period of deviance and rebellion against their elders in the same way that other adolescents around the world do. Freeman asserted that hormonal changes as

Margaret Mead with Samoan girl.

well as cultural influences have consequences for adolescent behavior everywhere. Samoan adolescents are not much different from adolescents elsewhere.

How could two anthropologists studying the same people arrive at such radically different conclusions? For example, instead of residing with a Samoan family, Mead lived with an American family and conducted interviews intermittently. On the other hand Freeman does concede that Mead had an incredible amount of energy and tried to find out as carefully as possible what and how these young females thought and behaved because they would frequently visit the back porch of her household. Although she was appointed by the Samoan chiefs as an important high status *taupou* (a ceremonial position as a village virgin), Freeman claimed that because she was a young woman, she did not interview many of the significant chiefs. Of the twenty-five females she interviewed, half were not past puberty and therefore could not serve as models of the transition from adolescence to adulthood.

Freeman argued that the major reason for Mead's misinterpretation of Samoan society was her extreme reliance on the model of cultural determinism of theorists such as Benedict. Thus, Mead's portrayal of Samoa as a society without adolescent problems supported the claims of her close colleagues at that time, who maintained that biology has had little influence on behavior. In contrast, Freeman emphasized an interactionist approach, which focuses on both biological and cultural influences. He argued that the biological changes that accompany adolescence inevitably affect adolescent behavior.

The Freeman-Mead debate remains a major controversy in anthropology. Supporters of Mead point out that Freeman studied Samoa years and even decades after Mead did. Because societies are not static, it is possible that Samoan values and lifestyles had changed by the time of Freeman's work. Freeman has two more recent books, *Margaret Mead and the Heretic: The Making and Unmaking of an Anthropological Myth* (1997) and *The Fateful Hoaxing of Margaret Mead* (1999), in which he emphasizes how Mead was strongly influenced by the ideas of cultural determinism. He believes that Mead overlooked any type of biological influences on behavior. However, other anthropologists of Samoa, such as Paul Shankman, note that Mead did not discount biology entirely; she merely rejected the extreme biological deterministic views of their time (Shankman 1998, 2000, 2001). In addition, Freeman tended to emphasize public morality or "ideal culture" based on what people said rather than what they actually did. Also, Freeman overlooked Mead's very precise study on Samoan social organization and culture that is still viewed as a classic intensive ethnographic work today by Samoan specialists (1934). Freeman was using a model of scientific investigation that emphasized the refutation of particular empirical claims that Mead was using (O'Meara 2004). Overall, the Mead-Freeman controversy resulted in a complex debate that fueled a lot of controversy within anthropology. As the controversy matured, a number of anthropologists refined their understanding of both the realities and myths about Samoan culture and gained more insight of the interactionist approach in assessing enculturation issues (Shankman 2001).

Childhood Acquisition of Cultural Knowledge

Despite limitations of early research on enculturation and culture and personality, pioneering women anthropologists such as Margaret Mead, Ruth Benedict, and others were the first to systematically examine the effects of childhood training on personality development. Male ethnographers had not paid much attention to this subject. This innovative research has resulted in a much improved understanding of the techniques of childhood training and enculturation throughout the world. Since then, a number of studies of childhood training by psychological anthropologists have contributed to this area of research.

Japanese Childhood Enculturation   Some contemporary ethnographic research projects focus on the type of childhood training and enculturation that influences the learning of basic concepts of a particular culture. One study, conducted by Joy Hendry (1992), focused on how children in Japan become enculturated. According to the Western stereotype, Japanese society is characterized as "collectivistic" rather than "individualistic." A related stereotype is that Japanese society is a "consensus," or "conformist," society, with everyone submitting to the norms of the group. Hendry's ethnographic research on whether these stereotypes are correct focused on how children learn their initial concepts of Japanese culture and adjust to group behaviors.

Hendry found that small children are extremely important in Japanese culture. Babies are afforded every possible individual attention. For example, many highly educated mothers give up their careers to dedicate themselves to full-time nurturing once a child is born. The child is to be kept in a secure, harmonious household. A tiny child is often strapped to a mother's back or front while the mother works, shops, and performs daily routines. Also, an adult will lie down with a child at bedtime until he or she falls asleep or in some cases sleeps all night with the child. From an American perspective, it appears that the child is totally indulged, but the child learns a great many routine tasks such as eating, washing, dressing, and toilet training through repetition until the child can do these tasks on his or her own.

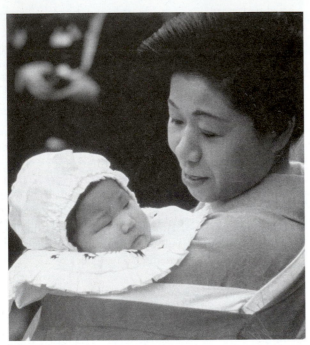

A Japanese mother with her baby.

During this early phase of enculturation, the child learns two basic cultural concepts: *uchi*, or inside of the house, including the people inside, and *soto*, the outside world. Human beings are categorized by these concepts, and various behaviors in a Japanese household, such as removing shoes before entering the house, reinforce the inside/outside dichotomy. *Uchi* is associated with safety, security, and cleanliness. Soto is where danger may lurk; big dogs, strangers, or even demons and ghosts may be outside. For the first few years of their lives, children play with siblings, cousins, and gradually with close neighbors. They are allowed to play in the immediate neighborhood from as early as 2 years of age if it is a safe environment, and the child begins to build up a new set of "inside" personal relations with neighbors who live nearby.

At the age of 4 or 5, the child is introduced to group life with outsiders in a kindergarten or day nursery. At first the children cry for a while and refuse to join in, but eventually they become involved with the new group of fellow kindergartners, and this becomes a new *uchi* group for them. They learn to cooperate with one another in the group and begin to develop an identity appropriate for group life. However, Hendry emphasizes that the children do not lose their individuality. Each child is treated as an individual by the teacher, who obtains a great deal of background knowledge about the child. (Parents fill out forms regarding their child's strengths and weaknesses, likes and dislikes, siblings, and other details.) In addition, teachers visit the child's home at least once during the academic year. Thus, along with learning to cooperate with their new *uchi* group, these children also become familiar with their own individuality and the individual characteristics of their peers. When engaging in group activities, whether in games, sports, learning activities, or other responsibilities, the children teach each other personal skills and abilities so that the entire group will benefit.

Hendry concludes that even though Japanese children learn to participate in many group-oriented activities, they do not completely lose their sense of individuality. Although Japanese society does not emphasize individualism in the same way U.S. society does, with its connotations of self-assertion and individual rights, Japanese children develop their own sense of self in respect to their individual talents and abilities. Linguistic anthropologist Patricia Clancy's study of Japanese language complements Joy Hendry's ethnographic study and demonstrates how language is used to accomplish the goals and behaviors for Japanese children (Clancy 1986).

One of the conclusions based on the new types of psychological anthropology studies such as Joy Hendry's is that children are not just passive recipients in the enculturation process. Instead, they are active contributors to the meaning and outcome of interactions with other members of society. As an example, in another ethnographic study, Bambi Schieffelin analyzed how Kaluli children in Papua New Guinea learn to decipher particular concepts and relationships for different social settings (1990). Kaluli children learn about the relationship *ade*. *Ade* behavior is a unique relationship between older sisters and younger brothers encouraged by mothers in early childhood. Using specific verbal routines, the younger brothers are socialized to appeal to an older sister for goods, services, and attention. The older sister "feels sorry for" her younger brother and shares food and nurtures him affectionately. Later, as children become older, they may use the *ade* relationship when they wish to elicit compassion and get something from an older sister. In other words, they learn to use the verbal routines appropriate to the *ade* relationship with older sisters who are always expected to give out of feelings of compassion (Schieffelin 1990). Thus, Kaluli children learn the content and meaning of this *ade* relationship in the course of specific interactions with older sisters and brothers, but this language and behavior is not used outside of these sibling relationships. Caregivers may give verbal instruction and enforce other norms of the culture, but the contributions of the children themselves in this process are extremely important.

These Kaluli children have to learn the routine of *ade* and the specific style of requesting (begging), and there is no room for innovation, but they learn it through observing its use, participating in interaction (and getting results), but they also have to learn the complementary demeanor of assertion, and begging is what kids do, though adults do it too. Kids have to learn various behavioral and linguistic strategies and learn to deploy them in appropriate social and cultural contexts.

This new perspective in psychological anthropology moves away from a simplistic conception of enculturation, which tended to emphasize children as passive recipients of culture. Modern psychological anthropologists emphasize a more sophisticated conception of enculturation that focuses on the interactive relationships between child and caregiver, child and siblings, child and peers, or child and outsiders. The child is viewed as an active agent in this new conception of enculturation. Children learn to choose and design appropriate responses to specific social situations and contexts as they are exposed to them. Psychological anthropologists are contributing to a better understanding of how children acquire cultural knowledge through exposure and active participation in everyday social interaction.

Psychoanalytic Approaches in Anthropology

Sigmund Freud

A number of psychological anthropologists have been influenced by the concepts and ideas of Sigmund Freud, the founder of psychoanalysis and psychiatry. Freud (1856–1939), a Viennese physician trained in the natural sciences, viewed human behavior as a reflection of innate emotional factors. His theory of human behavior emphasizes the importance of emotions in the development of an individual's personality. He tried to demonstrate that a great deal of emotional life is unconscious; that is, people are often unaware of the real reasons for their feelings and actions. Freud postulated that the personality is made up of three sectors: the *id*, *ego*, and *superego*.

Freud believed that all humans are born with unconscious, innate drives for sex and aggression. These unconscious desires are part of the **id**. According to Freud, these drives promote the seeking of immediate pleasure and the avoidance of pain. The id represents the basic needs of humans, needs that exist in the unconscious. Freud maintained that the id is rooted in the biological organism and is present at birth; the newborn is basically a bundle of needs. But the sexual and aggressive drives are often frustrated by society. This frustration often results in what Freud termed repression, wherein the energy based on these sexual and aggressive drives of the id is redirected into socially approved forms of expression.

Eventually, the second part of the personality, the *ego*, becomes differentiated from the id. The **ego** represents the conscious attempt to balance the innate pleasure-seeking drives of the human organism with the demands and realities of the society. The ego is the "conscious" part of the personality and is sometimes referred to as the "reality part" of the personality.

Finally, the human personality develops the superego, which is the presence of culture within the individual. The **superego** is based on the internalized values and norms of society, which create the individual's conscience. The superego develops first in response to parental demands, but gradually the child learns that he or she has to respond to the society and culture at large. For example, Freud hypothesized that all male children are driven by an unconscious desire to have an affectionate and sexual relationship with their mother. This unconscious desire leads to hostility toward their natural father, the authority figure within the family. Freud called this the Oedipus complex. This desire is frustrated by the morality and norms of society, the superego, and the enculturation process. These emotional

Critical Perspectives

THE ANTHROPOLOGY OF THE "SELF"

One topic that is currently inspiring a great deal of cross-cultural research is the issue of the individual, or the concept of the "person" within society. More specifically, many anthropologists are addressing the questions: Do people in different societies view themselves as "individuals," "selves," or "persons" who are separate from their social group? If not, can we assume that people in these societies are "self-motivated" or "self-interested" in pursuing various goals? We usually make this assumption to explain our own behaviors and those of other people in our own society. Can we use this assumption to explain the behavior of people in other societies?

In the West, we tend to regard people as individuals who feel free to pursue their self-interests, to marry or not to marry, and to do what they want with their private property. Individualism is stressed through cultural beliefs and ideologies that serve as a basis for our economic, social, political, legal, and religious institutions. But is this sense of individualism a "natural" condition, or is it a by-product of our distinctive social and historical development? One way of answering this question is through cross-cultural research. If we find that other people do not think in these terms, then we can assume that our thoughts about the self, mind, and individual are conditioned by our historical and cultural circumstances.

One early theorist who influenced modern anthropological research on these questions was Marcel Mauss, a French sociologist who argued that the concept of the "self" or "person" as separate from the "role" and "status" within society arose in relationship to modern capitalist society ([1938] 1985). Relying on the ethnographic research of anthropologists such as Franz Boas, he theorized that the concept of the individual person had developed uniquely in the West through the evolution of Roman law, Christian ideas of morality, and modern philosophical thought.

For example, according to Mauss, during the medieval period in Europe it would have been unheard of to think of an individual as completely separate from the larger social group. Medieval Christianity portrayed the individual as merely an element in God's creation, which was referred to as the "great chain of being." All elements in the universe were arranged in a hierarchy from God to angels, humans, animals, trees, rocks, and other inorganic materials. All these elements had a distinct value, depending on their distance from God. To modern Westerners, these views appear strange and outmoded. However, according to some anthropologists, our view of ourselves as independent from groups and environments may be just as strange.

Influenced by Mauss, French anthropologist Louis Dumont (1970) argued that modern Western notions of individualism differ from those of other societies such as India. In his book *Homo Hierarchicus*, he contrasted Western individualism with Indian Hindu conceptions that value social hierarchy. He pointed out that Hindu philosophy treats individuals as members of caste groups, which are linked to one another in a social hierarchy. Thus, from the Hindu vantage point, individuals cannot be thought of as separate from their social environment.

Francis Hsu, a Chinese-American anthropologist, maintained that the Chinese concept of self is radically different from that of the West (1981). Hsu argued that whereas individualism permeates all U.S. values and institutions, in China the individual is inclined to be socially and psychologically dependent on others. He contrasted the individual-centeredness of American society with the situation-centeredness of Chinese society. He concluded that the individual in China is strongly encouraged to conform to familistic and group norms.

Hsu argued that the situation-centeredness of Chinese society is partly responsible for its lack of economic and political development. In contrast, he believed that the individualism of American society has encouraged capitalist enterprise and democratic institutions. However, he also believed that the American concern for self and individualism has led to

rampant materialism and consumerism and a lack of concern for the overall good of society.

Dorinne Kondo makes a similar argument regarding the Western notion of the self in comparison to the Japanese conception of the self (1990). Kondo refers to the Western notion of the autonomous, private self that moves across different social contexts, whereas the Japanese self is always viewed in a relational, socially bounded context. When the Japanese participate in workplace and neighborhood activities embedded within networks and hierarchies, they cannot conceive of their private "self." Even within their households, individuals are constrained by their neighbors. On the other hand, do Westerners or Americans, as students or workers,

feel they have complete control of their own self and their destiny (De Munck 2000)?

As we can see psychological anthropologists differ over the degree in which culture influences the concept of the self. In some cases, these descriptions of different concepts of self may be exaggerations by anthropologists working in very different kinds of societies. Melford Spiro and other psychological anthropologists think that humans everywhere have similar concepts regarding the self (Spiro 1993). These different understandings reflect various assumptions and conclusions based on philosophical commitments, which need to be evaluated and criticized by anthropologists based on the most significant research findings available in

biological, cross-cultural, and specific findings within ethnographic research.

POINTS TO PONDER

1. To what extent are your views of yourself as a distinct individual influenced by prevailing social norms?

2. Do you think that people throughout the world hold similar views? Why or why not?

3. Do you agree with Hsu's analysis of the benefits and shortcomings of widespread individualism?

4. What would be the advantages and disadvantages of a system that emphasizes the overall society rather than the individual?

feelings become repressed, and the mature ego of the individual emerges to intervene between these desires and the dictates of society.

Freud's hypotheses were highly controversial in his own lifetime and remain so today. Although his theories are based on limited examples from his European medical and psychoanalytic practice, he extended his conclusions to include all of humanity. Freud's early scientific work was in neurology and brain science, and he believed that all of his findings regarding the human psyche would eventually be reduced to neurological patterns and development within the brain (1891). For example, Freud experimented with the drug cocaine himself in the early twentieth century, and although he abandoned the use of this drug because of its negative consequences, nevertheless his experiments did increase scientific findings about the effects of these drugs on the brain (Konner 2002). Freud's conceptions regarding enculturation have been modified by some modern anthropologists who study the role of childhood experiences in the formation of personality. However, his theories of emotional development and the role of the unconscious in personality represent significant contributions to anthropological research on enculturation.

Modern Psychoanalytic Anthropology

One of the most prominent contemporary anthropologists who uses a neo-Freudian approach in understanding human behavior is Melford Spiro. During his career, Spiro, a prodigious fieldworker, has done ethnographic research on the Ojibwa Indians, the Ifaluk people of Micronesia, the Israelis, and Burmese Buddhists. In all his fieldwork, he states that his principal objective has been to illuminate "the universal through an examination of the particular" (Spiro 1971).

Spiro maintains that human behavior cannot be adequately explained solely by environmental circumstances. He adopts some of Freud's concepts to explain such universal phenomena as aggression, sexuality, competition, and cooperation within society. In some of his early studies of the Ifaluk, he underscored the relationship among basic needs, cultural beliefs, and societal demands. For example, Spiro analyzed the Ifaluk belief in malevolent ghosts as a means of reducing interpersonal aggression and stimulating cooperation. Thus, according to Spiro (1952), the belief in harmful ghosts, an aspect of the superego that influences personality development, inhibits the expression of innate aggressive desires of the id.

One of Spiro's most recent works (1982) is a restudy of a classic ethnographic study by Bronislaw Malinowski of the Trobriand Islands. Malinowski did his ethnographic study in the 1920s, a time in which Freud's ideas were becoming popular. Malinowski discovered that in Trobriand society, the natural, or biological, father plays a minor role in the family. The mother's brother is the principal authority within the Trobriand family. Malinowski reported that tension exists between the male children and their maternal uncle, rather than between natural father and son. From these data, Malinowski claimed that the Trobrianders do not have the Oedipus complex. In other words, he challenged Freud's claims about the universal occurrence of this phenomenon.

Relying on Malinowski's data on Trobriand society, Spiro concluded that Malinowski ignored much evidence bearing on the relationships within the Trobriand family. One problem was that Malinowski focused on adolescent males, whereas Freud maintained that the Oedipus complex develops during the infantile stage of development. Furthermore, as Spiro indicated, Malinowski overlooked the continuing sexual relationship between the biological father and mother. Spiro suggested that this does create sexual jealousy and tension between a son and his natural father. From his neo-Freudian psychoanalytic perspective, Spiro hypothesized that Trobriand male children develop an Oedipus complex, just as do all male children throughout the world.

Spiro's psychoanalytic view does not represent the only view of enculturation in anthropology. Yet his use of psychoanalytic models in combination with ethnographic field methods to offer comprehensive hypotheses on the relationship among society, culture, and personality formation has been significant. Anthropologists inspired by the Freudian approach attempt to study the relationship among the unconscious thoughts, emotions, and motives of humans. In some cases they collaborate with psychiatrists to study dreams, symbols, fantasy life, interrelations among family members, and sexual relations (Paul 1989; Herdt and Stoller 1990).

Understanding Incest Avoidance and the Incest Taboo

One of the topics addressed by psychological anthropologists is incest. During their studies of interrelationships among family members and sexual relations in various societies, psychological anthropologists noted the widespread avoidance of incestuous behavior. They have developed various hypotheses to understand what are referred to as incest avoidance and the incest taboo. Freud offered a mythical explanation for the origins of the incest taboo in his book *Totem and Taboo* (1913). In this book Freud proposed that the incest taboo is a result of the Oedipus complex and the rivalry between fathers and sons. According to Freud, in the earliest family the sons rebelled against their fathers, resulting in what he referred to as "Primal Patricide." Having killed their fathers, the sons felt a sense of guilt, so they developed the incest taboo prohibiting sexual relations within the family.

Although anthropologists no longer take Freud's myth of the Primal Patricide seriously, a recent book by Robert Paul, *Moses and Civilization: The Meaning Behind Freud's Myth* (1996) indicates that Freud was struggling to understand the relationships between fathers and sons, men and women, and the family in modern Western civilization. There is no question that Freud's notions have had an enormous influence on thinking about the problems of incest avoidance and the incest taboo. Anthropologists have been studying these issues regarding incest and the family for a long period of time and have developed a number of different hypotheses to explain the worldwide prevalence of the incest taboo.

Incest involves sexual relations or marriage between certain relatives. **Incest avoidance** refers to the shunning of sexual relations and marriage between certain relatives. Incest avoidance is a universal phenomenon (Brown 1991). This appears to be valid for humans, and it is also widely found throughout the animal kingdom (Bischof 1972; Murray and Smith 1983: Pusey 2004). The **incest taboo** is based on strong cultural norms that prohibit sexual relations or marriage between certain

relatives. Although incest avoidance is found universally, incest taboos are not. Anthropologists find that some societies view incest with disgust and revulsion; these societies have strong prohibitions or taboos against incest. Yet in other societies, people view incest as such an incredulous and even laughable behavior that no taboo is called for (Van den Berghe 1979).

Marriage and sex between parent and child or brother and sister are forbidden in almost all societies, although certain exceptions do exist. Ancient Egyptians, Hawaiians, and Incas institutionalized incestuous brother-sister marriages within their ruling classes. This phenomenon is known as royal incest. The purpose of these practices was to maintain the ruling family's economic wealth and political power. For most people in most societies, however, marriages within the immediate family are forbidden.

Biological Explanations of Incest Avoidance

One ancient and widely held view of incest avoidance is that inbreeding within the immediate family causes genetic defects. This view is connected with the observation that abnormal or defective negative traits that are carried within the family would be accentuated by inbreeding.

The problem here is that inbreeding itself does not cause harmful genes to exist; it only perpetuates these harmful genes in a rapid fashion if they already exist within the immediate family. In fact, recent studies of cousin marriage have indicated that inbreeding actually produces mostly positive genetic influences. Obviously, as mentioned before, harmful genes can result in negative consequences in cousin marriages; however, according to the recent scientific findings in the human genome project, every individual has approximately 1,000 harmful genes out of about 30,000 genes. Anthropologists find that populations apparently can be highly inbred for many generations and survive quite well. Although harmful genetic consequences are found within some inbred populations, anthropologists seek alternative explanations of the universality of incest avoidance (Wolf and Durham 2004).

Marital Alliance and the Incest Taboo

Rather than focus on biological tendencies, some anthropologists have concentrated on the social consequences of inbreeding. In an early explanation, E. B. Tylor (1889) hypothesized that incest taboos originated as a means of creating alliances among different small-scale societies. Marriages outside of one's group create kinship alliances that encourage cooperation and improve chances for survival. Tylor coined the phrase "marry out or be killed out" to summarize his argument that if people did not create these social alliances, dire consequences would follow, including warfare among the different groups. Anthropologists Leslie White and Claude Levi-Strauss have presented variations of this functionalist hypothesis (White 1959; Levi-Strauss 1969). The problem with these hypotheses is that they explain the origins of marrying outside of one's group rather than incest taboos (Van den Berghe 1980; Wolf 2004).

Another type of explanation was proposed by Malinowski, who viewed the incest taboo as a mechanism that functions to sustain the family as an institution (1927). Malinowski argued that brother-sister, father-daughter, or mother-son marriages or sexual relations would generate status-role conflict and rivalry within the family, leading to dysfunctions and possible dissolution. The incest taboo thus serves to reduce family friction and conflict and to maintain harmony within the family. Obviously, this view is closest to the traditional Freudian perspective on the incest taboo.

Childhood Familiarity Hypothesis

Another explanation of the origin and perpetuation of incest avoidance is known as the *childhood familiarity hypothesis*, which proposes that siblings raised together in the family do not become erotically involved or sexually attracted to one another because of a biological tendency. Children living in close association with one another, however, would develop mutual sexual aversion and avoid incest.

A number of psychological anthropological studies appear to support this hypothesis. Arthur Wolf studied a marriage pattern in Taiwan called "minor marriage" (known locally as *sim-pua* marriage), in which a very young girl was adopted into the family of her future husband. The boy and the future bride were then raised in a sibling type of relationship. The purpose of this system was to allow the girl to adjust to her new family through a long association with her husband's kin. Wolf (1970, 2003, 2004) interviewed many people who were involved in these arranged relationships and found that most of them were dissatisfied both sexually and romantically with their spouses. Both males and females were inclined to have extramarital relations, and divorce rates were higher than normal. These conclusions appear to support the childhood familiarity hypothesis.

Another study, conducted in Israel, also presented evidence to support this hypothesis. When European Jews first settled in what was then known as Palestine in the early twentieth century, they established collective communities known as kibbutzim. Within these kibbutzim, children were separated from the family into peer groups of six to eight children to be raised and socialized together. Children in these peer-group settings had sibling-like relationships with one another.

To examine the childhood familiarity hypothesis, Israeli anthropologist Yonina Talmon (1964) studied the second generation of three kibbutzim.

These Israeli children are eating lunch on a kibbutz. Anthropologists find that children who are raised together on a kibbutz usually do not marry one another.

She discovered that there were no married couples who had known each other from peer groups in the kibbutzim. Although as small children these individuals may have shown a sexual interest in members of the opposite sex within their peer groups, this interest diminished after maturity. A later comprehensive study of 211 kibbutzim by anthropologist Joseph Shepher (1983) found that of 2,769 married couples, only 14 marriages were from the ranks of the peer groups. Moreover, every one of these 14 marriages had been dissolved through separation or divorce.

Incest Avoidance: Interactionist Perspectives

Today, most anthropologists agree that incest avoidance likely occurs for a variety of reasons. From an evolutionary perspective, the rule of marrying outside one's family would help to create alliances. It would also induce greater genetic diversity, thereby enhancing the adaptation and survival of different populations. In an extensive cross-cultural analysis of mating systems, Melvin Ember (1975) hypothesized that populations expanding as a result of agricultural development began to notice the spread of (not the creation of) harmful genes as a result of inbreeding and therefore created incest prohibitions. And, additionally, as Malinowski had suggested, incest avoidance would support family roles and functions.

The fact that incest does occur, coupled with the existence of institutionalized incestuous marriage practices in the royal families of some societies, indicates that incest avoidance cannot be reduced to a biological instinct. Humans are not biologically programmed to avoid incest in any mechanistic fashion. The most comprehensive explanation of incest has to take into account generalized biological tendencies along with sociocultural factors.

In a new refinement of the childhood familiarity hypothesis, Paul Roscoe (1994) offers an interactionist explanation of incest avoidance. He suggests that relatives who are raised in close association with one another develop strong emotional bonds, or kinship amity—culturally based values that lead to a sense of mutual support and intense feelings of affection. In contrast, sexual arousal and sexual relations are connected to some degree with aggressive impulses, which have a physiological and neurological basis. Thus, sexual-aggressive impulses are depressed between close kin, who have developed kinship amity. In addition, according to Roscoe's hypothesis, kinship amity can be extended to distant kin through enculturation, resulting in an incest taboo that prohibits sex between more distant relatives. Interactionist explanations such as Roscoe's, combining both biological and cultural factors, are producing insightful hypotheses regarding incest avoidance.

Despite the fact that incest avoidance is found universally and is likely tied to biological processes, many social workers and psychologists note that we appear to be in the midst of an epidemic of incest. By one estimate, 1 in 20 women may be victims of father-daughter sexual abuse (Russell 1986). Anthropologist Mark T. Erickson has been exploring this incidence of incest using a model based on evolutionary psychology and medicine (1999). He suggests that within contemporary societies, as the family unit has become more fragile with weaker kinship attachments, incest is likely to occur more frequently. In the cases of incest that do occur between father and daughter, the father is usually a person who has been sexually abused himself and has not developed close kinship and familial attachments with his children. An extreme lack of nurturance and mutual bonding between family members increases the likelihood of incest arising within families. Erickson's findings suggest that the incest avoidance biological processes can be stunted and distorted, leading to tragic results in contemporary societies.

Enculturation and the Sex Drive

Human sexuality is a subject that connects the biological and cultural aspects of the individual and culture. The sex drive, sexual maturation, and sexual activity have different meanings for individuals, depending on societal and cultural context. What are considered "normal" or "abnormal" or "deviant" patterns of sexuality differ from one society to another.

Anthropologists have studied enculturation and its consequences for sexual practices in varying societies. Like our biological drive of hunger, sex is a natural biological drive or urge for humans universally. However, this drive is channeled into certain directions through the process of enculturation.

Codes of Sexual Behavior

Societies differ with respect to how permissive or restrictive their codes or norms regarding sexuality are. Some societies approve of premarital and extramarital sexual relations, whereas others strictly segregate males from females to prohibit such relations. In some societies, sexual activity begins very early for both males and females to prepare for marriage. For example, with the Lepcha of Sikkim (a small kingdom north of India in the Himalayan Mountains), girls have their first sexual experience before puberty. In Lepcha society, sexual activity is considered as much a necessity as food or drink, and like food or drink, for the most part it does not matter from whom one receives it, though one is naturally grateful to those who provide it (Lindholm and Lindholm 1980). The Lepcha have a great deal of sexual freedom and appear to have very little sexual jealousy.

The antithesis of this permissive pattern of sexuality is found in some Arab societies of the Middle East. In Saudi Arabia, girls and women are strictly segregated from boys and men. Young girls begin wearing a cloak and veil at the age of puberty. Saudi Arabian society prohibits the mixing of males and females and to this end provides separate institutions for education, work, and other public facilities. In Saudi society, a family's honor is judged by its control over the sexuality of its daughters. Brides are expected to be virgins, and to guarantee this, families prevent daughters from interacting with boys. Sexual segregation and the dress code are strongly enforced by religious police in Saudi society.

Other highly restrictive attitudes and patterns of sexuality are found in societies such as the Inis Beag Islanders of Ireland, studied by anthropologist John Messenger (1971). Sex is never discussed openly at home or near children. Parents give no sexual instruction to children. Messenger reported that the Inis Beag people lack basic knowledge regarding sexual matters: For example, there seems to be a general ignorance of the ability of females to have orgasms; any expression of male or female sexuality is considered deviant; and it is believed that sexual activity weakens men. Females and males are separated at an early age. Dancing is permitted, but there is no touching or contact between males and females. Dirty jokes and nudity are strongly frowned upon. Messenger reports that there is little evidence of any premarital sex or any sexual foreplay between married people. Generally people marry very late in age, and there is a high percentage of celibate males in the population.

Homosexual Behavior

In exploring sexuality in other societies, psychological anthropologists have examined homosexuality by using a comparative, cross-cultural approach. Homosexuality in ancient societies such as that of the Greeks and Romans was a well-accepted pattern of behavior. Many societies have had institutionalized cultural roles for people who are not classified as either male or female. In the country of Oman, anthropologist Unni Wikan (1991) describes individuals known as *xaniths*, who are transsexuals and represent a third gender. In some islands of Southeast Asia such as Bali and Java, third-gender individuals are not only accepted but have important roles to play in the society (Brown 1976). In Thailand a third gender is represented by what are known as *kathoeys* (Nanda 2000; Jackson 1995; Barmé 2004). *Kathoeys* are primarily transsexual males who dress in women's clothes and take on a feminine role in Thai society. Many Buddhists in Thailand believe that one becomes a *kathoey* as a result of a *karmic* destiny influenced by one's reincarnation. This *karmic* destiny is inherited and is unalterable.

In some Native American Indian societies, certain males wore female clothing, and some devoted themselves to offering sexual services to male warriors. These individuals were referred to as *berdaches* by Europeans and were regarded as different from both males and females. These individuals, many of whom were homosexuals, also provided resources and took care of other subsistence activities for their neighbors and relatives in the society (Callender and Kochems 1983). Within these Native American societies, the distinction between homosexuals and heterosexuals did not exist in the same way it does in Western European and U.S. culture. The sexuality of this third gender was not central to their identity or role within society. Instead, the central characteristic of this third gender was the occupational role. Traditionally, these individuals did not face prejudice and discrimination and were accepted as a natural third gender within their society.

Anthropologist Serena Nanda (1990, 2000) has done an extensive ethnographic study of the *hijras* of India, who are viewed as neither men nor women. They are born as males but undergo an operation in which their genitals are surgically removed. This operation transforms them, not into females (because they cannot give birth), but into *hijras*, a third gender. The *hijras* are followers of a particular Hindu deity and earn their living by performing at various types of religious ceremonies. They dress like females and to some extent exaggerate feminine behavior, but they also indulge in certain male-only behaviors, such as smoking a *hookah* (water pipe) and cigarettes. Within the cultural context of Indian society, the *hijras* are considered neither deviant nor unnatural but rather simply an additional form of gender.

Anthropologists have described a variety of male homosexual practices among the highland societies of Papua New Guinea. Among peoples such as the Etoro and the Sambia, male homosexuality is incorporated into initiation rituals. In these societies there appear to be no distinctions among heterosexual, homosexual, or bisexual individuals. Gilbert Herdt (1987) describes how prepubescent Sambian males are initiated into male secret societies and engage in strictly homosexual activities with the older males of these societies. They are obligated to perform regular oral intercourse on the older males and believe that obtaining the gift of semen from their seniors will enable them to become strong, vigorous warriors. These boys are forbidden to engage in any heterosexual relationships for about ten years. Following this lengthy period, they marry and, from that time onward, take up heterosexual relationships with their wives, but then they have homosexual relationships with the young men undergoing their initiation puberty rites of passage. Though there is an enormous range of scientific evidence to suggest that homosexuality is an inherited disposition influenced by genes, neurological developments, and heredity, anthropologists continue to investigate both the biology and cultural aspects of this form of sexuality.

U.S. society has gone through different cycles of restrictiveness and permissiveness regarding cultural norms influencing sexual practices (D'Emilio 1988). In the early history of the United States, Puritan norms equated sexuality with sinful behavior. Later, in the nineteenth century, American society reinforced restrictive Puritan attitudes. But in the 1920s, a more liberal, permissive era of sexual attitudes developed. The 1950s proved to be once again a more restrictive period, but this was followed by the sexual revolution of the 1960s. U.S. society is extremely complex, and many different norms and attitudes are represented in respect to sexuality. The restrictive legacy of Puritanism still exists within some groups, as evidenced by the various legal statutes in some states regarding homosexual practices. The attempt to regulate sexual behavior by government is a U.S. practice that has been abandoned by most other Western governments.

Enculturation and Cognition

Psychological anthropologists have been exploring thinking processes, or cognition, among different peoples in various societies. One assumption held widely by nineteenth-century and early twentieth-century social scientists was that people in small-scale or so-called primitive societies have different forms of cognition from people in civilized societies. This assumption was challenged by a number of anthropologists, who focused on cognitive development from a cross-cultural perspective.

Structuralism

Following World War II, French anthropologist Claude Lévi-Strauss founded a field of study known as *structuralism*. The primary goal of structuralism is to investigate the thought processes of the human mind in a universal context; consequently, it is a field that overlaps psychological anthropology. Structuralists are interested in the unconscious and conscious patterns of human thinking. In one of his first major books, *The Savage Mind* (1966), Lévi-Strauss discussed how peoples living in small-scale societies use the same unconscious thinking and logical reasoning processes that people in

Claude Lévi-Strauss.

large-scale, complex societies do. He proposed that there is a universal logical form in human thought and cognition around the world.

Drawing on the field of linguistics, Lévi-Strauss argued that thinking is based on *binary oppositions.* In other words, humans classify the natural and social world into polar types (binary oppositions) as a stage of reasoning. For example, foods are classified as raw versus cooked or hot versus cold. From these binary contrasts, coherent patterns of thought are developed. In addition, he suggests that the fundamental binary structural distinctions between "nature" and "culture" are found in all societies. He demonstrated how religious mythologies universally invoke symbols that have a dualistic aspect between that of nature and culture. Lévi-Strauss focused on such diverse phenomena as kinship, mythology, cuisine, and table manners to discover the hidden structural logic underlying these diverse cultural ideas and practices. Within all of these practices and beliefs, Lévi-Strauss maintains that there are important logical and deep structural distinctions between nature and culture. Even though the rules and norms that structure these ideas and practices may appear arbitrary, Lévi-Strauss believed that this "deep universal structure" underlies these cultural phenomena. Thus, this universal structure of the mind produces similar thinking and cognition throughout the world.

Jean Piaget and Lev Vygotsky

Jean Piaget (1896–1980), a Swiss psychologist, spent more than a half-century studying the ways in which children think, perceive, and learn. His research has influenced the anthropological perspective on cognition and enculturation. Piaget believed that the process of thinking and reasoning was related to the biological process of neural changes that influence the brain. He used experiments that focused not only on what children learn but also on how they understand the world. Piaget identified four major stages of cognitive development: sensorimotor, preoperational, concrete-operational, and formal-operational. Piaget hypothesized that these stages reflect biological maturation as well as enculturation. As each child progresses through these stages, he or she acquires more information and begins to organize and perceive reality in new and different ways.

Piaget's Four Stages of Human Development   The first stage of human development in Piaget's scheme is the *sensorimotor stage*, in which a child experiences the world only through the senses in terms of physical contact. In this stage, which corresponds to approximately the first two years of life, the infant explores the world through touching,

Psychological anthropologists are studying the cognitive development of children everywhere in the world.

sucking, listening, and other direct contact. According to Piaget, at this first stage children may imitate the sounds of others, but they do not have the capacity to use symbols.

The second stage, the *preoperational stage*, refers to the level of cognitive development in which symbols, including language, are first used. During this stage, roughly ages 2 to 7, children begin to experience the world abstractly. This symbolic learning enables children to conceive of something without having direct contact with it. Children gain the ability to distinguish among their ideas of the world, dreams, fantasies, and objective reality. Yet at this second stage, children do not use symbols as adults do. They learn to attach meanings and names to objects in their specific environment, but they do not conceptualize the world in general terms.

In the third stage, the *concrete-operational stage*, children between ages 7 and 11 begin to use logic, connecting events in terms of cause and effect, and they learn to manipulate symbols in a more sophisticated manner. At this stage children are also able to put themselves in the position of another person and perceive a situation from another's point of view. This allows them to engage in complex activities such as games that involve a number of participants (including most team sports).

The fourth stage, known as the *formal-operational stage*, is the level of cognitive development characterized by highly abstract concepts and formal reasoning processes. At about age 12, children develop the capacity to think of themselves and the world in highly abstract terms rather than only in terms of concrete situations. They can envision alternatives to reality by proposing differing hypotheses for evaluation. In this final stage of cognitive development, which continues throughout adult life, children begin to use reasoning processes and abstract symbols to interpret and understand the world.

Piaget suggested that certain innate categories regulate and order our experience of the world. Although he was certainly aware that the learning of values, norms, and beliefs is not the same from society to society, he believed that humans everywhere progress in the same sequence through the various stages described above. He also recognized that the precise age at which each stage of

cognitive development is reached varies from individual to individual, depending on innate mental capacities and the nature of the enculturation experience.

Another Russian psychologist, Lev Vygotsky, followed the work of Piaget and emphasized the biological aspects of thinking and cognition, but because he was living in the Soviet Union he was influenced by the thinkers such as Karl Marx on how social relationships had an impact on thinking and behaving (Gopnik, Meltzoff, and Kuhl 1999; Konner 2002; Lima and Emihovich 1995). Vygotsky accepted some of the stages of cognitive development proposed by Piaget, however, he argued that the stages in these thought and reasoning developments did not represent sharp distinctions, but rather were more continuous and also were shaped by linguistic, social, and cultural contexts. For example, he thought that literacy could have an important influence on cognition and perception. One of his students, Alexander Luria, carried out experiments on this aspect of Vygotsky's psychology projects (Wertsch 1985; Lima and Emihovich 1995). Unfortunately, Vygotsky died as a young man of 38, and his students were forbidden to conduct further research on the relationship between biology and culture because the Soviet Union under Joseph Stalin banned the teaching of evolutionary biology because it conflicted with Marxist doctrines.

Piaget and Vygotsky and their research have influenced numerous psychological anthropologists and their approach to understanding cognition, the human mind, and enculturation. British anthropologist Maurice Bloch (1977, 1985) has suggested that many cultural universals are the result of biopsychological factors shared by all humans that interact with the practical conditions of the world. For example, Bloch postulates that all humans have intuitive capabilities to perceive time and space in the same way. Time and space are fundamental concepts that enable humans to adapt to the practical conditions of the world. These practical conditions include changes in seasons, climatic and environmental characteristics, and the overall effects of natural aging processes. In Bloch's view, people can learn to conceptualize time and space in radically different ways, depending on religious beliefs and worldviews. For example, in the Hindu tradition, people perceive time cyclically in relationship to the creation and destruction of the universe that takes place over millions of years. In the Judeo-Christian tradition, people perceive time in a more linear fashion from the time of creation to the present. However, in both the Hindu and Judeo-Christian cultures, in everyday, practical circumstances, people perceive time both cyclically and linearly in relation to the cycle of seasonal changes or the life cycle of an individual through biological aging.

Many other psychological anthropologists have been testing Vygotsky's and Piaget's theories throughout the world to determine whether their stages are indeed universal. As we will see shortly, their theories have had an enormous impact on contemporary explanations of cognition and thought within the field of cognitive anthropology. One conclusion emphasized in this research by psychological anthropologists is that we humans share very similar cognitive and reasoning processes whether we live in the forests of New Guinea or the city of New York. Yet, all our cognitive processes are influenced by the culture and language that we are exposed to as children and throughout our lives. All people use similar patterns of logic and develop an understanding of cause and effect relationships. People everywhere develop classification systems through similar processes of abstraction and generalization. The differences among cultural groups lie in the content of the values, beliefs, and norms of society.

Cognitive Anthropology and Evolutionary Psychology

A number of anthropologists have been pursuing the understanding of human psychology through the fields of cognitive anthropology and evolutionary psychology. **Cognitive anthropology** is the study of cognition and cultural meanings through specific methodologies to elicit underlying unconscious *schemas* or *taxonomies* that structure human thinking processes. Cognitive anthropology developed in the 1950s and 1960s through the systematic investigation of kinship terminologies within different cultures. However, more recently, cognitive anthropology has drawn upon the findings within the field of cognitive science, the study of the human mind based on computer modeling

(D'Andrade 1995; de Munck 2000). Cognitive anthropologists have developed experimental methods and various cognitive tasks to use among people they study in their fieldwork to better comprehend human psychological processes and their relationship to culture. Through cognitive anthropology we have learned that the human mind organizes and structures the natural and social world in distinctive ways.

For example, cognitive anthropologists have been doing research on how humans classify and perceive colors in the natural world. Color is a very complex phenomena for scientists and anthropologists. To physicists, color is determined by wavelengths of light. To the biologist, color involves the neural responses in the human eye and the brain and is related to the ability of humans to adapt and survive in nature. Color can also be symbolic and represent our feelings and emotions, and as we saw in Chapter 3 it varies from culture to culture. Early philosophers and scientists such as Aristotle, René Descartes, and the physicist Isaac Newton believed that there were seven basic colors. Later, anthropologists and linguists began to ask questions such as, Do people classify and categorize colors in an arbitrary manner based on their language and culture? Or do people classify, categorize, and perceive colors in similar ways throughout the world? Cognitive anthropologists Brent Berlin and Paul Kay have been studying the basic color terms of different societies since the 1960s. They analyzed the color-naming practices of informants from ninety-eight globally distributed language groups and found that societies differ dramatically in the number of basic color terms they possess, from two in some New Guinea tribes to eleven in English. They showed, however, that despite this difference, all color terms used by diverse societies follow a systematic pattern (1969).

A language with only two color terms will divide the color spectrum between white and black. If a language contains three terms, the spectrum will be black, red, and white. A language with four terms will have black, red, white, and either green, yellow, or blue. A language with six terms will have black, white, red, yellow, green, and blue. Language systems add basic color terms in a systematic progression until a maximum of eleven terms is reached.

Berlin and Kay suggest that this pattern indicates an evolutionary sequence common to all languages.

Red is adopted after white and black. In general, a language does not adopt a term for brown unless it already has six color terms. English, most Western European languages, Russian, Japanese, and several others add four color terms: gray, pink, orange, and purple, after brown is classified. Berlin and Kay correlate the evolution of color terms with the evolution of society. Societies with only two color terms have a simple level of technology, whereas societies with eleven basic color terms have a complex technology.

The evidence from Berlin and Kay's study suggests that color naming is not at all arbitrary. If color terms were selected randomly, there would be thousands of possible color systems. In fact, there are only thirty-three possible color-naming systems. Recently, Paul Kay reported that based statistical tests from more than a hundred languages in both industrial and nonindustrial societies demonstrated that there are strong universal tendencies in color classification and naming (2003). In other words color perception transcends culture and language.

However, other anthropologists and psychologists have done some research that indicates that color is influenced by language and culture. British anthropologists and psychologists Debi Roberson, Ian Davies, and Jules Davidoff did research among the Berinomo tribe of Papua New Guinea and found that they do not distinguish blue from green, but they do distinguish between shades of green (*nul* and *wor*) that are not shared by Western peoples. Also, these researchers found some tribal members who were trained could learn to distinguish blue from green unlike other members of the tribe (2000). Yet, these findings do not completely refute the empirical findings of Berlin, Kay, and other anthropologists. Although much more research needs to be done on the perception and classification of colors, these findings do not support the conclusion that color classification is completely arbitrary. Instead, all the vast majority of psychologists and anthropologists concur that the physiological basis of color vision is the same for all humans (and some primates) with normal color vision. On the other hand, anthropologists recognize that the mental and cognitive higher-order processing, and linguistic learning may have an influence on color perception, and as is well known, the symbolic representation and meaning of colors do vary from society to society (Sahlins 1976; Lucy and Shweder 1979).

In a more recent cognitive anthropological study, James Boster concluded that, as with colors, people from different societies classify birds in similar ways. Boster (1987) found that the South American Jivaro Indian population classified species of native birds in a manner corresponding to the way scientists classify these birds. To discover whether this pattern of classification was random, Boster had University of Kentucky students with no scientific training and no familiarity with South American birds classify these birds. The students did so with the exact criteria used by both the Jivaro Indians and the Western scientists. Most recently, two cognitive anthropologists working in Honduras found that insects were classified by Honduran farmers in the same way that scientists do worldwide (Bentley and Rodriguez 2001). Cognitive anthropologists such as Scott Atran (1990, 1998) and Cecil Brown (1984) have shown that plants and animals are categorized and classified in universally similar taxonomies. These taxonomies are ordered according to the distinctive morphological features of the various plants and animals in nature. Despite variant cultures in different regions of the world, the human mind appears to organize the natural world in non-arbitrary ways.

These findings in cognitive anthropology suggest that the human mind organizes reality in terms of **prototypes**, distinctive classifications that help us map and comprehend the world. If reality was inherently unorganized and could be perceived in any way, then color naming and animal and plant classification would be completely arbitrary. The results of this research support the notion that people the world over share certain cognitive abilities, and language and culture is as likely to reflect human cognition as it is to shape it. It suggests that evolution selected certain fundamental visual-processing and category-building abilities for humans everywhere (Lakoff 1987; Lakoff and Johnson 2000; D'Andrade 1995).

Cognitive anthropologists have discovered that not only do humans think in prototypes, but we also use *schemas* to help us understand, organize, and interpret reality. The concept of schemas was introduced by Jean Piaget to discuss a particular "cognitive structure which has reference to a class of similar action sequences" (de Munck 2000). Schemas are constructed out of language, images, and logical operations of the human mind in order to mediate and provide meaning to social and cultural reality. Thus, schemas are more complex than prototypes or taxonomic categories. And schemas may vary from one culture to the next. For example, the schema *writing* in English and *kaku* in Japanese have some similarities, and these terms are usually translatable between the languages. They both refer to making some marks with an implement across a surface. The schema writing in English, however, always entails the act of writing in a language, whereas *kaku* can refer to writing or doodling or drawing a picture (D'Andrade 1995). Cognitive anthropologists find that, like taxonomies, schemas are also organized into hierarchies and aid in our adapting and coping with cognitive and cultural complexities. Claudia Strauss is investigating how schemas are organized hierarchically in an analogous manner to how computers process data and information (1992). She has been investigating the interconnection of schemas within the individual mind and comparing them with how data are arranged, interconnected, and sorted within computers. These models from cognitive science and computer modeling are employed to gain insight into cultural values and beliefs within the mind.

In addition to prototypes, taxonomies, and schemas, cognitive anthropologists also investigate how *narratives* are used to coordinate thought processes. **Narratives** are stories or events that are represented within specific cultures. There are certain types of narratives, such as the story of Little Red Riding Hood, that are easily retained by an individual's memory and told over and over again within a society. Thus, certain forms of narrative have easily recognizable plots and can be distributed widely within a society (Sperber 1996). Other forms of narratives, such as a formal proof in mathematics or logic or evolutionary biological explanations in science, are much more difficult to distribute widely. Cognitive anthropologists are studying religious mythologies, folktales, and other types of narratives to determine why some spread quickly and are effortlessly transmitted and used to produce cultural representations that endure for generations. Cognitive anthropological research has been fruitful in providing interactionist models of the ways in which humans everywhere classify, organize, understand, interpret, and narrate their natural social and cultural environment.

Cognitive scientist Steven Pinker is described as one of the world's leading thinkers by Time *magazine, May 2004.*

A recent development that draws upon cognitive anthropology and attempts to emphasize the interaction of nature (biology) and nurture (learning and culture) in understanding and explaining enculturation, human cognition, and human behavior is the field known as **evolutionary psychology**. This field includes anthropologists such as John Tooby, Daniel Sperber, Pascal Boyer, Laura Betzig, Lee Cronk, Donald Symons, Robin Fox, Mark Flinn, Melvin Konner, and many psychologists, including Leda Cosmides, Patricia Kuhl, Susan Gelman, David Buss, Alison Gopnik, Steven Pinker, and Paul Rozin. Evolutionary psychology is a field that draws on ethnographic research, psychological experiments, and evolutionary theory to demonstrate how the human brain developed and how it influences thinking processes and behavior. These anthropologists question the traditional premise that the human mind is a passive instrument that soaks up the cultural environment like a sponge. Instead, they view the human mind as designed by evolution to actively adjust to the culture and environment.

They begin with the understanding of the effects of evolution during the long period of the Paleolithic that caused the emergence of a specific form of human brain. Evolutionary psychologists suggest that the mind and culture coevolved. They believe that natural selective forces must have shaped the mind and behavior. Consequently, because natural selective forces are highly specific, they hypothesize that the human brain is divided into specialized cognitive domains or modules, or independent units, which contain various functions that enabled our ancestral humans to adapt to Paleolithic conditions. These specific modules within the brain predispose humans to perceive, think, and behave in certain ways to allow for adaptation. In other words, there are genetically induced "evolved predispositions" that have consequences for human perception, thinking, emotions, and behavior today. For example, in Chapter 5 we review the research indicating that the human brain has a language-learning module enabling children to learn their language without learning the specific complex rules of grammar for communication.

Aside from the language-learning module, evolutionary psychologists, in a book entitled *The Adapted Mind* (1992) edited by Jerome Barkow, John Tooby, and L. Cosmides, have hypothesized that modules in the brain enable humans to understand intuitively the workings of nature, including motion, force, and how plants and animals function. The authors refer to psychological research that demonstrates how infants distinguish objects that move around (such as balls) from living organisms (such as people and animals) that are self-propelled. These anthropologists theorize that innate, specialized modules in the human brain help develop an intuitive understanding of biology and physics. Just as children learn their language without learning the formal grammatical rules, humans can perceive, organize, and understand basic biological and physical principles without learning formal scientific views. Children at very early ages have intuitive notions, or "theories," about persons, animals, plants, or artifacts. They have an intuitive understanding of the underlying properties and behavioral expectations of these phenomena from early stages of infancy. In addition, young children at two years old or so have the ability to comprehend how other people have intentions. In other words, these young children have an intuitive "theory of mind" and can determine how other people have thoughts and intend to use them in communication or behavior (Boyer 1998, 2001).

Evolutionary psychologists further contend that the mind uses different rules to process different types of information. For example, they suggest there are innate modules that help interpret and predict other people's behavior and modules enabling humans to understand basic emotions such as happiness, sadness, anger, jealousy, and love. In addition, these specialized modules influence male-female relationships, mate choice, and cooperation or competition among individuals.

In *The Adapted Mind,* anthropologist Jerome Barkow asks why people like to watch soap operas. He answers that the human mind is designed by evolution to be interested in the social lives of others—rivals, mates, relatives, offspring, and acquaintances. To be successful in life requires knowledge of many different phenomena and social situations, evolutionary psychologists argue, and innate predispositions influence how we sense, interpret, think, perceive, communicate, and imagine to enable adaptation and survival in the world.

Evolutionary psychologists tend to emphasize the commonalities and similarities in culture and behavior found among people in different parts of the world. Thus, they are interested in the types of human universals described by anthropologist Donald Brown (see Chapter 3). Although evolutionary psychologists do not ignore learning or culture, they hypothesize that innate modules or mechanisms in the brain make learning and enculturation happen.

Many evolutionary psychologists believe that some of the evolved predispositions that are inherited may not be as adaptive today as they were during the time of the Paleolithic. For example, humans during that period had to worry more about danger from wild animals and about getting enough salt and sugar to eat for survival, but such evolved predispositions may not help humans adapt to modern society.

Some anthropologists have criticized evolutionary psychology for not emphasizing the richness and complexity of cultural environments. At present, however, many anthropologists are using the methods of cognitive anthropology and evolutionary psychology to understand human nature and culture. The field of evolutionary psychology is in its infancy and will most likely grow to offer another interactionist perspective on human thought and behavior.

Enculturation and Emotions

One significant question asked by psychological anthropologists is to what degree enculturation influences emotions. Obviously, different language groups have different terms for emotions, but do the feelings of anger, happiness, grief, and jealousy vary from society to society? Do some societies have unique emotions? For example, Catherine Lutz, in her book *Unnatural Emotions: Everyday Sentiments on a Micronesian Atoll and Their Challenge to Western Theory* (1988) suggests that many of the emotions exhibited by the Ifaluk people in the Pacific islands are not comparable to American or Western emotions. She notes that the Ifaluk emotion words *song* (justifiable anger) and *fago* (compassion/love/sadness) have no equivalent in English emotion terms, and that anthropologists need to examine the linguistic and cultural context to interpret what emotions mean from culture to culture. Lutz argues that emotions cannot be understood universally based on biological factors. Or are, as some anthropologists maintain, human emotions the same throughout the world?

Psychological anthropologists have been conducting research on the topic of emotions since the early research of Benedict and Mead. As discussed earlier in the chapter, Benedict and Mead argued that each culture is unique and that people in various societies have different personalities and, consequently, different types of emotions. These different emotions are a result of the unique kind of enculturation that has shaped the individual's personality. In their view, the enculturation process is predominant in creating varying emotions among different societies. In other words, culture determines not only how people think and behave but also how they feel emotionally.

In contrast, other early psychological anthropologists focused on universal biological processes that produce similar emotional developments and feelings in people throughout the world. According to this perspective, emotions are seen as instinctive behaviors that stimulate physiological processes involving hormones and other chemicals in the brain. In other words, if an individual feels "anger," this automatically raises his or her blood pressure and stimulates specific muscle movements. In this view, emotional developments are part of the biology of humans universally, and thus emotions are experienced the same everywhere.

More recently, psychological anthropologists have emphasized an interactionist approach, taking both biology and culture into account in their studies of emotions (Hinton 1999). A study conducted by Karl Heider (1991) focused on three different ethnic groups in Indonesia. The three groups are the Minangkabau in West Sumatra, the Minangkabau Indonesians, and the Javanese. Heider systematically described the vocabulary of emotions that each of these groups used to classify their feelings of sadness, anger, happiness, fear, surprise, love, contempt, shame, and disgust, along with other feelings. Through intensive interviews and observations, Heider determined whether the vocabulary of emotions is directly related to specific emotional behaviors.

Following his ethnographic study, Heider concluded that four of the emotions—sadness, anger, happiness, and surprise—tend to be what he classifies as basic cross-cultural emotions. In other words, these emotions appear to be universally understood and stable across cultures. Other emotions, however, such as love, fear, and disgust, appear to vary among these societies. For example, love among the Minangkabau and Minangkabau Indonesians is mixed with the feeling of pity and is close to sadness. Fear is also mixed with guilt, and feelings of disgust are difficult to translate across cultural boundaries. Heider emphasizes that his study is preliminary and needs much more analysis and reanalysis; nevertheless, it is an interesting use of the interactionist approach to the study of emotions.

Daniel Fessler also explored how both biology and culture contribute to the development of human emotions (1999). Fessler did ethnographic work among the Bengkulu, an ethnic group in Sumatra, a major island in Indonesia. He discusses the importance of two emotions, *malu* and *bangga*, exhibited in many situations by the Bengkulu. Malu appears to be quite similar to "shame" in English. Bengkulu who feel *malu* withdraw from social interaction, stoop, and avert their gaze. People who feel *malu* are described as those who have missed religious services, didn't attend to the sick, didn't send their children to school, drank alcohol, ate during times of fasting, or violated other norms. *Bangga* is the linguistic expression of the emotion that people feel when they do something well and have had success, such as doing well in baking cakes, winning an election, hosting a large feast, being skilled in oratory, or feeling good about their physical appearance or house and furnishings. *Bangga* seems to be most similar to the emotion term "pride" in English. Fessler notes that malu and bangga appear to be exact opposites of one another, and both emotions provide individuals with an assessment of their relationship to the rest of the group. He suggests that these two emotions are universal and are found in all societies and that they have evolved in connection with attempts to coordinate one's mind and behavior for cooperation and competition within groups of people. Fessler emphasizes that these emotions may be displayed and elaborated in different ways in various cultures; they reflect a universal, panhuman experience.

In *Thinking through Cultures: Expeditions in Cultural Psychology* (1991), psychological anthropologist Richard Shweder emphasizes that ethnographic research on emotions has demonstrated the existence of both universals and culturally specific aspects of emotional functioning among people in different societies. He uses a piano keyboard as an analogy to discuss emotional development in children. Children have something like an emotional keyboard, with each key being a separate emotion: disgust, interest, distress, anger, fear, contempt, shame, shyness, guilt, and so forth. A key is struck whenever a situation such as loss, frustration, or novelty develops. All children recognize and can discriminate among basic emotions by a young age. However, as adults, the tunes that are played on the keyboard vary with experience. Some keys are not struck at all, whereas others are played extensively. Shweder concludes, "It is ludicrous to imagine that the emotional functioning of people in different cultures is basically the same. It is just as ludicrous to imagine that each culture's emotional life is unique" (1991, 252). Psychological anthropologists recognize that an interactionist approach that takes into account human biological factors and cultural variation is necessary to comprehend the enculturation process and emotional development.

Culture and Mental Illness

Another area of interest for psychological anthropology is the study of mental illness in different societies. The major concerns of these studies revolve around two questions: Is there a universal concept of "normal" and "abnormal" behavior? and Do mental illnesses differ in their symptoms or patterns in different societies? These questions serve as the basis for many ethnographic projects in different societies.

What Is Abnormal?

In the early twentieth century, one of the assumptions in the fields of psychiatry and psychology was that mental illness and abnormal behavior are universal. In other words, depression, schizophrenia, psychoses, and other mental disorders are essentially the same for all humans. For example, in the field of psychiatry, particular types of mental disorders were classified by specific symptoms. Thus, a *psychosis* was classified as a type of mental disturbance characterized by personality disorganization, disturbed emotional responses, and a loss of contact with reality. A *neurosis* was characterized as a nonpsychotic disorder marked by considerable anxiety for individuals, especially when they are involved in social interaction.

Psychological anthropologists such as Ruth Benedict challenged these classifications of mental illness in the 1930s. Benedict argued that all criteria of abnormality reflect the particular culture of the individual and must be understood within the context of that culture. In her classic book *Patterns of Culture* (1934), Benedict remarked:

> It does not matter what kind of "abnormality" we choose for illustration, those which indicate extreme instability, or those which are more in the nature of character traits like sadism or delusions of grandeur or of persecution, there are well described cultures in which these abnormals function with ease and with honor and apparently without danger of difficulty to the society. ([1934] 1959, 263)

In other words, Benedict questioned whether any type of absolute standards of "normalcy" as defined by Western preoccupations and categories were satisfactory criteria for mental health. Benedict described a situation in which an individual heard very loud voices, was plagued by dreams of falling off cliffs, and feared being devoured by swarms of yellow jackets. This individual went into a trance state, lay rigid on the ground, and shortly thereafter recovered and danced for three nights in a row. Although in Western society this individual would be treated as "abnormal," Benedict suggested that this behavior and thought was not unusual in some societies. The individual described was a type of medicine man or woman and was not only accorded respect but enjoyed tremendous prestige within the particular Native American tribe to which he or she belonged.

Ethnographic descriptions such as these demonstrate the difficulties of classifying mental illness across cultural boundaries. When the concept of abnormality is applied cross-culturally, it becomes an extremely vague concept. Behavior that is considered deviant in one society may represent a culturally acceptable form of behavior in another. The fields of modern psychiatry and psychology have been attempting to revise their classification of mental illnesses and often work with anthropologists on joint research projects to refine understandings of psychological disorders.

Culture-Specific Disorders

A number of ethnographic studies have focused on mental disorders that are unique to certain cultural settings. These culture-specific disorders include *latah*, *amok*, *windigo*, and *pibloktoq*. *Latah* has been described as a mental disorder in areas of Southeast and East Asia. In Southeast Asia, *latah* appears as a type of hysteria or fear reaction that afflicts women who become easily startled, resulting in compulsively imitating behaviors or shouting repetitive phrases that they have heard (echolalia). Sometimes this disorder is triggered by the word *snake* or by tickling. In the East Asian area of Mongolia, however, David Aberle (1961) described a form of *latah* that affects men. These men may be startled suddenly and put their hands into a fire, jump into a river, or begin to scream obscenities wildly.

Amok is a culture-specific disorder that is described in Malaysia, Indonesia, and parts of the Philippines. It is a disorder of middle-aged males following a period of withdrawal marked by brooding over a perceived insult. During this period, in which the individual loses contact with reality, he may suffer from stress and sleep deprivation and consume large quantities of alcohol. Then a wild outburst marked by rage occurs, with the individual attempting a violent series of murderous attacks. The man may pick up a weapon such as a machete and attack any person or animal in his path. These aggressive, homicidal attacks will be followed by prolonged exhaustion and amnesia (Bourguignon 1979). *Amok* appears to be a culturally sanctioned form of violent behavior viewed as an appropriate response to a specific situation in these Southeast Asian regions. (The Malay term *amok* has entered the English language, referring to wild, aggressive behavior, as in someone running *amok*.)

Another culture-specific disorder, formerly found among the males of the Chippewa, Cree, and Montagnais-Naskapi Indians in Canada, is referred to as the *windigo* psychosis. It is described as a disorder in which the affected individual becomes deeply depressed and begins to believe that he has been possessed or bewitched by the spirit of a *windigo*, a cannibal giant with a heart or entrails of ice. The individual may have symptoms of nausea, anorexia, and insomnia and may see other humans being transformed into beavers or other animals. As these hallucinations occur, the individual begins to have an overwhelming desire to kill and eat these humans (Barnouw 1985). This insatiable craving for human flesh has resulted in documented cases of homicide and cannibalism among some of these people (Marano 1982; Barnouw 1985).

The disorder *pibloktoq*, also referred to as Arctic hysteria, is found among Eskimo adults in Greenland and other Arctic regions. It may affect both men and women but has been described more frequently among women. The subject is initially irritable or withdrawn and then becomes violently emotional. The victim may scream as if terrified, tear off her clothes, run out into the snow, jump into fire, throw things around, and begin to "speak in tongues." After this period of excitement, the woman sometimes has convulsive seizures and then may fall asleep. On awakening she may be perfectly calm and have no memory of the incident. *Pibloktoq* usually has a high frequency in the winter, and a number of persons living in a small community may be afflicted with it during the cold months (Wallace 1972). Thus, it may be a more extreme form of what Americans sometimes call cabin fever.

A number of explanations have been put forth to explain these culture-specific mental disorders. For example, the *windigo* disorder has been attributed to the experience of starvation and famine conditions that can occur in the wintertime. Long ago, anthropologist Anthony Wallace (1972) suggested that a lack of calcium in the diet of Eskimos may partially explain the occurrence of *pibloktoq*. In these areas, the drastic annual variation in daylight may be partially responsible for these behavioral and emotional disturbances (Bourguignon 1979).

Some critics believe that these culture-specific disorders may just be different expressions of certain illnesses such as paranoid schizophrenia or other types of psychoses. Persecution ideas, hysteria, panic disorders, and other bizarre behaviors occur in all societies to one degree or another. There is a substantial body of evidence from various sources that certain types of depression and schizophrenia are caused by biochemical disorders that are genetically inherited (Myers 2004). International surveys by the World Health Organization have examined disorders such as schizophrenia around the world and have found some basic similarities in the symptom profiles (Marsella 1979). Psychological anthropologists have found, however, that the cultural beliefs and worldviews, family communication patterns, early childhood training, and particular life stresses of certain societies influence the content of these mental disorders (Goodman and Leatherman 1998). Conditions resulting in stress from homelessness, war, living in refugee camps, or other anxiety-producing or depression-inducing conditions can influence biological tendencies that may not appear in normal circumstances (Dressler 1991). The delusions, hallucinations, and other symptoms that occur with these disorders reflect wide-ranging economic, social, and cultural variations throughout the world. Psychological anthropologists are beginning to combine biological explanations with cultural variables to arrive at more comprehensive, interactionist explanations of mental illness and personality disorders.

The Limits of Enculturation

When we consider enculturation or socialization, we are confronted with this question: Are humans only robots who respond rigidly to the demands of their innate drives, genes, and the norms of their culture? If our behavior depends so much on the enculturation process, what becomes of human concepts such as freedom and free will? Do people in our society or other societies have any personal choice over their behavior, or is all behavior and thought shaped by innate drives and the norms of these societies?

Unique Biological Tendencies

In actuality, although enculturation plays a major role in producing personality and behavioral strategies within society, there are a number of reasons why enculturation is not completely determinative. First, people are born with different innate tendencies (not instincts) for responding to the environment in a variety of ways. Our individual behavior is partially a result of our own genetics and biological constitution, which influences our hormones, metabolism, and other aspects of our physiology. All societies have people who differ with respect to temperament because of these innate tendencies. Enculturation cannot produce people who respond only to environmental or cultural pressures in a uniform manner.

Individual Variation

Second, enculturation is never a completely uniform process. Enculturation experiences are blended and synthesized in unique ways by individuals. Even in the most isolated, small-scale societies, young people behave differently from their parents. Furthermore, not all people in a particular society are socialized or enculturated in exactly the same manner. As we have emphasized in the contemporary understanding of culture, anthropologists recognize that the vast amounts of information transmitted through enculturation often lead to variations in what children are taught in different families and institutions.

In addition, norms do not dictate behavior in any rigid manner. People in any society are always confronted with contradictory norms, and society is always changing, affecting the process of enculturation. Enculturation rarely provides people with a precise blueprint for the behavioral responses needed in the many situations they face.

Thus, enculturation is an imprecise process. People may internalize the general program for behavior—a series of ideal norms, rules, and cultural guidelines for action—but how these general principles apply in any specific set of concrete circumstances is difficult or impossible to specify. In some cases, people obey social and cultural rules completely, whereas in others they violate or ignore them. Enculturation provides the historically developed cultural forms through which the members of society share meanings and symbols and relate to one another. But in reality, people maneuver within these cultural forms, choosing their actions to fulfill both their own needs and the demands of their society.

SUMMARY

Psychological anthropologists attempt to understand similarities and differences in behavior, thought, and feelings among societies by focusing on the relationship between the individual and culture, or the process of enculturation. One question that psychological anthropologists focus on is the degree to which human behavior is influenced by biological tendencies versus learning. Today, most anthropologists have adopted an interactionist approach that emphasizes both biology and culture as influences on enculturation and human behavior.

Another related question is whether humans, as part of the animal kingdom, have instincts or genetically programmed behaviors that nonhuman animals have. Many nonhuman animals have closed instincts that rigidly structure their behavior patterns, allowing for survival and adaptation in specific environmental conditions. These closed instincts have been selected by environmental factors over millions of years of evolution.

It does not appear that humans have closed instincts. Instead, humans have the unique capacity for culture, which enables them to modify and shape their behavior to adapt to different environmental conditions. Without enculturation, humans are unable to think, behave, and develop emotionally in order to function in society.

The early studies of enculturation, called culture-and-personality studies, focused on culture as if it were an integrated type of personality. These early studies by pioneers such as Ruth Benedict and Margaret Mead provided some important data regarding enculturation processes, but they often exaggerated the significance of cultural determinants of human behavior. However, these efforts led to a more systematic examination of enculturation and childhood training. These studies have refined our understanding of childhood training in many different types of societies.

The theories of Sigmund Freud have had an influence on psychological anthropology. His model of enculturation and personality development has been used by a number of psychological anthropologists to investigate human behavior. In some cases, anthropologists collaborate with psychoanalysts to study dreams, sexual fantasies, family relations, and topics such as incest. Incest, incest avoidance, and the incest taboo have been studied thoroughly within anthropology, leading to insightful explanations for these phenomena.

Enculturation's relationship to sexual practices and norms has been a topic of research in psychological anthropology. A wide variation of sexual practices and norms in different parts of the world has been described. These practices and norms, including widely distributed patterns of homosexual behavior and acceptance of a third gender beyond male and female, indicate how enculturation influences the sex drive in human communities.

The relationship between enculturation and cognition has also been a field of study within psychological anthropology. Structuralist anthropology, developed by Claude Levi-Strauss, focuses on the relationship between culture and thought processes. Levi-Strauss hypothesized that the human mind is structured to produce underlying patterns of thinking that are universally based.

Psychologist Jean Piaget's and Lev Vygotsky's early studies on the development of cognitive processes have also influenced psychological anthropology. Many researchers are actively engaged in testing Piaget's and Vygotsky's model of cognitive development in different societies. Cognitive anthropologists have been drawing from the fields of computer modeling and psychological experimentation in laboratories to examine cognition. Evolutionary psychologists have hypothesized that humans have some genetically prepared predispositions that have a wide-ranging influence on enculturation, cognition, and human behavior. Their research has been a leading example of interactionist research in psychological anthropology.

Emotional development is another area of study in psychological anthropology. Researchers are trying to understand how emotions such as sadness, happiness, fear, anger, and contempt are similar and different from one society to another. Their findings indicate that there are both universal and specific cultural variations with respect to emotional development in different societies.

Psychological anthropologists have been exploring different forms of mental disorders in various societies. This type of research has led anthropology to challenge some of the typical classifications used in Western psychiatry and psychology to define mental disorders.

QUESTIONS TO THINK ABOUT

1. Discuss the differences between animal and human behavior. After reading this chapter, do you believe that humans have instincts?

2. What are some of the methods of enculturation used in your society? Give an example of how your own personality has been affected by enculturation.

3. Can anthropologists classify various cultures by identifying certain personality characteristics found among certain individuals, as did Ruth Benedict? Discuss the limitations of this approach.

4. Are cognitive and reasoning thinking processes universal among all people? What evidence do anthropologists have for agreeing or disagreeing with this opinion?

5. Are emotional expressions universal? To what extent are human emotions such as anger or jealousy similar or different around the world?

6. Describe a pattern of human behavior that you believe to be "normal" for your society but that might be considered "abnormal" in another society.

KEY TERMS

cognitive anthropology	incest	prototypes
drives	incest avoidance	psychological anthropologists
ego	incest taboo	superego
evolutionary psychology	narratives	
id	personality	

Chapter 5

Language

CHAPTER OUTLINE

CHAPTER QUESTIONS

- What is it that makes human languages unique in comparison with nonhuman animal communication?

- What does the research indicate about nonhuman animal communication?

- What do anthropologists conclude about the evolution of language?

- How do linguistic anthropologists study language?

- What have anthropologists learned about how children acquire their languages?

- What is the relationship between language and culture?

- How do anthropologists study the history of languages?

- What does the field of sociolinguistics tell us about language use?

- What other forms of communication do humans use aside from language?

In Chapter 3 we discussed how the capacity for culture enables humans to learn symbolically and to transmit symbols from generation to generation. **Language** is a system of *symbols* with standard meanings. Through language, members of a society are able to communicate with one another. It is an integral aspect of culture. Language allows humans to communicate with one another about what they are experiencing at any given moment, what they have experienced in the past, and what they are planning for the future. Like culture, the language of any particular individual exists before the birth of the individual and is publicly shared *to some extent* by the members of a society. People born in the United States are exposed to an English-speaking language community, whereas people in Russia learn the Russian language. These languages provide the context for symbolic understanding within these different societies. In this sense, language, as part of culture, transcends the individual. Without language, humans would have difficulty transmitting culture. Without culture, humans would lose their unique "humanity."

When linguists refer to language they usually mean spoken language. Yet spoken language is only one form of communication. **Communication** is the act of transferring information to others. As we will discover in this chapter, many nonhuman animals have basic communication skills. We will also discover that humans communicate with one another in ways other than through language.

Nonhuman Communication

Teaching Apes to Sign

Psychologists and other scientists have conducted a considerable amount of research on animal communication. Some of the most interesting and controversial research on animal communication has been done on chimpanzees and gorillas, animals that are close genetically, physiologically, and developmentally to humans. In 1966 psychologists Allen and Beatrice Gardner adopted a female chimpanzee named Washoe and began teaching her the American Sign Language (ASL, or Ameslan), a nonvocal form of communication used by the deaf. The ASL used by deaf humans is not an "artificial language" for deaf people. ASL is a complex language that evolved over 150 years in the United States and is very similar to spoken language with a complex grammar and abstract symbolic representations. After four years with the Gardners, Washoe was able to master over 150 signs. They reported that Washoe was able to combine signs together to invent new signs. This was truly a remarkable feat for a chimpanzee, and it challenged the traditional assumption that only humans have the capacity for using symbols (Gardner and Gardner 1969; Gordon 2004).

At the Yerkes Regional Primate Research Center at Emory University in Atlanta, Georgia, in the 1970s a chimpanzee named Lana was taught to communicate through a color-coded computer keyboard using *lexigrams* (graphic symbols). Researchers concluded that Lana was able to use and combine signs in the computer language. For example, she referred to a cucumber as a "green banana" and to an orange as an "apple that is orange" (Rumbaugh 1977). University of California Santa Barbara psychologists David and Ann Premack taught a chimpanzee named Sarah to manipulate plastic colored discs and different shapes to form simple sentences and ask for objects (Gordon 2004). Eventually, primatologist Roger Fouts, who had been Gardner's graduate student, took over the care of Washoe and spent some thirty years with her and other chimpanzees. During this period, Fouts observed Washoe communicating signs from the ASL with other chimpanzees. He has spent considerable time and research on chimpanzee communication abilities and linguistic capacities, recorded in his book *Next of Kin: What Chimpanzees Have Taught Me About Who We Are* (1997). He found that these chimps could produce category words for certain types of foods: celery was "pipe food"; watermelon was "candy drink"; and radish, a food first tasted by Washoe, was "hurt cry food." Also, when he introduced Washoe to a newly adopted chimpanzee named Loulis, Fouts signed in ASL, "I HAVE BABY FOR YOU." Washoe signed back "BABY, BABY, BABY!" and hooted for joy. In his book, Fouts argues that chimpanzee communication and linguistic capacities are very similar to that of human language capacities and differ only in *degree*.

In a widely publicized study in the 1970s, Francine Patterson taught Koko, a female gorilla, to use some 500 ASL words. Koko was billed as the world's first "talking" gorilla (Patterson and Cohn 1978; Patterson and Linden 1981). At the age of 4, Koko was given an intelligence test based on the Stanford–Binet Intelligence Scale and scored an 85, only slightly below the score of an average human child. Patterson contends that Koko even told stories about her violent capture in Africa. In addition, according to Patterson, Koko demonstrated the capacity to lie, deceive, swear, joke, and combine signs in new and creative ways. Koko also asked for and received a pet kitten to nurture (Gordon 2004).

Ape Sign Language Reexamined

These studies of ASL sign use by apes challenged traditional ideas regarding the gap between humans and other types of animals. They are not, however, without their critics. One source of criticism is based on work done at Columbia University by psychologist Herbert Terrace (1986). Terrace began examining the previous ape language studies by training a chimpanzee named Nim

Chimpsky (named after the well-known linguist discussed later, Noam Chomsky). Videotapes of the learning sessions were used to observe carefully the cues that may have been emitted by the trainers. Terrace also viewed the videotapes of the other studies on chimpanzee communication.

Terrace's conclusions challenged some of the earlier studies. Videotape analysis revealed that Nim rarely initiated signing behaviors, signing only in response to gestures given by the instructors, and that 50 percent of his signs were simply imitative. Unlike humans, Nim did not learn the two-way nature of conversation. Nim also never signed without expecting some reward. In addition, Nim's phrases were random combinations of signs. And Nim never signed to another chimpanzee who knew ASL unless a teacher coached him. Finally, the videotapes of the other projects showed that prompters gave unconscious signals to the chimpanzees through their body gestures.

Terrace's overall conclusions indicate that chimpanzees are highly intelligent animals who can learn many signs. They cannot, however, understand syntax, the set of grammatical rules governing the way words combine to form sentences. An English-speaking child can systematically place a noun before a verb followed by an object without difficulty. A chimpanzee cannot use these types of grammatical rules to structure sentences. Terrace concludes that although chimpanzees have remarkable intellectual capacities and excellent memories, they do not have the syntactical abilities of humans to form sentences.

Researcher Joyce Butler showing Nim the chimpanzee the sign for drink.

Terrace's work has not ended the ape language debate. Sue Savage-Rumbaugh has tried to eliminate the methodological problem of giving ambiguous hand signs to train chimpanzees at the Yerkes laboratory at Emory University. Terrace had suggested that the researchers such as Patterson and Rumbaugh were cuing their subjects with their own signs to respond to specific signs. In her book *Ape Language: From Conditioned Response to Symbol* (1986), Savage-Rumbaugh reports on a ten-year-old *bonobo*, or "pygmy," chimpanzee (a different species of chimpanzee than the common chimpanzee) named Kanzi, who learned to communicate with lexigrams, the graphic, geometric word-symbols that act as substitutes for human speech. Two hundred and fifty lexigrams are displayed on a large keyboard. At the age of 2½, Kanzi spontaneously reached for the keyboard, pointed to the lexigram for chase, and ran away. Savage-Rumbaugh observed him repeatedly touch the lexigram for chase and scamper off. By age six, Kanzi had mastered a vocabulary of ninety symbols.

In addition, Savage-Rumbaugh notes that Kanzi indicated that he understood spoken English words. She observed Kanzi listening to spoken words like a human child does. The preliminary research indicates that Kanzi could understand English words, even when produced by a speech synthesizer. Another astonishing revelation reported by Savage-Rumbaugh is that Kanzi appeared to have a crude command of syntax. He seemed to be able to use word order to convey meaning. On his own initiative, Kanzi requested activities in the order he desired them. For example, if he wanted to be chased and play-bitten, he first pressed the lexigram for chase, then bite. Savage-Rumbaugh reports that Kanzi could understand some 650 sentences. Rumbaugh concluded that Kanzi had learned to understand syntax (word order) and complex sentences and possessed a rudimentary linguistic capacity equivalent to a two-year-old child.

Psychologist Sally Boysen at Ohio State University and researchers Tetsuro Matsuzawa at Kyoto University in Japan have been doing research not only on language abilities of chimpanzees but also numerical abilities (Boysen and Bernston 1989; Matsuzawa 1985). These chimpanzees are reported to have learned how to count from zero to nine and also "read" Japanese characters (kanji) or English words. However, these researchers do not conclude that these chimpanzees have grammar or syntactical abilities. And, in a more recent book Sue Savage-Rumbaugh and her colleagues have claimed that Kanzi demonstrates the capacity for a "theory of mind," meaning that Kanzi can attribute "thoughts" and "intentions" within the mind of others, a capacity that most linguists and psychologists maintain that only humans have (Savage-Rumbaugh 1998; Gordon 2004).

However, Terrace suggests that the animal sign language studies are misguided. He is more concerned with how chimpanzees and gorillas think *without* language, because the complicated cognitive processes that are being studied in the trials reveals "a lot about the evolution of intelligence." He believes that these researchers are attempting to elicit "bits of language" from apes, who are preoccupied with performing only to obtain rewards (Gordon 2004).

Ethological Research on Ape Communication

In addition to laboratory research on animal communication, *primatologists* study the behavior of primates in their natural environment and have conducted a number of impressive field studies. **Ethologists**, scientists who study animal behavior, find that many types of animals have *call systems*—certain sounds or vocalizations that produce specific meanings—that are used to communicate for adaptive purposes. Animals such as prairie dogs, chickens, various types of monkeys, and chimpanzees have call systems.

In a primatological study of gorillas in central Africa, George Schaller isolated twenty-two vocalizations used by these primates. This compares with twenty vocalizations used by howler monkeys, thirty used by Japanese macaque monkeys, and nine used by gibbons (Schaller 1976). Like these other vocalizations, the gorilla sounds are associated with specific behaviors or emotional states, such as restful feeding states, sexual behavior, play, anger, and warnings of approaching threats. Infant gorillas also emit certain sounds when their mothers venture off. Schaller admits that some vocalizations were not accompanied by any specific type of behavior or stimulus.

Chimpanzee Communication: Jane Goodall The most impressive long-term investigation of chimpanzees in their natural environment was carried out by Jane Goodall, a primatologist who has been studying the chimpanzees of the Gombe Game Reserve in Africa since 1960. Goodall has gathered a great deal of information on the vocalizations used by these chimps. Her observations have shown that the chimpanzees use a great variety of calls, which are tied directly to emotional states such as fear, annoyance, and sexual excitement. She concludes that "the production of a sound in the absence of the appropriate emotional state seems to be an almost impossible task for the chimpanzee" (Goodall 1986, 125).

Goodall found that the chimps use "intraparty calls," communication within the group, and "distance calls," communication to other groups. Intraparty calls include pant-grunts directed to a higher-ranking individual within the group as a token of respect, and barks, whimpers, squeaks, screams, coughs, and other sounds directed toward other chimps in the immediate group. Distance calls serve a wider range of functions, including drawing attention to local food sources, announcing the precise location of individuals in the home territory, and, in times of distress, bringing help from distant allies. Further research is needed to discover whether the chimps use these vocalizations to distinguish among different types of foods and dangers in the environment.

Although primate communication in the wild indicates that they do not use symbolic language or anything close to ASL, nevertheless the laboratory studies that have trained chimpanzees and gorillas to use ASL clearly demonstrate that the gap between primates and human communication is somewhat similar. Whether they indicate that apes can use true human symbolic language remains undecided and controversial. Although recent neurological research on chimpanzees has shown that they have areas in their brain where linguistic capacities and potentialities are similar to that of humans, more research needs to be done on chimpanzee and primate communication to investigate this phenomena (Gannon et al. 1998; Small 2001; Gordon 2004). Most anthropologists and psychologists have concluded that apes show the ability to manipulate linguistic symbols when the symbols are hand gestures or plastic symbols. However, the

Jane Goodall with chimpanzees.

fact they do not have the capacity to transmit symbolic language beyond the level of a two-year-old human child does not mean that they are *failed humans*. Chimps are perfectly good at being chimps. It would appear that humans have much different sorts of linguistic capacities. Whether they are different in *degree* or in *kind* is a topic that has divided the primatologists, linguistic anthropologists, and psychologists into asserting differing claims based on their evidence in the field or the laboratory. We will explore this aspect of linguistic capacities in humans further later.

Currently, many of the primatologists, such as Roger Fouts and Jane Goodall, have turned their attention to saving and conserving the environments of chimpanzee and other primate populations that are increasingly in danger in their natural habitats. Over the past thirty years primate research taught humans a lot about how chimpanzees are individuals with capacities that differ little from our own. Primatologists have learned that chimpanzees have a great capacity to acquire a sophisticated gesture communication system. But more recently, these primatologists have embraced the ethical and moral implications of the findings and expressed them in their activism aimed at stopping the exploitation of all our fellow animals (Fouts and Mills

1997; Goodall 2004; Hart 2004). Looking back on how these primates were treated in many of the laboratory settings for research and taken out of their wild habitat has demonstrated that these animals were treated unfairly by most of their trainers. These primatologists are devoted to saving the natural habitats of these primates and actively working against using these animals for experimental purposes in inhumane manners. Goodall, Fouts, and other primatologists recognized that many of these animals were preyed upon by humans for both food and tourist souvenirs in their natural environments. As primatologists they are actively campaigning against the brutality in which these animals have been treated by their close kin, we humans. In a passage from *Descent of Man* (1871), Charles Darwin states "Our moral progress will not be complete until we extend our compassion to people of all races, then to the imbecile, the maimed, and other useless members of society, and finally to the members of all species." Although this nineteenth-century language seems crude with reference to the "imbecile" and "useless members of society" to our twenty-first-century ear, it reflects a morality that has been increasingly adopted by many primatologists and anthropologists today.

Animal Communication and Human Language

Both laboratory and field studies of animal communication offer fascinating insights into the question of what distinguishes human communication from animal communication. Many Western philosophers such as Plato or Rene Descartes have identified speech and language as the major distinction between humans and other animals. Modern studies on animal communication, however, suggest that the language gap separating humans from other animals is not as wide as it once appeared. These studies also indicate that fundamental differences exist between animal communication and human languages. The question is not whether animals can communicate, because we know that almost every animal can. The real question is: How does animal communication differ from human communication? In searching for an answer to this question, linguistic anthropologists have identified a number of distinctive characteristics of human languages. The four most important features are productivity, displacement, arbitrariness, and combining sounds (Hockett and Ascher 1964).

Productivity

Human languages are inherently flexible and creative. Users of human languages, even small children, can create sentences never heard before by anyone. There are no limits to our capability to produce messages that refer to the past, present, or future. We can express different thoughts, meanings, and experiences in infinite ways. In contrast, animal communication systems in natural settings are rigid and fixed. The sounds of animal communications do not vary and cannot be modified. The offspring of chimpanzees will always use the same pattern of vocalization as the parents. In contrast, the highly flexible nature of human languages allows for efficient and creative uses of symbolic communication. William von Humboldt, a nineteenth-century linguist, used the phrase "the infinite use of finite media" to suggest the idea of linguistic productivity (von Humboldt [1836] 1972; Pinker 1994).

Displacement

It is clear from field studies, and to some extent from laboratory studies, that the meaning of a sound or vocalization of a nonhuman animal is closely tied to a specific type of stimulus. For example, the chimpanzee's vocalization is associated with a particular emotional state and stimulus. Thus, a growl or scream as a warning to the group cannot be made in the absence of some perceived threat. Similarly, animals such as parrots and mynah birds can learn to imitate a wide variety of words, but they cannot substitute or displace one word for another. In contrast, the meanings of sounds in human languages can refer to people, things, or events that are not present, a feature called displacement. We can discuss things that are not in front of our visual or auditory capacities.

This capacity for displacement enables humans to communicate with one another using highly abstract concepts. Humans can express their objectives in reference to the past, present, and future. They can discuss spiritual or hypothetical phenomena that do not exist concretely. They can discuss past history through myth or specific genealogical relations. Humans can refer to what will happen after death through myth or theological concepts such as heaven or spiritual enlightenment. Displacement allows humans to plan for the future through the use of foresight. Obviously, this linguistic ability for displacement is interrelated with the general symbolic capacities that are shared by humanity, providing the basis of culture as discussed in Chapter 3. Symbolic capacities allow humans to manipulate abstract concepts to develop complex beliefs and worldviews.

Arbitrariness

The arbitrariness of sounds in a communication system is another distinctive feature of human languages. Words seldom have any necessary connection with the concrete objects or abstract symbols they represent. In English we say one, two, and three to refer to the numbers, whereas the Chinese say *yi*, *er*, and *san*. Neither language has the "correct" word for the numbers, because there is no correct word. "Ouch" is pronounced "*ay*" in Spanish and "*ishkatak*" in the Nootkan Indian language. A German shepherd dog does not have any difficulty understanding the bark of a French poodle. An English speaker, however, will have trouble understanding a Chinese speaker. A chimpanzee from West Africa will have no difficulty communicating with a chimpanzee from East Africa (although primatologists do find different behavior patterns such as tool making, nut cracking, and other behaviors among chimpanzees residing in different locales in Africa) (Mercader, Panger, and Boesch 2002).

Combining Sounds to Produce Meanings

We have mentioned that various animals have sounds that indicate different meanings in specific contexts. Human languages, in addition, have units of sound that cannot be correlated with units of meaning. Every human language has between twelve and sixty of these sound units, called *phonemes*. A **phoneme** is a unit of sound that distinguishes meaning in a particular language. For example, in English the difference between "dime" and "dine" is distinguished by the sound difference or phonemic difference between /*m*/ and /*n*/. English has forty-five phonemes, Italian has twenty-seven, and Hawaiian has thirteen (Farb 1974).

Nonhuman animals cannot combine their sound units to communicate new meanings; one vocalization is given to indicate a specific response. In contrast, in human languages the same sounds can be combined and recombined to form different meanings. As an illustration, the sounds usually represented by the English letters p, t, c, and a (the vowel sound in the word bat) have no meaning on their own. But they can be used to form words like pat, tap, cat, apt, act, tact, pact, and so on, which do have meanings. The Hawaiian language, with only thirteen sound units, has almost three thousand words consisting of different combinations of three sounds and more than five million words formed by combinations of six sounds. Phonemes that may have no meaning alone can be combined and recombined to form literally as many meaningful units (words) as people need or want. Primates and other animals do not have this ability.

Having defined these features of human language, we can discern fundamental differences between human and animal communication. However, some researchers working with chimpanzees

in laboratories are still not willing to label human languages as "true languages," as distinguished from "animal communication systems." They criticize what they refer to as the "anthropocentric" view of language—the view that takes human language as its standard. Because chimpanzees do not have the physical ability to form the sounds made by humans, it may be unfair to compare their language strictly in terms of vocal communication.

The Evolution of Language

Throughout the centuries, linguists, philosophers, and physical anthropologists have developed theories concerning the origins of human language. One early theory, known as the "bowwow" theory, maintains that language arose when humans imitated the sounds of nature by the use of onomatopoeic words, such as "cock-a-doodle-do," or "sneeze," or "mumble." Another theory associated with the Greek philosopher Plato argues that language evolved as humans detected the natural sounds of objects in nature. Known as the "ding-dong" theory, this argument assumed that a relationship exists between a word and its meaning because nature gives off a harmonic ring. For example, all of nature, including rocks, streams, plants, and animals, was thought to emit a ringing sound that could be detected by humans. The harmonic ring of a rock supposedly sounded like rock. Both theories have been discredited, replaced by other scientific and linguistic anthropological hypotheses concerning the evolution of language. When anthropologists study the evolution of language, they draw on evidence from all four fields of anthropology: physical anthropology, archaeology, linguistic anthropology, and cultural anthropology.

The Anatomy of Language

One distinction that needs to be understood when understanding the hypotheses put forward by anthropologists regarding the evolution of language is that there is a difference between *speech* and *language*. Speech is how we communicate with one another through oral/auditory mechanisms to convey our thoughts to one another. Language is the capacity to exchange symbolic abstract ideas with one another through writing and without sound. For thousands of years, according to the evidence anthropologists have about human communication, speech and oral/auditory messages were the only form of communication. Thus, the evolution of speech and language may be separate from one another to some extent (Clegg 2004).

As discussed earlier in the text, the evolution of hominids was accompanied by some degree of increase in brain size. The expansion of the hominid brain reflects the increasing size of the cerebral cortex, the part related to all of the higher functions of the brain, such as memory and symbolic and cultural capacities. Although many capacities of the human brain, including memory, learning, and other functions, are not completely understood by modern science, we do know that the cerebral cortex contains the billions of nerve cells needed for receiving, storing, and processing information.

The Human Brain and Speech   Other centers of the brain play important roles in the human capacity for language. The human brain is divided into two hemispheres. Although neither hemisphere is dominant and both play important roles in all functions, most human linguistic skills are more closely identified with one hemisphere. In general, the left hemisphere controls specialized functions related to linguistic abilities, and the right hemisphere controls functions related to spatial orientation and proportion. This is true even for the deaf person who uses sign language to communicate. One area of the brain that is located in the left hemisphere and that especially influences human language abilities is known as *Broca's area*; it is associated with the production of sound or pronunciation and with grammatical abilities.

Another area related to linguistic abilities is *Wernicke's area*, also located in the left hemisphere of the brain. Wernicke's area is associated with the ability to understand the meanings of words and sentences, or the semantics of language. This center of the brain is important for listening and reading. However, current anthropological research on primate brains, especially chimpanzees, has found that there are similar regions within their brains that control the use of their hands and mouths (Gannon et al. 1998).

Human Anatomy and Speech   Other anatomical and physiological features contribute to human

speech abilities. Although primates, especially the apes, have lips, mouths, and tongues, no primate other than humans has the physical anatomy for sustaining speech production. Human vocal organs form an irregular tube connecting the lungs, windpipe, and *larynx*, the voice box containing the vocal cords. Another vocal organ is the *pharynx*, the part of the vocal tract between the back of the tongue and the larynx extending into the nasal cavity. The larynx serves to hold air in the lungs and to control its release. These vocal organs work in conjunction with our tongue, lips, and nose to produce speech. The lungs force air through the pharynx, which changes shape to control the column of air. The nasal cavity, lips, and tongue can constrict or stop the flow of air at any point, enabling us to make vowel or consonant sounds. The organs involved in producing speech are illustrated in Figure 5.1.

Could Early Hominids Speak?   Some physical anthropologists are using complex computer programs and statistical procedures to compare the

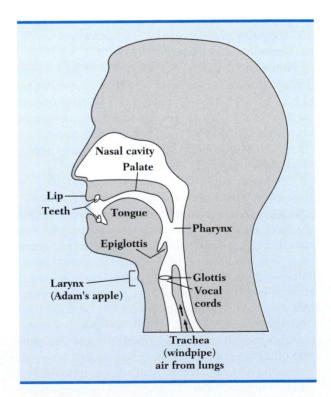

FIGURE 5.1   The physiology of speech making, which is unique to humans.

anatomy of primates, early hominids, and modern humans. Through this method, Philip Lieberman and Jeffrey Laitman proposed a hypothesis regarding the evolution of language. They suggested that australopithecines did not have the vocal tract needed to produce the range of vowels found in human language. In addition, they suggested that the cranium of early hominids such as Neandertals was much flatter and that the larynx was higher than that of modern *H. sapiens*. They concluded that Neandertals, archaic *Homo sapiens*, could not produce vowels such as a, i, and u, thus limiting their linguistic abilities (Laitman 1984; Lieberman 1991, Lieberman and McCarthy 1999). They hypothesized that the language capacity developed with the lowering of the larynx and changes in the cranium for modern *H. sapiens*. They went on to say that this reconfiguration of the vocal tract made breathing more difficult, increased the risk of death from choking, and crowded the teeth, which can lead to impacted wisdom teeth, so the advantages of having language must have outweighed the disadvantages caused by the change in anatomy.

More current hypotheses have emerged to question some aspects of this earlier hypothesis regarding the evolution of speech. For example, physical anthropologists Margaret Clegg and A. C. Aiello have found that death by choking or suffocation is extremely rare among humans and is usually due to improper feeding or insufficient medical care (2002). These anthropologists along with others have been reanalyzing the skeletal material associated with Neandertal and suggest that compared with earlier hominids such as *H. erectus,* the breathing apparatus, changes in facial characteristics, and vocal tract would have enabled Neandertal to speak (Clegg and Aiello 2002, 2004; Schepartz 1993, R. F. Kay et al. 1998). Furthermore, in contrast to Lieberman and Laitman's hypotheses regarding the inability of Neandertals to use certain vowel sounds, these newer hypotheses indicate that many modern human languages do not use or stress these particular "vowel" sounds (Pickett 1999).

This recent reanalysis of both primate and early hominid fossil evidence has given rise to a popular hypothesis regarding the evolution of language that suggests that australopithecines probably communicated through sign communication, vocal calls, and gestures. Linguistic capacity was most likely *not* present in the early hominids such as *H. habilis*. However, as *H. erectus* fossils indicate, they were fully erect and bipedal and they may have been able to speak, but again did not have the expansion of the brain that would be connected with language capacities, although their ability to manipulate tools may have resulted in preadaptations that may have resulted in future language capacities. These new hypotheses suggest that Neandertals would have the appropriate requirements in brain expansion and other physical anatomy that would have enabled them to speak. Eventually, these developments led to the increasing size of the cranium, resulting in the reorganization of the brain regions and neurological capacities that resulted in language capacities and the abstract, symbolizing power of language that is associated with modern humans (Clegg 2004).

Whatever the precise determinants of the evolution of language, it is difficult to identify the critical stage in the evolution from a simple, sign-based communication system to a more advanced symbolic form of language. It is, however, recognized that this capacity broadly expanded human capabilities for adaptation and creativity. Although anthropologists disagree with one another regarding the actualities and purpose of language capacities in humans, this capacity for language was probably the last major step in our biological evolution (Mithen 1996; Deacon 1997; Dunbar, Knight, and Power 1999). Since that time, human history has been dominated by *cultural* rather than *biological* evolution. This cultural evolution and the subsequent developments in adaptation and creativity could not have occurred before a fully evolved language capacity.

The Structure of Language

Linguistic anthropologists compare the structure of different languages. To do so, they study the sounds of a language (*phonology*), the words of a language (*morphology*), the *sentence structure* of a language (*syntax*), the meaning of a language (*semantics*), and the *rules* for the appropriate use of language (*pragmatics*). More than six thousand languages have existed throughout history, all of which have contained these five components, although the components vary considerably from one language to another.

Phonology

Phonology is the study of the sounds used in language. Although all human languages have both vowel and consonant sounds, no language makes use of all the sounds humans can make. To study phonetic differences among languages, linguists have developed the International Phonetic Alphabet (IPA), which enables linguists to transcribe all the sounds produced in the world's languages. Each sound is used somewhere in the world, although no single language contains all of them. Each language has its own phonetic inventory, consisting of all the sounds normally produced by its speakers, and also a phonemic inventory, consisting of the sound units that can produce word contrasts in the language. As we have already seen, human languages, which have only a limited number of sounds, can combine these sounds to produce complex meanings.

Linguists attempt to discover the phonemes, or contrasting sound-units of a language, by looking for what are called minimal pairs: words that are identical except for one difference in sound. For example, the English words lot and rot form a minimal pair; they are identical except for their beginning sounds, spelled *l* and *r*. The fact that English speakers recognize lot and rot as different words establishes that /*l*/ and /*r*/ are contrasting sound-units, or phonemes, in English. In contrast, when Japanese children acquire their native language they do not make a sharp categorical distinction between the /*l*/ and /*r*/ sounds. Japanese adult speakers do not hear the distinction between /*l*/ and /*r*/, even when they listen very carefully to English speakers. Recently, Patricia Kuhl and her Japanese colleagues have been studying how Japanese infants attend to different sounds of their own language and why they do not make distinctions between /*l*/ and /*r*/ (1996, 1997). This research suggests that as we are exposed to our language environment, the initial sounds that we detect as infants in our first language alters our neurological networks in our brains that have enduring effects on our ability to distinguish particular sounds within a language.

When linguistic anthropologists analyze the phonological system of a language, they attempt to organize the sounds, or **phones**, of the language into a system of contrasting phonemes. For example,

English speakers produce both a /*p*/ sound and the same sound accompanied by *aspiration*, a light puff of air, symbolized in the IPA as /*p*ʰ/; compare the difference between the *p* sounds in spy and pie. Because in English the sounds /*p*/ and /*p*ʰ/ never form a minimal pair and their pronunciation depends on their position in a word, these sounds are allophones of the same phoneme in English. In other languages, such as Aymara (spoken in Bolivia, Perú, and Chile), aspiration of consonants produces a phonemic contrast: compare Aymara /*hupa*/, which means *they*, with /*hup*ʰ*a*/, a kind of cereal. In Aymara, then, the sounds /*p*/ and /*p*ʰ/ belong to separate phonemes, just as /*l*/ and /*r*/ do in English, as we saw before. This illustrates the fact that the "same" sounds may be contrastive in one language and not contrastive in another. Also, what sounds like a /*b*/ to a native Spanish speaker sounds like a /*p*/ to a native English speaker. Obviously, neurological changes are occurring within the brain as a child acquires their native language.

In addition to aspiration, sounds may be modified in other ways, including nasality, pitch, stress, length of time the sound is held, and so on. Many Asian languages, such as Chinese and Thai, are *tonal*; that is, a word's meaning is affected by the tones (contrasting pitches) of the sounds that make up the word. Put another way, the tones of the language have phonemic value. To an English speaker's ear, a Chinese or Thai speaker sounds musical. For example, in Thai *may* can mean "new," "to burn," or "silk," depending on the tone used.

Pueblo Indians use many nasalized sounds to produce phonemic differences. Arabs use the back of the tongue and the throat muscles, whereas Spanish speakers use the tip of the tongue. The !Kung San or Ju/'hoansi of southern Africa have a unique manner of producing phonemic differences. They use a sharp intake of air to make clicks that shape meaning for them. Their language also requires more use of the lips to produce smacks than most other languages. The Ju/'hoansi language has been referred to as a "clicking language."

Most people are unaware of the complex physiological and mental processes required for pronouncing the sounds of their native tongue. Only through extensive phonetic and phonological analysis by linguists and anthropologists is this component of language understood.

Morphology

To study the words of human languages, anthropologists isolate the **morphemes**, the smallest units of a language that convey meaning. The study of morphemes is called **morphology**. Morphemes may be short, only a single phoneme; or they may be a combination of phonemes. They are the minimal building blocks of meaning and cannot be reduced further. *Bound morphemes* are those morphemes that cannot stand alone, such as suffixes and prefixes. For example, in English *s* is a bound morpheme that indicates the plural, and the prefix *un* is a bound morpheme meaning not. *Free morphemes*, in contrast, are independent units of meaning; they can stand alone, for example, as nouns, verbs, adjectives, or adverbs. Words such as boy, girl, happy, and close are free morphemes.

In any language, morphemes are limited in number, and languages differ in how these morphemes are used and combined. In contrast to many languages, English has complex rules governing the formation of plurals of certain words (for example, geese, mice, children, and shrimp). Some languages, such as Chinese, generally use one morpheme for each word. Other languages, such as the Eskimo (Inuit) languages, combine a large number of affixes to form words.

An important way that languages differ is the extent to which they use morphology to convey meaning. For example, in English we can say the girl sees the dog or the dog sees the girl. The nouns *girl* and *dog* do not change form, and only their position in the sentence indicates which is subject and which is object. But in Russian, *dyevushka videt sobaku* means that the girl sees the dog; the dog sees the girl is *sobaka videt dyevushku*. Note that the endings on the nouns show which is subject and object, even if the word order is changed: *Sobaku videt dyevushka* still means that the girl sees the dog.

Syntax

The **syntax** of a language is the collection of rules for the way phrases and sentences are made up out of words. For example, these rules determine whether a subject comes before or after a verb or whether an object follows a verb. Linguistic anthropologist Joseph Greenberg (1990) classified languages based on word order within sentences—that is, the location of the subject (S), the verb (V), and the object (O). He demonstrated that these components occur in six possible orders: VSO, SVO, SOV, VOS, OSV, and OVS. But, in fact, what Greenberg found in his cross-linguistic comparison is that usually just three patterns of word order occur: VSO, SVO, SOV. Since his study, other languages have been discovered with the VOS, OVS, and OSV forms, though the last two are extremely rare (Smith 1999).

Although most languages permit variation in syntax to allow for emphasis in expression, most linguists suggest that some innate universal capacities may influence word order. For example, the expression for the English sentence "The boy drank the water" can be found in all languages. Notice the variations in syntactical order among six different languages:

	S	V	O
English:	the bóy	dránk	the wáter
	S	V	O
Russian:	mál'c_ik	vy´pil	vódu
	V	S	O
Arabic:	s_áraba	lwáladu	lma-?a
	S	V	O
Hausa:	ya-ro-	yás_a-	ruwa-
	S	V	O
Thai:	dègchaaj	dyym	nàam
	S	O	V
Quechua:	wámbra	yakúta	upiárqan

(Hausa is a West African language. Quechua is a language of the ancient Incas and their modern descendants.)

The syntax of a language also includes rules for transforming one kind of sentence into another, for example, forming questions from statements. To form questions from statements, English has a rule that moves the auxiliary verb from its normal position in the sentence to a position at the front of the sentence. This rule allows us to take the statement Mary will study for the exam and, by moving will to the front, transform it into the question Will Mary study for the exam?

Semantics

Semantics is the study of the meaning of symbols, words, phrases, and sentences of a language. The field of semantics has led to important developments in linguistic anthropology. These linguistic anthropologists focus on the meaning of language as it relates to beliefs, concepts, and patterns of thought in different societies. A specialty has developed to account for the meaning of concepts and terms with respect to kinship terms and other cultural phenomena. This specialty, sometimes referred to as *ethnosemantics*, overlaps the field of cognitive anthropology introduced in Chapter 4.

Kinship Terms   The goal of ethnosemantics is to understand the meanings of words, phrases, and sentences and how members of other societies use language to organize things, events, and behaviors. For example, this type of analysis has been applied to kinship terminologies of many societies. It became increasingly clear to many anthropologists that they could not understand the kinship terms of other societies by simply translating them into English. English terms such as mother, father, brother, brother-in-law, cousin, aunt, and uncle treat the meaning of kinship terms differently from the kinship terms of other societies.

Some groups classify their kin with very precise terms for individuals, no matter how distantly they are related. English kin terms are fairly precise and distinct with respect to genealogical relatedness, yet English does not specify every kin relationship precisely. For example, English speakers do not distinguish between maternal and paternal uncles or aunts. Chinese kinship terminology, on the other hand, includes different terms for one's mother's brother and one's father's brother. There are separate terms for every sibling as well as for different cousins. This is an example of a highly descriptive kinship terminology. Other forms of kinship terminologies are highly generalized. In the Hawaiian kinship system, there is no specific term to parallel the English term father. Instead, the Hawaiians use one general term to classify their father and all male relatives in their father's generation. Some kinship terminologies, such as those of the Iroquois Indians, are intermediate between the descriptive and the generalized forms. The Iroquois have one single term for one's father and father's brother but two

separate terms for one's mother and one's mother's brother.

Ethnosemanticists or cognitive anthropologists worked out systematic methods to understand the kinship terminologies of many different societies by focusing on the distinctive common features of these terminologies (D'Andrade 1995). For example, in English there is a male and female contrast with every kin term except cousin. In addition, the feature of generation is designated in terms such as uncle and nephew, aunt and niece, and in these same terms we distinguish between ascending and descending generations. There is also a contrast between direct (same generation) and collateral (different generation) relatives. Great uncles and great aunts are collateral relatives, whereas brothers and sisters are direct relatives. Ethnosemanticists use these methods to analyze other forms of kinship terminologies in various societies.

Recently, a fascinating study by Larry Hirschfeld suggests that there are some universal aspects regarding the meaning of kinship terminology (1986, 1989). Hirschfeld found that children and adults assume that kinship terms refer to a "natural affinity" for their own genealogical relatives and families. Children appear to have an intuitive understanding of the relationship between kin terms and their relatives and family. Kinship terms are used to refer to people who share a common descent and an internal "essence." The family is based on a particular group of people and is different from a group of students in a class or other types of groups. Anthropologist Doug Jones has followed this model of linguistic research on kinship terms and also suggests that there is a "universal" aspect to kinship terminology found among all societies (1999, 2000, 2003, 2004). Other cognitive anthropologists continue to investigate kin terminologies and other cultural phenomena to seek out both similarities and differences among human groups (Bloch and Sperber 2003).

Language Acquisition

Although human infants are born with the ability to speak a language, they are not born preprogrammed to speak a particular language such as English. Just as infants are exposed to enculturation to absorb and learn about their culture, they

Children learning language on a computer.

must be exposed to the phonemes, morphemes, syntax, and semantics of the language within their culture. Linguistic anthropologists have examined this process, drawing on different hypotheses regarding language acquisition.

One of the earliest discussions in Western society on how humans learn their language came from the writings of the Catholic theologian Saint Augustine in his famous book *Confessions* (AD 400/1995). Augustine believed that as we hear our parents speak words and point to objects, we associate the words with the objects. Later, the empiricist philosopher John Locke (1632–1704) maintained a similar belief and suggested that the human mind at birth is like a blank tablet, a *tabula rasa*, and that infants learn language through habit formation. This hypothesis was further developed by behavioral psychologists such as B. F. Skinner in the twentieth century, who maintained that infants learn language through conditioned responses and feedback from their environment. An infant might babble a sound that resembles an acceptable word like *mama* or *daddy* and would then be rewarded for that response. Thus rewarded, the child would use the word *daddy* in certain contexts. According to Skinner, children learn their entire language through this type of social conditioning.

The Enlightenment French philosopher René Descartes (1596–1650) advocated a contrasting view of language learning. He argued that innate ideas or structures in the human mind provide the basis for learning language. Until the late 1950s, most linguists and anthropologists working on language assumed that Locke's model—and, by extension, Skinner's—was correct. However, by about 1960 evidence began to accumulate that suggested that, in fact, humans come into the world especially equipped not only to acquire language, but to acquire any human language.

Chomsky on Language Acquisition

The most influential modern proponent of Descartes's hypothesis is linguist Noam Chomsky. Chomsky is interested in how people acquire *grammar*, the set of rules that determine how sentences are constructed to produce meaningful statements. Most people cannot actually state the rules of their grammar, but they do use the rules to form understandable sentences. For example, in English young children can easily transform the active sentence "Bill loves Mary" into a passive sentence, "Mary is loved by Bill." This change requires much grammatical knowledge, but most English speakers carry out this operation without thinking about it. According to Chomsky, all children acquire these complex rules readily and do not seem to have difficulty producing meaningful statements, even when they have not been exposed to linguistic data that illustrate the rules in question. Furthermore, children are able to both produce and understand sentences they have never heard before. All this would be impossible, Chomsky claims, if acquiring language depended on trial-and-error learning and reinforcement, as Skinner had thought. In other words, Chomsky suggests that we are born with a brain *prewired* to enable us to acquire language easily; Chomsky often refers to this prewiring as *universal grammar*.

Universal grammar serves as a template, or model, against which a child matches and sorts out the patterns of morphemes and phonemes and the subtle distinctions that are needed to communicate in any language. According to Chomsky, a behavioristic understanding of language learning is too simplistic to account for the creativity and productivity of any human language. In his view, the universal structure of the human mind enables the child to acquire language and produce sentences never heard before. In addition, Chomsky and

Saving Languages

There are more than six thousand languages distributed throughout a population of more than 6 billion people in the world. As many linguistic anthropologists have noted, however, tens of thousands of languages have become extinct through the years. In Western Europe, hundreds of languages disappeared with the expansion of agricultural empires that imposed their languages on conquered peoples. For example, during the expansion of the Roman Empire for approximately a thousand years, many tribal languages disappeared as they were replaced by Latin. Currently, only forty-five native languages still exist in Western Europe.

When Columbus discovered the Americas, more than two thousand languages existed among different Native American peoples. Yet even in pre-Columbian America, before AD 1500, native languages were displaced by the expansion of peoples such as the Aztecs and Incas in Central and South America. As the Spanish and British empires expanded into these regions, the indigenous languages began to disappear even more rapidly. A similar process has been ongoing throughout Asia, Africa, and the Middle East.

The majority of people in the world speak one of the "large" groups of languages, such as

Mandarin Chinese (with more than 1 billion speakers), Spanish, or English. Most of the more than four thousand languages that exist are spoken in small-scale societies that have an average of five thousand people or so. For example, Papua New Guinea alone has perhaps as many as a thousand different languages distributed among various ethnic groups (Diamond 1993). Other islands in countries such as Indonesia may have as many as four hundred different languages. Yet in all of the areas of the Pacific and Asia, the "larger" languages are beginning to replace the "small" ones.

Some linguists estimate that if the present rate of the disappearance of languages remains constant, within a century or two our four thousand languages could be reduced to just a few hundred. For example, as young people in the Pacific islands begin to move from rural to urban regions, they usually abandon their traditional language and learn a majority tongue to be able to take advantage of educational and economic opportunities. As the media—television, radio, and newspapers, now the Internet—opt for a majority language, more people will elect to abandon their native languages. These are global processes that have resulted in linguistic homogeneity and the loss of traditional languages.

In North America and Alaska, there are some two hundred languages ranging from Inuit and Yupik among the native Alaskans to Navajo, Hopi, Choctaw, Creek, Seminole, Chickasaw, and Cherokee in other areas. However, most

of these languages are now on the verge of extinction. As Europeans began to expand and control North America and Alaska, they forced Native American children to speak the English language as a means of "civilizing" them. In many cases, Native American children were removed from their families and were forbidden to speak their native languages. In addition, most Native American peoples have had to learn English to adjust to circumstances in an English-language-dominated society. Thus, very few of the Native American languages are actively spoken.

Some people say that this process of global and linguistic homogenization and the loss of traditional languages is a positive development. As people begin to speak a common language, communication is increased, leading to improvements in societies that formerly could not unify through language. For example, in India, hundreds of languages existed before the British colonized the area. As the educated class in India (a small minority) began to learn and speak English, it helped provide a means of unifying India as a country. Many people say that for the purpose of developing commerce and political relationships, the abandonment of native languages is a good thing. Many businesspeople and politicians argue that multiple languages inhibit economic and political progress, and the elites of many countries have directly encouraged language loss.

A number of linguistic anthropologists, however, disagree with these policies. They may agree

that people ought to have some common language to understand one another, to conduct business, and to have common political goals. But, they argue, this does not have to mean eliminating minority languages. It requires only that people become bilingual or multilingual. In most societies throughout the world, including Western Europe, people routinely learn two or more languages as children. The United States and Japan are exceptional in being monolingual societies.

Linguistic anthropologists find from their studies that people who are forced to abandon their native languages and cultures begin to lose their self-esteem. Bilingualism would permit these people to retain their own language while simultaneously learning the majority language to be able to share in a common national culture.

The U.S. government is beginning to realize that bilingualism has a positive influence on community development among minority populations such as Native Americans. Recently, a number of educational programs have been funded under the U.S. Bilingual Education Act. This act encourages the development of English-speaking skills; however, it also offers instruction in the native languages. During the 1980s there were more than twenty Title VII projects serving Native American students from sixteen different language backgrounds. Through these government-sponsored programs, linguistic anthropologists have been actively engaged in both research and language-renewal activities among the Native American population (Leap 1988). These activities have led many younger Native Americans to become interested in studying their traditional languages, which may lead to improvements in classroom learning and inhibit high dropout rates among young students (Laughlin 2004).

Anthropologist Russell Bernard has promoted the value of maintaining the native languages of people through the use of micro-computers (1992). Anthropologists use computers to help develop writing systems and literature for native languages. Through this computer technology, anthropologists can help native peoples to produce literature in their own languages for future generations. Bernard emphasizes that this will enable all of humanity to profit from the ideas of these people. Bernard was able to establish a center in Mexico where the Indian population could learn to use computers to write in their native languages. Sixty Indian people have learned to write directly in languages such as Mixtec, Zapotec, Chatino, Amuzgo, Chinantec, and Mazataec. These native authors will use these texts to teach adults and children of their home regions to read. Projects such as these represent opportunities for anthropologists to apply their knowledge in solving important problems in U.S. society and beyond.

Noam Chomsky.

others who study language acquisition propose a *critical period*, between birth and roughly the onset of puberty, during which language acquisition must take place. If children are not exposed to language during that period, they may never be able to acquire it, or they may learn it only in a very rudimentary fashion. Chomsky believes that the human brain contains genetically programmed blueprints or *modules* for language learning, and he often refers to language acquisition as a part of children's "growth," not something they do but rather something that happens to them. In addition, Chomsky argues that there is a difference in *kind* between primate communication and human language capacities. He suggests in a well-known statement that "Olympic athlete broad-jumpers can *fly* some 30 feet in the air, but humans do not have the capacity to *fly* like chickens or other birds." The capacity for flying, like "language capacity," require a tremendous difference in physical and anatomical requirements.

Another important contribution of Chomsky's is the realization that human languages, despite their apparently great diversity, are really more alike than they are different. Anthropologists had previously assumed that languages could vary infinitely,

and there was no limit to what could be found in a human language. Chomsky and the researchers that followed him, in contrast, have catalogued many basic, underlying ways in which all languages are really the same. In this view, a hypothetical Martian linguist visiting Earth would probably decide that all humans speak dialects of human language. Note that this is somewhat parallel to the search for *cultural universals* described in Chapter 3.

Chomsky's model is referred to as generative grammar. In this view, speakers of a language generate their sentences from a set of rules, some of which we have discussed earlier. This model is extremely powerful, because many sentences can be generated with a relatively small number of rules operating on the lexicon, or vocabulary, of the language. For example, a very simple generative grammar for English might include the following rules:

S → NP VP (a sentence consists of a noun phrase plus a verb phrase)

VP → V (NP) (a verb phrase consists of a verb plus an optional noun phrase)

NP → Art N (a noun phrase consists of an article plus a noun)

N → girl, dog

Art → the, a

V → sees

With this simple set of rules we can generate sentences such as the girl sees the dog, a girl sees a dog, a dog sees the girl, the girl sees, and so on. Each time we add a noun or verb, we increase exponentially the number of sentences we can generate.

In the early years of generative grammar, Chomsky and others proposed an enormous number of complicated grammatical rules, including transformational rules, which had to be learned by children. But it soon became apparent that children could not, in the short time they take to acquire language, learn so many complex rules, and there has been a push more recently to simplify the generative model as much as possible. One of the more elegant outcomes of this trend has been the principles and parameters approach. One example of this is the head parameter, which determines whether the head of a phrase precedes or follows its complement (the only two possibilities). In English, for example, heads precede their complements, as illustrated here with the complements in brackets:

Verb + object	sees [the dog]
Preposition + object	over [the rainbow]
Noun + complement	President [of Mexico]
Adjective + complement	afraid [of spiders]

In other languages, like Japanese and Aymara, heads follow their complements (the rainbow + over; the dog + sees). Chomsky and others noticed that, as with the preceding English examples, this parameter tends to apply across all the possible phrase types in a language. In other words, English-speaking children don't have to acquire, separately, that verbs precede their objects and prepositions precede theirs. They only need to acquire one fact: The setting of the head parameter for English is head-initial. Once they know that, a number of apparently disparate facts about English fall into place. There is some evidence that children begin "setting" their head parameter very early, at around two years of age (Goodluck 1991).

Recently, there has been a push toward what Chomsky and some other linguists call *minimalism*, a search for ways to further simplify the model of universal grammar, and many of the former generative rules have disappeared completely. One that remains is the merge rule, which allows for constituents such as words to be joined together (for example, forming the noun phrase *the dog* from the separate article *the* and noun *dog*). Another rule that continues to be useful is the move rule mentioned earlier. In keeping with minimalism, these rules are very general; what can be joined together, and what can be moved and to where, are determined by properties of the constituents involved (Chomsky 1995, 2002).

Chomsky argues that languages have two separate modes of existence, which he calls *E-Language* and *I-Language*. E-Language is the "external" observable word and utterances that we make to one another as we communicate, with our specific vocabularies, dialects, nuances in our speech habits, and the circumstances and social context of our use of language. Other linguists refer to this as the *pragmatics* of language or, as we will see later, the subject of sociolinguistic studies. He believes that this E-Language is very difficult to study because it involves so many complex variables that make our everyday conversations and use of speech and writing almost impossible to comprehend. However, I-Language is an "internal" set of rules that children acquire to be able to communicate in their specific language that they are exposed to in Japan, America, or Uruguay. Chomsky suggests that no two individual children share exactly the same I-Language, although they will share some similarities with one another in order to be able to communicate. He also indicates that there will be differences between the I-Languages from one generation to another and that eventually results in the development of new languages in different areas of the world, the subject of the next section below (Chomsky 1986).

Creole Languages One source of evidence for Chomsky's model of innate universal grammar is research on specific types of languages known as *creole* and *pidgin* languages. Linguist Derek Bickerton has compared these two types of languages from different areas of the world. Pidgin and creole languages develop from cross-cultural contact between speakers of mutually unintelligible languages. A *pidgin* form of communication emerges when people of different languages develop and use a simple grammatical structure and words to communicate with one another. For example, in the New Guinea highlands, where many different languages were spoken, a pidgin language developed between the indigenous peoples and the Westerners.

In some cases, the children of the pidgin speakers begin to speak a *creole* language. The vocabulary of the *creole* language is similar to that of the pidgin, but the grammar is much more complex. There are more than a hundred known creole languages. Among them are the creole languages developed between African slaves and Europeans, leading to languages such as Haitian or Jamaican Creole. A Hawaiian creole language emerged after contact between English-speaking Westerners and native Hawaiians.

What is remarkable, according to Bickerton, is that all these languages share similar grammatical patterns, despite the lack of contact among these diverse peoples. For example, Hawaiian Creole uses the English word *walk* in a very different manner from standard English. The phrase *bin walk* means "had walked"; *stay walk* is continuing action, as in "I am walking" or "I was walking"; and "I bin stay walk" means "I had been walking." Although this phrasing might sound unusual to a person from England or the United States, it does conform to a clear set of grammatical rules. Very similar tense systems are found in all other creole languages, whatever their vocabularies or geographic origins.

Bickerton suggests that the development of creole languages may parallel the evolution of early human languages. Because of an innate universal grammatical component of the human mind, languages emerged in uniform ways. The prehistoric languages would have had structures similar to that of the creole languages. As languages developed in various types of environments with different characteristics, people evolved different vocabularies and sentence structures. Yet when societies are uprooted by cultural contact, the innate rules for ordering language remain intact. Bickerton's thesis suggests that humans do have some sort of universal linguistic acquisition device, as hypothesized by Chomsky (Bickerton 1985, 1999, 2002).

Ebonics as a Creole Language   A number of linguists have been doing research on *Ebonics*, a distinctive variety of American English spoken by some African Americans. The term Ebonics is derived from the words ebony and phonics, meaning "black sounds" (Rickford 1997). Ebonics is also known as Black English Vernacular (BEV), Black English (BE), African American Vernacular English (AAVE), and African American English (AAE). The majority of African Americans do not speak Ebonics; however, it is commonly spoken among working-class and, in particular, among adolescent African Americans. Linguistic anthropologists have suggested that Ebonics may have emerged as a creole language under the conditions of slavery in the United States. As slaves from Africa, captured from different areas and speaking an enormous variety of languages, were placed together on plantations in the American South, they developed a pidgin language to communicate. From this pidgin, the children may have created a systematic syntax and grammar, as they were at the critical stage of language learning. Just as Jamaican or Haitian Creole emerged in the Caribbean under the conditions of

slavery, a variety of creoles may have evolved in the United States. One form of an early creole still exists among African Americans off the coast of South Carolina and Georgia on the Sea Islands. This creole is known as Gullah. Other forms of creole speech may have been introduced by the large numbers of slaves coming from Jamaica or Barbados into the American South, or could have emerged within early communities of slaves within the United States. Ebonics may very well be a product of this early creolization.

Linguist John Rickford notes that Ebonics is not just the use of slang. There are some slang terms in Ebonics, such as chillin (relaxing) or homey (close friend), but there is a systematic grammar and pronunciation within the language. There are standard usages of sentences within Ebonics, such as He runnin ("He is running") or He be running ("He is usually running"), or He bin runnin ("He has been running for a long time and still is"). Other rules, such as dropping consonants at the end of words such as tes(t) and han(d), are evident in Ebonics. Rickford emphasizes that Ebonics is not just a lazy form of English. Ebonics is no more lazy English than Italian is a lazy form of Latin. These are different languages with systematically ordered grammar and pronunciation usages.

A controversy regarding Ebonics developed in Oakland, California, when the school board announced that they were going to recognize Ebonics as a separate language. The school board was committed to teaching American Standard English to the African American students. However, because of the prejudices and misunderstandings regarding Ebonics as "a lazy form of English," the Oakland school board set off a controversy all over the United States. Linguistic anthropologist Ronald Kephart has commented on this Ebonics controversy based on his extensive research on the study of creoles in the Caribbean (Monaghan, Hinton, and Kephart 1997). Kephart studied creole English on the islands of Carriacou and Grenada. He did research on young students who were reading in the creole language as well as learning standard forms of English. The children who read in the creole language were able to learn the standard forms of English more readily, and they enjoyed the process. Kephart suggests that the recognition of Ebonics by the school board in Oakland would help children learn American Standard English.

These children would appreciate the fact that the language they brought with them into the school was to be respected as another form of English, and they would develop more positive attitudes about themselves and not be treated as "illiterate" or "lazy" children. This would help promote more effective learning strategies and enable the students to master American Standard English in a more humane manner.

It appears that language acquisition depends on both biological readiness and learning. The ability to speak seems to be biologically programmed, whereas a specific language is learned from the society the child grows up in. Children who are not exposed to language during their "critical period" may not be able to learn to use language properly. Research such as Chomsky's provides for further advances in an interactionist approach to test hypotheses regarding language, biology, mind, and thought. Yet, in his most recent book on language (2002), Chomksy urges caution for linguists, cognitive scientists, psychologists, and anthropologists against making sweeping claims about the evolution of language, cognition, linguistic capacities, and culture. He notes that we are only in the initial stages of these investigations and we have much more research to do in the future.

A new interesting study of deaf children in Nicaragua conducted by linguistic anthropologists Ann Senghas and colleagues may be suggestive in understanding how language can develop from a gesture system to a full-fledged language with grammar, symbols, and meanings (Senghas, Kita, and Ozyurek 2004). These linguists studied three generations of deaf schoolchildren in Managua, Nicaragua. These deaf schools were established in 1977 and had many deaf children who interacted with one another. As we will see later in our discussion, all human languages exhibit very similar structural features. These deaf children were actually constructing linguistic rules from various gestures that they were using with one another over the years. The studies indicate that the pre-adolescent children have much better capacities to learn the new deaf language than the older children, thus indicating that there is a "critical stage" in the capacity for learning grammar, syntax, and rules of language. This study suggests that this deaf language invented by these Nicaraguan children developed from a gestural sign system to a more full-fledged

structured linguistic system. This linguistic study provides more confirmation of Chomsky's views on language acquisition and also the research on the transition from pidgin to creole languages previously described. It appears that children's brains are predisposed to learn the rules of complicated grammar and impose grammatical structure in innovative and productive ways. This study of deaf Nicaraguan children indicates that there is a biologically based language acquisition device that enables young children to learn and create extremely complex fundamental grammatical and linguistic systems with symbolic meanings understood by all of them.

Language, Thought, and Culture

In the early part of the twentieth century, Edward Sapir and Benjamin Whorf carried out studies of language and culture. Sapir was a prodigious fieldworker who described many Native American languages and provided the basis for the comparative method in anthropological linguistics. Whorf, an insurance inspector by profession and a linguist and anthropologist by calling, conducted comparative research on a wide variety of languages. Sapir and Whorf's research led their students to formulate a highly controversial hypothesis that differs dramatically from the theories of Chomsky and the ethnosemanticists of cognitive anthropologists and linguists.

The Sapir–Whorf Hypothesis

The **Sapir–Whorf hypothesis** suggests that there is a close relationship between the properties or characteristics of a specific language and culture and that these features of specific languages define experiences for us. In other words, although humans everywhere have approximately the same set of physical organs for perceiving reality—eyes to see, ears to hear, noses to smell—the human nervous system is bombarded with sensations of all kinds, intensities, and durations. These sensations do not all reach our consciousness. Rather, humans have a filtering device that classifies reality. This filtering device, according to the Sapir–Whorf hypothesis, is based on the characteristics of a specific language. In this view, certain features of language, in effect, provide us with a special pair of glasses that heighten certain perceptions and dim others, determining what we perceive as reality.

A Case Study: The Hopi Language To understand this hypothesis, we look at some examples given by Whorf. Whorf compared the grammar of English with that of the Native American Hopi language of the southwestern part of the United States. He found that the verb forms indicating tense differ in these two languages. English contains past, present, and future verb forms; the Hopi language does not. In English we can say, "I came home," "I am coming home," or "I will come home." The Hopi do not have the verb corresponding to the use of come (Whorf 1956). From this type of example, Whorf inferred that Hopi and English speakers think about time in fundamentally different ways. English speakers conceptualize time in a measurable, linear form,

Hopi female child with traditional hairstyle.

speaking of a length of time or a point in time. We say that time is short, long, or great. We can save time, squander it, or spend it.

To the Hopi, in contrast, time is connected to the cycles of nature. Because they were farmers, their lives revolved around the different seasons for planting and harvesting. The Hopi, Whorf argued, did not see time as a motion upon space (that is, as time passing) but as a getting later of everything that has ever been done. Whorf concluded that the Hopi did not share the Western emphasis on history, calendars, and clocks. From evidence such as this, Sapir and Whorf developed their hypothesis that the specific aspects of a language of a speaker provides a grid, or structure, that influences how humans categorize space, time, and other aspects of reality into a worldview. The Sapir–Whorf hypothesis is thus an example of *linguistic relativism* because it maintains that the world is experienced differently among different language communities.

Universals of Time Expression Anthropological linguist Ekkehart Malotki (1983) investigated the Sapir–Whorf hypothesis by reexamining the Hopi language. His research, based on many interviews with Hopi speakers, showed that, in fact, the Hopi calculate time in units very similar to those of native English speakers. He concluded that Whorf had exaggerated the extent to which specific linguistic features influence a people's perceptions of time and demonstrated that the Hopi do make linguistic distinctions between the past and the present based on tense form. In the Hopi language, tense is distinguished between future and nonfuture instead of between past and present.

In a recent book, anthropologist Hoyt Alverson (1994) investigated four different unrelated languages to determine how time is conceptualized. Alverson studied the metaphors and symbolic usages of time in the Mandarin language of the Chinese, the Hindi language of India, the Sesotho language of Africa, and English. He looked at 150 different linguistic usages of time from native speakers and showed that there are basic metaphors that universally underlie the conceptualization of time in any language. However, in different languages time may be conceptualized in one or more of five universal possibilities. For example, time is usually conceptualized as partible or divisible, or it can be expressed as either linear, circular, oscillating, or a causal force, or a spatialized relation to the human body. This study, along with Malotki's, suggested that all humans share a common cognitive framework when conceptualizing time. These findings undoubtedly have implications for humanity's genetic heritage, a universal cognitive evolution, and a common identity as a species.

Although these studies appear to have refuted the Sapir–Whorf hypothesis, most linguistic anthropologists agree that a relationship exists between language and thought. Rather than assert that language determines thought, they maintain that language influences the speaker's thinking and worldview. Some experts refer to this approach as a "weak" version of the linguistic relativity hypothesis.

Some contemporary researchers have looked for ways to reformulate the Sapir–Whorf hypothesis in the form of a more precise, testable hypothesis about the relationship between language, thought, and behavior. For example, John Lucy (1992) compared speakers of English and Yucatec Mayan to see if their languages led them to perform differently on tasks involving remembering and sorting objects. As predicted from the grammar of the languages, English speakers appeared to attend more closely to the number and also to the shape of the objects, while Mayan speakers paid less attention to number and more attention to the material from which the objects were made.

It is also true that specific languages contain the vocabulary needed to cope in particular environments. The need for a specific vocabulary in a society does not necessarily mean that language determines our perception of reality. After all, when a need to express some unlabeled phenomenon arises, speakers easily manufacture new words. English-speaking skiers, like Eskimos (Inuit), distinguish among several types of snow, speaking of powder, corn, and so on.

Language may also influence social perception. For example, many women in English-speaking societies have long objected to the use of man, men, or mankind to refer to humanity and he to refer to any person, male or female. They argue that the use of these masculine terms reinforces the idea that humanity is male and women are outsiders, the "second sex." Other gender-biased language occurs when words such as lady and girl are used in a demeaning manner to refer to women. In ad-

dition, the tradition of addressing females by the title Mrs. or Miss also reflects gender bias in English-speaking countries.

To help explain this presumed bias, another linguistic anthropologist, M. J. Hardman-de-Bautista (1978), has formulated the notion of linguistic postulates, distinctions that are made obligatorily in language and that also reflect distinctions central to culture. For example, in English, biological sex is marked on the third-person singular pronouns (she, he). This distinction between female and male permeates English-speaking culture in important ways, for example, in how children are socialized into appropriate behavior ("be a nice little girl; act like a lady; be a man," etc.). In the Aymara language of Peru and Bolivia, in contrast, the third-person pronoun is not marked for sex or number, so that Aymara jupa means "she/he/they." Instead, for Aymara, the relevant contrast is human versus nonhuman, and jupa cannot be used to refer to an animal, such as a dog or llama; instead, a different pronoun must be used. Aymara children are not taught to behave like "nice girls" or "good boys" but rather to behave "like human beings, not like animals." On the other hand, linguistic anthropologists who study Chinese or the Bantu languages of Africa find that despite the gender inequalities that are associated with these societies, the languages do not distinguish sex or gender in their pronoun usage. So, the features of specific languages do not always reflect the social conditions and values of a particular society. Linguistic anthropologists continue to investigate these issues of gender and language in different societies.

Historical Linguistics

Historical linguistics is the study of language change and the historical relationships among different languages. The research in historical linguistics tries to discover what kinds of changes occur in languages and why. Research on this subject began in the late eighteenth century when Sir William Jones, a British legal scholar, suggested that the linguistic similarities of Sanskrit, an ancient Indian tongue, to ancient Greek, Latin, German, and English indicate that all these languages were descended from a common ancestral language. It was discovered that all these languages are part of one family, the Indo-European family, and share certain words and grammar. For example, the English word three is trayas in Sanskrit, tres in Latin, treis in Greek, and drei in German (see Table 5.1). The similarity in Indo-European languages led some early anthropologists to conclude that all current languages could be traced to a single language family.

The Family-Tree Model

Modern historical linguists agree that they probably can never reconstruct the original language, but they still may be able to reach far back into history to reconstruct an early **protolanguage**, a parent language for many ancient and modern languages. Many linguists hold the view that all languages change in a regular, recognizable way and that similarities among languages are due to a historical relationship among these languages. In other words, people living in adjacent areas of the world would tend to share similar phonological, syntactical, and semantic features of their languages. For example, the Romance languages of French, Spanish, Portuguese, Italian, and Romanian developed from Latin because of the historic relationship with one another through the influence of the Roman Empire. This view is known as the family-tree theory of language change (see Figure 5.2).

Most recently, historical linguists have been working with archaeologists to reconstruct the Proto-Indo-European language. They have found that the Indo-European languages did spread within distinctive regions for certain societies. British archaeologist Colin Renfrew (1989) hypothesizes that the spread of the Indo-European languages was linked to the spread of a particular technology and material culture. He suggests that the Indo-European languages spread throughout Europe from an original homeland in Anatolia, today part of Turkey, as early cultures adopted intensive agriculture. Similarly, English is currently promoted throughout the world as the language of television, computers, and other features of Western technology.

Assessing Language Change

To reconstruct a family tree of languages, the linguist compares the phonological (sounds) and morphological (words) characteristics of different languages. Linguistic anthropologist Morris Swadesh (1964) developed a systematic method of assessing historical language change. His goal was to date the separation of languages from one another using a statistical technique known as glottochronology (from the Greek glotta, meaning "tongue," and chronos, meaning "time"). Swadesh reasoned that the vocabulary of a language would remain stable at some times but

Table 5.1	Comparative Word Chart of Indo-European Languages				
English	**Sanskrit**	**Latin**	**Greek**	**German**	**Old English**
To bear	Bhar	Ferre	Fero	Gebären	Beran
Father	Pitar	Pater	Patir	Vater	Fæder
Mother	Matar	Mater	Mitir	Mutter	Modor
Brother	Bhratar	Frater	Frater	Bruder	Brodor
Three	Trayas	Tres	Treis	Drei	Brie
Hundred	Sata	Centum	Ekaton	Hundert	Hund
Night	Nisitha	Noctis	Nikta	Nacht	Niht
Red	Rudhira	Ruber	Erithros	Rot	Read
Foot	Pada	Pedis	Podos	Fuss	Fot
Fish	Piska	Piscis	Ikhthis	Fisch	Fisc
Goose	Hamsa	Anser	Khin	Gans	Gos
What	Kwo	Quod	Ti	Was	Hwæt
Where	Kva	Quo	Pou	Wo	Hwær

Source: Table from *The Way of Language: An Introduction* by Fred West. Copyright © 1975. Reproduced by permission of Heinle & Heinle, a division of Thomson Learning. Fax 800-730-2215.

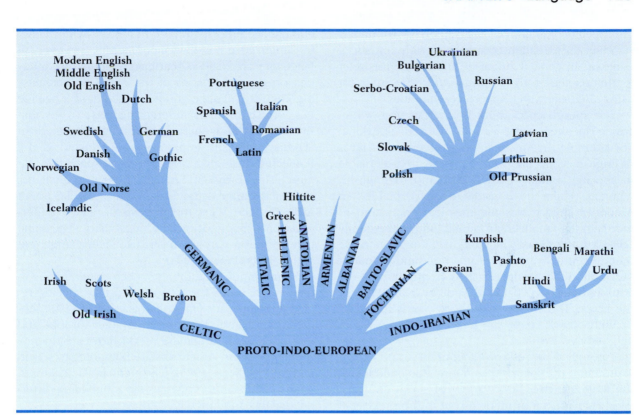

FIGURE 5.2 This family-tree model shows the relationships among the various Indo-European languages.

would change rapidly at others. Words for plants, animals, or technology would change quickly if the speakers migrated or came into contact with other groups. Swadesh thought, however, that a *core vocabulary* (words for pronouns and numbers, or for the body, earth, wood, and stone) would remain immune to cultural change. He thought that if we could measure the rate of retention of this core vocabulary, then we could measure the separation of one language from another.

By comparing core vocabularies from different languages, linguists found that on the average, 19 percent of this core vocabulary would change in a language in approximately 1,000 years. In other words, about 81 percent of the core vocabulary would be retained. From this formula, linguistic anthropologists have reconstructed languages and produced "family trees" of languages from around the world.

Through the study of language change, linguistic anthropologists have put to rest the idea that all current languages in the world can be traced to a single language family. Language change has been swift in some circumstances and gradual in others. Multiple borrowings, or the spread of vocabulary and grammar throughout the world, have affected most languages. Two linguistic researchers emphasize that many of the world's languages, including Russian, French, and English, have in their past development undergone radical change through language mixing (Thomason and Kaufman 1988). In their book, the researchers claim that in the same way that many creole languages have emerged (discussed earlier in the chapter), other languages have developed through intensive culture contact. Instead of development of language from one source, there apparently are different centers and regions of language change.

Sociolinguistics

Linguistic anthropologists have researched the use of language in different social contexts, a field known as *sociolinguistics*. The sociolinguist takes the speech community as the framework for understanding the variation of speech in different social contexts. In general, linguistic anthropologists refer to this as the study of *pragmatics*, the rules for using language within speech communities.

The speech community is a social unit within which speakers share various ways of speaking. For example, in American society certain patterns of English syntax and pronunciation are acceptable in specific contexts (American Standard English), whereas others are considered unacceptable. An American child may sometimes learn nonstandard words in the family environment, and, if the family considers them cute, the child may continue to use them. Eventually, however, the child moves out of the family into the larger speech community, encountering speech habits that differ from those of the home. If the child uses those words in school or with others, he or she will be reprimanded or laughed at.

Through a process of enculturation and socialization into the speech community, the child learns the language used in a variety of social contexts. Language plays a prominent role in the process of enculturation. American children learn the regional pronunciation and grammatical usages within their speech community.

Dialectal Differences in Spoken Language

A speech community may consist of subgroups that share specific linguistic usages within a larger common language family. If the linguistic usages of these subgroups are different but mutually intelligible, their language variations are called dialects. **Dialects** are linguistic differences in pronunciation, vocabulary, or syntax that may differ within a single language. For example, dialectal differences in American Standard English exist in the northeast, midwest, south, and southwest of the United States. In the southern United States, one might hear such grammatical items as "It wan't (or weren't) me," or pronunciation characteristics such as Miz for Mrs. and the frequent loss of r except before vowels: foah for four, heah for hear, and sulfuh for sulfur (West 1975).

Certain dialects of English are looked on as more prestigious than others, reflecting educational, class,

ethnic, race, and regional differences. When viewing language as a global phenomenon, however, all languages are dialects that have emerged in different locales and regions of the world. In actuality, the English language is not one standard language but consists of many different dialects. To say that British English is more "correct" than American Standard English simply because England is the homeland of English does not make sense to a linguist. The forms of English spoken in England, Australia, Canada, the United States, India, South Africa, or the West Indies have distinctive differences in pronunciation and vocabulary. The same generalization can be applied to many languages and dialects (Pinker 1994).

Some linguists studying speech communities in the United States have concluded that specific regional dialects are gradually disappearing. As people move from one region to another for jobs and education, and as television and movies influence speech patterns, Americans are beginning to sound more alike (West 1975). Through similar changes, many of the same processes are influencing different dialects and languages the world over.

Honorifics in Language

Sociolinguists have found that a number of languages contain honorific forms that determine the use of grammar, syntax, and other word usage. Honorific forms of language are used to express differences in social levels among speakers and are common in societies that maintain social inequality and hierarchy. Honorific forms can apply to the interaction between males and females, kin and nonkin, and higher- and lower-status individuals. For example, in many of the Pacific island societies such as Hawaii, a completely separate honorific vocabulary was used when addressing a person who was part of the royal family. People of lower rank were not allowed to use these forms of language among themselves.

In the Thai language, a number of different types of honorific pronouns are used in various social contexts. Factors such as age, social rank, gender, education, officialdom, and royal title influence which pronouns are used. For example, the first-person pronoun I for a male is *phom*, a polite form of address between equals. The pronoun for *I* shifts to *kraphom* if a male is addressing a higher-ranking government official or a Buddhist monk. It shifts to *klaawkramom* when a male is addressing the prince of the royal family. All together, there are thirteen different forms of the pronoun *I.* Similar differences exist for the other pronouns in Thai to express deference, politeness, and respect (Palakornkul 1972; Scupin 1988).

In the Japanese and Korean languages, honorific forms require speakers to distinguish among several different verb forms and address terms that indicate deference, politeness, or everyday speech. Different speech levels reflect age, gender, social position, and out-groupness (the degree to which a person is considered outside a particular social group) (Martin 1964; Sorensen 2005). Specifically, the Japanese distinguish between *tatemae* and *honne* in all of their linguistic expressions: *Tatemae* is a very polite form of expression used with strangers; *honne* is the expression of "real" feelings and can be used only with close friends and family.

Greeting Behaviors

The exchange of greetings is the most ordinary, everyday use of language and gesture found universally. Yet sociolinguistic studies indicate that these routine greeting behaviors are considerably complex and produce different meanings in various social and cultural contexts. In many contexts, English speakers in the United States greet one another with the word *Hi* or *Hello.* (The word *hello* originated from the English phrase *healthy be thou.*) Members of U.S. society also greet one another with questions such as "How are you?" or "How's it going?" or "What do you know?" or the somewhat popular but fading "Whassup?" In most contexts, these questions are not considered serious questions, and these exchanges of greetings are accompanied by a wave or a nod, a smile, or other gesture of recognition. They are familiar phrases that are used as exchanges in greetings. These greetings require little thought and seem almost mechanical.

Among Muslim populations around the world, the typical greeting between two males is the shaking of hands accompanied by the Arab utterance *As-salam ale-kum,* "May the peace of [Allah] be with you." This is the phrase used by Muslims even

Indian greeting of "Namaste."

in non-Arabic-speaking societies. The Qur'an, the sacred religious text of Muslims, has an explicit injunction regarding this mode of greeting for the male Muslim community (Caton 1986). A similar greeting of *Scholem aleicham,* "May peace be with you," is found among the Jewish populace throughout the world. In some Southeast Asian societies such as Vietnam, the typical greeting translates into English as "Have you eaten rice?"

All these greetings express a concern for another person's well-being. Although the English and Vietnamese greetings appear to be concerned with the physical condition of the person, whereas the Arab and Jewish phrases have a more spiritual connotation, they all essentially serve the same social purpose: They enable humans to interact in harmonious ways.

Yet there is a great deal more social information contained in these brief greeting exchanges than appears on the surface. For example, an English-speaking person in the United States can usually identify the different types of social contexts for the following greeting exchanges:

1. "Hi, Mr. Thomas!"
   "Hello, Johnny. How are you?"

2. "Good morning, Monica."
   "Good morning, sir."

3. "Sarah! How are you? You look great!"
   "Bill! It's so good to see you!"

4. "Good evening, Congressman."
   "Hello there. Nice to see you."

In greeting 1, the speakers are an adult and child; in 2, there is a difference in status, and the speakers may be an employee and employer; in 3, these speakers are close acquaintances; in 4, the second speaker does not remember or know the other person very well (Hickerson 1980).

The author of this text did a systematic sociolinguistic study of greeting behaviors found among different ethnic and religious groups in Thailand (Scupin 1988). Precise cultural norms determine the forms of greetings given to people of different status levels and ethnic groups. The traditional greeting of Thai Buddhists on meeting one another is expressed by each raising both hands, palm to palm, and lightly touching the body between the face and chest. Simultaneously, the person utters a polite verbal phrase. This salutation, known as the *waaj*

(pronounced "why"), varies in different social contexts. The person who is inferior in social status (determined by age and social class) initiates the *waaj*, and the higher the hands are raised, the greater the deference and politeness expressed. For example, a young child will *waaj* a superior by placing the fingertips above the eyebrows, whereas a superior returning a *waaj* will raise the fingertips only to the chest. A superior seldom performs a *waaj* when greeting someone of an inferior status. Other ethnic and religious groups such as the Muslims in Thailand use the *waaj* in formal interactions with Thai Buddhists, but among themselves they use the traditional Muslim greeting described previously.

Another form of Thai greeting found among Buddhists includes the *kraab*, which involves kneeling down and bowing to the floor in conjunction with the *waaj* in expressing respect to a superior political or religious official. The *kraab* is used to greet a high-ranking member of the royal family, a Buddhist monk, respected officials, and, traditionally, one's parents (Anuman-Rajadhon 1961; Scupin 1989). These deferential forms of greetings are found in other societies that maintain social hierarchies based on royal authority or political or religious principles.

Although greeting behaviors differ from one society to another, anthropologists find that all peoples throughout the world have a means to greet one another to establish a basis for social interaction and demonstrate their concern for one another's welfare.

Ethiopian Jewish males greeting each other. In many societies, males often greet each other with a kiss on the cheek.

Nonverbal Communication

In interacting with other people, we use nonverbal cues as well as speech. As with language, nonverbal communication varies in human populations, in contrast to the nonverbal communication of non-human animals. Dogs, cats, and other animals have no difficulty communicating with one another in nonverbal ways. Human nonverbal communication, however, is extremely varied. It is often said that humans are the only creatures who can misunderstand one another.

Kinesics

Some anthropological linguists study gestures and other forms of body language. The study of **kinesics** is concerned with body motion and gestures used in nonverbal communication. Researchers estimate that humans use more than 250,000 facial expressions. Many of these expressions have different meanings in different circumstances. For example, the smile indicates pleasure, happiness, or friendliness in all parts of the world. Yet in certain contexts, a smile may signify an insult (Birdwhistle 1970). Thus, the movement of the head, eyes, eyebrows, and hands or the posture of the body may be associated with specific symbolic meanings that are culturally defined.

Many types of nonverbal communication differ from society to society. Americans point to things with their fingers, whereas other peoples point with only their eyes, their chin, or their head. Shaking our head up and down means "yes" and from side to side means "no," but in parts of India, Greece, and Turkey the opposite is true. An "A-OK" sign in the United States or England means "you are all right," but it means "you are worth zero" in France or Belgium, and it is a very vulgar sign in Greece and Turkey (Ekman et al. 1984). Pointing to your

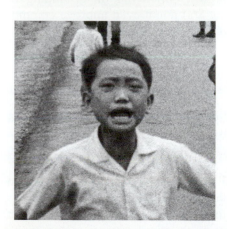

Some human facial expressions are based on universally recognized emotions.

head means "he or she is smart" in the United States, whereas it means "stupid" in Europe. The "V" sign of the 1960s meant "peace"; in contrast, in World War II England it meant "victory"; in Greece it is an insult. Obviously, humans can easily misunderstand each other because of the specific cultural meanings of nonverbal gestures.

Despite all these differences, however, research has revealed certain universal features associated with some facial expressions. For example, research by psychologist Paul Ekman and his colleagues suggests that there are some basic uniformities regarding certain facial expressions. Peoples from various societies recognize facial expressions indicating emotional states such as happiness, grief, disgust, fear, surprise, and anger. Ekman studied peoples recently contacted by Western society, such as the Fore people of Papua New Guinea (Ekman, 1973). When shown photos of facial expressions, the Fore had no difficulty determining the basic emotions that were being expressed. This research overlaps the psychological anthropology studies of emotions discussed in the previous chapter. Ekman has concluded that some universal emotional expressions are evident in certain facial displays of humans throughout the world.

Proxemics

Another nonverbal aspect of communication involves the use of space. **Proxemics** is the study of how people in different societies perceive and use space. Studies by the pioneering anthropologist in this area, Edward T. Hall (1981), indicate that no universal rules apply to the use of space. In American society, people maintain a different amount of "personal space" in different situations: We communicate with intimate acquaintances at a

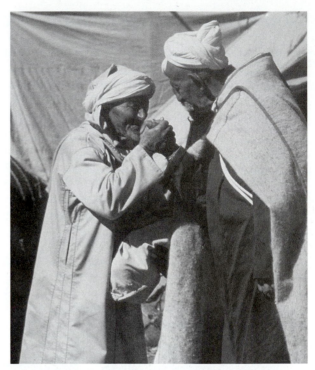

When communicating, Arab males stand at a closer distance to each other than do U.S. males.

range of about eighteen inches; however, with nonintimates, our space expands according to how well we know the person. In some other societies, people communicate at very close distances irrespective of the relationship among them.

Nonverbal communication is an important aspect of social interaction. Obvious gestural movements, such as bowing in Japan and shaking hands in the United States, may have a deep symbolic significance in certain contexts. The study of nonverbal communication will enrich our understanding of human behavior and might even improve communication among different societies.

SUMMARY

Language is a vital component of human cultural knowledge. It is the most important means of expressing and transmitting symbols and culture from one person to another. Language is the major means of communication for humans. A great deal of laboratory and field research is shedding light on how the closest related species to humans, the apes, can learn sophisticated sign communication.

Linguists have focused on some specific criteria that distinguish human languages from animal communication. All human languages have certain features such as productivity, displacement, arbitrariness, and combining sounds that set them apart from animal communication systems.

Linguistic anthropologists study the structure of language by studying sound patterns (phonology), the meaning of words (morphology), and how these meaningful units are put together in phrases and sentences (syntax). They also focus on the meaning (semantics) of different terms used to classify reality. Although there are many differences in how people in various societies use terms to describe kinship relations and physical phenomena, cognitive anthropologists have found some universals, such as the way people classify relatives. This suggests that humans have common biological capacities that determine how they perceive certain aspects of reality.

Linguistic anthropologists are interested in how language is acquired as an aspect of the enculturation process. The behaviorist model suggests that language is learned through positive and negative conditioning. In contrast, linguist Noam Chomsky suggests that all humans use an innate, or genetically encoded, capability for learning complicated syntax and grammar. Chomsky's model has led to research on languages such as creole languages.

Another topic explored in linguistic anthropology is the relationship among language, thought, and culture. An early hypothesis, known as the Sapir–Whorf hypothesis, suggested that specific features of language acts as a filter for the classification and perception of reality. This is known as linguistic relativism.

In reexamining the Sapir–Whorf hypothesis, anthropologists have concluded that the hypothesis exaggerates the extent to which language determines the perception of time, space, and other aspects of reality. Most modern anthropologists do not accept an extreme form of linguistic relativism as proposed by Sapir and Whorf's students.

Historical linguistics is the study of how languages are related to one another and how they have diverged from one another. Linguistic anthropologists have examined the historical relationships among languages. This research has helped understand the process of language change.

Sociolinguistics focuses on the relationship between language and society. Sociolinguists examine social interactions and the ways in which people use certain linguistic expressions that reflect the dialect patterns of their speech community. Researchers have found that many languages have nuances in linguistic usage such as greeting patterns or speech differences that vary according to age, gender, and status.

The study of nonverbal communication is also a rich field for linguistic anthropology. Although much nonverbal communication varies around the world, some forms can be understood universally. Anthropologists focus on the use of body language (kinesics) and the use of space (proxemics) to understand better how people supplement their spoken-language skills with nonverbal communication.

QUESTIONS TO THINK ABOUT

1. Suppose you are studying chimp communication. What limitations will you have in teaching the chimps a human language?

2. Give some examples of unique human linguistic abilities.

3. Provide some examples of phonemes, morphemes, syntax, and semantic aspects of language.

4. Do you agree with Skinner's or Chomsky's view of language learning? Why?

5. Can you think of any ways in which language influences culture, or vice versa?

6. What types of body language or gestures are universally understood?

KEY TERMS

communication
dialects
ethologists
kinesics
language

morphemes
morphology
phoneme
phones
phonology

protolanguage
proxemics
Sapir–Whorf hypothesis
semantics
syntax

Chapter **6**

Globalization and Culture

CHAPTER QUESTIONS

- What do anthropologists mean by globalization?

- From an anthropological perspective when did globalization begin?

- What are the major trends associated with globalization?

- Does globalization have positive or negative consequences for societies?

- What are the major theories used to explain globalization?

- How can contemporary anthropologists contribute to the understanding of globalization?

- What impact does globalization have on language and culture?

Globalization: A Contested Term

Anthropologist Richard Wilk has described on his web site what he terms "Globobabble" that has infected the discussions of contemporary trends presently. These terms include Globalacious, Globalasia, Globalatio, Globalemic, and Globaloney. He introduces his web site on globalization at Indiana University with his statement that "In this globalized global age, when everything has globated to the point where it is completely globulous, we obviously need some new vocabulary to describe the globish trends that are englobing us all" (http://www.indiana.edu/~wanthro/babble.htm 2000).

Just as with the concept of culture, discussed in Chapter 3, where we saw how contemporary anthropologists have a much more refined approach to this concept than fifty years ago, we are only at the early stages of developing a concept of globalization that could be shared by all anthropologists. Anthropologists have discovered that not all people share exactly the same form of culture or patterns of culture within the same society, and the same is true today with respect to the anthropological community in agreeing on a precise concept of globalization. Just as cultural values, beliefs, values, and norms are often in conflict among groups and individuals within a society, the term *globalization* is often a term that is contested and argued about by anthropologists. The term *globalization* is presently an imprecise "narrative" or "metaphor" for understanding what is occurring presently in the world within and among different societies. Generally speaking, anthropologists usually refer to **globalization** as the broad-scale changes and transformations that have resulted from the impact of industrialization and the emergence of an interconnected global economy with the spread of capital, labor (migration), and technology across national borders. Globalization continues to occur today through the increasing spread of industrial technology, including electronic communications, television, the Internet, and the expansion of multinational corporations into the non-Western world.

However, despite this general consensus, there has been an ongoing debate within anthropological circles as to when globalization actually began. Most anthropologists connected this process with the developments following the Industrial Revolution in Western Europe and the spread of these developments throughout many societies in the world. However, some anthropologists refer to globalization as developing during the 1500s within the period of Western Europe exploration and early colonization, whereas others link it to earlier time periods in East Asia, especially Chinese technological and economic developments prior to AD 1500 (Frank 1998). Some anthropologists identify elements of globalization in various areas in early history and prehistory and among "tribal cultures" (Friedman 1998).

Despite these differences among anthropologists, we all can recognize various elements of globalization within our everyday lives in the United States or any other society in the world. We recognize a remarkable acceleration in computer technological developments, migration trends, and changing communications with the Internet, e-mail, fax, television, and other media that have brought the societies in the world into what is sometimes referred to as a "global village" or "spaceship earth," a "world without walls." Thomas Friedman, a journalist who was educated in Arabic and Middle Eastern studies and reports on the Middle East and Asia, wrote a book about global trends called *The Lexus and the Olive Tree* (1999). Friedman emphasized the positive aspects of globalization with its integration of the world economy, financial markets, and pervasive international political coalitions and cooperation that was replacing the archaic one that dominated the world during the Cold War years. In that book Friedman made the famous statement that whenever two societies share a McDonald's they will not go to war against one another. However, Friedman's book was written prior to 9/11/2001 and the attack on the World Trade Center in New York City. This tragic episode of 9/11/2001 caused many Americans and Westerners to reflect on how globalization may not always bring the world closer together, but rather may result in severe political and cultural conflict.

In our everyday life we recognize globalization in our educational settings because there are many students from every area of the world in our universities

The 9/11 tragedy in New York City.

and colleges. In the United States we see professional athletic teams with Russians and East Europeans in hockey; Latin Americans, Caribbean peoples, Asians from Japan and Korea are on the professional baseball teams; Chinese players such as Yao Ming are joining athletes from the Dinka and Nuer groups of East Africa in pro basketball; and Tiger Woods, who is part Thai, part Chinese, part African American, and part American Indian, represents a truly multicultural individual who excels in international golf. When this textbook author goes to Asia to do ethnographic research, he turns on the television in hotels in Singapore, Indonesia, Malaysia, or Thailand and can view not only CNN and the BBC but also versions of MTV with their own traditions of music and dance, including hip-hop and rap music in India. So, these elements of globalization surround us in the United States and other areas of the world. Despite the differences and disagreements among social scientists and anthropologists over the precise meaning of the term, we surely are aware of these globalization processes around us.

Bill Gates.

Globalization: Technological and Economic Trends

In 1980 fewer than 2 million computers existed in the world, and nearly all of them were mainframes. There were 150 million computers by 1995, and the numbers have swelled considerably since that time (Strada 2003). Most of these computers are personal desktop or laptop computers, but major companies such as Microsoft and Intel were producing computer technology so rapidly that when an individual or company purchased one off the shelf, the technology was already obsolete. No one can keep pace with these rapid developments in computer chips and software. These computer technology trends are transforming the entire economies of the industrial economies into what many social scientists call **postindustrial societies**. These postindustrial societies have reduced the manufacturing sectors of their economies and developed high-tech computer hardware and software capacities based on information rather than "manual labor" that have had transforming effects on the global economy. As a result of these technological trends, Bill Gates has become one of the

richest multibillionaires in the world. The Internet was developed in the late 1960s through the U.S. Department of Defense. At first the Internet was developed to help scientists and engineers working on defense-related projects together to communicate research findings more easily to one another. However, the Internet today is used not just by scientists and academics for research or to download music, but by multinational corporations that have integrated the global economic developments among many societies.

These economic aspects of globalization are also readily visible to most people today. When consumers buy their clothing in the United States from the Gap, Walmart, Banana Republic, or other retailers, they find that most of it is produced in Asia, the Caribbean, Latin America, or islands in the Pacific. Automobile manufacturers such as Ford, Chrysler, and GM have plants all over the world, including China, Mexico, and Europe. These auto companies are now transnational corporations such as Daimler-Chrysler (German owned), and Ford and GM have joint production programs with Japanese and South Korean auto manufacturers such as Honda, Toyota, Mitsubishi, and Hyundai and have manufacturing plants in the United States,

Antiglobalization protestors.

Europe, Latin America, and Asia. The Honda Accord is produced in Ohio in the United States, but Dodge is produced outside of the United States. As we will discuss further in Chapter 16 on contemporary global trends, multinational corporations are continually merging together in large conglomerates to promote more economic efficiency and international manufacturing and marketing to enhance their revenues. For example, this textbook is produced by Pearson Publishing, a British-based corporation owned by a large communications and media company, Viacom, which owns many subsidiary companies such as Simon and Schuster, Prentice Hall, and Allyn and Bacon, who publish books and educational materials all over the world.

As we will see in Chapter 8 economics is studied by anthropologists in many areas of the world. Economic anthropologists study the production, distribution, and consumption of goods and services in different societies. Today, these economic anthropologists are focusing on how the economies of different societies are being transformed by these globalization factors. For example, the anthropologist Richard Wilk (mentioned earlier) has been doing extensive research on consumption and advertising of various products and services in the country of Belize (1995). His findings demonstrate that patterns of consumer behavior and cultural changes are rapidly changing the lifestyles of the people in Belize.

One important topic being studied by anthropologists today is what has been termed outsourcing. In later chapters we discuss the consequences of the relocation of manufacturing plants such as Nike in regions in Asia to enhance revenues and reduce the costs of labor for multinational corporations. Most recently, however, there has been a new trend in the relocation of white-collar service professional IT (information technology) jobs from the United States, Japan, and Europe to areas such as India and China. Many Americans and Westerners have been alarmed at the fact that many engineering, computer-related service jobs, chip design, tax form services, and telecommunications jobs are now being relocated to India or China. When Americans have a problem with their Microsoft Word documents, they call an 800 number for Microsoft and often talk to someone in China or India about how to solve these problems. As the cost has fallen for the development of fiber-optics cables that connect computers and telecommunication in Asia with Europe and America, engineers and other IT workers can use high-speed data transmission to produce software for companies within India and China. Economists predict that by 2015 the United States will shift some 3.3 million IT jobs to India. India is adding some 2 million college graduates a year, most of them with degrees in engineering and IT. The starting salary of a software engineer in India is $5,000 compared to twelve times that much for a U.S. entry-level engineer (Reich 2003).

There is an ongoing debate among economists, politicians, and corporate managers about the long-term costs and benefits of such outsourcing. New IT jobs are being produced in areas such as Bangalore or Delhi, India, for many Indians who learn how to speak with New England, Southern, Midwest, Canadian, or British-dialect English to serve their customers in the United States, Canada, Australia, or the U.K. Journalist Thomas Friedman has been reporting on outsourcing in India and China. In a recent report he states "When I was growing up, my parents used to say to me: "Finish your dinner—people in China are starving." I, by contrast, find myself wanting to say to my daughters: "Finish your homework—people in China and India are starving for your job" (2005). In his report filed from the city of Dalian in China, Friedman emphasizes that the Chinese are not making tennis shoes in Dalian; instead he notes that there are 22 universities and colleges with 200,000 students and that more than half will graduate with engineering or science degrees. Most students are also directed to study Japanese or English along with computer science. Friedman interviewed the mayor of Dalian, who told him that the rule of

the market economy is that jobs will flow to where the richest human resources and cheapest labor exist. The mayor went on to say that this was the same pattern for Japan at first. They began in the manufacturing sector, but eventually they moved to R & D (research and development) and other high-tech developments. He predicts that the same trend will develop in China. Chinese engineers will learn the process and steps of IT development and then eventually move to the design stage to innovate in high-tech. However, Friedman interviewed the president of the Chinese Academy of Engineering, who stated that the country will have to radically restructure their rote tradition of education to bring about these developments. And, anthropologists and other social scientists would also emphasize that the Chinese Communist Party will have to relinquish control over the Internet and other media to allow for the free flow of information to enhance these technological and economic changes (DeVoe 2005).

Anthropologists are investigating the results of these outsourcing trends for the societies in Asia and also whether they produce negative or positive developments in the global economy. Some economists—both conservative and liberal—believe that outsourcing is inevitable in a global market economy and will produce positive results in the

Outsourcing technical and service occupations from postindustrial societies to India and other areas is a major aspect of globalization today.

long term for the economies in all societies, while at the same time they are concerned about the *short-term* impact on the development of unemployment for highly educated sectors of the postindustrial societies and the effects on education and technological expertise. Will China and India move ahead of the Western postindustrial societies with more understanding of computer technology and the reduced costs of labor and increasing education in those societies? Yet, some economists note that outsourcing accounts for only a very minor fraction of the IT workforce of 10 million in the United States. Furthermore, as more outsourcing results in moving the standard IT jobs to China or India, the IT workers in the United States will be shifted toward more R & D operations resulting in more technological innovation (Reich 2003; Bhagwati 2004; Drezner 2004).

Ethnographic research on these outsourcing activities is now in progress in countries such as India and China. Anthropologists and international studies specialists are asking these Indians or Chinese about their training, background, socioeconomic status, and perceptions of this globalization and its impact on their own lives and culture. One of the findings by these anthropologists is that because outsourcing has played an important role in the economic boom occurring in China and India, many Chinese and Indians who live in the United States and Europe are returning in large numbers to their home countries. What began as a trickle in the late 1990s is now substantial: a trend in reverse migration from Europe and the United States to India and China. By one estimate, there are 35,000 "returned nonresident Indians" in Bangalore, India, alone.

Anthropologists and other international studies specialists are asking questions such as the following of the Chinese and Indians who are involved in these new IT hubs in Bangalore or Shanghai: Are they concerned about the loss of jobs in America or Europe? Do they purchase more American and European goods when they earn money in their new jobs? Are they becoming more individualistic in their consumption and tastes and challenging their governments to allow for more freedom? (Basi 2004; DeCosta and Sridharan 2004; Kabayashi-Hillary 2004; Heitzman 2004).

Some people stereotype anthropologists as doing ethnographic research on "tribal societies" or peasant farmers in the "Third World." However, today, many anthropologists are investigating communities such as corporate workers employed in the financial market area in multinational companies. A recent study by anthropologist Hirozaki Miyazaki reported on three years of ethnographic research in a large Japanese securities firm (2003). He observed how teams of workers known as "arbitrageurs" made decisions about trading financial instruments such as stocks, bonds, and other equities. He compared how these Japanese arbitrageurs had beliefs and cultural values that reflected their own culture, in contrast to the business culture of American investors. First, he observed that these Japanese traders made a virtue out of being second rather than first and focused on improvement rather than innovation in their investments without having the startup costs and capital investment that Western companies had developed to be "first." He suggests that this was an aspect of Japanese business culture that emerged in post–World War II Japan. In addition, the traders took advantage of gaps between prices for stocks in order to develop more efficient means of investment and to rely on models of the market economy to provide a system of "guessing" where economic trends would develop next. Instead of relying on innovation, these Japanese traders would develop economic decision models to "guess" how to improve their dividends.

Miyazaki emphasized that by guessing what the future is going to be next, these traders would enhance these possibilities by remaining excited about future prospects rather than becoming bored with their jobs. They remained optimistic rather than pessimistic about their economic predictions, and it helped them retain their positive attitudes even during declining financial conditions. Ethnographic research can shed light on these differences in investment strategies and provide useful insights about cross-cultural differences in economic decision making.

In another interesting case study, Theodore C. Bestor illustrates the globalization process in an essay entitled "How Sushi Went Global" (2003). He describes how the eating of raw fish, a Japanese dish, became sought after in the United States and Europe. The major sushi dish is made with bluefin tuna and is the most popular dish in Japan. Although Japanese colling was introduced to the

United States in the 1920s just as Japanese art and architecture were influencing the work of Frank Lloyd Wright and others, raw fish was not acceptable to Americans at that time. However, during the rise of Japan as an economic contender in the 1970s, the demand for tuna increased, while at the same time supplies in fishing areas in Japan were being depleted and restrictions on fishing areas within different countries were being enforced; thus, Japan began to search for new sources of their favorite dish. During the 1970s Americans began to experiment with sushi as a nouvelle cuisine, gourmet food and it grew in popularity along with other items such as cappuccino, espresso, lasagna, and other "healthy" dishes. During the 1980s there was a steep demand for bluefin tuna from the New England fishing grounds, and jumbo jets flew the tuna to the Japanese market.

Prior to the Japanese demand, the bluefin tuna was viewed by U.S. fisheries as a "trash fish." However, the total amount and price of Atlantic bluefin shipped to Japan increased dramatically in the 1980s and 1990s. The Japanese economy began to stagnate during the Asian fiscal crisis in the 1990s, and demand began to decline. However, the sushi craze took off in the United States and saved the industry. Other countries, such as Spain, Italy, Croatia, Tunisia, and Morocco, began to exploit the fisheries for bluefin tuna. Demand for sushi chefs from Japan developed in the United States and Europe. Thus, all these shifts in tastes, preferences, and desires drove globalization processes that interconnected and integrated the Japanese with many other countries throughout the world. As we see in this example, economics and technological transformations brought about by globalization cannot only fundamentally transform daily gourmet habits, but also result in migration, interconnections in communication and media, and the enhancement of the "global village."

Globalization: Theoretical Approaches

Three major theoretical approaches have been used to examine globalization: modernization theory, dependency theory, and world-systems theory.

Each has provided a model for analyzing the impact of globalization on industrial and nonindustrial societies.

Modernization Theory

The historical intellectual heritage of what is called modernization theory is associated with the prolific German scholar and sociologist Max Weber (1864–1920). To some extent, Max Weber was reacting to the earlier ideas of Karl Marx (discussion to follow) who argued that the "material conditions," including technology, environment, and the economy, determined or influenced the cultural beliefs and ideas of different people within a society. In contrast, Max Weber recognized that cultural values and beliefs had a very significant influence on the development of particular technological and economic conditions in a society. He focused on the interrelationship of cultural values to economic action and behavior. Weber's views on the modernization of society have influenced many economic, historical, sociological, and anthropological interpretations. He noted that all humans provided significance and meaning to their orientations, practical actions, and behavior in the world (Keyes 2003). The modernization theory absorbed Weber's theory and emphasized how ideas, beliefs, and values have transforming effects on practical activity within society. Societies are not just products of technology and a particular mode of production or economy, but of *culture*, which shaped and influenced the modes of thinking and significance for action within a society.

Using a broad cross-cultural and global approach, modernization theorists relying on Weber's model maintain that premodern and preindustrial societies were *traditional* in their worldview, whereas people in *modern industrial capitalist societies* endorsed rationality. While traditional societies were guided by sentiments and beliefs passed from generation to generation, modern societies embraced rationality, and used deliberate strategies, including scientific methods, to pursue efficient means to obtain particular goals. Like Weber, the modernization theorists argued that traditional cultural beliefs are swept away by the process of rationalization as a society modernizes. They view the rationalization of society as the historical change from a traditional worldview to scientific rationality as the dominant mode of human thought and action.

One of the most influential books that Weber wrote that later influenced the modernization approach to globalization was *The Protestant Ethic and the Spirit of Capitalism* (1904). In that work, Weber sought to understand the values that influenced the emergence of industrial capitalist society. Through a historical analysis he thought that the specific values of hard work, thrift, and discipline as exhibited within the Calvinist religious tradition in Europe in the seventeenth century resulted in a more rational, scientific, and efficient form of technological and economic conditions, ushering in the development of industrial capitalism, or modernity.

Despite the fact that Weber focused on the emergence of modernity, capitalism, and rationalization along with Calvinist traditions, he did not accept a unilineal ladder-like evolution of culture from traditional primitive to complex industrial societies as did some early anthropologists and sociologists. Instead, anthropologists today have re-evaluated Weber's cross-cultural understanding of global history and see that he recognized that economics and technology did not always follow a simple one-directional progressive path of development (Keyes 2003).

Modernization Theory and the Cold War

Although modernization theory had its roots in nineteenth-century Enlightenment ideas, as espoused by Max Weber and other social scientists, it became the leading model for understanding globalization in the 1950s in the context of the Cold War between the United States and the former Soviet Union. During that period, the two superpowers were competing for economic resources and the political allegiance of different nations. Modernization theory provided a model to explain how social and cultural change could take place in all societies through industrial capitalism.

One of the most influential proponents of modernization is the American economist W. W. Rostow, who was an advisor to presidents during the Cold War years. Rostow argued that although modernization occurred first in the West, it can occur in all societies, provided those societies meet certain preconditions. According to Rostow (1978), evolution

from traditional preindustrial societies to modern industrial societies takes place through five general stages:

1. *Traditional stage.* Premodern societies are unlikely to become modernized because of *traditionalism*—persisting values and attitudes that represent obstacles to economic and political development. According to modernization theorists, traditionalism creates a form of "cultural inertia" that keeps premodern societies backward and underdeveloped. Traditionalism places great significance on maintaining family and community relationships and sentiments, which inhibit individual freedom and entrepreneurial initiative.

2. *Culture-change stage.* One of the preconditions for modernization involves *cultural and value changes.* People must accept the belief that progress is both necessary and beneficial to society and to the individual. This belief in progress is linked to an emphasis on individual achievement, which leads to the emergence of individual entrepreneurs who will take the necessary risks for economic progress. Modernization theorists insist that these change in values can be brought about through education and will result in the erosion of traditionalism.

3. *Takeoff stage.* As traditionalism begins to weaken, rates of investment and savings begin to rise. These economic changes provide the context for the development of industrial-capitalist society. England reached this stage by about 1783 and the United States, by about 1840. Modernization theorists believed that this stage can be reached only through foreign aid to support the diffusion of education, which will reduce traditionalism and the transfer of industrial technology from capitalist societies into premodern societies.

4. *Self-sustained growth.* At this stage, the members of the society intensify economic progress through the implementation of industrial technology. This process involves a consistent reinvestment of savings and capital in modern technology. It also includes a commitment to mass education to promote advanced skills and modern attitudes. As the population becomes more educated, traditionalism will continue to erode.

5. *High economic growth.* This last stage involves the achievement of a high standard of living,

characterized by mass production and consumption of material goods and services. Western Europe and the United States achieved this stage in the 1920s, and Japan reached it in the 1950s.

This modernization model includes both noneconomic factors such as cultural values and economic behavior such as individualism and entrepreneurial behavior as preconditions for modernization. In fact, as seen in stage 2, the changes in attitudes and cultural values are the most important prerequisites for eliminating traditionalism and generating patterns of achievement. Thus, modernization theorists view cultural values and traditionalism as the primary reasons for the lack of economic development. The practical implication that derives from this model is that before a country should receive foreign aid, traditionalism and the values that support it must be transformed.

Like Rostow who drew on Max Weber, psychologist David McClelland (1973) maintained that a *need for achievement* represents the most important variable in producing the process of modernization. McClelland argued that this need for achievement is not just a desire for more material goods, but rather an intrinsic need for satisfaction in achieving success. He believed that this desire for achievement leads to increased savings and accumulation of capital. McClelland claimed to have found evidence for this need in some non-Protestant countries such as Japan, Taiwan, and Korea, as well as in Western countries.

First, Second, and Third Worlds The modernization model led to the categorization of societies into three "worlds": the First, Second, and Third Worlds. According to the modernization theorists, the **First World** is composed of modern industrial states with predominantly capitalist or hybrid economic systems. These societies became industrialized "first." Included in this group are Great Britain, Western Europe, Australia, Canada, New Zealand, Japan, and the United States. The **Second World** consists of industrial states that have predominantly socialist economies. It includes the former Soviet Union and many of the former socialist countries of Eastern Europe—for example, Poland and Hungary. The **Third World** refers to premodern agricultural states that maintain traditionalism. The

Third World encompasses the vast majority of the people in the world, including most of Latin America, Africa, the Middle East, and Asia.

Modernization Theory, Max Weber, and Contemporary Anthropology Max Weber began to have an influence on American and Western anthropologists following World War II when they began shifting focus from studying isolated "tribal" cultures to how modernization and social and economic change (globalization) were having an impact all over the world. One sociologist who influenced a number of anthropologists in the United States was the Harvard-based Talcott Parsons, who had translated Weber's works, such as the *Protestant Ethic and the Spirit of Capitalism*, into English. Parsons trained many social scientists in Weber's approach after World War II.

One of the most prominent anthropologists in the United States, Clifford Geertz, was deeply influenced by Talcott Parsons, Max Weber, and modernization theory during the 1950s and 1960s. He and many other social scientists, including economists, psychologists, sociologists, political scientists, and anthropologists, were trained in modernization theory by Parsons.

Geertz and a team of social scientists did fieldwork in Indonesia in the 1950s. Geertz's first major book, *The Religion of Java* (1960), was a classic ethnography based on his fieldwork in Indonesia. This ethnography is a detailed description and analysis of the complexities of religion in Indonesia, which is a mix of Islam, Hinduism, and animist spiritual traditions. His next major work, *Agricultural Involution* (1963), is an ecological and economic analysis of Indonesia, focusing on how Dutch colonialism had an impact on the prospects of economic development in this Asian country. In another ethnography of the same year, *Peddlars and Princes* (1963), Geertz compared the Javanese Muslim town of Modjokuto with the Balinese (Hindu-Buddhist) town of Tabanan to illustrate how cultural and religious values of various peoples influenced their economic development. He argued that there were some cultural values among some Muslim entrepreneurs that (as Weber had concluded) resulted in similarities to the "Protestant Ethic" in Western societies.

Eventually, Geertz became the pioneer of what became known as symbolic anthropology (described briefly in Chapter 3). This approach emphasized the study of the meaning of symbols, and in a famous phrase that drew on Weber, Geertz (1973) stated "that man is an animal suspended in webs of significance he himself has spun. I take culture to be those webs." Generally, symbolic anthropologists tend to emphasize Weber's interest in the meaning and significance of symbols by interpreting cultures as one would interpret a "text." However, they tend to neglect the other aspect of Weber's synthetic approach to understanding and explaining culture by attending to scientific and empirical causal accounts and explanations of human behavior and action.

Another sociologist and anthropologist trained in France, Pierre Bourdieu, reflected an appreciation and comprehensive understanding of Weber's synthetic approach to human behavior and culture. Pierre Bourdieu did ethnographic research in Algeria and France. In Algeria he described and analyzed the social and cultural conditions of the Berber or the people of the Kablia region of some 1,500 villages. Later in France he turned his attention to ethnographic research of the French university system and higher education. His most important theoretical ideas were developed in a book translated into English and called *Outline of a Theory of Practice* (1977). Bourdieu's approach to understanding culture and action reflected some of Weber's theoretical model and involved a synthetic blend of understanding both symbolic meaning and explaining human action, which he referred to as "practices." As Weber had emphasized the use of "ideal types" as a means of developing hypotheses to examine and interpret human thought and behavior, Bourdieu used the term *habitus* to refer to internal or subjective "dispositions" that became embedded with meaning through the enculturation process that shaped behavior and action. Bourdieu's theoretical approach partially based on Weber's models has provided inspiration for many contemporary anthropology ethnographic research projects (Keyes 2003).

Criticisms of Modernization Theory Modernization theory enabled anthropologists and other social scientists to identify various aspects of social and cultural change that accompany globalization. By the 1960s, however, modernization theory had

come under attack by a number of critics. One of the major criticisms is that the applied model of modernization has failed to produce technological and economic development in Third World countries. Despite massive injections of foreign aid and education projects sponsored by First World countries, most Third World countries remain underdeveloped. An *underdeveloped society* has a low gross national product (GNP), the total value of goods and services produced by a country.

Some critics view modernization theory as ethnocentric, or "Westerncentric." They believe that this theory promotes Western industrial-capitalist society as an ideal that ought to be encouraged universally. These critics argue that Western capitalist societies have many problems, such as extreme economic inequality and the dislocation of community and family ties, and they question whether a Western model of modernization is suitable or beneficial for all societies. They do not agree that all societies must emulate the West to progress economically.

Modernization theorists have also been criticized for citing traditional values as obstacles to technological and economic development in the Third World. Critics consider this an example of blaming the victim. They charge that this argument oversimplifies both the conditions in Third World countries and the process of industrialization as it occurred in the West. For example, anthropologists and historians have recognized that individual entrepreneurs in the West and in Japan had a great deal of economic freedom, which encouraged independent initiative. Both Europe and Japan experienced historical periods where their governments did not have systematic control over independent economic activities in local regions. Consequently, entrepreneurs had freedom to develop their technologies and trading opportunities. In contrast, many Third World people have a so-called need to achieve but lack the necessary economic and political institutions and opportunities for achievement.

Another criticism of modernization theory is that it neglects the factors of global economic and political power, conflict, and competition within and among societies. For example, the wealthier classes in Third World countries that have benefited from the new technology and other assets from the First World often exploit the labor of the lower classes. This conflict and division between classes may inhibit economic development. Modernization theorists also tend to view First, Second, and Third World countries as existing in isolation from one another.

One other major problem with the modernization theorists is that the terminology First, Second, and Third World countries is too simplistic today to account for the great diversity that anthropologists actually discover in these societies. Modernization theory was a product of Cold War politics, in which the capitalist West (the First World) was in global competition with the socialist East (the Second World), and the rest of the world (the Third World) was influenced by Cold War politics. However, as we see in Chapter 16, sweeping changes have been transforming the Eastern bloc countries, including those of the former Soviet Union, resulting in the dissipation of most Second World socialist societies. In addition, the phrase *Third World societies* tends to lump together many societies that are at different levels of socioeconomic development. For example, Saudi Arabia, rich in oil resources, cannot be compared with Bangladesh, which has very little natural resource wealth on which to draw. Some countries in the so-called Third World are much better off economically, with ten to twenty times the national wealth of other countries. Although the terms First, Second, and Third Worlds are still used in the media and elsewhere, we should be aware that this terminology is a legacy of the Cold War and is no longer relevant to an understanding of present-day societies.

Dependency Theory

Criticism of modernization theory led to a new approach that emerged primarily from the underdeveloped world. Known as **dependency theory**, this approach is a model of socioeconomic development that explains globalization and the inequality among different societies as resulting from the historical exploitation of poor, underdeveloped societies by rich, developed societies.

The historical roots of the dependency view of globalization are connected with the well-known German social philosopher Karl Marx (1818–1883). As mentioned previously, Marx argued that the

material things of life were primary, and cultural beliefs and concepts were secondary. Later, Marx wrote many tracts such as *Economic and Philosophic Manuscripts* (1844), *Das Kapital* (in English, *Capital*) (1867), which emphasized his philosophy of materialism sometimes referred to as historical materialism.

In Marx's historical materialist thesis he argued that economic realities, or what he termed the *mode of production*, which included the way a society organized its economy and technology, were the primary determinant of human behavior and thought. A second ingredient in Marx's historical materialist thesis was that all human history was driven by *class struggle*, perpetual conflicts between the groups who owned resources and had political power and those who owned very little and had very little political power. Marx, and his close collaborator Friedrich Engels, developed a sweeping *unilineal and global evolutionary scheme* (see Chapter 3) based on the different modes of production that societies had developed since early prehistory. The earliest mode of production was hunting and gathering, followed by the development of agriculture, succeeded by feudalism, which evolved into industrial capitalism. Each of these different modes of production was transformed by class conflicts and struggles, resulting in the successive stages of societal evolution.

Writing at the time of early industrialization and capitalism in Europe in the nineteenth century, Marx and Engels viewed these developments as causes of exploitation, inequality in wealth and power, and class struggle. They believed that a struggle was emerging between the bourgeoisie (owners of factories, mines, and other industries) and the proletariat (the working class) in industrial capitalist societies such as England, Germany, and the United States. They maintained that through this class conflict, new modes of production would develop, first socialism and, eventually, communism, which represented the end of class conflict, private property, poverty, economic exploitation, warfare, and power struggles.

Marx was convinced that a particular mode of production, referred to as the "base" of a society, significantly shapes other spheres of society such as religion. Religion, along with philosophy, ethics, and the arts, were called the "superstructure" of society, and represented ideologies, which reflected the inner tensions and interests of the class struggles and conflicts within any type of society. Specific ideologies become the dominant ruling ideas in a society organized by a particular mode of production.

Dependency theory was influenced by Marxism and is associated with theorists such as Andre Gunder Frank, who denied that underdevelopment is the product of the persistence of traditionalism in preindustrial societies as the modernization theorists maintained. These dependency theorists instead contend that wealthy industrialized capitalist countries exploit underdeveloped precapitalist societies for the cheap labor and raw materials needed to maintain their own industrial technologies. Through this process, impoverished underdeveloped countries became economic and political dependencies of wealthy industrialized capitalist countries.

Dependency theorists suggest that mercantilism increased the prosperity and economic and political power of Western nations at the expense of poor nations. Especially after 1870, following the early phases of industrialism, a new type of relationship developed between industrialized and nonindustrialized societies. As manufacturing expanded, the industrial nations' needs for raw materials increased. Also, changing patterns of consumption created more demands for new foodstuffs and goods such as tea, coffee, sugar, and tobacco from nonindustrialized regions. The availability of cheap labor in underdeveloped countries contributed to increasing wealth and profits in industrial nations. Thus, according to dependency theorists, the wealth and prosperity of the industrial capitalist countries was due largely to the exploitation of the underdeveloped world.

The need for raw materials, consumer goods, cheap labor, and markets led to increasing **imperialism**, the economic and political control of a particular nation or territory by an external nation. Although imperialism had developed among preindustrial agricultural states, it did not involve the whole world. In contrast, industrial countries such as Great Britain, the United States, France, Germany, the Netherlands, Belgium, Russia, and Japan divided the nonindustrialized areas into "spheres of economic and political influence." Most of the nonindustrialized regions became *colonies* that

An Indian farmer working in his fields. Marx believed that societies evolved through stages such as the Asiatic, in which the land was cultivated by peasant farmers.

exported raw materials and provided labor and other commodities for the industrialized nations.

Dependency theorists categorize the industrial capitalist countries as the *metropole* societies that maintain dependent *satellite countries* in the underdeveloped world. Through the organization of the world economy by the industrial capitalist societies, the surpluses of commodities produced by cheap labor flow from the satellites to the metropole. The satellites remain underdeveloped because of economic and political domination by the metropole. Despite the fact that many satellite countries have become politically independent from their former colonial rulers, the emergence of multinational corporations based in the industrialized capitalist societies has produced a new form of imperialism, *neoimperialism*. The industrial capitalist societies control foreign aid, international financial institutions such as the World Bank and the International Monetary Fund (IMF), and international political institutions such as the United Nations, all of which function to maintain their dominant position.

Criticisms of Dependency Theory Unlike modernization theory, the dependency approach demonstrates that no society evolves in isolation. By examining the interrelationships between the political economy in industrial capitalist and precapitalist countries, theorists showed conclusively that some aspects of underdevelopment are related to the dynamics of power, conflict, class relations, and exploitation.

Critics, however, have noted a number of flaws in the dependency approach. Generally, dependency theory tends to be overly pessimistic. It suggests that dependency and impoverishment can be undone only by a radical restructuring of the world economy to reallocate wealth and resources from wealthy industrial capitalist countries to impoverished precapitalist countries. Economic development, however, has occurred in some countries that have had extensive contact with industrial capitalist societies. Notably, Japan moved from an underdeveloped society to a wealthy industrial capitalist position after the 1950s. Other countries such as Taiwan and South Korea have also developed. In contrast, some poor societies that have had less contact with the industrial capitalist societies remain highly undeveloped.

Critics also point out that dependency theorists neglect the internal conditions of underdeveloped countries that may inhibit economic development. Rapid population growth, famine and hunger, the excessive control of the economy by centralized governments, and, in some instances, traditional cultural values may inhibit economic development.

World-Systems Theory

The perspective known as **world-systems theory** on globalization maintains that the socioeconomic differences and inequalities among various societies are a result of an interlocking global political economy. The world-systems model represents a response to both modernization and dependency theories. Sociologist Immanuel Wallerstein, who developed the world-systems approach, agrees with the dependency theorists that the industrial nations prosper through the economic domination and exploitation of nonindustrial peoples. His world-systems model (1974, 1979, 1980) places all countries in one of three general categories: *core, peripheral,* and *semiperipheral.* **Core societies** are the powerful industrial nations that exercise economic domination over other regions. Most nonindustrialized countries are classified as **peripheral societies**, which have very little control over their own economies and are dominated by the core societies. Wallerstein notes that between the core and peripheral countries are the **semiperipheral societies**, which are somewhat industrialized and have some economic autonomy but are not as advanced as the core societies (see Figure 6.1).

Unlike dependency theorists, Wallerstein believes that under specific historical circumstances, a peripheral society can develop economically. For example, during the worldwide depression of the 1930s, some peripheral Latin American countries, such as Brazil and Mexico, advanced to a semiperipheral position. Wallerstein also explains the recent rapid economic development of countries such as Taiwan and South Korea in terms of their favored status by core societies. Because the United States was in competition with the former Soviet Union and feared the emergence of communism in Asia, it invested huge amounts of technology and capital in Taiwan and South Korea.

Criticisms of World-Systems Theory Although Wallerstein's world-systems theory has some advantages over modernization and dependency theories, critics note some weaknesses (Shannon 1988). One criticism is that the theory focuses exclusively on economic factors at the expense of noneconomic factors such as politics and cultural traditions. In addition, it fails to address the question of why trade between industrial and nonindustrial nations must always be exploitative. Some theorists have noted that in certain cases, peripheral societies benefit from the trade with core societies in that, for example, they may need Western technology to develop their economies (Chirot 1986).

Although world-systems theory has been helpful in allowing for a more comprehensive and flexible view of global economic and political interconnections, it is not a perfected model. However, the terms used by Wallerstein, such as *core, semiperipheral,* and *peripheral,* have been adopted widely by the social sciences. These terms did offer an improvement by helping to classify different types of global interrelationships and substitute for the older terminology of *First, Second,* and *Third Worlds.*

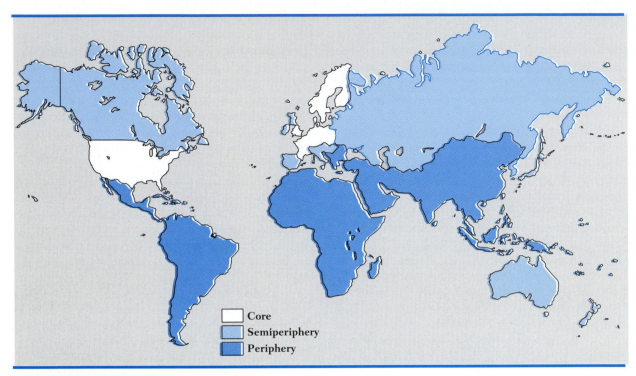

FIGURE 6.1(a) The world system around 1900.
Source: From *Macrosociology: An Introduction to Human Societies*, 4th ed., by Stephen K. Sanderson. Copyright © 1999. All rights reserved. Reprinted by permission of Allyn & Bacon.

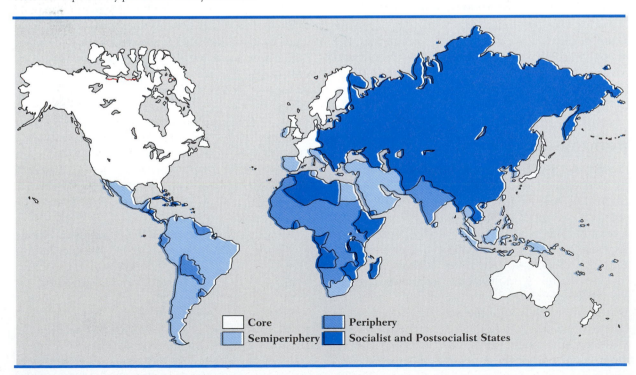

FIGURE 6.1(b) The world system, 2000.
Source: From *Macrosociology: An Introduction to Human Societies*, 4th ed., by Stephen K. Sanderson. Copyright © 1999. All rights reserved. Reprinted by permission of Allyn & Bacon.

Anthropological Analysis and Globalization

Eventually, ethnographic research has uncovered limitations to all three different approaches to globalization. Such labels as *traditional, modern, metropole-satellite,* and *peripheral* are too simplistic to classify realistically the diverse economic and cultural traditions in the world. As Max Weber's view suggested, anthropologists discovered that there are no predictable, unilineal, or unalterable patterns of societal evolution. For example, anthropologists today recognize that Marx's prediction regarding the evolution of socialist and communist stages of society from the capitalist stage is wrong. Historically, socialist and communist revolutions occurred in the former Soviet Union and China, which were by no means industrial-capitalist societies. The industrial societies that Marx had focused on, such as Great Britain and Germany, did not develop into what Marx conceived of as socialist or communist societies. They criticize the modernization, dependency, and world-systems theorists for neglecting the diverse precapitalist economic systems, specific histories, internal class relations, ethnic differences, political conditions, and dynamic cultural traditions.

Anthropologists at Work

Eric Wolf: A Global Anthropologist

Eric Wolf was born in Vienna, Austria, in 1923. After elementary school he went to *gymnasium,* a combined middle school and high school, in Czechoslovakia. At an early age, he was exposed to many diverse ethnic groups and nationalistic movements. His parents later sent him to England, where he first discovered the natural sciences. In 1940, he came to the United States to attend Queens College. He majored in a variety of subjects until he finally settled on anthropology. In 1943, he joined the U.S. Army and saw combat in Italy, returning with a Silver Star and a Purple Heart. After the war, he completed his studies at Queens College and then went on to graduate from Columbia University, where he studied with Ruth Benedict and Julian Steward. He did ethnological fieldwork in Puerto Rico, Mexico, and the Italian Alps.

Having been exposed to peasant groups during his childhood in Europe, Wolf focused his studies on the peasantry in different parts of the world. Through his fieldwork in areas such as Puerto Rico and Mexico, he became interested in how peasants adjust to global change. In a number of essays, he refined the analytical approach to understanding the peasantry. His early books include *Sons of the Shaking Earth* (1959), an overview of the historical transformations in Mesoamerica caused by Spanish colonialism; *Peasants* (1966), an analytic treatment of peasants throughout the world; and *Peasant Wars of the Twentieth Century* (1969), an examination of peasant revolutions.

Because of the success of his early books and his global perspective in his comprehensive *Europe and the People without History* ([1982] 1997), Wolf has exerted a tremendous influence on many anthropologists and other social scientists. *Europe and*

Eric Wolf.

the People without History won several awards. Wolf was awarded a grant from the MacArthur Foundation, frequently called the "genius" award. Candidates are recommended by 100 anonymous nominators, whose selections are reviewed by panels of experts. Recipients can spend the grant money as they wish on their own research projects. Wolf wrote another influential text called *Envisioning Power* (1999) about ideology and its relationship to political economy, global developments, and culture.

Eric Wolf died in March 1999, but his contributions to anthropological thought and his emphasis on the global perspective will endure forever within the profession.

Before the 1960s, many anthropologists were influenced by the modernization approach, which tended to view societies in isolation. Since the development of the dependency and world-systems perspectives, however, anthropologists have become more attuned to the global perspective. For example, an important book by the late Eric Wolf, *Europe and the People without History* (1997), reflected these developments in anthropological thought. Wolf espoused a global perspective by drawing on modernization, dependency, and world-systems approaches while criticizing all of them for their weaknesses. Anthropologists today evaluate the claims of all three approaches by combining in-depth historical information with cultural data gathered through ethnographic research. This strategy contributes to a more comprehensive understanding of the internal and external conditions that influence societal changes arising from globalization.

Globalization and the Fourth World

We discussed how the modernization theorists during the Cold War years divided the world into three major types of societies: the First, Second, and Third Worlds. However, anthropologists have done much research on what are sometimes referred to as the **Fourth World** societies, as an additional classification to the First, Second, and Third World categories. Other terms for these societies include native, indigenous, aboriginal, or first nation. As we will see in later chapters, extensive ethnographic research has provided us with considerable documentation concerning the changes resulting from globalization in these Fourth World societies.

The expansion of globalization often produced traumatic and violent changes in many of these Fourth World indigenous societies. These peoples were absorbed as subordinate ethnic groups in larger nation-states or in some cases became extinct. When absorbed, they usually were forced to abandon their traditional language and culture, a process anthropologists call **ethnocide**. In other situations, aboriginal peoples faced **genocide**, the physical extermination of a particular group of people. People such as the Tasmanians of Australia and also some Native American Indian groups were deliberately killed so that colonists could take their lands and resources. The attitudes of the Europeans toward these indigenous peoples reflected racism and ethnocentrism, which resulted in many massacres of these aboriginal peoples.

As in many other parts of the world there was a sense among white European Christians of themselves as civilized and "others" who were not. President Teddy Roosevelt, who often wrote of the winning of the West, observed, "Of course our whole national history has been one of expansion. That the barbarians recede or are conquered, with the attendant fact that peace follows their retrogression or conquest, is due solely to the power of the mighty civilized races which have not lost the fighting instinct, and which by their expansion are gradually bringing peace into the red wastes where the barbarian peoples of the world hold sway" (Drinnon 1980, 79).

Teddy Roosevelt found nothing wrong in even the most genocidal and barbaric American military actions. In December of 1864, an audience in a Denver theater applauded wildly as were displayed the results of the latest encounter between the civilized races and the others. The U.S. cavalry had surprised and massacred at least 150 Indian children, women, and old men. The braves had been away hunting. About the Sand Creek massacre Teddy Roosevelt said that "in even certain most objectionable details . . . it was on the whole as righteous and beneficial a deed as ever took place on the frontier" (Dyer 1980, 79).

Almost the entire West was ethnically cleansed of Indians in the same manner, by American soldiers acting on government orders to remove the "Red Devils" from their land by imprisoning them on reservations or killing them. As Teddy said, "I don't go so far as to think that the only good Indians are dead Indians, but I believe nine out of every ten are, and I shouldn't like to inquire too closely into the case of the tenth" (Dyer 1980, 86). As we see in the next chapter, these views represented the racist, genocidal attitudes of many educated Europeans as they took over the lands and colonized many areas of the world. We spend considerable time on the ethnographic research and the impact of globalization on these indigenous peoples in Chapters 9, 10, and 11.

Many Native American Indian reservations have extreme poverty conditions.

Pro- and Antiglobalization: An Anthropological Contribution

Throughout the world there have been both positive and negative appraisals of the process of globalization and its impact on societies throughout the world. International economist Jagdish Bhagwati authored a recent book, *In Defense of Globalization* (2004). In this book Jagdish notices that politicians in the United States on the right, such as Pat Buchanan, and on the left, such as Ralph Nader, have mounted political arguments against globalization. Buchanan emphasizes the negative effects of globalization on the U.S. economy, whereas Ralph Nader is against globalization, which he argues only serves corporate multinational capitalist interests and results in harmful and negative consequences for the environment and economy exploitation in underdeveloped societies. After many years of economic research in Asia and elsewhere on the developing global trends, Bhagwati suggests that both sides of this antiglobalization political crusade are extreme and that we need to empirically evaluate the realities of both positive and negative consequences of globalization. He urges a middle-of-the-road approach that is based on a pragmatic solution to deal with the impact of globalization.

For example, Bhagwati carefully evaluates the International Monetary Fund (IMF) and the World Bank and its policies that have an enormous influence on economic development in various societies. He indicates that the IMF and the World Bank has modified its policies drastically as a result of its problematic solutions in dealing with the Asian fiscal crisis of the 1990s.

Bhagwati suggests that globalization trends need to be studied to comprehend their effects on not only economic and environmental developments, but also pro- and antiglobalization ideologies on all sides of the political spectrum, migration and immigration policies, the role of NGOs (Non-Government Organizations), increasing inequality both within societies and between societies, workers' wages, child labor, prostitution, gender inequities, childcare and work issues, and constraints on the emergence of democratic institutions and civil society that can sustain positive and inhibit negative trends in globalization.

Cultural anthropologists and their research projects all around the world are perfectly situated to understand these aspects of globalization at the local level through their ethnographic findings. As we see in Chapter 16, "Contemporary Global Trends," these ethnographic research projects are aimed at assessing both the positive and negative aspects of globalization through empirical investigation of current environmental, demographic, and technological trends as well as economic, political, and religious developments that have emerged in many regions of the world. Obviously, during this historical time period, globalization has produced some high-stakes winners and losers among different countries and groups within countries. Everyone on the pro- and antiglobalization side concurs that there has been a widening of the wealth gap both within and among different societies. Therefore, within any society there are going to be those in favor of globalization trends and those opposed. As in the criticism of the modernization model as expressed before, many people in non-Western societies may resist the "excessive" aspects of individualism and free-market ideology that have emerged in the context of Western culture.

Many anthropologists refer to themselves as studying globalization "from below" by focusing on the people in local areas being affected by these multinational technological and international economic and political policies. In one major book authored by Rutgers political scientist Benjamin Barber called *Jihad vs. McWorld: Terrorism's Challenge to Democracy* (2001), he argues that globalization as represented by the spread of McWorld (McDonald's, MacIntosh computers, and Mickey Mouse) through many societies has resulted in Jihad (the term for "Holy War" in Arabic) by those who resist these global trends and therefore react in antagonistic ways, including terrorism of the sort that led to 9/11/2001. In his analysis, Barber suggests that McWorld has imposed a form of cultural homogeneity or domination in the media, individual consumption preferences, politics, religion, and other institutions in the world. The Jihad reaction (which is not limited to the Islamic world) includes many other non-Western local-level political and religious responses to McWorld cultural uniformity.

In another well-known analysis of globalization, Harvard political scientist Samuel Huntington wrote an influential book, *The Clash of Civilizations and the Remaking of the World Order* (1996), that continues to resonate with many people in the West and other regions of the world. Huntington argues that a unitary "Western civilization and culture" is at odds with "Islamic civilization and culture," "Hindu civilization and culture," and "Confucian civiliza-

tion and culture." Huntington argues that the societies with these Islamic and Asian cultures do not have the institutions for developing civil democratic societies, individualism, free markets, or other elements that will enable them to develop peaceful coexistence with Western culture. He envisions these cultural and regional blocs as fragmenting the world order and resulting in more conflict and instability throughout the world. Huntington's perspective has perpetuated a view that has been widely accepted within both the West and the Islamic world, especially after the tragedy of 9/11 and the aftermath of the United States–led invasion of Afghanistan and Iraq. Huntington has been an influential political advisor to the State Department and the U.S. government. The clash-of-civilization thesis has been used to develop foreign-policy strategies in the Islamic and Asian world since its initial publication.

However, cultural anthropologists who do current ethnographic research in the Islamic world or Asia (like this author) have problems with the sweeping generalizations perpetuated by Barber and Huntington. In contrast to these political scientists, who generally interview the political elites of these different countries and read the religious doctrines of these people, ethnographers live among these people on a day-to-day basis for years and observe and interview them. Cultural anthropologists do not just interview the political elites, but they also interview and observe the middle class, working class, peasants and rural villagers, religious clerics of all levels, and other indigenous people. We find a tremendous range of religious, ethnic, and political diversity as well as aspects of civil society within these regions. The views of Huntington and Barber are also based on antiquated understandings of "culture" as forms of fixed beliefs and values shared within a "homogeneous civilization." This understanding of fixed and widely shared "culture" is not found in non-Western societies (or any society) by cultural anthropologists. People in both non-Western, Islamic, or Asian (and Western) societies are constantly reinterpreting and transforming their cultural conceptions as they are exposed to rapid changes through the Internet, media, consumption patterns, and other results on globalization processes. Cultural anthropologists find that there is no "Islamic culture or civilization," or "Confucian culture or civilization," or "Asian culture or civilization," or "Western culture or civilization," despite the rhetoric that political and religious leaders espouse in these respective regions (Appadurai 1997; Eickelman 2001, 2002; Scupin 2003, 2004, 2005).

Additionally, cultural anthropologists find that globalization is not a one-sided dominated process stemming from the major industrialized capitalist or socialist countries, but rather it is a nuanced process of interactive relations between the local and global levels. As the late anthropologist Eric Wolf emphasized in his pioneering book on globalization *The People without History* (1997), mentioned before, ethnographers must attend to the study of local level processes as well as integrating an empirical understanding of the global trends that are incorporated at the local level. Sometimes, anthropologists refer to this as **glocalization**—absorbing and localizing the global—as an indicator of what this process entails. In later chapters, we investigate what these anthropologists have found through their ethnographic research on glocalization.

Globalization and Its Impact on Language and Culture

Many anthropologists are investigating the impact of globalization on language and culture in different regions of the world. For example, Asia, with the development of the Internet, is undergoing a transformation. Prior to the Internet, languages in Asia were primarily influenced by first the print media, especially newspapers and magazines. Eventually, with the development of the radio and then television, language shifts in Asian countries occurred as people listened to and watched how other people use the spoken language of their countries. However, when the Internet came more recently with globalization economic and technological developments, English, which has become much more of a global language, became more prominent in educational areas in China, India, Taiwan, Singapore, Japan, Indonesia, Malaysia, and other areas of Asia (Lindsay and Ying 2003). Although some Asians do view English as a form of linguistic imperialism or hegemony, it is recognized as the primary vehicle of economic and technological globalization.

Likewise, anthropologists—as discussed in different areas of this chapter—have focused on various changes occurring with economic and technological globalization and its consequences for cultural change. One concrete example from economic anthropologist Richard Wilk's studies of cultural consumption demonstrates more forms of individualistic tastes and preferences for goods and services (2004). In some respects, these new forms of individualistic consumption preferences have global cultural consequences for many areas of the world. In the United States, politicians and other civic leaders are contesting the rise of *excessive individualism,* which they perceive as eroding civic social bonds within communities. Some politicians and religious leaders view the family and community as very fragile, and the common ground of cultural values are viewed as eroding. With a fast-paced life, it has become very difficult for many overwhelmed Americans to find the time and space for the things that strengthen the bonds of trust and cooperation among citizens, jeopardizing the existence of institutions such as the PTA, the town hall meeting, and the ballpark. A legion of evidence indicates there has been a steady erosion of face-to-face interaction in American neighborhoods, civic organizations, and communities.

Membership in the vast majority of civic and fraternal organizations—from the Red Cross to scouting to women's clubs to fraternal groups of every sort—appears to be steadily declining. Regardless of the type of voluntary organization, whatever its area of interest or its beliefs, the trend appears undeniable. We seldom spend the time chatting over the back fence or playing cards as our parents did a generation ago. How can we account for this development and what is its significance?

Several interrelated factors appear to be of importance: the fast pace of modern life, the impact of geographic mobility, and the influence of growing numbers of women in the labor force. But, in addition, technological developments have privatized leisure-time activities. Products of globalization, including 200 channel cable televisions, CDs and DVDs, the Walkman, and the Internet all contribute to this process. Donning a virtual reality helmet to be entertained in isolation is the epitome of further diminishing face-to-face contact. Similar developments in the workplace such as voice mail

Critical Perspectives

GLOBALIZATION AND MCDONALD'S

When many people around the world think of globalization, the McDonald's fast-food restaurants come to mind. McDonald's (serving 20 million people a day around the world) represents to many people the projection and symbol of cultural hegemony or dominance of U.S. capitalism around the world. As mentioned in this chapter, the political scientist Benjamin Barber views McDonald's as an aspect of the McWorld (including MacIntosh computers and Mickey Mouse) that signals the cultural spread of globalization stemming from U.S. society. The triumph of the Big Mac and Hollywood films are viewed by some people as the negative signs that a country has become penetrated by the imperial domination of U.S. culture. However, when cultural anthropologists study the cultural spread and diffusion of McDonald's into the different societies of the world, they find that globalization is not a one-sided process and that like other external cultural elements, McDonald's restaurants are transformed and localized by the people within these societies.

This process of "globalization" of McDonald's occurs throughout the world. Harvard anthropologist James Watson edited a volume called *Golden Arches East: McDonald's in East Asia* that contains essays by cultural anthropologists who have studied how the "globalization" of McDonald's takes place in China, Japan, Korea,

and Taiwan (1997, 2004 (new second edition)). In this book UCLA anthropologist Yunxiang Yan describes how this globalization of McDonald's has emerged in China. Since McDonald's moved in as the iconic symbol of American culture and globalization in Beijing during the 1990s, it has been attractive to Chinese citizens not only because of its food, but also because of the ability of the citizens to consume popular cultural values stemming from America. Following the decline of the rigid Maoist orthodoxy and Communist ideology prior to the 1990s, McDonald's was perceived as a means of expressing freedom of choice in taste and lifestyle to many Chinese. Yunxiang Yan noted that other cultural values associated with American traditions also diffused into China along with the popular culture associated with the Big Mac, and these values were also absorbed and localized into Chinese society. For example, despite some resistance to American cultural hegemony by some of the Chinese, he interviewed others who said that the NBA games, Coca-Cola, Hollywood movies, and the Declaration of Independence all belong to the shared culture of all human societies (2002, 34).

The sociologist Peter Berger refers to this process observed by Yunxiang as the "sacramental consumption" of food that carries the cultural freight of individual freedom, democracy, and human

rights, which he also links with the eating of a Big Mac in the former Soviet Union (2002). Similarly, anthropologist Conrad Kottak refers to McDonaldization as a secular religion with a sacred text called an "Operations Manual" that has strong cultural resonance for many.

Anthropologists who study McDonald's in Japan, such as Tamotsu Aoki and Emiko Ohnu-Tierney, find similar glocalization processes at work. Emiko Ohnu-Tierney describes how prior to World War II, that even though meat had been available since the 1920s, most Japanese did not eat much of it at all. They ate primarily vegetables and seafood. However, after the U.S. occupation in Japan following the war, gradually some of the wealthier Japanese began to consume meat products, including beef (1999). Following the period of postwar affluence in Japan, they began to eat meat with gusto because it was associated with the Western civilization, science, technology, and culture being integrated into Japanese culture. Eventually, McDonald's came to Japan in the 1970s. By 1982 McDonald's was the most profitable fast-food company in Japan. McDonald's began a marketing campaign to target higher-income middle-class people who were benefiting from the growth of the Japanese economy by establishing its restaurants in the high-real-estate areas, such as the Ginza in Tokyo, and near train stations. With the introduction of McDonald's into Japan, eating habits were changed radically, as described by these anthropologists. The traditional form of lunch for most Japanese was the box lunch called *obento*. However, as Japanese customers came to eat lunch in McDonald's, they learned to hold the bread and meat in their hands, munching on their favorite teriyaki burger or *McChao* (chicken-fried rice), while standing (to appear more American) at the counters during their lunch breaks. Although other Japanese restaurants adopted the fast-food program for traditional dishes such as *ramen* Chinese noodles, take-out sushi, or *gyudon* (a bowl of rice topped with beef), McDonald's remained a very popular feature of Japanese cuisine.

Yet, since McDonald's entered Japan, a variety of restaurants have developed that have proliferated within the streets and markets of Japan. In a passage from anthropologists John McCreery and Ruth McCreery's descriptive scene of the Yokohama train station, there are two Italian restaurants (one of which appeals to health-conscious diners by labeling its offerings "natural Italian"), two Chinese restaurants (one offering market-stall dishes from Taiwan), a Russian tearoom, a Thai restaurant, and a beer hall whose menu features German sausages. One restaurant specializes in *omuraisu* (omelet rice), a Japanese culinary invention that consists of rice seasoned with ketchup, onions, and peppers,

wrapped in an omelet, and topped with curry, stew, or simply more ketchup. All these restaurants are filled with Japanese customers visibly enjoying their food.

Up two escalators and a short walk away is a busy street filled with young people, where the offerings include KFC, McDonald's, Starbucks, Haagen-Dazs, Shakey's Pizza, Mr. Donut, and a British pub. All are doing a thriving business—as are places offering Japanese-style dishes, *soba* (buckwheat) and *udon* (wheat) noodles, *unagi* (eel), *sushi* (raw fish) or other seafood on rice flavored with sweetened vinegar with *wasabi* (Japanese horseradish), soy sauce, and (to freshen the palate) slices of pickled ginger. One mustn't forget the *tonkatsu*, deep-fried pork cutlet served with rice, a bowl of *miso* (fermented soybean paste) soup, salty Japanese pickles, and a generous heap of chopped cabbage, or the *okonomiyaki*, do-it-yourself savory pancakes stuffed with all sorts of things and topped with dried bonito flakes, seaweed, and a dark brown savory sauce. Plus, of course, there are *tempura* (batter-fried seafood or vegetables) and *sukiyaki* (thin slices of beef sautéed in a heavy iron pan with *tofu* and vegetables).

Within a half-mile radius, one can also find Indian, Mexican, and Vietnamese restaurants. The McCreerys also indicate that as women and young people have become more active in the workplace and other areas of life, they depend more on take-out and fast food. (McCreery and McCreery

2005). Thus, it would appear that McDonald's actually opened the path for more multicultural and fast-food dining for many Japanese consumers.

Anthropologist Tulasi Srinivas has studied the McDonaldization process of globalization in India (2002). The major marketing obstacle that faced McDonald's in India was the image of a beef patty on a bun in the eyes of the majority of Hindu peoples, who maintain beliefs regarding the sacredness of cows. Srinivas noted that McDonald's invested a great deal of time and money to build appropriate kitchens in their restaurants that prevented the mixing of vegetarian foods with meat products. Eventually, McDonald's began to localize its foods by developing the Maharajah Mac, a type of Indian spiced hamburger, along with a vegetarian menu. However, this was not appealing to the majority of Indian consumers. Srinivas concludes that companies such as McDonald's, Pizza Hut, or KFC and the standardization and cultural homogenization of food that they represent do not become profitable in the multiethnic, pluralistic consumer atmosphere in India. Sociologist George Ritzer, in his provocative book *The McDonaldization of Society*, describes the standardized and homogenized commercialization of U.S. popular culture as lowering the level of sophistication wherever its long tentacles reach (1995). In contrast to the change reflected in Peter Berger's phrase "sacramental consumption" for

Ronald Bertapa *is a symbol of Buddhist, Hindu, and Islamic traditions in Indonesia.*

the former Soviet Union and China, Srinivas emphasizes that this aspect of the Big Mac does not apply to India because the Indian population resides in a pluralistic democratic nation. Thus, glocalization of McDonald's takes a much different form in India.

Finally, in a broad comprehensive essay accompanying his study of McDonald's in Indonesia, anthropologist Ronald Lukens-Bull demonstrates the process of glocalization, which has taken a different form in that country (2003). The Big Mac came to Jakarta, Indonesia, in 1990 and by 2003 there were 108 stores employing about 800 people. Lukens-Bull indicates that McDonald's is a prestigious and expensive form of dining for the vast majority of Indonesians. It is identified with an upwardly mobile middle class of consumers—young teens who wear jeans and watch a version of MTV Asia. In central Jakarta, the

major McDonald's—near the Hard Rock Café, Chili's, and movie theaters and department stores—has a large, forty-foot inflatable Ronald McDonald in a Buddhist- or Sufi Islamic–like meditative position. Local Indonesians refer to him as "Ronald Bertapa," the Meditating Ronald. *Ronald Bertapa* is a powerful syncretic symbol in Indonesia associated with the original Hindu-Buddhist traditions of Indonesia blended with the legends of the nine original Sufi saints who brought Islam to Indonesia.

Another Ronald McDonald statue in Bali appears to coopt the art and culture in order to market hamburgers to Western tourists. And one other Ronald McDonald figure in East Java was referred to as the "freedom fighter." This "freedom fighting" Ronald McDonald was pictured riding on a tank with friends waving the Indonesian flag celebrating the

independence from the Dutch. The multiplicity of symbols associated with McDonald's and its particular glocalization in Indonesia represents a cultural accommodation to external sources and also the ambivalence that those external sources reflect in various modes of discourse about modernity, Western influence, and its impact on Islamic culture in Indonesia.

POINTS TO PONDER

1. What do you see as the negative and positive aspects of the McDonald's restaurants moving into different societies of the world?

2. What does the adaptation of the new forms of McDonald's in different societies suggest about culture change?

3. If you were going outside of the United States to travel would you eat in a McDonald's restaurant and why?

and isolated work cubicles with computers also contribute to this individualistic trend.

The significance of these developments is undeniable. Global technology is driving a wedge between our individual or private interests and our collective or public interests. Most anthropologists recognize that the more global technology allows people to satisfy their own individual tastes, the greater the cost in the possible loss of social interaction that fosters ongoing and meaningful social relationships and face-to-face relationships, which are the very basis of any sense of community, any hope for well-integrated neighborhoods, and any expectation that families will remain intact and functioning.

Societies all over the world are being transformed by similar global economic and technological trends that influence traditional cultural beliefs and values. As different social arrangements are either more or less favorable to creating and protecting human connectedness, a final question arises. How do our American communities or any other communities in the world foster what anthropologists such as Pierre Bourdieu referred to as "social capital," the norms and networks of social engagement produced through social living that encourage cooperation and social trust? As we discuss in later chapters, anthropologists are doing ethnographic research on these new changes in culture that result from globalization (Hefner 1998).

SUMMARY

This chapter focuses on the process of globalization and the impact it has had on the world today. There is no widespread consensus within anthropology on what are the definitive aspects of globalization. However, many aspects of globalization are evident in the new rapidly changing high-tech economy and technology, the immigration of different peoples throughout the world, and the wide diffusion of culture through new forms of media. Anthropologists have been investigating different aspects of globalization and its effects on people's lives in many different societies. Various theories that are developments from early ideas of Max Weber and Karl Marx to explain the process of globalization have led to models such as modernization, dependency, and world systems theory. Anthropologists have drawn from these various theories and integrated their findings from local areas and are trying to understand how global changes are influencing the cultural developments that they study. Sometimes, anthropologists refer to this as "glocalization."

The modernization theorists developed the terminology of First, Second, and Third Worlds to divide up the planet's societies. However, today these simplistic categories do not apply to the complexity of socioeconomic and cultural developments. Anthropologists have added another term, the Fourth World, to distinguish those societies that were indigenous or native to the lands that they inhabit. These indigenous societies have had a very difficult time in confrontation with globalization and have usually been overwhelmed by this process. Dependency and world systems models have also been criticized as being too simplistic in accounting for the diversity of societies throughout the world.

Anthropologists are conducting in-depth ethnographic studies on the process of globalization and how it influences technological, economic, social, political, and religious developments in trying to understand how these processes have an impact on local communities. They also do research on language and the influence of globalization on the use of speaking, writing, and even cyberspace communications in different societies.

Some theorists in political science have developed generalized models of globalization that have produced both economic and political policies. Anthropologists find weaknesses in these models, as they do not discuss the nuances and subtleties of culture, ethnicity, religious beliefs, and local circumstances in different societies. Anthropologists continue to produce ethnographic studies that draw on both local data combined with an understanding of how global changes are occurring very quickly around the world.

QUESTIONS TO THINK ABOUT

1. What do anthropologists mean by the term *globalization*?

2. What do you see in your everyday life that results from the process of globalization?

3. What are the strengths and weaknesses in the three models of globalization in this chapter? What would you adopt or reject regarding these models?

4. What are some of the consequences of globalization on technology, the economy, and languages as observed by anthropologists?

5. How do anthropologists understand glocalization?

6. What are the weaknesses in the approaches of Benjamin Barber and Samuel Huntington's understanding of globalization?

7. What are the negative and positive aspects of globalization?

KEY TERMS

core societies

dependency theory

ethnocide

First World

Fourth World

genocide

globalization

glocalization

imperialism

peripheral societies

postindustrial societies

Second World

semiperipheral societies

Third World

world-systems theory

Chapter 7

Race and Ethnicity

Race, Racism, and Culture

As we saw in Chapter 2, physical characteristics such as skin pigmentation, nose shape, and hair texture have prompted people throughout history to classify humans into different "races." The word *race* is a loaded term in part because people use the word differently in different contexts to mean different things (MacEachern 2003). It can be used in census data or in other senses to refer to certain styles of music, dance, or literature. Biologists may employ the term *race* to refer to different species of plants and animals.

The term *races* appears to have been derived from the Latin root *ratio,* with a meaning similar to species or kind (of thing). However, as seen in Chapter 2, attempts to employ racial classifications for humans based on "scientific criteria" have foundered because they were too rigid to account for the tremendous variation within different so-called races. The majority of anthropologists today find dividing different populations into distinctive racial categories or classifications extremely problematic. Clearly, bounded racially distinct populations are not found in the real world. However, it cannot be denied that humans in both the past and present have used various racial classifications to categorize people and develop stereotypes about the behavior and mental abilities of different "racial categories." These categories have often been used throughout human history as the basis and justification of **racism**, the belief that some races are superior to other races. Racism can often result in discrimination and hostile acts toward different peoples and societies (Frederickson 2002).

Some fascinating and intriguing research in cognitive anthropology in France, in the United States by Lawrence Hirschfeld (1996), in Mongolia by Francisco Gil-White (2001), and in Thailand by Raymond Scupin (2005) indicates that all humans categorize races and ethnic groups using similar attributes to categorize different groups of people. Earlier, we saw how people throughout time and in different cultures classified different races and ethnic groups in *essentialist categories,* categories that assumed that there were physical and cultural features that were similar. Hirschfeld did laboratory studies of cognition of children in the United States and France and found that at very early ages children constructed prototypical, essentialist categories of different races. He concluded that these categories become more salient and are utilized more frequently if the society emphasizes racial differences within their culture. Francisco Gil-White found that when he gave cognitive tasks to Mongols in China to elicit thought about the differences among ethnic groups, they used essentialist categories to think about ethnic differences. Scupin used similar techniques among Chinese, Indian, Thai, and Malays in Thailand, and the data showed similar results (2005).

All these anthropologists emphasize *that there are no biological, essential features of distinctive races among human populations*. Yet despite these scientific findings, most people tend to utilize essentialist categories to categorize racial and ethnic groups. Based on this research and other similar cognitive research, it appears that humans everywhere tend to classify different populations in essentialist, stereotypical ways (Boyer 1994).

Ancient Classification Systems

Prior to the emergence of writing tradtions in ancient civilizations, archaeologists found evidence of racist classification of peoples through depictions of people in artistic design and rock paintings in Europe and many other areas of the world (Jochim 1998). All the ancient agricultual societies with written texts, including Egypt, Israel, Greece, Rome, India, China, the Islamic, and European civilizations, used early racial classifications that were essentialist folk taxonomies, informal and unscientific classifications based on skin color and other cultural characteristics (Barber 1999; Dikotter 1999; Gossett 1963; Snowden 1983; Craven 1997; Goring 1994; Lewis 1970). As early as 3,000 BC, the ancient Egyptians divided all human populations into one of four categories: red for Egyptians, yellow for people to the east, white for people to the north, and black for Africans to the south. However, it is unclear whether the Egyptians were using skin color as the basis of their classifications. Later, in the biblical book of Genesis, a similar classification scheme appears in a tale chronicling the distribution of the human population:

And the sons of Noah that went forth from the ark were Shem, Ham and Japheth:. . . these are the three sons of Noah: and of them was the whole earth overspread. (Genesis 9:18–19)

The descendants of Shem (the Semites) were the ancient Israelites. The descendants of Ham ventured to the south and the east, and the descendants of Japheth moved north. The word Ham originally meant "black" and referred to the black soil of the Nile delta, but its meaning was eventually changed to describe the skin color of Ham's descendants. According to the Bible, Ham had seen his father naked in a drunken sleep and was cursed and sent off to the south to become the father of the black people. At the end of Genesis, the descendants of Ham are condemned to be "servants of servants unto [their] brethren" (Genesis 9:25). Many Westerners subsequently cited this passage as the justification for an entrenched system of racial discrimination (Leach 1988).

In a recent essay by historian Benjamin Braude, he describes how the so-called Curse of Ham presented in the early prints of Johannes Gutenberg based especially on Martin Luther's teachings became the basis of a new understanding of the Old and New Testaments for Christians in America and Europe (1997). The new readings of Genesis 9 and 10 regarding the biblical account of Noah and his sons was reinterpreted in these new printings. However, there were many inconsistencies in these printings of the Old Testament. Thus, Cush, the son of Ham, was identified with the people of Ethiopia and Africa and was afflicted with the "curse." However, Cush spoke a "Semitic" language, which was identified at the time with "racist" notions of the "Semitic" race, the people associated with Noah's other son Shem. The sons of Japheth are associated with the peoples of Asia Minor and Central Asia. In addition, at the time of the Old Testament, the world was divided into only three continents (Asia, Africa, and Europe). Braude has examined many of the medieval and modern early European manuscripts and books on the Sons of Noah in Spain, France, and Europe and finds many different interpretations of this biblical tradition. For example, some of these early writings indicated that the blacks of Africa were the descendants of Cain, rather than Ham. Yet, Braude and other historians agree that these biblical ideas regarding the "Curse of Ham" were promoted by Christian Europeans and Americans, and within the Islamic civilizations to justify slavery and colonialism of African peoples in the United States, the Caribbean, Africa, and elsewhere (Braude 1997; Davis 1997; Vaughn and Vaughn 1997; Blackburn 1997; Sweet 1997; Kupperman 1997; Chaplin 1997; Lewis 1970).

By correlating physical characteristics with cultural differences, classification systems such as these assumed erroneously that populations that shared certain physical traits, especially skin color, also exhibited similar behaviors. These beliefs gave rise to many popular misconceptions and generalizations concerning the values, traditions, and behaviors of different peoples. Based on contemporary scientific research on DNA, genetics, linguistics, prehistory, historical, and anthropological data, there is no scientific evidence to substantiate the claims of any of these biblical beliefs about the sons of Noah (Olson 2002; Cavalli-Sforza, Menozzi, and Piazza 1994; Brooks 2004; Kittles and Weiss 2003).

The conceptual idea that one's physical characteristics are linked to mental abilities and behaviors was inherent within ancient Greek society. Philosophers such as Plato (427–347 BC) argued that there were different "essences" for different types of people. According to Plato, people were born with different types of souls, which gave them particular dispositions or essences. For example, he claimed that certain categories of people who had the specific *essences* were suited to be rulers, soldiers, farmers, or

slaves. Another Greek, Hippocrates (460–377 BC), the well-known medical specialist of ancient Greek society, developed a "humoral-environmental" essentialist theory to classify various peoples throughout the world. According to Hippocrates, there were four elements that constituted the universe: fire, air, earth, and water. These four elements were transformed into *humors,* or essences, that were present in all forms of life. One of the primary humors in humans was the type of blood inherited, which contained different distributions of the four elements that produced varying personality and behavioral dispositions among populations. Hippocrates maintained that the different populations of humanity had different essences and temperaments. For example, he claimed that the people of Asian descent were "gentle, well-fed, courageous," and could endure suffering. However, Asian people would not develop industrious habits because pleasure dominated their lives. These folk classifications of race were used to justify slavery, racism, and ethnocentrism in Greece. Aristotle, the famous philosopher of Greece, recommended to his student Alexander the Great to treat his conquered peoples as animals and plants because they were not humans as Greeks were (Wright 2000).

This type of classification based on the idea of inherited blood, essences, and humors continued to influence people during the medieval period in Western society and resulted in simplified stereotypes of behavior and temperament of people around the world. In the medieval period, it was accepted that there was a "Great Chain of Being," which posited natural essential categories based on a hierarchy established by God and nature. Eventually, social groupings based on blood, essences, and humors were placed within this hierarchy. By correlating physical characteristics with cultural differences, classification systems such as these assumed erroneously that populations that shared certain physical traits also exhibited similar patterns of behavior. These beliefs gave rise to popular misconceptions and generalizations concerning the values, traditions, and behaviors of differing peoples.

Modern Racism in Western Thought

Later, after the period of the 1500s in European society when explorers began to make contact with many peoples and cultures outside of Europe, various forms of "scientific racialism" began to replace the earlier medieval conceptions. The prior conceptual frameworks based on blood and humors influenced these models of scientific racism. As Europeans began to discover civilizations and cultures in the Americas, Africa, the Middle East, and Asia, they associated the skin color of many of the people in these non-Western societies with certain forms of essences, behavior, and mental developments. Europeans measured these civilizations in comparison with their own and thus designated them as "savage" and "barbaric." Because many of these people had a different skin color, they began to assume that the level of these civilizations had something to do with the skin color, essence, or race of these populations. Europeans began to rank the people they discovered according to skin color differences, with nonwhite peoples at the bottom. Thus, colonizing their lands and using them as slaves could occur freely. It was assumed by the Europeans that these people were no better than animals and that they needed Europeans to help civilize them.

The Spanish used the term *Negro* to describe the Africans in the 1500s. They used *claro*, or "light," for themselves. Following exploration and colonization by northern Europeans such as the Dutch, British, and Belgians, the term *white* was used to apply to their own skin color. Eventually, these folk classifications began to creep into the scientific attempts to classify different peoples.

For example, in one of the earliest scientific efforts to organize human variation into racial categories, the Swedish scientist Carolus Linnaeus constructed a taxonomy in 1758 that divided *Homo sapiens* into four races based on skin color: Europeans (white), North American Indians (red), Asiatics (yellow), and Africans (black). Yet his classification of humans was influenced by ancient and medieval theories and various ideas about European superiority. For example, he classified the American Indians with reddish skin as choleric, with a need to be regulated by customs. Africans with black skin were relaxed, indolent, negligent, and governed by caprice. In contrast, Europeans with white skin were described as gentle, acute, inventive, and governed by laws (Lieberman 2003).

In 1781, a German scientist, Johann Blumenbach, devised a racial classification system that is still sometimes used in popular, unscientific discussions of race. He divided humans into five distinct groups—Caucasian, Mongolian, Malay, Ethiopian, and Native American—corresponding to the colors white, yellow, brown, black, and red, respectively. Blumenbach based his racial typology primarily on skin color, but he considered other traits as well,

Neo-Nazi groups promote hatred against minorities in the United States and elsewhere.

Timothy McVeigh was motivated by racist beliefs to bomb the Federal Building in Oklahoma City.

including facial features, chin form, and hair color. Later, following the evolutionary ideas of Darwin and especially his cousin Francis Galton, a number of physical anthropologists in the United States and Europe such as Samuel Morton, Ernst Haeckel, Rudolph Virchow, and others began to assert that the Caucasian race had larger brains and higher intellectual capacities than non-Caucasians (Shipman 1994; Wolpoff and Caspari 1998; Lieberman 2003).

The major Enlightenment philosophers of Europe that influenced the U.S. political leaders and others such as Thomas Jefferson and Benjamin Franklin also held similar views regarding races. For example, Immanuel Kant wrote scientific treatises on how the African race (and others) were retarded and incapable of rational thought compared to the Europeans. In his essay "Of the Different Human Races," Kant relied on his close colleague, anthropologist Ernst Haeckel, biblical teachings regarding the sons of Ham, and other European philosophers and scientists such as Buffon to perpetuate the

views of innate racial inequalities in intelligence and also that different races could not and should not reproduce with one another (1775; Bernasconi 2001; Lott and Ward 2004). Of course, these ideas of race influenced Thomas Jefferson and other leaders who participated in the drafting of the U.S. Declaration of Independence and the U.S. Constitution, which emphasized the "Equality of Man," who were obviously excluding people such as African slaves, which many of them owned, and Native American Indians.

Eventually, these "scientific racialism" beliefs were used to rationalize slavery and the political oppression of various groups around the world. In nineteenth-century England, thinkers such as Herbert Spencer and Francis Galton believed that social evolution worked by allowing superior members of society to rise to the top, while inferior ones sank to the bottom. These views reinforced the false belief that particular groups of people, or races, had quantifiably different intellectual capacities.

In 1853 the French aristocrat Joseph Arthur de Gobineau published a work entitled *Essai sur l'inégalité des races humaines* (*Essay on the Inequality of the Races of Humanity*). In this work, Gobineau described the whole of human history as a struggle among the various "races" of humanity. He argued that each race had its own intellectual capacity, either high or low, and that there were stronger and weaker races. Gobineau promoted the conquest of so-called weaker races by allegedly stronger ones. He opened the book with the statement that everything great, noble, and fruitful in the works of humanity springs from the Aryan family, the so-called super race. The Aryans spread out to create, first, the Hindu civilization, then the Egyptian, Assyrian, Greek, Chinese, Roman, German, Mexican, and Peruvian civilizations (Banton 1998; Montagu 1997). Gobineau argued that these civilizations declined because of "racial mixing." These so-called scientific views of racism were later taken up by writers such as Houston Stewart Chamberlain in twentieth-century Europe, whose writings, in turn, influenced Adolph Hitler. Gobineau's ideas were the philosophical progenitors of Hitler's *Mein Kampf,* which promoted the notions of racial superiority and inferiority. In the 1930s, the Nazi "scientific racist" ideology, based on the presumed superiority of a pure "Aryan race," was used to justify the annihilation of millions of Jews and other "non-Aryan" peoples, such as Slavs and Gypsies in Europe.

What most Americans are not aware of is that many of Hitler's ideas about race came from sources in American society. In two recent major books on this topic by an American and a German historian who documented carefully the connections between early race notions in the United States based on correspondence between Hitler and authors in America reveals a connection between the United States and Hitler's campaign against inferior races (Black 2004; Kuhl 2002). In the book *War Against the Weak* by the American historian Edwin Black, he describes how, in Hitler's book *Mein Kampf*, he praised America's exclusionary immigration laws against the Chinese, non-Aryan Europeans such as Italians and Polish races. Hitler carefully studied American eugenics laws and programs allowing sterilization of the "unfit" on eugenic grounds. He wrote fan letters to leading American eugenicists, telling Madison Grant, for example, that his book *The Passing of the Great Race* (1904) was his "Bible." Grant had argued that all non-European, non-Aryan peoples were racially inferior and needed to be eliminated.

During the early twentieth century in America, many scientists both on the right and the left were sympathetic to eugenics ideas as perpetuated by Francis Dalton that called for the sterilization of people because of mental retardation, low IQs, and other physical handicaps. Dalton believed that society should encourage healthier people to reproduce and unhealthier ones to have fewer children. Many Americans were alarmed by increased immigration and by the huge growth of the native African American population, so America's elite discovered in eugenics a "scientific" basis for their belief in white, Northern European supremacy.

Thus, at the turn of the twentieth century, scientists with a can-do spirit and just enough knowledge of Mendelian genetics to be dangerous devised grand schemes to improve the American racial population. They would segregate, sterilize, and even eliminate those deemed "unfit"—as much as 10 percent of the population, some 14 million people who were classified as "inferior races and unfit people." This program was supported by the Carnegie, Harriman, and Rockefeller family foundations to promote Madison Grant's beliefs about the inferiority of non-Anglo, non-Aryan races, which were developed into eugenics policies to improve the American race.

Researchers were dispatched to mental asylums, prisons, hospitals, and poor towns to collect family histories of the supposedly unfit—which included the mentally ill, the disabled, epileptics, alcoholics, criminals, the immoral, and pretty much anyone else they wanted to throw in. These reports were collected at the Eugenics Record Office. Some 60,000 U.S. citizens were sterilized in these campaigns because they were deemed "unfit." In 1927 the Supreme Court laid the capstone on these laws with the notorious 1927 decision in *Buck v. Bell* affirming the sterilization of an unwed teenage mother. Drawing on statements of proeugenics medical personnel, the court decided not only that Carrie Buck was feeble-minded (she wasn't), but that her daughter was clearly doomed to abnormality (she wasn't). The supposed incapacity of Carrie Buck, her mother, and her infant daughter inspired Justice Oliver Wendell Holmes's famous conclusion: "It is better for all the world, if instead of waiting to execute degenerate offspring for crime, or to let them starve for their imbecility, society can prevent those who are manifestly unfit from continuing their kind . . . . Three generations of imbeciles are enough" (1927).

Later, based on the American eugenics campaign, sterilization laws sprang up throughout Northern Europe. German eugenicists, particularly captivated by the American notion of Nordic and Aryan supremacy, published textbooks based on American ideas, and Hitler read them. The Rockefeller Foundation funded eugenic experiments in Germany through the early 1930s. These recent books don't claim that American eugenics created Hitler's evil policies, resulting in the crimes against Jews, Gypsies, Poles, and others in Europe; however, the American policies did allow Hitler to medicalize, scientize, and sanitize his hatred, making it palatable for a mass audience in Germany. Although America committed violence in the name of eugenics, it never got close to mass murder in the way that Nazi Germany did. Yet, one of the books quotes an American leader supporting Nazi eugenics—"Hitler is beating us at our own game"—and even that dates to 1934, before Germany's worst crimes. However, when Americans did recognize what the Nazis were doing, most Americans wanted no part in this genocidal and eugenics campaign at all (Black 2004; Kuhl 2004).

Critiques of Scientific Racism

Prior to the Holocaust in Germany and within the context of the historical eugenics campaign in the United States, a number of scholars within the field of anthropology were subjecting these scientific racialistic beliefs to rigorous testing and evaluation. In the United States, anthropologist Franz Boas (1858–1943), who had migrated from Germany, led a concerted effort to assess these scientific racist ideas (Pierpoint 2004; Degler 1991; Baker 2004). Boas and his students took precise assessments of the physical characteristics of different populations, including cranial capacity and brain size. His research began to challenge the scientific racist views. The research demonstrated conclusively that brain size and cranial capacities of modern humans differ widely within all so-called races. This anthropological research resulted in findings that conclusively showed that there were no so-called superior or inferior races. Boas's research also confirmed that there was no direct link between race, brain size, cranial capacity, and intelligence levels.

Franz Boas in Eskimo clothing.

This pioneering research initiated a program of research among the four fields of anthropology, which has continued over the past century to challenge scientific racist beliefs wherever they appear. This research has demonstrated time and time again that racist beliefs have no basis in fact. Human groups never fit into such neat categories. For example, many Jewish people living in Europe during the Holocaust possessed the same physical features as those associated with the so-called Aryans. The physical anthropologists of Nazi ideology who advocated Aryan racist ideology found it difficult to define precisely which physical characteristics supposedly distinguished one race from another (Schafft 1999). At present, a number of groups such as the Pioneer Fund persist in supporting research that purports to demonstrate scientifically that races differ in brain size, mental abilities, and intelligence. Anthropologists are actively criticizing these erroneous views with sound, scientifically based research (Lieberman 2001, 2003).

Race and Intelligence

Intelligence is the capacity to process and evaluate information for problem solving. It can be contrasted with **knowledge**—the storage and recall of learned information. Heredity undoubtedly plays a role in intelligence; this is confirmed by the fact that the intelligence of genetically related individuals (for example, parents and their biological children) displays the closest correlation. Yet other factors also come into play. In no area of study have the varying effects of genes, environment, and culture been more confused than in the interpretation of intelligence.

Most scientists agree that intelligence varies among individuals. Yet it has been difficult to measure intelligence objectively because tests inevitably reflect the beliefs and values of a particular cultural group. Nevertheless, a number of devices have been developed to measure intelligence, most prominent among them the intelligence quotient (IQ) test, invented by French psychologist Alfred Binet in 1905. Binet's test was brought to the United States and modified to become the Stanford–Binet test. The inventors warned that the test was valid only when the children tested came from similar environments. Yet the IQ test is widely used today for tracking students in the U.S. educational system, sparking controversy among educators and social scientists alike. In a controversial book called *The Bell Curve: Intelligence and Class Structure in American Life* (1994), Richard Herrnstein and Charles Murray argue that research supports the conclusion that race is related to intelligence. Utilizing a bell-curve statistical distribution, they place the IQ of people with European ancestry at 100. People of East Asian ancestry exceed that standard slightly, averaging 103; people of African descent fall below that standard, with an average IQ of 90. Their findings imply that IQ scores are related to genetic differences among races.

A number of scientists have noted the faulty reasoning and flawed methods used by Herrnstein and Murray and others, who have inferred IQ differences between African Americans and European Americans or other so-called racial groupings. If there were truly differences in IQ between African Americans and European Americans—accurately reflected, genetically determined differences in intelligence between these two groups—then African Americans with more European ancestry ought to have higher IQ scores than those with less European ancestry. In a major IQ study of hundreds of African Americans that was based on blood testing to determine European ancestry, Scarr and Weinberg (1978) found no significant correlation between IQ scores and the degree of European admixture. More recent studies of ethnic groups around the world demonstrate that most of the documented racial differences in intelligence are a result of environmental factors (Sowell 1994, 1995).

Scholars have tracked IQ scores for various racial and ethnic categories from the early years of the twentieth century. For example, early immigrants to the United States from European nations such as Poland, Italy, and Greece, as well as from Asian countries, including China and Japan, scored ten to fifteen points below long-time U.S. citizens. However, people in these same ethnic categories today—Asian Americans, Polish Americans, Italian Americans, or Greek Americans—have IQ scores that are average or above average. Among Italian Americans, for example, average IQ rose by almost ten points in fifty years; among Polish and Chinese Americans, the rise was almost twenty points. It is obvious that as immigrants settled in the United States, their new cultural and environmental surroundings affected them in ways that improved their performance on IQ tests.

Among African Americans, northerners have historically scored higher than southerners on IQ tests by about ten points. Moreover, the IQ scores of African Americans who migrated from the South to the North after 1940 rose the same way they did among immigrants from abroad. Other studies indicate that middle-class African Americans score higher on IQ tests than do lower-class white Americans. These test scores indicate that cultural patterns matter. African Americans are no less intelligent than other groups but carry a legacy of disadvantage, with a cultural environment that discourages self-confidence and achievement. Most anthropological research on this topic indicates that when differences in socioeconomic status and other factors were controlled for, the difference between African Americans and European Americans was insignificant.

In Japan, a group of people known as the *burakumin,* who exhibit no major physical differences between themselves and other Japanese people but who have been subject to prejudice and discrimination for centuries in their society (see Chapter 13), tend to score lower on IQ tests than other Japanese (Molnar 1997). This difference indicates the strong influence of socioeconomic factors in measuring IQ tests. Additional studies show that educational enrichment programs boost IQ scores (Loehlin, Lindzey, and Spuhler 1975; Molnar 1997). Much research has determined that IQ scores increase within every generation of every population by three to five points, indicating the profound influence of social and educational conditions on IQ scores. The other major criticism of Herrnstein and Murray and like-minded theorists is that they reify the concept of race as if races were based on clear-cut and distinct genetic groups, ignoring the enormous variation within these so-called races.

Most psychologists agree that intelligence is not a readily definable characteristic like height or hair color. Psychologists view intelligence as a general capacity for "goal-directed adaptive behavior"—that is, behavior based on learning from experience, problem solving, and reasoning (Myers 1998). Although this definition of intelligence would be acceptable to most social scientists, we now recognize that some people are talented in mathematics, others in writing, and still others in aesthetic pursuits such as music, art, and dance. Because abilities vary from individual to individual, psychologists such as

Howard Gardner question the view of intelligence as a single factor in human makeup. Based on cross-cultural research, Gardner (1983) has concluded that intelligence does not constitute a single characteristic but rather amounts to a mix of many differing faculties. According to Gardner, each of us has distinct aptitudes for making music, for spatially analyzing the visual world, for mastering athletic skills, and for understanding ourselves and others—a type of social intelligence. Not surprisingly, Gardner concludes that no single test can possibly measure what he refers to as these "multiple intelligences."

The vast majority of anthropologists and other scientists concur with Gardner's findings that intelligence spans a wide and diverse range. The IQ test ranks people according to their performance of various cognitive tasks, especially those that relate to scholastic or academic problem solving. Yet it cannot predict how successfully a person will adapt to specific environmental situations or even handle a particular job. Throughout the world, people draw on various forms of intelligence to perform inventive and creative tasks, ranging from music composition to the development of efficient hunting strategies and other aesthetic and adaptive tasks. Before we call someone "intelligent," we have to know what qualities and abilities are important in that person's environment. Different sorts of cognitive abilities lead to success in a hunting and gathering society, an agricultural society, or an industrial society.

The Cultural and Social Significance of Race

Despite a century of anthropological research in genetics and DNA studies, physical measurements of crania, skin color, and other population data on the topic of race that has demonstrated that this term does not have any precise scientific validity and does not have the biological foundations it is assumed to have, proves that not only is the concept of race very significant in culture and folk classifications in the United States, it is as important throughout the world as well. For example, in Puerto Rico, an island colonized by the Spanish and later by the United States, racial classifications are used to categorize different people by skin color. Puerto Ricans use *blanco* to refer to whites, *prieto* to refer to blacks, and *trigueño* to refer to tan-skinned people. In Brazil, a complex racial classification uses different criteria with which to categorize people. Brazilians do not see or define races in the same way as people in the United States. An individual categorized as "black" in the United States might be categorized as "white" in Brazil (Harris 1964; Gil-White 2004).

Since the nineteenth century in the United States, there is what has been termed the **hypodescent concept** of racial classification. This means that in cases of racial mixture, offspring have the race of the parent with the lowest racial status. Because black Americans were considered to be a lower race, a person is considered black if he or she has a black ancestor anywhere in the family history. This is known as the **one-drop rule** of racial classification because it is based on the myth that one drop of "black blood" is sufficient to determine racial blackness. Thus, Americans with both white and black ancestry are usually classified as black and often encouraged to identify as black in personal and social contexts. In contrast, a person is classified as white if he or she has no black ancestry anywhere in his or her family history. This means that in order to be white, a person has to prove a negative, the absence of black ancestors.

Other racial categories such as *mulatto* (half black and half white), *quadroon* (one-quarter black and three-quarters white), and *octoroon* (one-eighth black and seven-eighths white) were developed to go along with this one-drop rule. Until the 1950s, in Louisiana it was illegal for a doctor to give a blood transfusion from a black person to a white person. Despite the fact that this notion of the one-drop rule is mythical and is based on false notions of "racial essences," these ideas still persist in some circles.

In contrast to the one-drop rule, Native Americans are treated differently in the United States. Because Native Americans have entitlements based on treaties and legislation, the U.S. federal government has sometimes imposed *blood quanta* rules of at least 50 percent ancestry from a particular tribe in order to be classified as a Native American. This rule has created considerable confusion both legally and socially for many Native American peoples.

The one-drop rule and blood quanta tests emphasize that the mythical ideas of *racial essences* are deeply embedded within the folk wisdom and culture of U.S. society. Similar folk conceptions are held about race in other societies. In Northern Ireland, both Protestants and Catholics say that they can identify members of the other group based on physical differences, despite their obvious physical similarities. Anthropologists have long recognized that although these folk conceptions of race are obviously based on arbitrary categories, they have a profound social and cultural significance in many societies.

Ethnicity

In Chapter 3 we discussed the concept of an *ethnic group,* which is a collectivity of people who believe they share a common history, culture, or ancestry. We also discussed how *ethnicity* is based on perceived differences in ancestral origins or descent and shared historical and cultural heritage. However, the terms *ethnicity* and *ethnic group* have had a long history of misinterpretation in Western culture. For example, anthropologist David Maybury-Lewis has noted that "ethnicity has a will-o'-the wisp quality that makes it extremely hard to analyze and not much easier to discuss" (1997, 59). He goes on to say that everyone knows that ethnicity has something to do with a kind of "fellow-feeling" that binds people together and makes them feel distinct from others. Yet it is difficult, if not impossible, he says, to say precisely what kind of feeling it is and why and when people will be affected by it. Under some circumstances, some people are willing to die on behalf of their ethnic group, whereas other people are not strongly preoccupied by their ethnicity in their everyday lives. In some circumstances, people will be classified as members of a particular ethnic group without feeling it or recognizing it themselves. Maybury-Lewis refers to the example of Native American "Indians," who were a diverse group of people before receiving that ethnic label "Indians" from Europeans. Also, the criteria for distinguishing ethnic groups require a complex interpretive process. At times, an ethnic group may be distinguished by language, in other cases by religion, and in other situations by skin color or a shared historical past. But it is also recognized that an ethnic group's shared past is open to reconstruction and reinterpretation in a variety of ways.

This chapter introduces the conceptions of ethnicity that have driven anthropological research and have led to a variety of insights into these complex questions.

One of the fundamental misconceptions in early Western perspectives on race and culture and later "scientific racist" views was the confusion between *race* and *culture.* Purported racial characteristics such as skin color, nose shape, or other traits were associated with particular "essences," which determined behavior and cultural attributes. These misunderstandings were also prevalent in the early usages of the word *ethnicity.* The Greek term *ethnos* (derived from *ethnikos*) was used to refer to non-Greeks, or to *other* peoples who share some biological and cultural characteristics and a common way of life. Later, the word *ethnos,* as used in the Greek New Testament, was associated with non-Jewish and non-Christian peoples and nations referred to as pagans, heathens, and idolaters (Simpson and Weiner 1989).

Eventually, in various European languages, the words *ethnic, ethnical, ethnicity, ethnique,* and *ethnie* corresponded to an association with "race" (Simpson and Weiner 1989). As the field of anthropology (including cultural anthropology or ethnology) developed in the nineteenth century, the usage of ethnology or ethnicity was associated with race. Thus, ethnological studies focused on the scientific investigation of the different "races of mankind." Race, language, and ethnicity were perceived as a fusion of physical and cultural traits by the Western scientists and anthropologists of the nineteenth century.

However, as emphasized before, one of the basic findings based on the research of Franz Boas and later anthropologists is that the "physical characteristics" of a specific group of people are not associated with any particular behavior or culture or language. In other words, one's language or culture is not inherited through biological transmission or genetics. Boas stressed that culture was far more significant in explaining how people in different ethnic groups behaved than any biological factors. One acquires his or her language and culture through *enculturation,* by learning the various language, symbols, values, norms, and beliefs in the environment to which one is exposed.

Since the 1960s, anthropologists and other social scientists have generally used the term *ethnicity* or *ethnic group* to refer to an individual's cultural heritage, which is separate from one's physical characteristics, as indicated in the definition at the beginning of this chapter.

In the modern definition, we emphasize both the objective and subjective aspect of ethnicity. The *objective aspect* of ethnicity is the observable culture and shared symbols of a particular group. It may involve a specific language or religious tradition that is maintained by the group, or it may be particular clothing, hairstyles, preferences in food, or other conspicuous characteristics. The *subjective aspect* of ethnicity involves the internal beliefs of the people regarding their shared ancestry. They may believe that their ethnic group has a shared origin, family ancestry, or common homeland in the past. In some cases, they may believe that their ethnicity has specific physical characteristics in common. This subjective aspect of ethnicity entails a "we-feeling," and a sense of community or oneness, or a distinction between one's own "in-group" versus an "out-group." It doesn't matter whether these beliefs are historically or scientifically accurate, genuine, or fictional. This subjective identification of individuals with an ideology of an (at least imagined) shared history, unique past, and symbolic attachment with a homeland are often the most important expressions of ethnicity (Smith 1986).

Thus, one's ethnicity is not innately determined by biology or purported racial characteristics. Despite early classifications of the "European race" or the "English, German, French, or Polish races," these differences among Europeans were not based on physical differences, but rather on linguistic and cultural variation. Likewise, there is no "African race." Rather, Africa is a continent or area of the world where hundreds of different ethnic groups reside that vary from region to region. The descendants of African slaves residing in the United States have a very different ethnicity than descendants of African slaves who live in the Caribbean Islands. In Asia, the differences among the Chinese, Japanese, Koreans, Thais, Indonesians, Vietnamese, Cambodians, or Laotians are not based on racial differences, but rather on ethnic differences. Although there may be some minor genetic differences among these populations, these genetic differences are slight and do not result in distinctive races. These ethnic groups have different languages, histories, and cultural traditions that create variation among

them. Because ethnicity is based on cultural characteristics, it is much more variable, modifiable, changeable, and—as we will see—more situational, than an identity based on physical characteristics.

Major Anthropological Perspectives on Ethnicity

The Primordialist Model Anthropologists have employed a number of different theoretical strategies to study ethnic groups and processes of ethnicity. One early model that developed in the 1960s is known as the *primordialist model*. The primordialist model of ethnicity is associated with anthropologist Clifford Geertz. Geertz attempted to describe how many Third World countries were trying to build nations and integrate their political institutions based on a "civil order"—a political system based on democratic representation processes rather than traditional ties of kinship or religion. However, as he indicates in the essay, this new civil order clashed with older traditional or "primordial" aspects of kinship, race, ethnicity, language, and religion (1963).

Geertz suggests that ethnic attachments based on assumed kinship and other social ties and religious traditions are deeply rooted within the individual through the enculturation process. He maintains that ethnic affiliation persists because it is fundamental to a person's identity. In this view, as people are enculturated into a particular ethnic group, they form deep emotional attachments to it. These emotional sentiments are sometimes evident through **ethnic boundary markers**, which distinguish one ethnic group from another. These ethnic boundary markers include religion, dress, language or dialect, or other visible symbols. But Geertz tends to focus on the intense internal aspects of ethnicity and the deep subjective "feeling of belonging" to a particular ethnic group. This is one of the strengths of the primordialist perspective on ethnicity. It emphasizes the meaning and significance that people invest in their ethnic attachments. Geertz emphasizes how the "assumed givens" are subjective perceptions of attributes such as blood ties and ancestry, which may or may not coincide with the actual circumstances of one's birth. Geertz went on to say that the primordial ties are experienced by the people of these new Third World nations, and that despite the introduction of new forms of civil political institutions and ideologies, these ethnic attachments endure and are at times obstacles, as new nations attempt to integrate their societies based on a new political civil order. He suggests that there is a basic conflict between the modern state and one's personal identity based on these primordial ties.

Another proponent of the primordialist model is Joshua Fishman. In an essay entitled "Social Theory and Ethnography," he says:

Ethnicity has always been experienced as a kinship phenomenon, a continuity within the self and within those who share an intergenerational link to common ancestors. Ethnicity is partly experienced as being "bone of their bone, flesh of their flesh, and blood of their blood." The human body itself is viewed as an expression of ethnicity, and ethnicity is commonly felt to be in the blood, bones, and flesh. It is crucial that we recognize ethnicity as a tangible, living reality that makes every human a link in an eternal bond from generation to generation—from past ancestors to those in the future. Ethnicity is experienced as a guarantor of eternity. (1980, 84–97)

The Circumstantialist Model Another model of ethnicity began to surface within anthropology during the 1960s based on research on multiethnic societies. *Ethnic Groups and Boundaries,* a book by anthropologist Frederick Barth, described a new approach to ethnicity (1969). In a number of case studies in this book, Barth noted the fluidity of ethnic relations in different types of multiethnic societies. Although ethnic groups maintain boundaries such as language to mark their identity, people may modify and shift their language and ethnic identity in different types of social interaction. He criticized a view of culture based on earlier anthropological research in small-scale societies that tended to treat ethnic groups as having discrete, impermeable boundaries. Barth emphasized the interaction between ethnic groups and how people identify with different elements of their own ethnicity and express or repress these elements and characteristics in different circumstances for economic, political, or other practical interests. This approach is sometimes referred to as the *instrumentalist approach* to ethnicity, but it has become known widely in anthropology as the *circumstantialist model* of ethnicity.

In the circumstantialist approach, Barth emphasizes how ethnic boundary markers such as language, clothing, or other cultural traits are not based on deeply rooted, enduring aspects of ethnicity. Ethnic boundaries are continually being revised, negotiated, and redefined according to the practical interests of actors. Ethnic boundaries are generated by the varying contexts and circumstances in which people find themselves. For example, in the United States, people of German descent may refer to themselves as German Americans to distinguish themselves from Irish Americans or Italian Americans. Should they happen to be among Europeans, however, these same people might refer to themselves simply as Americans. The circumstantialist model explains how people draw on their ethnic identity for specific economic, social, and political purposes. People strategically use their ethnic affiliations as the basis of collective political mobilization or to enhance their economic interests. Barth demonstrates how some people modify and change their ethnic identity when it is perceived to be advantageous for their own interests. They may emphasize the ethnic or racial identities of others or establish boundaries between themselves and others in order to define themselves differently and interact with others for political or economic purposes. Thus, in Barth's view, ethnicity is not fixed and unchanging but is instead fluid and contingent, as people strategically use, define, and redefine their ethnicity to respond to their immediate basic needs.

Barth's analysis of ethnicity illustrates how individuals within ethnic groups that adapt to specific types of economic and political circumstances in a multiethnic society may emphasize their shared identity as a means of enhancing cooperation with other members of the group. Throughout the world, individuals migrating to different areas often use ethnic ties as a means of social adjustment. Individuals may pursue political interests through ethnic allegiances. In numerous situations, people may manipulate ethnic traditions and symbols to their advantage.

This circumstantialist view of ethnicity also asserts that ethnicity will be displayed to a different degree by various ethnic groups. Ethnic traits will vary from one historical time to another, and group identity may shift from one generation to another. Ethnic groups are not stable collective entities. They may appear and vanish within a generation or less than a generation. Ethnic groups will come into being during different historical periods.

Ethnogenesis refers to the origins of an ethnic group. Ethnogenesis has taken place throughout the world in many different historical circumstances. For example, the English, Germans, French, and other major ethnic groups went through this process in Europe. They began to define themselves as distinctive ethnic groups, which is what is meant by ethnogenesis. Ethnogenesis is a continual, ongoing sociocultural and political process that began in prehistory and continues today for many people.

Over the years, most contemporary anthropologists have drawn from both the primordialist and circumstantialist models to explain or interpret ethnicity. Both models have clarified the nuances of ethnic identity throughout the world. The primordialist model has been extremely useful in substantiating the persistence of ethnicity, whereas the circumstantialist model has helped demonstrate how ethnic identity can be altered and constructed in various economic and political conditions. Today, many contemporary anthropologists occupy a middle ground between these positions because they pay close attention to the detailed manner in which ethnicity may be both primordial and circumstantial.

Anthropologists today investigate how societal conditions may impinge on how people define themselves ethnically. What are the ethnic categories that have enduring meaningfulness and purpose for people, and under what circumstances are those categories asserted, negotiated, reaffirmed, or repressed? Also, to what extent and to what ends are the elements of ethnicity "invented" and "imagined" by ethnic groups? Anthropologists have to provide a detailed understanding of the ethnogenesis of a particular ethnic group. How does an ethnic group come to construct a shared sense of identity? What are the particulars of this ethnic identity? Is most ethnicity tied to religion? Or is it based on common ancestors or shared myths of common history and territory? Furthermore, anthropologists find it necessary to understand the global and local economic and political dynamics and processes that affect ethnic relations in continually changing societies. Globalization, government policies, the labor market, urbanization, and other aspects of the political economy have a profound influence on how ethnicity is expressed in different societies.

Patterns of Ethnic Relations

Pluralism

In the book *Pluralism in Africa,* a number of anthropologists described a **plural society** as one in which different groups are internally distinguished from each other by institutional and cultural differences (Kuper and Smith 1969). Instead of one identical system of institutions shared within a society, a plural society consists of ethnic groups that differ in social organization, beliefs, norms, and ideals. Building on this framework, anthropologists have utilized the phrase *cultural pluralism* to describe how various ethnic groups maintain diverse cultures within one society. The example of the Amish in U.S. society exemplifies cultural pluralism. In contrast, *institutional pluralism* is the phrase used to refer to how different ethnic groups may have a similar culture but maintain separate institutions, including schools, churches, businesses, and other organizations within a society. These ethnic groups may share the same language, dietary practices, and subscribe to the same values and beliefs but have minimal social interaction with other ethnic groups. In the United States the Mormon religious community exemplifies this type of institutional pluralism.

Different forms of plural societies are based on the political order and legal institutions. In some forms of plural societies, ethnic groups not only are divided culturally and structurally, but they are also organized in highly unequal political relationships. We term such societies *radically plural* societies. In radically plural societies, a minority ethnic group rules other ethnic groups through coercion. The state or government rules as an agent to protect the interests of the dominant ethnic group. The subordinate ethnic groups are treated as "subjects" rather than "citizens." This results in an ethnic hierarchy, with the dominant ethnic group in control of the political, economic, and prestigious social positions within the society. Some radically plural societies evolved in early ancient agricultural civilizations. However, these forms of radically plural societies developed in more recent times under European colonialism in many parts of Latin America, the Caribbean, Africa, the Middle East, and Asia, as described in the last three chapters. These radically plural societies had a European elite that ruled through control of the political economy and the legal institutions of these colonized regions. Typically, these inegalitarian plural societies usually resulted in divisive ethnic conflict and strained ethnic relationships.

Other forms of plural societies, sometimes referred to as *consociational plural societies,* are based on more egalitarian relationships among ethnic groups. In these plural societies, the government protects the structural and cultural differences among the ethnic groups. These ethnic groups are formally recognized by the state and legal institutions to allocate political rights and economic opportunities proportionally. Each ethnic group has a great deal of political autonomy, and, in theory, there is no politically dominant ethnic group. In Europe, Switzerland is often used as an example of a plural society, where different ethnic groups have distinctive cultures, but they have parity or equality with each other. Switzerland consists of French, Italian, German, and Romansh ethnic groups, and they all have relatively similar political and economic opportunities. Another European country, Belgium, is also known as an egalitarian plural society, in which the population is divided into two major ethnic groups: the Dutch-speaking Flemish and the French-speaking Walloons. In such plural societies, ethnic groups have the legal and political right to maintain their own language, educational systems, and culture. A balance of power is often reached among the different ethnic groups according to a political formula that grants each group a proportional representation of the multiethnic population. As expected, cultural pluralism endures and remains stable in these ethnically egalitarian societies, resulting in relatively amicable relationships.

Many plural societies today fall between the inegalitarian radically plural and egalitarian consociational forms. Following decolonization in most of the countries of Latin America, Africa, the Middle East, and Asia, the radically plural forms of society were dislodged. The European elites were replaced by indigenous elites in these postcolonial societies. However, as we see in later chapters, these societies remained pluralistic because they comprised many different ethnic groups. In some cases, the indigenous elites represented one particular ethnic group and perpetuated a continuation of radically plural politics. In other situations, new indigenous-based governments developed policies to manage competition and rivalry among different ethnic groups. This resulted, under some conditions, in another form and pattern of interethnic relations known as assimilation.

Assimilation

Assimilation is a process of ethnic boundary reduction that may come about when two or more ethnic groups come into contact with each other. One or more ethnic groups adopt the culture, values, beliefs, and norms of another ethnic group. The process of assimilation results in similarity of culture and homogeneity among ethnic groups. As would be expected, assimilation occurs more easily when the physical and cultural characteristics of the different ethnic groups are more similar from the beginnings of contact. Anthropologists have been engaged in research to determine whether these general factors are valid in different societal and cultural contexts. But in order to refine their research, anthropologists distinguish different forms of assimilation: *cultural assimilation* and *biological assimilation.*

Cultural assimilation involves one ethnic group's adoption of the culture traits, including language, religion, clothing styles, diet, and other norms, values, and beliefs, of another group. Sometimes anthropologists use the term *acculturation* to refer to the tendency of distinct cultural groups to borrow words, technology, clothing styles, foods, values, norms, and behavior from each other. Generally, cultural assimilation and acculturation have slightly different meanings to anthropologists. Cultural assimilation involves a subordinate ethnic minority adopting *some* of the culture of another ethnic group, whereas acculturation refers to the overall adjustment and adaptation of the group to the dominant ethnic group. Obviously, the process of cultural assimilation or acculturation has been going on since the earliest days of humanity and continues today.

As groups came in contact with one another, they borrowed from each other's cultures. Anthropologists, however, find that cultural assimilation or acculturation can be a very complex process for many ethnic groups. These processes may vary, depending on government policies and other societal conditions. For example, some cultural assimilation

Guatemalan women wear particular types of clothing to exhibit their ethnic traditions.

may be voluntary, wherein a particular ethnic group may choose to embrace the culture of another group. Many ethnic groups who immigrate into a particular society adopt the culture of the ethnically dominant group to secure their political rights and economic prospects. In some societies, government and educational policies may encourage groups to assimilate the culture of the dominant ethnic group. During different historical periods, the policies of many governments such as the United States, France, Mexico, Nigeria, Israel, or China have promoted cultural assimilation on a voluntary basis within their societies.

Conversely, under some historical conditions, governments may require nonvoluntary, or *forced, cultural assimilation.* This is where the government forces ethnic groups to take on the culture of the dominant ethnic group of the society. Anthropologists sometimes refer to forced cultural assimilation as *ethnocide,* which implies the killing of the

culture of a particular ethnic group (see Chapter 6). Ethnocide demands an ethnic group to abandon their language, religion, or other cultural norms, values, and beliefs and adopt the culture of the dominant group. This process of ethnocide occurred in various ancient agricultural civilizations, such as Egypt, India, China, Rome, and the Aztecs. As these agricultural civilizations expanded and conquered territories and other ethnic groups, at times they forced these other ethnic groups to assimilate and adopt the culture of the dominant ethnic group.

This pattern of induced ethnocide was also prevalent during more modern forms of colonialism. For example, as Europeans colonized areas of Latin America, or the Japanese colonized areas in Asia such as Taiwan, or the United States colonized the region of North America, indigenous peoples were often forced to assimilate. This type of forced assimilation is usually extremely difficult for individuals. They have to forsake their own language and cultural traits to become a part of a different, often antagonistic set of values and beliefs. As was seen in earlier chapters, forced cultural assimilation and ethnocide continues to influence many contemporary patterns of ethnic relations.

Biological assimilation refers to the process of intermarriage and reproduction among different ethnic groups resulting in the development of a new ethnic group. This is also known as *amalgamation,* or the biological merging of formerly distinct ethnic groups. The process of biological assimilation has been taking place for thousands of years as different groups have been intermarrying and reproducing with each other. Usually intermarriage among ethnic groups occurs after a great deal of cultural and structural assimilation following extensive interethnic contact. Thus, ethnic boundaries have usually been extensively reduced, if not eliminated, when intermarriage takes place. The degree of biological assimilation may range from a society where there are no longer any cultural and biological distinctions among the population to societies where new forms of ethnicity develop. Historically, in the United States intermarriage among different European Americans (descendants of English, Irish, German, Italian, Polish) have reduced most meaningful ethnic boundaries. On the other hand, as is seen in Chapter 14 on Latin America and the Caribbean, new forms of ethnicity emerged as intermarriage took place among Europeans, native populations, and African slaves.

Anthropologists have identified three other patterns of ethnic interaction. One is **segregation**, or the physical and social separation of categories of people. Segregation was the policy of many southern states in the United States following the abolition of slavery until the civil rights movements of the 1950s and 1960s. **Jim Crow laws** were developed, which resulted in the creation of separate facilities and institutions for African Americans and white Americans. There were segregated schools, restaurants, drinking fountains, restrooms, parks, neighborhoods, and other areas. Until recently, the South African government had similar laws to segregate the races and ethnic groups within its legal constitution.

Another pattern of ethnic interaction is *ethnic cleansing,* the attempt to remove an ethnic group from its location and territory within a society. Recently, the Serbs attempted to bring about ethnic cleansing and remove ethnic groups such as the Bosnians from different regions of Yugoslavia. In East Africa, former ruler Idi Amin expelled East Indian immigrants from Uganda for economic and political reasons. Following the Vietnam War, in 1975 the Vietnamese government encouraged the migration of more than one million ethnic Chinese from their country. These people were abruptly eliminated as an ethnic minority, despite the fact that many had assimilated into Vietnamese society. In the past, the U.S. government removed Native Americans from their territories, a process of ethnic cleansing that resulted in reservation life for these ethnic groups.

Finally, the third pattern of ethnic interaction is known as *genocide,* the systematic attempt to kill and totally eliminate a particular ethnic group. Genocide may overlap with ethnic cleansing. In both the cases of the U.S. government and Native Americans and the Serbs and the Bosnians, removal policies were often combined with more deadly policies of genocide. When the British colonized Australia, native populations such as the Tasmanians were exterminated. There were 5,000 Tasmanians in 1800, but as a result of being attacked by the British, the last full-blooded Tasmanian died in 1876. In the settling of South Africa by the Dutch,

indigenous populations such as the Hottentots were systematically killed off. In the twentieth century, the most horrific forms of genocide befell European Jews and other ethnic groups under Adolf Hitler's reign of terror. The Nazi Party murdered about 6 million Jews and millions of other ethnic groups, including 6 million Polish people and many European gypsies. In Cambodia, the communist ruler Pol Pot killed as many as 2 million people (one-fourth of the population) in what have become known as the "killing fields." Ethnic minorities, such as people with Chinese ancestry or Muslims, were favored targets in this genocidal campaign (Kiernan 1988). In 1994, in the country of Rwanda in Central Africa, the majority ethnic group (the Hutus) slaughtered some half a million ethnic Tutsis within a few weeks. Although genocidal policies have been condemned by recognized moral standards throughout the world, they have occurred time and again in human history.

Ethnic Relations in the United States

To illustrate the dynamics of ethnic relations, we focus on U.S. society. We begin with an overview of the early English settlers to America, or the so-called WASP ethnic group, which provided the basic cultural heritage for U.S. society. In addition, we examine the patterns of non-WASP immigration from Europe in the nineteenth century and the consequences of this immigration for U.S. society.

WASP Dominance

The early European colonization of what was to become the United States begins with the so-called WASPs, or white Anglo-Saxon Protestants. The term *WASP* has come to refer to the ethnic group with a particular cultural and institutional complex that dominated U.S. society for generations. The British settlers were able to overcome their rivals—the French, Spanish, and Dutch in colonial America—and were free to develop their own form of culture. With the exception of the Native Americans and enslaved African Americans, four out of five colonial settlers in America were British Protestants. Smaller groups of settlers included Scots and Welsh, as well as Scotch-Irish (Protestants from Northern Ireland), Dutch, Germans, and Scandinavians. Although Anglo-American leaders such as Benjamin Franklin expressed fears of these non-English-speaking people with different cultures such as the Germans as taking over Anglo American culture, by the end of the seventeenth century, these early non-Anglo settlers assimilated, culturally and structurally, becoming a part of the core WASP ethnic group that became dominant.

WASP ethnicity became preeminent in the United States through the establishment of its language, symbols, and culture. The English language was the fundamental underpinning of the cultural legacy that was bestowed by the WASPs on American society. It became the acceptable written and spoken language for the building of the nation-state and country, and it represented the standard for creating ethnic identity in colonial America. English was the institutional language of education, politics, and religion among the WASPs. From the early establishment of WASP culture, the expectation held that any subsequent ethnic groups that came to America would have to learn the English language. This was the first stage of what has sometimes been referred to as *Anglo-conformity*.

Along with the English language, the WASP brought their basic fabric of the economic, legal, and political institutional framework for U.S. society. One of the primary reasons for colonization of North America by the British settlers was to extract raw materials and to produce new markets for England. Commercial capitalism, including the right to own private property, was brought to America by the English settlers. The initiatives for taking land from Native Americans, for developing European forms of agriculture—including the importation of slaves—and for sending raw materials across the Atlantic were all aspects of the market-oriented capitalism that was transported from England to America. Following the American Revolution, this market-oriented capitalism became the cornerstone of the expansion of the Industrial Revolution in the United States. As the principal ethnic group engaged in the development of commercial capitalism and the Industrial Revolution, the WASPs were able to dominate and manage the major economic capitalist institutions in U.S. society. At present, some 33 million people trace their descent to these English settlers.

New Ethnic Challenges for U.S. Society

The nineteenth century saw an enormous number of non-Anglos flowing in from other areas of the world that would begin to challenge the Anglo dominance of U.S. society. More than 30 million non-Anglo European immigrants would come to the United States in the nineteenth century. Many were non-Protestants, maintaining either Catholic or Jewish religious traditions. In addition, especially in respect to those ethnic groups from southern and eastern Europe, these people spoke different languages that were historically far removed from the English language. As we saw in our earlier discussion, many of these people were viewed as inferior, and there were exclusive immigration policies to keep them out of the United States.

German and Irish Americans

Since the seventeenth century, approximately 7 million people born in the area now known as Germany settled in North America. Currently, more Americans trace their ancestry to Germany than any other country. Although it is difficult to assess these numbers precisely, some 46 to 50 million Americans are descendants of Germans (2000 Census 2002) out of approximately 274 million people. Many of the German migrants entering the United States were urban-based peoples skilled in crafts, trades, or the professions. Some of these immigrants were German Jewish migrants who were adapting along with other Germans to the booming cities of New York, Cincinnati, St. Louis, Chicago, Pittsburgh, Milwaukee, Indianapolis, and Louisville. Located along waterways or railways, these were attractive sites for urban skills (Glazier 2003). Breweries, bakeries, distilleries, flour millers, tailor shops, print shops, surveying businesses, and plumbing stores were developed by these immigrants. A number of well-educated immigrants who had fled Germany for political reasons became important political activists and officials of the U.S. government. Thus, nineteenth-century German American ethnic communities included both skilled and unskilled laborers. Because of their numbers and the occupational diversity of their population, German Americans could develop extremely self-sufficient communities.

As the numbers of immigrants from Germany increased, rather than assimilating quickly into American society, many attempted to retain their ethnic identity, including their language, culture, and religious traditions. Many of these German immigrants wanted to conserve their ethnic and nationalist identity within the United States. Aside from German-language schools and churches, they began to establish ethnically based organizations such as music societies, theater clubs, beer halls, lodges, and political clubs. Through these organizations and institutions, as well as the private schools and churches in specific neighborhoods, various "Little Germanies" emerged in major cities such as St. Louis, Cincinnati, and Milwaukee. The endeavor to preserve German culture in the United States even led to a proposal to establish an exclusive German state in the Union (Adams 1993; Cornell and Hartmann 1998).

The major influx of Irish immigrants into the United States came during the nineteenth century. Today, some 33 million persons in the United States trace their ancestry to the Irish (2000 Census 2002). As the Irish Catholics settled in the United States, they adapted within many different types of occupations, skilled and professional. Because many of the Irish came with little education and capital, they were forced to take the lowest-wage jobs in factories, mines, mills, construction of railways and canals, and other unskilled occupations. For example, large numbers of Irish workers were employed in the construction of the Erie Canal in New York State. Later, Irish labor was used to build the intercontinental railroad across the United States. Others worked in foundries, railway locomotive factories and repair shops, furniture factories, boat-building shops, breweries, and other unskilled industries. Many Irish women began to work as domestic servants for WASP households or in the textile mills and factories in eastern cities such as New York and Boston.

As Irish and German immigration increased in the nineteenth century, xenophobic sentiments (fear of foreigners) helped usher in nativistic movements among WASPs. In particular, Roman Catholicism associated with the Irish was perceived to be untrustworthy. A political party known as the Know-Nothings developed. (They were known as Know-Nothings because party members were instructed to divulge nothing about their political program and to say they knew nothing about it.) Much of the Know-Nothing Party activity was aimed at the Irish, who were unwelcome because they were non-WASP and Roman Catholic. The Know-Nothing program aimed to elect only WASPs to political office, to fight against Roman Catholicism, and to restrict citizenship and voting rights to immigrants who had resided in the United States twenty-one years instead of the five years required by law. The Irish Catholics were perceived to be a "separate race" and were purported to have a distinctive biology that made them different from the WASPs. Members of the "Irish race" were perceived by the WASPs as undesirables who were immoral, unintelligent, uncouth, dirty, lazy, ignorant, temperamental, hostile, and addicted to alcohol. In cities such as Boston and New York, there were signs in storefronts, housing complexes, and factories saying "No Irish Need Apply."

During World War I and World War II, extensive anti-German prejudice and discrimination emerged within American society. As a reaction to these anti-German sentiments, rapid cultural assimilation began to dominate the German American communities. For example, German surnames and German business names were Anglicized.

Italian and Polish Americans

Many southern and eastern European ethnic groups—Greeks, Italians, Serbians, Hungarians, Bulgarians, Russians, Ukrainians, and Poles—began to immigrate to the United States between 1880 and 1915. The United States was undergoing an unprecedented economic and industrial transformation that demanded large reserves of labor. Industrial expansion in the garment industries, food processing, mining, construction, and other manufacturing and services offered opportunities for people from southern and eastern Europe. Approximately two-thirds of the foreign-born population that came into the United States during this period were from these regions.

Unlike the northern European groups such as the Germans or Irish, these new immigrants had languages and cultures that were far and away much different from those of prior immigrants. Today, more than 15 million Americans trace their ancestry to Italy (U.S. Census Bureau 2000). Many of the early Italian immigrants had come through a form of indentured labor known as the *padrone system*. A *padrone*, or boss, would recruit laborers in Italy, pay for their passage to the United States, and arrange work for them, mostly in construction. Other Italian immigrants came through "chain-migration," relying on kinship networks. As Roman Catholics, they used the church organizations and other voluntary mutual-aid societies to help them adapt to the new conditions in America. Because of these ties, eventually these immigrants began to perceive themselves as having a common identity as Italian Americans (Alba 1985). This new identity created the foundation for "Little Italys" in different urban areas such as New York, Boston, Chicago, and St. Louis.

Like many others from Europe, people from Poland were pushed and pulled by economic, political, and religious factors that influenced their decision to immigrate to America. Polish peasants (together with some members of the Polish middle class and intelligentsia) began to seek a new way of life in the United States. Letters from relatives and friends in America advertised high wages and employment opportunities in America. In addition, class, political, and religious oppression from occupying ruling empires propelled Polish immigration to America. Poles with sufficient funds could buy transatlantic tickets, whereas others depended on their relatives to provide kinship connections

through the process of chain migration for their re-settlement in America.

Although about 3 of every 10 migrants returned to Poland, today about 9 million Americans trace their descent to Polish ancestry (U.S. Census Bureau 2000). Many of the Polish immigrants were taken to coal-mining towns like Scranton, Wilkes-Barre, Windber, and Hazelton in Pennsylvania or the steel manufacturing cities of Pittsburgh and Cleveland. Other midwestern cities, such as Toledo, Milwaukee, Minneapolis, St. Louis, Chicago, and Detroit, attracted Poles who were seeking work in the mills, slaughterhouses, foundries, refineries, and factories. In 1920 Chicago had 400,000 Poles, New York, 200,000, Pittsburgh, 200,000, Buffalo, 100,000, Milwaukee, 100,000, and Detroit, 100,000 (Greene 1980). In these towns and cities, Polish immigrants founded neighborhoods and communities known individually and collectively as "Polonia" (Latin for Poland).

With the unprecedented immigration into the United States from southern and eastern Europe in the first two decades of the twentieth century, Italians and the Poles were subjected to severe discrimination and prejudice from many Americans. As we saw before, nativistic movements, beliefs in the superiority of the Anglo-Saxons, and anti-Catholicism were developing at this time. Like the Irish, the Italians and Poles were categorized by

An Italian American family.

many WASPs as a different "race" that was inferior intellectually and morally to the Anglo-Saxons. But this construction of an "Italian race" or "Polish race" was even more severely restrictive than that applied to the Irish. An Anglo-Saxon-based racialism, which was linked to "scientific racism" in the 1880s and 1890s, grew in the United States as a reaction to the immigration of southern and eastern European peoples. The "Italian race" and "Polish race," as well as other southern and eastern European "races" such as Jews, were classified as inferior in contrast to the northern European "races."

As mentioned before, IQ tests and literacy tests were also given to these early Italian and Polish migrants; as expected, these people scored lower than the "average" American. These IQ and literacy tests were used as purported scientific proof of these new immigrants' inferior intellect (Kamin 1974). These racist beliefs were promoted by the media and other "scientific" works of the time. Anglo-Saxon Americans were warned not to intermarry with Italians and Poles because it would cause the degeneration of the "race." The Italian and Polish "races" were identified with correlates of behavior such as jealous, overly emotional, rough, mean, dirty, lazy, and other negative characteristics.

Despite the racial prejudice and discrimination they faced, the German, Irish, Italian, and Polish American communities were able to adjust to their circumstances through organized efforts in economic and political activities. They joined unions and organized political parties to cope with discrimination and prejudice, and the second and third generations of these non-Anglo immigrants began to assimilate culturally into U.S. society.

The Melting Pot: Assimilation or Pluralism?

As we saw earlier, U.S. society was challenged dramatically by the massive immigration of non-Anglo populations in the nineteenth and early twentieth centuries. Questions were raised about whether German, Jewish, Irish, Italian, or Polish immigrants could really become "Americans." Nativistic groups such as the Know-Nothings and the American Protective Association directed prejudice and discrimination at these immigrants. This prejudice against

Catholicism and other ethnic traits, including language and purported race, eventually resulted in restrictive immigration policies. During this same period, state and local authorities began to restrict the use of languages other than English in schools and to require all teachers to be U.S. citizens. Government policies promoted the use of the public school system to "Americanize" and assimilate the various non-Anglo immigrants.

One of the popular manifestations of these policies of assimilation evolving in U.S. society was the concept of "The Melting Pot." This became the popular symbol of ethnic interaction in the United States during the early twentieth century. The term *melting pot* was associated with a play by a Jewish immigrant, Israel Zangwill, called *The Melting Pot,* which had a long run in New York in 1909. Zangwill's play focused on the life of a Jewish immigrant who believed that the Old World nationalities and languages ought to be forgotten in the United States and that all ethnic elements should fuse together in the creation of a new and superior American nationality and ethnicity (Gleason 1980). This was not a new idea, but it was popularized at this time as a response to anti-immigration and antiforeign attitudes of the nativist movements. The melting pot ideal implied that the new "American ethnicity" would represent only the best qualities and attributes of the different cultures contributing to U.S. society. It became a plea for toleration of the different immigrants as they poured into American society. It was assumed that the American ideals of equality and opportunity for material improvement would automatically transform foreigners into Americans. It also suggested that the Anglo or WASP ethnicity was itself being transformed into a more comprehensive, global type of an American ethnic identity.

Despite the tolerant tone, universal appeal, and openness of the metaphor of the melting pot, it still emphasized assimilation. The belief that immigrants must shed their European ethnic identity and adopt a "Yankee" ethnic identity was at the heart of this concept. The second generation of Germans, Jews, Irish, Italians, and Poles thus tended to assimilate into the Anglo-American culture of the majority. Economic, social, and political benefits accrued to these "white ethnics" upon assimilation. To pursue the American Dream, the white ethnics assimilated culturally and structurally into the fabric of American society. As older ethnic neighborhoods and communities declined, most white ethnics abandoned their traditional languages and cultures. The metaphor of the melting pot appeared to have some validity, at least for most of these white ethnics. A substantial number of white ethnics had sloughed off their ethnic traditions to adapt to American society. For example, many Jewish celebrities changed their names, including Tony Curtis (Bernie Schwartz), Doris Day (Doris Kapplehoff), and Kirk Douglas (Issur Daneilovitch) (Glazier 2003).

Along with this assimilationist trend in U.S. society, the crystallization of the race concept of "whiteness" was reinforced. Eventually, the people who came from Ireland, Germany, Italy, Poland, and other European countries became "white Caucasians," in contrast to other ethnic minorities (Jacobson 1998). For many Americans, "whiteness" became a new socially constructed category of race that differentiated these Europeans from non-Europeans in the United States. Native Americans, African Americans, Hispanic Americans, and Asian Americans were nonwhites and thereby were excluded from the institutional benefits and privileges of people with white identities. Although there were some who still referred to the Anglo-WASP racial category, the enlarged category of a "white identity" assigned to Europeans tended to become part of the racial consciousness of U.S. society.

African Americans

Although people of African descent have been involved in peopling and building civilization in the United States for as long as Europeans, there are various misrepresentations and stereotypes about African Americans that have been perpetuated by the media and held by many U.S. citizens. For example, contrary to these stereotypes, two-thirds of African Americans are working class and middle class and above and are not living in poverty conditions. Today, African Americans constitute about 13 percent of the population, or about 34 million people (2000 Census 2002).

The majority of African Americans trace their ethnic history to the slave-trading activities that brought approximately 500,000 West and Central Africans to the United States beginning in the seventeenth century. As we will see in Chapter 14, millions more were brought to Latin America and the

Caribbean. Slaves were chained together on sailing ships for a trip across the Atlantic Ocean, and many of them were killed by disease and filthy conditions aboard the European ships. The first slaves were auctioned off in 1619 in Jamestown, Virginia. Slavery was the foundation of the plantation system. Slavery was used both in the north and south United States prior to the American Revolution due to labor shortages. The first colony to legalize slavery was Massachusetts in 1641. The people of West and Central Africa were experienced farmers, skilled at iron smelting, cattle herding, and textile manufacture, and thus were viewed as valuable "commodities" by plantation owners (Brown 2003). Slave labor was used for the benefit of the white plantation owners to plant and harvest their crops from daybreak to sunset and even longer. Slave families were often divided when these humans were bought and sold in public auctions. Despite this attack against the family unit, most slaves practiced marriage and attempted to maintain the family as much as possible (Brown 2003). The southern laws

An African American family.

enabled owners to treat their slaves as property and to discipline them in any way they desired to produce obedience and productivity. Although some slaves managed to resist and rebel against their oppression, the military and political power mustered by their owners disallowed the slaves to have any real control over their destinies.

Anthropologist Melville Herskovits did extensive studies of African Americans in the United States. As a student of Franz Boas, he debunked many racist notions that maintained that African Americans were an inferior race (Brown 2003). Herskovits had a deep knowledge of African cultures and societies and demonstrated that African Americans were neither inferior nor a people without a past. He and other anthropologists provided a foundation for understanding the unique and substantial contribution that African Americans have made to U.S. society.

Not all African Americans were slaves. Some were "free blacks" who had earned their freedom by working in nonagricultural professions in the urban areas, primarily in the north. Many free blacks were descendants of runaway slaves or had purchased their freedom through their own labor. Many African Americans managed to adapt to their condition in the United States by maintaining their own Christian churches, which became the center for social life in their communities. Thus, the culture of African Americans was forged in both slave and free conditions (Brown 2003). They developed their own unique music and gospel singing that persists until the present, and they introduced many foods and agricultural and skilled techniques such as cattle herding that were brought from Africa.

Postslavery and Segregation Following the Civil War in 1865, the Thirteenth Amendment to the U.S. Constitution outlawed slavery. The Fourteenth Amendment granted citizenship to all people born in the United States. The Fifteenth Amendment, ratified in 1870, stated that neither race nor previous condition of slavery should deprive anyone of the right to vote. Despite these amendments to the Constitution, African Americans found that obstacles were created to prevent them from becoming equal citizens under the law. In particular, southern states began to disenfranchise blacks legally by passing state laws denying them access to equal education.

Laws that segregated U.S. society into two "racial castes" were referred to as *Jim Crow laws*.

If African Americans resisted segregation laws that upheld separate schools, restaurants, drinking fountains, restrooms, parks, churches, and other institutions, they were beaten and sometimes lynched. Between 1882 and 1927, almost 3,500 African Americans were lynched. Southern whites justified these lynchings as a form of social control. Organizations such as the Ku Klux Klan and the White Citizens Councils conducted lynchings, violence, and intimidation against African Americans. Tired of suffering these deprivations in the southern areas, many African Americans began to move to northern cities for newly developing jobs in industry and other enterprises. However, even in northern cities, African Americans often found prejudice and discrimination awaited them.

The Civil Rights Movement Following World War II, many African American males who had fought in segregated divisions for U.S. society recognized that they did not have the individual freedoms and equal opportunities for which they had fought. In the 1950s and 1960s many African Americans, sometimes assisted by white Americans, began to participate in a massive civil rights movement for individual freedoms and equal opportunities as idealized within the American Constitution. In southern towns and cities African Americans began what were called "sit-ins" in segregated restaurants, bus boycotts against segregated buses, and other protests led by leaders such as the Reverend Martin Luther King. The civil rights movement often faced brutal violence, bombings of black churches, arrests, and intimidation. Some African American leaders such as Malcolm X of the Nation of Islam and Eldridge Cleaver of the Black Panthers called for armed defense against police brutality and violence against their communities. As a result of the civil rights movement and other protests, a number of civil rights bills were passed that provided for more individual rights, equal opportunity, and the breakdown of the Jim Crow laws.

African Americans Today Despite the considerable gains of African Americans following the civil rights movement, a disproportionate number of their communities are in poverty when compared to white U.S. citizens. During the 1980s, earnings declined for many African Americans as factory jobs and other industries closed in the United States (Wilson 1980). Thus, African American unemployment, especially among young black teenagers, rose considerably. Although African Americans have made tremendous strides in educational achievement since the 1960s, black college graduates are still half of the average national standard in the United States. These factors have left many young African Americans in inner cities susceptible to crime, drug addiction, and other dysfunctional behaviors. The destiny of the African American community in the twenty-first century will inevitably be influenced by a continued struggle for equality and individual rights and against racism (Brown 2003; Shanafelt 2004).

Hispanic Americans

The 2000 Census reported that the Hispanic/Latino population has had the largest demographic increase compared with any other ethnic group in the United States. The Hispanic/Latino population is approximately 34.3 million people, or more than 13 percent of the U.S. population, which is larger in size than the African American populace (2000 Census 2002).

The terms *Hispanic* and *Latino* are umbrella terms that include many diverse people (Bigler 2003). They include descendants of Mexican Americans (20 million), Puerto Rican Americans (3.4 million), Cuban Americans (1.2 million), and smaller groups of Dominican Americans, Mayan Indians, Peruvians, and other Central and South American immigrants and their descendants. These Hispanics or Latinos comprise a cluster of distinct populations, each of which identifies with groups that are associated with different countries or regions of origin. Hispanics or Latinos do not constitute a particular "racial" group. Skin coloration, hair texture, facial features, and physical appearance vary considerably among and within these different populations.

Most of the U.S. Hispanic and Latino population live in the southwest. Following the Mexican American War (1846–1848), the U.S. government annexed the areas now known as California, Colorado, New Mexico, Nevada, Utah, most of Arizona, and Texas. This area was known as *Aztlan* (home of the original Aztecs) to the Mexican population and represented half of Mexican territory. The influx of Anglos into these regions following the gold rush and the development of ranching, mining, and other activities rapidly made the Mexicans minorities within these new states of the United States. Although

A Hispanic American family.

these Mexican minorities were promised equal rights if they chose to become American citizens, they were discriminated against by laws enacted by Anglo-dominated legislatures (Takaki 1990). They also faced assaults and lynchings similar to those abuses faced by African Americans. Many Mexican Americans lost their lands and found themselves surrounded by Anglo-Americans who maintained racist and ethnocentric views about the superiority of their own race and culture.

Eventually, as ranching and industrial development expanded in the southwest, many Mexican nationals were encouraged to immigrate to these U.S. regions to work as low-wage labor. Mexicans were paid much lower wages than Anglos to work in the mines or to plant and harvest the various crops of the region. The industries and ranches became dependent on this Mexican labor, and people moved back and forth across the border very easily. The unstated policy of the U.S. ranchers and industrialists was to have the Mexicans fulfill the demands of the labor market but to return to Mexico when the economy went sour. Thus, during the Great Depression of the 1930s, many Mexicans were rounded up and deported back to Mexico so that Euro-Americans could have their jobs. However, following World War II, Mexican labor was again in demand. This shortage resulted in what is known as the *Bracero* program, which allowed the United States to import Mexican labor to meet the demands of the economy (Bigler 2003).

Following the war, the U.S. government organized "Operation Wetback," which captured and deported some 3.8 million people who looked Mexican to Mexico. This was done without any formal legal procedures. Yet many U.S. ranchers and industrialists continued to encourage the movement of Mexican labor back and forth across the border. As a result of the *Bracero* program and the importation of temporary workers, the Mexican American population, both legal and illegal, began to increase after World War II.

Puerto Rican Americans   In contrast to Mexican Americans in the southwest, New York City and the northeast became the center for the Puerto Rican American community. Puerto Rico came under U.S. control following the Spanish-American War of 1898. In 1917, Puerto Ricans became U.S. citizens. As U.S. citizens, Puerto Ricans were eligible to migrate to the United States without any restrictions. Following World War II, as industrial expansion increased, many Puerto Ricans were recruited and enticed to work in the low-wage sector vacated by Euro-Americans who were moving to the suburbs. Most of them settled in New York, and the people sometimes referred to themselves as "Nuyoricans," many of whom reside in "Spanish Harlem." They believed that they were going to participate in the "American Dream" of upward mobility. Manufacturing jobs and related industries, however, were declining in the 1970s and 1980s in New York and other regions. Like many African Americans, Puerto Rican Americans were caught in the industrial and urban decline of this period. Better-paying unionized manufacturing jobs were disappearing, and combined with racism and discrimination, the Puerto Rican community encountered difficulties in achieving the American dream of upward mobility.

Cuban Americans   Prior to the Cuban revolution in 1959 led by Fidel Castro, a number of Cubans had migrated to the United States for economic opportunities. However, following the Cuban revolution, some 400,000 Cubans immigrated to the United States. The first wave of the Cubans after the revolution comprised middle- and upper-class families who were threatened by the Castro government. These people were highly educated professionals, government officials, and business people who brought capital and skills with them to the United States. Most of them settled in Miami, Florida, and became extremely successful in their adjustment to U.S. society. Many of them thought that they would return to Cuba to reestablish themselves after Castro was defeated (Bigler 2003).

During the Cold War, these Cubans were welcomed by the U.S. government as political refugees fleeing a communist regime. A second wave of Cuban refugees came during the 1980s, when Castro allowed people to freely leave Cuba to go to the United States. About 10 percent of these refugees were ex-convicts and mental patients, and they have had a much more difficult time adapting to conditions in U.S. society. Overall, although many Cuban Americans speak both English and Spanish, they have maintained the Spanish language and Cuban culture within the boundaries of U.S. society.

Hispanic Americans Today   As indicated earlier, aside from the Mexican, Puerto Rican, and Cuban Americans, many other individuals are included within the terms *Hispanic* and *Latino*. These Hispanic/Latino people were influenced by the civil rights movements of the 1960s. Although African Americans were at the center of the civil rights struggle, many Hispanic/Latino populations became involved in what some called the "Brown Power Movement." Civil rights activists such as Cesar Chavez, who led the United Farm Workers (UFW) struggle for Mexican American workers, began to challenge the inherent racism, prejudice, and discrimination against Hispanic/Latino Americans. Some Mexican Americans began to call themselves "Chicanos" as a means of challenging the hyphenated-American ethnic policies of assimilation and "melting pot" orientation of U.S. society. Mexican American activists began to refer to *Aztlan* as their original homeland. Puerto Rican American political activists also joined in many of the civil rights struggles against the assimilationist policies of the United States.

Today, the three largest Hispanic/Latino populations are concentrated in the southwest, northeast, and Miami, Florida. Four out of five Mexican Americans reside in the southwest, one-third of the Puerto Rican Americans live in New York City, and two-thirds of Cuban Americans live in the Miami area. But many others from the Dominican Republic, Nicaragua, El Salvador, Guatemala, Colombia, and other areas of the Caribbean, Central, and South America are arriving in U.S. cities. Many of these migrants are poor and unskilled and have taken low-wage jobs in the informal labor sector of the economy. Over one-quarter of all Hispanic/Latino Americans live below the poverty level, and the median family income of Hispanics is roughly half of that of Euro-Americans (Bigler 2003). Thus, the Hispanic/Latino communities face challenges as they confront this twenty-first century in the United States.

Asian and Arab Americans

Asian and Arab Americans represent highly diverse populations that arrived during the nineteenth and twentieth centuries in the United States. Asian Americans include people from China, Japan, Korea, the Philippines, Vietnam, India, Pakistan, and other countries. Arab Americans include people from Lebanon, Syria, Iraq, Egypt, Jordan, Yemen, and other Middle Eastern countries. The 2000 U.S. Census reports that there are approximately 11 million Asian Americans and about 2 million Arab Americans (2000 Census 2002).

An Asian American family.

During the mid-nineteenth century, Chinese immigrants came during the gold-rush economic boom in California. Many of the Chinese worked as "coolie labor" building railways and in other lower-status jobs shunned by whites. Japanese immigrants followed in the 1880s and found jobs as agricultural laborers, first in Hawaii and then in California (Benson 2003). Nativist white Americans viewed the immigration of the Chinese as a threat, resulting in mob violence against them. The Chinese were viewed as "The Yellow Peril" by these nativist white Americans. Eventually, the Chinese Exclusion Act was passed, the first federal law ever enacted solely on the basis of race or nationality. Although the numbers of Japanese immigrants were smaller and did not engender similar hostile legislation, in 1913 laws were passed in California restricting the amount of land that could be purchased by the Japanese.

Japanese Americans faced their greatest challenge after December 7, 1941, when Japan bombed Pearl Harbor. President Franklin D. Roosevelt signed laws that resulted in the internment of 110,000 Japanese Americans in military detention camps. This relocation meant selling their homes, furniture, and businesses on very short notice, and much of their property was confiscated. They were placed in crowded and dirty military prisons surrounded by barbed wire and armed guards. Not one of the Japanese Americans had been accused of any disloyal act, and two-thirds of the population were *Nisei*—U.S. citizens by birth. Very little action was taken against German or Italian citizens at this time. Thus, this legislation and its implementation were based partially on the racist views held by many white Americans.

Koreans and Filipinos came to Hawaii to work on the sugar and pineapple plantations. Following World War II and the Korean War of the 1950s, Koreans came as wives to U.S. military personnel and as independent businesspeople. Because the Philippines were acquired as a colony by the United States following the Spanish–American War of 1898, Filipinos were not subject to the same anti-immigrant, discriminatory laws faced by Chinese and Japanese populations. Thus, many Filipinos came to work in the agricultural fields in California and other West Coast states. Despite the lack of discriminatory legislation, a number of race riots directed at Filipinos broke out during the depression of the 1920s and 1930s. Several states also passed legislation against Filipino-white intermarriages (Benson 2003).

South Asians from India, Pakistan, and Bangladesh migrated to the United States during the twentieth century. In the early 1900s, Punjabi Sikhs migrated to northern and central California to work as agricultural laborers. Anthropologist Karen Leonard studied these Sikh migrants and found that many Sikh men intermarried with Mexican American women (1997). It was next to impossible to get a white Justice of the Peace to recognize a Sikh and white marriage. The first generation of children of these Sikh–Mexican American marriages learned Spanish and identified with their mother's cultural heritage. In the second generation, however, many of these children are beginning to identify with their father's Sikh traditions.

Following the Immigration and Nationality Act of 1965, which opened the doors for Asian immigration, Chinese, Korean, Filipino, Vietnamese (following the Vietnam War after 1975), and South Asian and Southeast Asian peoples arrived on U.S. shores. Aside from the Vietnamese, who came as political refugees, these Asian immigrants were seeking opportunities in the booming U.S. economy. Some were working-class people who did not know English and encountered problems in adjusting to their new homes. Others were highly skilled professionals or independent businesspeople who had a very successful adaptation to the U.S. way of life. Because of the success and higher incomes of this latter group compared to most other immigrants, Asian Americans have been labeled a "model minority." Many Asian Americans, however, resent this stereotype, because it tends to neglect the hard work and determination of these families despite racist attitudes and discrimination against them. This stereotype also neglects the problems and difficulties faced by working-class Asian Americans in U.S. society.

The Arab American communities are smaller than other nonwhite minorities and are often marginalized in discussions of ethnicity in the United States. The major problem encountered by Arab Americans is a monolithic negative stereotype of Arabs and the Islamic tradition. Despite the tremendous diversity within this population of 2 million people, many of whom are Christians, the prevalent stereotype of Arab Americans is based on fears of international

An Arab American family.

terrorism. This stereotype became heightened as a result of the September 11, 2001, attack on the World Trade Center. Following that event, many Arab Americans became alarmed that they would all be lumped together as threats to U.S. society. There was some violence directed at Arab Americans and Islamic mosques. Many Arab Americans were arrested following 9/11 and were detained and released without substantial evidence of any links with terrorist networks. The negative stereotype of the Arab and a misunderstanding of their religion and history, as depicted in textbooks and the Western media, is the major problem that affects the Arab American communities in the United States.

Cultural Pluralism

Beginning in the late 1950s and 1960s, the *melting pot* metaphor was challenged by many non-European ethnic groups. African Americans, Hispanic Americans, Native Americans, Asian Americans, and other non-European ethnic groups demanded equal rights and opportunities for their respective communities. Non-European ethnic groups asserted that, because of their skin color and other cultural elements, they were not as "meltable" as European ethnic groups. Some civil rights leaders, such as Martin Luther King, Jr., rejected the assimi-

lationist policies of U.S. society and called for a plural society, where different ethnic groups could retain their culture and heritage but have equal rights and opportunities like other Americans.

The demand for cultural pluralism became a dominant trend in ethnic relations in the 1960s in U.S. society. Various non-European ethnic groups emphasized a pride in their own unique history, experience, and culture. "Black Power" among African Americans, "Brown Power" among Hispanic Americans, and "Red Power" among Native Americans became the rallying anthems for cultural pluralism in America. Rather than emphasizing the melting pot as an ideal, non-European groups suggested that America should be a "salad bowl" or better yet, a "stir fry," which implied that everyone could maintain his or her own distinctive culture and ethnicity and still contribute to American society.

Multiculturalism in the United States

In the 1950s during the Cold War, the United States opened its doors for political refugees from communist countries such as Hungary and Cuba. Later, during the civil rights movement and demands for more cultural pluralism in the United States, a new

APPLYING ANTHROPOLOGY

Multiculturalism in U.S. Society

As we have seen in this chapter, since the nineteenth century, the population of the United States has become more ethnically and culturally diverse. In addition, during the past forty years, there has been a significant growth in the population of peoples of non-European ancestry. The population of the United States is approximately 284 million. Ethnic minorities are increasing their proportion of this total very rapidly.

As a response to this multiculturalism, federal, state, and local governments in the United States have encouraged the development of programs to prepare people to live in this new type of society. For example, at least twenty-two states have developed guidelines to implement a multicultural approach in their educational systems. These guidelines have resulted in changes in curriculum and the content of textbooks to attempt to fairly portray the ethnic and cultural groups that compose the country's multicultural heritage.

Some anthropologists have become involved in trying to solve some of the problems that have resulted from these new ethnic and demographic trends. These applied anthropologists have been using knowledge from different cultures to educate people in different types of institutions in the United States. For example, applied anthropologists have been providing intercultural training workshops in schools, hospitals, police departments, businesses, and other community settings where different ethnic groups are interacting with one another. These anthropologists are using their ethnographic knowledge about different cultures of the world to help people from different ethnic and religious backgrounds understand one another.

For example, the author of this textbook was called on to help direct an intercultural workshop for a police department in a rural area of Missouri that had recently experienced the immigration of ethnic minorities from urban areas. The police department had had no experience in dealing with African Americans and Hispanic Americans. The workshop was intended to overcome some of the problems that had developed between the police department and the new ethnic communities. It included an introduction to what anthropologists have discovered regarding prejudice and discrimination on a worldwide basis and how some societies have resolved these problems. It also provided cultural background about ethnic minorities in the United States and demonstrated examples of communication and value differences that can create conflict between ethnic groups.

Applied anthropologists have been working with educators and education researchers in a number of areas regarding multiculturalism in U.S. society. They have contributed to curriculum development projects aimed at multicultural education and have also provided cultural background information to help educators adapt their teaching to the specific needs of ethnic minority children.

However, many applied anthropologists have become aware of some inherent problems with these multicultural education programs. Cultural ideas can be applied overzealously by educators. Anthropologist Jacquetta Hill-Burnett discovered that teachers would sometimes use cultural information regarding Puerto Rican Americans to stereotype children in the classroom (1978). Another researcher found a similar tendency in teachers of Eskimo and Indian children in Alaska (Kleinfeld 1975). Thus, anthropologists have to provide cultural information for use in the multicultural settings, but they must also be extremely cautious to avoid broad generalizations about cultural differences that can be used as the basis of ethnic stereotypes. One of the major lessons that anthropology has to teach is that despite being part of an ethnic or cultural group, individuals differ from one another.

immigration law in 1965 opened the doors again for immigration into the United States from different areas of the world. During the past forty years there has been a significant growth in the population of peoples of non-European ancestry. A decline in the birth rate of the majority of the white population of European descent, coupled with new trends in immigration and higher birth rates of ethnic minorities, is changing the ethnic landscape of U.S. society.

As indicated by Figure 7.1, recent immigration from Europe to the United States represents a tiny fraction compared with immigration from Latin America and Asia. The ethnic diversity of non-European immigrants to the United States is remarkable. Among the Asians are Filipinos, Koreans, Chinese, Japanese, Vietnamese, Laotians, Cambodians, Thais, Indians, and Pakistanis. From Latin America come Central Americans from El Salvador, Guatemala, and Mexico and people from other countries of South America. And from the Middle East and Africa come Palestinians, Iraqis, Iranians, Lebanese, Syrians, Israelis, Nigerians, and Egyptians.

Like the nineteenth-century immigrants from Europe, the majority of these immigrants have come to the United States seeking economic opportunities, political freedom, and improved social conditions. The United States has truly become much more of a multicultural society. A movement known as **multiculturalism** developed as an extension of the demand for cultural pluralism in U.S. society. As a result of this multiculturalist movement, federal, state, and local governments in the United States have encouraged the development of educational programs to prepare people to live in this new type of society.

Multiculturalism has led to revision of the curricula in educational programs throughout the United States. Instead of focusing narrowly on a Eurocentric or an Anglocentric version of history, history texts were revised to include discussions of non-European ethnic groups and their contributions to U.S. history. Bilingual education was developed to extend equal education for those students not proficient in English. The ongoing multicultural movement emphasizes that there is no one model type

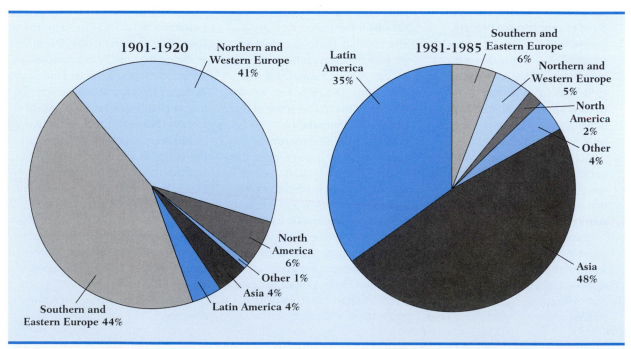

FIGURE 7.1   Legal immigrants admitted to the United States by region of birth.
Source: Leon F. Bauvier and Robert W. Gardner, "Immigration to the U.S.: The Unfinished Story." *Population Bulletin,* 40(4). Washington, DC: Population Reference Bureau, Inc., 1986 and U.S. Census Bureau, *Statistical Abstract of the United States: 1998.* Reprinted by permission of the Population Reference Bureau.

of "American." Cultural pluralism is endorsed fully, and the multiculturalist movement tends to suggest that there are no significant costs for retaining one's ethnic heritage.

The movement for multiculturalism views cultural and ethnic differences as positive. It downplays any kind of competition or conflict among ethnic groups. Rather, the emphasis is on encouraging tolerance and cooperation among different ethnic groups. The hope is that as students become more ethnically literate and more educated about ethnic groups, they will be able to appreciate and tolerate other people from different ethnic backgrounds. In addition, they will be able to make personal decisions that would affect public policy, promoting a more harmonious form of ethnic and race relations in the United States.

Ethnonationalism

In Chapter 6 we discussed how globalization has had an impact on culture, language, and also national identity for many people throughout the world. In Chapter 13 in our discussion of what anthropologists have learned about industrial societies, we find that *nationalism*—a set of symbols and beliefs providing the sense of belonging to a single political community—developed along with industrialism in Europe and elsewhere. Before the development of nationalism, the primary focus of loyalty was to the local community, a particular ruler, ethnicity, religion, and the family (Gellner 1983; Anderson 1991). However, as nationalism has emerged in these societies, minority ethnic groups sometimes view the imposition of language, culture, and the political system of the majority ethnic group as a form of cultural hegemony. To contest and resist this cultural hegemony, these ethnic groups may want to secede and develop their own ethnically based nation-states. These ethnic secessionist developments are often called **ethnonationalist movements**. Many other indigenous people and ethnic minorities have expressed their identity in nationalistic terms without actually having an existing nation-state.

As Chapters 9, 10, 11, 12, 13, 14, and 15 show, many ethnonationalist movements have emerged in areas of the world that were once colonized by Europeans. Ethnonationalist movements played a

role in the struggle against European colonialism and globalization. Leaders such as Mohandas Gandhi in India, Jomo Kenyatta in East Africa, and Simon Bolivar in Latin America mobilized new forms of ethnonationalism in order to free themselves from European colonialism. After independence, these new, postcolonial societies had to form nation-states that incorporated disparate ethnic communities and cultures. In some instances, during the colonial period some ethnic groups had prospered more than others, and this disparity often resulted in postcolonial states in which the dominant ethnic group imposed their particular culture and language. Many of these postcolonial states still have a very weakly developed sense of nationalism because ethnic minorities perceive their own local interests and culture as being undermined by the dominant ethnic group.

Another variation of the postcolonial ethnonationalist movement occurred with the downfall of the former Soviet Union and its satellite countries in Eastern Europe. Various ethnic minorities— Latvians, Estonians, Lithuanians, Belarusians, Ukrainians, Georgians, Turkmens, Uzbeks, Tajiks, and others—began to accentuate their ethnic identities and regional nationalism as the Soviet empire began to collapse in the late 1980s. Historically, the Soviet Union was administered by fifteen Soviet Socialist Republics that contained "autonomous Republics" defined by ethnic groups or nationalities. However, under the orthodox Marxist ideology that provided the foundation for Soviet political policies, ethnic groups were supposed to "wither away" and be replaced by a Soviet "superethnicity." This was an attempt by the Soviet political elite to use its own version of nationalism, based on a political creed, to produce a civil polity (Banks 1996; Gellner 1988). In reality, none of these autonomous regions were allowed political rights and were strictly controlled by Soviet authorities in Moscow. Members of ethnic groups were subject to deportation or exile, and their boundaries were manipulated by the Soviet state.

In most cases, contrary to Marxist dogma, the various ethnic minorities did not abandon their cultural, linguistic, and religious traditions as expected. As the Soviet system began to disintegrate, a variety of ethnonationalist movements developed among these various ethnic minorities throughout the empire. In the aftermath of the dissolution of the Soviet Union, these ethnonationalist aspirations resulted in myriad newly independent countries. In Eastern Europe, as the communists lost their authority over Hungary, Czechoslovakia, Bulgaria, Romania, Poland, Yugoslavia, and East Germany, ethnonationalist movements materialized, which have had major consequences for these regions. For example, deep tensions between the ethnic Czechs and Slovaks led to the division of the former Czechoslovakia. Much more tragic results transpired in Yugoslavia, when Serbs, Croats, Bosnians, and other ethnic groups turned against one another in genocidal warfare.

In general, globalization processes have been a major factor in the appearance of many of these ethnonationalist movements (Friedman 1994). At times, regional and ethnic identities are accentuated in a response to, and as a defense against, the growing impact of the wider world on their lives. As we saw in our discussion of globalization processes in the last chapter, this process is sometimes perceived as a "McWorld" tendency that stems from the United States. The communications media—including television, film, and the Internet—are diffusing particular forms of culture as globalization has an impact on all areas of the world. One of the responses to these globalizing trends is a reassertion and revitalization of people's own ethnic and local identity (sometimes referred to as "Jihad"), leading to ethnonationalist movements. Many ethnic groups view these globalizing trends as a menacing process that tends to obliterate their own cultural traditions. Today, as later chapters show, there are various ethnonationalist movements: Mayan ethnonationalism in Mexico and similar movements among the Igbo, Yoruba, and Hausa in Nigeria, Africa, the Sikhs in India, and native Hawaiians in the United States. Undoubtedly, these ethnonationalist movements will become a prevalent aspect of social and political life in the twenty-first century.

Neo-Racist Movements in the United States and Elsewhere

In 1999, 21-year-old Benjamin Smith spent the July 4th weekend cruising in his car in Chicago and central Indiana areas shooting at African Americans, Orthodox Jews, and Asians. In this three-day shooting spree two were killed and nine were

wounded before Smith shot and killed himself during a police chase. The African American killed was Rick Birdsong, a former basketball coach at Northwestern University. He was jogging with his children when he was shot in the back. Won Joined Soon, a Korean graduate student at Indiana University, was killed outside of a Korean church.

Benjamin Smith was a former member of the World Church of the Creator, which is currently led by Matt Hale of East Peoria, Illinois. Hale refers to himself as Pontifus Maximus and teaches that only white Anglo-Saxons are true human beings, descendants of Adam and Eve. Jews are believed to be illegitimate offspring of Eve and Satan, and African Americans and other people of color are descendants of inferior non-Adamite anthropoids called "mud people." The church believes that the United States should be "cleansed" of all Jews and nonwhites. The church's Web site features a discussion of the mental inferiority of African Americans. Most recently, Matt Hale was convicted in conspiring to murder a federal judge who disagreed with his policies and propaganda with some of his racist followers and was convicted to 27 years in prison. The FBI had his conversations about this murder plan on tape (2004).

Although groups such as the World Church of the Creator are small, with only a few thousand members, their influence seems to be on the rise. For many years, most anthropologists and other social scientists believed that racism and ethnic conflict were going to decline. Unfortunately, however, more extremist racist and ethnic groups have emerged in many parts of the world within the past decade. For example, in the former East Germany there has been a rise of a neo-Nazi movement among German youth who resent the immigration of nonwhites into their society. Other neo-racists groups in the United States influenced by a book called the *Turner Papers* led people such as Timothy McVeigh and other militia members to destroy the Oklahoma federal building, killing hundreds of innocent Americans because they believed the U.S. government was supporting the invasion of non-Anglo peoples to take over American society (Scupin 2003).

Unfortunately, a small minority of anthropologists have joined a Canadian psychologist Philip Rushton to attempt to perpetuate these neo-racialistic views in a book entitled *Race: The Reality of Human*

Differences (Sarich and Miele 2004). In this book these anthropologists claim that "scientific research" can be used to confirm that populations of different skin colors and physical attributes can be classified into different categories of "biological races." They go on to argue that these different races have distinctively different IQs and intelligences and Africans fall at the bottom in intelligence. IQ tests are given to African peoples who have had a very limited education and have been subjected to racial prejudice and discrimination for years in South Africa. Another book by former television producer Jon Entine makes similar claims about the "reality" of biological races in his book *Taboo: Why Black Athletes Dominate Sports and Why We're Afraid to Talk about It* (2000). Currently, anthropologists who understand the genetic, DNA, and molecular data and the geographical and physical attributes of human populations, along with the history and cultural conditions of these populations in Africa and elsewhere that have resulted in low IQ tests, are presenting devastating criticisms of this book based on good scientific evidence (MacEachern 2003; Brooks, Jackson, and Grinker 2004; Olson 2002). It is unfortunate to see that some anthropologists and others have begun to perpetuate these scientific racialistic views among the public within the United States because it does reinforce earlier conceptions of racialistic differences that anthropologists have been engaged in debunking with sound scientific evidence for more than a hundred years.

SUMMARY

Race and culture were misunderstood for many centuries in Western society. As Europeans explored the world, they confused the culture and behavior of different peoples with superficial physical traits such as skin color. Eventually, this led to distortions within early scientific classifications of human racial groups. In addition, scientific racist beliefs began to dominate Western society, resulting in tragic human events such as the Holocaust in Nazi Germany. Anthropologists have been engaged in criticizing scientific racist beliefs in the past and the present by using sound evidence and rigorous examination of indicators such as IQ tests. Despite the useless scientific enterprise of classifying races throughout the world, societies continue to use folk taxonomies of race to distinguish different people. These folk taxonomies have profound social and cultural meaning for societies around the world.

Another confusion that developed within Western societies and other areas of the world is the identification of race with culture. Anthropologists have used the term ethnic group or ethnicity to distinguish ethnicity from race and are actively engaged in studying ethnic relations in different regions of the world.

Contemporary anthropologists have been doing research on race and ethnic relations in U.S. society. The history of U.S. race and ethnic relations was defined by the WASPs (white Anglo-Saxon Protestants), who instituted the language, the political culture, and the religious culture in American society. Other Europeans who immigrated to the United States included Irish, Germans, Italians, and Polish ethnic groups. These groups became known as the "White Ethnics." African Americans arrived in the United States as slaves and have struggled for their political rights for centuries. Hispanic Americans are a diverse group that includes Mexican, Cuban, and Puerto Rican Americans, all of whom maintain distinctive cultural traditions in the United States. Asian and Arab Americans are also represented in multiethnic America. Although the myth of the melting pot has worked better for white Americans, policies involving multicultural practices and values aimed at recognizing the contributions of all Americans now permeate U.S. society. Unfortunately, racism, ethnocentrism, prejudice and discrimination continue to plague the United States and other societies throughout the world. Anthropologists have devoted themselves to explaining these issues regarding race, ethnicity, and the problems resulting from folk and popular conceptions of these issues by sound empirical, and scientific research.

QUESTIONS TO THINK ABOUT

1. What was the basis of race classification in ancient societies?

2. What were the basic criticisms of racism developed by anthropology?

3. What are some examples that represent the difference between race and ethnicity?

4. What can we learn from primordialist and circumstantialist approaches to ethnicity?

5. How do patterns of assimilation and pluralism differ in various societies?

6. What can we learn from the ethnic group adaptations in U.S. society?

7. What is the basis of ethnonationalist movements today?

8. What are some of the current neo-racist movements in the world and the U.S. today?

KEY TERMS

assimilation

biological assimilation

cultural assimilation

ethnic boundary markers

ethnogenesis

ethnonationalist movements

hypodescent concept

intelligence

Jim Crow laws

knowledge

multiculturalism

one-drop rule

plural society

racism

segregation

INTERNET EXERCISES

1. Review the Web site titled "The Death of Scientific Racism" at **http://shadow.autono.net/sin001/race.htm**. How does the author of this Web site dismiss the concept of the heritability of IQ? How do the conclusions of this Web site compare to this chapter in the textbook?

2. Question: How does the Census Bureau define race and ethnicity? For the answer to this question, go to that section in the following Web site: **http://www.census.gov/Press-Release/www/2001/raceqandas.html**. How does this definition compare to anything you have read in the book? Could this legal definition used by the U.S. government cause any harm to groups or individuals? Why does our government classify people in such a way?

Chapter **8**

Analyzing Sociocultural Systems

CHAPTER OUTLINE

ETHNOGRAPHIC FIELDWORK

Ethnographic Research and Strategies / Ethics in Anthropological Research / Analysis of Ethnographic Data

UNIVERSALS AND VARIABLES STUDIED BY CULTURAL ANTHROPOLOGISTS

SUBSISTENCE AND THE PHYSICAL ENVIRONMENT

Modern Cultural Ecology / Biomes / Subsistence Patterns and Environments

DEMOGRAPHY

Fertility, Mortality, and Migration / Population and Environment / Population and Culture

TECHNOLOGY

Anthropological Explanations of Technology

ECONOMY

The Formalist Approach / The Substantivist Approach / Contemporary Economic Anthropology

SOCIAL STRUCTURE

Components of Social Structure / The Family / Marriage / Gender / Age

POLITICAL ORGANIZATION

Types of Political Systems / Decision Making in a Political System / Warfare and Feuds / Law and Social Control

RELIGION

Myths / Rituals / Religious Specialists / Religious Movements / Cognition and Religion

CROSS-CULTURAL RESEARCH

CHAPTER QUESTIONS

- How do cultural anthropologists study society and culture?

- What are the universals and variables that cultural anthropologists rely on to do their fieldwork?

- What are the strengths and limitations of the cross-cultural approach?

As we discussed in Chapter 3, at times anthropologists use the term *sociocultural system* as a combination of the terms *society* and *culture* in analyzing their data. We also saw that there are some basic cultural universals that are found in all societies (Brown 1991). This chapter provides insight on how anthropologists do research on the universal characteristics of sociocultural systems. These universal features of sociocultural systems are usually analyzed by anthropologists as *variables*. Immediately, this terminology suggests that these universals can *vary* within different sociocultural systems, and this is just what anthropologists have discovered in their research. Thus, there are basic universal similarities among all humans, and yet within different societies, these universal features can exhibit tremendous variations. In order to investigate universals *and* variations, anthropologists must utilize both a scientific and humanistic perspective as discussed in Chapter 1. In accounting for patterns of relationships found within a sociocultural system, anthropologists use *both* scientific causal explanations and humanistic interpretations of cultural beliefs.

In this chapter we examine the universal conditions and variable features that are investigated by anthropologists, including environmental, demographic, technological, economic, social-organizational (social structure, family, marriage, age, gender relations), political, and religious variables. Anthropologists use the *holistic approach* to analyze sociocultural systems, which means demonstrating how all of these universals and variables interact and influence one another. Although the term "system" is used, it is employed in a highly "metaphorical manner." It does not suggest that sociocultural systems are somehow running "above" like some computer system in human affairs. Humans are not just automatons being driven by some mechanical "cultural system." Rather, humans as individuals are actively involved in managing, shaping, and modifying their culture from within these so-called systems.

In later chapters, we examine different types of sociocultural systems to illustrate the interconnections of these variables. This chapter presents a broad overview of the basic universals and variables that anthropologists investigate when explaining the similarities and differences in societies. Various concepts and terms used by anthropologists to examine variables are also introduced. This will prepare you to evaluate the results of ethnographic findings discussed in later chapters.

Ethnographic Fieldwork

In Chapter 1 we introduced the subfield of anthropology known as cultural anthropology. This subfield focuses on the ethnographic study of contemporary societies all over the world. To prepare for ethnographic fieldwork, the anthropologist must be well grounded in the different theoretical perspectives of anthropology that are discussed within different chapters. This background knowledge is especially important for developing a research design for the fieldwork.

A *research design* is the formulation of a strategy to examine a particular topic and specifies the appropriate methods for gathering the richest possible data. The research design must take into account the types of data that will be collected and how those data relate to existing anthropological knowledge. In the research design, the cultural anthropologist has to specify what types of methods will be used for the investigation. Typically, the cultural anthropologist develops the research design, which is then reviewed by other anthropologists, who recommend it for funding by various government or private research foundations.

Before going into the field for direct research, the cultural anthropologist analyzes available *archival data,* including photos, films, missionary reports, business and government surveys, musical recordings, journalistic accounts, diaries, court documents, medical records, birth, death, marriage, and tax records, and landholding documents. These data help place the communities to be studied in a broad context. Historical material in the archives help the cultural anthropologist evaluate the usefulness of the observations and interviews he or she will document. Archival data can enrich the sources of information that fieldworkers obtain once they get to the field. They must also read the published anthropological, historical, economic, sociological, and political science literature on the geographic region they are heading toward.

Ethnographic Research and Strategies

After receiving funding and obtaining the proper research clearances from the country in which the subjects of the research are located, the cultural anthropologist takes up residence in that society to explore its institutions and values. This is the basis of the *participant observation* method, which involves learning the language and culture of the group being studied and participating in its daily activities. Language skills are the most important asset that a cultural anthropologist has in the field.

One of the major means of learning about culture and behavior is through direct observation, sometimes referred to as *naturalistic observation.* Naturalistic observation consists of making accurate descriptions of the physical locale and daily activities of the people in the society. This may involve creating maps or at least being able to read maps to place the society's physical location in perspective. It may also involve more intensive investigation into soil conditions, rates of precipitation, surveys of crops and livestock, and other environmental factors. Naturalistic observation also involves accurate and reliable records of the cultural anthropologist's direct observations of human social interaction and behavior.

Some cultural anthropologists use what is called *time-allocation analysis* to record how much time the people in the society spend in various activities: work, leisure, recreation, religious ceremonies, and so on. For example, Allen Johnson (1975) did a systematic time-allocation study of the Machiguenga Indians, who live in the Andes Mountains in Peru. He found that men worked 4.6 hours per day and women worked 4.2 hours per day in the production and preparation of food. Women spent 2.1 hours and men spent 1.4 hours per day in craft production. Men were involved in trade and wage work, and women did housework and child-care activities. The total amount of labor time allocated for this work was 7.6 for men and 7.4 for women. This type of time-allocation study can be useful in assessing how different societies use their time in various activities.

Key Informants   Usually the cultural anthropologist learns about the society through trusted *key informants*, who give the cultural anthropologist insight into the culture's patterns (Powdermaker 1966; Wax 1971; Agar 1980). These informants become the initial source of information and help the cultural anthropologist identify major sources of data. Long-term collaboration with key informants is an integral part of quality ethnographic research.

The cultural anthropologist tries to choose key informants who have a deep knowledge of the community. These informants are usually "native cultural anthropologists" who are interested in their own society. They may serve as tutors or guides,

answering general questions or identifying topics that could be of interest to the cultural anthropologist. They often help the cultural anthropologist establish rapport with the people in the community. In many situations, the people may not understand why the cultural anthropologist is interested in their society. The key informant can help explain the cultural anthropologist's role. In some cases, the key informant may become involved in interviewing other people in the community to assist the cultural anthropologist in collecting data. The relationship between the key informant and the cultural anthropologist is a close personal and professional one that usually produces lifelong friendship and collaboration.

Interviews   Cultural anthropologists use a number of *unstructured interviews*, which may involve open-ended conversations with informants, to gain insights into a culture. These unstructured interviews may include the collecting of life histories, narratives, myths, and tales. Through these interviews, the cultural anthropologist may also find out information on dispute settlements, legal transactions, political conflicts, and religious and public events. Unstructured interviewing sometimes involves on-the-spot questioning of informants.

The strength of this type of interviewing is that it gives informants tremendous freedom of expression

Anthropologist Richard Lee interviewing the !Kung San (Ju/'hoansi).

in attempting to explain their culture (Bernard et al. 1986). The informant is not confined to answering a specific question that is designed by the cultural anthropologist. The informant may, for example, elaborate on connections between certain beliefs and political power in the community. Fredrik Barth (1975, 2002) discovered through his informant among thc Baktaman people of New Guinea that when young males go through their initiation ceremonies, they are introduced to the secret lore and sacred knowledge of the males who are in authority. Thus, cultural beliefs are transmitted along with political authority. Barth found that this secretive sacred knowledge was often arcane and ambiguous. As these young Baktaman males went through each stage of the ritual, the knowledge became much more mysterious and ambiguous. It appeared that the most important feature of the ritual was the reinforcement of clder authority and group bonding. Without his informant's help, Barth might not have paid attention to this relationship between belief and the transmission of authority.

Following this unstructured interviewing, the cultural anthropologist focuses on specific topics of interest related to the research project. In some cases, the cultural anthropologist then begins to develop structured *interviews*. Structured interviews systematically ask the same questions of cvery individual in a given sample. The cultural anthropologist must phrase the questions in a meaningful and sensitive manner, a task that requires knowledge of both the language and the cultural lifestyle of the people being studied.

By asking the same type of question of every individual in a given sample, the cultural anthropologist is able to obtain more accurate data. If the cultural anthropologist receives uniform answers to a particular question, then the data are more likely to be reliable. If a great deal of variation in responses is evident, then the data will be more unreliable or may indicate a complex issue with many facets. The structured interview helps assess the validity of the collected data. By asking people the same type of question, the cultural anthropologist attempts to gain more quality control over his or her findings. This type of data quality control must be a constant aspect of the cultural anthropologist's research strategy. However, as we discussed in Chapter 3, contemporary anthropologists concur that there is always a great deal of variation in cultural beliefs,

values, and norms in every society. Thus, one cannot portray a simplistic account of "a culture" in the same way that anthropologists did in the 1930s, 1940s, and 1950s.

To develop an effective questionnaire, the cultural anthropologist must collaborate with her or his informants. This is tedious and difficult methodological work, but it is necessary if the cultural anthropologist is to understand the workings of the society.

If the society is large, the cultural anthropologist must distribute the questionnaire to a random sample of the society. A **random sample** is a representative sample of people of different ages, genders, economic and political status, and other characteristics within the society. In a random sample, all the individuals in the society have an equal chance of being selected for the survey. If the cultural anthropologist draws information from only one sector of the population—for example, males or young people—the data may be biased. This shortcoming would limit the ability of the cultural anthropologist to develop a well-rounded portrait of the society.

Quantitative and Qualitative Data Through the structured interviews, the cultural anthropologist gathers basic **quantitative data**: census materials, dietary information, income and household-composition data, and other data that can be expressed as numbers. This information can be used as a database for developing a description of the variations in economic, social, political, and other patterns in the society. For example, dietary information can inform the cultural anthropologist about the basic health and nutritional problems that the society may have. Quantitative data provide background for the cultural anthropologist's direct and participant observations and further open-ended interviews with the individuals in the society. Sometimes this objective, quantitative data is referred to as an aspect of the *etic* perspective of the anthropologist. The **etic perspective** is the outsider's objective, quantifiable data that is used to scientifically analyze the culture of a society. *Etic* is derived from the term *phonetics* in linguistics, which are the sounds of a language.

Most of the data achieved through participant observation and interviewing are **qualitative data**, nonstatistical information that tends to be the most important aspect of ethnographic research. Qualitative data include descriptions of social organization, political activities, religious beliefs, and so on. These qualitative data are often referred to as part of the **emic perspective**, the insider's view of their own society and culture. The term *emic* is derived from the word *phonemics* in linguistics, which refers to the sound units of language that have "meaning" for the speakers of the language (see Chapter 5). For example, as we discussed in Chapter 3, the religious beliefs of some societies have influenced their cultural preferences for various foods. Islamic and Jewish cultural traditions prohibit the eating of pork, and orthodox Hindus encourage meatless, vegetarian diets. This type of *emic*, qualitative data about a society helps the cultural anthropologist understand the *etic*, quantitative data. Ordinarily, both etic quantitative and emic qualitative data are integral to ethnographic research. Although there are considerable philosophical differences among anthropologists over the precise criteria in which emic and etic knowledge differ, most agree that the insider's emic understandings and perceptions of their culture differ from the outsider's etic views to some degree. The cultural anthropologist strives to understand the culture from both the outsider's and insider's perspective in their ethnographic descriptions.

Cultural anthropologists have a number of different methods for recording qualitative data. The best-known method is *field notes*, which are the systematic recording of observations or interviews into a field notebook. Cultural anthropologists should have some training in how to take useful field notes and how to manage them for more effective coding and recording of data. An increasing number of cultural anthropologists now use the computer as a means of constructing databases to manage their field notes. They select appropriate categories for classifying the data. For example, a cultural anthropologist may set up specific categories for kinship terms, religious taboos, plants, animals, colors, foods, and so on. These data can then easily be retrieved for analysis. Some cultural anthropologists rely on tape recorders for interviews, although they recognize the problems such devices present for producing valid accounts. Most ethnographic fieldworkers utilize photography to record and help document their findings. Cultural anthropologists must use extreme caution when using these technologies, however, for in some cultures people are very sensitive about being recorded or photographed.

Today, many anthropologists use video cameras when gathering primary data. Video recording is one of the most exciting recent developments in anthropology and has stimulated a new area of anthropological research known as visual anthropology. The visual documentation of economic, social, political, and ritual behavior sometimes reveals intricate patterns of interaction in a society—interactions that cannot otherwise be described thoroughly. One drawback to video recording, however, is that people who know they are being filmed frequently behave differently from the way they would normally. This may distort the cultural anthropologist's conclusions. On the other hand, the video can be used to present playbacks to informants for comments on the recorded behaviors. William Rittenberg, who did studies of Buddhist rituals in villages in central Thailand, often played back his video recordings of rituals to members of the community. The informants, including the Buddhist monks, would view the recordings and offer more elaborate explanations of the meanings of the ritual. These strategies frequently help the cultural anthropologist gain a more comprehensive understanding of the culture.

Culture Shock Ethnographic fieldwork can be a very demanding task. Cultural anthropologists sometimes experience **culture shock**, a severe psychological reaction that results from adjusting to the realities of a society radically different from one's own. A cultural anthropologist enculturated in the United States who may have to eat unfamiliar foods such as reptiles or insects, reside in uncomfortable huts in a rainforest, or observe practices that may not occur within their own society could experience culture shock. Of course, the actual degree of culture shock may vary depending on the differences and similarities between the society studied and the anthropologist's own society. The symptoms may range from mild irritation to surprise or disgust.

Usually after the cultural anthropologist learns the norms, beliefs, and practices of the community, the psychological disorientation of culture shock begins to diminish. Part of the challenge for anthropologists is adjusting to a different society and gaining a much better perspective on one's own society. In fact, most anthropologists report considerable culture shock upon returning from another society to back home. They will never again view their own society and culture in the same light. The adjustment process of culture shock out in the field and returning from the field enables cultural anthropologists to understand themselves and their own society better.

Ethics in Anthropological Research

Cultural anthropologists must not only be trained in appropriate research and analytical techniques, they must also abide by the ethical guidelines of their discipline. In many instances, cultural anthropologists conduct research on politically powerless groups dominated by more powerful groups. When cultural anthropologists engage in participant observation, they usually become familiar with information that might, if made public, become harmful to the community or to individuals in the community. For example, when researching isolated or rural communities, cultural anthropologists might come across certain economic or political behavior or information that could be used by government authorities. This information might include the specific sources of income for people in the community or whether they participate in political opposition to the government. Whenever possible, cultural anthropologists attempt to keep such information confidential so as not to compromise their informants or other sources of data.

Most ethnographic reports do not include the real identities of informants or other people. Cultural anthropologists usually ensure their informants' anonymity, if at all possible, so that these individuals will not be investigated by their governments. Sometimes cultural anthropologists use pseudonyms (fictional names) to make identification difficult. Cultural anthropologists also attempt to be frank and open with the population under study about the aims of the research. At times this is difficult because the community does not understand the role of the cultural anthropologist (Kurin 1980). Out of courtesy, the cultural anthropologist should give the community a reasonable account of what he or she wants to do.

In general, cultural anthropologists do not accept research funding for projects that are supposed to be clandestine or secretive. Although this type of research has been conducted by some anthropologists in the past (especially during World War II), contemporary anthropologists have adopted a code of ethics that reflects their grave reservations about undercover research (Wax 2003; Gellner 2003).

Analysis of Ethnographic Data

The results of ethnographic research are documented in a descriptive monograph referred to as an *ethnography*. In writing the ethnographic description, the cultural anthropologist must be extremely cautious. The accumulated field notes, photos, perhaps video or tape recordings, and quantitative data from survey sources must all be carefully managed to reduce bias, distortion, and error. The cultural anthropologist must analyze these data, making sure to cross-check the conclusions from a variety of sources, including informants, censuses, observations, and archival materials. In addition, the cultural anthropologist should plainly distinguish the views of the people being studied from his or her interpretation of those views.

Universals, Independent, and Dependent Variables

Culture, society, and human behavior are not just a random array of occurrences that develop without rhyme or reason. They are the result of universal features and interacting variables that influence the human condition. In analyzing a sociocultural system, anthropologists frequently find that different universals and specific variables interact with one another. The interaction of two variables is called a **correlation**. For example, a particular society may experience both population increases and a high incidence of warfare. This does not necessarily mean that the population growth causes the warfare, or vice versa; it simply means that both conditions exist within the society. To determine whether a causal relationship exists between these variables would require further investigation, including, in many cases, comparisons with other societies. Further research may indicate that the relationship between population and warfare is a spurious correlation; that is, two variables occur together, but each is caused by some third variable.

Alternatively, research may indicate that in a certain society the rate of population growth does influence the frequency of warfare. In such cases the anthropologist might hypothesize that population increases cause the high incidence of warfare. This hypothesis could then be tested and evaluated by other anthropologists.

In determining cause-and-effect relationships, anthropologists distinguish between independent and dependent variables. An **independent variable** is the causal variable that produces an effect on another variable, the **dependent variable**. In the previous example, population growth would be the independent variable because it determines the incidence of warfare, which is the dependent variable.

In actuality, this example of determining causal relationships is far too simplistic. Anthropologists recognize that no aspect of culture and society can be completely explained by any single cause or independent variable. They rely instead on hypotheses that are *multidimensional*, in which many variables interact with one another. This multidimensional approach must be kept in mind when considering the specific variables explored by cultural anthropologists in their study of different societies. The multidimensional approach is linked with the holistic perspective in anthropology; that is, the attempt to demonstrate how sociocultural systems must be understood through the interconnections among universals and specific variables.

Universals and Variables Studied by Cultural Anthropologists

The major variables and universal features of sociocultural systems include subsistence and the physical environment, demography, technology, the economy, social structure (including family and marriage, and gender and age relations), political organization, and religion. Although this is not a complete list of the universals and specific variables studied by cultural anthropologists, it provides the general framework for understanding different societies. An explanation of these universals and specific variables follows, to help you understand the discussions of different types of societies considered in the rest of the book.

Subsistence and the Physical Environment

Living organisms, both plant and animal, do not live or evolve in a vacuum. The evolution and survival of a particular species is closely related to the type of physical environment in which it is located. The speed of a jackal or an arctic fox has evolved in relationship to the predators and prey found in East Africa or the Arctic. The physical characteristics of the orchid plant make it highly suitable for surviving in a tropical environment. The environment affects the organism directly and, as Charles Darwin noted, affects the passing on of certain adaptive characteristics that enable these life forms to survive and reproduce in their particular surroundings.

Biologists use the term *adaptation* to refer to the process in which an organism adjusts successfully to a specific environment. Most organisms adapt to the environment through the physical traits that they inherit. Like other creatures, as we have seen in Chapter 2, humans have adapted to their respective environments through physical changes in body size and shape, blood groups, skin coloration, and biological traits. Humans, however, adapt to their specific environments primarily through *culture*. By any measure, humans have been the most successful living forms in terms of adapting physically and culturally to different types of environments. Humans occupy an extraordinary range of environments, from the tropics to the Arctic, and have developed cultural solutions to the various problems that have arisen in these different regions. Anthropologists have been studying these adaptive strategies and cultural solutions to explain both the similarities and differences among societies.

Modern Cultural Ecology

The term *ecology* was coined by German biologist Ernest Haeckel in the nineteenth century from two Greek words that mean "the study of the home." **Ecology** is the study of living organisms in relationship to their environment. Here we are defining environment broadly, to include both the physical characteristics and the forms of life found in a particular region. In biology, ecological studies focus on how plant and animal populations survive and reproduce in specific environmental niches. An **environmental niche** refers to the given set of ecological conditions that a life form uses to make a living, survive, and adapt.

There is a branch of anthropology known as **cultural ecology**, the systematic study of the relationships between the environmental niche and culture. Anthropologists recognize that all humans can adjust in extremely creative ways to different environments. Nevertheless, humans, like other organisms, are universally connected to the environment in a number of ways. Just as the environment has an impact on human behavior and society, humans have a major impact on their environment. Modern cultural ecologists examine these dynamic interrelationships as a means of understanding different societies.

Biomes

In their studies of different environments, cultural ecologists use the concept of a *biome*. A **biome** is an area distinguished by a particular climate and certain types of plants and animals. Biomes may be classified by certain attributes, such as mean rainfall, temperature, soil conditions, and vegetation, which support certain forms of animal life (Campbell 1983). Cultural ecologists investigate the relationship between specific biomes and human sociocultural systems. Some of the different biomes that will be encountered in this text are listed in Table 8.1.

Table 8.1	A Listing of the Various Biomes Discussed in the Text, along with Their Major Characteristics			
Biome	**Principal Locations**	**Precipitation Range (mm/year)**	**Temperature Range (hr °C) (daily maximum and minimum)**	**Soils**
Tropical rainforest	Central America (Atlantic coast) Amazon basin Brazilian coast West African coast Congo basin Malaya	1,270–12,700 Equatorial type; frequent torrential thunderstorms	Little annual variation Max. 29–35 Min. 18–27	Mainly reddish laterites
	East Indies Philippines New Guinea N. E. Australia Pacific islands	Tradewind type; steady, almost daily rains No dry period	No cold period	
Tropical savanna	Central America (Pacific coast) Orinoco basin Brazil, S. of Amazon Basin N. Central Africa East Africa S. Central Africa Madagascar India S. E. Asia Northern Australia	250–1900 Warm-season thunderstorms Almost no rain in cool season Long dry period during low sun	Considerable annual variation; no really cold period *Rainy season (high sun)* Max. 24–32 Min. 18–27 *Dry season (low sun)* Max. 21–32 Min. 13–18 *Dry season (higher sun)* Max. 29–40 Min. 21–27	Some laterites; considerable variety

(continued)

Table 8.1	A Listing of the Various Biomes Discussed in the Text, along with Their Major Characteristics—Continued			
Biome	**Principal Locations**	**Precipitation Range (mm/year)**	**Temperature Range (hr °C) (daily maximum and minimum)**	**Soils**
Temperate grasslands	Central North America Eastern Europe Central and Western Asia Argentina New Zealand	300–2000 Evenly distributed through the year or with a peak in summer Snow in winter	*Winter* Max. -18–29 Min. -28–10 *Summer* Max. -1–49 Min. -1–15	Black prairie soils Chestnut and brown soils Almost all have a lime layer
Temperate deciduous forest	Eastern N. America Western Europe Eastern Asia	630–2300 Evenly distributed through year Droughts rare Some snow	*Winter* Max. -12–21 Min. -29–7 *Summer* Max. 24–38 Min. 15–27	Gray-brown podzolic Red and yellow podzolic
Northern coniferous forest	Northern N. America Northern Europe Northern Asia	400–1000 Evenly distributed Much snow	*Winter* Max. -37– -1 Min. -54– -9 *Summer* Max. 10–21 Min. 7–13	True podzols Bog soils Some permafrost at depth, in places
Arctic tundra	Northern N. America Greenland Northern Eurasia	250–750 Considerable snow	*Winter* Max. -37– -7 Min. -57– -8 *Summer* Max. 2–15 Min. -1–7	Rocky or boggy Much patterned ground permafrost

Source: Adapted from W. D. Billings, *Plants, Man, and the Ecosystem*, 2nd ed. ©1970. Reprinted by permission of Brooks/Cole, an imprint of the Wadsworth Group, a division of Thomson Learning. Fax 800-730-2215.

Subsistence Patterns and Environments

In U.S. society, when we have the urge to satisfy our hunger drive, we have many options: We can go to a local fast-food restaurant, place money into a machine to select our choice of food, or obtain food for cooking from a grocery store or supermarket. Other societies have different means of obtaining their food supplies. Cultural anthropologists study **subsistence patterns**, the means by which people in various societies obtain their food supplies. As we see in later chapters, the amount of sunlight, the type of soil, forests, rainfall, and

mineral deposits all have an effect on the type of subsistence pattern a particular society develops. The specific biome and environmental conditions may limit the development of certain types of subsistence patterns. For example, arctic conditions are not conducive to agricultural activities, nor are arid regions suitable for rice production. These are the obvious limitations of biomes and environmental conditions on subsistence patterns.

The earliest type of subsistence pattern—known as foraging or hunting-gathering—goes back among early hominids to perhaps 2 million years ago. This pattern of subsistence, along with others such as horticulture, pastoralism, various types of intensive agriculture, and developments in agribusiness in industrial societies, is introduced in subsequent chapters. As we shall see, these subsistence patterns are not only influenced by the environment but also directly affect the environment. In other words, as humans transform their subsistence pattern to adapt to the environment, the environment is also transformed to varying degrees depending on the type of subsistence pattern developed. The interaction between subsistence pattern and environment has become an extremely important topic in anthropology and has a direct bearing on how human-environmental relationships may be modified in the future.

Demography

Demography is the study of population and its relationship to society. Demographers study changes in the size, composition, and distribution of human populations. They also study the consequences of population increases and decreases on human societies. Demographic anthropology has become an important specialty in anthropology.

Much of the research in demographic anthropology is concerned with the quantitative description of population. Demographic anthropologists design censuses and surveys to collect population statistics on the size, age and sex composition, and increasing or decreasing growth of population of a society. After collecting these data, demographic anthropologists focus on three major variables in a population: fertility, mortality, and migration.

Fertility, Mortality, and Migration

To measure **fertility**—the number of births in a society—demographic anthropologists use the **crude birth rate**; that is, the number of live births in a given year for every thousand people in a population. They also measure **mortality**—the incidence of death in a society's population—by using the **crude death rate**; that is, the number of deaths in a given year for every thousand people. In measuring the **migration rate**—the movement of people into and out of a specified territory—demographic anthropologists determine the number of in-migrants (people moving into the territory)

and the number of out-migrants (people moving out of the territory). They then use these numbers to calculate the **net migration**, which indicates the general movement of the population in and out of the territory.

To assess overall population change, demographic anthropologists subtract the crude death rate from the crude birth rate to arrive at the *natural growth rate* of a population. The natural growth rate is usually the major indicator of population change in a society. By adding the rate of migration, these anthropologists are able to calculate total population change.

Rates of fertility, mortality, and migration are also influenced by a number of other variables. **Fecundity**—the potential number of children that women in the society are capable of bearing—has an influence on fertility rates. Fecundity varies, however, according to the age of females at puberty and menopause, nutrition, workload, and other conditions in the societies and individuals being studied.

Life expectancy is the number of years an average person can expect to live. A particularly important component of the life expectancy rate in a society is the **infant mortality rate**—the number of babies per thousand births in any year who die before reaching the age of 1. When the infant mortality rate is high, the life expectancy—a statistical average—decreases. In many countries throughout the world, **childhood mortality rates**—the number of children who die before reaching the age of 5—is a major problem. Disease, nutrition, sanitation, warfare, the general standard of living, and medical care are some of the factors that influence mortality, life expectancy, and infant and child mortality rates.

Migration is related to a number of different factors. In many instances, migration is *involuntary*. For example, the Cajun people of Louisiana are descendants of French people who were forced out of Canada by the British in the 1700s. Migration can also be *voluntary*. This type of movement is influenced by what demographers refer to as *push-pull factors*. **Push factors** are those that lead people to leave specific territories; examples are poverty, warfare, and political instability. **Pull factors**, such as economic opportunity, peace, and political freedom, are powerful incentives for people to move to other societies.

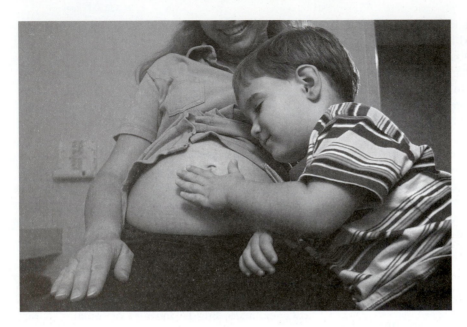

Fertility trends are studied by anthropologists to determine how populations are increasing or decreasing.

Population and Environment

Demographic anthropologists study the relationship between environments (specific biomes) and population. One variable they investigate is **carrying capacity**—the maximum population that a specific environment can support. This concept refers to the environment's potential energy and food resources that can be used to support a certain number of people. Some environments contain food and energy resources that allow for substantial population increases, whereas other environments contain only limited resources. For example, in the past, desert and arctic biomes had carrying capacities that severely limited population increases. In contrast, various river valley regions containing water and fertile soils permitted opportunities for greater population size. As we see in later chapters, the development of mechanized agriculture, fertilizers, and synthetic pesticides increases the carrying capacity for many different environments.

Population and Culture

Demographic anthropologists examine not only the relationship between environment and population but also cultural values, beliefs, and practices that affect fertility, mortality, and migration rates. In some societies, religious beliefs encourage high birth rates. In others, political authorities institute programs to increase or decrease population growth. One recent area of anthropological research involves gathering data and developing hypotheses on decisions concerning the "costs and benefits" of having children and the consequences of these individual decisions on fertility. Anthropologists also investigate strategies of population regulation, such as birth-control techniques. These topics and others on research in demographic anthropology are introduced in later chapters.

Technology

The term *technology* is derived from the Greek word *techne*, which refers to art or skill. When we hear this term, we usually think of tools, machines, clothing, shelter, and other such objects. As defined by modern anthropologists, however, **technology** consists of all the human techniques and methods of reaching a specific subsistence goal or of modifying or controlling the natural environment. Technology is cultural in that it includes methods for manipulating the environment. But technology is also the product of those methods that are important in changing the environments in which humans live, work, and interact. Thus, technology consists not merely of physical tools but also of cultural knowledge that humans can apply in specific ways. In societies in which people use technologies such as bows and arrows, canoes, plows, penicillin, or computers, the cultural knowledge needed to construct, design, and use these materials is extremely important.

To sustain life, human societies need to produce and allocate goods and services to provide food, clothing, shelter, tools, and transportation. **Goods** are elements of material culture produced from raw materials in the natural environment, ranging from the basic commodities for survival to luxury items. The commodities for survival may include axes and plows for clearing land and cultivating crops. Luxury commodities include such items as jewelry, decorative art, and musical instruments. **Services** are elements of nonmaterial culture in the form of specialized skills that benefit others, such as giving spiritual comfort or providing medical care. Goods and services are valued because they satisfy various human needs. To produce these goods and services, societies must have suitable technologies.

Anthropological Explanations of Technology

As we saw in an earlier section of the text, in the nineteenth century, anthropologists such as E. B. Tylor and Lewis Morgan constructed a unilineal scheme of cultural evolution in which societies progressed from the simple, small-scale societies of "savages" to the more complex industrial technologies of modern civilizations. In the twentieth century, these simplistic views of technological evolution were rejected through detailed ethnographic research. Anthropologists in the 1950s and 1960s such as Leslie White, Julian Steward, and other anthropologists—who became known as *cultural materialists*—came to view technology as one of the primary factors of cultural evolution. White defined technology as an energy-capturing system made up of energy, tools, and products—that is, all the material means with which energy is harnessed, transformed, and expended (1959). These anthropologists viewed technology as a basic and primary source of sociocultural change. They argued that we cannot explain different technological developments in society with reference to "values." Instead, technology must be viewed as a method designed to cope with a particular environment. Therefore, variations in environment, or habitat, could account for the differences between, say, the Inuit (Eskimo) and the Australian aborigine societies.

White's views on technology, as well as the views of other cultural materialists, have been criticized as a rigid form of "technological determinism." Although the cultural materialists see sociological, ideological, or emotional factors as conditioning or limiting the use or development of technology, these factors exert little influence on sociocultural systems compared to technology's dominant role. Anthropologists are currently evaluating this cultural materialist hypothesis to determine whether technology is a primary variable in societal development or whether a number of factors work in conjunction with technology to condition societal developments and evolution. So far, anthropologists have concluded that technology alone does not result in cultural change and transformation, but rather cultural values, beliefs, and practices interact with technology to create changes. For example, the Old Order Amish people reject modern technology because of their significant religious beliefs and cultural values. Technology has to be understood with respect to the cultural context in which it is accepted, rejected, or modified by human communities.

Economy

Like other animals, humans universally require food and shelter. In addition, humans have special needs for other goods and services, ranging from hunting materials to spiritual guidance. As we have seen, these goods and services are produced through technology. The **economy** of a society consists of the social relationships that organize the production, exchange, and consumption of goods and services. **Production** is the organized system for the creation of goods and services. **Exchange** is the process whereby members of society transfer goods and services among one another. **Consumption** is the use of goods and services to satisfy desires and needs. We are going to examine these three different components of the economy in subsequent chapters in various forms of society.

Anthropologists have found that the economy is closely connected with the environment, subsistence base, demographic conditions, technology, and division of labor of the society. The **division of labor** consists of specialized economic roles (occupations) and activities. In small-scale societies, the division of labor is typically simple, and in large-scale societies it is extremely complex. In the twentieth century, ethnographic descriptions of different types of societies have generated two perspectives on economic systems: the *formalist* and *substantivist* approaches.

The Formalist Approach

The formalist view maintains that all economic systems are fundamentally similar and can be compared with one another. Formalists assume that all people act to maximize their individual self-interest and gains. In other words, all humans have a psychological inclination to calculate carefully their self-interest. Formalists hypothesize that people do not always choose the cheapest and most efficient strategies to carry out their economic decisions, but they do tend to look for the best "rational" strategy for economic decision making.

Formalists hold that the best method for studying any economy is to employ the same general theories developed by economists. Formalists collect quantitative data and interpret these data by using sophisticated mathematical models developed by economists. They focus on such economic variables as production and consumption patterns, supply and demand, exchange, and investment decisions. One classic formalist study, by anthropologist Sol Tax (1953), focused on economic decision making in Guatemalan Indian communities. Tax analyzed the economic transactions in the traditional markets of these communities. He concluded that although the economy was undeveloped, the people made the same types of economic decisions as people in the developed world. Tax referred to these Indians as "penny capitalists."

The Substantivist Approach

The substantivist approach draws its supporting hypotheses from twentieth-century ethnographic studies. Substantivists maintain that the ways of allocating goods and services in small-scale societies differ fundamentally from those of large-scale Western economic systems. Thus, the social institutions found in small-scale societies or larger agricultural societies produce economic systems that are fundamentally different from the market economies of Western societies. According to substantivists, preindustrial economies are not driven by the motive of individual material gain or profit, as are industrial economies. They argue that the economy is *embedded* in the sociocultural system, including the kinship systems, values, beliefs, and norms of the society. These substantivists also argue that modern capitalist societies are *embedded* within an economy based on market exchange. Other precapitalist societies have other forms of exchange, such as reciprocity and redistribution. We focus on these other forms of exchange in later chapters. In general, substantivists emphasize that precapitalist societies had different forms of logic and processes than the market exchange economies of capitalist societies.

Contemporary Economic Anthropology

Most anthropologists today do not identify exclusively with the formalist or the substantivist perspective; instead, they recognize the contributions of both perspectives to our knowledge of economic systems (Wilk 1996; Gudeman 1986; Bloch and Parry 1989). Modern anthropologists investigate the different patterns of production, ownership, distribution, exchange, and consumption in relationship to ecological, demographic, and cultural factors, which influence economic choices, risk, and consumption preferences. They collect quantitative economic data along with more qualitative cultural data (*emic*-insider's understandings) to explain the workings of economic choices and systems. As we see in later chapters, most economic anthropologists are not as concerned with how precapitalist societies organized their economies; rather, they are more concerned with how precapitalist economies change as they are influenced by globalization and contact with the global market economy. In addition, many anthropologists are using psychological experiments based on game theory or other models to assess how people make their economic decisions (Boyd and Richerson 2004; Gil-White and

Heinrich). These new psychological experiments tend to demonstrate that human economic decision making is not wholly based on rational calculations, but rather is influenced by "emotional" factors regarding choices and preferences. In later chapters we discuss the empirical data gathered by anthropologists about different types of economic systems and how they are affected and dramatically influenced by global change.

Social Structure

All inorganic and organic things, from planets to living cells, have a structure; that is, they consist of interrelated parts in a particular arrangement. Buildings, snowflakes, amoebas, and the human body all have a certain structure. A book has a certain structure consisting of rectangular printed pages, binding, and a cover. All books have a similar structure, although the characteristics of different books can vary significantly.

Anthropologists use the image of structure when they analyze different societies. Societies are not just random, chaotic collections of people who interact with one another. Rather, social interaction in any society takes place in regular patterns. As we discussed in Chapter 4, through the process of enculturation, people learn the norms, values, and behavioral patterns of their society. In the absence of social patterns, people would find social life highly confusing. Anthropologists refer to this pattern of relationships in society as the **social structure**. Social structure provides the framework for all human societies, though it is not a static, determining influence on decision making and choice by individuals.

Components of Social Structure

One of the most important components of social structure is *status*. **Status** is a recognized position that a person occupies in society. A person's status determines where he or she fits in society in relationship to everyone else. Status may be based on or accompanied by wealth, power, prestige, or a combination of all of these. Many anthropologists use the term **socioeconomic status** to refer to how a specific position is related to the division of labor, the political system, and other cultural variables.

All societies recognize both *ascribed* and *achieved* statuses. An **ascribed status** is one that is attached to a person from birth or that a person assumes involuntarily later in life. The most prevalent ascribed statuses are based on family and kinship relations (for example, daughter or son), sex (male or female), and age. In addition, in some societies ascribed statuses are based on one's race or ethnicity. For example, as we see in a later chapter, skin color was used to designate ascribed status differences in South Africa under the system of apartheid.

In contrast, an **achieved status** is one based at least in part on a person's voluntary actions. Examples of achieved statuses in the United States are one's profession and level of education. Of course, one's family and kinship connections may influence one's profession and level of education. George W. Bush's or John Kerry's educational level and status are interrelated to their family of birth. However, these individuals had to act voluntarily to achieve their status.

Closely related to status is the concept of social *roles*. A **role** is a set of expected behavior patterns, obligations, and norms attached to a particular status. The distinction between status and role is a simple one: You "occupy" a certain status, but you "play" a role (Linton 1936). For example, as a student you occupy a certain status that differs from that of your professor, administrators, and other staff. As you occupy that status, you perform by attending lectures, taking notes, participating in class, and studying for examinations. This concept of role is derived from the theater and refers to the parts played by actors on the stage. If you are a husband, mother, son, daughter, teacher, lawyer, judge, male, or female, you are expected to behave in certain ways because of the norms associated with that particular status.

As mentioned, a society's social statuses usually correspond to wealth, power, and prestige. Anthropologists find that all societies have inequality in statuses, which are arranged in a hierarchy. This inequality of statuses is known as **social stratification**. The degree of social stratification varies from one society to another, depending on technological, economic, and political variables. Small-scale societies tend to be less stratified than large-scale societies; that is, they have fewer categories of status and fewer degrees of difference regarding wealth, power, and prestige.

Anthropologists find that in some societies wealth, power, and prestige are linked with ownership of land or the number of animals acquired. In our society, high status is strongly correlated with the amount of wages or salary a person receives or how much property in the form of stocks or other paper assets is held. Exploring the causes of differing patterns of social stratification and how this stratification relates to other facets of society is an important objective of an ethnographic study.

The social structure of any society has several major components that anthropologists look at when analyzing a society. These components are discussed in the following sections on family, marriage, gender, and age.

The Family

Many years ago, in a comprehensive cross-cultural study, George Murdock (1945) found that all societies recognize the family. Thus, the family is a *universal* feature of humans. Anthropologists define the **family** as a social group of two or more people related by blood, marriage, or adoption who live or reside together for an extended period, sharing economic resources and caring for their young. Anthropologists differentiate between the *family of orientation*, the family into which people are born and receive basic enculturation, and the *family of procreation*, the family within which people reproduce or adopt children of their own (Murdock 1949). The family is a social unit within a much wider group of relatives, or *kin*. As we see in later chapters, kinship relationships beyond the immediate nuclear family play a significant role in most societies throughout the world. Anthropologists study kinship relationships along with the family to fully comprehend how individual thought and behavior is influenced by these interacting aspects of human communities.

Although variations exist in types and forms, as mentioned before, George Murdock found that the family is a universal aspect of social organization. The reason for the universality of the family appears to be that it performs certain basic functions that serve human needs. The primary function of the family is the nurturing and enculturation of children. The basic norms, values, knowledge, and worldview of the culture are transmitted to children through the family.

Another function of the family is the regulation of sexual activity. Every culture places some restrictions on sexual behavior. Sexual intercourse is the basis of human reproduction and inheritance; it is also a matter of considerable social importance. Regulating sexual behavior is therefore essential to the proper functioning of a society. The family prohibits sexual relations within the immediate family through the incest avoidance behaviors, as discussed in Chapter 4.

Families also serve to protect and support their members physically, emotionally, and often economically from birth to death. In all societies people need warmth, food, shelter, and care. Families provide a social environment in which these needs can be met. Additionally, humans have emotional needs for affection and intimacy that are most easily fulfilled within the family.

The two major types of families found throughout the world are the *nuclear* and *extended* families. A typical **nuclear family** is composed of two parents and their immediate biological offspring or adopted children. George Murdock believed that the nuclear family is a universal feature of all societies (1949). What he meant by this was that all societies have a male and female who reproduce children and are the core of the kinship unit. However, as we see in later chapters, the nuclear family is not the principal kinship unit in all societies. In many societies the predominant form is the **extended family**, which is composed of parents, children, and other kin relations bound together as a social unit.

Marriage

In most societies the family is a product of **marriage**, a social bond sanctioned by society between two or more people that involves economic cooperation, social obligations, rights, duties, and sometimes culturally approved sexual activity. Two general patterns of marriage exist: **endogamy**, which is marriage between people of the same social group or category; and **exogamy**, marriage between people of different social groups and categories.

A marriage may include two or more partners. **Monogamy** generally involves two individuals in the marriage. Though this is the most familiar form of marriage in Western industrial societies, it is not

A wedding in India.

the only type of marriage practiced in the world. Many societies practice some form of **polygamy**, or *plural marriage* involving a spouse of one sex and two or more spouses of the opposite sex. There are two forms of polygamy: **polygyny**, marriage between one husband and two or more wives, and **polyandry**, marriage between one wife and two or more husbands. Although the majority of the world's population currently practices monogamy, polygyny is a common form of marriage and is associated with 80 percent of human societies, many of which have relatively small populations (Murdock 1981a, b). Polyandry is the rarest form of marriage, occurring in only 0.5 percent of all societies. Although typically marriages involve the uniting of males and females, a number of societies have homosexual marriages that are recognized socially and legally (Stone 2000). As we will see, anthropologists have developed hypotheses regarding why certain forms of marriage develop within particular sociocultural systems.

Gender

Gender relationships are another important component of the social structure of a society. Typically, when anthropologists discuss relationships between males and females in a society, they distinguish between *sex* and *gender*. **Sex** refers to the biological and anatomical differences between males and females. These differences include the primary sexual characteristics—the sex organs—and secondary sexual characteristics, such as breasts and wider hips for females and more muscular development of the upper torso and extensive body hair for males. Note that these are general tendencies, to which many exceptions exist. That is, many males are smaller and lighter and have less body hair than many females. Nevertheless, in general, males and females are universally distinguished by physiological and anatomical differences.

In contrast to sex, most anthropologists view *gender* as based on a cultural rather than biological distinction. **Gender** refers to the specific human traits attached to each sex by a society. As members of a particular society, males and females occupy certain statuses, such as son, daughter, husband, wife, father, and mother. In assuming the gender roles that correspond to these different status positions, males are socialized to be "masculine," and females are socialized to be "feminine." Anthropologists find that definitions of masculine and feminine vary among different societies. Presently, some anthropologists do recognize that the boundaries between sex and gender may vary depending on how people within the society culturally construe these categories. In other words, in some cases, the boundaries between sex and gender are "fuzzy" rather than distinctly defined in some societies (Yanagisako and Collier 1990).

Gender and Enculturation One major issue regarding gender is the degree to which enculturation influences male and female behavior. To study this issue, anthropologists focus on the values, beliefs, and worldviews that may influence gender roles. They also observe the types of activities associated with young boys and girls. In many societies, boys and girls play different games as an aspect of enculturation. For example, in U.S. society, boys are traditionally encouraged to participate in aggressive, competitive team sports, whereas girls have not traditionally been encouraged to do so. Cultural values and beliefs that affect gender roles are found in other societies as well.

Gender and the Division of Labor A basic component of the division of labor in most societies is the assigning of different tasks to males and females. In studying this phenomenon, anthropologists focus on the issue of whether physical differences between males and females are responsible for these different roles. To address this issue, they ask a number of questions: Is there a universal division of labor based on sex? Does physical strength have anything to do with the work patterns associated with gender? Do child care and pregnancy determine or influence economic specialization for females? To what degree do values and beliefs ascribed to masculine or feminine behavior affect work assignments?

Gender and Status Another important issue investigated by anthropologists is the social and political status of males and females in society. As is discussed in a later chapter, some early anthropologists such as Lewis Morgan believed that females at one time had a higher social and political status than males, but through time that pattern was reversed. Anthropologists currently focus on how the status of males and females is related to biology, the division of labor, kinship relations, political systems, and values and beliefs.

Although sex characteristics are biologically determined, gender roles vary in accordance with the technological, economic, and sociocultural conditions of particular types of societies. In later chapters we explore some recent studies by anthropologists who have broadened our understanding of the variation of gender roles among a wide range of societies.

Age

Like kinship and gender, age is a universal principle used to prescribe social status in sociocultural systems. The biological processes of aging are an inevitable aspect of human life; from birth to death our bodies are constantly changing. Definite biological changes occur for humans in their progress from infancy to childhood to adolescence to adulthood and to old age. Hormonal and other physio-logical changes lead to maturation and the onset of the aging process. For example, as we approach old age, our sensory abilities begin to change. Taste, eyesight, touch, smell, and hearing begin to diminish. Gray hair and wrinkles appear, and we experience a loss of height and weight and an overall decline in strength and vitality. Although these physical changes vary greatly from individual to individual and to some extent are influenced by societal and environmental factors, these processes are universal.

The biology of aging, however, is only one dimension of how age is related to the social structure of any specific culture. The human life cycle is the basis of social statuses and roles that have both a physical and a cultural dimension. The cultural meanings of these categories in the life cycle vary among different societies, as do the criteria people use to define age-related statuses. The definitions of the statuses and roles for specific ages have wide-ranging implications for those in these status positions.

Age and Enculturation As people move through the different phases of the human life cycle, they continually experience the process of enculturation. Because of the existence of different norms, values, and beliefs, people in various societies may be treated differently at each phase of the life cycle. For example, the period of enculturation during childhood varies among societies. In the United States and other industrialized societies, childhood is associated with an extensive educational experience that continues for many years. In many preindustrial societies, however, childhood is a relatively short period of time, and children assume adult status and responsibilities at a fairly young age.

Another factor influenced by aging in a society is how individuals are viewed at different ages. How is "old age" defined? For example, in many societies old age is not defined strictly in terms of the passage of time. More frequently, old age is defined in respect to changes in social status, work patterns, family status, or reproductive potential (Cowgill 1986). These factors influence how people are valued at different ages in a society.

Age and the Division of Labor Another societal factor that is influenced by the aging process is the economic role assumed by a person at different stages of the life cycle. Children everywhere are

An elderly Japanese woman accepts assistance at a grocery store.

exposed to the technological skills they will need to survive in their environment. As they mature, they assume specific positions in the division of labor. Just as male and female roles differ, the roles for the young and old differ. For example, in some preindustrial societies, older people occupy central roles, whereas in others they play no important role at all. In industrial societies, the elderly generally do not occupy important occupational roles.

Age and Status Age is one of the key determinants of social status. People are usually assigned a particular status associated with a phase of the life cycle. The result is **age stratification**, the unequal allocation of wealth, power, and prestige among people of different ages. Anthropologists find that age stratification varies in accordance with the level of technological development. For example, in many preindustrial societies, the elderly have a relatively high social status, whereas in most industrial societies the elderly experience a loss of status.

One of the most common ways of allocating the status of people at different ages is through *age*

grades. **Age grades** are statuses defined by age, through which a person moves as he or she ages. For example, the age grades in most industrial societies correspond to the periods of infancy, preschool, kindergarten, elementary school, intermediate school, high school, young adulthood, middle age, young old, and old old (Cowgill 1986). Each of these grades conveys a particular social status.

Age Status and Rites of Passage Anthropologists have done considerable research on the **rites of passage**, rituals associated with the life cycle and the movement of people between different age-status levels. Almost all cultures have rites of passage to demarcate these different stages of the life cycle. Arnold Van Gennep (1960), a Belgian anthropologist, wrote a classic study of different rites of passage throughout the world. He noted similarities among various rites connected with birth, puberty, marriage, and funerals. According to Van Gennep, these rites of passage are characterized by three interconnected stages: *separation*, *marginality*, and *aggregation*.

The first phase, *separation*, transforms people from one age status to another. In this phase, people leave behind the symbols, roles, and norms associated with their former position. The second phase, referred to as *marginality*, places people in a state of transition or a temporary period of ambiguity. This stage often involves separating individuals from the larger society to undergo traditional ordeals or indoctrination. The final phase is *aggregation*, or incorporation, when individuals assume their new status.

The best-known examples of these rites of passage are various religious rituals associated with adolescence, such as the confirmation rituals associated with Catholicism and the *bar mitzvah* rituals in Judaism. In later chapters we encounter examples of different rites of passage. The importance of these rites as an aspect of aging, status, and enculturation are explored there.

Political Organization

In the early twentieth century, German sociologist Max Weber introduced definitions of political power and authority that have since been adopted and modified by cultural anthropologists. Weber defined

political power as the ability to achieve personal ends despite opposition. In this sense, political power can be based on physical or psychological *coercion*. Weber perceived this type of political power as *illegitimate*, in that it is unacceptable to most members of a society. According to Weber, the most effective and enduring form of political power is based on **authority**, power generally perceived by members of society as legitimate rather than coercive.

A brief example will illustrate the difference between illegitimate and legitimate power. If a large country invades and conquers a smaller one, the occupied people generally will not consider their new rulers to be legitimate. Thus, the rulers must rely on coercion to enforce their laws and to collect payments in the form of taxes or tributes. In contrast, most U.S. citizens voluntarily comply with the tax laws. Although they may complain, they perceive their government as representing legitimate authority. Although physical coercion and force might be used to arrest some people who refuse to pay their taxes, in the majority of cases such actions are not necessary.

Types of Political Systems

The general categories used by anthropologists to describe political systems are band, tribe, chiefdom, and state. In the next chapter we describe band societies associated with hunter-gatherers. A **band** is the least complex—and most likely the oldest—form of political system. Political institutions in band societies are based on close kinship relations within a fairly small group of people. In Chapter 10, we discuss **tribes** as more complex societies with political institutions that unite larger groupings of people into a political system. Generally tribal societies developed along with food production. Tribes do not have centralized, formal political institutions, but they do have **sodalities**, groups based on kinship, age, or gender that provide for political organization. For example, in some tribal societies of Papua New Guinea, secret male societies function as political institutions.

In Chapter 11 we will discuss **chiefdom** political systems, which are more complex than tribal societies in that they are formalized and centralized. Chiefdoms establish centralized, legitimate authority over many communities through a variety of complex economic, social, and religious institutions. Despite their size and complexity, however, chiefdoms are still fundamentally organized by kinship principles. Although chiefdoms have different levels of status and political authority, the people within these levels are related to one another through kinship ties.

Chapter 12 will discuss the evolution of **states**, which are political systems with centralized bureaucratic institutions to establish power and authority over large populations in distinctive territories. State systems are not based on kinship. State bureaucracies govern society on behalf of ruling authorities through procedures that plan, direct, and coordinate highly complex political processes. State political systems range from the early bureaucratic political units of agricultural societies such as ancient Egypt and China to the modern industrial societies of the United States, Japan, the former Soviet Union, and European nations.

These various institutions and practices of these types of societies are discussed in the next several chapters. Nevertheless, it must be emphasized here that this classification does not represent a single scheme of political evolution for the entire world. The archaeological and ethnographic data demonstrate again and again that a stage-by-stage development or evolution from band to tribe to chiefdom to state did not occur in all areas. These classifications are to be used only as categories to organize the vast amounts of data accumulated by anthropologists. As with all models, the boundaries separating the various categories are somewhat arbitrary and fuzzy.

Decision Making in a Political System

An important topic in the study of a society is the day-to-day, individual decision making and competition for power and authority. In studying this topic, anthropologists may focus on *fields* or *arenas* within a society. A field is an area in which political interaction and competition take place (Bourdieu 1977). It may involve a part of a society, or it may extend beyond the boundaries of a society. For example, a field could be a whole tribe, a chiefdom, a state, or several of these units. A political arena is a more local, specific area in which individual actors or small groups compete for power and authority. An arena may be made up of factions, elites, or political parties in a society. Another aspect of political anthropology is the focus on how political succession occurs within different societies. In other words, who inherits or is appointed or elected to political offices or roles within a society. As we will see, various strategies are developed in different societies to determine who gains political power and authority.

Warfare and Feuds

The study of politics includes political conflicts within and among societies. Two major forms of conflicts are warfare and feuds. Anthropologists define **warfare** as armed combat among territorial or political communities. They distinguish between *internal warfare*, which involves political communities within the same society or culture, and *external warfare*, which occurs among different societal groups. A **feud** is a type of armed combat occurring within a political community and usually involves one kin group taking revenge against another kin group (Otterbein 1974; Kelly 2003). Anthropologists examine the different biological, environmental, demographic, economic, social, political, and other cultural variables that influence warfare and feuds.

Law and Social Control

Another aspect of political anthropology is the study of law and social control. As discussed in Chapter 3, one aspect of nonmaterial culture is the normative dimension, sometimes referred to as an *ethos*. All societies maintain an ethos that encourages certain behaviors and prohibits others. This ethos, along with the society's values, makes up the moral code that shapes human behavior. The particular ethos of a society represents an attempt to establish social control through various internal and external mechanisms. The internal mechanisms of social control are built into the enculturation process itself. Through enculturation, people learn the specific norms regarding society's expectations. Thereafter, those who violate these norms frequently experience emotional and cognitive discomfort in the form of guilt. Thus, internalized norms can shape and influence people's behavior, even in the absence of constraints from other people.

Despite these internal mechanisms, however, individuals frequently violate norms. For a variety of reasons, including biological influences on behavior, enculturation does not bring about perfect social control in a society. Hence, in addition to internal mechanisms, societies use external mechanisms to enforce norms. External mechanisms take the form of sanctions: rewards (positive sanctions) for appropriate behaviors, and punishments (negative sanctions) for inappropriate behaviors.

Societies vary with respect to both the nature of their moral code and the types of external sanctions used to enforce the moral code. What one societal group considers deviant or unethical may be acceptable to another group. Divorce is an acceptable solution for severe marital conflicts in the United States. In Italy and Ireland, however, despite recent legislation that allows divorce, many still view it as an unethical pattern of behavior.

In large, complex social groups, sanctions are usually highly formalized. Rewards can take the form of public awards, parades, educational or professional degrees, and banquets. Negative sanctions include fines, imprisonment, expulsion, and sometimes death. In small-scale societies, sanctions tend to be informal. Examples of positive sanctions are smiles, handshakes, pats on the back, hugs, and compliments. Negative sanctions include restricted access to certain goods and services, gossip, frowns, impolite treatment, and ostracism.

Law as Formalized Norms and Sanctions   Anthropologists define *laws* as clearly defined norms, violations of which are punished through the application of formal sanctions by ruling authorities. In the 1960s, cultural anthropologist Leopold J. Pospisil attempted to distinguish law from other social norms, based on his research among the Kapaukan tribe of New Guinea. He specified four criteria that must be present for a norm to be considered a law: (1) authority, (2) intention of universal application, (3) obligation, and (4) sanction (1967). To institutionalize legal decisions, a society must have members who possess recognized authority and can therefore intervene to settle disputes. These authorities must be able to enforce a verdict by either persuasion or force. Their verdicts must have universal application; that is, these decisions must be applied in the same manner if a similar situation arises in the future. This distinguishes

South Korean students and police control.

legal decisions from those based purely on political expediency.

Obligation refers to the status relationships among the people involved in the conflict. If status relationships are unequal, the rights, duties, and obligations of the different parties can vary. Legal decisions must attempt to define the rights and obligations of everyone involved and to restore or create an equitable resolution of the conflict. Finally, punitive sanctions must be applied to carry out the legal decision. More recently in ethnographic studies, anthropologists have abandoned any simplistic universalistic aspect that defines law from norms. Presently, anthropologists study the language, symbolism, and discourse used in society to distinguish legal sanctions along with historical and global developments that have an influence on legal processes. A new journal called the *POLAR* (*Political and Legal Anthropology Review*) features many articles by anthropologists as they study legal processes in many different countries of the world.

Religion

As we saw in Chapter 2, archaeologists have discovered some limited evidence of religious beliefs and practices associated with archaic *Homo sapiens*, or Neandertals, that date back to 100,000 years ago. Religion is a cultural universal, although specific beliefs and practices vary significantly from one society to another. For example, some religions are based on the worship of an all-knowing, all-powerful supreme being, whereas others have many deities, and some may have no deities at all. The term religion itself is derived from a Latin term *religio* that had different meanings in Western history. In some cases it referred to a "transcendent" experience that individuals had beyond normal everyday social life, but at other times it referred to "superstition" or "piety" (Saler 1993). It has been extremely difficult for anthropologists to define religion with a simple formula because it varies so much from one region and culture to another (Scupin 2000; Saler 1993; Boyer 2001; Crapo 2003).

Humans learn their religious traditions through the process of enculturation. Religious convictions are, therefore, shaped by the historical and social situations in which a person lives. For example, a person enculturated in ancient Greece would most likely have believed in many deities, among whom Zeus was the most powerful.

In studying the anthropology of religion, a critical point must be understood: Anthropologists are not concerned with the "truth" or "falsity" of any particular religious belief. As anthropology is partially based on the scientific method, the field of anthropology is not competent or able to investigate supernatural or metaphysical questions that go beyond empirical data. Rather, anthropological research on religion focuses on the relationship of doctrines, beliefs, and other religious questions to aspects of cognition, emotions, and society. Most anthropologists recognize that religious faith is not a testable proposition that can be analyzed by science or logic. Faith is beyond empirical findings that can be uncovered by scientific investigation. The major questions posed by anthropologists are: How do religious beliefs become established within a society? How do religious beliefs affect, relate to, and reflect the cognitive, emotional, and sociocultural conditions and concerns of a group of people?

In addition, anthropologists often use the humanistic-interpretive approach when analyzing religious beliefs, symbols, and myths. Clifford Geertz (1973, 90) offered a sophisticated definition of religion to use as a tool in this humanistic-interpretive mode of understanding religion:

> A religion is a system of symbols which acts to establish powerful, pervasive, and long-lasting moods and motivations in men by formulating conceptions of a general order of existence and clothing these conceptions with such an aura of factuality that the moods and motivations seem uniquely realistic.

Let us examine this definition more closely. Central to any religion is a "system of symbols" that includes all sacred objects, ranging from Christian crucifixes, Native American "medicine pouches," and Buddhist relics, to sacred myths such as "Genesis" or the "Ramayana" of Hinduism. These symbols produce "moods," such as happiness and sadness, and "motivations" that provide direction or ethical goals in a person's life. Hence, religious symbols enhance particular feelings and dispositions, creating an intense sense of awe in individuals. This sense of awe is induced through the use of sacred symbols in rituals and other religious performances to create an atmosphere of mystery going beyond everyday experience. But religious symbols also create and reaffirm a worldview by "formulating conceptions of a general order of existence." This worldview provides meaning or purpose to life and the universe. A religious worldview helps people discern the meaning of pain and suffering in the world. Sacred myths help people make sense of the world and also explain and justify cultural values and social rules. One problem with Geertz's definition of religion is that it does not regard the great deal of diversity of cultural beliefs, worldviews (a questionable concept), symbolic meanings, and the multiplicity of practices and variation within any religious tradition— something that Geertz himself has recognized recently (2000). In other words, as we emphasized in earlier chapters, presently anthropologists are more aware that the concept of culture used in the past is not useful in understanding different religions or civilizations.

Myths

The study of the religious traditions includes the analysis and interpretation of myths. **Myths** consist of a people's assumed knowledge about the universe and the natural and supernatural worlds, and humanity's place in these worlds. In Chapter 2, we presented some basic myths or cosmologies regarding the creation of the universe. All societies have such sacred myths. Anthropologists focus on a number of questions regarding myths: Why do myths of a particular type exist in different societies? What is the relationship between myths and other aspects of sociocultural systems? Are myths distortions of historical events? Or, as Geertz suggests earlier in the chapter, do myths provide a blueprint for comprehending the natural and social world for a society? What are the functions of myths? How are myths interpreted and reinterpreted by different people within the society?

Rituals

The final portion of Geertz's definition—that these systems of symbols act to clothe those conceptions in "such an aura of factuality that the moods and motivations seem uniquely realistic"—attempts to deal with the question often asked about religious belief: How do humans come to believe in ideas about spirits, souls, revelations, and many unsupportable or untestable conceptions? Geertz's answer to this question is that religious rituals in which humans participate create an "aura of factuality." It is through ritual that deeper realities are reached. Religion is nonempirical and nonrational in its search for truth. It is not based on conclusions from scientific experience but is "prior" to experience. Religious truth is not "inductive," providing evidence for metaphysical explanations. It symbolically and abstractly evokes the ultimate concerns of humans. Through ritual activities these symbolic and abstract nonempirical truths are given meaning.

Religious **rituals** consist of repetitive behaviors that communicate sacred symbols to members of society. Examples of religious rituals are the Catholic Mass, Jewish Passover rites, and the Native American sweat lodge rites, which include prayer, meditation, and other spiritual communication. Anthropologist Edmund Leach (1966) emphasized that religious rituals communicate these sacred symbols and information in a condensed manner. He noted that the verbal part of a ritual is not separable from the behavioral part and that rituals can have different symbolic meanings for people in a society. In other words, religious rituals convey a unique, personal, psychological experience for every individual who participates.

Religious Specialists

One important area of research in the anthropology of religion is the study of religious specialists in different societies. Every society has certain individuals who possess specialized, sacred knowledge. Such individuals officiate over rituals and interpret myths. The type of religious specialist varies with the form of sociocultural system. **Shamans** are usually part-time religious practitioners who are believed to have contact with supernatural beings and powers. They do not have a formalized official status as religious practitioners in their respective societies. As we see in later chapters, shamans are involved in various types of healing activities, treating both physical and psychological illnesses. Aside from their religious functions, they participate in the same subsistence activities and functions as anyone else in their society. Anthropologists also use terms such as native healer, medicine man, and medicine woman to refer to these practitioners.

The terms **priest** and **priestess** refer to full-time religious specialists who serve in an official capacity as the custodians of sacred knowledge. In contrast to shamans, priests and priestesses are usually trained through formal educational processes to maintain religious traditions and rituals. Priests and priestesses are usually associated with more complex sociocultural systems.

Religious Movements

Another topic of interest in the anthropology of religion is the analysis of religious movements. In early approaches of the social sciences, religion was

viewed simply as an outcome of certain economic or political conditions in society. It was assumed that as society developed modern economic and political institutions, religious traditions would disappear. Religion was viewed as a peripheral element that served only to conserve society as a static system. Today, however, some anthropologists have begun to analyze religious beliefs and worldviews as major variables that induce societal change. For example, cultural anthropologists studying Islamic fundamentalist movements have concluded that in the Middle East, religion is a major force for social change. These new modes of understanding and explaining religious movements are analyzed in subsequent chapters.

Cognition and Religion

In Chapter 4 we introduced the fields of cognitive anthropology and evolutionary psychology. Cognitive anthropologists Pascal Boyer and Scott Atran have drawn on these two fields in order to explore religion. In Boyer's book *Religion Explained: The Evolutionary Origins of Religious Thought* (2001) and Atran's book *In Gods We Trust: The Evolutionary Landscape of Religion* (2002), these anthropologists both recognize the importance of the humanistic-interpretive approach in understanding religion, but they also want to explore the scientific-causal aspects of religion and the universal aspects of religion everywhere. These anthropologists investigate questions such as: Why does religion matter so much in people's lives everywhere? Are there any common features of religion? Why do certain types of religious beliefs develop rather than other types? Drawing on a vast range of cross-cultural data, these anthropologists suggest that evolution and natural selection have designed the human mind to be "religious." Although there is a tremendous diversity of religious traditions throughout the world, some types of religious beliefs have more resilience and are retained and culturally transmitted by humans more than others. In all societies, children are exposed to various religious beliefs and practices. But, as Atran and Boyer emphasize, because of specific predispositions and intuitions within our evolutionary-designed mind, certain forms of religious beliefs and concepts have exceptional relevance and meaning for humans.

Based on an enormous amount of data in experimental psychology, Atran and Boyer examine

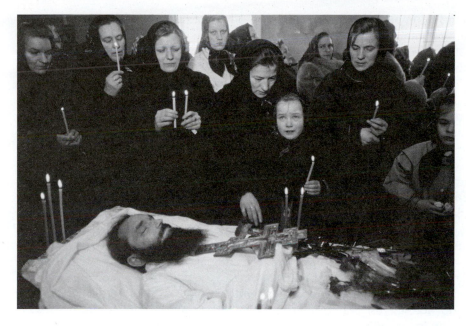

One function of religion is to help people cope with major events and crises, such as death.

what types of intuitive knowledge become evident to children. For example, Boyer indicates that cognitive experiments indicate that if a young child learns that a specific type of animal gives birth to offspring in a particular manner, they will intuitively understand that other types of animals within the same species will give birth in the same manner. They do not have to be exposed to every type of experience in order to develop this intuitive knowledge and make inferences and predictions about various natural phenomena. It appears that, as humans, we build upon mental templates such as ANIMAL, PLANT, PERSON, ARTIFACT, or TOOL. These templates become the basis of inferential and intuitive knowledge that we use to comprehend the world. Children know that objects such as tools or artifacts do not move around or give birth like animals. Boyer does not claim that children are born with these mental templates, but rather, as the mind develops, the child will acquire these templates from an interaction between innate predispositions and a normal environment. Just as children who are not isolated from language acquire their linguistic skills and abilities readily within a normal speaking environment (see Chapter 5), they also develop their intuitive knowledge to make inferences about the world. These inferential systems and intuitive insights do not just enable children to comprehend the natural world. They also provide specialized mechanisms to intuitively understand and empathize with other people's

minds and adjust behaviorally and morally to the social world. Children at an early age learn that other persons have thoughts and intentions, and they can rely on these intuitions to engage in social and moral relationships with other people.

In contrast to the intuitive knowledge and inferences that become a reliable basis for comprehending the natural and social world, both Atran and Boyer emphasize that religious beliefs and knowledge are mostly counterintuitive. Religious spirits and gods have properties that normal people do not have. Although most humans treat religious spirits and gods as persons, they are radically different from what our intuitions tell us about persons. For the most part, they do not eat, grow old, or die; they can even fly through space, become invisible, change shape, and perceive our innermost thoughts. Gods and spirits become invisible partners and friends of people, but these spiritual beings are unlike normal persons. These spiritual agents can be at several places at one time and have full access to our innermost thoughts and specific behaviors and actions. Some societies have a concept of a god that knows everything. Children at an early age and adults understand that normal persons do not have these capacities for knowledge.

These counterintuitive abilities of spirits and gods, including their full access to our thoughts and specific behaviors, are "attention-grabbing" for humans throughout the world. Spiritual agents who have this full access to knowledge become extremely relevant in understanding human social and moral conditions. Beings that can know our innermost thoughts and all of our behaviors resonate with our social and moral intuitions. Thus, religious beliefs and concepts become widespread and plausible in all societies because of the way human cognition is organized and designed. Beliefs in witches, ancestral spirits, and angry or beneficent gods become easily represented in all cultures because they are dependent on our human cognitive capacities and intuitive understandings of the natural and social world. These religious phenomena activate and trigger our human cognitive capacities and intuitive abilities, which results in the universal distribution of certain types of spiritual beliefs and concepts.

Both Atran and Boyer explain why religious beliefs have become so powerful throughout human prehistory and history. They do not suggest that there is a specialized area of the brain, or "religious instinct," that is a religious center that handles god-related or spiritual-related thoughts. In addition, they do not suggest that there are specific people who have exceptional religious abilities and were responsible for establishing religious beliefs and practices. Religion, like other everyday matters in our natural and social circumstances, does not require special capacities. Rather, religious beliefs and concepts become relevant to humans everywhere because they readily coincide with our cognitive capacities and intuitive and inferential abilities. These religious beliefs and concepts are likely to have a direct effect on people's thoughts, emotions, and morality. In addition, religious beliefs are different from scientific theories in that they don't easily assimilate with our cognitive dispositions and intuitions. Religious beliefs have commonalities such as spiritual agents that have full access to our innermost thoughts, concepts of life after death, and concepts of morality all over the world, and most likely have a long evolutionary history. Other religious beliefs may have developed in the past, but they did not have the cognitive resilience or sustaining power of the ones known today, and they disappeared. The religious beliefs that still exist have a central relevance to many people and are extremely powerful and converge with their cognitive capacities and abilities. In some cases, people give up their lives or kill others based on their particular religious beliefs.

Atran's and Boyer's exploration of the interconnection between human cognition and religious expression has contributed toward anthropological hypotheses about our cognitive capacities and links between biological and psychological developments and our religious life. Many other cognitive anthropologists are following in these studies to support or negate these hypotheses.

Cross-Cultural Research

This chapter has focused on the analysis of universals and variables and their interconnections within specific societies. Although the primary objective of ethnographic research is to improve our understanding of a particular sociocultural system, another aim is to provide a basis for comparing different societies and to offer general explanations for human behavior. Specific ethnographies provide the necessary data for this type of cross-cultural research. This cross-cultural research is usually referred to as ethnological research. Anthropologists use ethnological research to further explore the universal and specific cultural conditions that influence the development of societies throughout the world.

Cross-cultural research has been an ongoing project in anthropology for the past hundred years or so. Recently, a great deal of ethnographic data has been computerized in the Human Relations Area Files, commonly known as the HRAF. The HRAF contains descriptive ethnographic data on more than 300 societies. Initiated by George P. Murdock of Yale University, it is made up of original ethnographic descriptions classified for cross-cultural research purposes. Murdock incorporated data on 862 societies in his *Ethnographic Atlas* (1981b) and on 563 societies that cover the major geographic regions of the world in his *Atlas of World Cultures* (1981a). These ethnographic databases enable scholars to retrieve information quickly and can be used for statistical and computerized cross-cultural research. These databases are extremely valuable sources for assessing the differences and similarities among cultures. Cross-cultural studies allow anthropologists to make distinctions between behaviors that are culture specific and those that are universal. These distinctions help anthropologists provide general explanations for human behavior. In doing so, these studies help fulfill the major goals of anthropological research.

Cross-cultural methods have some limitations, however. One major weakness is that some cultural anthropologists in the past may not have taken historical circumstances into account when describing the particular conditions in a society. This omission may have led to a static, unchanging portrait of the society studied. For example, the description of the economic practices of people in Africa, Asia, or the Pacific Islands may not make sense outside of a specific historical context. These societies had historical relationships with other societies outside of their own cultural boundaries, and these relationships resulted in changes in the particular economic practices observed by the cultural anthropologist. In later chapters of this text we explore why cultural anthropologists must understand the historical context of different societies that they study so that they can fully comprehend the behavior being observed.

Another problem with cross-cultural studies lies with faulty ethnographic reporting, which can produce unreliable data, contributing in turn to a distorted image of the society being studied. Consequently, anthropologists approach cross-cultural research with caution. Contemporary anthropologists who use these data must review the work of their predecessors who gathered the basic information to assess its validity. Through careful examination of the original data in the HRAF and other cross-cultural databases, modern anthropologists will make further progress toward formulating sound generalizations regarding the cultures of humankind.

SUMMARY

Cultural anthropologists conduct fieldwork in different societies to examine people's lifestyles and behavior. They describe societies in written studies called ethnographies, which focus on behavior and thought among the people studied. Cultural anthropologists must use systematic research methods and strategies in their examination of society. Their basic research method is participant observation, which involves participating in the activities of the people they are studying.

In their analyses of sociocultural systems, anthropologists investigate cause-and-effect relationships among different variables. They use a multidimensional approach, examining the interaction among many variables to provide explanations for the similarities and differences among societies. Anthropologists explore the interaction between the environment and subsistence practices. They examine the biomes of different regions to determine the influence of environment on societal development. They investigate fertility, mortality, and migration to detect changes in demographic conditions. They also investigate the relationship between cultural values and population. Technological and economic variables are assessed in the analysis of society and culture. The technology and economy of a society produce distinctive differences in the division of labor. Anthropologists find that technology and economic conditions are also influenced by cultural values and norms.

Another area of research is social structure, including the family, marriage, kinship, gender, and age. These components of social structure are related to the division of labor and other cultural conditions. Anthropologists explored different types of political organizations and legal systems. Through detailed ethnological research and cross-cultural comparisons, anthropologists have found that specific types of political and legal systems have been influenced by various societal conditions. To analyze different forms of political systems, anthropologists classify societies into bands, tribes, chiefdoms, and states.

The anthropology of religion is devoted to the examination of diverse religious beliefs and worldviews. Myths, rituals, religious specialists, and religious movements are explored in relationship to other aspects of society. Some anthropologists use the humanistic-interpretive method to understand the symbols, myths, rituals, and meaning of religious practices. Other anthropologists focus on the universality of religion and how it is linked with human psychological processes.

Many ethnographic data have been coded for computer use in cross-cultural studies. These cross-cultural studies can be employed to develop general explanations regarding human behavior in specific societies and across cultural boundaries.

QUESTIONS TO THINK ABOUT

1. What are some of the things that a cultural anthropologist has to do to prepare herself or himself for fieldwork?

2. What are some of the research goals of demographic anthropologists as they relate to fieldwork? Why is a demographic perspective important in anthropological research?

3. Do you think that technology is the primary, basic source of sociocultural change? Do values play any role in sociocultural change?

4. What are the basic components of the economy and the division of labor?

5. What are the basic components or patterns of family and marriage from an anthropological view?

6. Have you ever gone through a rite of passage? If so, what was it? Have you experienced more than one? Pick one rite of passage that you have experienced and describe it in terms of Van Gennep's stages of separation, marginality, and incorporation (aggregation).

7. What is the difference between legitimate and illegitimate political power? Give an example of each.

8. Review Clifford Geertz's definition of religion. What do you think are the strengths or weaknesses of his definition?

9. What are the benefits and limitations of conducting cross-cultural research?

KEY TERMS

achieved status
age grades
age stratification
ascribed status
authority
band
biome
carrying capacity
chiefdom
childhood mortality rate
consumption
correlation
crude birth rate
crude death rate
cultural ecology
culture shock
demography
dependent variable
division of labor
ecology
economy
emic perspective
endogamy
environmental niche

etic perspective
exchange
exogamy
extended family
family
fecundity
fertility
feud
gender
goods
independent variable
infant mortality rate
life expectancy
marriage
migration rate
monogamy
mortality
myths
net migration
nuclear family
political power
polyandry
polygamy
polygyny

priest
priestess
production
pull factors
push factors
qualitative data
quantitative data
random sample
rites of passage
rituals
role
services
sex
shamans
social stratification
social structure
socioeconomic status
sodalities
states
status
subsistence patterns
technology
tribes
warfare

Chapter **9**

Band Societies

CHAPTER OUTLINE

CHAPTER QUESTIONS

- What are some of the stereotypes and images about hunter-gatherer societies?

- How are the environments of the modern foraging or band societies different from those of the Paleolithic?

- What are the distinguishing features of the population, economy, social life, political systems, and religious traditions of band societies?

- How has globalization influenced the band societies throughout the world?

Basic Questions about Band or Hunter-Gatherer Societies

In Chapter 2, on human evolution, we discussed the Paleolithic period (Old Stone Age) and discussed the emergence of hunting and gathering as a means of subsistence that goes back to at least 1 million years ago. As the next chapter shows, food production as a subsistence pattern developed relatively recently, about 12,000 to 10,000 years ago. Thus, for almost 99 percent of humanity's life span, humans lived as foragers. This lifestyle has been the most enduring and persistent adaptation humans have ever achieved. Therefore, band societies have been the basic type of sociocultural system for perhaps as long as 1 million years. In this chapter we discuss what anthropologists have learned from their ethnographic studies about contemporary hunting and gathering societies or band societies. When archaeologists do studies of the artifacts found during the Paleolithic to understand the human past, they often look to the ethnographic studies of modern hunter-gatherers. As we will see, most contemporary **hunter-gatherer societies**, with their relatively small groups, low population density, highly nomadic subsistence strategies, and loosely defined territorial boundaries, have social organizations that tie kin (related individuals) together and foster unity within and among groups. Constant circulation of material goods in such societies not only enhances and maintains kin ties through mutual obligations but also inhibits the accumulation of wealth by any individuals in the society. This enables these societies to remain **egalitarian**—societies that have very small differences in wealth among individuals. There are no rich or poor in most of these societies.

Also, the most common form of political organization among ethnographically documented hunter-gatherer societies is the **band**, a fairly small group of people tied together by close kinship relations. A band is the least complex form of political system—and most likely the oldest. Typically, as we will see, each band is politically independent of the others and has its own internal leadership. Most of the leaders in the bands are males, but females also take on some important leadership roles. Leaders are chosen because of their skills in hunting, food collecting, communication, decision making, or other personal abilities. Political leaders, however, generally do not control the group's economic resources or exercise political power as they do in other societies, and there is little, if any, social stratification between political leaders and others in the band. In other words, band societies are highly *egalitarian*, with no major differences between those with and those without wealth or political power. Thus, leaders of bands must lead by persuasion and personal influence rather than by coercion or withholding resources. Leaders do not maintain a military or police force and thus have no definitive authority.

Although it is tempting to draw a similar picture of Paleolithic, Old Stone Age hunters, the analogy is not without limitations. The archaeological record of the Paleolithic is consistent with small kin-based groups. Yet archaeological information on Paleolithic hunter-gatherers suggests that their subsistence strategies varied substantially and probably included the beginnings of some of the complexity, socioeconomic inequality, and more sedentary lifestyle that characterize more recent periods (Price and Brown 1985; Jochim 1996). In addition, anthropologists have also found a vast range of different subsistence and technological developments among contemporary hunter-gatherer societies throughout the world (Kelly 1995). And as Chapter 11, on *chiefdoms* shows, there are some

hunting-gathering societies that were *settled* and *not nomadic* and evolved a much more complex economic, social, and political culture primarily because of the environmental and demographic conditions that existed in some areas of the world.

Also, as discussed at the end of this chapter, the contemporary hunting-gathering societies are not living "fossils" of the Old Stone Age but are *fully modern humans just like you and me*. In contrast to Paleolithic hunting-and-gathering societies who resided in nearly *all* the major biomes and environments of the world, contemporary band societies exist only in limited, marginal environments, those that are not suitable for intensive agriculture. In addition, and most importantly, these modern human band societies are enmeshed in the process of globalization, which has had dramatic consequences for their lifestyle. And, these contemporary hunter-gatherer societies have been in contact with outsiders such as the agricultural societies surrounding them for many years (Bailey et al. 1989). Thus, what we learn from contemporary band societies is nothing comparable to some "pristine" Paleolithic Stone Age society and culture.

As we saw in Chapter 7 on race and ethnicity, most nineteenth-century Western (and non-Western) scholars, scientists, politicians, and others, including anthropologists, had very racist and ethnocentric beliefs about "savages," "barbarians," and culturally inferior peoples with low intelligence throughout the world. Reflecting the views of the time period in the nineteenth century, Mark Twain considered the Shoshone Indians of the Great Basin in Nevada as "the wretchedest type of mankind I have ever seen up to this writing" (Farb 1969; Wright 2000). Charles Darwin also had some of the same nineteenth-century prejudices and racist beliefs about these hunter-gatherer societies. When Darwin observed the Yahgan and Ona in Tierro Del Fuego at the southern end of South America, he wrote in a letter "I feel quite a disgust at the very sound of the voices of these miserable savages" (Wright 1994, 2000).

Sometimes these views are still perpetuated about these contemporary hunting and gathering societies in Africa, Asia, and South America. However, after the nineteenth century, as we saw in Chapter 7, many anthropologists began to do extensive scientific research on race and culture and began to systematically refute these racist and ethnocentric conceptions. In addition, in the twentieth century, cultural anthropologists began to conduct long-term ethnographic research among these people and discovered that the people within these societies have very complex beliefs and a tremendous amount of cultural knowledge about the plants, animals, medical techniques, and environments in which they have been living. As mentioned in Chapter 7, on race and IQ differences, the vast majority of contemporary anthropologists and psychologists concur that there are intelligence differences within all societies based on different inherited capacities and abilities (see pages 162–164). Therefore, contemporary hunters and gatherers are *modern peoples like us* who have adapted to more extreme, marginal environmental and ecological conditions than we have in modern societies. And, we have also learned that some people from these band societies (such as some members of the Shoshone Native American Indians) have become educated in different areas of the world today to become computer scientists, engineers, and even anthropologists. Their intelligence or intellectual capacities have not inhibited them from learning new languages, mathematics, and other modern technologies.

However, the basic question still arises in many people's minds: If these hunting and gathering peoples are generally as intelligent and modern as we in the industrialized and more advanced societies of the world, why did they not develop more complex technologies and subsistence strategies where they lived? In other words, from our contemporary perspective in our advanced high-tech world, why did these hunter-gatherers continue to rely on their "antiquated" techniques and social life for coping in their environments? Why didn't they develop computers and other high-tech accouterments in their societies as we have in our own? If race had anything to do with the development of complex societies, why have anthropologists found that Native American Indians who originated in "Asia" (and have genetics similar to other Asian peoples) have many different forms of sociocultural complexity, including band, tribes, and chiefdom societies in different regions of North America, but did not develop complex agricultural societies like some of the Native American Indians in Central America such as the Maya or the Inca of South America or the Chinese? As we see in this chapter and the later chapters on other preindustrial societies, contemporary ethnographic research

has demonstrated that part of the reason for the perceived lack of technological and cultural development is due to the geographical, environmental, ecological, and historical circumstances that have influenced the development of these societies and cultural traditions.

For example, with respect to the geographical and ecological factors that have had an influence on the development of certain forms of technological and sociocultural conditions in sub-Saharan Africa, prehistoric North and South America, some areas of the Pacific islands, and Asia, Jared Diamond's book *Guns, Germs, and Steel: The Fates of Human Societies* (1997) has influenced many anthropologists. Diamond did many years of ecological research on the plants, animals, and cultures of the Pacific islands of Papua New Guinea, and he draws on an enormous range of data from geographic, ecological, archaeological, and historical data to help illuminate why the Eurasian continent that includes areas of Europe, Russia, and China had some definite geographical and ecological advantages that resulted in the development of complex societies in that continental region, compared to others such as sub-Saharan Africa, prehistoric North and South America, the Pacific islands, and elsewhere. He notes that the Eurasian continent had early connections with the Near East or Fertile Crescent areas of the Nile and Tigris-Euphrates rivers (see Chapter 12) that contained species of plants and animals such as wheat, barley, oats, sheep, cattle, goats, pigs, horses, and others that were easily domesticated for the development of complex agricultural societies. These ideas spread rapidly across the Mediterranean areas of Greece and Rome and other areas of Europe and beyond.

In contrast, the area of Africa, the Pacific island areas such as Australia, and the Americas had very *few species* of animals and plants that could be domesticated and had major geographical obstacles such as large tropical rain forests and deserts and infertile land that inhibited the development of agriculture or the rapid diffusion, or spread of technologies and ideas from one area to the next. These factors limited the technological and sociocultural developments of different areas of the world, whereas other areas had more geographical and ecological advantages that fostered more complex technological and sociocultural developments. Although some archaeologists and anthropologists have refined Diamond's understanding of these developments in different areas of the world, they concur that these geographical and environmental factors did have an enormous influence on technological and sociocultural developments for pre-industrial societies.

You will notice that in this chapter we refer to hunter-gatherers in both the past and present tenses. As a result of contacts with other peoples, many traditional practices and institutions of band societies have been transformed. The past tense is used to describe these traditional phenomena. Those traditions that have managed to persist into the present are discussed in the present tense.

Modern Foraging Environments and Subsistence

During the last 10,000 years, hunting-gathering, band, or **foraging societies** have grown fewer and fewer and are now restricted to marginal environments. Deserts, tropical rain forests, and arctic areas are considered **marginal environments**, because *until recently* too much labor and capital were needed to irrigate deserts, slash down tropical forests for agriculture, or cultivate crops in the Arctic. Consequently, those few foraging or hunter-gatherer societies that adjusted to these marginal environments managed to exist in relative isolation from surrounding groups. Figure 9.1 shows the locations of the major hunter-gatherer societies that still exist.

Deserts

Various cultural-ecological studies have been done with foragers surviving in desert environments. One long-term study focuses on the !Kung San or Ju/'hoansi of the Kalahari Desert in southwestern Africa. The San occupied southern Africa for thousands of years along with another, biologically related population known popularly as the Hottentots, or Khoi. Archaeologist John Yellen (1985) located prehistoric sites in the Kalahari that have been dated to well over 11,000 years ago. This evidence suggests that the !Kung San had been residing in this region before agriculture spread to the surrounding region.

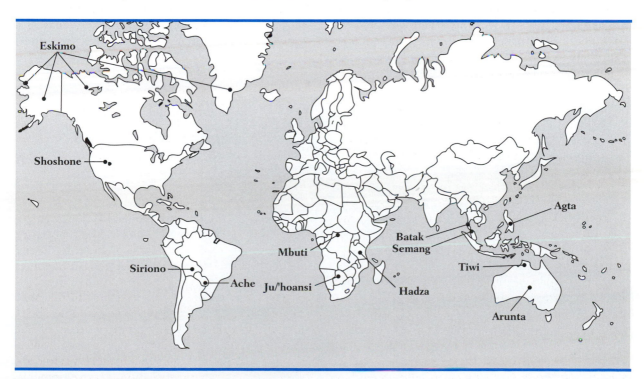

FIGURE 9.1   Hunter-gatherer societies discussed in this chapter.

Most historians and archaeologists agree that the processes of migration and culture contact with surrounding societies have affected the !Kung San, and the "modern" !Kung San do not represent a pure remnant of Paleolithic society. The frequency of interaction of San accelerated with European expansion and settlements throughout southern Africa in the eighteenth century (see Chapter 14). The San people (Bushmen) of southern Africa consist of close to 100,000 people who reside in six countries (Angola, Botswana, Namibia, South Africa, Zambia, and Zimbabwe). Most of the San people reside in the countries of Botswana and Namibia in the Kalahari Desert and consist of different populations such as the G/ui San, !Xo San, the Kua, or Ju/'hoansi San (Hitchcock 2004). Currently, the Ju/'hoansi San in Botswana and Namibia have been studied by anthropologists for almost 70 years. Their population is approximately 7,000 people within this San populace.

Richard Lee, who has studied the Ju/'hoansi San from the 1960s through the present, gives a comprehensive picture of their food-gathering and dietary practices. At the time he studied them in the 1960s and early 1970s, between 60 and 80 percent of the Ju/'hoansi San diet consisted of nuts, roots, fruit, melons, and berries, which were gathered by the women. Meat from hunting was less common,

providing only 20 to 30 percent of the diet. To procure this diet, the Ju/'hoansi San did not need to expend enormous amounts of time and energy. In fact, Lee estimated that Ju/'hoansi San adults spent between two and three days each week finding food. Women often were able to gather enough in one or two days to feed their families for a week, leaving time for resting, visiting, embroidering, and entertaining visitors. Males spent much of their leisure time in ritual activities, including curing ceremonies (Lee 1972b, 1979, 1993).

Other foraging societies existed in various arid and semiarid desert biomes, an example being the Great Basin Shoshone, a Native American Indian group. Shoshone males hunted and trapped game, and Shoshone females gathered seeds, insects, and assorted vegetation. Both males and females harvested wild pinyon nuts, which the women mixed with seeds and insects and ground into flour for cooking.

Many of the Australian Aborigines were hunter-gatherers living in deserts that made up one-third of the continent. One group, known as the Arunta, lived in the interior desert region. They subsisted on the various species of animals and plants found in their habitat. Women and children gathered seeds, roots, snails, insects, reptiles, burrowing rodents, and eggs of birds and reptiles. Arunta males specialized

The Ju/'hoansi San people of the Kalahari Desert.

in hunting larger game such as the kangaroo, the wallaby, the large, ostrichlike emu, and smaller birds and animals. Ethnographic studies indicate that Aborigines spent four to five hours per day per person in gathering food (Sahlins 1972).

Tropical Rain Forests

Foragers have also adapted to the marginal environments of tropical rain forests. In the central African country of Congo, formerly Zaire, a group of foragers known as the Mbuti "Pygmies" (the term Pygmy has a long history going back to ancient Egypt and is considered a pejorative term by these native people today) resides in the luxuriant Ituri rain forest. The first evidence of the Mbuti peoples came from early Egyptian accounts of an expedition into the Ituri forest. From other archaeological data, it appears that the Mbuti have inhabited this region for at least 5,000 years.

The late Colin Turnbull (1983), who did ethnographic research among the Mbuti in the 1960s, did some in-depth ethnographic research on these people. He found that the division of labor among the Mbuti resembles that of other hunting-and-gathering groups. Males hunt elephants, buffalo, wild pigs, and other game, and females gather vegetation. The entire group, including females and children, however, is involved in the hunting endeavor. Mbuti males set up nets to capture the game, after which they stand guard with spears. Youths with bows and arrows stand farther back from the nets to shoot any game that escapes, and women and children form semicircles to drive the game into the nets. More independent hunting is done by older males and youths, who may wander off to shoot monkeys and birds.

Some recent DNA evidence suggests that these native people of Africa were some of the earliest migrants out of Africa into the regions of Asia such as the Andaman islands near the Indian continent, New Guinea, and Australia. The anthropologist Arthur Radcliffe-Brown did research among the Andaman hunter-gatherer populations in the early twentieth century and collected hair samples from them. Modern geneticists have used these hair samples to extract DNA samples and demonstrate a connection between the Andamanese people,

people of south New Guinea and Australia, and these African groups during the ice ages about 35,000 to 40,000 years ago. Archaeologist Peter Bellwood indicates that the archaeological evidence coincides with these genetic findings (2004). This recent hypothesis gives support to the "Out of Africa" hypothesis discussed in Chapter 2.

Another hunting-gathering people, known as the Semang, inhabit the tropical forests of the Malaysian and Thai peninsula. They live in the foothills and lower slopes of dense rain forests that have exceptionally heavy precipitation. Although in the past the Semang may have hunted large game such as elephants and buffalo, they abandoned large-game hunting when they took up the blowgun instead of the bow and arrow (Keyes 1995). Today, Semang males fish and hunt small game. However, Semang subsistence depends primarily on the gathering of wild fruits and vegetables, including yams, berries, nuts, and shoots collected by females.

Arctic Regions

Survival in arctic conditions has inspired considerable creative adjustments by groups of foragers popularly known as the Eskimo. Most Eskimo refer to themselves as the Inuit, because Inuit is the major language of these people. The other major language of the Eskimo family is Yupik, spoken in Southwest and Central Alaska (and Southeastern Siberia). Early Inuit culture has been dated to at least 2500 BC. Some Inuit live in northwestern Alaska near the Bering Sea, and others live in the arctic regions of northern Canada, extending eastward all the way to Greenland. The northwestern Alaska Eskimo hunt sea mammals such as bowhead whales, seals, and walruses. Interior groups such as the Netsilik in central Canada, who were studied by cultural anthropologist Asen Balikci and others, hunt caribou (large reindeerlike animals), musk oxen, an occasional polar bear, seals, and birds. They also fish in nearby bays.

Because vegetation historically was scarce in arctic regions, it was a prized food. For example, after killing the caribou, male hunters ate the animal's stomach so as to obtain the valued undigested vegetation. Although their diet consisted primarily of meat, the Inuit generally satisfied their

Inuit hunter.

basic nutritional requirements of carbohydrate, protein, and vitamins from eating berries, green roots, fish, and fish oil. They preferred cooked foods, but boiling food over fires fueled by blubber oil was slow and expensive; consequently, the Inuit ate most of their food raw.

The division of labor among the Inuit was unlike that of most other foraging societies. Because of the scarcity of vegetation, women were not specialized collectors. However, during the summer season, males and females gathered larvae, caribou flies, maggots, and deer droppings that contained vegetation.

Mobility and Subsistence

No matter what their particular environment, most band societies share one characteristic: mobility. As food and other resources become scarce in one site, the groups have to move on to another. The Mbuti Pygmies, for example, reside in certain areas during the rainy season and other areas during other seasons, depending on the supply of game (Turnbull 1983). The Ju/'hoansi San moved frequently in pursuit of resources. During the winter dry season, they congregated in large groupings around several watering holes, but during the rainy season the groups dispersed into small units. The Ju/'hoansi San moved when subsistence required (Lee 1969). Most Inuit groups also have to move during different seasons to pursue game and other resources. For example, the northwestern Alaska Eskimos move from the coastal areas into the interior regions during the summer seasons to hunt herds of caribou.

These nomadic behaviors are not arbitrary or spontaneous. Rather, they are carefully planned to minimize labor while providing vital resources. These patterns of mobility represent an admirable appreciation and intimate knowledge of the environment in which these foragers reside.

Optimal Foraging Theory

One of the ways in which anthropologists attempt to study the subsistence and foraging practices of hunter-gatherers is referred to as optimal foraging theory. Optimal foraging theory is used to try to predict what potential foods the foragers should exploit, if they are to make the most efficient use of time and energy. It also is used to predict what foods would be avoided because exploiting them would take up time and energy that could be used more efficiently for procuring other foods. The theory assesses the immediate costs and benefits of utlizing different subsistence strategies.

One of the most extensive uses of optimal foraging theory was that of Kristin Hawkes, Kimberly Hill, and James O'Connell, a team of anthropologists who studied the Ache hunter-gatherers of the tropical rain forests of Paraguay in South America (1982). These anthropologists found that optimal foraging theory tended to predict the types of foods procured by the Ache. They started by having the Ache rank the kinds and types of foods that they foraged. Then, the anthropologists carefully observed what foods were actually procured. For example, they observed that the Ache picked oranges rather than killing monkeys most of the time. Though oranges give a lower yield in calories than monkeys, the processing time was much shorter for oranges than monkeys. The anthropologists calculated that the average return from Ache hunting was 1,115 kilocalories per hour per person. But when they picked oranges, the individuals' average return rose to 4,438 kilocalories per hour. Therefore, oranges were a much more profitable and efficient food to exploit. The Ache told the anthropologists that monkeys were not worth hunting because they were not fat enough. However, when they came across a monkey, they would kill it for food. The Ache tended to make the kinds of decisions one would expect according to optimal foraging calculations. This study, along with other optimal foraging studies, demonstrates that hunter-gatherers make very efficient use of their environment for subsistence purposes.

Foragers and Demographic Conditions

As we have seen, modern foragers live in marginal environments and travel from location to location. The requirement of mobility to procure resources has had a major effect on demographic conditions in these societies. Unlike food producers, hunters and gatherers must depend on the naturally occurring food resources in their territories. These food resources determine and limit excessive population growth. Generally, the population densities of foragers are extremely low as measured in relation to the limited carrying capacity of their environments.

Demographic studies such as those done by cultural anthropologists Richard Lee, Nancy Howell, and Patricia Draper on the Ju/'hoansi San have enabled anthropologists to make certain generalizations concerning demographic conditions among modern foragers. Population size among the Ju/'hoansi San was carefully controlled in a number of ways. According to Lee (1979), the Ju/'hoansi San tried to control the number of people who could be supported in specific territories and provide sufficient resources. Having too many people leads to shortages of resources, whereas having too few people leads to ineffective foraging strategies. Despite their attempts to control their population in various ways at different times, like all people, they misjudged and sometimes paid the ultimate price for overpopulation.

Fissioning

One of the most important means of limiting population growth for foragers is *fissioning*. **Fissioning** is the movement of people from one group to another or fragmenting the group into smaller units when the population begins to increase and food or other material resources become scarce. Resource scarcity creates population pressure in the form of hardships and problems that emerge as the biome's resources become overtaxed. In such cases, the typical response is for a portion of the population to migrate to other geographic regions. Fissioning was most likely the primary means of population control for Paleolithic foragers and to some extent explains the worldwide expansion of the human species.

Fissioning is practiced by modern foragers to a limited extent. Its success depends on the presence of unoccupied land into which the excess population can expand. In situations where an increasing population is surrounded by other populations and fissioning is not possible, conflict between groups becomes likely, although sometimes fusion, or groups combining with one another, occurs (Hammel and Howell 1987).

Infanticide and Geronticide

Another means of population control in some foraging societies is **infanticide**, the deliberate abandonment or killing of infants, usually immediately after birth. Infanticide has been well documented in foraging societies. Physical anthropologist Joseph Birdsell (1968) hypothesized that infanticide is a means of spacing children. Because a woman can carry only one child in her arms at a time as a nomadic gatherer, there is a need to space childbirth. Typically, childbirth was spaced at intervals of four years. However, Nancy Howell reported 6 cases out of 500 births, and thus infanticide among the San was not as common as earlier anthropologists such as Birdsell believed it was (1979). It was only practiced if the child was severely deformed or in some other way physically challenged or if a mother had a child that was being nursed and could not sustain an additional child to feed.

Most cases of infanticide in these foraging societies appear to be decisions made by individuals in response to famine conditions or to anticipated food and material scarcities (Harris and Ross 1987). Infanticide in some of these societies is also associated with the birth of twins (supporting two children might be difficult or impossible) and with genetically abnormal infants.

One popular legend about the Eskimo (Inuit) indicated that **geronticide** (the killing of old people) was very frequent. However, more recent ethnographic research indicates that this practice was never universal among the Eskimo. It was common in some parts of their range but more so among the Inuit (Greenland to Northern Alaska) than the Yupik (western and southwestern Alaska). Even among the Inuit, some groups found the practice repugnant. Where it was practiced, geronticide was rare except during famines. As long as there was enough food to go around, everyone got their share, including the relatively unproductive. Given that the usual diet consisted of fairly dependable catches of caribou, fish, and sea mammals, many years could pass between episodes of scarcity. Considering the dangers of hunting, the old and infirm who weren't expected to hunt could outlive a hunter in his prime.

On the other hand, when food did run short among the Inuit, the old and sick may have been perceived as a drain on the community. They may have been abandoned to die. The victim might be taken out in the wilderness and left there, or the whole village might pick up and move away while the old person slept. On the other hand, if the villagers were unexpectedly restored to prosperity, they would return to welcome the abandoned person back into the community. Most of what has been called geronticide is better called assisted suicide. Assisted suicide was common throughout the range inhabited by Yupik and Inuit alike. In times of famine or hardship, older Inuit often believed they were a burden and asked their younger relatives to kill them. Similar requests could be made by any individual, young or old, for any number of reasons: pain, grief, or clinical depression. The person who was asked to help was obligated to comply even if they had misgivings (Oswalt 1999).

Some hunting-gathering societies also practiced *invalidicide* (the killing of sick or disabled people). The sick received care as long as there was any hope of recovery. When hope faded, care ceased and they were left to die. Like geronticide, it was rare in most areas except during famine.

Fertility Rates

Other lines of demographic research investigate the relatively slow rate of population growth for foraging societies. Some anthropologists are testing demographic hypotheses on the relationship among nutrition, physiological stress, breast-feeding, and rates of fertility (Howell 1979; Lee 1979). The purpose of these studies is to determine whether biological factors rather than cultural practices such as infanticide may induce low fertility rates and thus slow population growth for foragers.

For example, Nancy Howell's research on the Ju/'hoansi San indicates that a low-caloric diet and the high energy rate needed for female foraging activities may postpone the occurrence of menarche, the onset of menstruation at puberty, which does not appear in San females until a mean age of 16.6 years (Howell 1979), compared with 12.9 years in the United States (Barnouw 1985). The low body weight of San females, whose average weight is 90 pounds, also influences the late onset of menarche. This slower rate of maturation may be related to the low fertility of the San.

Other studies have suggested that breast-feeding contributes to low fertility rates. Breast-feeding stimulates the production of prolactin, a hormone that inhibits ovulation and pregnancy (McKenna, Mosko, and Richard 1999). San women breast-feed their infants for three to four years. Considering the workload and general ecological conditions San women must deal with, this prolonged nursing may produce a natural, optimal birth interval, or spacing of children (Blurton Jones 1986, 1987). This factor, along with sexual abstinence, abortion, infanticide, and delayed marriage, may be evidence of early forms of fertility control in prehistoric foraging societies.

Technology in Foraging Societies

In Chapter 2, we discussed the evolution of technology during the Paleolithic period. The crude stone tools of the Lower Paleolithic gave way to the more sophisticated stone tool complex of the Upper Paleolithic. As humans migrated across the continents, technology became specialized, enabling populations to adjust to different types of environments.

Until recently, anthropologists believed that many modern hunter-gatherers had limited technologies. Nineteenth-century anthropologists thought that these limited technologies reflected a simplicity of mind and lack of skill. Modern anthropologists, in contrast, regard these technologies as highly functional in particular ecological conditions. These band societies also enhanced many clever techniques and their technology was not completely "static" in development. More importantly, remember that technology does not refer just to tools or artifacts; it also includes the cultural knowledge that has to be maintained by the society. All foraging peoples have an extensive knowledge of their environmental conditions and of the appropriate means of solving technological problems in these environments.

Desert foragers such as the Ju/'hoansi San use small bows and arrows and spears. Australian Aborigines did not have the bow and arrow, but they used the well-known boomerang (which did not return to the thrower), spears, and spear-throwers for hunting in desert areas. Some of the Australian Aborigines developed fishhooks for harvesting eels in various streams and canals that increased their potential for resources. In tropical rain forests, foragers make traps, snares, and sometimes nets such as those used by the Mbuti. The Mbuti also make

fire-hardened wooden spears and arrow tips for hunting. Some foraging groups, like the Semang, use the blowgun for hunting game. Most of the desert and rain forest foragers use natural poisons to make their hunting more efficient. In some cases, the foragers take various types of poisons from plants and place the poisons in streams to kill fish. In other cases, they put poison on the tips of their arrows to kill game.

As we have seen, fruit and vegetable gathering is at least as important as hunting in foraging societies. In the desert and tropical rain forest, the implements for gathering are uncomplicated. The cultural knowledge needed for gathering, however, is profound. The people need to know where to find the plants, when to find them during different seasons, which plants are edible, which plants are scarce or plentiful, and so on. In most cases, gathering food is the responsibility of women and children. The typical tool is a simple sharpened stick for digging up tubers or getting honey out of hives. Sometimes foragers also use net bags, bark, wooden bowls, or other natural objects to carry nuts, seeds, water, or fruit. For example, San women used large ostrich eggs to hold and carry water.

An extremely complex foraging technology was created by the Inuit (Eskimo) to procure animal food resources. The classic Inuit technology has

A hunter using a blowgun in the rain forest.

evolved over the past 3,000 years and includes equipment made from bone, stone, skin, wood, and ice. Inuit technology also includes kayaks, dogsleds, lances, fish spears, bows and arrows, harpoons with detachable points, traps, fishhooks, and soapstone lamps used with whale and seal oil for heating and cooking. Unlike the desert and rain forest foragers, who wear very little clothing, the Eskimo people have developed sophisticated techniques for curing hides from caribou and seals to make boots, parkas, and other necessary arctic gear. However, again, one cannot simply categorize all of these "Eskimo" hunting-gathering societies into one simple "band" form of society. As Timothy Earle and Allen Johnson indicate in their cross-cultural research, another group of "Eskimo," the Tareumiut, are closely related linguistically to other groups but adopted a whale-hunting subsistence strategy with large *umiaks* or boats that enabled them to develop a much more complex sociocultural system that allowed them to endure long hard winters more comfortably than other Inuit (2000).

Economics in Foraging Societies

Despite the vast differences in physical environment, subsistence, and technology, most foraging societies have very similar economic systems. The major form of economic system identified with these societies is called the **reciprocal economic system** (Sahlins 1972). A reciprocal economic system is based on exchanges among family groups as a means of distributing goods and services throughout the society. The basic principle underlying this system is **reciprocity**, the widespread sharing of goods and services in a society. One reason for this system of reciprocal exchange is that the consumption of food and other resources is usually immediate, because there is very little storage capacity for any surplus. Thus, it makes sense to share what cannot be used anyway.

Reciprocity

The many descriptions of economic transactions and exchanges in foraging societies have led anthropologist Marshall Sahlins to distinguish three types of reciprocity: generalized, balanced, and negative (1965, 1972).

Generalized Reciprocity Generalized reciprocity is based on the assumptions that an immediate return is not expected and that the value of the exchanges will balance out in the long run. The value of the return is not specified, and no running account of repayment of transactions is calculated. Although generalized reciprocity exists in all societies—for example, in the United States when parents pay for their offspring's food, clothing, and shelter—in foraging societies these transactions form the basis of the economic system.

Anthropologists used to refer to generalized reciprocity as a *gift* to distinguish it from trade or barter. Neither altruism nor charity, however, accurately describes these transactions. Rather, these exchanges are based on socially recognized family and kinship statuses. Because such behaviors are expected, gratitude or recognition is usually not required. In fact, in this form of reciprocity it might be impolite or insulting to indicate that a return is expected. For example, among the San and Eskimo foragers, a "thank you" for food or other services is interpreted as an insult (Freuchen 1961; Lee 1969). Generosity is required in these small-scale societies to reduce envy and social tensions, promote effective cooperation, distribute resources and services, and create obligations.

Examples of generalized reciprocity occur among foragers like the Ju/'hoansi San, Mbuti, and Inuit (Eskimo). Aside from food, which is shared with everyone in the group, the San have a generalized exchange system known as *hxaro*, which not only circulates goods but also—and primarily—solidifies social relationships by creating mutual obligations among related kin (Lee 1993). The *hxaro* system involves exchanging goods ranging from weapons to jewelry. Constant circulation of these material goods not only enhances and maintains kin ties through mutual obligations but also inhibits the accumulation of wealth by any individuals in the society. This enables these societies to remain egalitarian, which refers to societies that have very small differences in wealth among individuals. There are no rich or poor in these types of societies.

Balanced Reciprocity A more direct type of reciprocal exchange with an explicit expectation of immediate return is **balanced reciprocity**. This form of reciprocity is more utilitarian and more like trade and barter than is generalized reciprocity. The material aspect of the exchange is as important as the social aspect. People involved in these transactions calculate the value of the exchanges, which are expected to be equivalent. If an equal return is not given, the original donor may not continue the exchange relationship. Balanced reciprocity is usually found in contexts of more distant kinship relations. Because most exchanges and transactions in modern foraging societies take place among close kin, balanced reciprocity is practiced less frequently than is generalized reciprocity.

Negative Reciprocity Sahlins (1972) defined **negative reciprocity** as the attempt to get something for nothing. Negative reciprocity means no reciprocity at all. It may involve bargaining, haggling, gambling, cheating, theft, or the outright seizure of goods. In general, negative reciprocity is least common in small-scale foraging societies, in which kinship relations predominate.

Exchange and Altruism In foraging societies, where reciprocity reigns, people may appear to outsiders as naturally generous, altruistic, and magnanimous. But as Lee noted in reference to the economy of the !Kung San or Ju/'hoansi:

> If I had to point to one single feature that makes this way of life possible, I would focus on sharing. Each Ju is not an island unto himself or herself; each is part of a collective. It is a small, rudimentary collective, and at times a fragile one, but it is a collective nonetheless. What I mean is that the living group pools the resources that are brought into camp so that everyone receives an equitable share. The !Kung and people like them don't do this out of nobility of soul or because they are made of better stuff than we are. In fact, they often gripe about sharing. They do it because it works for them and it enhances their survival. Without this core of sharing, life for the Ju/'hoansi would be harder and infinitely less pleasant. (1993, 60)

It appears that these hunting-and-gathering peoples are no more noble or less "materialistic" than other people (Hayden 1993). Rather, the conditions of their existence have led them to develop economic practices that enable them to survive in their particular habitat. As humans, it appears that we reciprocate with one another in all societies. The strategy of "I'll scratch your back and you scratch mine" is found everywhere. And, in a small-scale foraging society where trust can be generated among everyone, reciprocity becomes highly generalized.

Collective Ownership of Property

In the nineteenth century, Lewis Morgan proposed that early economic systems associated with small-scale societies were communistic. In his book *Ancient Society* ([1877] 1964), Morgan claimed that during the early stages of cultural evolution, the productive technology and economic resources were shared by everyone in the society. As indicated earlier, Morgan's views shaped and influenced the ideas of Karl Marx in his vision of early communist and future communist societies. Today, Morgan's views appear too simplistic to account for the vast range of economic systems found in small-scale societies.

Ethnographic data indicate that hunting-and-gathering societies have differing forms of property relations, which reflect their particular ecological conditions. Among some groups, such as the Ju/'hoansi San, the Eskimo, and the Western Shoshone, where resources are widely distributed, cultural anthropologists report that there are no exclusive rights to territory (Durning 1992). Although specific families may be identified with a local camp area, territorial boundaries are extremely flexible, and exclusive ownership of resources within a territory is not well defined. For example, among the Ju/'hoansi San, sacred sites were frequently associated with territories that contained various resources such as water, wild plants, shade trees, fuel wood, and other items for tool making and were said to be owned by individual families (Hitchcock 2004). Yet few restrictions were placed against other families or groups in using these resources. Many foraging groups may have rights of temporary use or rights to claim resources if needed, but not "once-and-for-all" rights that exist in modern capitalist societies (Bloch 1983).

However, in other foraging societies, such as that of the Owens Valley Paiute Indians who resided near the edge of the Great Basin region in the American West, exclusive rights to territory were well defined and defended against outsiders. The Paiute were heavily dependent on pinyon nuts, which were concentrated in one area and were a more predictable source of food than game animals. Specific territorial ties and exclusive rights to land carrying these resources became important for bands and families. The defense of these resources was economically beneficial to the Paiute. In a comparison of territorial rights among different hunter-gatherers, anthropologists Rada Dyson-Hudson and Eric Smith (1978) found that the greater the predictability and concentration of resources within a particular region, the more pronounced were the conceptions of private ownership and exclusive rights to territory among foragers.

Other forms of private property in foraging societies are associated with individuals—pets, ornaments, clothing, and items of technology such as bows, knives, scrapers, and blowguns. Such items are usually regarded as a form of private personal property over which the person who owns them has certain rights.

The Original Affluent Society?

Until the 1960s, the traditional picture of foraging societies was that of people with limited technologies who were at the mercy of a harsh environment. It seemed that in these dire environmental circumstances, people had to work constantly to survive. In the 1960s, however, anthropologists began to draw on ethnographic studies to produce a much different image of hunter-gatherer societies. Modern cultural anthropologists gathered basic data on the types of production systems that hunter-gatherers use, the amount of time they spend in production and subsistence, the role of mobility in their adaptation, and how long they live.

The ethnographic data reported in Lee and DeVore's work indicate that contemporary foraging societies usually have an adequate and reliable food base. Lee (1972a, b; 1979; 1993), for example, has argued that the Ju/'hoansi San diet was nutritionally adequate. The data also indicate that these foragers expended minimal labor to provide for their basic physical needs. Finally, the life expectancy in these societies turns out to be much greater than was once thought. These findings have led some anthropologists to refer to foragers as "original affluent societies" or "leisured societies" (Sahlins 1972). Sahlins, for example, argued that the worldview and cultural values of foragers differ radically from that of capitalist societies. He

suggested that the sharing-oriented economy of people such as the Ju/'hoansi San demonstrates that the forager's needs are few and are easily satisfied by a relatively meager amount of labor time. In Sahlins's view, foragers do not value the accumulation of material goods in the same way that people in modern capitalist societies do.

It is obvious that for populations that have to maintain a nomadic lifestyle, the accumulation of resources would be unproductive. Material possessions would be burdensome when trekking across the ice of the Arctic or through the dense rain forests. Without a way to store large quantities of food, it would be irrational to accumulate food resources only to have them spoil.

Further evidence of the affluence of foragers is drawn from the demographic conditions for these groups. For example, Lee argued that the composition of the Ju/'hoansi San population demonstrates that these people were not on the edge of starvation. Ten percent of the individuals surveyed by Lee were over 60 years of age, "a proportion that compares favorably to the percentage of elderly in industrialized populations" (Lee 1968, 36). The blind, senile, or disabled continued to be supported by the Ju/'hoansi. The system of reciprocal exchanges thus ensures the survival of these individuals.

The Affluence Hypothesis Challenged

Some recent anthropological research, however, has challenged the notion of the original affluent societies. Although the San and similar groups may spend only a few hours each day and a few days each week bringing in basic food resources, they must also spend time making tools, weapons, and clothing; processing and cooking food; planning for future foraging activities; solving disputes; healing the sick; and raising children (Konner 2002). In other words, we can view the Ju/'hoansi San and other foragers as affluent only if we restrict our definition of work to the actual quest for food.

The study of the Ache, foragers mentioned earlier who live in the rain forest of eastern Paraguay, illustrates the shortcomings of the affluence hypothesis. A team of cultural anthropologists analyzed Ache subsistence activities (Hill et al. 1985).

They discovered that Ache males spend forty to fifty hours a week in the quest for special kinds of food. Time-allocation studies such as these challenge the notion that all foragers spend minimal time in pursuit of food resources.

Furthermore, recent medical research has challenged Lee's arguments that the Ju/'hoansi San diet is nutritionally sound. Although the diet is well balanced in respect to carbohydrates, proteins, and fats, the overall caloric intake of the San appears to be inadequate. The small physical size of the San may be due to the fact that mothers usually have not supplemented nursing with additional food intake for infants more than six months old. Moreover, the entire San population has suffered from seasonal food shortages and starvation (Konner 2002).

This recent research on the Ju/'hoansi San does not totally refute the overall hypothesis regarding the original affluent societies. In general, it appears that in some cases, especially in the tropical rain forest, groups like the Mbuti and the Semang have an abundance of vegetables and fruits. In contrast, groups such as the Shoshone or the Ache have to expend much more time in securing basic resources. When there is a ready presence of resources, relative affluence is possible. But when these items are absent or less plentiful, subsistence becomes much more demanding.

Another factor that influences the relative affluence of foraging societies is the ability to preserve resources over a period of time. Although most of these societies did not store food, groups such as the Eskimo had limited storage capacities. Some Eskimo groups dug holes beneath the permafrost so that they could store meat. The storage of meat, berries, and greens enabled the Eskimo to maintain a certain amount of affluence even in winter. They thus had a steady, reliable source of meat and vegetation as a base for subsistence activities.

Social Organization in Foraging Societies

The fundamental social organization in foraging societies is based on family, marriage, kinship, gender, and age. The two basic elements of social organization for foraging populations are the nuclear family and the band. The **nuclear family** is the small family unit associated with procreation: parents and offspring. The nuclear family appears to be most adaptive for hunting-gathering societies because of the flexibility needed for the location and easy distribution and exchange of food resources and the other exigencies of hunting (Fox 1967; Pasternak 1976).

A Baka Pygmy couple in West Africa.

The most common type of band is made up of a related cluster of nuclear families ranging in size from 20 to 100 individuals. At times, in societies such as the desert-dwelling Shoshone Indians, the bands may break up into nuclear families to locate food and other resources. Under other circumstances, several families may cooperate in hunting and other foraging activities. In some instances, bands may contain up to four or five (sometimes more) **extended families**, in which married children and their offspring reside with their parents. These multifamily bands provide the webs of kinship for foraging societies, enabling them to cooperate in subsistence and economic exchanges.

The specific number of people in a band depends on the carrying capacity of the natural environment. Most foraging groups had a range of 20 to 100 people. Foragers in the desert, the Arctic, and the tropical rain forest all lived in small multifamily bands residing in separate territories. Typically, band organization is extremely flexible, with members leaving and joining bands as circumstances demand. Personal conflicts and shortages of resources may encourage people to move into or out of bands. In some cases, when food or water resources are scarce, whole bands may move into the territories of other bands.

Marriage and Kinship

Although a number of foraging groups practice *polygyny*, marriage between one male and two or more females, the most common type of marriage found in foraging societies is monogamy. Marriages are an important means of cementing social relationships. In some cases, betrothals are arranged while the future spouses are still young children. Typically, the girl is much younger than the male. For example, Ju/'hoansi San girls are often married between the ages of 12 and 14, whereas males may be 18 to 25 years old or older.

Although these marital arrangements are regular features of foraging societies, it does not mean the couple easily accepts these arranged marriages. A San woman expressed herself on her first marriage:

When I married my husband Tsau I didn't fight too hard, but I cried a lot when I was taken to sleep in his hut. When the elders went away I listened carefully for their sleeping. Then, when my husband fell asleep

and I heard his breathing, I very quietly sat up and eased my blanket away from his and stole away and slept by myself out in the bush.

In the morning the people came to Tsau's hut and asked, "Where is your wife?" He looked around and said, "I don't know where my wife has gone off to." Then they picked up my tracks and tracked me to where I was sitting out in the bush. They brought me back to my husband. They told me that this was the man they had given to me and that he wouldn't hurt me.

After that we just lived together all right. At first when we slept under the same blanket our bodies did not touch, but then after a while I slept at his front. Other girls don't like their husbands and keep struggling away until the husbands give up on them and their parents take them back. (Lee, 1993, 83)

Marriage Rules Marital arrangements in foraging societies are intended to enhance economic, social, and political interdependence among bands and to foster appropriate band alliances. To do this, rules are established to determine who may marry whom. Many of these rules concern marriages among cousins. A common marriage rule found in foraging societies is referred to as *cross-cousin marriage*. A **cross cousin** is the offspring of one's father's sister or one's mother's brother. In effect, a cross-cousin marriage means that a male marries a female who is his father's sister's daughter or his mother's brother's daughter.

In addition, foraging societies frequently have rules of residence that specify where the married couple must reside. Most band societies practice **patrilocal residence**, in which the newly married couple resides with the husband's father. Thus, if a man marries a woman from a different band, she must join her husband's band. In such societies, the patrilocal residence rule and cross-cousin marriage combine to create a system called *restricted marital exchange*, in which two groups exchange women (Levi-Strauss 1969). The purpose of this system is to foster group solidarity by encouraging kinship alliances.

The kinship diagram in Figure 9.2 gives a visual model of the social structure in some foraging societies. In the diagram, Ego is used as a point of reference, and kinship relationships are traced from Ego's offspring, parents, grandparents, and other relatives. Note that Ego has married his father's sister's daughter (his cross-cousin on his father's

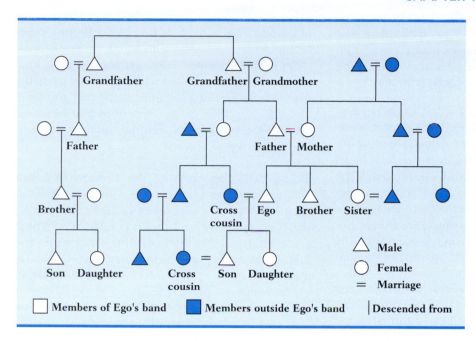

FIGURE 9.2 Kinship and marriage patterns in hunting-and-gathering societies.

side). Because of the rule of patrilocal residence, Ego's father's sister had to move to another band with her husband. Therefore, Ego is marrying outside his own band.

Like Ego, Ego's wife's brother has married a woman outside his band. In keeping with the cross-cousin rule, their daughter has married Ego's son. Ego's daughter will eventually marry someone from another band. Through the rules of cross-cousin marriage and patrilocal residence, this restricted exchange develops strong networks of interfamily and interband kinship relations. These kin networks widen over the generations, expanding reciprocal economic, social, and political relationships.

Brideservice Some foraging societies practice **brideservice**, in which a male resides for a specified amount of time with his wife's parents' band. The rule of residence that requires a man to reside with his wife's parents is called **matrilocal residence**. Among the Ju/'hoansi San, brideservice can last eight to ten years, and the husband and wife don't return to the husband's father's band for residence (the patrilocal rule) until after several children are born (Lee 1993). The husband will help his wife's band in their subsistence activities, which helps consolidate both economic and social ties between the two bands. Another reason the Ju/'hoansi San practice brideservice is that females are not sex-

ually mature at the time of their marriage. San girls who marry before their menarche are not expected to have sexual intercourse with their husband. Thus, the brideservice period coincides with female maturation. But brideservice also functions to reinforce the kinship and reciprocal ties between bands.

Other Marital Patterns among Foragers Not all foraging societies conform to the marital patterns just described. For example, most Inuit (Eskimo) marriage involved no preferred rules regarding cousin marriage or rituals and ceremonies sanctioning the new couple's relationship. Traditionally, the man and woman simply begin residing with each other. To some extent, the Eskimo view this marriage arrangement as a pragmatic and utilitarian relationship for economic and reproductive purposes (Balikci 1970).

Another aspect of Inuit marriage is the well-known tradition of wife exchange. In some cases, males established partnerships with other males that include having sexual intercourse with each other's wives. Usually it is clear that both the men and the women involved make decisions about this. However, cultural anthropologist Ansen Balikci records cases wherein wives were threatened and intimidated if they did not want to participate (1970). One of the most important aspects of wife exchange was the interregional social networks established among these families. In addition, the children produced from these exchanges were considered siblings, which further enhanced the development of kinship obligations and reciprocity.

Divorce   In most cases, divorce is easily accomplished in hunting-and-gathering societies. For example, Ju/'hoansi San divorces, which are most frequently initiated by the wife, are simple matters characterized by cordiality and cooperation. The divorced couple may even live next to one another with their new spouses. Because there are no rigid rules or complex kinship relations beyond the nuclear family to complicate divorce proceedings, the dissolution of a Ju/'hoansi San marriage is a relatively easy process (Lee 1993).

Divorce was also frequent and easily obtained among the Eskimo (Balikci 1970). As with the San, one reason for this was the lack of formal social groups beyond the nuclear family. Another reason was the absence of strict rules governing marriage and postmarital residence. Significantly, divorce did not necessarily lead to the cutting of kin ties. Even if an Eskimo couple separated, and this happened for nearly 100 percent of the marriages studied, the kin ties endured (Burch 1970). Sometimes the couple reunited, and the children of first and second marriages became a newly blended family. Thus, divorce frequently extended kin ties, an important aspect of sociocultural adaptation in severe arctic conditions.

Gender

Gender as an aspect of social structure in foraging societies is an extremely important area of ethnographic research. Cultural anthropologists have been examining the interrelationships among gender, subsistence, economic, and political patterns.

Gender and the Division of Labor   Considerable ethnographic research has demonstrated that gender roles in foraging societies are strongly related to the basic division of labor. Prior to recent ethnographic research on foraging societies, anthropologists believed that male subsistence activities, especially hunting and fishing, provided most of the food resources. However, as we have seen, in some of the foraging societies such as the Ju/'hoansi San, the Semang, and Mbuti, women are providing most

of the food, because gathering and collecting vegetation is the primary means of securing food (Martin and Voorhies 1975; Dahlberg 1981). One cross-cultural analysis based on all of the available evidence for foraging societies in the past and present indicates that males have typically obtained most of the meat-foods through hunting and fishing (Ember 1978).

Biological Explanations of the Division of Labor
One question posed by modern cultural anthropologists is: Why is the division of labor in foraging societies so strongly related to gender roles? There are several possible answers to this question. The first is that males hunt and women gather because males are stronger and have more endurance in the pursuit of large game. Another possibility is that because women bear and nurse children, they lack the freedom of mobility necessary to hunt (Friedl 1975). A third answer is that gathering, especially near a base camp, is a relatively safe activity that entails no potential dangers for women who are either pregnant or caring for children (Brown 1970b).

There is evidence for and against each of these theories. We have seen, for example, that in some foraging societies men and women are involved in both hunting and gathering. In addition, women often perform tasks that require strength and stamina, such as carrying food, children, water, and firewood. Thus, gathering resources is not a sedentary or leisurely activity. Based on this evidence, anthropologist Linda Marie Fedigan (1986) has proposed that heavy work and child-care activities may not be mutually exclusive, as was previously thought.

Many research questions pertaining to gender roles and subsistence among foragers remain for future anthropologists. Much of the recent evidence suggests that gender roles and subsistence activities are not as rigid as formerly thought. Among the Batak foragers of the rain forests of Malaysia and the Agta in the Philippines, both men and women perform virtually every subsistence task (Estioko-Griffin and Griffin 1978; Endicott 1988). Women among the Agta go out into the forest to kill wild boars just as the men do. The Tiwi of Australia and the Hadza foragers of East Africa demonstrate this same pattern (Goodale 1971; Woodburn 1982). In these cases, it appears that the subsistence strategies for both males and females are open, and behavior is flexible.

Female Status Closely related to gender roles and subsistence is the question of the social status of women. Empirical data suggest that gender relations tend to be more *egalitarian*—men and women having more or less equal status—in foraging societies than in other societies (Friedl 1975; Shostak 1981; Endicott 1988, Lepowski 1993; Ward 2003). This may reflect the substantial contributions women make in gathering food.

Richard Lee notes, for example, that as a result of their important role in economic activities, Ju/'hoansi San women participate equally with men in political decision making (1981). Ju/'hoansi San women are treated respectfully, and there is little evidence of male domination or the maltreatment of females. A similar generalization could be applied to the Mbuti, Semang, and Agta as well as to most of the other foragers. This hypothesis suggests, however, that in societies in which female contributions to the food supply are less critical or less valued, female status is lower. For example, among some of the Eskimo and other northern foraging groups for whom hunting is the only subsistence activity, females do not gather much in the way of resources for the family. Consequently, those societies tended to be more **patriarchal**, or male dominated, in political and economic matters (Friedl 1975; Martin and Voorhies 1975; Lepowski 1993; Ward 2003).

Clearly, equality between males and females in foraging societies is not universal. In some groups, such as the Ju/'hoansi San and Agta, women have more equality, whereas in others such as the traditional Eskimo, females have a lower status. Even in the most egalitarian groups, males tend to have some inherent cultural advantages. In some cases, meat is viewed as a more luxurious and prestigious food and enhances the male status. In addition, males are more likely to become the political and spiritual leaders in foraging societies. When considering gender relations in a broad, cross-cultural perspective, however, foragers tend to have much more equality than do most other societies.

Age

Like kinship and gender, age is used in virtually all foraging societies as a basis for assigning individuals their particular status in the social hierarchy. Patterns of age stratification and hierarchy vary considerably from society to society, depending on environmental and cultural conditions. Age is also a primary aspect of the division of labor in foraging societies.

Children and Rites of Passage The period of childhood among foragers is a time of playful activity and excitement. But it is also a time when children learn their basic subsistence activities, economic responsibilities, and political roles. In his studies of the Mbuti Pygmies, Turnbull (1963, 1983) has provided us with a thorough account of childhood in a foraging society.

At the age of 3, the Mbuti child enters the *bopi*, a tiny camp about a hundred yards away from the main camp, which might be considered a playground. Older children and adults do not enter the bopi. Within the bopi, all the children are part of an age grade and are equal to one another and remain so throughout the rest of their lives. It is the area in which children become enculturated and learn the importance of age, kinship, and gender, and the activities associated with these statuses.

Within the bopi are noncompetitive play activities for boys and girls. Many of these activities reinforce the rules of hunting and gathering. The elders bring the children out of the bopi to show them how to use nets to hunt animals. Children also play house to learn how to take care of their households later in life. Before the age of puberty, boys and girls quit going into the bopi and join the main camp with older youths. When they reach puberty, Mbuti males and females have separate, informal rites of passage. The puberty ritual, known as the *Elima* for Mbuti females, occurs at the first menstruation, which is an occasion for great rejoicing because it is a sign that the girl is ready for marriage and motherhood. For a month the girl resides in a special hut with her agemates, and she is watched over by an older female. The girl learns the special songs of the *Elima* and occasionally appears in front of the hut while young men sit outside to admire the girls. At this time, the females sing the *Elima* songs, and the boys sing in response in a form of flirtation. Through their participation in the *Elima* ritual, the Mbuti males demonstrate their readiness for adulthood and marriage.

Older people are taken care of by the group in band societies.

The Roles of the Elderly In foraging societies, old age tends to be defined less in terms of chronology and more in terms of some change in social status related to involvement in subsistence or work patterns, or becoming grandparents (Glascock 1981). In all societies, however, the onset of old age is partially defined in terms of the average life span. The general demographic and ethnological data on foraging societies indicate that definitions of "old age" vary from 45 to 75 years old.

An early study of aging hypothesized that in hunting-and-gathering societies, older people wield little power and have low status (Simmons 1945). This argument was based on the assumption that, because foraging societies had few material goods that older people controlled and could use as leverage with the younger generation, old age represented a loss of status. This hypothesis suggested that the status of older people is correlated with subsistence and economic activities. As foraging people age and decline in strength and energy, their subsistence contribution may be limited, thereby diminishing their status.

Most of the current ethnographic data, however, do not support this hypothesis. In an early account of foragers in the Andaman Islands off the coast of India, for example, A. R. Radcliffe-Brown ([1922] 1964) described the reverence and honor given to older males. Among the Mbuti Pygmies, age is a key factor in determining status, and the elders make the most important economic and political decisions for the group. Despite the fact that young people sometimes openly ridicule older people, the elders are able to dominate Mbuti society because of their cultural knowledge (Turnbull 1983).

Anthropologists who have studied the Ju/'hoansi San point out that though there was little material security at old age, the elderly were not abandoned and had a relatively high status (Thomas 1958; Lee 1979). Despite the fact that older people do not play a predominant productive role in subsistence activities, they are able to remain secure because of close kinship ties. Through reciprocal exchanges within the economic system of these foraging societies, older people are able to maintain a relatively secure existence.

Anthropologists find that older people in foraging societies generally have a higher status than do younger people. Because of their accumulated knowledge, which is needed for subsistence activities, political decision making, and intellectual and spiritual guidance, older people tend to be respected and are treated with a great deal of deference. Human memory serves as the libraries of these societies and is important for the preservation of culture and the transmission of knowledge. Cultural and historical traditions are memorized and handed down from generation to generation. Control of information is one important basis of esteem for the elderly in nonliterate societies.

In general, the evidence indicates that only in cases of extreme deprivation are the elderly in foraging societies maltreated. In their investigation of the treatment of the elderly in a wide variety of foraging societies, researchers concluded that practices directed against the elderly, such as abandonment, exposure, and killing, occur only under severe environmental circumstances, in which the elderly are viewed as burdens rather than assets (Glascock 1981). These practices have been documented for groups ranging from the Eskimo to the Siriono, but these cases appear to be exceptional.

In most foraging societies, the young have moral obligations to take care of the elderly.

Child-Care Activities Turnbull (1983) has remarked that one of the significant universal roles of elderly grandparents is babysitting. While the parents in foraging societies are involved in subsistence chores like hunting and collecting, grandparents often are engaged in child-care activities. Among the Ju/'hoansi San and the Mbuti, elderly grandparents care for small children while the children's mothers are away on gathering activities. The elderly teach the grandchildren the skills, norms, and values of the society. Reflecting on the Mbuti Pygmy elders, who spend time in storytelling and reciting myths and legends, Turnbull indicates that this role is the primary function of the Mbuti elderly in the maintenance of culture. In most foraging societies, this is the typical pattern for relationships between the young and the old. Recently, anthropologist Kristen Hawkes (2004) studied how the "Grandmother Effect" and the longer life span of women have had significant survival value in childcare and nurturing the young children in foraging societies.

Political Organization in Foraging Societies

Just as the band is the fundamental element of social organization in most hunting-and-gathering societies, it is also the basic political unit. As we saw in the discussion of social organization, bands are tied together through kinship and marriage, creating reciprocal economic and social relationships throughout the community. Each band, however, is politically independent of the others and has its own internal leadership. Most of the leaders in the bands are males, but females also take on some important leadership roles. Leaders are chosen because of their skills in hunting, food collecting, communication, decision making, or other personal abilities.

Political leaders generally do not control the group's economic resources or exercise political power as they do in other societies, and there is little, if any, social stratification between political leaders and others in the band. In other words, typically band societies are highly egalitarian, with no fundamental differences between those with and those without wealth or political power. Thus, leaders of bands must lead by persuasion and personal influence rather than by coercion or withholding resources. Leaders do not maintain a military or police force and thus have no definitive authority.

In recent extensive cross-cultural studies of the political processes of hunting-gathering societies, Christopher Boehm (1993, 1999) developed an imaginative hypothesis to explain the lack of political power and domination in these egalitarian societies. Boehm suggested that there is a pattern of reverse dominance in these societies, which keeps anyone from becoming coercive or politically dominating the group in any manner. Reverse dominance ensures that the whole group will have control over anybody who tries to assert political power or authority over them. Reverse dominance is practiced through criticism and ridicule, disobedience, strong disapproval, execution of offenders or extremely aggressive males, deposing leaders, or outright desertion (an entire group leaving a particularly dominant leader). Boehm finds that reverse dominance and related political processes are widespread in band societies, reinforcing patterns of egalitarianism.

In a related hypothesis, Peter Gardner (1991) suggests that foraging societies tend to have strong cultural values that emphasize individual autonomy. Like Boehm, Gardner suggests that hunter-gatherers dislike being dominated and disdain conforming to norms that restrict their individual freedom. From reviewing many cases of band societies, Gardner indicates that the cultural values promoting individual autonomy enable these people to sustain their egalitarian way of life while promoting flexibility in their behavior, a distinguishing feature of foraging societies.

Characteristics of Leadership

In most cases, individuals in hunting-and-gathering societies do not seek out leadership roles, because there are few benefits or advantages in becoming a leader. Leaders do not accrue power or economic resources in these egalitarian societies. They do, however, have a tremendous responsibility for the management of the band. In a classic essay in political anthropology, Claude Levi-Strauss (1944) described the band leader of the Nambikuara of South America as entirely responsible for selecting the territories for procuring game; ordering and organizing hunting, fishing, and collecting activities; and determining the conduct of the band in relation to other groups in the region. Yet Levi-Strauss emphasized the consensual aspect of this leadership pattern. The leader has no coercive power and must continuously display skill in building consensus within the band to provide political order.

A quotation from a Ju/'hoansi San leader sums up the pattern of leadership among hunter-gatherer societies: "All you get is the blame if things go wrong." Morton Fried (1967) notes a remark frequently heard from band leaders: "If this is done it will be good." These remarks indicate the lack of authority that leaders of bands have in these societies. Levi-Strauss (1944), however, states that some people in all societies desire the nonmaterial benefits such as prestige that can be gained through assuming leadership responsibilities. Therefore, despite the lack of political power or material benefits, foraging leaders may be motivated by other cultural concerns.

Another characteristic of band political leadership is that it is transient; leaders of bands do not hold permanent positions or offices. This informal leadership pattern adds to the weakness of centralized political authority in band societies. Informal leadership is somewhat situational in that it varies according to circumstances; the band will call on the appropriate type of leader when dealing with a specific type of activity. In some bands, for example, certain individuals may be good at solving disputes within the band or between bands. These individuals may be chosen to deal with such problems when they arise. In general, then, band leadership is diffuse and decentralized.

This minimal pattern of leadership also involves an informal type of political succession. Most hunting-and-gathering societies have no definitive rules for passing leadership from one individual to another. Rather, leadership is based on personal characteristics. It may also be based on supernatural powers that the individual is believed to possess. When an individual dies, his or her influence and authority also die. This lack of rules for succession emphasizes the decentralization of political power and authority in band societies.

Warfare and Violence

Contemporary foraging societies generally engage in very limited warfare. However, Melvin and Carol Ember's cross-cultural research indicates that foragers were engaged in frequent warfare in the past (1992). And increasing archaeological evidence suggests that foragers in the past may have been involved in extensive warfare (Keely 1996; LeBlanc 2003). Most of the ethnographic evidence, however, suggests that warfare among foragers took the form of sporadic violence rather than continual fighting (Kelly 2000). One factor that limited warfare was that almost the entire population was engaged in the day-to-day hunting and collecting of food, so no long-term fighting could be sustained. Also, the lack of centralized political institutions to implement large-scale military mobilization inhibits the development of intense or frequent warfare. No standing armies with specialized warriors can be organized for continual warfare.

The Tiwi of Australia provide a classic case of "restrained" warfare among foraging populations (Hart, Pilling, and Goodale 1988). War parties of thirty men from two different bands, each armed with spears and wearing white paint symbolizing anger and hostility, met in an adjoining territory. The dispute had originated because some of the males from one band had apparently seduced females from the opposing band. In addition, the senior males of one of the bands had not delivered on their promise to bestow daughters to the other band—a deliberate violation of the norms of reciprocal marital exchange. Both sides first exchanged insults and then agreed to meet with one another on the following day to renew old acquaintances and to socialize. On the third day, the duel resumed, with males throwing spears in all directions, resulting in a chaotic episode in which some people, including spectators, were wounded. Most of the battle, however, involved violent talk and verbal, rather than physical, abuse. Although variations on this type of warfare existed among the Tiwi, warfare generally did not result in great bloodshed.

Richard Lee described conflict among the Ju/'hoansi San, which involves fights and homicides. Lee (1993) found twenty-two cases of homicide by males and other periodic violence, usually related to internal disputes over women. As Eric Wolf (1987, 130) comments: "Clearly the !Kung are not the 'Harmless People' that some have thought them to be: They fight and sometimes injure other individual !Kung." Robert Kelly did a broad cross-cultural survey of warfare and violence in band societies and concluded that although violence did occur it did not involve sustained vengeance and enduring warfare between family band groupings, rather it involved individual cases of revenge that were brief (2000). The next chapter shows that warfare and violence develops in a much more sustained manner when more complex descent groups develop in tribal societies.

Anthropologist Bruce Knauft (1988) has summarized several generalizations concerning violence in foraging societies, which coincides with Kelly's hypothesis. First, these societies lack a competitive male-status hierarchy; in fact, there is a strong tendency to discourage this type of interpersonal competition. Status competition among males is a major source of violent conflict in other types of societies. Second, in contrast to many other societies, public displays of interpersonal violence are not culturally valued among foragers. Instead, these societies seek to minimize animosities. Finally, because of the emphasis on sharing food and other resources, rights to property are not restricted. All these factors serve to reduce the amount of violence in these societies.

Conflict Resolution

Because of the lack of formal government institutions and political authority, social control in foraging societies is based on informal sanctions. One basic mode of conflict resolution that occurs frequently among groups such as the Ju/'hoansi or San is for the people involved to move to another band. Thus, the flexibility of band organization itself is an effective means of reducing conflict. Furthermore, the economic and social reciprocities and the frequent exchanges among bands also serve to reduce conflicts. These reciprocal ties create mutual obligations and interdependencies that promote cooperative relationships.

Nevertheless, violations of norms do lead to more structured or more ritualized means of conflict resolution in foraging societies. Among the Mbuti, for example, age groups play specific roles in the conflict-resolution process. Children play an essential role in resolving conflicts involving misbehavior such as laziness, quarreling, or selfishness. Children ridicule people who engage in these behaviors, even if these people are adults. Young children excel at this form of ridicule, which usually is sufficient to resolve the conflict.

When these measures do not succeed, the elders in the group assert their authority. They try to evaluate the dispute carefully and show why things went wrong. If necessary, they walk to the center of the camp and criticize individuals by name, although they frequently use humor to soften their criticism. Through this process, elders reinforce the norms and values of Mbuti society (Turnbull 1983).

The Eskimo Song Duel   Another example of dispute resolution is the Eskimo song duel. The song duel was often used to resolve conflicts between males over a particular female. Because Eskimo society lacks specific rules of marriage, males would sometimes accuse others of wife stealing. In these types of conflicts, the two males encountered each other in front of a large public meeting. They then insulted each other through improvised songs, and the crowd resolved the conflict by selecting a winner. With the declaration of a winner, the dispute was resolved without the use of any formal court system or coercion (Hoebel [1954] 1968). Other methods of conflict resolution among the Eskimo included wrestling and punching matches. (An excellent recent film made by the Canadian Inuit people themselves called *Anarajuat: The Fast Runner* shows some of the punching and wrestling matches among the Inuit.)

Religion in Foraging Societies

The religions associated with modern foragers are based on oral traditions referred to by the religious studies scholar Mircea Eliade (1959) as "cosmic religions." Cosmic religions are intimately associated with nature. The natural cycle of seasons; inorganic matter such as rocks, water, and mountains; and other features of the natural environment are invested with sacred significance. All foraging societies have sacred places associated with the landscape where they live. These sacred spots are often marked or painted with petroglyphs (rock paintings) that identify the spiritual significance of the territories of these peoples. Spirit and matter are inseparable. In addition, cosmic religions are not identified with any particular historical events or individuals, as are the "literate" religious traditions of Judaism, Islam, Christianity, Buddhism, and Hinduism.

The sacredness of the natural environment is sometimes expressed in a form of **animism**, the belief that spirits reside within all inorganic and organic substances. Yet, as applied to the metaphysical conceptions in the Ju/'hoansi or San, the Australian Aborigine, or Mbuti cultural systems, the label animism appears too simplistic. Concepts of a god or gods are found in combination with animistic beliefs.

The Dreamtime

An illuminating example of a cosmic religion among foragers is the Australian Aborigine notion of dreamtime (Stanner 1979). The dreamtime exists in the "other world," the world associated with the time of creation, where a person goes in dreams and visions and after death. It is believed that at the time of creation, the ancestors deposited souls of all living forms near watering holes, and eventually these souls or spirits were embedded in all matter, from rocks and water to trees and humans. The unification of all substance and spirit was a byproduct of the work of these ancestral beings. All of these spirits come to the world from the dreamtime; the birth of the universe is like a fall from the dreamtime.

The Aborigines believe that the ancestral beings still exist in the dreamtime, where they act as intermediaries between that world and the profane, everyday world of human affairs. The ancestral beings intervene in life, controlling plant, animal, and human life, and death. This fundamental belief provides explanations for pain, joy, chaos, and order in human life. The dreamtime is a fundamental and complex conception that embraces the creative past and has particular significance for the present and future.

According to Aborigine conceptions, life without the dreamtime is extremely unsatisfactory. The invisible side of life can become visible through rituals, ceremonies, myths, art, and dreams. Aborigines believe that through these activities they can communicate with their ancestral beings. This belief is reflected in Aborigine rites of passage. In initiation

ceremonies it is believed that the individual moves farther and farther back into the dreamtime. In puberty rituals, which for males included circumcision, *subincision* (the cutting of the penis lengthwise to the urethra), and other bloodletting actions, the individual is dramatically moved from one status to another through contact with the dreamtime. The rite of passage at death moves the individual into the invisibility of the dreamtime.

The dreamtime also conveys certain notions of morality. According to Aborigine traditions, the ancestral beings originally lived like other humans and had the capacity for being both moral and immoral, both good and evil (Stanner 1979). The immoral behavior of the dreamtime beings is highlighted to accentuate what is proper and moral in human affairs. Thus, this religion creates a moral order, which functions to sustain social control in the physical world. Although the dreamtime ancestors do not directly punish human wrongdoers, they have provided a blueprint for proper behavior with respect to obligations, reciprocities, and social behavior in general.

Eskimo Religion

The Inuit (Eskimo) maintain a traditional religious belief system that involves curers or healers who control and manipulate the supernatural world. In contrast to some of the "literate" religious traditions, Inuit religion did not assume the existence of an omnipotent supreme being. The Inuit did believe that every living creature possesses a soul or spirit that is reincarnated after death. They believed that the souls of deceased individuals remain in the vicinity of the living. The Inuit did not maintain a belief in an afterworld, or heaven, in which these souls congregate after death. Rather, they believed that these souls remain close to the natural world. The spirits of animals allow themselves to be hunted and are constantly reincarnated in other animal forms, to be hunted again to ensure the Inuit way of life.

Within these general conceptions of spirituality, the Inuit believe in *soul loss*, in which a person's soul is taken from the body as a result of unforeseen circumstances. Soul loss causes mental and physical illness for the individual. It is often believed that the soul has been stolen by another spirit. The Inuit coped with these situations through shamanism.

Two major forms of shamanism are found in Inuit culture. One form is hereditary, passed on through either parent. The more common variety involves people who receive shamanistic powers through direct contact with the supernatural, usually through dreams, visions, or hallucinations. In most cases, the shamans are male, however, some Inuit females can also become shamans. In the Bering Straits area, Inuit male and female shamans are believed to be able to own dead souls and spiritual beings called *tunghat*. Typically, the more spirits and souls these shamans own can increase their spiritual status. The shamans are believed to be able to journey to the realm of the dead souls and spiritual beings to induce changes in the weather, or cure the sick, or ensure the prosperity and reincarnation of animals (Lowenstein 1993).

People usually go through an extensive training period before they can begin practicing as a shaman. Eskimo shamans learn various relaxation and meditation techniques to induce trance states. They also learn methods of healing, curing, and exorcism. These techniques are used to produce group emotional experiences to enhance spiritual growth. In many cases, the shamanistic performances work effectively in curing illnesses or resolving emotional problems. Undoubtedly, in certain instances the Eskimo beliefs and cultural conceptions surrounding shamanism trigger certain states of mind that produce positive psychological and even physical consequences, such as overcoming illness and injuries.

Art, Music, and Religion

The art of foraging societies is intimately related to nature. Animals, plants, humans, and other components of the natural environment are the major subjects. This naturalistic art also has a religious significance, as nature and spirit are viewed as inseparable. Rock paintings with highly symbolic images of natural phenomena are found in most foraging societies. It is believed that this art is sacred and can be used to make contact with supernatural sources.

Traditional Inuit (Eskimo) art products include many items made from ivory, one of the few rigid materials available in the Arctic. Human and animal figurines, which were worn as amulets to enhance supernatural powers and practices, dominate Eskimo artistic output. The Eskimo also carve masks in ivory (or sometimes wood) for use by their shamans.

The music of foraging societies is generally divided into recreational (folk or popular) and religious music. The Mbuti, for example, have no instrumental music, but they have many songs and dances. In their vocal music they have a precise sense of harmony, giving each singer one note to produce at a given moment. This leads to a harmonic pattern that is passed around a circle of people. This technique is often used in Mbuti recreational music.

The sacred music of the Mbuti is much more important than their recreational music, and much of it is linked to the *Elima* rites of passage discussed earlier. In the *Elima*, young girls and boys sing back and forth to one another in harmony. Other sacred songs are sung by males only. The intensity of the singing builds so as to reach the spirit of the rain forest. One of the hunters goes off into the forest to echo the song of his fellows, so that the spirit may be sure to hear it. As in most societies, Mbuti ritual music usually has a standardized form, with little improvisation allowed. Ritual music helps sustain the cultural and spiritual traditions of the people. The lyrics of the music emphasize the sacred symbols that are maintained in Mbuti society. As the group chants the music together, a sense of sacredness is created in the community.

Music and religion are inextricably bound within the shamanistic rituals of the Inuit (Eskimo). In the shamanistic performances, a drum is used to enhance the rhythmic songs. The shaman's songs are simple, chant-like recitations that have no actual words. Short phrases are repeated again and again. The drumming and song chants are used to establish contact with the spirits. Anthropologist Rodney Needham (1967) suggested that the use of instruments such as the drum in shamanistic rituals not only heightens the spiritual atmosphere of the ceremony but also affects psychological (and neurological) processes that produce altered states of consciousness in individuals.

Globalization and Its Impact on Band Societies

Vanishing Foragers

As seen earlier in this chapter, most contemporary bands, or foraging societies, have survived in marginal environments: deserts, tropical rain forests, and arctic regions. Because these lands are not suitable for agriculture, foragers lived in relative isolation from surrounding populations. Following the emergence of industrial states and the extensive globalization induced by industrialism (see Chapter 6), these former marginal areas became attractive as unsettled frontiers with low population densities and bountiful natural resources such as land, timber, energy resources, minerals, and other valuable products. Industrial states have expanded into these regions in search of energy supplies and resources such as oil and minerals in the deserts and arctic areas, and land and timber from the tropical rain forests. As discussed in Chapter 6 on globalization, one result of this process has been increased contact between globalization processes and foraging societies, often with tragic results such as *ethnocide,* the destruction of the local culture and sometimes even *genocide.*

The Ju/'hoansi Foragers

The bands of the African deserts and tropical rain forests have been devastated by confrontations with expanding industrial states and globalization. The Ju/'hoansi San people of the Kalahari Desert, who, before the 1950s, had little contact with industrialized nations, are now caught in the midst of forced change. Many of the Ju/'hoansi San live in Botswana and Namibia, which for many years were controlled by the more industrialized country of South Africa. Beginning in the 1960s, the South African government began to expand into the Kalahari Desert. In the process it restricted the Ju/'hoansi San hunting territories and attempted to resettle them in a confined reservation at Tjum!kui, which represented only 11 percent of their ancestral land (Hitchcock et al. 1996; Hitchcock 2004). It further attempted to introduce the Ju/'hoansi San to agriculture—the cultivation of maize, melons, sorghum, and tobacco—and cattle raising. Because of the unsuitability of the land and inadequate water supplies, however, these activities have not succeeded. Consequently, the Ju/'hoansi San have become increasingly dependent on government rations of corn, salt, sugar, and tobacco.

In both Botswana and Namibia, the only economic opportunities for Ju/'hoansi San males are menial chores, clearing fields, and building roads. The government initially paid Ju/'hoansi San laborers with mealie (ground corn), sugar, or tobacco, but eventually switched to money. The introduction of this cash economy transformed traditional relationships in Ju/'hoansi San society. People who previously had embraced a reciprocal exchange system that enhanced their kinship and social ties now had to adjust to a system in which resources were managed for one's own family. Conflicts arose between those who wanted to share and others who were forced to become self-interested and hide resources even from their own kin.

In some of the areas where the Ju/'hoansi San were settled, population began to increase. This is a typical consequence of a shift from a foraging to a settled life. With increased crowding came epidemics, particularly tuberculosis, that claimed many lives. Moreover, in response to the rapid transformation of their lifestyle, many Ju/'hoansi San resorted to frequent drinking. Much of their newly acquired cash from employment went into alcohol consumption, and alcoholism became a problem for many.

Other Ju/'hoansi San males at the Tjum!kui reservation were recruited by the South African military to engage in campaigns during the 1960s and 1970s against the South-West African People's Organization (SWAPO), guerrilla insurgents who opposed the South African regime. The Ju/'hoansi San were valued as soldiers because they were good trackers and courageous fighters. Most of them, however, were unaware of the geopolitical strategies and racist policies of the South African government. They were simply attracted to military service by the promise of high wages.

Richard Lee believed that this involvement in the South African military increased the amount of violence in Ju/'hoansi San society. Lee documented only twenty-two cases of homicide among all the Ju/'hoansi between 1922 and 1955. In contrast, seven murders were recorded in a single village known as Chum!kwe during the brief period from 1978 to 1980, a major increase (Lee 1993). According to Lee, the aggressive values and norms associated with militarism increased the tendency toward violence in Ju/'hoansi San society.

The confinement to the reservation and the restriction from hunting and gathering subsistence resulted in the reduced access to protein, foods and other items for reciprocal exchanges, a decline in handicraft production, and rising dissatisfaction and frustration by the Ju/'hoansi San people toward the outsiders and the government that controlled their land (Hitchcock and Biesle 2002). In addition, increasing health and social problems, including higher suicide and murder rates, alcoholism, more patriarchal control and abuse of women, and increases in sexually transmitted diseases, including HIV/AIDs infections, have resulted in higher mortality rates (Hitchcock 2004).

Finally, in 1998 in Namibia the Ju/'hoansi San established what is known as a conservancy to oversee the wildlife resources in the region. It is a block of communal land on which people can utilize the wildlife resources and make decisions about land use. This conservancy, called NYAE NYAE, has been successful in producing income for the group and giving assistance for conservation projects. Recently, however, a number of refugees have flooded into Namibia from an ongoing war in neighboring Angola, which has created problems for resettling these populations in the Kalahari region. To some degree, these refugees threatened the conservancy projects in Namibia (Biesle and Hitchcock 2002a).

The Dobe Ju/'hoansi

Lee (1993) also studied the situation of the Ju/'hoansi San of the Dobe area, who have not had to make the same types of adjustments as the Ju/'hoansi San, who were settled on the confined reservation. Generally, Ju/'hoansi San of the Dobe area were not subjected to the same expansive South African policies as the other Ju/'hoansi San. For example, the Ju/'hoansi in Dobe have not been recruited into the South African army, nor has the government funded settlement reservations. However, Lee found that by the 1970s, the Ju/'hoansi Dobe were beginning to adopt agriculture and herding. Although agriculture continues to be a very risky proposition in the desert area, herding and livestock production is beginning to become a viable source of income for the Dobe Ju/'hoansi.

Lee described how Ju/'hoansi Dobe males also began to migrate outside their own territories to work in South African mines for $18 to $25 a month. Upon returning home after months of working in the mines, they spent much of their cash wages on a home brew. This pattern of drinking increased the tendency toward alcoholism among some Ju/'hoansi Dobe.

The introduction of a cash economy disrupted traditional Ju/'hoansi Dobe patterns of egalitarianism and reciprocity. The availability of manufactured goods such as soap, foodstuffs, kerosene, and clothing led to the decline of indigenous technologies and crafts. Drinking, violence, and conflict increased. These problems heightened anxieties

among the Ju/'hoansi Dobe, as they realized how dramatically their traditional lifestyle had changed. However, even in the late 1990s, much of the ethos of sharing and egalitarianism endured in spite of all the changes, giving some indications of the resilience of this way of life.

In 2001, the Botswana government moved toward restricting the land use rights of the San people. The government announced that the local people would no longer have legal rights to exploit natural resources in the Central Kalahari. They have taken steps to cut off the San water supplies and are restricting their subsistence hunting activities. The native people have said they will resist this intrusion with their bows and arrows. Some suspect that the area's rich diamond deposits are the real motivation for moving these people off their land (Biesle and Hitchcock 2002b).

The Mbuti Pygmies

The late Colin Turnbull examined two cases of African foragers who have faced decimation through forced cultural change. Turnbull did the major ethnographic study, discussed in Chapter 15, of the Mbuti Pygmies of the Ituri rain forest of the Congo, formerly Zaire. He noted (1963, 1983) that the Pygmies had been in contact with outsiders for centuries but had chosen to retain their traditional hunting-and-gathering way of life. During the colonial period in what was then the Belgian Congo, however, government officials tried to resettle the Mbuti on plantations outside the forest.

Following the colonial period, the newly independent government of Zaire continued the same policies of forced resettlement. In the government's view, this move would "emancipate" the Pygmies, enabling them to contribute to the economy and to participate in the national political process (Turnbull 1983). The Pygmies would become national citizens and would also be subject to taxation. Model villages were built outside the forest with Mbuti labor. Convinced by government officials that they would benefit, many Mbuti at first supported these relocation projects.

The immediate results of this resettlement, however, were disastrous. Turnbull visited the model villages and found many of the Mbuti suffering from various diseases. Because the Mbuti were unaccustomed to living a sedentary life, they lacked

The Mbuti Pygmies have been traumatically influenced by globalization processes.

knowledge of proper sanitation. Turnbull found that the Mbuti water had become contaminated, and the change of diet from forest products to cultivated crops had created nutritional problems.

More recently, globalization has had other effects on many of the Mbuti people. In 1992, international pressure resulted in the government creating an area called Okapi Faunal Reserve or "green zone" to conserve the rain forest and indirectly to preserve the Mbuti way of life. The law protecting the reserve decreed that poaching protected animals like elephants, leopards, chimpanzees, and gorillas was forbidden (Tshombe 2001). However, the "green zone" has not been protected due to the extreme political and institutional crises faced by the Democratic Republic of the Congo. This region has been besieged by civil wars and the erosion of political control and stability. Due to this weakening of the state, immigrants began to flow into the Ituri forest to clear land for agriculture, which resulted in the rapid deterioration of the soil. Multinational companies continued logging throughout the forest area, and elephant poaching increased with the killing of about a hundred elephants between 1998 and 2000.

One of the most devastating consequences in the Ituri forest came from the introduction of coltan mining (Harden 2001). Coltan is a mineral that is found in the forests of the Congo near where the Mbuti live. Coltan is refined in the United States and Europe into tantalum, which is a metallic element that is used in capacitors and other electronic components for computers, cell phones, and pagers. The electronics and computer industries are heavily dependent on coltan. Many of the Mbuti have been recruited by the mining industry to dig for coltan. They chop down great swaths of the rain forest and dig large holes in the forest floor to dig out this vital mineral, which is used in electronic equipment far away from the Ituri forest. The Mbuti use pick and shovel to dig out this mineral, which was worth $80 a kilogram in the early part of 2001. They could earn as much as $2,000 a month, which represented more cash wages than the Mbuti had ever seen. Thousands of other immigrants began to pour into the area to take advantage of this new profitable mineral needed by the high-tech businesses of the postindustrial societies.

This encounter between the high-tech world and the Ituri forest resulted in painful circumstances for the Mbuti people. First, the mining created major environmental damage to the rain forest where these people depended on hunting and gathering. The streams of the forest were polluted, trees were cut down, and the large holes in the ground for coltan mining ruined the environment. The growing migrant population began to poach and kill the lowland gorillas and other animals for food. Lowland gorillas have been reduced to fewer than one thousand, and other forest animals were overhunted.

Along with the increase of the population in the mining camps came prostitution, the abuse of alcohol, conflict, exploitation by outside groups, and the spread of diseases such as gonorrhea.

Additionally, by the spring of 2001, the price of coltan fell from $80 to $8.00 a kilogram. A slump in cell phone sales and the decrease in the high-tech economy created a glut of coltan on the global market, which had consequences for the people of the rain forest. Mining camps that had ravaged the rain forest were still filled with migrants, prostitutes, and some of the Mbuti people, but many of the people abandoned these mining camps. However, many of the Mbuti have not returned to their traditional hunting-and-gathering way of life. Many of them lost the land that sustained their way of life. The weakness of the state, civil wars, and ethnic conflict surrounding the Mbuti enabled outsiders to take over their forest land. Globalization resulted in ecological damage and social and cultural dislocations for the Mbuti people in a very short period of time.

In the last chapter of this text we discuss the field of applied anthropology, which attempts to utilize the knowledge that anthropologists have acquired about other societies to help solve some of the problems and developments that have occurred as a result of globalization. We emphasize the fact that anthropologists not only use the scientific and other investigative methods to examine and understand other societies but also are actively involved in assisting in the solution of economic and nutritional problems resulting from globalization as well as human rights issues. As seen before, the globalization process has created many new difficulties for foraging societies. Most anthropologists argue that these indigenous peoples should be able to make free and informed choices regarding their destiny, instead of being coerced into assimilating to the wider globalization pressures surrounding them (Hitchcock 1988; Bodley 1990). As previously discussed, many nonstate societies have tried to resist domination by outside powers but generally lacked the power to do so successfully.

In some cases, anthropologists assisted these peoples in their struggles. A number of anthropologists have set up foundations to collect money to aid indigenous peoples in their struggles against governments and economic interests who demand their territory. At Harvard University, anthropologists under the guidance of David Maybury-Lewis formed an organization known as Cultural Survival that seeks to aid these indigenous societies in their confrontations with industrial and global pressures. Robert Hitchcock, a student of Richard Lee, has become an internationally known advocate of the human rights of indigenous peoples such as the Ju/'hoansi. Hitchcock's anthropological research is aimed at a more comprehensive understanding of these foraging societies as well as assisting their economic and political efforts in their continuing struggle and confrontation with the external aspects of globalization processes (Hitchcock 2003). It is hoped that these efforts by anthropologists such as Maybury-Lewis, Hitchcock, and many others will enable the foraging societies to cope successfully in their future adaptation to globalization.

Robert Hitchcock and other anthropologists who have been doing ethnographic research among the San peoples of the Kalahari region for many years illustrate how good scientific and empirical research findings can be combined with ethical and human rights advocacy to aid in the plight facing these indigenous societies from the new problems of globalization. We will address this question regarding how anthropologists are combining good scientific studies with the improvement in human rights in our final chapter of this textbook on Applied Anthropology.

SUMMARY

Unlike the hunter-gatherers, or foragers, of the Paleolithic period, most modern foraging societies have adapted to marginal environments: deserts, tropical rain forests, and arctic regions. The subsistence patterns of band societies in these environments require a mobile, nomadic lifestyle. Foragers must move frequently to procure their basic food resources.

Population growth among foragers within specific territories is minimal. This slow growth rate is due to fissioning and other practices that minimize the number of individuals within a territory. Cultural anthropologists have been studying foragers to determine whether low fertility rates are due to biological or cultural factors. The technology of foragers is refined to enable adjustments to the practical needs of their environmental conditions. They have developed economic patterns that depend on reciprocity and resource sharing to produce cooperative behavior. Generally, a foraging economy does not depend on private property but rather on kinship and family ownership.

The social organization of foraging societies is based on kinship, age, and gender. Kinship relations are maintained among different multifamily bands through marriage. Generally, people marry outside their own band. Gender relations are related to the division of labor; in most societies men hunt and women gather. To some extent, this division of labor determines the status of females. Age is also an important determinant of status in foraging societies. As individuals move through the life cycle, they learn more about their society. As they reach old age, they are respected for their knowledge and teaching skills.

Political organization is limited in foraging societies. There is no formal, centralized political authority. Leadership is based on personal qualities and is not permanent. Although violence exists, usually among males, warfare is infrequent and restrained because of the limited political organization.

Religion in foraging societies is based on a unity between spiritual and material forces. Healers and shamans are the religious specialists who serve the people's spiritual needs. The art forms found among foragers reflect the spiritual aspects of their culture. The most common subjects are components of the natural environment, including plants, animals, and human beings. Globalization has had dramatic negative consequences for most foraging or band societies presently. Anthropologists are actively involved in assisting these people in their political struggle for more autonomy and choice as they encounter these new globalization processes.

QUESTIONS TO THINK ABOUT

1. What can we learn from studying hunter-gatherer societies that might help us understand and interpret life in industrial societies today?

2. How can the study of contemporary foragers provide us with an understanding of Paleolithic lifestyles?

3. What types of economic exchange would you expect to find in hunter-gatherer societies? Are the individuals in foraging societies more altruistic, magnanimous, and generous, or are they no more noble than other peoples?

4. Is private ownership of land a universal concept that applies to all societies? How much variation in "ownership" is found among forager groups?

5. Evaluate the hypothesis that in societies in which female contributions to the food supply are less critical or less valued than male contributions, female status is lower.

6. Would you rather be involved in warfare as a member of a forager society or as a member of an industrial nation? Why?

7. How are forager religions different from your own? Are there any similarities?

8. How has globalization influenced band societies? Do you see any positive aspects of globalization presently for these societies? What do you think will happen to these societies in the future?

KEY TERMS

animism
balanced reciprocity
band
brideservice
cross cousin
egalitarian
extended families

fissioning
foraging society
generalized reciprocity
geronticide
hunter-gatherer society
infanticide
marginal environments

matrilocal residence
negative reciprocity
nuclear family
patriarchal
patrilocal residence
reciprocal economic system
reciprocity

Tribes

CHAPTER QUESTIONS

- What problems do anthropologists encounter in trying to use the term *tribe* to classify various societies?

- What are the basic environmental, demographic, technological, and economic features associated with tribal societies?

- Compare the complexities of social organization in tribal societies with those in band societies.

- What are the differences in gender relations in tribal societies compared to those in band societies?

- What are the characteristics of tribal political relationships?

- What are the unique expressions of religion, art, and music among tribal peoples?

- What has been the impact of globalization on tribal societies?

- How are some tribal peoples resisting globalization?

The Concept of Tribe
in Anthropology

In Chapter 8 we introduced the typologies that anthropologists use to classify different forms of political systems. For example, hunter-gatherer societies

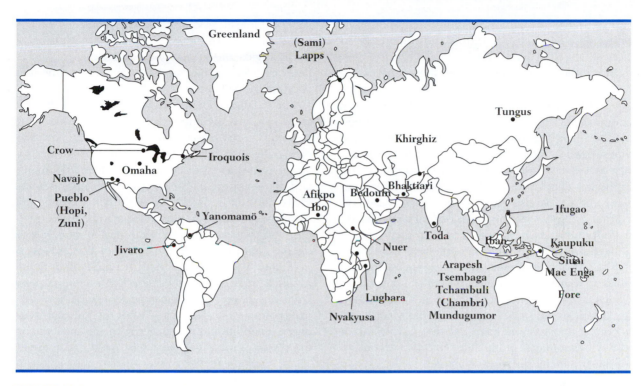

FIGURE 10.1 This map highlights many tribal societies, including those discussed in this chapter.

are classified as band political systems. The term *tribe* is used loosely to characterize *two* different types of subsistence systems: *horticulturalist* and *pastoralist*. Unlike hunting-and-gathering societies, tribal societies are *food-producing groups* that depend on the limited domestication of plants and animals. Figure 10.1 shows the distribution of tribal societies around the world. Politically, *tribes* are usually defined as noncentralized sociocultural systems in which authority is diffused among a number of kinship groups and associations. These characteristics of tribes are explored in this chapter.

Some anthropologists, most notably the late Morton Fried (1967, 1975), have objected to the use of the term *tribe* to characterize these societies. The word *tribe* is derived from the Latin term *tribus*, which was used by the Romans to refer to certain peoples who were not technologically advanced. Fried claimed that the term is often applied to a particular group by a more powerful group and usually has a pejorative connotation.

One aspect of Fried's criticism has created some theoretical controversy in anthropology. Fried argued that tribal organization is not an evolutionary stage emerging from the simpler stage represented by the foraging society, as most anthropologists had maintained. He suggested that, for the most part, tribes are usually "secondary" developments that evolve through contacts with other societies. This contact occurs when large, complex state societies, both agricultural and industrial, create tribal groups through the process of subjugation and domination. In many cases, these tribal groups become subjugated ethnic minorities in state societies.

Fried's criticisms have sensitized most anthropologists to the vagueness of the term *tribe*. In the past and sometimes currently, the term has been used haphazardly to refer to an enormous range of societies that have almost nothing in common. As we see in this chapter, there is a tremendous range of environments, social structures, political, religious, and other features that do not fit "neatly" into the concept of the "tribe." Despite these reservations, the term is still used to categorize the many different types of horticulturalist and pastoralist societies and to denote a form of political complexity and evolutionary development that bridges the gap between bands and centralized societies (Lewellen 1983).

The same types of stereotypes that many people have had in the past and sometimes still have, about the racial inferiority, low intelligence, and cultural inferiority of indigenous or aboriginal peoples such as foragers, were used and still sometimes persist about "tribal people and societies." Just as we saw in the discussion of band societies in the last chapter, since the twentieth century cultural anthropologists have done extensive ethnographic fieldwork among these tribal societies and have found that the people have a tremendous understanding of their environments and have a normal range of intelligence that compares with other modern humans. Many of these people in tribal societies among North and South American Indians, or Melanesia, or other regions of the world have become educated and have become physicians, attorneys, engineers, politicians, and also anthropologists. So, again, the question arises for many people in advanced industrial societies, Why did these tribal societies not develop more complex developed technologies and sociocultural systems? It is obvious that it does not have anything to do with "race" or "intelligence," because many of these North American Indians in tribal societies had similar genetic and biological traits as other Asians, but they did not develop civilizations such as in China or elsewhere in Asia. What is the explanation for their "perceived lack of technological and sociocultural complexity"?

Anthropologists have been inspired by Jared Diamond's book *Guns, Germs and Steel: The Fates of Human Societies* (1997), where he emphasizes how geographical and ecological conditions gave enormous advantages to some areas of the world, such as the Eurasian continent, which had the "package of domesticated animals and plants" that diffused and spread across Europe and other areas very rapidly without major geographic boundaries such as mountains, tropical rain forests, and deserts. This resulted in tremendous advantages for Greece, Rome, and other complex societies in the development of agricultural civilizations. Archaeologists and other anthropologists have been refining Diamond's hypotheses with extensive research on these issues in different areas of the world, but they concur with the general findings of his approach regarding the

lack of domesticated animals and plants, as well as geographical barriers that restricted the diffusion of technologies and ideas from one area to another in many regions of the world such as the Americas and the Pacific Islands.

For example, Diamond has done extensive research in the Melanesian Islands of Papua New Guinea, which is discussed in this chapter. The peoples in this region were fairly isolated from other societies until the 1930s, when Australians, Germans, and other Europeans began to explore the islands. There are hundreds of different tribes and different languages in this region because many of these people were separated by geographical boundaries in the mountain and highland areas and lowland areas. In addition, just as in North, Central, and South America or Australia, these people of Papua New Guinea had very few domesticated plants and animals compared to the Near East or the Eurasian continent. In addition, there were no metals available in the region, unlike the Near East or Eurasian areas. These ecological, geographical, and historical circumstances give us a better understanding of why tribal peoples have not developed more complex sociocultural systems than any views about the lack of intelligence or racial inferiority.

Environment and Subsistence for Horticulturalists

Horticulture is a form of agriculture in which people use a limited, nonmechanized technology to cultivate plants. One major type of horticulture is known as *slash-and-burn cultivation*. This system was once widespread but today is found primarily in tropical rain forests. Approximately 250 million people throughout the world currently engage in slash-and-burn cultivation (Moran 1982).

Slash-and-burn cultivation involves the production of food without the intensive use of land, a large labor force, or complex technology. As generally practiced, it is a cyclical process that begins with clearing a tract of land by cutting down the trees and then setting fire to the brush. The burned vegetation and ashes remain, and the nutrients from them are unlocked and sink into the soil. After the land is cleared and burned, various crops are planted. In most cases, women and children spend a great deal of time weeding and tending the gardens. Typically, after the crops are planted and harvested for several years, the garden plot is left fallow (unplanted) for three to fifteen years, and the cultivators must shift to a new location.

People who practice slash-and-burn cultivation must maintain a delicate balance with their environment. If the plot is not left fallow and is cultivated too often, grasses and weeds may colonize the area at the expense of forest regrowth. The land then becomes useless or overexploited. Some horticulturalists have recleared their land too often and brought devastation to some forest environments; others have been able to reside in one location for almost a century (Carneiro 1961). In general, compared with foragers, slash-and-burn horticulturalists are less nomadic and more sedentary.

Amazon Horticulturalists: The Yanomamö

One South American tribal group, known as the Yanomamö, practices slash-and-burn cultivation. Napoleon Chagnon studied the Yanomamö for more than thirty years. Approximately 80 to 90 percent of their diet comes from their gardens (Chagnon 1997). Yanomamö males clear the forest, burn the vegetation, and plant the crops; the females (and sometimes children) weed the garden and eventually harvest the crops. Generally, the Yanomamö do not work on subsistence activities for food production more than three to four hours per day. A Yanomamö garden lasts for about three years from the time of the initial planting; after this period, the garden is overrun with scrub vegetation, and the soil becomes depleted.

Early cultural ecologists assumed that slash-and-burn cultivators are forced to relocate because the soil becomes exhausted. Chagnon, however, has shown that Yanomamö decisions to move are not based simply on soil depletion. In fact, as the soil begins to lose its capacity to support crops, the Yanomamö make small adjustments, such as extending a previous garden or clearing a new tract of land near the old one. Chagnon discovered that major population movements of the Yanomamö are due instead to warfare and political conflict with neighboring groups. Thus, a sedentary life in these Amazonian societies is not simply a product of ecological conditions; it also involves strategic alliances and political maneuvers designed to deal with human populations in nearby communities (Chagnon 1997).

Although horticulture is the primary subsistence activity of many Amazonian tribes, hunting, fishing, and gathering typically supplement this activity. The Yanomamö gather wild foods, especially palm fruits and a variety of nuts, pods, tubers, mushrooms, and honey. They hunt game birds and a number of animals. In addition, they collect toads, frogs, and many varieties of insects.

A tropical forest in the first stages of slash-and-burn horticulture.

New Guinea Horticulturalists: The Tsembaga

As mentioned in the introduction to this chapter, the Melanesian Islands of Papua New Guinea have many tribal horticulturalist populations, some of whom were not contacted by Western society until the 1930s. Archaeologists have traced early horticultural developments in highland New Guinea to 7000 BC (White and O'Connell 1982). One group, the Tsembaga Maring, has been studied thoroughly by the late anthropologist Roy Rappaport (1984).

The Tsembaga live in two river valley areas surrounded by mountains. They cultivate the mountain slopes with their subsistence gardens. Tsembaga males and females clear the undergrowth from the secondary forest, after which the men cut down the trees. When the cut vegetation dries out, it is stacked up and burned. The women then plant and harvest crops, especially sweet potatoes, taro, manioc, and yams; 99 percent of the Tsembaga diet by weight consists of vegetables, particularly these root crops. The Tsembaga also domesticate pigs, but these animals are usually consumed only during certain ritual occasions.

Horticulturalists in Woodland Forest Areas: The Iroquois

In the past, many Native American Indian groups such as the Iroquois, who resided in the eastern woodland region of North America, practiced horticulture. Actually, the term Iroquois was a French use of a Basque term that translates as "killer people," because they were involved in much warfare with other tribes and then with the Europeans when they arrived. The people themselves use the native Seneca word *Haudenosaunee*, which means "the Longhouse people," because they lived in large, long houses described later (Sutton 2004). The *Haudenosaunee* included five major tribes: the Mohawk, Seneca, Onondaga, Oneida, and Cayuga. They were first studied by the nineteenth-century anthropologist Lewis Morgan, and he relied on his Seneca Indian informant Ely Parker (see Chapter 3, pages 58–61). These tribes lived in the upper New York State region, where rivers such as the St. Lawrence and Hudson drain into the area, providing fertile ground for horticultural activities. These horticultural practices probably appeared between 2300 and 1000 BC and were adopted as a regular subsistence system around AD 400 (Fagan 2000) Eventually, the native peoples of this region began to raise maize and other crops along with local wild species. Most archaeologists have concluded that this horticultural pattern of maize, beans, and squash originated in Mesoamerica and then extended across the regions of North America, spreading out to the Ohio River valley areas and eastward to Native American groups such as the Iroquois.

The Iroquois constructed their villages with longhouses in the center of the settlement. (Longhouses were large, multifamily houses built with upright posts that supported horizontal poles for rafters. Large slabs of bark, laced together with cords of plant fiber, covered the framework.)

Iroquois males cleared the primary forest around the village and burned the cut litter. In the spring the women planted fifteen varieties of maize, beans, squash, and other crops, which they later harvested and processed. The Iroquois left part of the primary forest standing so that deer, squirrels, fox, and bear were available for hunting. The forest also provided nuts, berries, and many species of wild plants.

After harvesting the crops in the fall, the men would concentrate their subsistence activities on game such as deer and bear. In the spring, while the women planted crops, the men fished in the many lakes and rivers and also captured birds. Like many other slash-and-burn cultivators, the Iroquois farmed their fields until the fields were no longer fertile, after which they cleared new fields while the old ones lay fallow. After a generation or so, depending on local conditions, the fertile fields were located far enough away from the village that the entire community moved so that it could be closer to the gardens.

Environment and Subsistence for Pastoralists

In central Asia, the Middle East, North and East Africa, South America, Northern and Southern Europe, and highland Tibet there were—and, in some cases, still are—**pastoralists**, groups whose subsistence activities are based on the care of domesticated animals. The use of herd animals differs from group to group, and again we as anthropologists find

Bedouin pastoralist with camels in the Middle East.

with foragers or bands, they find a great deal of variation among pastoralist tribes (Salzman 2004). The Bedouins (the Arabic term for "camel breeders") of Arabia and North Africa, for example, use the camel mainly for transportation; they use the hair for tents, caravans, and other purposes and only sometimes consume the meat. Other pastoralist groups, such as the Saami (Lapps) of Scandinavia, have in the past completely depended on caribou, deriving most of their food and other vital resources from them. In South America, some tribal pastoralists in the Andes mountains bred llamas and alpaca for transportation and wool for clothing. Other pastoralist tribes, such as the Basseri, Qashqai, and Bahktiari of Iran, have a complex of animals, including horses, donkeys, sheep, goats, and cattle, that they maintain and herd for their livelihood. Although some pastoralists may have small gardens, most of them have only their herd animals for subsistence purposes. These domesticated animals provide food such as milk, butter, blood, and meat, wool and hair for clothing, bone and horn for tools and weapons, skin for making leather, traction for loads and plows, transportation, travel, warfare, recreation, and ritual (Salzman 2004).

The care of herd animals requires frequent moves from camp to camp and sometimes involves long migrations. Some groups, such as the Tungus of Siberia, who are reindeer pastoralists, trek more than 1,000 miles annually. The Basseri, Qashqai, and Bahktiari of Iran, with their complex of animals, migrate seasonally through mountainous regions hundreds of miles from winter pastures to highland pastures (Barth 1961; Beck 1991; Garthwaite 1983; Salzman 2004). These pastoralist migrations are not aimless; the groups know the layout of the land and move to territories that contain specific grazing pastures or waterholes during different seasons. Other pastoralist tribes are more settled, such as the Turkman of northeast Iran, but migrate once in awhile because of political conflict with the government (Irons 1974; Salzman 2004).

East African Cattle Complex

In an area stretching from southern Sudan through Kenya, Uganda, Rwanda, Burundi, Tanzania, Mozambique, and into parts of South Africa, various pastoralists herd cattle as their means of subsistence. Most of these groups do not depend entirely on their cattle for subsistence needs, but they plant gardens to supplement their food resources. These pastoralist groups include the Maasai, the Nuer, Karimojong, Pokot, Sebei, Samburu, and the Dinka.

The Nuer Anthropologist E. E. Evans-Pritchard (1940, 1951, 1956) conducted a classic study of a pastoralist group called the Nuer. The Nuer reside along the upper Nile River and its tributaries in southern Sudan. Because of the flatness of this region, the annual flooding of the Nile during the rainy season, and the heavy clay soils, the Nuer spend the wet season on high, sandy ground, where they plant sorghum, a cereal grass used for grain. This horticulture is very limited, however, because strong rainfall, as well as elephants, birds, and insects, destroy the crops. Therefore, cattle are the most important subsistence resource for the Nuer.

The Nuer view cattle herding with a great deal of pride. In the dry season they move with their cattle into the grassland areas. The cattle transform the energy stored in the grasses, herbs, and shrubs into valuable subsistence products. Yet, as is true of other herders in this area, the basis of the Nuer subsistence is not consumption of cattle. Rather, they depend heavily on the blood and milk of their animals. Every few months during the dry season, the cattle are bled by making small incisions that heal quickly. The Nuer boil the blood until it gets thick, roast it, and then eat it. The cows are milked morning and night; some of the milk is used to make butter. The Nuer slaughter their old cattle, which then calls for elaborate ceremonies or sacrifices.

Demographics and Settlement

Generally, as humans developed the capacity to produce food through the domestication of animals and plants, the carrying capacity of particular territories increased to support a greater population density than had been possible for band societies. Whereas foraging populations had to live in small bands, tribal societies became much more densely populated. According to Murdock's (1967) cross-cultural tabulations, the median size of horticulturalist societies ranges from 100 to more than 5,000 people in specific territories, and pastoralists have a median size of 2,000 people in particular niches. Some tribal populations have denser populations in large regions in which villages are connected through economic, social, and political relationships.

Compared with most foraging societies, tribal societies are relatively settled within fairly well-defined territories. As mentioned earlier, horticulturalists are somewhat mobile, having to move to fertile lands every so often, but they generally settle in one locale for a number of years.

Of course, many pastoralist societies are nomadic, but their wanderings are limited to specific pastures and grasslands to care for their animals. Because pastoralists move seasonally from pasture to pasture, they place less intense population pressure on each area. Population densities for pastoralists range from one to five persons per square mile of land; however, in the richly endowed grassland environment of central Asia, the Kalmuk Mongols maintain an average density of about eighteen people per square mile. In general, pastoralist populations are denser than are those of foragers, but in many cases, both are spread thinly over the land (Sahlins 1968b; Salzman 2004).

Like foraging societies, both horticulturalist and pastoralist societies experience slow population growth because of limited resources. To regulate their populations, tribal societies have adopted the same strategies as bands, especially fissioning. Other cultural practices designed to control population growth include sexual abstinence, infanticide, abortion, and a prolonged period of nursing.

Technology

The whole range of tribal technologies is extremely broad and varies among differing populations depending on whether they are horticulturalists or pastoralists and to what types of environments they have had to adapt. Technological innovations found in tribal societies include woodworking, weaving, leather working, and the production of numerous copper ornaments, tools, and weapons.

Horticulturalist Technology

Horticulturalist groups used sharpened digging sticks and sometimes wooden hoes to plant small gardens. Slash-and-burn horticulturalists such as the Yanomamö and the Iroquois used crude stone or wooden axes to fell the primary forest. It sometimes took weeks for a small group of males to cut down a wooded area for a garden.

Many horticultural societies have also developed technologies to aid in hunting and fishing to supplement their horticultural activities. For example, some Amazonian peoples, such as the Jivaro of Ecuador and Peru, often use blowguns, which propel poison darts up to forty-five yards, to kill monkeys and birds deep in the forest (Harner 1972). The Yanomamö use large, powerful bows, sometimes five to five and half feet long, and long arrow shafts with a splintered point, dipped in *curare*, a deadly poison (Chagnon 1997). Amazonian horticulturalists also mix poisons into local waters, causing the fish to rise to the surface in a stupefied condition; they are then gathered for food (Harner 1972; Chagnon 1997).

The woodland Iroquois tribes used both the blowgun and the bow (called the self-bow) and arrow to hunt game in surrounding forests. The Iroquois carefully selected light wooden branches for arrow shafts, dried them to season the wood, and then smoothed them with stone and bone tools. To make the arrow twist in flight, they took feathers from eagles, turkeys, and hawks, which they then attached with a glue made from animal tissues, sinew, or horns. Arrowheads were made from wood, stone, horn, antler, shell, or raw copper (Garbarino 1988).

Horticulturalists such as the Pacific Islanders, who were not slash-and-burn farmers and resided in more permanent locations, tended to have a more elaborate technology. In addition to the simple digging stick used to cultivate the irrigated gardens, they had many other sophisticated tools and utensils. Although the Pacific Islanders had no metals or clay for pottery, they had many specialized kinds of shell and woodworking tools for making jewelry, knives, rasps, and files.

Pastoralist Technology

The mobility required by the pastoralist lifestyle prevented these groups from using an elaborate technology. Pastoralists such as the Mongols and the Bedouins carried all of their belongings with them in their yearly migrations. Their technologies aided them in these mass movements; for example, they had saddles for their horses and camels, weapons for hunting, equipment for taking care of their livestock and processing food, and tents that could be moved during migrations. Other pastoralists such as the Nuer of East Africa constructed huts of thatch in permanent locations that served as home bases where a certain number of people remained during the migration season.

Economics

As in hunting-and-gathering societies, *reciprocity* is the dominant form of exchange of economic resources in tribal economic systems. All three forms of reciprocity—generalized, balanced, and negative—are used by tribal societies. *Generalized reciprocity* tends to occur within close kinship groupings. Balanced and negative reciprocity occur among more distant kinship groupings. One example of balanced reciprocity occurs among the Yanomamö, who maintain a system of trade and feasting activities with other villages. One village will host a feast, inviting another village to attend. During the feast, the villagers exchange tools, pots, baskets, arrows, dogs, yarn, and hallucinogenic drugs. The feast activities sustain intervillage cooperation, marital exchanges, and political and military alliances (Chagnon 1997). The villagers calculate these transactions and exchanges very carefully to determine exact equivalencies. If an equal return is not given, then the original donor village will discontinue the exchange relationship. This may lead to hostilities and perhaps warfare between the villages.

Money

Unlike foragers, some tribal societies engage in monetary exchange, that is, transactions that involve money. **Money** is a medium of exchange based on a standard value. According to economists, money has four functions:

1. It enables people to pay for a good or service, and then it circulates to allow for subsequent purchases.

2. It serves as a uniform standard of value for goods and services within a society.

3. It has a store of value; that is, its standard of value does not fluctuate radically from one time to another.

4. It serves as a form of deferred payment; that is, it can express a promise to pay in the future with the same standard value. (Neale 1976)

Economic anthropologists classify money into two types: *general-purpose money* (or multipurpose money) and *limited-purpose money* (or special-purpose money). General-purpose money serves all four of the above functions. It can be used as a medium of exchange for most of the goods and services in society. Limited-purpose money, in contrast, is restricted to the purchase of certain goods and services. The paper currencies used in the United States and other industrial societies are examples of general-purpose money. In contrast, most tribal societies that practice monetary exchange use limited-purpose money.

Peoples in some of the Pacific Islands and other coastal areas have used a variety of shells to conduct trade relations. In other tribal societies, livestock, cloth, salt, feathers, animal teeth, and, sometimes, women functioned as money. This type of money was used for specialized exchange circumstances. For example, the Siane of New Guinea exchanged food for other subsistence goods, and luxury items such as bird feathers were exchanged only for other luxury items. Another separate level of exchange took place with respect to prestige items such as certain forms of shell necklaces (Salisbury 1962).

Property Ownership

Ownership of property, especially land for horticulturalists and animals for pastoralists, takes on significance in tribal societies that it does not have in band societies. The concept of property ownership becomes more clearly defined in tribal societies and is based on a web of social relations involving rights, privileges, and perhaps duties and obligations regarding the use of a particular piece of land, a herd of animals, or other objects.

In tribal societies, exclusive right to use property is rare. With some exceptions, property rights in tribal societies are generally invested in family and wider kinship groupings. Usually tribal families have use rights to farmland, pastures, animals, and other items. The property of tribal societies is transferred to families through inheritance; individual access to property, however, is largely determined by status. In other words, in tribal societies, an individual gains certain rights, privileges, and obligations with respect to property through inheriting a particular status position. Status in tribal societies is usually determined by kinship, age, and gender, as we discuss later in the chapter.

Property rights in tribal societies are not completely static with respect to statuses. Rather, they may fluctuate according to the availability of basic resources. If land is plentiful in a specific tribe, for example, outsiders who need land may be granted rights to use the land. On the other hand, if there is a shortage of land, rights to that property may become more narrowly defined and may be defended if the land is intruded on. Grazing land for pastoralists or arable land for horticulturalists may become limited, and, if so, use rights may be defined more exclusively for particular family and kinship groupings. In contrast to foraging societies, in tribal societies warfare frequently results from encroachments on more narrowly defined property.

Tribal societies generally possess certain types of personal property. Horticulturalists typically have more personal property than do pastoralists, because they are generally more sedentary. Because of the demands of a nomadic life, pastoralist property tends to be portable (saddles, tents, and similar objects), whereas much horticultural property tends to be immovable, like housing structures and land. Because families based on large kin groupings own most tribal property, individuals generally do not have the opportunity to amass concentrations of wealth. The limited technological capabilities and reciprocal economic system of tribal societies also restrict the capacity of individuals to accumulate large stores of wealth. Consequently, tribal societies tend to be egalitarian with respect to the ownership of property.

Social Organization

Tribal societies differ from foraging societies in that tribal peoples produce most of their subsistence foods through small-scale cultivation and the domestication of animals. The evolution of food-producing subsistence corresponds to the development of new forms of social organization. As is true among foragers, social organization among tribes is largely based on kinship. Rules concerning kinship, marriage, and other social systems, however, are much more elaborate in tribal societies, which have to resolve new types of problems including denser populations, control of land or livestock, and, sometimes, warfare.

New and diverse forms of social organization have enabled tribal societies to adjust to the new conditions of food production. Unlike foragers, who sometimes have to remain separate from one another in small, flexibly organized bands, food producers have had to develop social relationships that are more fixed and permanent. Tribal social organization is based on family, the descent group, gender, and age. The social organization of tribal societies is much more complex than that of band societies.

Families

The most common social grouping among tribal societies is the *extended family*. Most extended families consist of three generations—grandparents, parents, and children—although they can also contain married siblings with their spouses and children. Compared with the nuclear family, the extended family is a larger and more stable social unit that is more effective in organizing and carrying out domestic economic and subsistence activities (Pasternak 1976). Even the extended family, however, cannot satisfy the complex needs of tribal societies for cooperation, labor, and reciprocity. To meet these needs, tribal groups have developed even more "extended" types of social organization, based on both kinship and nonkinship principles.

Descent Groups

One of the more extended social groupings that exist in tribal societies is the **descent group**. A descent group is a social group identified by a person to trace actual or supposed kinship relationships. Descent groups are the predominant social unit in tribal societies.

One major type of descent group is based on lineage. Anthropologists define **lineages** as descent groups composed of relatives, all of whom trace their relationship through *consanguineal* (blood) or *affinal* (marriage) relations to an actual, commonly known ancestor. Everyone in the lineage knows exactly how she or he is related to this ancestor.

Unilineal Descent Groups

Unilineal descent groups are lineage groups that trace their descent through only one side of the lineage or through only one sex. The most common type of unilineal descent group is a ***patrilineal descent group***, or *patrilineage*, composed of people who trace their descent through males from a common, known male ancestor (see Figure 10.2, top). Patrilineal descent groups are the predominant form of lineage in tribal societies (Pasternak 1976).

Another form of unilineal descent group is the **matrilineal descent group**, or *matrilineage*, whose members calculate descent through the female line from a commonly known female ancestor (see Figure 10.2, bottom). Matrilineal descent groups occur most frequently in horticultural societies, although they are not the most common organization. Matrilineal descent is found among a small number of North American tribal societies such as the Iroquois, Hopi, and Crow; among a number of tribes in throughout central and south Africa; and among a few peoples who live in the Pacific Islands.

One very rare type of unilineal grouping is based on *double descent*, a combination of patrilineal and matrilineal principles. In this type of social organization, an individual belongs to both his or her father's and mother's lineal descent groups. Several African tribal societies, such as the Afikpo Igbo in Nigeria, have a double-descent type of social organization (Ottenberg 1965).

Ambilineal Descent Groups One other form of descent group is known as ambilineal descent. An **ambilineal descent group** is formed by tracing an individual's descent relationships through either a male or a female line. The members of these groups are not all related to each other through a particular male or female. Therefore, technically, this form of descent group is not unilineal. Usually, once an individual chooses to affiliate with either the father's or mother's descent group, he or she remains with that descent group. Because each individual may choose his or her descent group, the ambilineal system offers more opportunity for economic and political strategizing. This choice frequently takes into account the relative economic

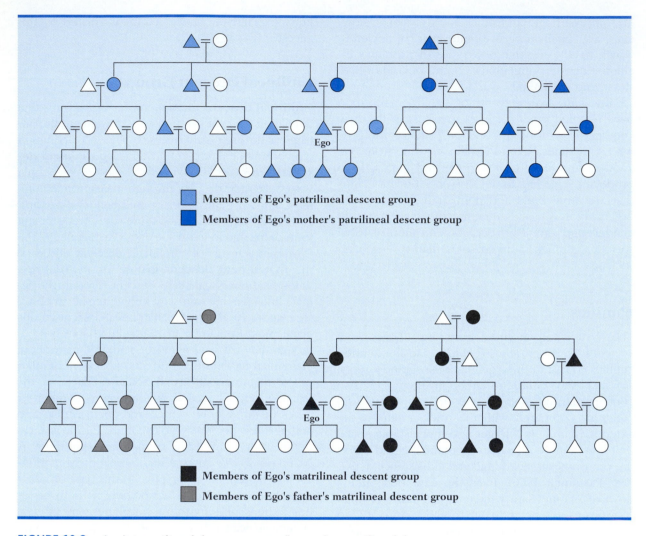

Members of Ego's patrilineal descent group
Members of Ego's mother's patrilineal descent group

Members of Ego's matrilineal descent group
Members of Ego's father's matrilineal descent group

FIGURE 10.2 (top) A patrilineal descent system; (bottom) a matrilineal descent system.

resources or political power of the two family groups.

Bilateral Descent A number of tribal societies practice **bilateral descent**, in which relatives are traced through both maternal and paternal sides of the family simultaneously. This type of descent system does not result in any particular lineal descent grouping. For that reason, it is not too common in tribal societies. In those cases in which bilateral descent is found among tribes, a loosely structured group known as a *kindred* is used to mobilize relatives for economic, social, or political purposes. **Kindreds** are overlapping relatives from both the mother's and father's side of a family that an indi-

vidual recognizes as important kin relations (see Figure 10.3). In U.S. society, for example, when a person refers to all of his or her relatives, that person is designating a type of bilateral kindred. This bilateral kindred, however, has no functional significance in U.S. society compared to its role in a tribal society.

Clans A **clan** is a form of descent group whose members trace their descent to an unknown ancestor or, in some cases, to a sacred plant or animal. Members of clans usually share a common name but are not able to specify definitive links to an actual genealogical figure. Some clans are *patriclans*, a group distinguished by a male through whom

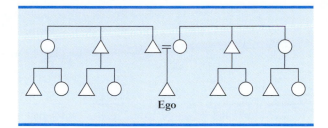

FIGURE 10.3 A kindred consists of relatives from both sides of a family that Ego recognizes as important kin relations.

descent is traced. Other clan groupings are *matriclans*, whose descent is traced through a female. Some tribal societies have both clans and lineages. In many cases, clans are made up of lineages that link their descent to an extremely vague person or sacred spirit. In such a system, clans are larger groupings, consisting of several different lineages.

Phratries and Moieties Other more loosely structured groups found in tribal societies include phratries and moieties. **Phratries** are social groupings that consist of two or more clans combined. Members of phratries usually believe they have some loose genealogical relationship to one another. **Moieties** (derived from the French word for "half") are composed of clans or phratries that divide the entire society into two equal divisions. In some cases, such as among the Hopi, the moiety divisions divide the village in half. People have to marry outside their own moiety. In addition, each moiety has specific functions related to economic and political organization and religious activities. Wherever phratries and moieties are found in tribal societies, they provide models for organizing social relationships.

Functions of Descent Groups

Descent groups provide distinctive organizational features for tribal societies. They may become corporate social units, meaning that they endure beyond any particular individual's lifetime. Thus, they can play a key role in regulating the production, exchange, and distribution of goods and services over a long period of time. Family rights to land, livestock, and other resources are usually defined in relation to these corporate descent groups.

Descent Groups and Economic Relationships
Descent groups enable tribal societies to manage their economic rights and obligations. Within the descent groups, individual nuclear families have rights to particular land and animals. In most cases, horticultural tribes inherit their rights to land owned by their entire lineage. The lineage allocates the land to members of the lineage through what anthropologists (and attorneys) call *usufruct* rights or corporate rights to the land. Among some more advanced patrilineal horticulturalist peoples, land is sometimes transmitted from generation to generation through an eldest male, an inheritance pattern known as **primogeniture**. Another, less common, pattern is **ultimogeniture**, in which property and land are passed to the youngest son.

In horticultural societies, separate families within patrilineages have joint rights to plots of land for gardening. For example, among the Yanomamö, villages are usually made up of two patrilineages; families within these lineages cultivate their own plots of land (Chagnon 1997). In this sense, the Yanomamö patrilineage is a like a corporate group. The transmission of status, rights, and obligations through these patrilineages occurs without constant disputes and conflicts. In these tribal societies, land is usually not partitioned into individual plots and cannot be sold to or exchanged with other descent groups.

Iroquois tribal society was based on matrilineal corporate groupings. Matrilineages among the Iroquois resided together in longhouses and had collective rights over tools and garden plots. These matrilineages were also the basic units of production in the slash-and-burn cultivation for maize and other crops. Property was inherited through matrilineal lines from the eldest woman in the corporate group. She had the highest social status in the matrilineage and influenced decision making regarding the allocation of land and other economic rights and resources (Brown 1970a).

Sometimes in societies with bilateral descent, kindreds are the basic labor-cooperative groups for production and exchange. People living in bilateral societies can turn to both the mother's and father's side of the family for economic assistance. The kindred is thus a much more loosely structured corporate group. The kindred is highly flexible and allows for better adaptation in certain environmental circumstances.

A depiction of a traditional Iroquois person.

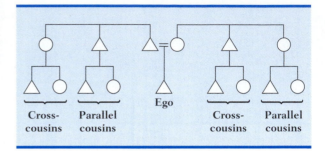

FIGURE 10.4   Different types of cousin marriage.

Marriage

Corporate descent groups play a role in determining marital relations in tribal societies. Like foragers, most tribal peoples maintain exogamous rules of marriage with respect to different corporate groups, meaning people generally marry outside their lineage, kindred, clan, moiety, or phratry. Marriages in tribal societies are guided by rules that ensure the perpetuation of kinship ties and group alliances.

Some tribal societies practice different forms of cousin marriage, which are illustrated in Figure 10.4. For example, among the Yanomamö, a pattern called double cross-cousin marriage and patrilocal residence, in which a newly married couple resides with the husband's parents, is practiced among patrilineages in different villages. Males in one patrilineage, in effect, exchange sisters, whom they may not marry, with males of other patrilineages. When

the sons of the next generation repeat this form of marriage, each is marrying a woman to whom he is already related by kinship. The woman whom the man marries is both his father's sister's daughter and his mother's brother's daughter. The woman is marrying a man who is both her mother's brother's son and her father's sister's son. This form of patrilineal exogamous marriage is common in many tribal societies. It is a type of restricted marriage exchange that helps provide for the formation of economic and political alliances among villages.

Some patrilineal tribal societies, including several in Southeast Asia, prefer a more specific rule of *matrilateral cross-cousin marriage*. In this system, males consistently marry their mother's brothers' daughters. This produces a marital system in which females move from one patrilineage to another. More than two lineages are involved in this system. The patrilineages become specialized as either wife givers or wife takers. In an example with three lineages—A, B, and C—anthropologists have noted cycles of marital exchange. Lineage B always gives women to lineage A but takes its wives from lineage C (see Figure 10.5). Claude Levi-Strauss (1969) refers to this type of marital system as general exchange, in contrast to restricted exchange, which is practiced between two lineages.

Another form of cousin marriage found in some patrilineal societies is **parallel-cousin marriage**, in which a male marries his father's brother's daughter. Unlike the other forms of cousin marriage, parallel-cousin marriage results in endogamy—marriage within one's own descent group (see Figure 10.6). This form of marriage is found among the Bedouin and other tribes of the Middle East and North Africa.

Polygyny   Cross-cultural research has demonstrated that *polygyny*, in which a male marries two or

Yanomamö people.

more females, occurs most frequently in tribal societies. In a classic cross-cultural study, anthropologists Kay Martin and Barbara Voorhies (1975) emphasized that polygyny is an ecologically and economically adaptive strategy for tribal populations. The more wives an individual male has, the more land or livestock he will control for allocation and exchange. This leads to an increase in both the labor supply and the overall productive value of the household. In addition, wealth in many of these tribal societies is measured in the number of offspring. Reproducing children for one's descent group is viewed as prestigious, and the children also become productive members of the household.

Anthropologist Douglas White (1988) and John Hartung (1982) did extensive cross-cultural research on polygyny. They describe one widespread type of polygyny as a wealth-enhancing form of marriage in which elder males accumulate several wives for productive labor, which increases their wealth. Strongly correlated with this wealth-enhancing polygyny is the ability to acquire new land for expansion. As new land becomes available, the labor produced by cowives is extremely valuable. According to White and Hartung, this wealth-enhancing form of polygyny is also related to warfare and the capture of wives. In their research, White and Hartung found that tribal warfare often involved the capture of women from other groups as a major means of recruiting new cowives for elder males.

In addition to increasing wealth, polygyny enables certain individuals and lineages to have a

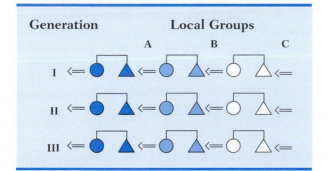

FIGURE 10.5 Matrilateral cross-cousin marriages among three lineages.

FIGURE 10.6 Patrilateral parallel-cousin marriage.

large number of children. For example, roughly 25 percent of Yanomamö marriages are polygynous. One sample group of twenty Yanomamö political leaders had 71 wives and 172 children among them (Chagnon and Irons 1979). One Yanomamö individual named Shinbone had 11 wives and 43 children (Chagnon 1997).

Bridewealth Exchange   Among many tribal societies, marriages are accompanied by an exchange of wealth. The most common type of exchange, particularly among patrilineal societies, is called **bridewealth**, which involves the transfer of some form of wealth, sometimes limited-purpose money like shells or livestock, from the descent group of the groom to that of the bride. Bridewealth is not a commercial exchange that reduces a bride to a commodity; that is, the bride's family does not "sell" her to her husband's family. Bridewealth serves to symbolize and highlight the reciprocities and rights established between two descent groups through marriage. In a patrilineal society, the bride becomes a member of a new corporate group that acquires access to her labor and, eventually, to her offspring. In return, the husband's kin group has certain responsibilities toward the wife. The bridewealth reflects these mutual rights and obligations and compensates the bride's family for the loss of her labor and her reproductive potential. Once the bridewealth is paid, any children she has belongs to the groom's family. Thus, it helps to forge an alliance between the two kin groups. One cross-cultural study of marriage transactions suggests that bridewealth exchanges in tribal societies relate to the need to introduce new female labor into the household, the transmission of property, and the enhancement of status for males (Schlegel and Eloul 1988). Failure to pay the bridewealth usually leads to family conflicts, including the possible dissolution of the marriage.

Polyandry   Not all tribal societies are polygynous. Some practice monogamy, and a few practice polyandry. *Polyandrous marriage* appears as a systematic pattern only in formerly tribal societies in the Himalayan regions of northern India and Tibet, and, until recently, among the Todas of southern India. The most common type of polyandry is fraternal polyandry, in which brothers share a wife.

The Toda were a buffalo-herding, pastoralist tribe of approximately 800 people. Traditionally, parents arranged the marriages when the partners were young children. When a Toda girl married a specific individual, she automatically became a wife of his brothers, including those who were not yet born. Through patrilocal residence rules, the wife joined the household of the husband. There was little evidence of sexual jealousy among the cohusbands. If the wife became pregnant, the oldest male claimed paternity rights over the child. The other cohusbands were "fathers" in a sociological sense and had certain rights regarding the child, such as labor for their households. Biological paternity was not considered important. The most prevalent explanation for the development of polyandry among the Toda was that female infanticide was practiced, leading to a scarcity of females (Rivers [1906] 1967; Oswalt 1972; Walker 1986).

Among other cases of polyandry such as in the Himalayan areas, a lack of land and resources fostered this practice. Nancy Levine found that among the Nyinba of northwestern Nepal, the ideal form of marriage is a woman who marries *three brothers from another family* (1988; Boyd and Silk 2003). This enables one husband to farm the land, another to herd livestock, and a third to engage in trade. Levine discovered that the males in these marriages were very concerned about the paternity of their own children in these polyandrous marriages and favored close relationships with their own offspring, just as would be predicted by an evolutionary psychology hypothesis (see Chapter 4).

The Levirate and Sororate   The corporateness of descent groups in some tribal societies is exemplified by two rules of marriage designed to preserve kin ties and fulfill obligations following the death of a spouse. These rules are known as the levirate and the sororate. The **levirate** is the rule that a widow is expected to marry one of her deceased husband's brothers. In some societies, such as the ancient Israelites of biblical times or the contemporary Nuer or Tiv tribe, the levirate rule requires a man to cohabit with a dead brother's widow so that she can have children, who are then considered to be the deceased husband's. The essential feature of the levirate is that the corporate rights of the deceased husband and the lineage endure even after the husband's death. The **sororate** is a marriage rule that dictates that when a wife dies, her husband is expected to marry one of her sisters.

Both the levirate and sororate provide for the fulfillment of mutual obligations between consanguineal (blood) and affinal (marital) kin ties after death. Reciprocal exchanges between allied families must extend beyond the death of any individual. These marital practices emphasize the crucial ties among economic, kinship, and political factors in tribal societies.

Postmarital Residence Rules in Tribal Societies

Anthropologists find that the rules for residence after marriage in tribal societies are related to the forms of descent groups. For example, the vast majority of tribal societies have patrilineal descent groups and patrilocal rules of residence. Another, less frequent, pattern of postmarital residence is matrilocal residence, in which the newly wedded couple lives with or near the wife's parents. Yet another rule of residence found in matrilineal societies is known as avunculocal, in which a married couple resides with the husband's mother's brother.

Causes of Postmarital Residence Rules

From studying the relationships between postmarital residence rules and forms of descent groups in tribal societies, anthropologists have found that residence rules often represent adaptions to the practical conditions a society faces. The most widely accepted hypothesis states that rules of postmarital residence usually develop before the form of descent groups in a society (Fox 1967; Keesing and Strathern 1998; Martin and Voorhies 1975). For example, limited land and resources, frequent warfare with neighboring groups, population pressure, and the need for cooperative work may have been important factors in developing patrilocal residence and patrilineal descent groups. The purpose of these male-centered rules of residence and descent may have been to keep fathers, sons, and brothers together to pursue common interests in land, animals, and people.

What, then, creates matrilocal rules and matrilineal descent? One explanation, based on cross-cultural research by Melvin and Carol Ember (1971), proposes that matrilocal rules developed in response to patterns of warfare. The Embers suggested that societies that engage in internal warfare—warfare with neighboring societies close to home—have patrilocal rules of residence. In contrast, societies involved in external warfare—warfare a long distance from home—develop matrilocal residence rules. In societies in which external warfare takes males from the home territory for long periods of time, there is a strong need to keep the women of kin groups together. The classic example used by the Embers is the Iroquois, whose males traveled hundreds of miles away from home to engage in external wars, and this produced matrilocal residence and matrilineal descent.

Marvin Harris (1979 extended the Embers' hypothesis to suggest that matrilocal rules and matrilineal descent emerge in societies in which males are absent for long periods, for whatever reason. For example, among the Navajo, females tended sheep near their own households, and males raised horses and participated in labor that took them away from their homes. The Navajo had matrilocal residence and matrilineal descent.

Generalizations on Marriage in Tribal Societies

It must be emphasized that descent, marriage, and residence rules *are not static* in tribal societies. Rather, they are flexible and change as ecological, demographic, economic, and political circumstances change. For example, tribal groups with rules of preference for marriage partners make exceptions to those rules when the situation calls for it. If a tribal society has norms that prescribe cross-cousin or parallel-cousin marriage and an individual does not have a cousin in the particular category, various options will be available for the individual.

There are usually many other candidates available for an arranged marriage. As anthropologist Ward Goodenough (1956) demonstrated long ago, much strategizing goes on in tribal societies in determining marital choice, residence locales, and descent. Factors such as property and the availability of land, animals, or other resources often influence decisions about marital arrangements. Often, tribal elders will be involved in lengthy negotiations regarding marital choices for their offspring. These people, like others throughout the world, are not automatons responding automatically to cultural norms. Kinship and marital rules are ideal norms, and these norms are often violated.

Divorce   Among tribal peoples, especially those with patrilineal descent groups, divorce rates may be related to bridewealth exchanges. One traditional view suggested that in patrilineal descent societies with a high bridewealth amount, marriages tend to be stable. In Evans-Pritchard's (1951) account of Nuer marriage, he noted that one of the major reasons for bridewealth is to ensure marital stability. In lineage societies, the man's family pays a bridewealth in exchange for the rights to a woman's economic output and fertility. The greater the bridewealth, the more complete is the transfer of rights over the woman from her own family to that of her husband. The dissolution of a marriage, which requires the return of bridewealth, is less likely to occur if the bridewealth is large and has been redistributed among many members of the wife's family (Gluckman 1953; Leach [1953] 1954; Schneider 1953). In contrast, when the bridewealth is low, marriages are unstable, and divorce is frequent.

As Roger Keesing (1981) has pointed out, however, this hypothesis raises a fundamental question: Is marriage stable because of high bridewealth costs, or can a society afford to have high bridewealth only if it has a stable form of marriage? Keesing's own theories concerning divorce focus on rules of descent. In general, societies with matrilineal descent rules have high divorce rates, whereas patrilineal societies have low rates. In matrilineal societies, a woman retains the rights to her children and so is more likely to divorce her husband if he misbehaves. Among the matrilineal Hopi or Zuni, for example, a woman has only to put a man's belongings outside her house door to secure a divorce. The husband then returns to his mother's household, and the wife and children remain in the wife's household (Garbarino 1988).

Marriages in matrilineal descent groups tend to be less enduring than those in patrilineal groups because of the clash of interests (or corporate rights) over children. When a woman's primary interests remain with her lineage at birth and the people of her descent group have control over her and her children, her bond to her husband and his lineage tends to be fragile and impermanent (Keesing 1975). In contrast, in patrilineal societies, the wife has been fully incorporated into the husband's lineage. This tends to solidify patrilineal rights over children, leading to more durable marital ties.

Gender

Gender is an extremely important element of social structure in tribal societies. Cross-cultural ethnographic research on tribal societies has contributed to a better understanding of male-female relations. Anthropologists are interested in the interrelationships among gender roles, subsistence practices, female status, patriarchy, and sexism in tribal societies.

Gender and Enculturation: Margaret Mead's Study
Although nineteenth-century anthropologists addressed the question of gender roles, their conclusions were largely speculative and were not based on firsthand ethnographic research. In the twentieth century, anthropologists went into the field to collect information concerning the roles of males and females. The first landmark ethnographic study of gender roles was carried out by Margaret Mead and involved three New Guinea societies: the Arapesh, the Mundugumor, and the Tchambuli. Mead's study was published in 1935 and was titled *Sex and Temperament in Three Primitive Societies*.

Mead described these three tribes as having totally different types of gender roles. Among the *Arapesh*, males and females had similar attitudes and behavior. Mead described both sexes as unaggressive, cooperative, passive, and sensitive to the needs of others. Based on U.S. standards of the time, Mead described the *Arapesh* as feminine. In contrast, Mead described *Mundugumor* males and females as aggressive, selfish, insensitive, and uncooperative, much like the U.S. stereotype of masculinity. The *Tchambuli*, according to Mead, represented a complete reversal of U.S. conceptions of gender roles. *Tchambuli* females were dominant politically and economically, whereas males were submissive, emotionally dependent, and less responsible. Females were the breadwinners and the political leaders, and they engaged in warfare. Males stayed near the domestic camp and cared for children. One of their primary activities was artistic work such as dancing, painting, and jewelry making. Hence, by U.S. standards, *Tchambuli* women were masculine, and *Tchambuli* men were feminine.

Mead concluded that societies can both minimize and exaggerate social and cultural differences between males and females. She argued that gender differences are extremely variable from society to society. Mead's study challenged the status quo in U.S. society regarding gender-role stereotypes. It also appealed strongly to the emerging feminist movement because it asserted that culture, rather than biology, determines (and limits) gender roles. *Tchambuli* women became an important symbol for the feminist movement in the United States during the 1960s.

Mead's Study Reappraised After restudying the Tchambuli (who actually call themselves the *Chambri*) during the 1970s, anthropologist Deborah Gewertz (1981) concluded that Mead's description of the reversal of gender roles was not a completely accurate hypothesis. Although Gewertz concludes that Mead was essentially valid in her descriptions and observations, she didn't stay long enough to see what was happening to the Chambri. According to Gewertz, Mead had viewed the Chambri at a time when they were going through a unique transition. For example, in the 1930s the Chambri had been driven from their islands by an enemy tribe. All their physical structures and artwork had been burned. Consequently, the Chambri men were engaged near the domestic camps in full-time artwork and rebuilding at the time Mead conducted her study. Mead assumed that these were typical activities for males, when, in fact, they were atypical. After assessing her ethnographic data carefully, Gewertz concludes that the Chambri are not the complete reverse of male and female gender roles that Mead had described. Gewertz found that the

Deborah Gewertz with the Chambri people.

Chambri males allocate and control the distribution of goods and valuables and hence are dominant politically and economically, despite the fact that females produce most of the goods.

Gewertz's reevaluation of Chambri gender-role patterns challenges the hypothesis presented by Mead regarding the tremendous flexibility of gender roles in human societies. Although Gewertz notes that cultural values do influence gender roles, a complete reversal of the male-female role was not evident in the Chambri case. Like many anthropologists of the era of the 1930s, Mead did not take account for the complex regional histories that influenced gender roles in these New Guinea tribal societies.

Patriarchy Despite Mead's conclusions concerning gender roles among the *Tchambuli*, most modern anthropologists agree that a pattern of matriarchy, in which females regularly dominate males economically and politically, is not part of the archaeological, historical, and ethnographic record (Bamberger 1974; Friedl 1975; Ortner 1974, 1996; Stone 2000). (Also see the box "Matriarchal Societies" in Chapter 12.) With some exceptions, most tribal societies tend to be patriarchal. Anthropologists have offered many hypotheses to explain the prevalence of patriarchy.

Sociobiologists and evolutionary psychologists view patriarchy in tribal societies as a consequence of innate reproductive strategies, leading to enhanced reproductive fitness. In this view, males are unconsciously motivated to reproduce with as many females as possible to increase their chances of reproductive success. As we have seen, some tribal males have many more children than others. These reproductive strategies involve competition among males for females. According to this model, this male competition, in turn, leads to political conflict and increases in warfare. These factors produce the patterns of patrilocality, patrilineality, polygyny, and patriarchy in tribal societies (Van den Berghe and Barash 1977; Chagnon and Hames 1979; Chagnon 2000). Another biologically based view suggested by Steven Goldberg is that males are always dominant in society because male hormones cause them to compete more strongly than women for high status and dominance (1993).

Instead of referring to supposed innate biological drives, cultural materialists like William Divale and Marvin Harris (1976) maintain that patriarchy and gender hierarchy are caused by the scarcity of resources and recurring warfare in tribal societies. In general, when material resources are scarce, especially in horticultural societies, warfare between competitive tribes is prevalent. Because most warriors are male, both the status and the power of males in these societies become intensified. For example, warfare is an endemic feature of life for some tribes in the Amazon and in New Guinea. For these reasons, a male-supremacy complex develops. However, despite the fact that Harris and Divale argue against innate biological drives, they do agree that some biological influence plays a role in the emergence of patriarchy because they contend that males are universally more aggressive and superior warriors than women.

Patriarchy and Sexism in Tribal Societies Other anthropologists emphasize that although biological or material considerations may contribute to male domination, the cultural values used to define "female" are extremely important in the maintenance of tribal patriarchies. In other words, in many tribal societies, female roles have much less prestige than male roles. Many tribal societies adhere to mythologies, beliefs, and ideologies that justify male domination and female subordination. These mythologies, beliefs, and ideologies reinforce **sexism**—prejudice and discrimination against people based on their sex. Many patrilineal horticultural societies of New Guinea, for example, seclude females from males during menstruation because they believe that menstruating females are unclean and will harm the community. Menstrual blood was often associated with witchcraft or the production of harmful potions; therefore, precautions, taboos, and regular contacts with women were prohibited. Women were often thought to be radically different physically and psychologically from males, and their bodily fluids and essences were dangerous and evil (Lindenbaum 1972). These male anxieties, mythical beliefs, and prejudices frequently led to discriminatory practices against females. For example, most tribes in New Guinea have rules of residence that separate husbands and wives into different houses, and young boys are taken from their mothers and segregated into men's houses.

In many of these tribal societies, women are excluded from political and sacred ritual activities as well as from military combat. This limitation results in the cultural definition of males as the primary gender that ensures the survival of society. Because of these views, women in many of these tribal societies are often subjected to social subordination, sexual segregation, excessive domination, and systematic physical abuse (Lindenbaum 1972; Chagnon 1997). At times, they are deprived of material resources during pregnancy, denied the same access to food as males, and physically mutilated. Sexist ideologies are often used to justify these practices.

Yet there is variation among tribal societies. Based on ethnographic research among the Vanatinal tribal people of Papua New Guinea, Maria Lepowsky reports that there is very little ideology of male dominance and no prohibitions regarding contact with women who are menstruating (1993). Lepowsky argues that the women among the Vanatinal are respected and treated as equals with the men. Vanatinal women can gain prestige through trading and exchanging valuables. Nevertheless, these women are not allowed to hunt, fish, or make war. Vanatinal men control and retain power over the mobilization of warfare and threats of violence. Thus, Vanatinal society is not a perfectly gender-egalitarian society. Another factor has played a role in understanding gender roles and taboos in Papua New Guinea in that to some extent the anthropologists overemphasized the male interpretations of these taboos against women without taking into consideration the voices of women. In some cases, the women viewed the men's semen as just as polluting as the men viewed their menstrual blood (Keesing and Strathern 1998).

Gender, Subsistence, and Female Status A number of anthropologists have proposed that, as in foraging societies, the status of women in tribal societies depends on their contributions to subsistence activities. As we have seen, both males and females are involved in horticultural production. Males usually clear the ground for the gardens, whereas women weed and harvest the crops. In cross-cultural surveys of tribal horticultural societies, women actually contribute more to cultivation activities in horticultural societies than do men (Martin and Voorhies 1975; Goody 1976). Nevertheless, patriarchy reigns in conjunction with a sexist ideology in most of these tribal groups. In some matrilineal horticultural societies, however, the status of females tends to be higher.

Female Status in Matrilineal Societies In matrilineally organized societies such as the Iroquois, Hopi, and Zuni of North America, women have considerable influence in economic and political decision making. Also, the mothers and sisters of the wives in matrilineages can often offer support in domestic disputes with males. In addition, rights to property—including land, technology, and livestock—are embodied in the matrilineages. In general, however, males in matrilineal societies hold the influential positions of political power and maintain control over economic resources. In most matrilineal societies, the mother's brother has political authority and economic control within the family. Thus, matrilineality does not translate into matriarchy.

The Iroquois: Women in a Matrilineal Society The Iroquois offer a good example of the status of females in matrilineal societies. The families that occupied the Iroquois longhouses were related through matrilineages. The senior women, their daughters, and the daughters' children, the brothers, and the unmarried sons built the longhouses. Although husbands lived in the longhouses, they were considered outsiders. The matrilineages of the longhouse maintained the garden plots and owned the tools in common. These matrilineages planted, weeded, and harvested the corn, beans, and squash. The Iroquois women processed, stored, and distributed all of the food and provisioned the men's war parties. The men were highly dependent on the food supplies of the women.

The elder matrons in these matrilineages had the power to appoint the sachem, a council leader of the Iroquois political system. A council of fifty sachems governed the five different tribes of the Iroquois confederacy. Often they appointed their younger sons to this position and would rule until their sons were older. Women could also influence decisions about peace and warfare and determine whether prisoners of war should live or die (Brown 1970a).

Clearly, as the Iroquois case indicates, women influenced the political and economic dynamics in some matrilineal societies. In their cross-cultural survey, Martin and Voorhies (1975) found that the status of women is higher in horticultural societies that practice matrilineal descent. In many of these matrilineal societies, males developed political power only if they had strong support from the relatives of their wives. Nevertheless, these findings also indicate that in the matrilineal societies, males still exercise political authority and assume control over key economic resources. In these societies, women may be held in high regard, but they are still economically and politically subordinate to men.

Age

As mentioned in Chapter 8, all societies have age grades, groupings of people of the same age. Within an age grade, people learn specific norms and acquire cultural knowledge. In some tribal societies, age grades have become specialized as groupings that have many functions.

Age Sets In certain tribal societies of East Africa, North America, Brazil, India, and New Guinea, specialized age groupings emerged as multifunctional institutions. In some tribal societies, age grades become much more formalized and institutionalized as age sets. **Age sets** are corporate groups of people of about the same age who share specific rights, obligations, duties, and privileges within their community. Typically, people enter an age set when they are young and then progress through various life stages with other members of the set. The transition from one stage of life to the next stage of life within the age set is usually accompanied by a distinctive rite of passage.

Age Sets and Age Grades among the Tribal Pastoralists A number of tribal pastoralists of East Africa, such as the Karimojong, the Masai, the Nuer, the Pokot, the Samburu, and the Sebei, have specialized age-set and age-grade systems that structure social organization. The Sebei, for example, have eight age-set groups, each of which is divided into three subsets. The eight groups are given a formal name, and the subsets have informal nicknames. Sebei males join an age set through initiation, in which they are circumcised and exposed to tribal secret lore and indoctrination.

The Sebei initiations are held approximately every six years, and the initiation rituals extend over a period of six months. Those who are initiated together develop strong bonds. Newly initiated males enter the lowest level of this system, the junior warriors. As they grow older, they graduate into the next level, the senior warriors, while younger males enter the junior levels. Groups of males then progress from one level to the next throughout the course of their lifetime (Goldschmidt 1986).

The most important function of the Sebei age sets is military. The members of the age set are responsible for protecting livestock and for conducting raids against other camps. In addition, age sets are the primary basis of status in these societies. Among the most basic social rankings are junior and senior military men and junior and senior elders. All social interaction, political activities, and ceremonial events are influenced by the age-set system. The young males of other East African pastoralists such as the Maasai or Nuer go through similar painful initiation rites of passage at puberty that move them from the status of a child to that of a warrior adult male, and they live separately from other younger and older people (Evans-Pritchard 1951; Spear and Waller 1993; Salzman 2004). The corporate units of age sets provide for permanent mutual obligations that continue through time. In the absence of a centralized government, these age sets play a vital role in maintaining social cohesion.

The Elderly Among tribal pastoralists and horticulturalists, older people make use of ownership or control of property to reinforce their status. Societies in which the elderly control extensive resources appear to show higher levels of deference toward the aged (Silverman and Maxwell 1983). The control of land, women, and livestock and their allocation among the younger generations are the primary means by which the older men (and sometimes older women, in matrilineal societies) exercise their power over the rest of society. In many cases, this dominance by the elderly leads to age stratification or inequalities.

The system in which older people exercise exceptional power is called **gerontocracy**—rule by elders (usually male) who control the material and reproductive resources of the community. In gerontocracies, elderly males tend to monopolize not only the property resources but also the young women in the tribe. Access to human beings is the greatest source of wealth and power in these tribal societies. Additionally, older males benefit from the accumulation of bridewealth. Through these processes, older men tend to have more secure statuses and economic prerogatives. They retire from subsistence and economic activities and often assume political leadership in tribal affairs. In this capacity they make important decisions regarding marriage ties, resource exchanges, and other issues.

Gerontocratic tribal societies have been prominent in the past and are in the present. Among the ancient Israelites—once a pastoralist tribe—the elders controlled the disposition of property and marriages of their adult children, and the Bible mentions many examples of tribal patriarchs who were involved in polygynous marriages. In a modern pastoralist tribe—the Kirghiz of Afghanistan—the elderly enjoy extensive political power and status gained partially through the control of economic resources. In addition, the elders are thought to be wise, possessing extensive knowledge of history and local ecological conditions as well as medical and veterinary skills crucial to the group's survival (Shahrani 1981). Thus, the possession of cultural knowledge may lead to the development of gerontocratic tendencies within tribal societies.

Political Organization

Like band societies, tribal societies have *decentralized political systems*, in which authority is distributed among a number of individuals, groups, and associations. Political leadership is open to any male (especially older males) in the society and is usually based on personal abilities and qualities.

Sodalities

Although anthropologists recognize that tribes are the most varied of all small-scale societies, Elman Service ([1962] 1971) attempted to distinguish the tribe from the band by referring to the existence of sodalities (associations). In tribal societies, two types of sodalities exist: kinship sodalities, including lineages and clans, and nonkin sodalities, voluntary and involuntary associations. Kinship sodalities are the primary basis for political organization in tribal societies. Nonkin sodalities, such as age sets, village councils of elders, male secret societies, and military societies, also have political functions and are mostly voluntary associations that cut across kinship ties by creating alliances outside the immediate kin groups.

In both horticulturalist and pastoralist societies, descent groups such as lineages and clans are the most common political sodalities. Intravillage and intervillage politics are based on these groups, through which alliances are created that assist in maintaining peaceful and harmonious relationships within the tribe. As we have seen, these descent groups are instrumental in carrying out reciprocal exchanges involving bridewealth, women, and other goods, and they are often the only basis for maintaining order. Kinship is the primary basis for political activities and processes in tribal societies.

How Leaders Are Chosen

In horticulturalist and pastoralist societies, political leaders are recruited from within descent groups. As in band societies, however, these leaders do not have much coercive power and formal authority. Although many tribes engage in warfare, political leadership tends to be almost as weak and diffuse as it is in band societies. A number of anthropologists hypothesize that this decentralized and limited form of political leadership is due to the constant movement involved in slash-and-burn cultivation and to the nomadism associated with pastoralism (Evans-Pritchard 1940; Vayda 1961; Sahlins 1968b; Lindholm 2002). They suggest that permanent, long-term settlement in one locale is needed for the development of an effective, centralized form of political authority.

Village Headman Some horticultural groups like the Yanomamö select a village headman. To become an effective leader, this individual must be "generous" and be able to motivate feasting and exchange activities among different lineages in the village. To become generous, the individual must cultivate more land, which requires more productive labor. These headman have larger gardens than the average family and can offer feasts and food to villagers to demonstrate their generosity. One way to be more productive is to have more

wives. As we have seen, the Yanomamö leaders are polygynous. Thus, polygynous marital relations enable a Yanomamö headman to sustain his generosity and political status.

The Yanomamö headman has no recognized authority to enforce political decisions in the group; he has to lead more by example than by coercion (Chagnon 1997). He must persuade people to obey the norms of the village, and he gives advice and suggestions on subsistence, economic, and ritual matters. Among the Ndembu horticulturalist tribe studied by Victor Turner, a village headman has to be aggressive, but it has to be balanced by tact, generosity, and the ability to serve as a mediator of conflicts (1957).

Big Man Another style of political leadership and organization found among some horticultural groups, particularly in Melanesia, is the *big-man* system. One of the most detailed descriptions of this system was compiled by anthropologist Douglas Oliver (1955), who did fieldwork in the Solomon Islands among the Siuai tribe. According to Oliver, the aspiring Siuai big man has to collect as many wives as possible to form kinship alliances with other descent groups. In addition, he must accumulate a large number of pigs and grow taro (an edible root crop) to feed them. Most of this productive labor is carried out by the man's wives. When a man has enough pigs, he has a pig feast, in which he attracts followers while humiliating rival big men. If the leader is able to recruit a few hundred men through the "generosity" demonstrated by the feast, these followers may begin to build a "clubhouse" to demonstrate their political commitment to the big man.

The big-man political organization of the Siuai is both formidable and fragile. It is formidable in that the pig feasts can enable a man to attract more and more followers and thus more power. This system provides the basis for political and war-making alliances. The big man is also able to command and sometimes coerce other people. At the same time, the political loyalties of the followers of the big man are not long-lasting; the lineage of the big man does not assume any of his political power or authority. With the death of the big man, the entire political organization collapses, and loyalties and allegiances shift to another or several other big

A "big man" of a tribe in New Guinea.

men, who compete through pig feasts for political supporters. Hence, the big man, like the hunter-gatherer leader, cannot pass on power or build permanent structures of authority.

There has been much more recent extensive ethnographic research on the big-man systems of Papua New Guinea that suggests that it is very diverse in different regions. This system of tribal politics cannot be reduced to a simplistic model. In some regions, the big man can consolidate alliances through the exchange of surplus crops and pigs maintained by the labor of women at feasts with many individuals, while in other regions, the resources may be more limited to sustain these alliances. For example, in a more recent study of the Wola tribe of the southern highlands of Papua New Guinea, anthropologist Paul Sillitoe indicates that male-female relationships in the big-man system are more egalitarian and interdependent than

described in earlier studies (2001). Other recent ethnographic research also supports these findings in these political systems (Strathern and Stewart 2000). Typically, the women do provide more labor in the raising of pigs, but they also gain some recognized prestige from the feasting activities, resulting in more egalitarian and interdependent relationships among men and women.

Pastoralist Tribal Politics

Pastoralist tribal groups tend to have similar political organizations, depending on the degree of their nomadic lifestyle. Some pastoralist societies depend on the agricultural societies within their region and are not completely self-sufficient. In these groups, leadership tends to become more permanent and centralized. For example, among the Basseri, a nomadic pastoralist group in Iran, leadership was vested in the *khan*, who was a strong force in decision making within the tribe (Barth 1961). Yet, in reality, the power and authority of the khan was extremely limited, and they had to rule from consensus (Salzman 2000, 2004). It appears that in tribal pastoralist societies, the greater the degree of nomadic independence, isolation, and self-sufficiency of a group, the more diffuse and egalitarian is its political leadership (Lindholm 2002).

Segmentary Lineage Systems One traditional form of political organization found among such groups as the Nuer of East Africa and the Bedouins of Arabia is the segmentary lineage system. A segmentary lineage system is a type of political organization in which multiple descent groups (usually patrilineages) form at different levels and serve political functions. This system reflects a complex, yet flexible, arrangement of lineage groups. Among the Nuer, for example, the patrilineages are identified with particular territories in the tribal area. These patrilineages have both maximal lineages, which include descendants who trace their ancestors back through many generations, and minimal lineages, segments of the maximal lineage whose descendants trace their ancestry back only one or two generations. Minimal lineages are nested within the maximal lineage, and all members of the lineage can link themselves directly to the same maximal blood ancestor.

Complementary Opposition The segmentary lineage system is composed of the various patrilineages, both maximal and minimal, that can be united for military or political purposes. The process by which alliances are formed and conflicts are resolved in this system is referred to as complementary opposition. **Complementary opposition** is the formation of groups that parallel one another as political antagonists. To understand this process, imagine a village with two different maximal lineages. We will call the maximal lineages A and B; the minimal lineages within A we will call A1 and A2; and the minimal lineages within B we will call B1 and B2 (see Figure 10.7).

Now imagine that a member of B2 commits an offense against a member of B1. A feud may erupt, but it will usually be settled within the maximal lineage (B) to which both minimal lineages belong. However, should B2 commit an offense against A2, a different process unfolds. Both A2 and A1 will unite in opposition to B2, which in turn will join with B1. The result is a large-scale feud between maximal lineages A and B. This process can extend beyond the lineages to an entire population. For example, in the event of an outside attack, all of the maximal lineages will unite to defend the tribe.

In the process of complementary opposition, then, kinspeople may be allies under one set of circumstances and enemies under another. Through this process, the segmentary lineage system can achieve political goals without any definitive type of centralized leadership, such as kings, chiefs, or headmen. The philosophy behind complementary opposition is summarized in an old Bedouin proverb:

> Me against my brother
> I and my brother against our cousins
> I and my brother and my cousins against non-relatives
> I and my brother and my cousins and friends against the enemies in our village
> All of these and the whole village against another village. (Murphy and Kasdan 1959)

Many other pastoralist societies have maintained segmentary lineage systems. For example, during their nomadic pastoralist existence prior to the establishment of the kingdom of Israel, the ancient Israelites appear to have been organized on the basis of segmentary lineages without any centralized political institutions. (In the Bible, patrilineal groups are referred to as *families*.)

Among segmentary lineage societies, feuds frequently erupt between lineages and result in retaliation or compensation without the imposition of force by a centralized authority. If a member of a particular lineage kills a member of another lineage, the victim's lineage may seek blood revenge. To prevent this blood revenge, the Nuer attempt to reduce the tension between the victim's and the murderer's lineages. In Nuer society, an individual known as the *leopard skin chief* sometimes provides sanctuary for a murderer and attempts to negotiate compensation with the victim's lineage. In some instances, compensation takes the form of cattle, a desired possession that can be used as bridewealth.

Again, increasing understandings by contemporary anthropologists have demonstrated that the segmentary lineage system is not a *static-fixed structure* or cultural belief system that determines political alliances and consolidation. Instead, it needs to be seen as a structure that is often drawn upon by individuals to produce political coalitions and negotiations for compensation in varying ecological, economic, and social circumstances (Salzman 2004; Lindholm 2002).

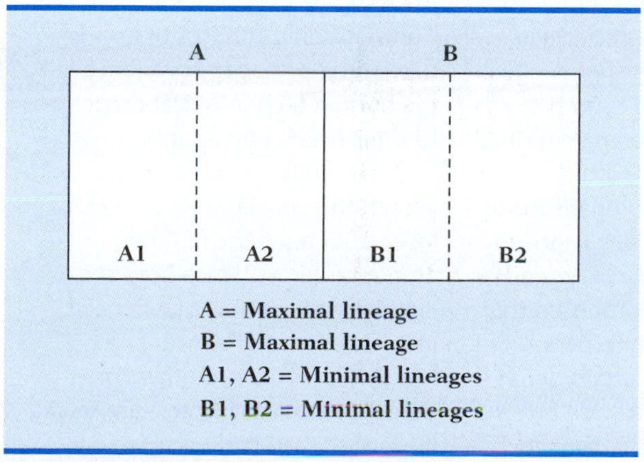

Explaining Tribal Warfare

Both internal and external warfare are far more common among tribes than among foragers. This does not suggest that all tribal societies were

A = Maximal lineage
B = Maximal lineage
A1, A2 = Minimal lineages
B1, B2 = Minimal lineages

FIGURE 10.7 Model of segmentary lineage system.

Critical Perspectives

HUMAN AGGRESSION: BIOLOGICAL OR CULTURAL?

Throughout history, humans have been confronted with questions about violence and aggression. Enlightenment philosophers such as Thomas Hobbes and Jean-Jacques Rousseau wrote about primitive societies in the state of nature, which they believed revealed the "natural" inclinations of humans. In *Leviathan* (1656) by Hobbes, humans were characterized as naturally violent, and life in primitive societies was described as "nasty, brutish, and short." Hobbes believed that the cultural lifestyle of primitives was devoted to a "war of all men against all men." He argued that only a strong state could coerce people to be peaceful. In contrast, Rousseau, in *Social Contract* (1762), argued that primitive societies were peaceful, harmonious communities. He classified these people as "Noble Savages." He claimed that the onset of civilization was the corrupting force that resulted in warfare and conflict within these societies.

One of the problems with both of these competing frameworks for understanding human nature is that they were based on superficial, fragmentary, and stereotypical depictions of small-scale societies. They drew on the stories, myths, and legends of explorers, missionaries, and government officials of that time to describe the native peoples of America and elsewhere. During the twentieth century, with the development of systematic ethnographic studies of indigenous societies, anthropologists began to build a better understanding of violence, aggression, and warfare in these societies.

In today's world of mass media, we are constantly confronted with accounts of violence and aggression, ranging from sports brawls to assaults and murders to revolutions and wars. The seeming universality of aggression has led some people to conclude with Hobbes that humans are "naturally" violent. Or is Rousseau more correct in his view that the development of civilization and its various corruptions caused once-peaceful societies to become warlike and aggressive? What are the causes of human aggression? Is violence inbred, or is it learned? Not surprisingly, anthropologists and other social scientists have been examining these questions for decades, often arriving at conflicting conclusions. Some tend to be more Hobbesian, whereas others are more Rousseauian. To some extent, these disputes concerning the origins of violence reflect the biology-versus-culture debate.

Some psychologists and ethologists attribute warfare and violence to humans' psychobiological genetic heritage. For example, ethologist Konrad Lorenz developed an elaborate biological hypothesis based on comparisons of human with animal behaviors. In his widely read book *On Aggression* (1966), Lorenz proposed that during humanity's long period of physical evolution, certain genes were selected that provide humans with an aggressive instinct, which has survival value for the species. He argued that this instinct evolved through natural selection because of intergroup warfare and competition. Lorenz noted that nonhuman animals usually do not kill within their species and that aggression among males within species is highly ritualized and rarely leads to death. Male deer, wolves, and other social animals fight each other, but this fighting establishes a hierarchy of dominant and submissive males and therefore helps to ensure order within the group. Thus, nonhuman animals have an instinct for inhibiting aggression that is activated by ritualized fighting behavior.

According to Lorenz, humans, in contrast, have evolved as physically weak creatures without sharp teeth, claws, beaks, or tremendous strength. Therefore, the instinct for inhibiting violence was not selected for the human species. According to Lorenz, this accounts for the prevalence of warfare in human societies and makes humans highly dangerous animals. Compounding this loss of instinctual inhibitions against violence is the human technological capacity to produce deadly weapons.

Many anthropologists challenged this concept of a universal instinct for aggression. Citing ethnographic evidence from sociocultural systems that experienced little violence, Ashley Montagu, Marshall Sahlins, and others proposed that cultural factors are more important than biological factors in determining or influencing

Napoleon Chagnon.

aggression (Montagu 1968; Sponsel 1998, Sussman 2000). These anthropologists argue that human behavior can be shaped and influenced in many ways. Humans can be extremely violent or extremely pacific, depending on the prevailing cultural values and norms. In general, these anthropologists were more Rousseauian in their approach, arguing that external forces such as industrial societies and globalization had an effect on tribal or small-scale societies.

During the 1980s, the controversial anthropologist Napoleon Chagnon hypothesized that aggression is related to strategies that have to do with reproduction and increasing one's ability to have more children. This sociobiological view of warfare and aggression has been challenged by other anthropologists. Though anthropologists such as Chagnon, influenced by sociobiology, denied the existence of an aggressive instinct, they agreed that humans possess an innate capacity or predisposition for violence. Violent behavior can be triggered by a number of factors that threaten humans' capacity to survive and reproduce, including scarcities of resources, excessive population densities, and significant ecological developments.

Sociobiologists and evolutionary psychologists do, however, acknowledge that the norms and values of a particular sociocultural system can either inhibit or enhance aggressive tendencies. Thus, the same pressures that would lead to warfare in one society might be resolved without violence in a society with a different set of values.

In this chapter, we saw that warfare is much more prevalent in tribal societies than in the hunting-gathering bands of the last chapter. Tribal societies such as the horticulturalist Yanomamö, some North American Indian tribes, or the pastoralist Nuer are more frequently involved in violence and aggression. And this violence and warfare appears to have developed prior to the influence of colonialism and outside global pressures. This suggests that the cultivation of crops and the domestication of animals as food sources by these tribal societies is related to the origins of warfare as well as the cultural norms and values (Ember and Ember 1992). Territories and land become more important within these tribal societies. Yanomamö lineages are important as social units that defend territories against raids and thefts of crops. Likewise, Nuer lineages defend their cattle against theft or raids. Most of the tribal societies are engaged in these defensive strategies involving warfare. Yet, as we saw in Chapter 9, band or hunter-gatherer societies have very limited warfare in their societies (though they do have homicide and violence).

Currently most anthropologists concur that human aggression and violence results "partially" from both biological and cultural factors, although they continue to disagree about the relative importance of whether it is an inherent aspect of biology or genetics or our evolution. There is an ongoing debate among primatologists about the level of violence and aggression in chimpanzee and gorilla societies. Contrary to Lorenz's theories about nonhuman animals having no incidence of violence, primatologists have much more evidence of some violence and aggression from their ongoing studies (Goodall 1986; Wilson and Wrangham 2003; Wilson and Waller 2004). However, other studies indicate that this aggression and violence within nonhuman primate populations is due to some extent to human intervention in their natural habitats (Hart and Sussman 2005). Anthropological research on the origins of aggression and violence has raised some basic questions concerning human nature and behavior and continues to be an important area of research on this topic.

POINTS TO PONDER

1. If cultural norms and values can promote violence, can they also eliminate or sharply reduce it?

2. Can you foresee a society (or a world) in which conflicts and problems are resolved peacefully? Or will violence always be with us?

3. Given the complex relationships among various cultural and biological factors, what concrete steps can a society take to reduce the level of aggressive behavior?

engaged in warfare, and there very well may have been long interludes in which tribes did not engage in warfare (Otterbein 2000). Apparently, at least in some cases, tribal warfare was exacerbated by external political processes resulting from globalization (Ferguson and Whitehead 1992). We return to these globalization pressures and their consequences for some of these tribal societies at the end of this chapter. Generally, anthropologists reject the notion that humans are by nature aggressive and warlike, possessing a definitive "biological instinct for violence" (see the box "Human Aggression: Biological or Cultural?"). Instead, most theories of warfare focus on environmental, demographic, and other external political and cultural factors.

Among horticulturalist societies, members of one village frequently raid other villages for territory, women, or, occasionally, headhunting (removing the head of a slain enemy and preserving it as a trophy). In a detailed analysis of warfare among the Mae Enga of highland New Guinea, anthropologist Mervyn Meggitt (1977) noted that land shortages and ecological conditions are the most important causes of warfare. The Mae Enga, numbering more than thirty thousand, are organized into phratries, clans, and localized patrilineal groups. Meggitt distinguishes among different types of warfare involving phratries, clans, and patrilineages.

Phratry warfare involving the entire tribe is mostly ceremonial and serves to display status and prestige between big men and males. Phratry warfare is extremely limited. Interclan and interlineage internal warfare, however, is vicious and ongoing, with conquering kin groups seizing the land of the conquered patrilineages. Meggitt noted that 58 percent of cases of internal warfare were over land, and in 74 percent of the cases, the victors incorporated some or all of the land of the victims. The Mae Enga themselves interpret their internal warfare as a consequence of population growth in relation to the scarcity of land for cultivation.

The Yanomamö and Protein Shortages Cultural materialists Divale and Harris (1976) explain warfare among the tribal Yanomamö in terms of ecological factors. They view the internal warfare of the Yanomamö as an indirect means of regulating population growth. Divale and Harris suggest that the Yanomamö institutions and values that relate to intervillage warfare emerge from the group's cultivation practices and nutritional deficiencies. They hypothesize that the Yanomamö expand their cultivation because they experience protein shortages. Thus, the intensification of warfare in which villages raid one another's game reserves is an adaptive Yanomamö response or mechanism that indirectly and unintentionally serves to inhibit population growth. The limited protein supplies are inadequate to support larger populations.

Other anthropologists have rejected the protein-shortage explanation of Yanomamö warfare. Napoleon Chagnon and Raymond Hames (1979) measured the amount of protein consumed in different Yanomamö villages and encountered no clinical signs of shortages. Furthermore, they discovered that some villages that consumed high amounts of protein engaged in warfare as frequently as villages that consumed low amounts.

Sociobiological Hypotheses of Tribal Warfare Anthropologist William Durham (1976) offered an evolutionary sociobiological hypothesis of tribal warfare. An example of his model is his study of the Mundurucu of the Amazon, who had a reputation for continual warfare and headhunting against other tribes. Although Durham did not rule out competition for resources and land as explanations for warfare, he hypothesized that, ultimately, warfare is an adaptive reproductive strategy. In Durham's view, tribal warfare is a means of increasing *inclusive fitness* or reproduction success for related kin-groups on a tribal level in competition with other tribal populations in the region. In other words, if the population of a rival tribe is reduced, one's own tribe may increase its rate of survival and reproduction. Durham believed that increasing the number and survival of offspring (one's own genes) into the next generation is the underlying motivation for tribal warfare. He is not suggesting that this was a conscious evolutionary process, but rather an underlying strategy that resulted in reproductive success for various tribal populations.

Multidimensional Explanations of Tribal Warfare All the preceding hypotheses view tribal warfare as having in some way an adaptive function for society or individuals within society. But many critics say that although population pressure, competition for land and livestock, and reproductive success may help explain tribal warfare, these variables need to be combined with cultural factors such as honor, prestige, and the enhancement of male status.

Anthropologist Walter Goldschmidt (1989) noted in an essay that males in tribal societies are induced to go to war against other groups through institutionalized religious and cultural indoctrination. Although in some tribal societies warriors are given material rewards such as women or land, in most cases, nonmaterial rewards such as prestige, honor, and spiritual incentives are just as important. Most likely, this generalization applies to all societies that engage in warfare.

Law and Conflict Resolution

Tribal societies that have no centralized political institutions for addressing internal conflicts must, for the most part, rely primarily on informal and formal sanctions to resolve conflicts. Because tribes have larger, more settled populations and more complex kinship networks than do bands, they cannot resolve disputes merely by having people move to another location. Thus, many tribal groups have developed more formalized legal techniques and methods of conflict resolution.

In general, tribal societies have no formal courts and no lawyers. However, ethnologists have found in such societies some individuals, usually older males, who are highly skilled in negotiation and conflict resolution. These individuals may become mediators who help resolve disputes among clans, lineages, and other descent groups. One example of a mediator is the Nuer leopard skin chief, who attempts to restore amicable relations between Nuer patrilineages after a homicide. It is important to note that the chief has no authority to enforce legal decisions, a pattern typical of mediators in tribal societies. These mediators preside over the litigation procedures, but the final decision can be reached only when a consensus is achieved among the different descent groups.

Ordeals Another, more formalized, legal mechanism found in some tribal societies is known as the *ordeal*. Anthropologist R. F. Barton described a classic case of an ordeal among the Ifugao, a horticulturalist tribe of the Philippines (1919). An Ifugao individual accused of a transgression who wanted to claim innocence might submit to an ordeal. Barton described several types of ordeals found among the

A Nuer leopard skin chief. These individuals are basically mediators who help resolve conflicts by building a consensus. They do not have the power to coerce other people.

Ifugao. In one type, referred to as the hot-water ordeal, a person had to reach into a pot of boiling water to pull out a pebble and then replace it. In another, a red-hot knife was lowered onto a person's hand. If the party were guilty, his or her hand would be burned badly; if innocent, it would not be. If there were two disputants, they both had the hot knife lowered onto their hands. The one burned more severely was judged to be the guilty party. A third type of ordeal among the Ifugao involved duels or wrestling matches between the disputants.

A *monkalun*, or arbiter, supervised all of these ordeals. The Ifugao assumed, however, that spiritual or supernatural intervention was the ultimate arbiter in these cases and that moral transgressions would be punished, not by the *monkalun*, but by cosmic religious forces and beings who oversee the social and moral order of Ifugaoan life. The *monkalun* interpreted the evidence and acted as an umpire in deciding the guilt or innocence of an individual.

Oaths and Oracles Some tribal societies use oaths and oracles to arrive at legal decisions. An **oath** is an attempt to call on a supernatural source of power to sanction and bear witness to the truth or falseness of an individual's testimony. Some tribal groups rely on **oracles**, individuals or sacred objects believed to have special prophetic abilities, to help resolve legal matters. Individuals who are believed to have oracular or prophetic powers are empowered to make legal decisions. One example is the Azande, a tribal group in East Africa described by Evans-Pritchard (1937). The Azande used oracles to help decide criminal cases.

In general, ordeals, oaths, and oracles are more common among tribal societies with weak authority structures, in which power is widely diffused throughout the society. Individuals in these societies lack the authority to enforce judicial rulings and therefore do not want to accept the full responsibility for making life-and-death decisions that would make them politically vulnerable (Roberts 1967).

Religion

Given the immense diversity from tribe to tribe, it is very difficult to generalize about tribal religions. Like hunter-gatherer religions, tribal religions tend to be *cosmic religions*; that is, the concepts, beliefs, and rituals of these religions are integrated with the natural environment, seasonal cycles, and all living organisms. Animism and shamanism are common religious traditions.

Animism and Shamanism in South America

The mingling of animism and shamanism is evident among some South American tribes. Some of these tribes use the extracts of certain plants for shamanistic practices. The Yanomamö, for example, use a hallucinogenic snuff called *ebene* to induce visual and auditory hallucinations during which it is believed an individual will have direct contact with the spirit world. The *ebene* powder is blown through a bamboo tube into the nostrils to gain contact with the *hekura* spirits. These spirits, numbering in the thousands, are believed to reside in trees, rocks, and even within people's chests. Through the use of *ebene*, Yanomamö shamans fall into trances, enabling them to attract and control the *hekura* for various purposes.

The Jivaro of Ecuador use a tealike drink, *natema*, which enables almost anyone to achieve a trance state. *Natema* is concocted by boiling vines to produce a hallucinogenic drink containing alkaloids, which are somewhat similar to LSD and mescaline. Among the Jivaro, approximately one out of every four males is a shaman. Any adult, male or female, who desires to become such a practitioner simply gives a gift to an experienced shaman, who, in turn, gives the apprentices a drink of *natema* as well as some of his own supernatural power in the form of spirit helpers. The spirit helpers, or darts, are believed to be the major causes of illness and death. Some Jivaro shamans send these spirit helpers to infect enemies. Others gain the ability to cure illnesses through the use of their clairvoyant powers (Harner 1972).

Witchcraft and Sorcery

Many tribal societies practice witchcraft and sorcery. Evans-Pritchard, in a classic ethnographic study of the Azande tribe, referred to **witchcraft** as a belief in an innate, psychic ability of some people to harm others, whereas **sorcery** is a magical strategy in which practitioners manipulate objects to bring about either harmful or beneficial effects (1937). Contemporary anthropologists regard this distinction as too clear-cut and view the belief in occult powers to be much more culturally variant, ambivalent, and diffuse in meaning to be subject to this type of precise definition.

Anthropologists perceive witchcraft and sorcery as strategies for people to understand bad luck, illness, injustice, and other misfortunes that they cannot otherwise explain. Sorcerers and witches in tribal societies of Africa and Melanesia are often described as insatiably hungry individuals who eat others by absorbing their reproductive powers, children, sexual fluids, and flesh (Patterson 2000). Witches and sorcerers are usually connected with kinship and descent, because these are all-important aspects of tribal society. In many cases, families are directing supernatural assaults upon one another. Witches and sorcerers may manipulate spirits to inflict diseases or use poisons on other individuals or families. Many tribal peoples perceive the cosmos as composed of various spirits that can affect human lives. Although these peoples accept cause-and-effect explanations for most occurrences, certain phenomena such as pain and suffering do not seem to have "natural" causes. These phenomena are therefore explained in terms of witchcraft and sorcery.

The Role of Witchcraft In Evans-Pritchard's study of the Azande, witchcraft played a role in all aspects of life. Any misfortunes that could not be explained by known causes, such as the lack of game or fish or crop failure, were attributed to witchcraft. The Azande believed that a person became a witch because of an inherited bodily organ or blackish substance known as *mangu*. The identity of a witch was even unknown to the individual who had this *mangu*. A male could inherit it only from another male, a female only from another female. The identity of a witch was determined by a "poison oracle." A carefully prepared substance called *benge* was fed to a bird, and a yes-or-no question was put to the oracle. Whether the bird survived or died constituted the answer to whether someone was a witch. After a witch died, the Azande performed autopsies to determine whether witchcraft was carried in a family line.

Anthropologist Clyde Kluckhohn (1967) analyzed witchcraft beliefs among the Navajo Indians of the southwestern United States. Navajo witches were considered despicable monsters. The Navajo believed that the witches could transform themselves into animals. In these werewolflike transformations, they ate the meat of corpses and made poisons from dried and ground human flesh, especially that of children. These poisons were thrown into houses of enemies, buried in cornfields, or placed on victims. Fatal diseases were believed to result from the poisons. The Navajo had antidotes (the gall of an eagle, bear, mountain lion, or skunk) to forestall witchcraft activity, and they usually carried these antidotes with them into public situations.

Kluckhohn learned that the Navajo believed witchcraft was related to economic differences. The Navajo thought that those who had more wealth had gained it through witchcraft activities such as grave robbing and stealing jewelry from the dead. The only way a person could refute such an accusation was to share his or her wealth with friends and relatives. Thus, Kluckhohn hypothesized that the belief in witchcraft had the effect of equalizing the distribution of wealth and promoting harmony in the community.

The Role of Sorcery In tribal groups in Africa, New Guinea, and North America, sorcery is also used to influence social relationships. Among many tribes, one form of sorcery is used to promote fertility and good health and to avert evil spells. Another type is used to harm people whom the sorcerer hates and resents. In some cases, sorcery is used to reinforce informal sanctions.

One example of how societies use sorcery to explain misfortunes is provided by Shirley Lindenbaum's (1972) study of various New Guinea tribes. Among the Fore people, sorcery is often used to explain severe illnesses and death, whereas in other tribal groups, such as the Mae Enga, sorcery is not important. In particular, the Fore accuse sorcerers of trying to eliminate all women in their society, thereby threatening the group's survival. At the time of Lindenbaum's fieldwork, the Fore were faced with an epidemic disease that was devastating their population. This epidemic disease was found to be a variant of Creutzfeld–Jakob's disease (mad cow disease), which the Fore were infected with as a result of eating human brains (Diamond 1997). In this traumatic situation, Lindenbaum found that sorcery aided in explaining fundamental survival questions.

Familistic Religion

In addition to animism, shamanism, witchcraft, and sorcery, tribal religions are intertwined with corporate descent groupings, particularly clans and lineages. Recall that clans are descent groups with fictive ancestors. Many of these clan ancestors are spiritual beings, symbolically personified by a deceased ancestor, animal, or plant found in specific environments. For example, among many Native American tribes, lineage groupings such as clans, moieties, and phratries divide the society into different groupings. Each group is symbolized by a particular animal spirit, or **totem**, which the group recognizes as its ancestor. Among the various totems are eagles, bears, ravens, coyotes, and snakes. There are as many tribal spirits or deities as there are constituent kin groupings. Although each grouping recognizes the existence of all the deities in the entire tribe, the religious activities of each group are devoted to that group's particular spirit.

Ghost Lineage Members among the Lugbara The Lugbara of Uganda, Africa, illustrate the familistic aspect of tribal religion (Middleton 1960). The Lugbara believe that the dead remain as an integral part of the lineage structure of their society. Ancestors include all the dead and living forebears of a person's lineage. The spirits of the dead regularly commune with the elders of the lineages. Shrines are erected to the dead, and sacrifices are offered to ensure that the ancestors will not harm people. At the shrines it is believed that people have direct contact with their ancestors, especially during the sacrifices.

A Lugbara elder explained the relationship between the dead and the living:

> *A ghost watches a man giving food at a sacrifice to him. A brother of that ghost begs food of him. The other will laugh and say "Have you no son?" Then he thinks, "Why does my child not give me food? If he does not give me food soon I shall send sickness to him." Then later that man is seized by sickness, or his wife and his children. The sickness is that of the ghosts, to grow thin and to ache throughout the body; these are the sicknesses of the dead.* (Middleton 1960, 46)

Art and Music

Art in tribal societies has both utilitarian and ceremonial functions. The expressive art of the tribes of Papua New Guinea and of the U.S. Southwest is used to decorate utensils such as baskets, bowls, and other tools. It is also deeply connected with religious and sacred phenomena. Various tribes in the interior highlands of Papua New Guinea use body decorations as their principal art form, whereas the tribal peoples in the coastal regions make large, impressive masks that symbolize male power. These tribes also use various geometric

A Katchina doll. The Katchina dolls represent some of the forms of artistic production of the Pueblo Indians of the Southwest.

designs to decorate their ceremonial war shields and other paraphernalia.

The Pueblo Indians of the U.S. Southwest, such as the Hopi and Zuni, use distinctive designs in their artworks to represent a harmonious balance among humans, nature, and the supernatural. The groups create colorful sand paintings that are erased after the ceremony is completed. In addition, they make masks and dolls to be used in the *katchina* cult activities. *Katchinas* are spiritual figures that exercise control over the weather, especially rainfall, which is particularly important in this arid region. *Katchina* art is used in various dance ceremonies and is believed to help produce beneficial weather conditions. Because clay is abundant in the southwest, the Pueblo Indians developed elaborate pottery with complex geometric motifs and animal figures representing different tribal groups in the area.

Musical Traditions

Music and musical instruments vary from one region to another. For example, various sub-Saharan African tribes produce a vast range of musical instruments, including drums, bells, shells, rattles, and hand pianos. The musical instruments are heard solo and in ensembles. The hand piano, or *mbira*, is a small wooden board onto which a number of metal keys are attached. The keys are arranged to produce staggered tones so that certain melodic patterns can be improvised. Along with the instrumentation, singing is used in many cases to invoke specific moods: sadness, happiness, or a sense of spirituality (Mensah 1983).

Native American tribal musical traditions also vary from region to region. The musical instruments consist primarily of percussive rattles and drums. The drumming is done with a single drumstick, although several drum players may accompany the drummer. The traditional tribal music includes spiritual hymns, game songs, recreational dance music, war dance music, and shamanistic chanting. Most of the songs, even the game and recreational songs, are inseparable from sacred rituals related to crop fertility, healing, and other life crises. Nearly all of the music is vocal, sung by choruses. Many of the song texts contain extensive use of syllables such as "yu-waw, yu-waw, hi hi hi, yu-wah hi." These songs help to create a hypnotic spiritual consciousness that produces an appropriate sacred atmosphere (McAllester 1983, 1984).

Globalization and Its Impact on Tribes

Tribes in Transition

The process of globalization that began with increased contact between societies throughout the world has dramatically affected many horticulturalist and pastoralist tribes. For example, many Native American Indian societies suffered serious disruptions as a result of European colonization into the Americas. The Spanish, French, Dutch, and British came to the Americas in search of precious metals, furs, and land for settlement. Each of these countries had different experiences with the indigenous peoples of North America. But wherever the Europeans settled, indigenous tribes were usually devastated through depopulation, deculturation, and, in many cases, physical extinction.

North American Horticulturalists

The collision of cultures and political economies between Native American Indians and Europeans can be illustrated by the experiences of the Iroquois of New York State. The traditional horticulturalist system of the Iroquois was described before. British and French settlers established a fur trade with the Iroquois and nearby peoples during the late 1600s. French traders offered weapons, glass beads, liquor, and ammunition to the Iroquois in exchange for beaver skins. Eventually, the Iroquois abandoned their traditional economy of horticulture supplemented by limited hunting to supply the French with fur pelts. The French appointed various *capitans* among the Iroquois to manage the fur trade. This resulted in the decline of the tribe's traditional social and political order (Kehoe 1995; Sutton 2004).

Meanwhile, the intensive hunting of beaver led to a scarcity of fur in the region, which occurred just as the Iroquois were becoming more dependent on European goods. The result was increased competition between European traders and various Native Americans who were linked to the fur trade. The Iroquois began to raid other tribal groups, such as the Algonquins, who traded with the British. Increasing numbers of Iroquois males were drawn into more extensive warfare (Blick 1988). Many other Native American tribal peoples also became entangled in the economic, political, and military conflicts between the British and French over land and resources in North America.

The Relocation of Native Americans Beginning in the colonial period, many Native American tribes were introduced to the European form of intensive agriculture, with plows, new types of grains, domesticated cattle and sheep, fences, and individual plots of land. The white settlers rationalized this process as a means of introducing Western civilization to indigenous peoples. However, whenever Native Americans became proficient in intensive agriculture, many white farmers viewed them as a threat. Eventually, following the American Revolution, the government initiated a policy of removing

Native Americans from their lands to open the frontier for white settlers. A process developed in which Native Americans were drawn into debt for goods and then pressured to cede their lands as payment for these debts.

Ultimately, the U.S. government developed the system of reservations for resettling the Native American population. Under Andrew Jackson in the 1830s, many southeastern tribal groups were resettled into western regions such as Oklahoma. In many cases, Native American Indians were forcibly removed from their land, actions that colonists justified as a way of bringing Western civilization and Christianity to these peoples. The removal policies led to brutal circumstances such as the Trail of Tears, in which thousands of Shawnees and Cherokees living in Georgia and North Carolina were forced to travel hundreds of miles westward to be resettled. Many died of starvation and other physical deprivations on this forced march.

The patterns of land cession were repeated as white settlers moved westward. European Americans justified these behaviors through the concept of Manifest Destiny, the belief that they were responsible for extending the benefits of Western civilization throughout the continent. Military force frequently was used to overcome Indian resistance.

In 1890, Native Americans held title to 137 million acres of land. By 1934, these holdings had been reduced to 56 million acres. After suffering the dispossession of most of their lands, the majority of Native Americans were forced to live on reservations, most of which were unsuitable for agriculture. Lack of employment opportunities led to increased impoverishment for many of these people. The Bureau of Indian Affairs (BIA) oversees the reservations. Before 1934, Native Americans were viewed as wards of the state, and the BIA established Indian schools to introduce "civilization" to Native American children. The BIA was empowered to decide whether Native Americans could sell or lease their land, send their children to boarding schools, or practice their traditional religion.

Native North American Indians in the Twentieth Century
Based on a survey of archaeological materials and fossil evidence, anthropologists have assessed and estimated how dramatic the population decline precipitated by colonization and settlement was. Estimates based on these studies indicate that there were from 8 to 18 million Native American Indians in North America prior to European contact (Sutton 2004; Ubelaker 1992, Reddy 1992; Stannard 1992). But by 1890, when Native Americans made their last stand at Wounded Knee, South Dakota, their population had declined to about 250,000, a reduction of about 95 percent. This trend reflects the effects of warfare, forced marches, loss of traditional lands, and diseases such as smallpox, measles, influenza, and tuberculosis, to which Native American Indians lacked immunity (Diamond 1997).

In the twentieth century, the Native American population increased to about 2 million. Approximately two-thirds of the Native Americans live on reservations, and most of the remaining one-third reside in major metropolitan areas. Native Americans are far below the average American in income and education.

Today, multinational corporations want to develop the reserves of coal, oil, natural gas, and uranium on Native American reservation lands, such as the Hopi and Navajo territories. Other companies have been making lucrative offers to lease Native American lands to be used as garbage landfills and toxic-waste dumps. These monetary offers have produced splits within Native American communities. Some favor the offers as a means of combating poverty, whereas others condemn mining or any other commercial activity as a desecration of their sacred land. Many other Native American Indian communities have developed casinos as a source of income for their people. These issues have caused splits in the communities and present difficult decisions for Native American Indians.

South American Horticulturalists

In the Amazon rain forests of South America, tribal peoples such as the Yanomamö, the Jivaro, and the Mundurucu are facing dramatic changes resulting from globalization. Beginning in the 1950s, European and American missionaries representing different Christian denominations began to settle in the Amazon region and competed to "civilize" peoples such as the Yanomamö. In Venezuela the major missionary group is the Salesians, a Catholic missionary order. The missionaries attempted to persuade Yanomamö communities to reside in their mission stations. The missionaries set up schools and teach the Yanomamö new methods of agriculture and train them to spread these ideas among others. With the building of highways and increased settlement in the Amazon rain forest—developments sponsored by the Brazilian government—the Yanomamö became increasingly exposed to influenza, dysentery, measles, and colds. In some regions, almost 50 percent of the population have fallen victim to these diseases (Kellman 1982).

One consequence of contact with the outside world was the Yanomamö's adoption of the shotgun for hunting in the forest. The Yanomamö originally obtained shotguns from the missionaries or other employees on the missions. Initially, Yanomamö hunters who knew the forest very well became proficient in obtaining more game. In time, however, the game in the rain forest grew more scarce. Consequently, the Yanomamö had to hunt deeper and deeper into the rain forest to maintain their diet. In addition, as indicated by cultural anthropologist Raymond Hames (1979a), the Yanomamö had to expend much more labor in the cash economy to be able to purchase shotguns and shells to continue hunting. Additionally, some Yanomamö began to use the shotgun as a weapon in warfare and political intimidation and raiding others.

Recent Developments among the Yanomamö

The Amazon rain forest is experiencing new pressures. Prospectors, mining companies, energy companies, and government officials interested in industrial development are eager to obtain the gold, oil, tin, uranium, and other minerals in the 60,000 square miles of forest straddling the Brazilian and Venezuelan borders, where the Yanomamö live. A 1987 gold rush led to the settlement of at least 40,000 prospectors in Yanomamö territory. The prospectors hunt game in the forest, causing scarcities and increased malnutrition among the Yanomamö. Clashes between prospectors and the Yanomamö have led to many deaths. In August 1993, gold miners massacred Yanomamö men, women, and children in Venezuela. After the attack, a Yanomamö leader described the massacre: "Many miners surrounded the lodge and started to kill Yanomamö. The women were cut in the belly, the breasts and the neck. I saw many bodies piled up" (Brooke 1993; Chagnon 1997).

Alarmed by these developments, concerned anthropologists, missionaries, and Brazilians have formed a committee to reserve an area for the Yanomamö to practice their traditional way of life. The Brazilian government and business leaders opposed this proposal, but eventually, the government alloted 8,000 square miles of land, which became known as Yanomamö Park. The land, however, was subdivided into small parcels that were impossible to defend against outsiders. In 1995 officials of the National Brazilian Indian Foundation (FUNAI) assured Napoleon Chagnon that there were no more than a few hundred illegal miners in the Yanomamö area, and they were systematically trying to find and expel them (Chagnon 1997). However, there are still news reports from Brazil indicating that more gold miners are infiltrating the area.

In Brazil, the drive toward economic development and industrialization has stimulated the rapid and tragic changes affecting the Yanomamö. The survival of the 9,000 Yanomamö in Brazil is in question. Their population has declined by one-sixth since the gold rush began in 1987. In contrast to Brazil, the Venezuelan government has been developing more humane and effective policies toward the Yanomamö natives. In 1991, then Venezuelan President Carlos Andres Perez took action to develop a reserve for the Yanomamö of some 32,000 square miles of rain forest as a "special biosphere" or national park that would be closed to mining and other development (Chagnon 1997). Then, in 1992, the Venezuelan government designated the Venezuelan Amazonas as a new state in its national political structure. State governments are being given more control over their own populations and resources. The resources of the new Amazonas state will probably include mineral wealth and tourism. Thus, the Yanomamö of Venezuela will become increasingly drawn into contact with outsiders. Whether this will mean more tragedy and epidemic diseases and economic problems for these natives is a question that can be answered only in the future (see the box "Controversy in El Dorado" in Chapter 17).

Pastoralist Tribes

Pastoralists have also been subjected to expanding industrial societies. The adaptive objectives of pastoralists tend to be at odds with the primary aims of state societies. Because of their nomadic way of life, pastoralists cannot be easily incorporated and controlled by state societies. They are not usually subject to the same processes of enculturation as settled peoples. They don't attend schools, and they may place their tribal loyalties above their loyalties to the state. Rapid change among pastoralist societies is evident in some Middle Eastern countries.

Middle Eastern Pastoralists: The Bedouins Anthropologist Donald Cole (1984) conducted research on the Bedouins of Saudi Arabia, groups of nomadic pastoralists. Cole focused on one particular group, the Al-Murrah, a tribe of 15,000 who live in the extreme desert conditions of Rub al-Khali. Traditionally, Al-Murrah subsistence was based on caravan trade, which depended on the care of camels and other animals. The Al-Murrah traded commodities with oasis centers for dates, rice, and bread. On average, they traveled about 1,200 miles annually during their migrations across the desert. They were also an autonomous military force, conducting raids and warfare.

The attempt to incorporate the Bedouin population into the Saudi state has been an ongoing process, going back to the early phases of state formation in the Arabian peninsula during the age of Muhammad (AD 622–632). As Cole indicates, this process of settling and controlling the Bedouins accelerated following the emergence of the modern petroleum industry. To facilitate this process, the Saudi government drafted Al-Murrah males into their national guard. The principal leader of the Al-Murrah, the emir, has been recognized by the Saudi government as the commander of this national guard unit. The government gives the emir a share of the national budget, and he distributes salaries to the tribespeople. Thus, the emir has become a dependent government official of the Saudi state.

The traditional subsistence economy based on nomadism and the care of herds of animals appears to be at an end. Camels are being replaced by pickup trucks. Bedouins are settling in cities and participating in the urban economy. All of the formerly self-sufficient Bedouin communities are being absorbed into nation-states throughout the Arabian peninsula.

The Qashqa'i Cultural anthropologist Lois Beck (1986, 1991) has written in-depth ethnographic accounts of how globalization has influenced the Qashqa'i pastoralist tribe of Iran. The Qashqa'i reside in the southern part of the Zagros Mountains. Beck emphasized that the Qashqa'i "tribe" was to some degree a creation of state processes within Iran. In other words, the Qashqa'i tribe was not a self-contained entity but rather was formed through the long-term process of incorporating tribal leaders into the Iranian nation-state. During different historical periods, the state offered land and political protection to the Qashqa'i in exchange for taxes. Through that process, the Qashqa'i leadership was able to maintain some autonomy. Eventually, the Qashqa'i political system became increasingly centralized around an economic and political elite. This is an example of how tribes may be formed as a result of an expansionist state political system.

As with other pastoralist societies, the Qashqa'i relationship with the central government in Iran was not always beneficial. During the 1960s, the Iranian government under Shah Pahlavi wanted to modernize and industrialize Iran rapidly with Western support (see Chapter 15). The government viewed the Qashqa'i as resisting modernization and used military force to incorporate them. This policy resulted in the establishment of strong ethnic boundaries between the Iranians and the Qashqa'i. The Qashqa'i began to emphasize their own ethnic identity and to demand more autonomy.

In the initial stages of the Iranian Revolution led by Ayatollah Khomeini, the Qashqa'i joined demonstrations against the shah. Following the revolution, however, the Qashqa'i found themselves subject to patterns of discrimination and repression similar to those they had endured under the shah. Because they never accepted the revolutionary doctrines of the Khomeini regime, they were considered a threat to the ideals of the state. Consequently, Khomeini's Revolutionary Guards harassed the Qashqa'i. Thus, Qashqa'i autonomy and local authority continued to erode under the pressures of the nation-state of Iran.

East African Pastoralists and Globalization

Earlier, we discussed pastoralists of East Africa such as the Nuer, the Maasai, Dinka, and others who maintain cattle-keeping on the savannah. Many of these East African tribes are now caught within the interregional net of globalization and disaster. A series of regional wars have broken out in East Africa as a by-product of colonialism, ethnic rivalry, and political competition within the last decade. For example, in the Republic of Sudan, a war between the Muslim north and the Christian south, has affected the Nuer and Dinka tribes that reside in the southern area. Nuer tribal peoples have been recruited into the Sudanese People's Liberation Army to fight against the north. Weapons have flowed into their society and have become new luxury items. Instead of cows being exchanged through reciprocal ties between kinsmen, weapons are now used as a source of wealth and money (Hutchinson 1996). These guns began to displace the traditional power relationships within the communities. The Nuer and other groups use their cattle to obtain guns and ammunition from different military factions. If these tribal people do survive in the warfare, many of them become displaced migrants living in poverty in urban areas and refugee camps. Globalization has brought tragedy to most of these once self-sufficient autonomous tribal pastoralists.

Forms of Resistance among Tribal Peoples

Revitalization among Native Americans

Native American Indian societies developed a number of revitalization movements as defensive strategy in their confrontation with European colonialism and increasing globalization. One type of movement was associated with a particular prophet who was able to mobilize the population both politically and spiritually. In the Pueblo groups of the southwest, a prophet leader known as Popé organized a rebellion against the Spanish rulers in 1680. The Pueblo tribes attacked the Spanish, killed the Catholic priests in the missions, and attempted to reinstitute Pueblo traditions. Twenty years later, Spanish troops based in Mexico defeated this movement and reasserted their authority over the region.

Other Native American prophets such as Handsome Lake, Pontiac, Tecumseh, and Chief Joseph combined traditional religious values with military activities to resist European and American expansion into their territories. Eventually the U.S. military defeated all of these leaders (Sutton 2004).

The Ghost Dance   One of the best-known revitalization movements was the Ghost Dance movement of the late 1800s. The Ghost Dance spread through the region of Nevada and California, across the Rocky Mountains to Plains groups such as the Cheyenne, Arapaho, and Sioux. The movement became associated with the prophet Wovoka, a Paiute who was believed to have received spiritual visions of the future during an eclipse of the sun. Wovoka taught that if the Native American people did the Ghost Dance, a hypnotic dance with spiritual meanings, the whites would disappear, and a train would come from the east with the ghosts of recently deceased Native Americans, signaling the restoration of Native American autonomy and traditions. Wovoka stressed nonviolent resistance and nonaccommodation to white domination (Kehoe 1989; Scupin 2000).

Among the groups influenced by the Ghost Dance were the Lakota Sioux, who had been forced to reside on five reservations in South Dakota. In 1890, the Lakota Sioux leader, Kicking Bear, introduced a special shirt, called a "ghost shirt," that he claimed would protect the Sioux from the bullets of the white soldiers. The wearing of the ghost shirts precipitated conflicts between the U.S. military and the Sioux, culminating in a massacre of almost two hundred Sioux at Wounded Knee, South Dakota, on December 29, 1890. Following that confrontation, Sioux leaders such as Kicking Bear surrendered to the U.S. military.

Among the most common refrains of the Ghost Dance songs were:

My children,/When at first I liked the whites,/I gave them fruits,/I gave them fruits. (Southern Arapaho)
The father will descend/The earth will tremble/Everybody will arise,/Stretch out your hands. (Kiowa)
We shall live again./We shall live again. (Apache) (Rothenberg, 1985: 109–110)

These Ghost Dance songs and dances are heard among the Native Americans up to the present. For example, in February 1973, Wounded Knee once

Big Foot's frozen body after the Massacre of Wounded Knee in 1890.

again became the site for a violent confrontation between the Plains Indians and the U.S. military forces. Led by the Lakota Indians, Russel Means, and spiritual leader Leonard Crow Dog, the Pine Ridge Indian reservation at Wounded Knee was taken over by the organization known as AIM, the American Indian Movement. AIM accused the tribal government leaders of political and economic corruption and demanded justice and civil rights for all Native Americans. Leonard Crow Dog led a Ghost Dance ritual during the seventy-day occupation to create solidarity and spiritual renewal among the Sioux at Wounded Knee. In addition, the Sun Dance ritual was also conducted at Pine Ridge in 1973. Fire fights between AIM and the FBI and U.S. forces were common throughout the longest siege in American history since the Civil War. The events of 1973 at Wounded Knee represented the frustration and resentment of many Native Americans regarding their conditions after a century of subordination by the U.S. government. The Ghost Dance led by Leonard Crow Dog symbolized the spiritual resurgence and religious renewal of contemporary Native Americans on the Plains.

More recently, Ron His Horse Is Thunder, president of Sitting Bull College and a descendant of Lakota Sioux Chief Sitting Bull, who was killed by agents of the U.S. Army in 1890, has been leading many of the young Native American Indians on a long horseback ride called the Chief Big Foot Memorial Ride to remind them of their painful history in U.S. society (Fedarko 2004). This use of history as an illustration of the ongoing revitalization movement related to the Ghost Dance that anthropologists and Native American Indian activists and scholars are describing as a means of understanding how globalization continues to have an impact on these indigenous societies.

The Peyote Cult Another form of revitalization movement developed among Native Americans on one Oklahoma reservation in the 1880s. It was also a nonviolent form of resistance, based on a combination of Christian and Native American religious beliefs. The movement is referred to as the peyote cult. Peyote, the scientific name of which is *Lophophora williamsii*, is a mild hallucinogenic drug contained in the bud of a cactus, which is either chewed or drunk as tea. It is a nonaddictive drug. Traditionally, for thousands of years peyote has been used in some Native American rituals for inducing spiritual visions, especially in the southwestern desert areas around the Rio Grande in both Mexico and North America. A number of Navajo Indians in the Southwest became involved in the ritual use of peyote (Aberle 1966). During their incarceration on the Oklahoma reservation, some of the Comanche, Kiowa, and other Plains Indians began to combine biblical teachings with the peyote ritual (Steinmetz 1980). The ritual took place in a tepee, where the participants surrounded a fire and low altar and took peyote as a form of communal sacrament to partake of the "Holy Spirit." Eventually, the peyote cult grew in membership and was legalized on the Oklahoma reservation as the Native American Church in 1914. It has spread throughout at least fifty other Native American tribes, and approximately 250,000 Indians are associated with the NAC (Sutton 2004; Smith and Snake 1997).

Melanesia and New Guinea: The Cargo Cults

As various Europeans colonized the islands of Melanesia, the native peoples' lives were forever transformed. The Dutch, French, British, and Germans claimed different areas as colonies. The Dutch, from their colonial base in Indonesia, took over the western half of New Guinea. It is now known as Irian Jaya and is a province of the country of Indonesia. In the 1880s, German settlers occupied the northeastern part of New Guinea. In the 1890s, gold was discovered in New Guinea, and many prospectors from Australia and other places began to explore the region. At the beginning of World War I in 1914, the Australians conquered the German areas. During World War II, the Japanese, Australians, and U.S. troops fought bitter battles in New Guinea. After the war, Australia resumed administrative control over the eastern half of the island until 1975, when Papua New Guinea was granted political independence. Today, the country of Papua New Guinea (PNG) occupies the eastern half of the island of New Guinea and has about 4 million people.

The colonization of Melanesia and Papua New Guinea was both a dramatic and traumatic experience for native peoples as they faced new systems of economics with the introduction of cash wages, indentured labor, plantations, taxation, new forms of political control, and the unfathomable technologies and apparently fabulous riches of the Europeans. Prospectors, traders, and soldiers during the world wars created a highly unstable and unpredictable environment for Melanesian natives. One of the reactions to this rapid change took a religious and spiritual form. These Melanesian religious responses to Western impact were often loosely labeled as revitalization movements and were called "cargo cults," which was a form of millenarian religious movement.

Beginning in the nineteenth century and continuing up to the present, these millenarian cult movements spread throughout many areas of Melanesia. Generally, in New Guinea the coastal or seaboard peoples were contacted first by Europeans, and by the end of the nineteenth century, they were subjected to intensive pressures from the outside world. The highland peoples were contacted much later and were not fully penetrated by the Europeans and Australians until after the 1930s. Many native peoples referred to the European or Australian goods that were loaded off ships or aircraft as *kago*, translated by anthropologists as "cargo." The native peoples became aware of a dazzling array of goods, such as steel axes, matches, medicines, soft drinks, umbrellas, and, eventually, jet planes and helicopters. Because these native peoples had no exposure to industrial production, they did not see how these Western goods were manufactured. Many, therefore, believed that these goods were generated through spiritual forces, which delivered cargo to humans through spiritual means. Many of the tribal groups of this region attempted to discover the identity of the cargo spirits and the magical-ritual techniques used by Westerners to induce the spirits to deliver the particular commodities.

One New Guinean man who led a millenarian cult movement is known as Yali. Yali had lived in the coastal area of New Guinea, and in the 1950s the Australians recognized him as an important future leader of his people. He had been a World War II war hero fighting with the Allies against the Japanese. The Australians took Yali to Australia to show him how the industrial goods were produced. Nevertheless, Yali maintained the belief that there must be a supernatural cause or divine intervention for the ability of Westerners to be able to produce cargo. He originated a millenarian cult movement known as Wok bilong Yali (Lawrence 1964) and began to preach in hundreds of villages throughout New Guinea about the need to develop spiritual techniques to duplicate the white man's delivery of cargo. Over the years of this movement, Yali's teaching ranged from recommending close imitation of the Europeans to opposing white culture and returning to traditional rituals to help deliver the cargo. Although Yali openly rejected the millenarian cult movements' beliefs, after his death in 1973 many of his followers began to teach that Yali was a messiah equivalent to the white man's Jesus. In their religious literature they propagated these ideas of messiah-ship by using Yali's sayings to help develop a religious movement that was an alternative to Christianity.

However, some of the millenarian cult movements combined traditional rituals with Christian beliefs in the hope of receiving the material benefits they associated with the white settlers. One movement, described by Paul Roscoe (1993), developed among the Yangoru Boiken of Papua New Guinea. It merged some of the millennial teachings of Canadian missionaries from the Switzerland-based New Apostolic Church (NAC). Roscoe describes how those in the movement believed that on Sunday, February 15, 1981, Yaliwan, a leading spiritual and political leader, was going to be crucified, ushering in the millennium. The villagers believed that the earth would rumble, hurricanes would arrive, the mountains would flash with lightning and thunder, and a dense fog would cover the earth. Afterwards, Yaliwan would be resurrected as the native counterpart of Jesus, and the two Jesuses would judge the living and the dead. They believed that the whites and native members of the NAC would usher in a new "Kingdom of Rest," described as an earthly utopian paradise with an abundance of material goods and peaceful harmony between native peoples and whites. The millennial teachings of the NAC were interpreted and integrated with traditional Yangoru beliefs of spirits of the dead and other magical practices. Some of the traditional aboriginal beliefs had millenarian aspects, promising the Yangoru economic prosperity and political autonomy. Therefore the NAC missionary teachings based on millenarian views were easily integrated with the traditional beliefs of the Yangoru. Though the crucifixion did not take place, millenarian movements continue to have some influence on religious and political affairs in Papua New Guinea.

Various anthropologists have attempted to explain the development of the millenarian cult movements of Melanesia. One early explanation by anthropologist Peter Worsley (1957) viewed these millenarian cults as rational attempts at explaining unknown processes that appeared chaotic to the natives. The myths and religious beliefs of the cults also helped mobilize political resistance against colonialism. The cults provided an organizational basis for political action for the various Melanesian tribes. Groups who spoke different languages and maintained separate cultures joined the same religious cult, which enabled them to form political organizations to challenge European and Australian colonial rule. Other explanations rely on more spiritually based phenomena emphasizing how the cargo cults represent the resurgence of aboriginal religious thought, which is more creative and authentic than that of the newer missionary religions that came to Melanesia.

Today most anthropologists recognize that these millenarian cult phenomena are extremely varied. As they learn more about cult movements in different regions of Melanesia, they discover that some have millenarian aspects while others do not. Some integrate aboriginal beliefs and practices with the teachings of Christianity, a form of *syncretism*, while others feature a revival of the aboriginal elements and a rejection of the Christian teachings. A few of the movements have developed into vital political movements and even violent rebellions, whereas others tend to have a purely spiritual influence. Anthropologists agree that the analysis of these cults is a fruitful area of investigation, and much more needs to be documented through interviews, historical examination, and intensive ethnographic research.

As is obvious, globalization processes have had dramatic consequences for these different forms of tribes in various regions of the world. In most cases, it has resulted in negative consequences such as depopulation, epidemic diseases, increases in warfare (though there was much warfare prior to globalization also), and loss of political autonomy and control over their future. As among band societies discussed in the last chapter, many anthropologists are not only engaged in ethnographic studies of these population, but are also supporting human rights issues, economic and educational projects to enhance the ability of these people to become more informed about what comes along with globalization and increasing contact with the outside world. In addition, as many of these people in these tribal societies become educated they themselves are asserting more political autonomy and striving to cope with their new status through new forms of political and religious movements.

SUMMARY

Most anthropologists use the term *tribe* to refer to peoples who rely on horticulture, which is a limited form of agriculture, or pastoralism, which involves the maintenance of animals, for their basic subsistence. Most horticulturalists reside in tropical rain forests, whereas most pastoralists reside in eastern and northern Africa and the Middle East.

The population of tribal societies is larger than that of foragers because they have more abundant food supplies. The economic patterns of tribal societies are based on reciprocal exchanges, although some groups have developed special-purpose forms of monetary exchanges for certain goods. Property ownership is based on large kinship groups.

Social organization varies widely from region to region. Large extended families are the norm. Anthropologists generally find that tribal societies have extensive descent groups consisting of many extended families known as lineages (patrilineages and matrilineages), clans, phratries, and moieties that are multifunctional and corporate in nature.

Marriage in tribal societies tends to be polygynous and usually involves bridewealth exchanges. Marriage bonds are the basis of descent-group alliances among villages. Marital practices such as the levirate and sororate tend to cement social ties among descent groups in tribes.

Despite some early research that indicated women had a fairly high status in tribal societies, modern anthropologists find that patriarchy prevails in most tribes. At times, patriarchy is associated with sexism and the maltreatment of women. Anthropologists have been investigating the relationship among subsistence, warfare, and biology to explain the prevalence of patriarchy in tribal societies.

Age is another important feature of social organization in tribal society. In some tribes, age sets are the basis of economic, political, and religious organization. As people age in tribal societies, they often become more powerful, and in some cases gerontocratic societies arise.

Tribal political organization is usually decentralized and lacks permanent political offices. In horticulturalist tribes, village headmen and big men often organize and arrange intervillage political activities. In pastoralist tribes, the lack of centralized leadership often leads to segmentary lineage systems based on the consolidation of kinship principles to resolve feuds and disputes.

Warfare tends to be more prevalent among tribal societies than among foragers. Anthropologists have investigated the causes of tribal warfare by drawing on ecological, demographic, economic, and biological factors. Most anthropologists agree that no one of these factors explains tribal warfare, and they must use cultural variables such as honor, status, and glory to offer comprehensive explanations.

Religion in tribal society consists of animism, shamanism, witchcraft, and sorcery. These practices and beliefs help to explain illness, bad luck, and various crises. In addition, tribal religion is often familistic, with beliefs in ancestor worship and spirits that commune with the living members of descent groups.

Today, all of these tribal societies are being dramatically impacted by the new developments related to globalization in their various regions. This has usually resulted in many negative consequences for their indigenous societies and people. However, many of the anthropologists and the people in these communities are striving toward a renewal of political and religious autonomy that will hopefully result in a more successful accommodation to these new global transformations.

QUESTIONS TO THINK ABOUT

1. What are some of the demographic differences one finds between foragers and food producers such as pastoralists and horticulturalists? Why do you think these differences exist?

2. Discuss the concept of property ownership in tribal societies. How does it differ from what generally occurs in band societies?

3. What is a descent group? What forms do descent groups take? What are some of their functions?

4. Discuss the functions of a descent group in managing the economic rights and obligations of a tribal society. Use specific examples to illustrate your points.

5. Why do you think a society would have marriage rules such as the levirate and sororate?

6. What are some of the explanations given for the fact that anthropologists have not found any truly matriarchal societies in the archaeological, historical, or ethnographic records?

7. What forms of political organization are found in tribal societies? What are some of the reasons that have been offered to explain these types of organization? How do these types of political organization differ from those found in forager groups?

8. How are descent groups associated with tribal religious practices?

9. What have been the results of globalization in these tribal societies?

KEY TERMS

age sets

ambilineal descent group

bilateral descent

bridewealth

clan

complementary opposition

descent group

gerontocracy

horticulture

kindreds

levirate

lineages

matrilineal descent group

moieties

money

oath

oracles

parallel-cousin marriage

pastoralists

patrilineal descent group

phratries

primogeniture

segmentary lineage system

sexism

sorcery

sororate

totem

ultimogeniture

unilineal descent groups

witchcraft

Chapter 11

Chiefdoms

CHAPTER OUTLINE

CHAPTER QUESTIONS

- What characteristics of an environment are conducive to the development of chiefdom societies?

- How is the political system of chiefdoms related to the economic system?

- How does the social structure of chiefdom societies compare to egalitarian societies?

- In what ways are the legal and religious traditions of chiefdoms different from those of tribal and band societies?

- How has globalization had an impact on chiefdom societies?

- Can we learn anything from the traditional aboriginal societies in the world?

The Concept of the Chiefdom

Like the term *tribe*, the term *chiefdom* has caused a certain amount of confusion outside anthropology. A major reason for this is that chiefdoms have little to do with what people commonly refer to as "chiefs." For example, in Chapter 11 we discussed the Nuer leopard skin *chief*. The Nuer, however, are not classified as a chiefdom society. In addition, many Native American Indian societies had leaders who were usually referred to as "chiefs," although these societies were usually *tribes* rather than *chiefdoms*. In the past, Western explorers, missionaries, and government officials used the label "chief" to describe any individual who held a leadership role in a non-Western, stateless society. But as we have learned in our previous discussions of band and tribal societies, political leadership was ususally widely diffused in these groups, and many of these societies did not have permanent systems of leadership, but rather they had loosely decentralized systems.

In contrast to this common usage, anthropologists use chiefdom to refer to a form of complex society that is intermediate between the band and tribal societies (discussed in Chapters 9 and 10) and the formally organized bureaucratic state societies (discussed in Chapters 12 and 13). A **chiefdom** is a political economy that organizes regional populations in the thousands or tens of thousands through a hierarchy of leaders, or chiefs. Typically, **chiefs** own, manage, and control the basic productive factors of the economy and have privileged access to strategic and luxury goods. These leaders are set off from the rest of society by various cultural practices and symbols, such as clothing, jewelry, specialized language, and social status. Thus, chiefdom societies are not *egalitarian* in the sense that band and tribal societies are.

Another reason that the term *chiefdom* is often unclear is that chiefdom societies vary greatly with respect to political, economic, and cultural forms. Hence, even anthropologists frequently disagree about which societies should be classified as chiefdoms. Some consider the chiefdom to be a subcategory of the tribe, whereas others view it as qualitatively different from tribes and bands (Service [1962] 1971; Sahlins 1968b; Earle 1997). Anthropologists have designated two different forms of chiefdoms: one is a centralized political system with localized chiefs who control economic, social, political, and religious affairs; a second is more decentralized, with centers of political power and authority distributed throughout a region and chiefs having control over different local arenas. Although most anthropologists now recognize the limitations of the term *chiefdom* as it is applied to a vast range of societies in different circumstances, most also consider it a valuable category for cross-cultural and comparative research.

As with tribal and foraging societies, hundreds of chiefdoms existed during at least the past 12,000 years of human history. Chiefdoms were widespread throughout Polynesia, including the islands of Hawaii, Tahiti, and Tonga. They also flourished in parts of North, Central, and South America, North Africa and the Middle East, sub-Saharan Africa, the Caribbean, Southeast Asia, and in Europe during the days of the Roman Empire. Today, however, very few of these chiefdoms remain as autonomous societies. Therefore, the past tense is used to discuss most of these societies. Not surprisingly, a great deal of the research on chiefdoms is based on archaeological and historical documentation.

The transition to a chiefdom society from a prior form of society is not well documented in any part of the world. But through comparisons with tribal and foraging societies, anthropologists have developed various hypotheses to explain this transition. The central question is how one particular descent group (or several descent groups) managed to gain advantages or monopolies of resources over other descent groups. In other words, how did social stratification and economic inequality emerge from the egalitarian economic and political processes found in tribal or foraging societies?

Stereotypical Images of Chiefdom Peoples: The Case of the Pacific Islands

As seen in our earlier chapters on bands and tribes up until the twentieth century, many people in both Western and non-Western regions of the world, including scientists, scholars, politicians, anthropologists, and others, had racist and ethnocentric views of people within these societies and believed they had low intelligence and racial traits that kept them undeveloped compared with industrialized or more advanced societies. If as has happened today, many of the Native Hawaiians or other Polynesian peoples, Native American Indians, or other people who were living in chiefdom societies have become doctors, lawyers, computer scientists, biologists, and anthropologists, why were those chiefdoms lacking in advanced technologies or more developed societies?

Again, Jared Diamond's book *Guns, Germs, and Steel: The Fates of Human Societies* (1997) has inspired anthropologists to refine and do further research on these issues. Diamond has a chapter in the book that focuses on sociocultural developments in different areas of the Pacific Islands that have been studied by anthropologists for many years. In some Pacific Island areas such as Australia, the peoples were organized as bands and lived as hunter-gatherers, whereas in Papua New Guinea, the people domesticated some plants such as yams and raised pigs, as we saw in the last chapter, and became tribally organized societies. However, the people that eventually migrated to the islands of Polynesia, such as Tahiti, Samoa, Hawaii, and the Easter Islands, developed multifaceted sociocultural societies known as chiefdoms with extremely sophisticated monument and sculpture constructions, extensive centralized economic and political systems, and elaborate temples with full-time priests, musicians, and others who officiated and performed through highly complex rituals. Diamond indicates that each one of these different island areas had plant and animal resources, ecological conditions, climate, and geographical conditions that either enabled complex sociocultural developments or inhibited the emergence of these developments. Again, the island of Australia—as noted in the chapter on band societies—contained very few animals and plants that could be domesticated and had very few areas of arable land for agricultural developments. Papua New Guinea had a little more, whereas the islands of Polynesia had an enormous array of rich and varied landscapes with ecological resources that enabled much more potential for sociocultural complexity. As we shall see in the descriptions of chiefdoms, ecological, demographic, economic, social, political, and religious factors all influenced the development of chiefdom societies. We begin with a description of the environments and subsistence activities of different chiefdoms.

Environment, Subsistence, and Demography

Most chiefdom societies have occupied ecological regions that contain abundant resources, usually more abundant than the resources in the areas inhabited by band and tribal societies.

Pacific Island Chiefdoms

In the area known as Polynesia, which extends eastward from Hawaii to New Zealand and includes Samoa, Tahiti, and Tonga (see Figure 11.1), various chiefdoms existed. The arable land on these Pacific Islands is very fertile, and the soil is covered by a dense forest growth. Rainfall is plentiful, and the average temperature is 77°F year-round. Tahiti is a typical example of a Polynesian island on which most of the people resided on the coastal flatlands.

One important aspect of subsistence for the Tahitian people was the bountiful harvest from the sea. Fish and shellfish accounted for a substantial portion of their diet. The coconut palm, which grows abundantly even in poor soil, provided nourishment from its meat and milk, as well as oil for cooking. The breadfruit plant was another important foodstuff; if fermented, breadfruit can be stored in pits for long periods of time.

Like many other chiefdom societies, the Tahitians practiced intensive horticulture, in which one improves crop production by irrigating, fertilizing, hoeing, and terracing the land. Through intensive horticulture (and near-perfect weather conditions), the Tahitians were able to make efficient use of small parcels of arable land. Although this type of agriculture demanded labor, time, and energy, the agricultural yields it produced were much greater than those produced by tribal peoples who practiced slash-and-burn horticulture.

The Tahitians' most important crops were taro, yams, and sweet potatoes. Supplementing these crops were bananas, plantains, sugar cane, and gourds. Protein requirements were met by the consumption of seafood and such animals as domesticated pigs, chickens, and, on occasion, dogs. (The Polynesians did distinguish between dogs that were kept as pets and those that were used for food.) The native peoples of Hawaii, Samoa, Easter Island, and Cook Island had essentially the same ecological setting for the development of a highly productive subsistence strategy.

African Chiefdoms

Anthropologist Jacques Maquet (1972) suggested that a very high proportion of precolonial African societies were chiefdoms. These savanna chiefdom societies included peoples such as the Kpelle of Liberia, the Bemba of Zambia, and the Luba and Songhe of central Africa. These chiefdoms developed in the dry forest, the woodland savanna, and the grassy savanna. In the savanna regions, the use of intensive horticulture, including the use of hoes, produced a surplus of crops consisting of cereals such as sorghum, millet, cassava, and maize and

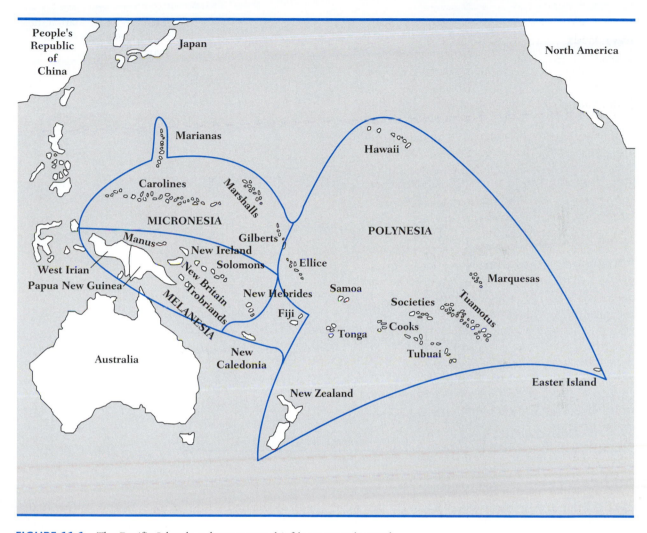

FIGURE 11.1 The Pacific Islands, where many chiefdoms were located.

legumes such as peas and beans. Archaeologists have determined that sorghum, rice, and millet were cultivated as far back as 1000 BC (McIntosh and McIntosh 1993). Generally, these chiefdoms were more decentralized and power was diffused widely throughout wide-ranging areas by localized leadership (McIntosh, 1999).

Native American Chiefdoms

The Mississippi Region One prehistoric ecological region in North America where various chiefdom societies flourished was the region along the Mississippi River extending from Louisiana northward to Illinois. One of the primary cultural centers of

the North American chiefdoms was the Cahokian society, located near where the Mississippi and Missouri rivers come together. This area contained extremely fertile soil and abundant resources of fish, shellfish, and game animals. The Cahokian people also practiced intensive horticulture, using hoes and fertilizers to produce their crops. The Cahokian chiefdom society emerged around AD 950 and reached its peak by about 1100. At that point, it had evolved into an urban center with a population of about 20,000 people.

The Northwest Coast Another region in North America that contains a vast wealth of natural resources is the area of the Northwest Coast. This

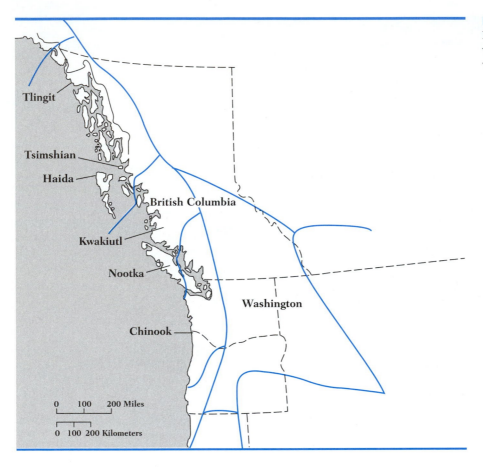

FIGURE 11.2 Map of the Northwest Coast showing where various chiefdoms were located.

area is bounded by the Pacific Ocean on the west and mountain ranges on the east. Numerous groups, such as the Haida, Tlingit, Tsimshian, Kwakiutl, Bella Coola, Bella Bella, Nootka, Makah, and Tillamook, lived in this region (see Figure 11.2). These societies are usually categorized as chiefdoms, although they do not fit the ideal pattern as neatly as do the Polynesian societies (Lewellen 1983). Although there were some differences in respect to subsistence and adaptation for each group, the patterns were very similar for the entire region.

One of the major reasons the Northwest Coast groups do not fit as well into the chiefdom category is that they were essentially hunters and gatherers and did not practice any horticulture or agriculture. Because of their economic, social, and political features, however, they have been traditionally characterized as chiefdoms. The unique ecological conditions of the northwest region enabled these societies to develop patterns not usually associated with the hunters and gatherers discussed in Chapter 8. Instead of residing in marginal environments as did many foragers, these peoples lived in environments rich with resources.

The ecological conditions on the Northwest Coast were as ideal as those of the Pacific Islands. The climate was marked by heavy rainfall, and the mountain barrier to the east sheltered the region from cold winds from the continent. The region could, therefore, support rich forests of cedar, fir, and other trees. Game such as deer, bears, ducks, and geese were plentiful, and berries, roots, and other plants were easily harvested. The most important food resources, however, came from the coastal and inland waters. Streams and rivers were filled every fall with huge salmon, which were smoked and dried for storage, providing a year-round food source. The coastal waters supplied these groups with shellfish, fish, and sea mammals such as seals, sea otters, and porpoises.

An artist's recreation of the Cahokia Mound around AD 1200.

The environments of the Pacific Islands, the Mississippi region, and the Northwest Coast of North America produced what is known as **regional symbiosis**. In regional symbiosis, a people reside in an ecological habitat divided into different resource areas; groups living in these different areas become interdependent. People in one region may subsist on fishing, in another region, on hunting, and in a third region, on cultivation. These groups exchange products, thus establishing mutual dependency.

Demography

Anthropologists hypothesize that population growth is an important factor in the centralized administration and social complexity associated with chiefdoms (Carneiro 1967; Dumond 1972). Chiefdom populations, which range from 5,000 to 50,000 people, frequently exceed the carrying capacity of the region (Drennan 1987; Johnson and Earle 2000). Population growth leads to an increased risk of shortages of food and other resources. To maintain adequate resources, these societies give certain individuals the power and authority to organize systematically the production and accumulation of surplus resources (Sahlins 1958; Johnson and Earle 2000).

Technology

Chiefdom societies developed technologies that reflected their abundant and varied natural resources. Although the Polynesians relied primarily on digging sticks for **intensive horticulture**, they also had many specialized tools—including tools to cut shells and stones—for making jewelry, knives, fishhooks, harpoons, nets, and large canoes. Likewise, the Cahokian society had an elaborate technology consisting of fishhooks, grinding stones, mortars and pestles, hoes, and many other tools.

Housing

The dwellings used in chiefdom societies varied over regions, depending on materials available. The traditional Pacific Island houses of Tahiti and Hawaii were built with poles and thatched with coconut leaves and other vegetation. The island houses needed repair from time to time but generally were long-lasting dwellings. Similarly, the Cahokian people built firm housing by plastering clay over a wood framework. In the Northwest Coast villages, people lived in houses made of cedar planks, which were some of the most solid houses constructed in all of America before European colonization. In all these chiefdom societies, the housing structures of the chief's family were much more elaborate, spacious, and highly decorated than those of other people.

Political Economy

Because the economic and political aspects of chiefdom societies are so strongly interrelated, we discuss the variables together. As we shall see, as political centralization emerged in chiefdom societies, the economic system came under control of the chiefly elite.

Food Storage

One aspect of the economy that often played a key role in chiefdom societies was the storage of food. For chiefdoms to exist, resources had to be abundant, and people needed a technology for storing and preserving these resources. Food storage was a key variable in the ability of a society to become economically productive, creating the potential for economic and political stratification. Although there were occasional instances of food storage in some nomadic hunter-gatherer societies in marginal environments, food storage was not common among foragers or tribal societies (Testart 1988).

The Northwest Coast Native Americans provide an example of food-storage methods practiced by chiefdoms. These societies experienced two different seasonal cycles: in the summer, the groups engaged in fishing, hunting, and gathering; during the winter season, little subsistence activity occurred. During the winter these peoples lived on stored food, particularly smoked and preserved salmon. In these circumstances, certain descent groups and individuals accumulated surpluses, thereby acquiring a higher position in the society.

Property Ownership

Property ownership developed when a powerful individual, a chief, who was the head of a lineage, a village, or a group of interrelated villages, claimed exclusive ownership of the territory within the region. To use the land, other people had to observe certain restrictions on their production and turn over some of their resources to the chiefs.

In chiefdom societies, property ownership tended to become more closely identified with particular descent groups and individuals. For example, on the Northwest Coast, fishing sites with large and predictable runs of salmon tended to be owned and inherited by particular corporate kin groups. As another example, specific chiefs among the Trobriand Islands owned and maintained more or less exclusive rights to large canoes that were important in regional trade.

Political Aspects of Property Ownership Anthropologists differ over how much exclusive ownership the chiefs had over their realm. As we shall see later in the chapter, the political authority of a chief did have some limitations. Accordingly, the claim to exclusive rights over the territories may, in some cases, have been restricted. For example, among the Kpelle of Liberia in West Africa, the land was said to be owned formally by the paramount chief (the highest-ranking chief), who divided it into portions for each village in the chiefdom. These portions were then distributed in parcels to families of various lineages. Once land was parceled out, it remained within the lineage until the lineage died out. In this sense, the paramount chief was only a steward holding land for the group he represented (Gibbs 1965). Among the Trobriand Islands, in theory, a *dala*, a corporate matrilineal kin group comprised of some sixty-five persons, owned their own land for cultivating yams and other crops for exchange. However, a *dala* leader (a son within the matrilineage) had effective control over the access and allocation of crops from the land (Weiner 1976).

The Evolution of Chiefdoms

A number of anthropologists, including the late Elman Service, hypothesized that in some cases chiefdom societies emerged because of regional symbiosis (Service [1962] 1971). Because particular descent groups were strategically located among territories with different resources, these groups played a key role in the exchange and allocation of resources throughout the population. Eventually, some of the leaders of these descent groups became identified as the chiefs or centralized leaders. In other words, by regulating the exchange of resources, the chiefs held these formerly autonomous regions together under a centralized administration. In a detailed account of the evolution of chiefdoms, Service (1975) used cultural ideology as well as ecological variables to identify certain individuals and descent groups as chiefs. He argued that particular individuals and their descent group were recognized as having more prestige and status. A consensus thus emerged within the society regarding who became chiefs.

Based on his research of Polynesian chiefdoms, archaeologist Timothy Earle (1977, 1997) challenged the hypothesis that chiefdoms emerged through regional symbiosis. By analyzing the ecological conditions and reconstructing exchange networks in Hawaii and other Polynesian locations, Earle found that commodity exchanges were much more limited and did not involve large-scale exchanges among specialized ecological regions as described by Service and others. Exchanges were localized, and most households appear to have had access to all critical resources.

Earle (1987, 1997) suggested that the key factor in the evolution of chiefdoms was the degree of control over vital productive resources and labor. In the case of Hawaii, with population growth, land became a scarce commodity, and competition for the limited fertile land developed. Chiefs conquered certain agricultural lands over which they claimed exclusive rights. Other people received use rights to small subsistence plots in return for their work on the chief's lands. This system permitted the chiefs to exercise much more extensive control over resources and labor. According to Earle, in contrast to the paramount chief as the steward of the land, these chiefs not only had "title" to the land but also effectively controlled the labor on the land. Thus, the chiefly families had a great deal of power and authority over other people.

Economic Exchange

Chiefdom societies practiced a number of different types of economic exchange. Two basic types of exchange are reciprocal exchanges and redistributional exchanges.

Reciprocal Exchange Like all societies, chiefdoms engaged in reciprocal exchanges. One classic case of balanced reciprocal exchange occurred among the Trobriand Islanders, as described by Bronislaw Malinowski ([1922] 1961). The Trobrianders, intensive horticulturalists who raised yams and depended heavily on fishing, maintained elaborate trading arrangements with other island groups. They had large sea canoes, or outriggers, and traveled hundreds of miles on sometime dangerous seas to conduct what was known as the *kula* exchange.

The Kula Exchange The **kula** was the ceremonial trade of valued objects that took place among a number of the Trobriand Islands. In his book *Argonauts of the Western Pacific* ([1922] 1961), Malinowski described how red-shell necklaces and white-shell armbands were ritually exchanged from island to island through networks of male traders. The necklaces traditionally traveled clockwise, and the armbands traveled counterclockwise. These necklaces and armbands were constantly circulating, and the size and value of these items had to be perfectly matched (hence, balanced reciprocity). People did not keep these items very long; in fact, they were seldom worn. There was no haggling or discussion of price by any of the traders.

Trobriand males were inducted into the trading network through elaborate training regarding the proper etiquette and magical practices of the *kula*. The young men learned these practices through their fathers or mothers' brothers and eventually established trading connections with partners on other islands.

A more utilitarian trade accompanied the ceremonial trade. Goods such as tobacco, pottery, coconuts, fish, baskets, and mats were exchanged through the Trobriand trading partners. In these exchanges, the partners haggled and discussed price. Malinowski referred to this trade as secondary trade, or **barter**, the direct exchange of one commodity for another. He argued that the ceremonial *kula* trade created emotional ties among trading partners and that the utilitarian trade was secondary and incidental. Because of this argument, Malinowski is often referred to as one of the first substantivist economic anthropologists (see Chapter 8). He hypothesized that the economic production and exchange of utilitarian goods were embedded in the social practices and cultural norms of the *kula* exchange, which was noneconomic.

Some anthropologists, however, hypothesized that the ceremonial trade was only the ritual means for conducting the more utilitarian transactions for material goods. Annette Weiner (1987) reanalyzed the *kula* trade and, in her interviews with older informants, found that Malinowski had overlooked the fact that certain armbands or necklaces, known as *kitomu*, were owned by the chiefs. The *kitomu* could be used for bridewealth payments, funeral expenses, or to build a canoe. In other words, they were more like money. At times, a chief would add some *kitomu* into the *kula* transactions to attract new partners and new wealth. These chiefs would take economic risks with these shells to accumulate valuable private profits. If a chief gained a new partner through these transactions, he would be able to gain more wealth. If he was not able to gain new partners, however, he could lose some of his investments.

Thus, Weiner viewed the *kula* not as a system of balanced reciprocity but rather as a system of economic competition in which certain traders tried to maximize social and political status and to accumulate profits. Although the *kula* exchanges emphasized the notions of equality and reciprocity, this was, in fact, an illusion. In actuality, trading partners tried to achieve the opposite—to gain ever-larger profits and status.

Malinowski overlooked the fact that the trade items of the *kula* exchange, referred to as "wealth finances," were critically important in establishing a chief's social status and personal prestige. For example, only the chiefs were able to control the extensive labor needed to construct outrigger canoes, by means of which the trade was conducted. Thus, the chiefs benefited enormously from the *kula* exchange (Earle 1987; Johnson and Earle 2000).

Redistributional Exchange   The predominant form of economic exchange in chiefdom societies, and one that is not usually found in band and tribal societies, is **redistributional economic exchange**, which involves the exchange of goods and resources through a centralized organization. In the redistributional system, food and other staples, such as craft goods, are collected as a form of tax or rent. The chiefs (and subsidiary chiefs) redistribute some of these goods and food staples back to the population at certain times of the year. This system thus assures the dispersal of food and resources throughout the community through a centralized agency.

Potlatch   A classic example of a chiefdom redistributional system was found among the Native Americans of the Northwest Coast. Known as the *potlatch*, it was described at length among the Kwakiutl by Franz Boas (1930) and was later interpreted by Ruth Benedict (1934).

The term **potlatch** is a Chinook word translated loosely as "giveaway." In a potlatch, local leaders gave away large quantities of goods and resources in what appeared to be a highly wasteful manner. Potlatches were held when young people were introduced into society or during marriage or funeral ceremonies. Families would prepare for these festive occasions by collecting food and other valuables such as fish, berries, blankets, and animal skins, which were then given to local leaders in many different villages. In these potlatch feasts, the leaders of different villages competed in giving away or sometimes destroying more food than their competitors. Northwest Coast Indians believe that the more gifts that were bestowed on the people or destroyed by a chief, the higher the status of that chief.

Benedict interpreted the potlatch feasts and rivalry among chiefs as the result of their megalomaniacal personalities. To substantiate this view, she presented this formal speech made by a Kwakiutl chief (1934, 191):

I am the first of the tribes, I am the only one of the tribes. The chiefs of the tribes are only local chiefs. I am the only one among the tribes. I search among all the invited chiefs for greatness like mine. I cannot find one chief among the guests. They never return feasts. The orphans, poor people, chiefs of the tribes! They disgrace themselves. I am he who gives these sea otters to the chiefs, the guests, the chiefs of the tribes. I am he who gives canoes to the chiefs, the guests, the chiefs of the tribes.

Despite the apparent wastefulness, status rivalry, and megalomaniacal personalities suggested by Benedict, contemporary anthropologists view the potlatch feasts as having served a redistributional exchange process. For example, despite the abundance of resources in the Northwest Coast region, there were regional variations and periodic fluctuations in the supply of salmon and other products. In some areas people had more than they needed, whereas in other regions people suffered from frequent scarcities. Given these circumstances, the potlatch helped distribute surpluses and special local products to other villages in need (Piddocke 1965).

Marvin Harris (1977) argued that the potlatch also functioned to ensure the production and distribution of goods in societies that lacked ruling classes. Through the elaborate redistributive feasts and conspicuous consumption, the chiefs presented themselves as the providers of food and security to the population. The competition among the chiefs meant that both the haves and the have-nots benefited from this system. According to Harris, this form of competitive feasting enabled growing chiefdom populations to survive and prosper by encouraging people to work harder and accumulate resources.

Redistribution in Polynesia   Another classic example of redistribution appears in the historical records of native Polynesian societies. In societies such as Tahiti and Hawaii, people who were able to redistribute goods and resources among various villages and islands emerged as leaders. After crops were harvested, a certain portion (the "first fruits of the harvest") was directed to local village leaders and then given to higher-level subsidiary chiefs who were more centrally located. These goods were eventually directed toward the paramount chiefs, who redistributed some of them back to the population during different periods of the year (Sahlins 1958; Kirch 1984). Along with coordinating exchanges, the chiefs could also decree which crops were to be planted and how they were to be used.

Redistributional exchange economies are similar to reciprocal economic systems in that they involve transfers of goods and other resources among related villagers. A major difference between the two systems is that the latter is predominant in societies that are highly egalitarian, whereas in the chiefdom societies that have redistributional economic systems, rank and status are *unequal*.

Within a redistributional system, local leaders and related individuals not only have a higher status and rank but are also able to siphon off some of the economic surplus for their own benefit. This inequality creates a **hierarchical society** in which some people have access to more wealth, rank, status, authority, and power than do other people. This redistributional exchange system among the Polynesian chiefdoms has been referred to as an early form of taxation (Johnson and Earle 2000). Thus, many anthropologists and other scholars have referred to these societies as "kleptocracies," meaning that the chiefs at the top were draining off the resources from others to enhance their own economic and political power (Diamond 1997).

Political Authority among Chiefdoms   Whereas the political structures of bands and tribes were impermanent and indefinite, chiefdom political structures were well defined, permanent, and corporate. In chiefdoms the leadership functions were formalized in the institutionalized office of chief, with the personal qualities of the chief being unrelated to

Many of the Northwest Coast chiefdoms use the potlatch for redistributing goods and resources.

the responsibilities and prerogatives of the office. (An **office** refers to the position of authority assigned to a person.) In most cases, the chief's office had clearly defined rules of succession. The office of the chief existed apart from the man who occupied it, and on his death the office had to be filled by a man from a similar chiefly family. This system differed markedly from the big-man system found in some tribes, in which leadership positions were attached to particular individuals based on personal characteristics. Tribal societies had no hereditary rules of succession; the big man's authority could not be passed on to his sons or to other kin.

In many of the Polynesian chiefdoms, the rule of succession was based on **primogeniture**, in which the eldest son assumed the status (and realm) of the father. This form of political succession is prevalent in other chiefdom societies as well. The rule of primogeniture helped to avoid a power struggle when the chief died, and it provided for continuity for the overall political (and economic) system (Service 1975).

As is evident from our previous discussions, the chiefs had a great deal of control over both surplus prestige goods and strategic resources, including food and water. This control enhanced chiefly status, rank, and authority, ensuring both loyalty and deference on the part of those from lower descent groups. In addition, it enabled the chiefs to exercise a certain amount of coercion. They could recruit armies, distribute land and water rights to families, and sentence someone to death for violating certain societal norms.

Limits on Chiefly Power   Nevertheless, chiefs did not maintain absolute power over their subjects. They ruled with minimal coercion based on their control over economic production and redistribution, rather than on fear or repression. This political legitimacy was buttressed by religious beliefs and rituals, which are discussed later.

A Case Study: The Trobriand Islands   The political systems of the Pacific Island societies had varying degrees of chiefly authority. Chiefly authority was more limited among the Trobrianders than among the Hawaiians and Tahitians. The Trobriand chief had to work to expand his arena of power and status and prevent other chiefs from destroying or

diminishing his ancestral rights (Weiner 1987). Much economic and political competition existed among the chiefs of matrilineal descent groups. A Trobriand chief gained rights, legitimacy, and authority through descent. That authority, however, also depended on what the chief accomplished in the way of redistribution and giving feasts to furnish food and other resources. Generosity was, therefore, one of the most important aspects of Trobriand chieftaincy. If generosity was not demonstrated, the chief's power, authority, and legitimacy diminished. Chiefs were frequently replaced by other, more generous people within the chiefly family.

A Case Study: Hawaii and Tahiti   The aboriginal Hawaiian and Tahitian chiefdoms tended to be more fully developed than those of the Trobrianders. For example, Hawaiian society was divided into various social strata composed of descent groups. The highest-ranking noble strata, known as *ali'i*, were district chiefs and their families. Within the highest-ranking descent groups, the eldest son (or daughter) inherited the political and social status of the father. Above the *ali'i* were the paramount chiefs, or *ali'i nui*, who ruled over the islands.

The paramount chiefs and district chiefs were treated with reverence and extreme deference. They were carried around on litters, and the "commoners"—farmers, fishermen, craftsworkers, and "inferiors"—had to prostrate themselves before the nobles. Thus, political legitimacy and authority were much more encompassing than in the Trobriand case.

This does not mean, however, that the Hawaiian or Tahitian chiefs had absolute or despotic power. In fact, most of the evidence indicates that the political stability of Tahitian and Hawaiian chiefdoms was somewhat delicate. There were constant challenges to the paramount and district chiefs by rival leaders who made genealogical claims for rights to succession. These rivals would marry women of chiefly families, combined with the manipulation of genealogical status, to challenge a paramount chief's leadership. In many cases, paramount chiefs had to demonstrate their authority and power not only through the redistribution of land, food, and prestige goods but also through warfare against rival claimants. If a paramount chief was unable to hold his territorial area, challengers could increase their political power, and the political legitimacy of the paramount chief might diminish substantially. Permanent conquest by rival chiefs over a paramount chief resulted in a new ranking system in which the lineage of the conquering group supplanted that of the paramount chief. When this occurred in Hawaii, the paramount chief's descent group became sacrificial victims to the new ruler's deities (Valeri 1985). Thus, conquest did not result in the complete overthrow of the society's political structure. Rather, it consisted of revolts that minimally reordered the social and political ranking order. The basic fabric of the chiefdoms was not transformed; one noble lineage simply replaced another.

In some cases, the chiefs tried to institutionalize a more permanent basis of power and authority. For example, chiefs occasionally meted out a death sentence for those accused of treason or of plotting to overthrow a chief. Yet this use of force was rarely displayed. Despite the fact that authority was centralized, political legitimacy was based ultimately on consensus and goodwill from the populace rather than military coercion. Polynesian chiefs could normally expect to command a majority of the labor and military needed in their domains simply by occupying their political office. But if things were going badly, if the chief were not fair and generous in redistribution or settling disputes, armed revolts could begin, or political struggles would erupt—not to overthrow the political or social order but to substitute one chief for another.

Warfare Warfare among chiefdom societies was more organized than among bands or tribes, primarily because the political and economic mechanisms in chiefdoms were more centralized and formalized. In many cases, chiefs were able to recruit armies and conduct warfare in a systematic manner.

Anthropologist Robert Carneiro (1970) views warfare as one of the decisive factors in the evolution of chiefdoms. The objective of many chiefs was to extend their chiefdom regionally so as to dominate the populations of surrounding communities and thereby control those communities' surplus production. As chiefdoms expanded through warfare and conquest, many of the people in the conquered territories were absorbed into the chiefdom. In certain cases, these chiefdoms succeeded because of their technological superiority. In many

other cases, such as in Polynesia, they succeeded because the surrounding communities were circumscribed by oceans and had no choice but to become absorbed by the conquering chiefdom.

Social Organization

In Chapter 8, we discussed the concept of social stratification, the inequality among statuses within society. Chiefdom societies exhibit a great deal of stratification. They are divided into different **strata** (singular: stratum), a group of equivalent statuses based on ranked divisions in a society. Strata in chiefdom societies are not based solely on economic factors but rather cut across society based on prestige, power, and generalized religious conceptions.

Rank and Sumptuary Rules

Chiefdom societies are hierarchically ranked societies. The various families and descent groups—households, lineages, and clans—have a specific ascribed rank in the society and are accorded certain rights, privileges, and obligations based on that rank. Social interaction between lower and higher strata is governed by sumptuary rules. **Sumptuary rules** are cultural norms and practices used to differentiate the higher-status groups from the rest of society. In general, the higher the status and rank, the more ornate the jewelry, costumes, and decorative symbols. Among the Natchez, Native Americans of the Mississippi region, the upper-ranking members were tattooed all over their bodies, whereas lower-ranking people were only partially tattooed (Schildkrout and Kaeppler 2004).

Some of the Pacific chiefdoms had sumptuary rules requiring that a special orator chief instead of the paramount chief speak to the public. The highest paramount chiefs spoke a noble language with an archaic vocabulary containing words that commoners could not use with one another. Other sumptuary rules involved taboos against touching or eating with higher-ranking people. Sumptuary rules also set standards regarding dress, marriage, exchanges, and other cultural practices. In many of the chiefdoms, social inferiors had to prostrate themselves and demonstrate other signs of deference in the presence of their "social superiors."

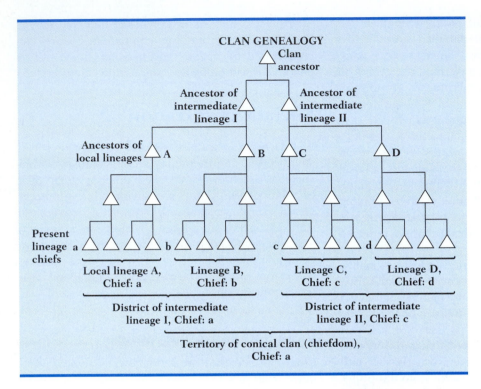

CLAN GENEALOGY

Clan ancestor

Ancestor of intermediate lineage I

Ancestor of intermediate lineage II

Ancestors of local lineages A   B   C   D

Present lineage chiefs a b   c d

Local lineage A, Chief: a

Lineage B, Chief: b

Lineage C, Chief: c

Lineage D, Chief: d

District of intermediate lineage I, Chief: a

District of intermediate lineage II, Chief: c

Territory of conical clan (chiefdom), Chief: a

FIGURE 11.3   Model of a conical clan.
Source: From *Tribesmen* by Sahlins, Marshall D. © 1968. Reprinted by permission of Prentice-Hall, Inc., Upper Saddle River, NJ.

Symbols of inequality and hierarchy were thoroughly ingrained in most of these societies.

A Case Study: Polynesia and Stratified Descent Groups   The ethnohistoric data on the Polynesian Islands contain some of the most detailed descriptions of social stratification within chiefdom societies. The ideal basis of social organization was the conical clan (see Figure 11.3), an extensive descent group having a common ancestor who was usually traced through a patrilineal line (Kirchoff 1955; Sahlins 1968b; Goldman 1970). Rank and lineage were determined by a person's kinship distance to the founding ancestor, as illustrated in Figure 11.3. The closer a person was to the highest-ranking senior male in direct line of descent to the ancestor, the higher his or her rank and status. In fact, as Marshall Sahlins (1985) suggested, the Hawaiians did not trace *descent* but *ascent* toward a connection with an ancient ruling line.

Although Polynesian societies reflected a patrilineal bias, most had ambilineal descent groups (Goodenough 1955; Firth 1957). Senior males headed local descent groups in the villages. These local groups were ranked in relation to other larger, senior groups that were embedded in the

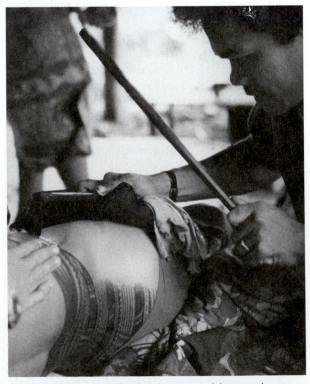

Tattooing in the Pacific Islands was used frequently to symbolize status relationships.

conical clan. Because of ambilateral rules, people born into certain groups had the option of affiliating with either their paternal or maternal linkages in choosing their rank and status. In general, beyond this genealogical reckoning, these chiefdom societies offered little in the way of upward social mobility for achieved statuses.

Marriage

As in tribal societies, most marriages in chiefdoms were carefully arranged affairs, sometimes involving cousin marriages from different descent groups. People who married outside of their descent group usually married within their social stratum. In some chiefdom societies, however, marriages were sometimes arranged between higher-strata males and females of lower strata. Anthropologist Jane Collier (1988) noted that women in chiefdom societies that emphasized hereditary rank tended to avoid low-ranking males and tried to secure marriages with men who possessed more economic and political prerogatives.

One chiefdom in North America illustrates a situation in which marriage provided a systematic form of social mobility for the entire society. The Natchez Indians of the Mississippi region were a matrilineal society divided into four strata: the Great Sun chief (the eldest son of the top-ranking lineage) and his brothers; the noble lineages; the honored lineages; and the inferior "stinkards." All members of the three upper strata had to marry down to a stinkard. This resulted in a regular form of social mobility from generation to generation. The children of the upper three ranks took the status of their mother, unless she was a stinkard.

If a woman of the Great Sun married a stinkard, their children became members of the upper stratum. If a noble woman married a stinkard man, their children became nobles. However, if a noble man married a stinkard, their children would drop to the stratum of the honored status. Through marriage, all stinkard children moved up in the status hierarchy.

Although this system allowed for a degree of mobility, it required the perpetuation of the stinkard stratum so that members of the upper strata would have marriage partners. One way the stinkard stratum was maintained was through marriage between two stinkards; their children remained in the inferior stratum. In addition, the stinkard category was continually replenished with people captured in warfare.

Endogamy Marriages in chiefdom societies were both exogamous and endogamous. Although marriages might be exogamous among descent groupings, the spouses were usually from the same stratum (endogamy). These endogamous marriages were carefully arranged so as to maintain genealogically appropriate kinship bonds and descent relations in the top-ranking descent group. Frequently, this involved cousin marriage among descent groups of the same stratum. Among Hawaiian chiefs, rules of endogamy actually resulted in sibling marriages, sometimes referred to as royal-incest marriage. One anthropologist categorized these sibling marriages as attempts to create alliances between chiefly households among the various Hawaiian Islands (Valeri 1985).

Polygyny Many of the ruling families in chiefdom societies practiced polygyny. Among the Tsimshian of the Northwest Coast, chiefs could have as many as twenty wives, usually women from the high-ranking lineages of other groups. Lesser chiefs would marry several wives from lower-ranking lineages. In some cases, a Tsimshian woman from a lower-ranking lineage could marry up through the political strategies of her father. For example, a father might arrange a marriage with a high-ranking chief and his daughter. All these polygynous marriages were accompanied by exchanges of goods that passed to the top of the chiefly hierarchy, resulting in accumulations of surplus resources and wives (Rosman and Rubel 1986). Among the Trobriand Islanders, male chiefs traditionally had as many as sixty wives drawn from different lineages. High rates of polygyny in the high-ranking strata flourished in many chiefdom societies.

General Social Principles

Among chiefdom societies, the typical family form was the extended family, with three generations living in a single household. In the Pacific region, for example, the basic domestic unit was usually made up of a household with three generations; in some cases, two or three brothers with their offspring were permanent residents of the household.

The households in a specific area of a village were usually part of one lineage. The extended-family household was usually the basic economic unit for subsistence production and consumption in chiefdom societies.

Postmarital residence varied among chiefdoms. Patrilocal, matrilocal, and ambilocal types of residence rules were found in different areas. The ambilocal rule, found in many chiefdoms of the Pacific, enabled people to trace descent to ancestors (male or female) who had the highest rank in the society. This flexibility enabled some individuals to attain access to property, privileges, and authority in spite of the inherent restrictions on status mobility in chiefdom societies (Goodenough 1956).

Gender

Typically, gender relations were highly unequal in chiefdom societies, with males exercising economic and political dominance over females. Bridewealth payments, along with arranged marriages, enabled men to claim rights to the labor of children and women. This practice was particularly significant among the highest-status descent groups. A woman's chances of success depended entirely on the rank of her siblings and parents. Higher-ranking males frequently married women with low-ranking brothers who wanted to control and manage their marital relations, labor, and potential offspring.

If a woman was fortunate enough to be born or marry into a high-ranking descent group, her ascribed or achieved status was secured. Anthropologist Laura Klein described how some high-ranking women among the Tsimshian Indians were able to maintain very high status in their society (1980). According to Sahlins (1985), some wives of high-ranking chiefs in traditional Hawaiian society married as many as forty males (a type of royal polyandry) to maintain their high status. Thus, the women of the ruling stratum had a higher status than men or women from other strata. Yet, generally, men controlled and dominated economically and politically in chiefdom societies.

Age

In many chiefdom societies, senior males had much more authority, rank, and prestige than other people. As in some tribal societies, this form of inequality produced gerontocratic systems. As people—especially in the higher-ranking descent groups—aged, they received more in the way of status, privileges, and deference from younger people. Because senior males controlled production, marriages, labor, and other economic activities, they became the dominant political authorities. Senior males also possessed special knowledge and controlled sacred rituals, reinforcing their authority. One of their major responsibilities was to perpetuate the beliefs that rank depended on a person's descent group and that status was hereditary. As in some of the tribal societies, the combination of patriarchy and gerontocracy resulted in cultural hegemony, the imposition of norms, practices, beliefs, and values that reinforced the interests of the upper stratum. This cultural hegemony will become more apparent in the discussion of law and religion in chiefdom societies.

Slavery

Earlier in the chapter, we noted that chiefdoms frequently engaged in systematic, organized warfare. One consequence of this warfare was the taking of captives, who were designated as slaves. Slavery in chiefdoms generally did not have the same meaning or implications that it did in more complex state societies, and it usually did not involve the actual ownership of a human being as private property. In this sense, it was very different from the plantation slavery that developed later in the Americas. With some exceptions, most of the slaves in chiefdoms were absorbed into kin groups through marriage or adoption and performed essentially the same type of labor that most people did. Nevertheless, in contrast to the more egalitarian band and tribal societies, chiefdom societies did show the beginnings of a slave stratum.

We have already mentioned an example of a chiefdom slave system in our discussion of the Natchez. Recall, however, that upper-ranking members were obliged to marry members of the stinkard stratum; thus the Natchez did not have a hereditary slave population.

One exception to these generalizations involves some of the Northwest Coast Indians, who maintained a hereditary slave system. Because marrying a slave was considered debasing, slavery became an inherited status (Kehoe 1995). The children of slaves automatically became slaves, producing a permanent slave stratum. These slaves—most of them war captives—were excluded from ceremonies and on some occasions were killed in human sacrifices. In addition, they were sometimes exchanged, resulting in a kind of commercial traffic of humans. Even in this system, however, slaves who had been captured in warfare could be ransomed by their kinfolk or could purchase their own freedom (Garbarino 1988).

Law and Religion

Legal and religious institutions and concepts were inextricably connected in chiefdom societies. These institutions existed to sanction and legitimize the political economy and social structure of chiefdoms. They played a critical role in maintaining the cultural hegemony discussed earlier.

Law

As with political economy, mechanisms of law and social control were more institutionalized and centralized in chiefdom societies. As we discussed earlier, in bands and tribes social norms were unwritten, and social conflicts were resolved through kinship groups, often with the intervention of a leader who was respected but lacked political authority. In contrast, the authority structure in chiefdoms enabled political leaders to act as third-party judges above the interests of specific kin groupings and to make definitive decisions without fear of vengeance. Chiefs had the power to sanction certain behaviors by imposing economic fines or damages, by withholding goods and services, and by publicly reprimanding or ridiculing the offending parties. Chiefs could use their economic and political power to induce compliance. They were not just mediators; rather, they engaged in **adjudication**, the settling of legal disputes through centralized authority.

Within chiefdoms, a dispute between kin groups was handled in the same way it was handled in band and tribal societies—through mediation by the groups. Chiefdoms differed substantially from these other societies, however, in their treatment of crimes against authority. These crimes were of two general types: direct violations against a high-ranking chief,

and violations of traditional customs, norms, or beliefs, injuring the chief's authority (Service 1975). Such crimes carried severe punishments, including death. The reason for such severe punishments is that these crimes were perceived as threatening the basis of authority in the chiefdom system.

Religion

Religious traditions in chiefdom societies were in some respects similar to the cosmic religions described for the band and tribal societies. That is, they reflected the belief that the spiritual and material aspects of nature could not be separated from one another. Religious worldviews were oriented to the cyclical pattern of the seasons and all other aspects of nature. The natural order was also the moral and spiritual order. The religious concepts in chiefdom societies were based on oral traditions perpetuated from generation to generation through elaborate cosmological myths. The most dramatic difference between chiefdom religions and band and tribal religions is the degree to which chiefdom religions legitimized the social, political, and moral status of the chiefs.

A Case Study: Law and Religion In Polynesia Nowhere was the relationship between law and religion clearer than among the Polynesian Island chiefdoms. Hawaiian chiefs, for example, were believed to be either gods or sacred intermediaries between human societies and the divine world. Hawaiian chiefdoms have been referred to as **theocracies**, societies in which people rule not because of their worldly wealth and power but because of their place in the moral and sacred order. The political and legal authority of Hawaiian, Tonga, and Tahitian chiefs was reinforced by a religious and ideological system known as the **tabu** system, which was based on social inequalities. Social interaction in these societies was carefully regulated through a variety of tabus. Elaborate forms of deference and expressions of humility served to distinguish various strata, especially those of commoners and chiefs.

Religious beliefs buttressed the tabu system. The Polynesians believed that people are imbued with cosmic forces referred to as **mana.** These spiritual forces were powerful and sometimes dangerous. They were inherited and distributed according to a person's status and rank. Thus, paramount chiefs had a great deal of mana, subsidiary chiefs had less, and commoners had very little. Violations of certain tabus—for example, touching a member of a chiefly family—could bring the offender into contact with the chief's mana, which was believed to cause death.

These magical forces could also be gained and lost through a person's moral actions. Thus, the success or failure of a chief was attributed to the amount of mana he controlled. This was also reflected in the economic and political spheres, in that a chief who was a good redistributor and maintained order was believed to possess a great amount of mana. On the other hand, if things went badly, this reflected a loss of magical powers. When one chief replaced another, the deposed chief was believed to have lost his powers.

Shamanism

Shamanism was practiced in many chiefdoms and has been thoroughly described among the Native American Indian groups of the Northwest Coast. Like other social institutions, shamanism reflected the hierarchical structure of these societies. The shamans became the personal spiritual guides and doctors of the chiefs and used their knowledge to enhance the power and status of high-ranking chiefs. For example, it was believed that the shamans had the ability to send diseases into enemies and, conversely, to cure and give spiritual power to the chief's allies.

In addition, shamans danced and participated in the potlatch ceremonies on behalf of the chiefs (Garbarino 1988). One widespread belief throughout the Northwest Coast was in a "man-eating spirit." These groups believed that an animal spirit could possess a man, which transformed him into a cannibal. During the potlatch ceremonies, shamans would dance, chant, and sing, using masks to enact the transformation from human to animal form to ward off the power of the man-eating spirit. Through these kinds of practices, shamans could help sanction the power and authority of the high-ranking chiefs. The chiefs demonstrated their generosity through the potlatch, whereas the shamanistic ceremonies exhibited the supernatural powers that were under the control of the chiefs.

By associating closely with a chief, a shaman could elevate both his own status and that of the chief. The shaman collected fees from his chiefly clients, which enabled him to accumulate wealth. In some cases, low-ranking individuals became shamans by finding more potent spirits for a chief. No shaman, however, could accumulate enough wealth to rival a high-ranking chief (Garbarino 1988).

Human Sacrifice

Another practice that reflected the relationships among religion, hierarchy, rank, and the legitimacy of chiefly rule was human sacrifice, which existed in some—but not all—chiefdoms. Among the Natchez Indians, for example, spectacular funerary rites were held when the Great Sun chief died. During these rites, the chief's wives, guards, and attendants were expected to sacrifice their lives, feeling privileged to follow the Great Sun into the afterworld. Parents also offered their children for sacrifice, which, they believed, would raise their own rank. The sacrificial victims were strangled, but they were first given a strong concoction of tobacco, which made them unconscious. They were then buried alongside the Great Sun chief in an elaborate burial mound.

Human sacrifice was also practiced in the Polynesian region. In Hawaii there were two major rituals: the *Makahiki*, or so-called New Year's festival, and the annual rededication of the *Luakini* temple, at which human sacrifices were offered (Valeri 1985). Some of the sacrificial victims had transgressed or violated the sacred tabus. These victims frequently were brothers or cousins of the chiefs who were their political rivals. It was believed that these human sacrifices would help perpetuate the fertility of the land and the people. Human sacrifice was the prerogative of these chiefs and was a symbolic means of distinguishing these divine rulers from the rest of the human population. Such rituals effectively sanctioned the sacred authority of the chiefs.

Art, Architecture, and Music

Compared with band and tribal societies, chiefdom societies had more extensive artwork, which reflected two different tendencies in chiefdom societies: a high degree of labor organization and the status symbols associated with high-ranking chiefs. One of the most profound examples of the artwork

Totem pole—Native artwork of the Northwest Coast.

covers 16 acres, and is built of earth, clay, silt, and sand. It took perhaps 200 years to construct. This flat-top mound is surrounded by hundreds of smaller mounds, some conical in shape, others flat-topped. Although the Cahokian society collapsed around AD 1450 (before European contact), archaeologists know from other remaining Mississippian chiefdom societies such as the Natchez Indians that the flat-topped mounds were used chiefly for residences and religious structures, whereas the conical mounds were used for burials.

Another example of the labor and status associated with chiefdom art forms comes from the Northwest Coast Native Americans. These groups produced totem poles, along with decorated house posts and wooden dance masks. The carved, wooden totem poles and house posts were the ultimate status and religious symbols, indicating the high social standing and linkages between the chiefs and the ancestral deities. Typically, a totem pole was erected on the beach in front of a new chief's house, which had decorated house posts. The symbolic messages transmitted through these poles expressed the status hierarchies in these societies (Marshall 1998).

Music

We have already mentioned the important shamanic dances that accompanied the potlatch activities of the Northwest Coast chiefdoms. Most of the traditional music of chiefdom societies exemplified the interconnections among sociopolitical structure, religion, and art. The traditional music of Polynesia is a good example of these interconnections. Although work songs, recreational songs, and mourning songs were part of everyday life, formal music was usually used to honor the deities and chiefs (Kaeppler 1980). In western Polynesia, on the islands of Tonga, Tikopia, and Samoa, much of the traditional music consisted of stylized poetry accompanied by bodily movements and percussion instruments such as drums.

In some ceremonies, formal poetic chants were sung in verses. In other contexts, people sang narrative songs, or *fakaniua*, describing famous places, past events, and legends, accompanied by hand clapping in a syncopated, complex rhythmic pattern.

The traditional formal musical style of eastern Polynesia, including the Hawaiian Islands, also

of a chiefdom society is found on Easter Island. Between 800 and 1,000 monumental stone figures known as *moai* have been discovered there. These figures vary in height from less than 2 meters to almost 10 meters (about 30 feet) and weigh up to 59 metric tons. After sculpting these figures in quarries, laborers dragged them over specially constructed transport roads and erected them on platforms. This project called for an extensive, region-wide labor organization. The symbolic design of the Easter Island statuaries evokes the power, status, and high rank of the chiefs of Easter Island (Kirch 1984).

The large mounds associated with the Cahokian chiefdom complex also represented extensive labor projects and a hierarchical society. Different types of earthen mounds surrounded the city of Cahokia. In the center of the city was a large, truncated, flat-top mound. This mound is 100 feet high, consisted of complex, integrated systems of poetry, rhythm, melody, and movement that were multifunctional but were usually related to chiefly authority. The Hawaiians had a variety of musical instruments, including membranophones made of hollow wooden cylinders covered with sharkskin, mouth flutes, rhythm sticks, and bamboo tubes. In contrast to performers of the other islands, traditional Hawaiian musical performers and dancers were highly organized and trained in specially built schools under the high priests. The major function of the Hawaiian performers was to pay homage to the chiefs and their ancestral deities through religious chants and narrative songs.

Globalization and Its Impact on Chiefdom Societies

Chiefdoms in Transition

Some chiefdoms experienced a fate similar to that of many of the other nonstate societies we have just discussed in prior chapters. For example, when the Canadian European settlers, followed by their military and political apparatus, confronted the Northwest Coast Native American Indian chiefdom societies such as the Nootka and the Kwaikuitl, they did not have any understanding of the functions and uses of the redistributional exchange system known as the potlatch. The European Canadians viewed these practices as wasteful, destructive, and anticapitalistic. Chiefs giving away large amounts of resources at large potlatch feasts were perceived as extremely dysfunctional. The Canadian government banned these practices in the 1880s and used military force against the Indian groups that were not cooperative. Eventually, the traditional salmon-fishing activities of these native chiefdoms were overcome by the more industrialized forms of fishing and canning factories introduced through the American and Canadian multinational firms. This, along with the epidemics introduced by Europeans resulted in both depopulation and economic decline. Common problems such as malnutrition and alcoholism found among many societies disrupted by rapid global transitions remain systematic among these Native American chiefdoms (Sutton 2004). Yet, many of these people of the Northwest Coast chiefdoms have restored their traditional potlatch feasting activities and are becoming more educated and adept at dealing with the new global trends. They are building new beautiful museums and re-learning their traditional art forms, including the building of the totem poles and other artistic works. This represents a new cultural and religious revitalization among these people.

The Hawaiian Islands

Anthropological and historical research has shown that chiefdoms, most likely because they were more centrally organized, developed complex *state* organizations themselves following Western contact. The historical development of Polynesian chiefdoms such as in Tahiti and Hawaii illustrates the evolution of state organization that occurred as a result of contact with the global economy.

Before contact with the West, Hawaii contained eight inhabited islands with a population of about 600,000. As described before, paramount chiefs, who maintained a redistributional exchange economy, ruled through a belief in their divine authority. The Hawaiian Islands were contacted by the English expedition of Captain Cook in 1778, and the islands were eventually penetrated by traders, whalers, missionaries, and other outsiders. The impact of the Western encounter resulted in a unique religious "revolution" when compared with other aboriginal societies we have discussed in earlier sections.

Cook's expedition on the part of the British, which began in the 1760s, set the stage for the colonization of the Pacific. At the time of Captain Cook's discovery of Hawaii, the major paramount chief on the island of Hawaii was engaged in warfare with the chief of the island of Maui, who had already incorporated the islands of Oahu and Molokai under his chieftaincy. The reaction to Cook's arrival during this period was shaped by the aboriginal religious culture. He appeared during the time of Makahiki, a time of religious-based human sacrifices, and he was perceived as someone extremely powerful, perhaps as a *god* or at the least an important foreign chief. There is a heated debate among anthropologists who have investigated the historical records of Cook and other British explorers along with ethnohistorical accounts from native Hawaiians today about whether

Cook was perceived as "God," and killed for religious or cosmological reasons or whether he was killed for political purposes by the natives (Sahlins 1985, 1995; Obeyesekere 1992). Anthropologists do concur that both the native accounts and the British historical records indicate that the distribution of Cook's bones coincide with him as being treated as a sacrificial victim (Sahlins 1995).

Later, a man by the name of Kamehameha, who was a nephew of the Hawaiian chief, made a considerable reputation as a fearless warrior in the Maui campaign. When the chief of Hawaii died, Kamehameha became his successor. Because the island of Hawaii offered good anchorage and became a vital strategic point of contact with Europeans, Kamehameha had an advantage over any other rivals in trading with European ships. The Hawaiians began to trade their products such as sandalwood with Europeans, and in exchange, Kamehameha received guns and light cannon. Eventually, he was able to employ European help in conquering most of the other islands of Hawaii and transformed the Hawaiian chiefdoms into a unified, centralized military kingdom or state.

Kamehameha died in 1819 and was succeeded by his son Liholiho, later known as Kamehameha II. Since Western contact, Hawaii continued to be heavily influenced by Western culture. A number of traditional taboos of the Hawaiian culture were being violated on a regular basis. Some of the Hawaiian women became involved in sexual and romantic relationships with Westerners and openly ate with men, violating traditional taboos (Ortner 1996; Sahlins 1995). Some of the commoner people began to trade openly with Europeans, which also violated traditional norms and taboos, causing tension between the rulers and commoners. Seeing practical advantages for trade with the Europeans and rule over their kingdom, in 1819 Liholiho, the new ruler, and other members of the royal family began to deliberately flout the most sacred traditional taboos of their ancient religion. The royal family began to systematically dismantle the aboriginal religious traditions and practices, which represented a revolutionary transformation in religious thought and culture for Hawaiian society. This transformation of religion was accomplished prior to the coming of Christian missionaries to Hawaii. This religious revolution was resisted by some of the more conservative people of Hawaii,

and Liholiho had to arm his forces to defeat the more conservative faction within the kingdom. This Hawaiian revolution appeared to be an intentional strategy on the part of the ruling family to enhance their political control over the military kingdom.

The sandalwood trade declined in the 1830s and was replaced by the whaling industry, which began to dominate commerce in Hawaii. Because the island was located in the vicinity of a major whaling area of the Pacific, New England whalers used Hawaii as an important base for provisioning and relaxation. However, during the 1830s, various companies began to develop sugar plantations in Hawaii, which eventually became successful, resulting in the influx of more Europeans, including various Christian missionaries from the United States. Many of the missionaries were themselves sugar planters or were connected with sugar planters. Private property was introduced, and land was commodified for sale. As the sugar plantations were developed, substantial native Hawaiian land was lost to the planters. Additionally, the native Hawaiians were subjected to devastating epidemics introduced by the Westerners. Whooping cough, measles, influenza, and other diseases led to rapid depopulation among the native peoples. As Hawaii became increasingly incorporated into the U.S. political economy during the nineteenth and twentieth centuries, the native population declined to a small minority of about 40,000 people. This depopulation resulted in a labor shortage for the sugar planters, who began to import labor from the Philippines, Japan, and China. In 1893, the United States, backed by American Marines, who represented the families of the missionaries and plantation owners such as Sanford Dole (founder of Dole pineapples), overthrew the Hawaiian monarchy. Five years later Hawaii was annexed as a colony of the United States.

Following U.S. colonization, the Hawaiian islands were dominated by U.S. global political and economic interests, and the native Hawaiian population became a marginal group in their own islands. Eventually, through more contact with Western societies, the Pacific Islands such as Hawaii and Tahiti experienced depopulation, deculturation, forced labor, and increased dependency on the global economy. The American and European settlers imported labor from Asia, introduced the system of private property, abolished the traditional patterns of authority, and incorporated the islands into colonial empires. As these islands were integrated into colonial systems, the people were forced to adjust to the conditions of the global economy.

Through missionary schooling and activities, the native Hawaiian people were forbidden to speak their native language or practice any of their traditional religious or cultural activities, which were deemed to be barbaric and uncivilized. These policies led to societal and cultural disintegration for the native population. Combined with the growing Asian population and new settlers from North America who were rapidly developing the sugar economy, and the expansion of mass tourism to Hawaii from the mainland United States, the small modern Hawaiian population began to lose not only its native lands but also its cultural and ethnic identity (Friedman 1992).

A Hawaiian Religious Renaissance

As U.S. corporate capitalism and tourism became the dominant form of economy in Hawaii, every aspect of the traditional Hawaiian culture was affected. At present, the tourist industry generates close to 40 percent of Hawaii's income. Tourists crowd the hotels, restaurants, streets, highways, beaches, golf courses, and parks throughout Hawaii. The advertising industry attempts to promote the image of Hawaii as a romantic and exotic paradise setting where tourists can enjoy the traditional dancing, music, and culture of "primitive" peoples. Ads show skimpily clad women and men dancing before fires on near-deserted beaches. The tourist industry is trying to preserve the traditional culture of Hawaii because it is "good for business."

However, native Hawaiians have begun to resist the marketing of their culture. Beginning in the 1970s, with a growing awareness of their marginal status in the U.S. political economy and more familiarity with the civil rights movement in the mainland United States led by various minorities, many Hawaiians have launched a movement known as the Hawaiian Renaissance. The Hawaiian Renaissance manifested itself as a resurgence of interest in aboriginal Hawaiian culture, including the traditional language and religious beliefs. The movement is fundamentally antitourist. Many contemporary native Hawaiians who are part of the new movement understand that their traditional culture has been mass-marketed and mass-consumed. They feel that their traditional culture has been overly

Many Native Hawaiians are beginning to emphasize their traditional ethnic heritage. In 1993, a march was held to commemorate the 100th anniversary of the Native Hawaiian monarchy.

commercialized, and they resent the tourist industry for selling the Hawaiian tradition.

Some of the spiritual elements of the native religious beliefs have been reintroduced and revitalized in the context of the Hawaiian Renaissance movement. For example, a number of native Hawaiians have become involved in environmental activism. In doing so, they draw on traditional religious beliefs. They are attempting to prohibit the destruction of the rain forests and other natural settings by developers. The native peoples emphasize a spiritual renewal and refer to traditional Hawaiian gods and goddesses that are associated with the natural areas in order to protect these areas from destructive tourist and commercial forces. In some areas, the native Hawaiians are restoring some of the ancient temples, or heiaus. Native Hawaiians can be seen making offerings to the god Pele at the rim of Halemaumau Crater in the Hawaii Volcanoes National Park. Some aboriginal young people complain about their parents' conversion to Christianity and the negative views expressed by Westerners about their traditional culture and religion. However, most important, the revitalization of their religious culture is part of an overall attempt to preserve their heritage and reclaim their cultural identity and selfhood. As these native peoples of Hawaii were subjected to overwhelming and traumatic cultural change, they found that they were marginalized in their own land. After losing their land, their autonomy, and their culture, these native Hawaiians have been involved in reconstructing and reinvigorating some of their aboriginal spiritual beliefs as a means of repossessing their cultural identity (Friedman 1995).

Interestingly, many of these young native Hawaiians who are turning toward their cultural, religious, and ethnic traditions also intermingle these traditions with cultural global trends that arrive from the United States and other areas of the world, as do many other people presently. For example, what was called "hotel hula" dancing for tourists has recently been combined with elements of hip-hop music of African Americans in the United States or popular music associated with Madonna, Britney Spears, or others. (Similar trends are evident among Native American Indian groups and other indigenous peoples throughout the world, a topic that needs more ethnomusicological research by anthropologists.)

Ethnic and Race Trends in Hawaii and the Pacific

There are new trends developing in the Hawaiian islands and other Pacific islands regarding ethnic and racial identity. Just as we discussed in Chapter 7 on race, people like Tiger Woods whose Thai, African American, Chinese, Native American Indian, and Irish descent demonstrate the complexity of race and ethnic classification, the peoples of Hawaii and the Pacific Islands are equally beset with difficulties of classifying themselves and others into distinct ethnic and race categories. In particular, young people on census forms in the United States designate more than one race, whether they are Hispanic Americans or Hawaiians. In Hawaii, some 259,000 reported more than one race and 42 percent of that population was under 18, and of the total Hawaiian population of 1,211,537, only 24 percent were under 18 (Census 2000, Summary File, 2). Although some people have referred to Hawaii as a "model" of multiracial and multiethnic relationships, there is a very nuanced system of racial and ethnic stratification visible to anthropologists and sociologists who study the area (Edles 2004; Buck 1993). Native Hawaiians will refer to "exploitative *haoles*" (whites), and "uppity Japs" or *kanaka*, contrasting themselves as people with a special *aloha* spirit that is harmonious, gentle, and cooperative. Thus, just as in other areas of the world, people use folk categories of "race" to stereotype and categorize one another, and at times this results in ethnic tension and even discrimination.

A Lost Opportunity?

As Brian Fagan noted in his book *Clash of Cultures* (1984b), which surveys the disappearance of many nonstate societies, the same confrontations between incompatible cultural systems were played out in many parts of the world during the late nineteenth century and continue to this day in the Amazon rain forests and other remote areas such as the Pacific Islands. Some government officials and businesspeople in industrial countries view the drastic modifications that took place and are taking place among prestate societies as necessary for the achievement of progress. This view is, of course, a continuation of the nineteenth-century unilineal view of cultural evolution, which overestimates the beneficial aspects of industrial societies. Depopulation, deculturation, fragmentation of the social community, increasingly destructive warfare, unemployment, and increases in crime, alcoholism, and degradation of the environment are only some of the consequences of this so-called progress. As Fagan (1984b, 278) emphasized:

> Progress has brought many things: penicillin, the tractor, the airplane, the refrigerator, radio, and television. It has also brought the gun, nuclear weapons, toxic chemicals, traffic deaths, and environmental pollution, to say nothing of powerful nationalisms and other political passions that pit human being against human being, society against society. Many of these innovations are even more destructive to non-Western societies than the land grabbing and forced conversion of a century and a half ago.

As we discussed in previous chapters and this one, these prestate societies were not idyllic, moral communities in which people lived in perfect harmony with one another and their environment. Warfare, sexism, infanticide, slavery, stratification, and other harmful practices existed in many of these societies. Nonstate societies are not inherently *good*, and industrial societies are not inherently *evil*. Both types of societies have advantages and disadvantages, strengths and weaknesses. There are benefits associated with industrial societies, such as hospitals, better sanitation, and consumer goods, that bring comfort and enjoyment, but nonstate societies also have benefits to offer to industrial societies.

Anthropological research has begun to alert the modern industrial world to the negative implications of the rapid disappearance of first nation peoples—specifically, the loss of extensive practical knowledge that exists in these populations. In the nineteenth-century view (and sometimes even in twenty-first-century discourse), nonstate societies were described as backward, ignorant, and nonscientific. Ethnological research, however, demonstrates that these peoples have developed a collective wisdom that has contributed practical benefits for all of humankind.

Native American Knowledge

In a book titled *Indian Givers*, anthropologist Jack Weatherford (1988) summarized the basic knowledge, labor, and experience of Native American peoples that have contributed to humankind's collective wisdom. Native American Indians introduced 300 food crops to the world, including potatoes and corn. Their experiments with horticultural diversity generated knowledge regarding the survival of crops in different types of environments. They recognized that planting a diversity of seeds would protect the seeds from pests and diseases. Only recently have farmers in the industrialized world begun to discover the ecological lessons developed by Native Americans.

The medical knowledge of Native American Indians, which is based on experience with various plants and trees, has benefited people throughout the world. Weatherford uses the example of quinine, derived from the bark of the South American cinchona tree, which is used to treat malaria. Ipecac was made from the roots of an Amazonian tree as a cure for amoebic dysentery. Native Americans treated scurvy with massive doses of vitamin C, using a tonic made from the bark and needles of an evergreen tree. They also developed treatments for goiter, intestinal worms, headaches (with a medication similar to aspirin), and skin problems.

The lesson from Weatherford's book is that without the contributions of Native American societies, humankind may not have acquired this knowledge for years. As globalization brings about the disappearance of many of these nonstate societies and peoples, humanity risks losing a great deal of knowledge. For example, as we saw in the last chaper, as the Amazon rain forests are invaded and destroyed by governments and multinational interests, not only do we lose hundreds of species of plants and animals, but we also lose the indigenous societies with their incalculable knowledge of those species. Thus, it is in humanity's best interests to abandon the view that deculturation, subjugation, and—sometimes—the extinction of nonstate societies represent a form of progress.

The most difficult issue that faces anthropologists, government officials, and aboriginal peoples is how best to fit traditional patterns in with the modern, industrial world. The fact that these nonstate societies were, and are, almost powerless to resist the pressures from global economic and political forces creates enormous problems. Multinational corporations, national governments, missionaries, prospectors, and other powerful groups and institutions place these indigenous societies in vulnerable circumstances. How will nonstate societies withstand these pressures and continue to contribute to humankind?

Preserving Indigenous Societies

Most anthropologists argue that indigenous peoples should be able to make free and informed choices regarding their destiny, instead of being coerced into assimilating (Hitchcock 1988, 2005; Bodley 1990). As previously discussed, many nonstate societies have tried to resist domination by outside powers but generally lacked the power to do so successfully. In some cases, anthropologists assisted these peoples in their struggles. As we saw, anthropologists such as Napoleon Chagnon and David Maybury-Lewis have set up foundations such as Cultural Survival based at Harvard University to collect money to aid indigenous peoples in their struggles against governments and economic interests who demand their territory.

Also, since the 1970s, many indigenous peoples themselves have become active in preserving their way of life. For example, at a 1975 assembly on the Nootka, a Northwest Coast American Indian chiefdom on Vancouver Island, the World Council of Indigenous Peoples was founded. Fifty-two delegates representing indigenous peoples from nineteen countries established this council, which has become a nongovernmental organization of the United Nations (Fagan 1984b). The council endorsed the right of indigenous peoples to maintain their traditional economic and cultural structures. It emphasized that native populations have a special relationship to their languages and should not be forced to abandon them. It further stressed that land and natural resources should not be taken from native populations. Perhaps this new political awareness and activism will enable these cultures to exercise greater control over their future economic, political, and cultural adjustments in the modern world.

SUMMARY

Chiefdoms are intermediate forms of societies between tribal and large-scale state societies. They tend to consist of more centralized economic and political sociocultural systems than those of foragers or tribes. In the past, they existed in many parts of the world, including the Pacific Islands, Africa, the Americas, and Europe.

Chiefdoms usually had greater populations and more extensive technologies than did tribes. The political economy of chiefdoms was based on redistributional economic exchanges, in which the upper stratum, the chiefly families, had greater access to wealth, power, and political authority than did other people. There were, however, many limitations on chiefly political authority and property ownership. Because many of these chiefdoms did not have regular police or a recruited military, the chiefs had to rule through popular acceptance rather than through coercion.

The social organization of chiefdom societies consisted of lineages, clans, and other descent groups. Yet unlike tribal societies, these descent groups were ranked in strata based on their relationship to a chiefly family. Marriages were frequently endogamous within a particular stratum. Many chiefdoms practiced polygyny, especially in the upper stratum. Gender relations in chiefdom societies tended to be patriarchal, although females in the chiefly stratum often had a high status. Senior males, especially in the upper stratum, often dominated chiefdom societies, resulting in a form of gerontocracy. Although slavery emerged in some chiefdom societies, it generally was not based on commercial exchanges of humans.

Law and religion were intertwined with the sociopolitical structure of chiefdom societies. Law was based on adjudication of disputes by chiefly authorities, especially in cases that threatened the chief's legitimacy. These laws were backed by supernatural sanctions such as the tabu system of Polynesia, which reaffirmed chiefly authority.

The traditional art and music in chiefdom societies were also intended as a form of homage to the legitimacy of the chiefs and their ancestral deities.

Anthropologists have been doing research on the influence of globalization on chiefdom societies at present. They find that there are some that have adapted more successfully than others. This research on globalization has demonstrated that many of these native cultures are disappearing, but also some have resisted globalization influences and want to restore their cultural traditions. Peoples in the Polynesian Islands and American Indian chiefdoms on the Northwest Coast are restoring their museums and struggling against some of the negative global changes that have influenced them. Some of them have become very successful in their efforts to revive and restore their cultural and ethnic heritage, although they often realize that the political struggle for human rights, land, and other demands for sovereignty and autonomy will need more effective strategies in the future.

QUESTIONS TO THINK ABOUT

1. How and why did chiefdoms come into existence? That is, how did economic inequality and social stratification arise from egalitarian foraging and tribal societies? What factors may have been involved in this change?

2. Aside from the prestige factors associated with the potlatch among the Northwest Coast Indians, what other functions did these ceremonies have, and what were the implications?

3. What role did kinship and descent play in the social structure of a chiefdom?

4. What was the role of trade and exchange in chiefdom societies? Give some specific examples of how goods were acquired and transferred from one individual to another.

5. How and why did the practices of reciprocity and redistribution in chiefdoms differ from the way they functioned in bands and tribes? What factors affected the way exchanges took place?

6. Describe the social structure of a chiefdom. What were the specific social rankings, and how were they determined?

7. How has globalization influenced chiefdom societies?

8. Should we be concerned about the disappearance of traditional aboriginal societies? Why or why not?

KEY TERMS

adjudication
barter
chiefdom
chiefs
hierarchical society
intensive horticulture
kula

mana
office
potlatch
primogeniture
redistributional economic
    exchange
regional symbiosis

strata
sumptuary rules
tabu
theocracies

Chapter 12

Agricultural States

CHAPTER OUTLINE

CHAPTER QUESTIONS

- What are some of the most important factors and influences that have resulted in the emergence of intensive agriculture and complex state societies?

- How do the demographic characteristics of agricultural societies differ from those of small-scale societies?

- What are the features of the different forms of political economy that can be found in agricultural societies?

- What is the relationship among family, gender, and subsistence in agricultural societies?

- How does social stratification in agricultural societies differ from that in more egalitarian societies?

- What are the characteristics of law, warfare, and religion in agricultural state societies?

As discussed in earlier chapters, throughout much of their prehistory humans have relied on hunting wild animals and gathering wild plants. This period of primary hunting-gathering is referred to as the Paleolithic period, as discussed in Chapter 9. During the Neolithic period, discussed in Chapter 10, beginning about 12,000 years ago, new patterns of subsistence developed involving the domestication of plants and animals and the emergence of tribal societies: horticulturalists and pastoralists. About 5,000 years ago or so, as we discussed in Chapter 11, some peoples became settled in regions with abundant resources and developed complex chiefdom societies. Archaeologists and historians have discovered increasing technological capacities and more social complexity during this extended period of the Neolithic era. As a result, many peoples developed **intensive agriculture**, the cultivation of crops by preparing permanent fields year after year, often using irrigation and fertilizers. In contrast to horticulture, intensive agriculture enables a population to produce enormous food surpluses to sustain dense populations in large, permanent settlements.

In some regions, beginning as much as 5,500 years ago, the intensification of agriculture was accompanied by the appearance of complex agricultural states. Anthropologists use the term *state* to describe a wide range of societies that differ structurally from bands, tribes, and chiefdoms. The major difference between *state* and *prestate societies* is a bureaucratic organization (or government). The first states developed with the intensification of agriculture and are referred to as agricultural states. The other type of state society—industrial states—are examined in Chapter 13.

As we will see, major agricultural states are sometimes referred to as agricultural civilizations. Although anthropologists disagree on the precise scientific meaning of **civilization**, the term loosely implies a complex society with a number of characteristics, including dense populations located in urban centers; extensive food surpluses; a highly specialized division of labor with economic roles other than those pertaining to agricultural production; a bureaucratic organization or government; monumental works, including art and engineering projects that involve massive labor; and writing systems for record keeping and religious texts. Figure 12.1 shows the location of some early agricultural states.

A number of important geographical and ecological features resulted in large-scale agricultural civilizations in some areas of the world, whereas other areas did not have those features. For example, agriculture developed around the major river valleys of the Near East in Mesopotamia and Egypt, but there were no such areas in sub-Saharan Africa. In addition, some areas, such as the Near East and Europe, had domesticated animals such as sheep, cattle, goats, and horses, whereas neither sub-Saharan Africa nor the Americas had many domesticated animals (Diamond 1997). Therefore, geographical and ecological advantages have played an important role in where agricultural civilizations developed. Also, some areas did not have geographical barriers such as mountains, rain forests, or deserts that inhibited the flow of agricultural patterns from one area to another. The Near East and Europe were contiguous with one another, and technology and agricultural patterns diffused quickly throughout these regions. The Mediterranean Sea enabled the cultures of Greek and Rome to have considerable contact with the diffusion of

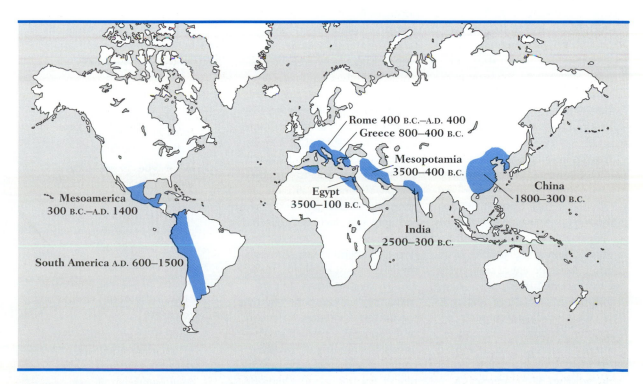

FIGURE 12.1   Map of major agricultural states.

Critical Perspectives

CONTACTS BETWEEN TWO WORLDS?

The structural similarities of Egyptian pyramids to those of Native American Indian civilizations have fostered theories about contact between the Near East and the Americas. For example, one idea promoted in the sixteenth century was that the indigenous peoples of the Americas were the descendants of the so-called Lost Tribes of Israel. Another theory proposed that the ancient continents of Atlantis and Mu connected the continents of America and Europe, enabling people to migrate between the two. In a speculative book entitled *American Genesis* (1981), Jeffrey Goodman proposes that all populations throughout the world are related to an original population located in California, which he asserts was the original Garden of Eden. Goodman contends that from this location, humans inhabited the Americas and crossed the continents of Atlantis and Mu to enter Europe and Asia. Zoologist Barry Fell (1980) has proposed that America was settled by colonists from Europe and North Africa sometime between 3000 and 1000 BC. In an even more radical vein, popular writer Erich Von Daniken (1970) has argued that extraterrestrial beings colonized the Americas and left behind the ideas for the development of civilization.

Archaeologists and physical anthropologists who have analyzed the question of early contacts between continents are skeptical of these theories. As we saw in Chapter 2, the consensus regarding the peopling of the Americas is that migrations occurred across the Bering Strait from Asia. All the dental evidence and skeletal remains indicate that Native Americans have the same physical characteristics as Asians. There have been no archaeological discoveries connecting ancient Israelites or any other societies with those of the Americas. In addition, geologists have not found any evidence of any lost continents such as Atlantis and Mu. Certainly, archaeologists have not identified any evidence of spaceships.

The similar pyramid construction in the Near East and the Americas, in addition to other evidence, has led to some interesting hypotheses regarding transoceanic contacts. A number of serious scholars of diffusionism have offered hypotheses that are still being evaluated by archaeologists. Anthropologist George Carter (1988) has suggested that plants and animals spread from Asia to America before the age of Columbus. Evidence such as pottery design, artwork, and plants has led some archaeologists to hypothesize pre-Columbian diffusion across the Pacific (Jett 1978). Most archaeologists have not collected enough convincing data to confirm these hypotheses. Although similarities exist between the Near East and Native American pyramids, they appear to be based on the universal and practical means of monument construction: There are a finite number of ways to construct a high tower with stone blocks. For this reason, children from widely different cultural settings often construct pyramids when playing with blocks.

Archaeologist Kenneth Feder (1999) reviewed many of the myths, mysteries, and frauds that have been perpetrated about the past. He thinks that many people are prone to believe these speculations rather than accept the scientifically verified evidence. Because the past cannot be experienced directly, people are drawn to speculative accounts of what occurred. This does not mean that anthropologists have absolutely disproved their findings about such phenomena as connections between the two worlds. Anthropologists, however, must rely on the precise evaluation of hypotheses to substantiate their explanations of whether there were any contacts between these areas.

POINTS TO PONDER

1. What ideas have you heard regarding connections between civilizations?

2. What types of evidence would convince you of connections between civilizations? How would you go about assessing information about these ideas?

3. What would it take to convince you that extraterrestrial creatures brought civilization to earth?

4. What does an extraterrestrial origin imply about the abilities of humans to develop their own civilizations?

ideas and agricultural patterns from Egypt and the Near East. Other areas of the world were not as fortunately located.

In this chapter, we examine some of the general characteristics associated with traditional agricultural states. Contemporary developments in specific world areas are explored in later chapters on globalization in Latin America, Africa, the Caribbean, the Middle East, and Asia. Once traditional agricultural states, these regions are now undergoing significant change. As with bands, tribes, and chiefdoms, the agricultural states discussed in this chapter no longer exist in the same form as in the past. The political economy, social organization, and religious traditions that emerged, however, have had consequences that persist up to the present.

Demography

After the transition to intensive agriculture, population began to increase dramatically along with an increase in agricultural production, enabling people to settle in large urban areas. These population increases produced conditions that led to higher mortality rates. Poor sanitation coupled with the domestication of confined animals led to frequent epidemics that affected both animals and humans. The overwhelming fossil and ethnographic evidence suggests that pre-Neolithic or Paleolithic peoples had fewer health problems and less disease than did Neolithic peoples. This debunks the notion that evolution always results in progress for humans, a nineteenth-century belief. Disease, warfare, and famines all contributed to higher mortality rates in agricultural societies than those found in bands, tribes, or chiefdoms. The majority of paleoanthropological and archaeological studies also suggest that life expectancy decreased with the development of intensive agriculture (Hassan 1981; Harris and Ross 1987; Cohen 1994, Robbins 2002).

Despite increased mortality rates and decreased life expectancy, populations continued to grow at a significant rate because of increased fertility rates. Undoubtedly, higher birth rates reflected the socioeconomic benefits associated with increased family size in agricultural civilizations. Children provided additional labor for essential agricultural tasks, such as planting, caring for animals, and harvesting, thereby freeing adults for other labor, such as processing food and making clothing. The actual costs of rearing children were relatively low in agricultural states in which increased agricultural yields produced surplus foods to support large

Large-scale monument buildings, like this Teotihuacan pyramid, required a ruling elite that organized peasants to provide labor to the state.

families. Clothing and shelter were manufactured domestically and were, therefore, inexpensive.

In addition, the mortality rates, particularly infant mortality rates, encouraged parents to have more children to ensure that some would survive into adulthood. Moreover, children were viewed as future assets who could take care of their parents in later life. In addition to the socioeconomic motives of parents, the political dynamics in agricultural civilizations encouraged high fertility rates. All of the agricultural states promoted the ideal of having large families (Harris and Ross 1987). These societies depended on a large labor force to maintain their extensive agricultural production and military operations. Policies favoring *pronatalist* population policies, or high birth rates, frequently were backed up by religious ideologies.

Technology

One major factor that contributed to the evolution of agricultural states was the development of a more sophisticated technology. To some extent, this represented modifications of existing technologies. For example, stone tools such as axes, hammers, knives, and scrapers were refined for more prolonged use. Increased knowledge of metallurgy enabled some agricultural peoples to create more durable tools. For example, copper, tin, and iron ores were smelted and cast into weapons, armor, ornaments, and other tools. Many technological innovations were dramatically expressed in myriad artwork and monumental constructions, exemplified by such massive structures as the Pyramid of the Sun at Teotihuacan in Mexico, which rises

Critical Perspectives

HISTORY AND THEORY IN ANTHROPOLOGY: DIFFUSIONISM

An anthropological theory that used the comparative method to explain why different societies are at different levels of development is called *diffusionism*. Diffusionism, which developed in the early part of the twentieth century, maintains that societal change occurs when societies borrow cultural traits from one another. Cultural knowledge regarding technology, economic ideas, religious views, or art forms spreads, or diffuses, from one society to another. There were two early schools of diffusionism: the British version associated with G. Elliot Smith and William J. Perry, and the German version associated with Father Wilhelm Schmidt.

of Egypt. Smith and Perry were specialists in Egyptian culture and had carried out research in Egyptology for a number of years. From this experience they concluded that all aspects of civilizations, from technology to religion, originated in Egypt and diffused to other cultural areas. To explain the fact that some cultures no longer had cultural traits from Egypt, they resorted to an ethnocentric view, maintaining that some cultures had simply become "degenerate." That is, in contrast to the civilized world, the lesser developed peoples had simply forgotten the original ideas borrowed from Egypt.

followers argued that several early centers of civilization had existed, and that from these early centers cultural traits diffused outward in circles to other regions and peoples. In German this view is referred to as the *Kulturkreise* (culture circles) school of thought. In explaining why some primitive societies did not have the characteristics of civilization, the German school, like the British diffusionists, argued that these peoples had simply degenerated. Thus, diffusionist views, like the unilineal evolutionary views, represent ethnocentric perspectives of human societies outside the mainstream of Western civilization.

BRITISH DIFFUSIONISM

The British school of diffusionism derived its theory from research on the ancient agricultural civilization

GERMAN DIFFUSIONISM

The German school of diffusionism differed somewhat from that of the British. Schmidt and his

THE LIMITATIONS AND STRENGTHS OF DIFFUSIONISM

Early diffusionist views were based on erroneous assumptions more than 200 feet in the air and covers some 650 square feet.

Agricultural Innovations

Technological innovations were of key importance in increasing crop yields in agricultural states. Humans in various world areas developed specialized techniques to exploit local natural resources more efficiently. Initially, water had to be transported by hand, but later civilizations crafted devices such as the *shaduf*, a pole-and-lever device that is believed to have originated in southwest Asia more than 4,000 years ago. Many of the "Old World" civilizations in southwest Asia, the Nile Valley, India, and the "New World" civilizations in the Americas created complicated irrigation systems that extended the amount of land that could be cultivated.

Old World agricultural civilizations reached a pivotal point with the advent of the plow, with which farmers could turn soil to a much greater depth than had previously been possible, radically transforming it by reaching deeper into the soil to replenish it with nutrients. The plow thus enabled agricultural peoples to utilize fields on a more permanent basis and occupy the same land for many generations.

The first plows were modifications of the hoe and were probably pulled by the farmers themselves. Eventually, oxen were harnessed to the plows, and farmers gained the ability to cultivate large plots. Then, as people forged innovations in metallurgy, wooden-tipped plows were replaced by

regarding humankind's innovative capacities. Like the earlier unilineal theorists in the nineteenth century discussed in Chapter 3, they maintained racist assumptions about the inherent inferiority of different non-Western peoples. The diffusionists assumed that some people were not sufficiently innovative to develop their own cultural traits.

Another limitation of the diffusionist approach is its assumption that cultural traits in the same geographical vicinity will inevitably spread from one society to another. Anthropologists find that diffusion is not an inevitable process. Societies can adjoin one another without exchanging cultural traits. For example, as we saw in Chapter 3, generations of Amish people in the United States have deliberately maintained their traditional ways despite being part of a nation in which modern technology is predominant.

However, diffusionism as a means of understanding societal development does have some validity. For example, diffusionism helps explain the emergence of the classical civilizations of Egypt, Greece, Phoenicia, and Rome. These peoples maintained continuous contact through trade and travel, borrowing many cultural traits from one another, such as writing systems. Today, through globalization we have the spread and diffusion of cultural ideas, beliefs, and technology very rapidly. In many areas of the world, one can view MTV and American films, eat McDonald's hamburgers, or watch Japanese anime films, contact others through the Internet and email to exchange ideas, and outsource jobs; and multinational companies do business almost everywhere in the world. Thus, diffusion is an important aspect of globalization today and represents a means of understanding technological, economic, social, and cultural change.

POINTS TO PONDER

1. What are the problems with the early British and German diffusionist models?

2. What are some of the positive aspects of understanding cultural diffusionism today?

3. Can you provide any good examples of diffusionism that you have seen in your own culture?

plows made first of bronze and then of iron. Oxen-drawn, iron-plowed agriculture spread widely, transforming civilizations throughout the Old World.

Early New World civilizations never used the plow. Instead, they devised a wide variety of other agricultural innovations in response to particular environmental settings. For example, in the Oaxacan Valley in Mexico, the people practiced pot irrigation, in which farmers planted their crops near small, shallow wells and used pots to carry water to their fields (Flannery 1968). More complicated irrigation techniques undergirded agriculture in other American agricultural states. In both the highland and lowland regions of Mesoamerica, the Mayan civilization (300 BC–AD 1500) created agricultural technology to support densely populated urban centers. Because no evidence of intensive agriculture had been discovered, archaeologists initially hypothesized that the Maya lived in widely dispersed villages with ritual centers consisting of relatively few inhabitants. However, using more careful study techniques, researchers have proved that the Maya devised sophisticated irrigation systems throughout lowland areas, which provided food for the large urban centers.

The Diffusion of Technology

In today's multicultural societies, we take the diffusion, or exchange, of technological innovations for granted and, indeed, archaeologists have uncovered evidence that certain ideas—such as iron technology and plow agriculture—diffused over large areas during ancient times. However, the fact remains that before AD 1500, most regions of the world were comparatively isolated, and technological innovations were not spread as readily as today.

Certain areas experienced greater technological advances than did others. For example, the Near East, China, and parts of India had made remarkable technological and scientific achievements compared with those of Europe (Diamond 1997). Among the major innovations identified with China alone were paper making, movable-type printing, paper money, guns and gunpowder, compasses, underwater mining, umbrellas, hot-air balloons, multistage rockets, and scientific ideas concerning the circulation of blood and the laws of motion

(Frank 1998). Little was known of these technological and scientific developments in Western societies until much later.

Political Economy

The scale of state organization varied in agricultural civilizations. In some areas, there existed large-scale bureaucratic empires that organized and controlled wide-ranging territories. Examples are centralized governments in the Near Eastern empires such as Mesopotamia and Egypt; Rome, which controlled an empire that incorporated more than 70 million people throughout its long period of domination; China, in which a large centralized bureaucracy managed by government officials ruled over perhaps as many as 100 million people; and American empires such as those of the Mayas and Aztecs, which ruled over millions of people.

In contrast, state societies in Africa, India, and Southeast Asia were much less centralized and had less authority over adjacent regions. Anthropologist Aidan Southall (1956) applied the term *segmentary states* to African states in which the ruler was recognized as belonging to an appropriate royal segmentary lineage but had only symbolic and ritual authority over outlying regions. Centralized bureaucratic structures in such states did not effectively control outlying peripheral areas. Anthropologist Clifford Geertz (1980) used the term **theater state** to refer to the limited form of state society in Southeast Asia. The power of the theater state was mostly symbolic and theatrical, with many ceremonies to demonstrate the political legitimacy of the regime. The power and authority of the theater state have been compared with the light of a torch, radiating outward from the center and gradually fading into the distance, merging imperceptibly with the ascending power of a neighboring sovereign (Geertz 1980). Another anthropologist, Stanley Tambiah, used a model to characterize two different forms of state societies: *galactic polity* and *radial polity* (1976). A **galactic polity** is a type of state that rules primarily through religious authority and cosmologies, whereas the **radial polity** is a state that rules more directly through government and military officials that have more centralized control over various provinces and regions. Although Tambiah initially applied this model to explain states and kingdoms in South and Southeast Asia, it is now widely used by archaeologists and others to interpret and explain various regions such as the Maya civilizations in Mesoamerica (Lucero 2003).

Feudalism, a decentralized form of political economy based on landed estates, existed in agricultural civilizations during different historical periods. Although anthropologists and historians have indicated that there is a tremendous difference among forms of feudalism in various societies, there are some similarities. To some extent, some of these feudal regimes were very similar to the chiefdom societies discussed in Chapter 11. Usually, as in Western history, feudal regimes resulted from the breakdown of large-scale centralized states. Feudal political economies emerged at various times in Western Europe and Japan. In these systems, lords, like chiefs, were autonomous patrons who owned land and maintained control over their own military (knights and *samurai*) and demanded labor and tribute from their serfs. Political power varied from a highly decentralized form of authority (the nobles) to a more centralized form (a king or emperor). For example, during the Tokugawa period in Japan (1600–1868), the *daimyo* (lords) had to reside in the central capital, Edo (present-day Tokyo), for a year to demonstrate loyalty to the ruler, or *shogun*. This represented a more centralized form of feudalism.

The Division of Labor

The creation of substantial food surpluses, along with better food-storing technologies, led to new forms of economic relations in agricultural states. Many people could be freed from working in the fields to pursue other specialized functions. Hundreds of new occupations developed in the urban centers of agricultural states. Craftsworkers produced tools, clothing, jewelry, pottery, and other accessories. Other workers engaged in commerce, government, religion, education, the military, and other sectors of the economy.

This new division of labor influenced both rural and urban areas. Farm laborers were not only involved in essential food production, they also turned to craft production to supplement their income. Over time, some agricultural villages began to produce crafts and commodities not just for their own consumption, but for trade with other villages and with the urban centers. Through these activities, rural villages became involved in widespread trading alliances and marketing activities.

Property Rights

Despite the complex division of labor in agricultural states, the major source of wealth was arable land. In effect, the ownership of land became the primary basis for an individual's socioeconomic position. The governing elite in most of the agricultural states claimed ownership over large landholdings, which included both the land and the peasant or slave labor that went with it (Brumfiel 1994).

Two major forms of property ownership predominated in agricultural states, depending on whether they were large-scale centralized states or decentralized feudal states. Eric Wolf (1966) identified one type of property ownership in which a powerful government claimed ownership of the land, appointed officials to supervise its cultivation, and collected the surplus agricultural production. In the other type of system, a class of landlords who owned the land privately inherited it through family lines and oversaw its cultivation. In certain cases, peasants could own land directly and produce surpluses for the elites. Agricultural states thus developed major inequalities between those who owned land and those who did not. Bureaucratic and legal devices were developed by the elite to institute legal deeds and titles, and land became a resource that was bought, sold, and rented.

A new form of economic system known as the tributary form became predominant. **Tribute**, in the form of taxes, rent, or labor services, replaced economic exchanges based on kinship reciprocity or chiefdom redistribution. Wolf (1997) referred to this as a **tributary mode** of production, in contrast to the *kin-ordered mode* of production of nonstate societies. Under these conditions, a hierarchy emerged in which the elite who resided in the urban centers or on landed estates collected tribute, and the peasants, who cultivated the land, paid tribute to this elite (Wolf 1966, 1982, 1997).

The Command Economy versus the Entrepreneur

In the large-scale centralized states, a form of **command economy** emerged, wherein the political elite controlled production, prices, and trading. Some agricultural states became expansive world empires that extracted tribute and placed limits on people's economic activities. State authorities controlled the production, exchange, and the consumption of goods within the economies of these bureaucratic empires. Although private trade and entrepreneurial activities did occur at times within these bureaucratic empires, it was rare (Brumfiel 1994). For example, China and Rome attempted to organize and control most aspects of their economy by monopolizing the production and sale of items like salt and iron.

In the less centrally organized agricultural states, more independent economic activity was evident. For example, during the feudal periods in western Europe and Japan, the lack of a dominating elite that organized and managed the economic affairs of the society enabled more autonomous economic production and exchange to occur at the local level. Entrepreneurs had freedom to develop and innovate within the context of feudal political economies. This was a key factor in the later economic development of these regions.

The Peasantry

Peasants are people who cultivate land in rural areas for their basic subsistence and pay tribute to elite groups. The socioeconomic status of the peasantry, however, varied in agricultural societies. As we have seen, rights to land differed between the bureaucratic empires and the less centralized societies. In most agricultural states, elites claimed rights to most of the land, and the peasantry in the rural areas paid tribute or taxes as a type of rent (Wolf 1966, 1997). In other cases, the peasants owned the land they cultivated; nevertheless, they still paid tribute from their labor surplus or production. In the case of feudal Europe, the peasants, or serfs, were bound to the estates owned by lords, or nobles.

Whatever their status, all peasants had to produce a surplus that flowed into the urban centers. It is estimated that this surplus, including fines, tithes, and obligatory gifts, represented at least half of the peasants' total output (Brumfiel 1994; Sanderson 1999). Also, in the bureaucratic civilizations such as Egypt and Teotihuacan, the peasantry provided much of the compulsory labor for large-scale government projects such as massive irrigation works and pyramids. Although research on peasants has demonstrated that they were often able to evade some of these obligations or contrived to hide some of their surpluses, most were subject to burdensome demands from the elites.

The Moral Economy Despite the domination of the peasantry by the agricultural state or by landlords, at times and different circumstances, the peasantry developed norms that emphasized community cooperation in production, distribution, consumption, and exchange in the village. These norms led to what some anthropologists have referred to as a moral economy for the peasantry. This **moral economy** involved sharing food resources and labor with one another in a reciprocal manner to provide a form of social and economic insurance so that individual families would not fall into destitution (Scott 1976; Boyd and Richerson 2002). Peasant families would exchange labor with each other to aid production of crops. In addition, rituals and festivals occurred at which peasants were encouraged to donate and exchange food and goods to be distributed throughout the community. Although the moral economy of the peasantry was not always successful, and individual families did become impoverished, in many cases it did help sustain the viability of the village community.

Trade and Monetary Exchange

As previously discussed, the production of agricultural surpluses and luxury items in agricultural states resulted in a great deal of internal and external trade. This trade included raw materials for production, such as copper, iron ore, obsidian, and salt. Long-distance trade routes over both land and sea spanned immense geographical areas. Through constant policing, governing elites enforced political order and military security over these trade routes. In turn, this protection led to the security and maintenance of extensive road networks that aided commercial pursuits. For example, the Romans constructed roads and bridges that are still in use today (Stavrianos 1995).

Women play an important role in markets in agricultural societies.

Extensive caravan routes developed in areas such as the Near East and North Africa. The Bedouins, Arabic-speaking pastoralists, used camels to conduct long-distance trade, carrying goods from port cities in the Arabian peninsula across the desert to cities such as Damascus, Jerusalem, and Cairo. In Asia, other caravan routes crossed the whole of China and central Asia, with connections to the Near East. In the Americas, long-distance trade developed between Teotihuacan and the Mayan regions.

In conjunction with long-distance trade, monetary exchange became more formalized. In the Near East (and probably elsewhere), foodstuffs such as grains originally could be used to pay taxes, wages, rents, and other obligations. Because grains are perishable and bulky, however, they were not ideal for carrying out exchanges. Thus, general-purpose money, based on metals, especially silver and copper, came into use. The sizes and weights of these metals became standardized and were circulated as stores of value. At first, bars of metal were used as money, but eventually smaller units of metal, or coins, were manufactured and regulated. After developing printing, the Chinese began to produce paper money as their medium of exchange.

The Rise of Merchants and Peripheral Markets

One result of the development of a formalized monetary system was the increased opportunity for merchants to purchase goods not for their own consumption but to be sold to people who had money. Merchants made up a new status category of people who, although below the elites, often prospered by creating demands for luxury goods and organizing the transportation of those goods across long distances. Much of the trade of the Near Eastern empires, followed by the Greek, Roman, Byzantine, and Islamic Mediterranean commercial operations, was stimulated by merchants who furnished imported luxury goods from foreign lands for consumption by internal elites (Wolf 1982). Sometimes, as in the case of the Aztecs, the merchants of these empires also doubled as spies, providing information to governing authorities regarding peoples in outlying regions.

With increasing long-distance trade and other commercial developments, regional and local marketplaces as well as marketplaces in the urban areas began to emerge. Foodstuffs and other commodities produced by peasants, artisans, and craftsworkers were bought and sold in these marketplaces. In early cities such as Ur, Memphis, Teotihuacan, and Tikal, markets were centrally located, offering both imported and domestically manufactured items as well as food. In addition, marketplaces arose throughout the countryside. A steady flow of goods developed from villages to counties to regional and national capitals.

Although many goods were bought and sold in these regional markets, the vast majority of people—that is, the peasantry—did not receive their subsistence items from these markets. Nor were people engaged full time in producing or selling in these marketplaces (Bohannon and Dalton 1962). The regional and local markets existed only as a convenient location for the distribution of goods. In many cases, the activity was periodic. For example, in medieval Europe, traveling fairs that went from city to city enabled merchants to bring their local and imported goods to be bought and sold.

Goods were bought and sold in markets through a system known as haggling. Haggling is a type of negotiation between buyer and seller that establishes the price of an item. The buyer asks a seller how much he or she wants for an item, the seller proposes a figure, and the buyer counters with a lower price, until a price is finally agreed on.

Social Organization

Because agricultural states were more complex and more highly organized than prestate societies, they could not rely solely on kinship for recruitment to different status positions. Land ownership and occupation became more important than kinship in organizing society. In highly centralized agricultural societies, the state itself replaced kin groups as the major integrating principle in society.

Kinship and Status

Nevertheless, as in all societies, family and kinship remained an important part of social organization. In elite and royal families, kinship was the basic determination of status. Royal incest in brother-sister marriages by both the Egyptian and Incan royalty shows the importance of kinship as a distinctive means of maintaining status in agricultural societies. The typical means of achieving the highest statuses was through family patrimony, or the inheritance of status. Access to the highest ranks was generally closed to those who did not have the proper genealogical relationships with the elite or the nobility.

The Extended Family   The extended family was the predominant family form in both urban and rural areas in most agricultural states. Family ties remained critical to most peasants; typically, the peasant extended family held land in common, and the members of the family cooperated in farm labor. To some extent, intensive agricultural production required the presence of a large extended family to provide the necessary labor to plant, cultivate, and harvest crops (Wolf 1966; Stone 2000). Large domestic groups had to pool their resources and labor to maintain economic production. To induce this cooperation, generalized reciprocal economic exchanges of foodstuffs, goods, and labor were maintained in these families.

Other Kinship Principles   In a cross-cultural survey of fifty-three agricultural civilizations, Kay Martin and Barbara Voorhies (1975) found that 45 percent had patrilineal kin groupings, another 45 percent had bilateral groupings, and 9 percent had matrilineal groupings. In some Southeast Asian societies, such as Burma, Thailand, and Cambodia, bilateral descent existed along with kindred groupings. In some circumstances, these kindreds provided domestic labor for agricultural production through reciprocal labor exchanges. Families connected through kindreds would regularly exchange labor for the transplanting or harvesting of rice crops.

Family Structure among the Nayar   One matrilineal society, the Nayar in the state of Kerala of southern India, had unusual marriage practices that produced a remarkably different type of family structure. They practiced a visiting ritualized mating system called the *sambandham* (joining together) (Gough 1961; Fuller 1976; Stone 2000). Once every ten years or so, the Nayar would hold this ceremony to "marry" females of one matrilineage to males of another matrilineage. At the ceremony, the male would tie a gold ornament around the neck of his ritual bride. After seclusion for three days, sexual intercourse might or might not take place, depending on the girl's age. After this the couple would take a ritual bath to purify themselves of the pollution of this cohabitation. After the ceremony, the male had no rights regarding the female. Later, the female could enter a number of marriages with males of her same caste or usually a higher caste, a marriage practice called *hypergamy*, and have children. Women could not marry men of a lower caste. The Nayar system was unusual because none of the husbands resided with the female. A husband would visit the wife at night but did not remain in the household. The matrilineal group assumed the rights over her and her children. Because the women could have more than one spouse, the society was polyandrous; however, because the males could also have more than one spouse, the Nayar were also polygynous. Thus, the household family unit consisted of brothers and sisters, a woman's daughter and granddaughters, and their children. The bride and her children were obliged to perform a ceremony at the death of her "ritual" husband.

From the Western viewpoint, the Nayar marital arrangement might not seem like a family because it does not tie two families together into joint bonds of kinship or even husband-wife bonds. In addition, males had very little biological connection to their children. This system, however, was a response to historical circumstances in southern India. Traditionally, most Nayar males joined the military. In addition, the land owned by the matrilineal group was worked by lower-caste, landless peasants. Thus, children were not even working on the land for their families. Therefore, young Nayar males had no responsibilities to the matrilineal group and were free to become full-time warriors (Mencher 1965). Recent ethnographic research on the Nayar has demonstrated that there is little remaining of this former unusual marriage system, and the matrilineal system has become increasingly patrilineal with a shift to a nuclear family and husband-wife monogamy (Fuller 1976; Menon 1996).

Marriage

The significance of social ties in agricultural states is evident in the form of marriage practices found in these societies, all of which have economic and political implications. Because of these implications, the selection of marital partners was considered too important to be left to young people. Marriages were usually arranged by parents, sometimes with the aid of brokers, who assessed the alliances between the extended families with respect to landed wealth or political connections to the elite. This was especially the case among the political elite, such as in Roman society (Stone 2000). In some cases (for example, China), arranged marriages were contracted when the children were young (see Chapter 4). As in chiefdom societies, elite marriages were frequently endogamous. Peasants, however, generally married outside their extended families and larger kin groups.

Dowry and Bridewealth   Most agricultural states practiced some form of marital exchange involving land, commodities, or foodstuffs. In Asia and some parts of Europe, the most common type of exchange was the **dowry**—goods and wealth paid by the bride's family to the groom's family. In this sense, the dowry appears to be the reverse of bridewealth, in which the groom's family exchanges wealth for the bride. The dowry was used as a social exchange between families to arrange a marriage contract. Upon marriage, the bride in an Indian, European, or Chinese family was expected to bring material goods into her marriage.

In a cross-cultural comparison, Jack Goody (1976, 1983) found that bridewealth occurs more frequently in horticultural societies, whereas the dowry is found in complex, agricultural societies. In Europe and

Asia, intensive agriculture was associated with the use of plows and draft animals, high population densities, and a scarcity of land. Goody hypothesized that one result of the dowry system was to consolidate property in the hands of elite groups. As commercial and bureaucratic families expanded their wealth and increased their status, these groups began to move from bridewealth to dowry. As bridewealth was a means of circulating wealth among families through creating alliances between the groom's and bride's families, the dowry served to concentrate property and wealth within the patrilineal line of families. Elites in India, China, and Greece relied on this form of marital exchange.

Although dowry exchanges were most significant in the upper socioeconomic groups in which wealth and status were of central significance, they were also supposed to be customary among the peasantry. Bridewealth was not unknown in peasant society. In both northern and southern India, bridewealth became more common among the lower socioeconomic classes. In the poorest families, there was little to be inherited anyway, and the actual exchanges were mainly for the costs of the wedding feast and for simple household furnishings.

Polygyny   In contrast to prestate societies, polygyny was rare in agricultural states, except among the elite. In some cases, the rulers of these state societies in Asia, the Middle East, Europe, and elsewhere had large harems, in which many different women were attached to one ruler. The royal households of many agricultural states had hundreds of women at the disposal of the rulers. The Thai, Nepalese, and other South and Southeast Asian kingdoms had royal families with many women attached to the king's palace quarters and households (Tambiah 1976; Bennett 1983). Many of the European kings had extensive polygynous households, even after Christianity had developed norms against such forms of marriage (Stone 2000). Elite males who were wealthy were able to keep mistresses or concubines in addition to their wives. For example, many elite Chinese males kept concubines or secondary wives, despite laws against this practice. Other agricultural states had similar polygynous practices for individuals in high-ranking socioeconomic positions. In addition, many of the marriages were endogamous, marriage within the same high-caste or upper-class category, similar to that of the chiefdom societies discussed in Chapter 11.

For most of the populace, however, monogamy was the primary form of marriage. Economist Ester Boserup (1970) has argued that the general absence of polygyny in societies with plow agriculture is due to the lack of land that could be accumulated by adding wives to one's family. Similarly, Goody (1976) hypothesized that in agricultural societies where land is a scarce commodity, peasants cannot afford the luxury of polygyny. Obviously, wealth and status influenced the type of marriage patterns found in agricultural civilizations.

Divorce   For the most part, divorce was rare in agricultural civilizations. The corporate nature of the extended family and the need for cooperative agricultural labor among family members usually led to normative constraints against divorce. In addition, marriage was the most important vehicle for the transfer of property and served as the basis for alliances between families and kin groups. Thus, families tended to stay together, and enormous moral, political, and social weight was attached to the marriage bond. In India, marriage was considered sacred, and therefore divorces were not legally permitted. Similar norms were evident in the feudal societies of Europe, where Christianity reinforced the sanctity of the family and the stability of marriage.

For women, however, marriage offered the only respectable career or means of subsistence. Most women faced destitution if a marriage were terminated. Thus, few women wanted to dissolve a marriage, regardless of the internal conflicts or problems. This pattern reflects the unequal status of males and females.

Gender, Subsistence, and Status

The transition to intensive agriculture affected the subsistence roles of both males and females. Martin and Voorhies (1975) noted that in agricultural systems the amount of labor that women contributed to actual production of food declined. For example, the adoption of plow agriculture greatly diminished the need for weeding, a task that was primarily taken care of by women. They hypothesized that as women's role in agriculture decreased, their

social status decreased accordingly. Thus, agricultural civilizations were even more patriarchal than were tribes or chiefdoms. Women were viewed as unable to contribute toward the household economy, and for the most part they were confined to cooking, child rearing, and caring for the domestic animals. They had little contact outside their immediate families.

Martin and Voorhies (1975) emphasized that a definite distinction arose in agricultural states between men's and women's roles. Women were restricted to *inside* (domestic) activities, whereas males were allowed to participate in *outside* (public) activities. In general, women were not allowed to own property, engage in politics, pursue education, or participate in any activity that would take them outside the domestic sphere. Since Martin and Voorhies did their research, a number of feminist anthropologists have questioned the simplistic dichotomy between the domestic and public realms for gender roles. In some cases, the domestic domain encompassed some of the activities of the public sphere, and vice versa. However, they have agreed that this distinction has helped analyze gender in most agricultural societies (Lamphere 1997; Ortner 1996). Generally, most studies concur that the female role was restricted in many of these societies.

Female Seclusion   This highly restricted female role in many agriculture societies was reflected in a number of cultural practices. For example, China adopted the tradition of foot binding, which involved binding a young female child's feet so her feet would not grow. Although this practice was supposed to produce beautiful feet (in the view of Chinese males), it had the effect of immobilizing women. Less of a handicap for upper-class females, who did not have to participate in the daily labor requirements of most women and were carried around by servants, foot binding was also practiced by the peasantry during various periods, which meant that peasant women had to work with considerable disabilities.

Similarly, many areas of the Near East, North Africa, and southern Asia practiced *purdah*, a system that restricted women to the household. **Purdah** is a Persian word translated as "curtain" or "barrier." In this system, women had to obtain permission from their husbands to leave the house to

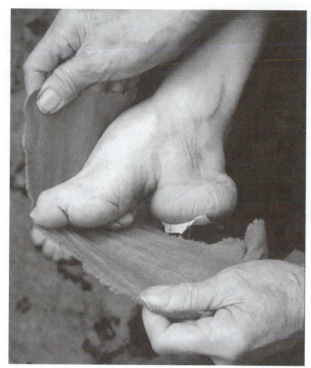

The binding of women's feet in traditional agricultural China led to results shown in this photo.

visit families and friends. In some of these regions, a woman had to cover her face with a veil when in public (Beck and Keddie 1978; Fernea and Fernea 1979). Female seclusion was one of the ways in which males tried to control the paternity of the children that they were raising.

Patriarchy and Sexism Sexist ideology developed in agricultural states as a means of reinforcing the seclusion of women. In many agricultural societies, females were viewed as inherently inferior and dependent on males. The so-called natural superiority of males was reinforced in most of the legal, moral, and religious traditions in agricultural states, including Confucianism, Islam, Hinduism, Judaism, and Christianity. For example, a daily Orthodox Jewish prayer for men says:

"Blessed art thou, O Lord our God, King of the Universe, that I was not born a gentile.
Blessed art thou, O Lord our God, King of the Universe, that I was not born a slave.
Blessed art thou, O Lord our God, King of the Universe, that I was not born a woman."

The New Testament text also supported patriarchal attitudes toward women. In Ephesians (5:22–24), it states "Wives be subject to your husbands, as to the Lord. For the husband is the head of the wife as Christ is the head of the church. As the church is subject to Christ, so let wives also be subject in everything to their husbands."

Many passages from the Qu'ran of the Islamic tradition (as we see in Chapter 15) and Hindu, Buddhist, and other religions developing in the agricultural societies throughout the world endorsed patriarchal attitudes and cultural values. In many of these agricultural societies, males were viewed as more intelligent, stronger, and more emotionally mature. In addition, many of these societies viewed women as sexually dangerous; women caught having premarital or extramarital sex were punished severely, in some cases by execution by stoning, as mentioned in Leviticus in the Old Testament. In contrast, males were permitted to engage in extramarital affairs or have many wives or mistresses.

Variations in the Status of Women The role and status of women in agricultural civilizations varied by region. For example, in some areas where soil conditions were poor, both male and female peasants had to work together in the fields to produce for the household, which tended to create more gender equality. In most Southeast Asian countries, such as Thailand and Cambodia, both males and females worked together in rice cultivation. In some cases, land was divided equally among all children, regardless of gender, indicating that in these societies females had relative equality with males. Although in these countries, women were mostly confined to the domestic sphere and to household tasks, they played an important role in decision making and financial matters within the rural communities (Keyes, 1995; Van Esterik 1996; Winzeler 1996; Scupin 2005).

Anthropologists have discovered other exceptions regarding the role and status of peasant women in public in some agricultural civilizations. In China, Mesoamerica, and West Africa, many women participated as sellers in the marketplaces, taking some of the surplus produce or crafts made

Critical Perspectives

WERE THERE MATRIARCHAL STATES?

As mentioned in earlier chapters, anthropologists have not found any substantive archaeological or ethnographic evidence for the existence of matriarchal societies. There are, of course, societies that have matrilineal social organization, in which one traces descent through the mother's side of the family. But as we have discussed (see Chapter 10), matriliny does not translate into a matriarchal society in which women would have economic and political dominance over males. Within societies organized by matrilineal descent, such as the Iroquois Indian societies discussed in Chapter 10, males tend to dominate in political and economic affairs. Women may have a more active role in these areas, but patriarchy exists as the prevalent gender pattern in these matrilineal societies.

However, the belief that there were once matriarchal societies that were overcome by male-dominated, warlike societies has a long history in the West. For example, after examining Greek and Roman mythology, law, religion, and history, the German lawyer Johann Jacob Bachofen wrote an influential book called *Das Mutterrecht (The Mother-Right)* published in 1861. Bachofen suggested that matrilineal kinship combined with matriarchy was the first form of human evolutionary development. He reasoned that since no child could determine its paternity, kinship, descent, and inheritance could be recognized only through women. Bachofen argued that women dominated these early primitive societies both economically and politically. Anthropologist John MacLellan developed this same theme in his book *Primitive Marriage: An Inquiry into the Origin of the Form of Capture in Marriage Ceremonies* (1865). A number of other scenarios of this evolution from matriarchy to patriarchy were published in books in Europe.

Using similar reasoning, Lewis Henry Morgan, an early American anthropologist (see Chapter 3), reinforced this Victorian view of ancient matriarchal societies. Based on his ethnographic study of Iroquois Indian society and other sources, Morgan argued in his famous book *Ancient Society* (1877) that there must have been an early stage of matriarchal society. He studied kinship terms from different areas of the world to substantiate this view. Morgan suggested that a patriarchal stage of evolution replaced an earlier form of matriarchy as more advanced forms of agriculture developed. In his understanding, matriarchal societies were based on the communal ownership of property and polyandry (females married to two or more males). He argued that patriarchy evolved along with the concept of private property and ownership. Morgan suggested that males invented the institution of monogamy in order to ensure their paternity of their children. This enabled them to pass their private property on to their male heirs.

Europeans Karl Marx and Friedrich Engels became enthusiastic about Morgan's ideas in *Ancient Society*. Engels wrote about the connection between the evolution of private property and the emergence of patriarchal societies in his book *The Origin of the Family, Private Property, and the State* in 1884. This book, along with other writings by Marx and Engels, provided the intellectual foundation of the socialist and communist movement in the nineteenth and twentieth centuries. Following Morgan, Marx and Engels believed that revolutionary change in the economy caused by the evolution of advanced forms of agriculture resulted in men taking control of the politics from women. As men gained control over herd animals and farmland, they also instituted the marriage pattern of monogamy, in which females pledged lifetime fidelity to one man. This institution assured males of the paternity of their own children. Engels referred to this commitment as "the world historical defeat of the female sex." He and Marx argued that the institution of the patriarchal family and monogamy became the basis of treating females as property and commodities, demonstrated in existing rituals such as the "giving away of the bride by the father to the groom" in Western wedding ceremonies. Women became servants of men and provided sustenance to support male authority and wealth accumulation in capitalist societies. Marx and Engels believed that Victorian sexist attitudes and male chauvinism had been developed to assure male authority and paternity. They believed that the global transformation from matrilineal and matriarchal societies into patrilineal and patriarchal societies established one of the integral components resulting in exploitative capitalist societies.

Other important thinkers of the twentieth century such as Sigmund Freud (see Chapter 4) transmitted these ideas regarding early matriarchal societies. One European archaeologist, the late Maria Gimbutas, proposed that early "matristic" societies were once the predominant form of society in ancient Europe (1982, 1991). She argued that in the period she calls "Old Europe" (between 6500 and 3500 BC), peaceful, sedentary villages existed where men and women formed equal partnerships with one another. Gimbutas drew upon a number of types of artifacts to make her case. Based on art, architecture, figurines, ceramic pottery, marble, gold, grave goods, and other artifacts, she suggested that the culture of "Old Europe" was based on the belief in a Great Mother Goddess and other goddesses. According to Gimbutas, a "queen-priestess" ruled and maintained control over this matrifocused religious tradition. She found no evidence of weapons or warfare from that time period. Thus, she challenged the assumption that warfare is endemic and universal in human societies. In addition, Gimbutas argued that these societies were completely egalitarian, with no classes, castes, slaves, and, of course, no male rulers.

According to Gimbutas, "Old Europe" began to be invaded by tribal horse-riding pastoralists known as the Kurgan by 4400 BC. These Kurgan pastoralists were male-dominated and were associated with the earliest forms of Indo-European languages. These Indo-European Kurgans from the Eurasiatic steppes developed religious traditions and mythologies that reflected a warrior cult. They maintained a pantheon of male gods representing the sun, stars, thunder, and lightning, and they were associated with warriorlike artifacts such as daggers and axes. Eventually, the Kurgan introduced iron plows that were used to cultivate the land. This technological innovation altered forever the relationship between males and females in European society. Males with plows and draft animals supplanted the female-oriented forms of cultivation. As the Kurgan society replaced the "Old Europe," women were relegated to the domestic aspect of subsistence activities. According to Gimbutas, the mythical and ideological culture perpetuated by the Kurgans continued until the beginnings of Christianity in Europe and beyond.

Recently, archaeologist Lynn Meskell has criticized the picture of Old Europe and the Kurgan culture presented by Maria Gimbutas (1995). Meskell notes that since the nineteenth century, there has been a recurrent interest in the notion of original, matriarchal Mother Goddess societies. This view has been perpetuated in some of the ecofeminist and "New Age" religious literature. Meskell argues that these "New Age" feminists utilize Gimbutas to ground their movement in a utopian vision of the past. She suggests that the current interest in the Mother Goddess "gynocentric" theories of prehistory serve as vehicles for attempting to overturn patriarchal institutions in today's societies. However, Meskell suggests that these gynocentric views are based on inadequate scholarship and actually damage the positive aspects of gender research in anthropology. She and many other archaeologists note that Gimbutas neglected a tremendous amount of data and artifacts that would demonstrate the fallibility of her thesis. Numerous artifacts such as artwork indicating the prevalence of male deity figurines were dismissed in Gimbutas' data collection. Artifacts indicating warfare, human sacrifice, and fortifications are abundant throughout the archaeological record dated within Gimbutas' "Old Europe" period. And the view of Kurgan patriarchal domination of this once-peaceful matristic society is too simplistic to explain the complexities of European archaeology. Meskell concludes that the belief that there were distinctive stages of matriarchal and patriarchal societies is a remnant of the Victorian past. She argues that these simplistic views do not do justice to interpretations in archaeology or feminist anthropological and gender studies in the twenty-first century.

Of course there were agricultural societies that worshipped female goddesses and maintained mythologies about matriarchal societies. In fact, there were agricultural societies that had females who held important leadership and political roles, such as the famed Cleopatra. Yet the evidence from archaeology and ethnography suggests that female political supremacy and domination over the economy did not exist. Despite Cleopatra's political authority, a male elite clearly controlled the economy and politics in ancient Egypt.

As we saw in this chapter, the status of women in most of the agricultural societies in the past, including the goddess-worshipping ones, was very low. Both males and females have used mythologies and beliefs about early matriarchies throughout history.

Nineteenth-century males used these beliefs to justify the status and authority of what they believed to be more evolved and advanced "patriarchal" institutions. Today, some women in the ecofeminist and "New Age" movements use these myths to perpetuate their vision of a utopian society. Many contemporary anthropologists, both male and female, argue that the terms patriarchy and matriarchy are too limited as dichotomies to assess the position of women in many societies of the world. For example, in a new ethnography based on eighteen years of study in Minangkabau, Indonesia, by University of Pennsylvania anthropologist Peggy Sanday called *Women at the Center: Life in a Modern Matriarchy* (2002), she challenges the framework and stereotype of many Western peoples who believe that the religion of Islam consistently subordinates women with its patriarchal traditions. She finds that in Indonesia, the cultural beliefs about women have always been relatively egalitarian and these beliefs have resisted any attempt at subordinating women in this society. Thus,

anthropologists are working all over the world to refine their approach to gender issues and investigating various global changes influencing gender change. In addition, one of the major goals of anthropology is to enhance and improve the rights of women and men throughout the world (see Chapter 17). But to do so, we must have an accurate assessment of what the archaeological and ethnographic record tell us. Without this accurate assessment, we cannot either further our knowledge of humanity or aid in the improvement of the human condition.

POINTS TO PONDER

1. What kind of data would be needed to infer a true matriarchal society in the past?

2. What are the strengths and weaknesses of the belief in an early matriarchal society?

3. Could there ever be a truly matriarchal society? If so, how could one develop?

4. What has this Critical Perspectives box taught you about analyzing anthropological data?

in the village to the marketplaces. This activity was generally restricted to older women whose children were grown, however; but in some cases the role of market woman did lead to higher status. Many of these women participated in the public sphere but were still segregated from male political activities. Moreover, these women had to perform their domestic chores as well as their marketplace activities.

Social Stratification

As previously mentioned, agricultural civilizations were highly stratified, and social mobility was generally restricted to people with elite family or kinship backgrounds. Thus, sometimes anthropologists classify these societies as **closed societies**, in that social status was generally *ascribed* rather than *achieved*. For example, in traditional Chinese society, people born outside the emperor's family had two paths to upward mobility. One route was to be born into the gentry—the land-owning class that made up about 2 percent of Chinese families. The second route was to become a mandarin—a Chinese bureaucrat and scholar—by becoming a student and passing rigorous examinations based on classical Confucian texts. Although in theory this option existed for all males, in fact it was restricted to families or clans that could afford to spend resources for educating a son (DeVoe 2005).

The Caste System

India and some areas connected with Hindu culture such as Nepal developed a much more restrictive form of social inequality known as the caste system. A **caste** is an endogamous social grouping into which a person is born and in which the person remains throughout his or her lifetime. Thus, an individual's status in a caste system is ascribed, and movement into a different caste is impossible. The Indian caste system evolved from four basic categories, or *varnas*, that were ranked in order from Brahmans (priests) to Ksaitryas (warriors) to Vaisyas (merchants) to Sudras (laborers). Hence, the caste into which a person was born determined that person's occupation. In addition, people were required to marry within their caste. Although contact among members of different castes was generally discouraged, the castes were interrelated through various mutual economic exchanges and obligations known as the *jajmani* system. We discuss how the process of globalization is influencing the caste structure found in India and elsewhere in Chapter 15.

Slavery   Another form of social inequality and ascribed status was slavery. Slavery tends to increase as a society increases its productive technology, as trade expands, and as states become more centrally organized (Goody 1980; Van den Berghe 1981). For example, the Mediterranean empires of the Greeks, Romans, Arabs, and Turks used vast numbers of slaves in galleys, monument construction, irrigation works, plantation agriculture, and major public works projects.

Slave systems differed from one society to another. The Greeks and Romans reduced the status of the slave to a subhuman "thing" that was considered an instrument or tool, differing from inanimate tools only by the faculty of speech (Worsley 1984). Indigenous African kingdoms practiced large-scale slavery in which nobles owned hundreds of slaves (Goody 1980). Most of these slaves worked on plantations or in the household, although some became advisers and administrators for nobles. Although African slavery involved the capture and sale of human beings, eventually the slaves could be incorporated into the kinship groups.

In a comprehensive review of indigenous Asian and African slavery, anthropologist James Watson (1980) referred to *open* and *closed* forms of slavery. The indigenous African form of slavery was open in that slaves could be incorporated into domestic kinship groups and even become upwardly mobile. In contrast, the slave systems of China, India, Greece, and Rome were closed, with no opportunities for upward mobility or incorporation into kinship groups.

The two different types of slavery were correlated with specific demographic conditions and political economies. In societies such as Africa or Thailand, where land was relatively abundant and less populated, more open forms of slavery developed (Goody 1971; Turton 1980). In these societies, the key to power and authority was control over people rather than land. In political economies such as Greece, Rome, China, and India, where land was scarce and populations much more dense, closed forms of slavery emerged. The key to power and wealth in these societies was control over land and labor.

Racial and Ethnic Stratification

Related to slavery and a rigid social hierarchy was a pattern not found in nonstate societies: racial and ethnic stratification. Although "race" is not a scientifically useful concept (see Chapters 2 and 7), the term is often used to differentiate people according to skin color or other physical characteristics. In contrast, as we saw in Chapter 7, **ethnicity** refers to the cultural differences among populations, usually based on attributes such as language, religion, clothing, lifestyle, and ideas regarding common descent or specific territory.

As agricultural states expanded into surrounding environments, a variety of perceived "racially" and ethnically different peoples were incorporated into the growing empires. Some of these groups were band, tribal, or chiefdom societies that spoke different languages and maintained different cultural or ethnic traditions. Once conquered or absorbed, they frequently found themselves under the rule of a particular dominant ethnic group. In many cases, the dominant group ascribed subordinate social and cultural statuses to them. Sometimes the conquered group became slaves. In other cases its members were viewed as "racially" or ethnically inferior and were given only limited opportunities for upward mobility. Thus, many ethnic and racial minorities were identified as subordinate classes and stigmatized as inherently inferior.

With the intensification of social stratification in agricultural states, social distance between the ruling elite and the rest of the population was accentuated not only by rights to land, wealth, and power but also by restrictive sumptuary laws. For example, among the Aztecs, patterns of deference and demeanor between the rulers and the ruled were highly formalized. The Aztec nobility were distinguished by clothing and jewelry, and they were believed to be vested with divine status (Berdan 1982). Aztec commoners were required to prostrate themselves before the emperor and were not permitted to speak to him or look at him. Similar patterns of deference and social etiquette developed throughout the agricultural societies in the Old and New World.

Law

Agricultural states formalized legal decisions and punishments not only through laws but also through court systems, police, and legal specialists such as judges. In many of these societies, law became highly differentiated from customs, norms, tradition, and religious dogma (Vago 1995). Writing systems enabled many of these societies to keep records of court proceedings.

The first recognized codified laws originated in the Near Eastern civilization of Babylon. The Babylonian code of law, known as the Laws of Hammurabi, was based on standardized procedures and precedents for dealing with civil and criminal offenses. Other agricultural states, such as China, Rome, and India, developed formalized legal systems, including court systems. Morton Fried (1978) used evidence from the Hammurabi codes to

An Aztec scene painting.

demonstrate that these laws reinforced a system of inequality by protecting the rights of the governing class while keeping the peasants in a subordinate status. In other words, the codes of Hammurabi were designed to allow those in authority to have access to scarce resources.

In contrast, some anthropologists emphasized the benefits of codified laws for the maintenance of society (Service 1978b). They argued that the maintenance of social and political order was crucial for agricultural states. Serious disruptions would have led to the neglect of agricultural production, which would have had devastating consequences for all members of society. Thus, legal codes such as the Hammurabi codes, the Talmudic laws of the Israelites, the laws of Manu of India, the Confucianist codes of China, and the Roman imperial laws benefitted the peasants by maintaining social order, which made possible greater agricultural production.

Obviously, both of these perspectives provide useful insights into the role of law in agricultural states. Ruling elites developed these codified legal systems, but they also functioned to control crime and institute political order.

Mediation and Self-Help

Despite the emergence of codified systems, the practice of mediation and self-help in the redress of criminal offenses did not completely disappear. Rolando Tamayo demonstrated, for example, that these practices continued centuries after the development of the Greek state (Claessen et al. 1985). In addition, oaths, oracles, and ordeals remained as methods for determining legal decisions in many agricultural civilizations.

A Case Study: Law in China The legal system of China evolved through various dynasties, culminating in the complex legal codes of the Han dynasty (206 BC–AD 220). Chinese criminal codes specified punishments for each offense, ranging from blows with a cane to execution by strangulation, by decapitation, or even by slow slicing. Punishments also included hard labor and exile. Chinese civil law included rules on agricultural property, family, and inheritance.

Decisions involving civil law frequently were left to arbitration between the disputants in the local community. In this sense, many legal decisions depended on self-regulation of small groups. Use of written laws and the court system was generally restricted to cases that affected society as a whole. County magistrates familiar with the legal codes administered the law and recorded the decisions, which served as precedents for future cases. A hierarchy of judicial bodies from the county magistrates to the imperial court served as courts of appeal for serious cases. Despite the existence of a highly formalized court system, however, most scholars concur that Chinese law was weak. Because local magistrates had hundreds of thousands of people under their jurisdiction and the police force was weak, law enforcement was ineffective at the local level. Basic law enforcement relied instead on informal processes and sanctions administered by community leaders (Clayre 1985).

Warfare

Warfare was an integral aspect of agricultural state development. The state emerged, in most cases, as a result of conflict and competition among groups that eventually led to domination by a ruling group. Thus, with the emergence of state societies, warfare increased in scale and became much more organized. As governing elites accumulated more wealth and power, warfare became one of the major means of increasing their surpluses. Archaeologist Gordon Childe (1950), a conflict theorist, maintained that the ruling class in agricultural societies turned its energies from the conquest of nature to the conquest of people.

One cross-cultural study of external warfare by Keith Otterbein found that the capacity for organized warfare is much greater in agricultural state societies than in band and tribal societies. State societies usually have a centralized political and military leadership as well as professional armies and military training. In addition, surpluses of foodstuffs and luxury items frequently attract outside invaders, particularly nomadic pastoralists. Otterbein (1994) concluded that the primary motivation for warfare in state systems was to gain political control over other people. In the feudal societies of Western Europe and Japan, professional classes of knights and samurai protected the interests and resources of nobles. In addition, these warrior classes were used to wage offensive warfare against neighboring estates to increase landholdings and the supply of manpower.

Religion

As state societies emerged, cultural elements such as political power, authority, and religion became much more closely intertwined. The religious traditions that developed in most of the agricultural states are referred to as ecclesiastical religions, in which there is no separation between state and religious authority. Generally, all people in the political jurisdiction are required to belong to the religion, and there is little toleration for other belief systems.

Ecclesiastical Religions

Major ecclesiastical religious traditions emerged in agricultural civilizations around the world. Mesopotamia, Egypt, China, Greece, Rome, Mesoamerica, and South America developed some of the earliest **ecclesiastical religions**. These religious traditions were limited to the specific territory of these societies and were intimately tied to their particular state organization. The Mesopotamian, Egyptian, Confucian (Chinese), Greek, Roman, Mayan, Aztec, and Incan religious traditions integrated both political and religious functions for their own people. The Aztec religion emerged between the fourteenth and sixteenth centuries CE in the city they called Tenochtitlan, in the central valley region of present-day Mexico (Carrasco 2002; Fagan 1998). The Aztecs have moved from northern regions of Mesoamerica and conquered this region. They called the ancient city of Teotihuacan (100 BCE) that had been built years earlier the "Abode of the Gods." Teotihuacan was divided into four major quarters that had extensive pyramids, courtyards, residences, and craft industry factories producing pottery, weapons, and other goods. In the center of the city stood the Temple of Quetzacoatl, the most important temple for the Aztecs. Aztec rituals were led by the temple priests and included fasting, offering of flowers, foods, and cloths for sacrifices, as well as a variety of types of human sacrifices. The Maya and other Mesoamerican states had similar religions and rituals. In the ecclesiastical religions in many agricultural states such as Egypt, the Aztecs, Maya, China, Greece, and Rome, the government officials were often the priests who managed the rituals and maintained the textual traditions for these people.

Universalistic Religions

Other religious traditions that developed in early agricultural societies became **universalistic religions**, consisting of spiritual messages that were believed to apply to all of humanity rather than just to their own cultural heritage. There are two major branches of universalistic religions: One emerged in the Near East and led to the formation of the historically related religions of Judaism, Christianity, and Islam; the other developed in southern Asia and resulted in Hinduism and Buddhism.

These universalistic religious traditions are sometimes known as the great religious traditions. Although they began as universalistic traditions, in many cases they evolved into ecclesiastical religions identified with specific political regions. For example, many European nations established particular Christian denominations as state official religions.

Divine Rulers, Priests, and Religious Texts

Most of the early ecclesiastical religions taught that their rulers have divine authority. For example, the rulers of Mesopotamia and the pharaohs of Egypt were believed to be divine rulers upholding the moral and spiritual universe. Various Greek and Roman rulers attempted to have themselves deified during different historical periods. In South and Southeast Asia, political rulers known as *rajahs* were thought to have a semidivine status that was an aspect of their religious traditions. Even during later times in agricultural Europe, kings were believed to inherit their rule from God and sanctioned their rule through Christian traditions of "divine right."

Ecclesiastical religious traditions are based on written texts interpreted by professionally trained, full-time priests, who became the official custodians of the religious cosmologies and had official roles in the political hierarchy. They presided over state-organized rituals called **rites of legitimation**,

Great Giza pyramid of Egypt. Some early anthropologists believed that all civilizations stemmed from ancient Egypt.

which reinforced the divine authority of the ruler. In these rituals, the priests led prayers, chants, and hymns addressed to the kings and the various deities (Parrinder 1983; Fagan 1998). As in chiefdom societies, religion sanctified and legitimized the authority of political leaders.

One of the major functions of the priests was to standardize religious beliefs and practices for the society. Individualistic religious practices and beliefs were viewed as threatening to state authorities. For example, among the Maya, state authorities perceived the shamanistic practice of taking hallucinogens to control spirits as too individualistic. As the ecclesiastical religion developed, only the Mayan priests were allowed to take mind-altering drugs. Priests managed the use of these hallucinogens on behalf of state-organized ritual activities (Dobkin de Rios 1984).

The Collapse of State Societies

Perhaps no aspect of early agricultural states is more intriguing than the question of why many of them ceased to function. As discussed in the chapter opening, no agricultural states exist today in the same form that they did prior to AD 1500. Lost ruins, palaces hidden in tropical forests, and temples buried beneath shifting sand captivate the attention of archaeologists and the public alike. These images grip our attention all the more because of the lusterless prospect that the downfall of these ancient societies offers insight into the limitations of our own civilization. As Joseph Tainter (1990, 2) notes: "Whether or not collapse was the most outstanding event of ancient history, few would care for it to become the most significant event of the present era."

In looking at their demise, it is important to note that many early agricultural states were exceedingly successful. They flourished in many different world areas for hundreds of years. The ancient Egyptian Old Kingdom, which spanned a period of almost 1,000 years, is particularly notable, but many lasted longer than the 200-odd years the United States has been in existence. The apparent success of these states makes the reasons for their collapse all the more enigmatic. What accounts for the loss of centralized authority; the decline in stratification and social differentiation; the interruption of trade; and the fragmentation of large political units that seem to document the end of many different civilizations? These features extend beyond the end of specific governments or political systems; rather, they seem to reflect the breakdown of entire cultural systems.

Possible Reasons for Collapse

In examining the downfall of complex societies, writers have posited many different theories. Among the earliest were notions that collapse was somehow an innate, inevitable aspect of society, to be likened to the aging of a biological organism. Plato, for example, wrote that "since all created things must decay, even a social order . . . cannot last forever, but will decline" (quoted in Tainter 1990, 74). Although romantically appealing, such interpretations lack explanatory value and cannot be evaluated by empirical observation.

More recent scholars and archaeologists have sought a more precise understanding of the factors that contributed to collapse. Many theories have focused on the depletion of key resources as a result of human mismanagement or climatic change. In an agricultural state, conditions that interfered with or destroyed the society's ability to produce agriculture surplus would have had serious consequences. If the society was unable to overcome this depletion, collapse would result. Reasons such as this have been posited as contributing to the collapse of complex societies such as Mesopotamia (Adams 1981), Egypt (Butzer 1984), and Mesoamerica (Haas 1982). In some cases, researchers have suggested that resource depletion may be the result of sudden catastrophic events such as earthquakes, volcanic eruptions, or floods, which have an impact on agricultural lands as well as other resources (Fagan 2004). One of the most well-known theories of this kind links the destruction of Minoan civilization in the Mediterranean to the eruption of the Santorini volcano on the island of Thera (Marinatos 1939).

Other theories have suggested that conditions within societies have led to collapse. Many of these theories stress the tension or conflict resulting from social stratification. For example, mismanagement, excessive taxes, demands for food and labor, or other forms of exploitation by a ruling class are seen as instigating revolts or uprisings by the disaffected peasant class. Without the support of the peasants, the political system cannot function and the state collapses (Yoffe 1979; Guha 1981; Lowe 1985).

Alternatively, some researchers have viewed collapse as the result of the societies' failure to respond to changing conditions. For example, the late anthropologist Elman Service (1960, 97)

argued: "The more specialized and adapted a form in a given evolutionary stage, the smaller its potential for passing to the next stage." Underlying this interpretation is the assumption that successful adaptation to a particular environmental or cultural setting renders a society inflexible and unable to adapt to changing conditions. In this setting, less complex societies with greater flexibility overthrew older states.

Anthropologist Joseph Tainter notes in a survey that most of the models that have been presented focus on specific case studies, not on the understanding of collapse as a general phenomenon. He points out that most researchers assume that the decline in complexity associated with collapse is a catastrophe: "An end to the artistic and literary features of civilization, and the umbrella of service and protection that an administration provides, are seen as fearful events, truly paradise lost" (Tainter 1990; 197). Tainter argues that, in reality, collapse represents a logical choice in the face of declining returns. When people's investment in complexity fails to produce benefits, they opt for disintegration.

Anthropological explanations concerning the collapse of agricultural states can be evaluated in light of ethnographic, historical, and archaeological evidence. Upon surveying information from different states, it appears that reasons for collapse are exceedingly complex. The specific manifestation varies in individual settings, just as the specific features that define states differ. Adequate appraisal is dependent on the existence of a great deal of information about the society under study, including its technological capabilities, population, agricultural yields, internal and external warfare, and climatic conditions in the region. The difficulty involved in assessing competing models is perhaps best illustrated by the fact that very different hypotheses have often been used to explain the decline of the same society. Anthropologists are committed to offer more comprehensive explanations of the collapse of various agricultural societies using more refined and sophisticated technologies and methods as they develop in the future.

As stated in the beginning of this chapter, no agricultural state exists today in any part of the world in the same way it did prior to AD 1500. In Chapters 14 and 15, we discuss how contemporary globalization trends beginning with European colonialism in the 1500s and onward have resulted in dramatic transformations in these various agricultural societies presently. We need to understand conditions of these agricultural societies as much as possible to offer more comprehensive explanations of globalization and its impact on these societies today.

SUMMARY

The development of agricultural societies resulted from the expansion of the Neolithic period that involved the domestication of plants and animals, which provided a more reliable food supply and thus allowed for population growth, the emergence of cities, the specialization of labor, technological complexity, and many other features that are characteristic of agricultural states. Anthropologists and geographers have found that various ecological conditions such as large river valleys and plants and animals that were easily domesticated were more conducive to the rise of agricultural states and developments than others.

States are societies that have bureaucratic organizations, or governments. State societies emerged with the development of intensive agriculture.

The demographic conditions of agricultural civilizations included a rise in mortality rates along with increases in fertility rates. Agricultural states often encouraged high fertility rates to raise population levels for political purposes. The technological developments associated with agricultural societies represented dramatic innovations in metallurgy, shipbuilding, paper making, printing, and many scientific endeavors.

The political economy of agricultural states varied from region to region. In some areas, large-scale, centralized empires emerged, such as in China and Egypt. In other areas, smaller-scale states developed that did not have complete political control over outlying regions. After the fall of some centralized states in Europe and Japan, a type of decentralized political economy known as feudalism developed.

Different forms of property relations developed, depending on whether an agricultural state was centralized or feudal. In the centralized states, property was owned and administered by the government, whereas in feudal regimes lords and nobles owned their estates. Long-distance trade and government-regulated monetary exchange systems developed in agricultural societies. Within the context of long-distance trade and monetary exchange, merchants and markets emerged.

The social organization of agricultural states consisted of extended families and other descent groups, including lineages, clans, and kindreds. Marriages in agricultural societies were arranged by parents and based on political and economic considerations. In contrast to prestate societies, polygyny (except among the elite) and bridewealth were not widespread among agricultural state societies. Instead, monogamy and dowry exchanges were the major patterns. Divorce was infrequent.

Gender relations became more patriarchal in agricultural societies, possibly reflecting the reduced participation of females in agricultural labor. Females were largely confined to the domestic sphere, and various patterns of female seclusion developed in many of these societies, although variations in the status of women appeared in some of these agricultural states.

Social stratification in agricultural societies was based on class, caste, slavery, and racial and ethnic stratification. Some of these societies have been described as closed societies, with little opportunity for social mobility. Formalized legal systems developed, codifying laws administered by courts and government authorities. However, self-help and mediation were also used to resolve disputes.

Ecclesiastical religions developed in agricultural societies, with full-time priests, religious texts, and concepts of divine rulers associated with particular state societies. Some universalistic religious traditions developed in the Near East and Asia. Archaeologists continue to offer explanations of what led to the collapse of various agricultural states in differing regions of the world by examining factors such as ecological conditions, climatic factors, internal and external warfare, and many other conditions. Although no agricultural states remain intact today, many of the earlier cultural traditions and practices such as religious cosmologies and beliefs have resonance for billions of people throughout the world.

QUESTIONS TO THINK ABOUT

1. How do agricultural states differ demographically from small-scale societies such as bands, tribes, and chiefdoms?

2. Discuss some of the technological innovations developed in agricultural states.

3. How do segmentary states and theater states differ from the Aztec, Roman, and Chinese empires?

4. How do property rights differ in agricultural states from those in forager and tribal societies?

5. What are some of the advantages of having an extended family organization in an agricultural state, as opposed to an autonomous nuclear family?

6. Are marriage patterns and social ties in agricultural states independent of economic and political considerations? If so, why? If not, what are some of the economic and political implications of marriage patterns and other social ties?

7. Discuss the relationships among gender, subsistence, and status in agricultural states. How does the picture that emerges differ from the one for any of the following groups: (1) foragers, (2) tribes, or (3) chiefdoms?

8. According to Morton Fried, codified laws reinforce a system of inequity by keeping peasants subordinate while allowing those in power to have access to scarce resources. Elman Service provides a different perspective. What is Service's perspective?

9. How does religion interact with state power and bureaucratic authority in agricultural civilizations? Give examples of the relationship between the state and religion in these agricultural societies.

KEY TERMS

caste
civilization
closed societies
command economy
dowry
ecclesiastical religions
ethnicity

feudalism
galactic polity
intensive agriculture
moral economy
peasants
purdah
radial polity

rites of legitimation
theater state
tributary mode
tribute
universalistic religions

Chapter **13**

Industrial States

CHAPTER OUTLINE

THE COMMERCIAL, SCIENTIFIC, AND INDUSTRIAL REVOLUTION

Modernization

ENVIRONMENT AND ENERGY USE

DEMOGRAPHIC CHANGE

The Demographic Transition / Urbanization

TECHNOLOGY AND ECONOMIC CHANGE

Technology and Work / The Division of Labor / Economic Exchange / Perspectives on Market Economies / The Evolution of Economic Organizations / Capitalist Consumer Societies

SOCIAL STRUCTURE

Kinship / Family / Marriage / Gender / Age

SOCIAL STRATIFICATION

The British Class System / Class in the United States / Class in Japan and the Former Soviet Union / Ethnic and Racial Stratification

POLITICAL ORGANIZATION

Political Organization in Socialist States / Industrialism and State Bureaucracy

LAW

Japanese Law

WARFARE AND INDUSTRIAL TECHNOLOGY

RELIGION

Religion in Socialist States / Religion in Japan

CHAPTER QUESTIONS

- What were some of the historical changes that resulted in the Industrial Revolution?

- What are some of the energy-use patterns and technological changes associated with industrial societies?

- What are the characteristics of the economy in industrial societies?

- How did the Industrial Revolution influence the status and role of family, gender, and age?

- Why are industrial societies considered to be more "open" in social stratification than pre-industrial societies?

- What are the characteristics of politics, law, and warfare in industrial societies?

- What are the consequences of industrialization for religion in industrial societies?

The *Industrial Revolution* is the term used to describe the broad changes that occurred during the latter part of the eighteenth century in Europe. However, the roots of these dramatic changes in the structure and organization of society were there much earlier. This chapter considers the causes of the Industrial Revolution and its consequences for the states in which it occurred. This is an extremely important topic, because it emphasizes how anthropologists interpret and explain the development of the Industrial Revolution in Europe, rather than in other regions of the world. Traditionally, most cultural anthropologists did research on preindustrial societies, as discussed in Chapters 9 through 13. However, many cultural anthropologists have turned their attention to doing ethnography in the industrial regions of the world, including Europe, Russia, the United States, Canada, Australia, and Japan. These cultural anthropologists have to take a highly interdisciplinary approach, drawing on the work of historians, economists, political scientists, and sociologists. The chapter uses much of the research of these other disciplines, as well as the studies of cultural anthropologists.

An **industrial society** uses sophisticated technology based on machinery powered by advanced fuels to produce material goods. A primary feature of industrial societies in comparison with preindustrial societies is that most productive labor involves factory and office work, rather than agricultural or foraging activities. This pattern has produced new forms of economic organization and social-class arrangements. In terms of political organization, industrial societies became the first well-developed **nation-states**—political communities that have clearly defined territorial borders dividing them from one another. All modern industrial nation-states exercise extensive political authority over many aspects of the lives of their citizenry through the application of formalized laws and a centralized government.

The Commercial, Scientific, and Industrial Revolution

One of the traditional explanations of why Europe succeeded in developing the Industrial Revolution and that other societies did not is that Europeans were superior to other people mentally and intellectually. Anthropologists do not accept this claim of European mental and intellectual superiority. This idea has a long history that is connected with racist beliefs that go back deep into Western history (see Chapter 7 on race). These racist views believe that other races of people were cognitively deficient and incapable of developing advanced technology, and that is why Europe was the center of the rise of industrial society. Again, anthropologists have refuted the basis of these racist arguments through systematic biological, archaeological, and cultural research throughout the world (see Chapters 2 and 7).

The influential book by Jared Diamond called *Guns, Germs, and Steel: The Fate of Human Societies* (1997), mentioned in earlier chapters and which draws on an enormous amount of geographical, archaeological, and anthropological research, demonstrates that the European Industrial Revolution did not develop as the result of the "unique" genius, intelligence, or particular superior cultural values of Europeans, but as an unpredictable sequence of prehistoric and historical processes. As mentioned in

Chapter 12, most of the plants and large mammals that could be domesticated existed in the Near East, and this pattern of plant and animal domestication spread into the Eurasian continent that included China and Europe. Europe, the Near East, and the Asian land mass were contiguous with one another. Harvests were abundant, and domesticated animals enabled the Near Easterners, Europeans, and Asians to develop cities with large populations, governments, specialized economic systems, and writing systems, as described in Chapter 12. In addition, there were no major obstacles such as geographical barriers—for example, rain forests—or large mountain barriers that inhibited the spread and diffusion of this agricultural package across the Near East and Mediterranean areas to the Eurasian continent. Centuries later, the Europeans developed the technological knowledge and political power to conquer other areas of the world that did not have these resources. For example, as mentioned in Chapter 12, Africa and the Americas lacked easily domesticated species of animals for agriculture. The Near Easterners, Europeans, and Asians developed resistance to certain diseases as a result of living with domesticated animals such as cattle and pigs for many years. The diffusion of agriculture and domesticated animals happened quickly in Europe and Asia because, unlike Africa and the Americas, there were no substantial geographic barriers such as oceans, deserts, and rain forests. This gave Europe the edge in the initial beginnings of the Industrial Revolution. China was almost to the same point of development in the 1600s, but for historical and political reasons China did not begin to expand beyond its boundaries. Consequently, Europe, not China, became the center of the Industrial Revolution during that period.

Anthropologists address the question of why Europe was the center of the Industrial Revolution by drawing on a wide range of historical sources from many regions of the world. A global perspective is the only way of trying to answer this question. Anthropologists such as Jack Goody (1996) and Eric Wolf (1997) have adopted this global perspective and have examined the interrelationships between the non-European world and Europe to provide answers to this question.

A major factor leading to the emergence of industrial states in European society was the increased contact among different societies, primarily through trade. Although, as discussed in the last chapter, long-distance trade was present in agricultural states, the major regions of the world were relatively isolated from one another. Trade was conducted in Asia, the Near East, Europe, Africa, and internally within the Americas before AD 1500, but the difficulties of transportation and communication inhibited the spread of ideas, values, and technology among these regions. Although Europeans had contact with non-Europeans through religious wars such as the Crusades and the travels of adventurers such as Marco Polo, they did not engage in systematic relations with non-Europeans until after the year 1500.

The upper class and royalty of agricultural European society encouraged long-distance trade as a means of accumulating wealth. Their principal motivation was to build a self-sufficient economy as a basis for extending their centralized government. This type of economic system is often referred to as *mercantilism*. **Mercantilism** is a system in which the government regulates the economy of a state to ensure economic growth, a positive balance of trade, and the accumulation of gold and silver. One key mercantilist strategy was for the government to grant monopolies to trading companies so that these companies could accumulate wealth for the home country. The European upper classes were also attempting to compete with the Islamic and Asian trade that predominated in the East. These elites formed an alliance with merchants to support their endeavors (Wolf 1997). Thus, for example, during the fifteenth and sixteenth centuries, the rulers of Spain and Portugal sponsored private traders who explored the world to search for wealth. These expeditions eventually established ports of trade in Africa, the Americas, and Asia.

Eventually European countries such as the Netherlands, Great Britain, France, and Russia became mercantile competitors with Spain and Portugal. They formed private trading companies such as the British East India Company, which were subsidized by the government. These companies were given special rights to engage in trade in specific regions. In turn, they were expected to find both sources of wealth and luxury goods that could be consumed by the ruling classes.

One result of this mercantilist trade was the beginning of global unity (Chirot 1986; Wolf 1997). European explorers visited every part of the globe. An enormous diffusion of plants, animals, humans,

technology, and ideas took place among Europe, America, and the rest of the world. Cultures from every region of the world began to confront each other. These encounters led to new patterns of trade, political developments, and the transmission of beliefs, ideas, and practices. European traders backed by military force began to compete with other traders from the Middle East and Asia. Soon, through the use of military force, European trade came to displace the Asian and Islamic trading empires. As economic wealth began to amass in Europe, through the accumulation of gold, silver, and other commodities from the Americas, Asia, Africa, and the Middle East, the political center of power also swung to Europe. These economic and political changes were accompanied by major transformations in non-Western societies. These changes in non-Western societies are discussed in later chapters.

The global diffusion of philosophical and practical knowledge provided the basis for the scientific revolution in the West. Ideas and technology that were developed in the civilizations of China, India, the Middle East, Africa, and the Americas provided the stimulus for the emergence of scientific enterprise in Europe. Eventually, scientific methods based on deductive and inductive logic (see Chapter 1) were allied with practical economic interests to provide the basis for the Industrial Revolution in Europe. But again, many of the ideas and technological developments that gave rise to the Industrial Revolution in Europe had emerged earlier in agricultural civilizations in other regions of the world. The scientific revolution would not have developed in Europe without the knowledge of scientific and mathematical concepts previously developed in India, the Middle East, and Asia.

The notion that there was a unique European miracle that was associated with the so-called white race is a fallacy. The idea that Europeans were superior geniuses who were capable of developing the industrial civilization is also a fallacy. Without the diffusion of knowledge and technologies from other regions of the world, Europe would not have been able to develop the Industrial Revolution. Slowly and gradually, over a period of some 400 years, the combination of scientific and commercial alliances in Europe produced dramatic consequences that transformed economic, social, and political structures through the process of **industrialization**—the adoption of a mechanized means of production to transform raw materials into manufactured goods.

Modernization

The overall consequences of the Industrial Revolution are often referred to as **modernization**—the economic, social, political, and religious changes related to modern industrial and technological change. Modernization was not an overnight occurrence. It took more than 400 years, from 1600 on, to develop in the West, and modernity remains an ongoing process. It depended on the commercial transformations brought about through years of mercantilism that led to the accumulation of capital for investment and the gradual diffusion of practical knowledge and scientific methods that engendered technological innovations.

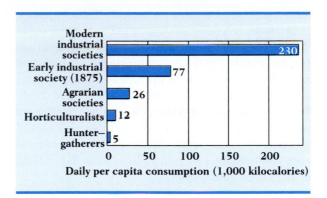

FIGURE 13.1 Energy consumption among the various types of societies. Note the dramatic increase in consumption in the modern industrial societies. *Source:* Adapted from Earl Cook, "The Flow of Energy in an Industrial Society," *Scientific American* 224(3) (1971): 136. Reprinted by permission of the Estate of Bunji Tagawa.

Environment and Energy Use

In earlier chapters, we saw how the availability of resources affects levels of political and economic development. States and chiefdoms emerged in areas with abundant resources, whereas other environments could support only bands and tribes. Environmental conditions also had an influence on the early phases of industrialization. Industrial societies still depended heavily on agricultural production to meet basic food requirements, but through industrialization, agricultural production itself was transformed. The major natural-resource requirements for industrial societies are based on harnessing new sources of energy, especially fossil-fuel energy.

In Chapter 3 we discussed Leslie White's attempt to explain sociocultural evolution in terms of energy use. He suggested that sociocultural evolution progressed in relationship to the harnessing of energy. A number of anthropologists, including anthropologist John Bodley (1985), attempted to quantify White's ideas. He suggested that sociocultural systems can be divided into *high-energy cultures* and *low-energy cultures*, and that these categories have implications for the evolution of society. For example, before the Industrial Revolution, no states used more than 26,000 kilocalories per capita daily, and tribal hunters and farmers used between 4,000 and 12,000. These societies are classified as low-energy cultures. In contrast, early

industrial societies using fossil fuels almost tripled their consumption of energy to 70,000 kilocalories. Later phases of industrialization in high-energy cultures such as the United States experienced a quadrupling of energy consumption. Energy use and expenditure have risen dramatically in all industrial societies (see Figure 13.1).

In the low-energy, preindustrial societies, human and nonhuman animal labor was the chief source of energy, supplemented by firewood, wind, and sometimes waterpower. In contrast, in high-energy societies, fossil fuels such as coal, natural gas, and petroleum became the primary energy sources. During the early phases of the Industrial Revolution, societies in Europe and America relied on fossil fuels found in their own territories, but they eventually began to exploit resources from other regions. In later chapters we examine the consequences of these patterns of high-energy use on the different environments of the world.

Demographic Change

One major consequence of the early phases of the Industrial Revolution was a dramatic increase in population. The major reasons for this were technological developments in agriculture and transportation that enabled farmers to grow more food and transport it to areas with food scarcities. In addition, scientific advances led to the control of some infectious diseases, such as the bubonic plague, diphtheria, typhus, and cholera, which had kept death rates high in preindustrial societies. As death rates declined, birth rates remained high. The combination of lower death rates with high birth rates produced major population increases of about 3 percent annually. Europe's population grew from about 140 million in 1750 to 463 million in 1914 (Staviranos 1995).

The Demographic Transition

During later phases of industrialization (especially since the 1960s), population growth began to decline in societies like England, Western Europe, the United States, and Japan (Population Reference Bureau 1986). Demographers refer to this change as the **demographic transition**, in which birth rates and death rates decline. In contrast to preindustrial societies, in which high birth rates were perceived as beneficial, in industrial societies many people no longer see large families as a benefit. One reason for this view is the higher costs of rearing children in industrial societies. In addition, social factors such as changing gender relations—more women in the workforce and the reduction in family size— have contributed to lower fertility rates. (These social factors are discussed later in this chapter.) Increased knowledge of, and access to, family planning and contraceptives helped people to control family size. Even in Roman Catholic countries that discourage family planning and birth control, individuals are controlling the size of their families. For example, the Roman Catholic country of Italy has one of the lowest fertility rates in the world.

Italy has one of the lowest fertility rates in the world.

Urbanization

Population increases, coupled with the movement of workers from farms to factories, resulted in the unprecedented growth of urban centers (see Table 13.1). During the nineteenth century, the populations of cities such as London, Paris, and Chicago soared into the millions. By 1930, one-fifth of all humanity, or approximately 415 million people, lived in urban areas (Mumford 1961; Stavrianos 1995). One of the major factors causing rapid urban growth was the increasing need for labor in the machine-based factory system. Factory towns like Manchester, England, grew into large industrial centers connected to financial and communications districts.

Table 13.1	Population in Selected Industrial Cities	
City	1995 (thousands)	2015 (projected) Density
Tokyo	26,959	28,887
New York	16,332	17,602
Los Angeles	12,410	14,217

Source: Reprinted from *The World Almanac and Book of Facts 1999.* Copyright © 1998 World Almanac Education Group. All rights reserved.

Technology and Economic Change

Industrialization was fueled by a series of technological innovations that occurred after the middle of the eighteenth century. The major change was a movement from human and animal labor to mechanical, or machine, labor. More recently, through science, engineering, and commerce, technological innovations ranging from automobiles to electronics to computers have continued to transform industrial societies. These technologies have not only made communication and transportation more efficient but have also contributed to a vast international global economic network in which all societies can interact. Through the Internet, the World Wide Web, e-mail, fax, telephones, television, and satellite transmissions, societies are increasingly linked to a global economy.

Technology and Work

The technological revolution transformed basic work conditions. The factory system imposed a new work pace and led to a new form of discipline for laborers. Factory and mine workers were organized around the machine's schedule, and work became increasingly time-oriented. Most work

in the early factories was highly routinized and repetitious.

Preindustrial workers had some control over the quantity and quality of their products and the pace of their labor, but early industrial workers had little control over these matters. Karl Marx, a major critic of industrial capitalism, saw that industrial workers were estranged and alienated from their work conditions and that they viewed their labor as meaningless and beyond their control.

The Division of Labor

The division of labor in industrial economies is much more complex than it is in preindustrial economies. Industrial economies have three identifiable sectors, which correspond to the division of labor. The **primary sector** represents the part of the industrial economy devoted to the extraction of raw materials and energy; it includes agriculture, lumber, fishing, and mining. The **secondary sector** includes the factories that take the raw materials and process them for consumption. The **tertiary sector**, sometimes referred to as the *service sector*, includes the financial and banking industries and other industries, such as automobile repair, communications, health care, computer services, government, and education.

Large metropolitan urban areas are typical in industrial societies.

In the first phases of industrialization, most of the labor force was engaged in the *primary sector*, extracting raw materials for industrial production. Further mechanization of industry led to an increase of the labor force in the *secondary*, or manufacturing, sector. These workers are the manual, or "blue-collar," workers. Finally, in the advanced phases of industrialization, an increasing percentage of the labor force has become located in the *tertiary* sector, or various service industries.

Currently, in the most advanced industrial societies—such as the United States, the United Kingdom, Japan, Germany, Canada, and Australia— the *tertiary sector* is the largest and most rapidly expanding component of the economy. Some sociologists refer to these societies as *postindustrial societies*, because more people are employed in service and high-technical computerized occupations than in manufacturing. Information is the key component of a postindustrial economy, because people must acquire a great deal of technical knowledge to function effectively, and educational requirements for many jobs have increased substantially. Sometimes postindustrial societies are referred to as *postfordism*, the type of society that was manufacturing-based like Henry Ford's auto company in the early twentieth century in the United States. To meet the demands of a postindustrial economy, an increasing percentage of the population attends college (and graduate and professional schools), and computer skills have been integrated into the educational curriculum. With their capacity to process and manipulate vast amounts of data, computers have become essential in these societies. Anthropologists are doing extensive ethnographic research on the development of this postindustrial society in numerous societies everywhere (McCreery 2000; McCreery and McCreery 2005; Denoon et al. 2001; Lewellen 2002; Harvey 1990).

Economic Exchange

Like other types of societies, industrial states engage in reciprocal and redistributional economic exchanges. Reciprocal exchanges, such as Christmas gifts and gifts of funds for college tuition, frequently occur within the family. The graduated income tax in U.S. society represents one form of redistributional exchange in which income is collected from some people and flows back to society. Taxes also represent a form of tributary economic exchange, which is characteristic of agricultural states.

Market Economies   In addition to these activities, industrial states developed a new pattern of exchange based on a market economy. A **market economy** is a pattern of economic exchange based on the value of goods and services determined by

The New York Stock Exchange represents the peak development of a market-driven economy.

the supply and demand of items such as commodities, land, and also labor. The evolution of the market economy, linked with industrial technological developments, radically changed the way goods and services are produced and exchanged in industrial societies. Goods and services are assigned monetary value and are bought and sold with general-purpose money. The prices of these goods and services depend on the supply and demand of the goods and services on the world market.

Moreover, in the market economy the basic factors of production—land, labor, and capital—are assigned monetary prices and are bought and sold freely in the marketplace. Thus, rather than kinship or prominent leaders, market forces determine the general process of economic exchange.

In agricultural societies, goods and services were bought and sold in regional or local markets. These markets, however, were not based on market exchange; instead, buyers and sellers met and haggled over the price of goods. This is a type of nonmarket price determination. In contrast, in industrial societies, buyers and sellers do not have to meet face to face. Buyers can compare prices from different sellers, and the prices themselves are established according to supply and demand. Impersonality and lack of haggling between buyer and seller are the general patterns in market exchanges.

Perspectives on Market Economies

Market forces based on the supply and demand of land, labor, and capital began to drive economic production, exchange, and consumption in industrial societies. The market process, which determined the prices of these factors of production, exerted tremendous influence over all aspects of these industrializing societies. The new economic forces and processes were described by the "father of modern economics," Adam Smith. In his book *The Wealth of Nations* ([1776] 1937), Smith argued that both buyers and sellers would reap rewards from market exchange and competition, because prices would be lower for consumers and profits higher for sellers. The result would be increased prosperity for all segments of society. Smith viewed the market economy as a mechanism for promoting progress.

In contrast, 100 years later, Karl Marx offered a gloomier picture of industrial societies. Marx focused on how the market economy determined the price and organization of human labor, bringing about misery for millions of people. Marx believed that industrial capitalist societies must be transformed to a new form of socialist society in which the factors of production would not be driven by the market but would be controlled by the *state* to ensure an even division of profits among all classes.

Eventually, both capitalist and socialist forms of industrial societies developed in different regions of the world. To highlight some of the variations of industrial societies, we next examine the development of capitalism and socialism in some of these regions.

Capitalism As is evident from the previous discussion, the Industrial Revolution was intricately connected with the emergence of capitalism in Western societies. **Capitalism** is an economic system in which natural resources as well as the means of producing and distributing goods and services are privately owned. Capitalist societies share three basic ideals: first, the factors of production are privately owned, and an emphasis on private property has become the standard incorporated into all economic, legal, and political documents of capitalist societies; second, companies are free to maximize profits and accumulate as much capital as they can; third, free competition and consumer sovereignty are basic to all economic activities. Ideally, people are free to buy and sell at whatever prices they can to satisfy their own interests. Also, government regulation of economic affairs is usually discouraged.

Capitalism in the United States Capitalism spread into North America following the settling of colonies by British and other European peoples. The English had incorporated major portions of North America as a colony during the mercantile period. But eventually, the Americans, whose ancestors had originally been colonists, began to control their own economic and political destinies, which led to the American Revolution of the late eighteenth century. Following independence, capitalist economic development and industrialization proceeded rapidly in the United States. Bountiful natural resources provided the raw materials for factory production, and millions of immigrants arrived from Europe, providing a source of cheap labor for factories. The U.S. economy grew quickly, and by 1894 the nation had the world's fastest-growing economy.

Despite the ideals of pure capitalism, which discouraged government regulation of the economy, the U.S. government actively encouraged industrial economic expansion through state subsidies, protective tariffs, and other policies. For example, the government promoted the development of a nationwide railroad system by providing large financial incentives, rights to land, and subsidies to individual capitalists. In addition, through the Homestead Act of 1862 free land was given to people who wanted to settle frontier regions.

By the late nineteenth century, rapid economic expansion had produced a new moneyed class that held a great proportion of assets. A relatively small number of people controlled a large number of industries and other commercial enterprises of finance and capital. The wealthiest 1 percent of the population owned about one-third of all capital assets (wealth in land or other private property). Economic expansion also spurred the growth of a large middle class that exerted a powerful influence on both the economic and political structure of U.S. society.

Capitalism in Japan   As we discussed in the last chapter, Japan was an agricultural feudal society from the period of the first *shogunate* in the twelfth century until about 1870, after which it rapidly industrialized. Following a period of historical isolation from the West during the Tokugawa period (1600–1870), Japan was forced to open its doors to outside powers such as the United States. The Japanese recognized the technological advancements of the Western world, and, to avoid being colonized like other Asian countries, they rapidly modified their society to accommodate industrial capitalism. But the socioeconomic and political conditions that made possible rapid capitalist development existed before Japan's intensive contact with the West.

For example, during the isolated period of the Tokugawa period, internal trade and entrepreneurial developments flourished in highly developed urban centers such as Tokyo and Kyoto. Moreover, Japan had a highly educated class of *samurai*, who were in a position to bring about innovations in society (Befu 1971; McCreery and McCreery 2006).

Following the opening of Japan to the West, the Japanese abandoned the feudal system and centralized their government under the Meiji emperor. With help from Western advisers (1868–1911), the Meiji government introduced a mandatory education system and modern military technology. The government also took concrete steps to help introduce capitalism (Geertz 1963b; McCreery and McCreery 2005). It taxed the peasants to raise money for industrialization and subsidized certain entrepreneurial families, the *zaibatsu*, who gained control of the major industrial technologies. Families such as the Mitsubishi family were encouraged to invest in needed industries to compete with Western interests. Thus, the government developed key industries in Japan by cooperating with private interests and families.

Socialism   A different type of economic system developed in some industrial societies as a historical response to capitalism. **Socialism** is an economic system in which the state, ideally as the representative of the people, owns the basic means of production. Although individuals may own some consumer goods such as housing and automobiles, they are not allowed to own stock in corporations or wealth-generating property related to the production of capital goods. Socialism evolved as a response to the considerable economic inequalities that existed in capitalist societies. To create more economic equality and less exploitation of working people, socialist philosophers promoted ideals that contrasted with those of capitalism. Socialist ideals maintained that meeting the population's basic needs takes precedence over the enrichment of a small number of people.

Socialism in the Former Soviet Union   In contrast to Marx's predictions that socialist revolutions would occur in industrial societies, socialism initially developed in Russia, which was primarily agricultural and feudal. From about AD 1000, the basic form of land tenure in Russia was based on the mir, or peasant commune, which was linked to feudal estates to which the serfs provided labor (Dunn and Dunn 1988). During the nineteenth century, feudalism was abolished, and the serfs were freed from the estates. The Russian economy, however, remained largely dependent on wheat exports and Western capital (Chirot 1986; Gellner 1988; Ensminger 2002).

As in Japan, the Russian elites realized that they had to industrialize quickly if they were to survive.

Soviet factory workers in the 1930s were mobilized by the state to develop heavy industry.

The central government subsidized industrialization by taxing the peasantry heavily and importing European industrial technology. As a result, Russia gradually began to industrialize. However, the new economic burdens on peasant society, a military defeat by the Japanese in 1905, and the widespread suffering produced by World War I severely weakened the government of the emperor, or czar. The result was the Russian Revolution of 1917.

Under the leadership of Vladimir Lenin, the new Soviet state implemented a number of policies designed to create a more egalitarian society that would meet the basic needs of all the people. All wealth-generating property (the means of production) was placed under government control. The government collectivized agriculture by taking land from landowners and distributing the peasant population on collective, state-controlled farms. State authorities systematically regulated all prices and wages. In addition, the government—through a centralized system of Five-Year Plans—initiated a policy of rapid industrialization to try to catch up with the West.

Hybrid Economic Systems To some extent, neither capitalism nor socialism exists in pure form according to the ideals espoused by their leading theorists. Government intervention in the economy exists in both types of economic systems. In some industrial societies such as Sweden, and to a lesser extent in Western Europe and England, a hybrid form of eco-

nomic system referred to as democratic socialism developed. In these societies, the key strategic industries that produce basic capital goods and services are government owned, as are certain heavy industries such as steel and coal and utilities such as telephone companies. At the same time, much of the economy and technology is privately owned, and production takes place for private profit. Some politicians and citizens support this mixed hybrid form of economy in the United States, whereas others resist it vehemently. On the other hand, some of the hybrid economic systems such as Sweden are beginning to move away from these mixed systems and introduce more privatization to reduce economic, social, and medical costs for their governments.

The Evolution of Economic Organizations

As industrial economies developed in capitalist, socialist, and democratic-socialist societies, the major economic organizations increased in size and complexity. In capitalist societies, family businesses grew into corporations, which were established as legal entities to raise capital through the sale of stocks and bonds. Eventually, these corporations increased their economic holdings and were able to concentrate their ownership on the society's major technology. Through expansion and mergers, they came to dominate economic production and exchange. The result was **oligopoly**, in which a few giant corporations control production in major industries. For example, in the United States in the early 1900s, there were thirty-five domestic automobile companies, but by the 1950s only three remained. This process of corporate expansion ushered in a phase of capitalism known as **monopoly capitalism**, a form of capitalism dominated by large corporations that can reduce free competition through the concentration of capital. This concentration of capital enables oligopolies to control prices and thereby dominate the markets.

In socialist societies such as the former Soviet Union, in which private ownership of technology was prohibited, the government controls and manages the major economic organizations. The equivalent of the large capitalist corporation is the state-owned enterprise that has some degree of financial autonomy, although government authorities established production goals. The majority of state enterprises were still small or medium in size, but the enterprises of the former Soviet state became more concentrated (Kerblay 1983; Ensminger 2002). These enterprises followed the production aims established by the various ministries, which were ultimately controlled by Communist Party officials.

Multinational Corporations In the capitalist, socialist, and hybrid economic systems, corporations increased in size to become large multinational corporations with enormous assets. **Multinational corporations** are economic organizations that operate in many different regions of the world. Multinational corporations are based in their home countries but own subsidiaries in many other countries. For example, American-based I.T.T., a multinational corporation with more than 400,000 employees, has offices in 68 different countries. Although approximately 300 of the 500 largest multinational corporations are based in the United States, others, such as Unilever, Shell, and Mitsubishi, are based in England, Western Europe, and Japan,

respectively. The socialist societies of the former Soviet Union and former Eastern European countries had large state-owned multinational corporations that coordinated their activities through what was known as Comecon (a committee that coordinated multinational activities worldwide).

The evolution of the multinational corporation has had tremendous consequences for the global economy. Anthropologist Alvin Wolfe proposed that multinational corporations are beginning to evolve into supranational organizations that are stronger than the nation-state (1977, 1986). Reed Riner (1981) described how various multinational corporations are interconnected in the world global economy. The top CEOs in the various multinational corporations sit on one another's boards of directors. In addition, the multinational corporations are increasingly involved in joint ventures, consolidating their capital assets and technologies to produce goods and services throughout the world. We consider the effects of these multinational corporations in different societies in later chapters.

APPLYING ANTHROPOLOGY

Studying Industrial Corporations

The image of cultural anthropologists is changing. The typical image of a cultural anthropologist is of a person dressed in a safari jacket copying detailed notes from an informant in a tropical region of the world. However, another role for cultural anthropologists has developed recently. In attempting to cut costs and improve productivity and competitiveness, many American and multinational corporations have begun to hire cultural anthropologists to do studies of

the "natives" in the factory or in middle and upper management. In the past, corporations usually hired efficiency experts such as industrial engineers and industrial psychologists to help design their policies and work systems. But those programs usually involved little input and feedback from the employees themselves. In many cases, the implementation of the policies resulted in inefficient and unproductive practices (Garza 1991).

Cultural anthropologists study corporate life through participant observation and in-depth interviews with employees. These studies focus on gathering information about the corporate culture: the corporate norms, values, and practices that can be described only through these anthropological

techniques. John Seely Brown, former director of Xerox Corporation's Palo Alto Research Center, has admitted that the cultural anthropologist of corporate life can deliver dramatic improvements in productivity. He goes on to say that "companies have to go beyond industrial psychology and reengineer the business process. They have to work from the bottom up. And anthropology is the field most attuned to that" (Garza 1991).

In the mid-1980s, Xerox set out to devise more efficient and less costly methods to train its service technicians. Julian Orr, an anthropologist, was hired to determine whether Xerox could do its training more productively. Orr used participant research methods, taking the service training and

Capitalist Consumer Societies

Another major change in industrial capitalist societies and the development of multinational corporations is the extent of production and consumption of consumer goods (Wilk 2000). After the twentieth century, and especially after World War II, corporations in the United States and other capitalist countries began to engage in extensive marketing to create demand for a plethora of consumer goods, including automobiles, home appliances, televisions, and other products. Corporations launched advertising campaigns targeting children and young people as potential consumers for these products. Major investment in advertising and marketing campaigns to create demand for consumer goods was promoted through the media, especially television. Eventually, cartoons and amusement parks such as Disneyland became vehicles for promoting toy products and other goods for young people. Television and media advertising, along with easy credit, created enormous demand for various consumer goods in these capitalist societies. These patterns of consumption

have resulted in extensive global ecological, economic, and cultural changes. We discuss some of the global consequences of capitalist consumer societies in the chapter on contemporary global changes (Chapter 16).

Social Structure

The impact of industrialization on kinship, family, gender, aging, and social status has been just as dramatic as it has been on demography, technology, and economic conditions.

Kinship

Kinship is less important in industrialized states than in preindustrial societies. New structures and organizations perform many of the functions associated with kinship in preindustrial societies. For example, occupational and economic factors in most cases replace kinship as the primary basis of social status; a person no longer has to be part of

going out on jobs himself to discover factors that affected the job. In the field, Orr found that the repair work was not the main job. Instead, he discovered that most of the service calls stemmed from customers who did not know how to run the machines rather than from technical breakdowns. Thus, the most important part of the job involved communication skills. Orr reasoned that service technicians ought to be trained as teachers who can explain the technicalities of the new machines to customers who are using them. Through participant-observation research methods, cultural anthropologists such as Orr can suggest remedies for improving relationships between companies and their clients.

Cultural anthropologists are also being hired to bring their understanding of different cultures and their specialized research techniques to bear on the problems of multinational corporations. One study by anthropologist Margo L. Smith (1986) observed fifteen multinational corporations based in Chicago to determine what types of employees were selected for overseas assignments in foreign cultural environments and what types of cross-cultural skills these employees needed. She found that very few of the companies recognized the need for cross-cultural training for employees to be sent overseas on short-term assignments. Companies usually provided culture and language training for upper-management

personnel who were going to be assigned for more lengthy periods. Smith advised that the companies underestimated the importance of language and culture skills, even for short-term assignments. Employees with short-term assignments represent the company's interests abroad as much as do those with longer-term assignments and may jeopardize the success of various projects by behaving improperly and saying something that could be interpreted as offensive to the local people.

General Motors hired anthropologists Elizabeth Briody and Marietta L. Baba to do research on overseas assignments. These anthropologists found that whereas upper management was promoting overseas assignments as a means of achieving improved business skills and managerial techniques, executives in the North American car and truck units discouraged the idea. The cultural anthropologists discovered that GM's North American operation was run separately from the company's overseas subsidiaries and that within GM's corporate culture, employees perceived the North American operation as GM's elite. Therefore, a position overseas was perceived as a lower-status position. Many of the people who worked overseas were placed on slower career paths. In contrast, in some component divisions of GM such as Delco, top executives were frequently assigned overseas and were viewed as valuable assets to the company.

Briody and Baba recommended that GM adopt a policy whereby managers assigned overseas would be given specific agendas that would lead to improvements in domestic car operations. For example, they could learn techniques from Europe on design, engineering, and manufacturing that could improve U.S. plants. They also suggested an exchange program to replace those sent overseas with a foreign counterpart. These exchanges would result in an improved understanding of global manufacturing, productivity, and competition.

A number of anthropologists are now directly employed in corporations or with market research firms to find out about consumer preferences for different products. A company may want to know which type of advertising has successfully attracted consumers and which segment of a population represents the most promising market for future sales. Why do certain products appeal to some ethnic, age, or sex groups and not others? Why do some advertising campaigns result in higher sales than others?

Anthropologist Steve Barnett, who headed a cultural-analysis group at Planmetrics, a Chicago consulting firm, directs a number of projects related to business research (Lewin 1986). Aside from directing research on management-union relations and other business-related topics for various corporations, Barnett also does marketing research and gathers information on consumer preferences. He emphasizes participant observation in his research methods. For example, to report on consumer patterns of teenagers for fast-food chains, Barnett directs student researchers who participate in teen activities.

As corporations become more experienced with international business and strive to become more productive and competitive both domestically and internationally, anthropologists will increasingly be drawn into consulting and research roles. Anthropological research techniques and cultural knowledge have helped corporations throughout the world solve some of their practical problems. Perhaps future anthropologists may want to think about combining their course-work with some business and management courses to prepare for these new projects in anthropology.

an aristocratic or elite family to have access to wealth and political power.

However, generally as states industrialized, newly emerging middle-class families began to experience upward economic and social mobility, and economic performance, merit, and personal achievement, rather than *ascribed* kinship relationships or birthright, became the primary basis of social status. Of course, kinship and family background still have a definite influence on social mobility. Families with wealth, political power, and high social status can ensure that their children will have the best education. And, *nepotism* families who are related by kin in small-scale businesses and other enterprises, including the political system in industrial and postindustrial societies, still play an important role. For example, the Roosevelt, Kennedy, and Bush families retain their role in political power and authority in U.S. society. These families provide their offspring with professional role models and values that emphasize success. They also maintain economic and political connections that enhance their offspring's future opportunities. Hence, their children have a head start over children from lower socioeconomic categories. But kinship alone is not the fundamental determinant of social status and rank that it had been in most preindustrial societies.

Family

In Chapter 8 we discussed the various functions of the family: socializing children, regulating sexual behavior, and providing emotional and economic security. In industrial societies, some of these functions have been transformed. The major transformation has been the diminishing importance of the extended family and the emergence of the smaller nuclear family. Some basic functions, such as reproduction and the primary care and socialization of children, are still performed in the nuclear family.

The family's economic role has changed dramatically. In industrial societies the family is no longer an economic unit linked to production. The prevalence of wage labor in industrial societies has been one of the principal factors leading to the breakdown of the extended family and the emergence of the nuclear family (Wolf 1966; Goody 1993). The extended family in peasant societies maintained cooperative economic production on the land. When employers began to hire individual workers for labor in mines, factories, and other industries, the extended family as a corporate unit no longer had any economically productive function.

Another factor leading to the diminishing importance of the extended family has been the high rate of geographical mobility induced by industrialization. Because much of the labor drawn into factories and mines initially came from rural areas, workers had to leave their families and establish their own nuclear families in the cities. Land tenure based on the extended family was no longer the driving force it had been in preindustrial societies. In addition, as manufacturing and service industries expanded, they frequently moved or opened new offices, requiring workers to relocate. Thus, the economic requirements of industrializing societies have had the effect of dissolving the extended family ties that had been so critical in preindustrial societies.

Historians, sociologists, and anthropologists have studied the disintegration of the extended family in industrial England, Europe, and North America for decades (e.g., Goode 1963, 1982, 1993; Stone 2000). Although the large extended patrilineal group families gradually broke down during the medieval period in Europe, a pattern of smaller kin-group families

During the early phases of industrialization, rural women, including these women who worked in the Lowell textile mill, often had to leave their rural extended families and, when married, formed nuclear families residing in urban areas.

and bilateral descent (tracing descent through both sides of the family) emerged throughout Europe. Although a similar process occurred in Russia and Japan, to some extent it was delayed in those countries. For example, in Russia, the nuclear family began to replace the extended family following the emancipation of the serfs (Kerblay 1983). Yet anthropologists have noted that the nuclear family is not the ideal norm in Russian society. Surveys indicate that the Russians do not consider it proper for older parents to live alone and that many consider the grandfather to be the head of the family. These ideal norms reflect the older traditions of the extended peasant family in Russia (Dunn and Dunn 1988).

In Japanese society, the traditional family was based on the *ie* (pronounced like the slang term "yeah" in American English). The *ie* is a patrilineal extended family that had kinship networks based on blood relations, marriage, and adoption (Befu 1971; Shimizu 1987; McCreery and McCreery 2005). The *ie* managed its assets in land and property as a corporate group and was linked into a hierarchy of other branch *ie* families, forming a *dozoku*. The *dozoku* maintained functions similar to those of the peasant families of other agricultural societies. With industrialization and now postindustrialization in Japan, the rurally based *ie* and *dozoku* began to decline, and urban nuclear families called the *kazoku* began to develop (Befu 1971; Kerbo and McKinstry 1998; McCreery and McCreery 2005). The shift from the *ie* and *dozuku* to the *kazoku* has been very sudden and recent, and many older people in Japan have not really adjusted to this recent change.

Despite the general tendency toward the breakup of the extended family in industrialized societies, specific groups and regions in these societies may still retain extended family ties. For example, extended, peasant-type families exist in the rural regions such as Uzbekistan, Azerbaijan, and Georgia, which were formerly part of the Soviet Union (Kerblay 1983). Similar tendencies can be found in rural British, European, and Japanese societies. Even in the urban areas of nations such as the United States and Great Britain, some ethnic groups maintain extended family ties. In the United States, some African Americans, Latinos, Arab Americans, and Asian Americans enjoy the loyalty and support of extended family ties to enhance their economic and social organization within the larger society (Stack 1975; Macionis 2004; Brown 2003; Bigler 2003; Benson 2003).

Marriage

One of the major changes in marriage in industrialized societies is that it has become much more individualized; that is, the establishment of the union has come to involve personal considerations more than family arrangements. This individualistic form of marriage is usually based on *romantic love*, which entails a blend of emotional attachment with physical and strong sexual attraction. Some anthropologists have hypothesized that erotic attraction and romantic love existed in preindustrial societies and was universal (Fisher 1992; Jankowiak and Fischer 1992), and there are many ethnographic descriptions of couples falling in love in both prestate and agricultural state societies. The classical litera-

ture of China, Arabia, India, Greece, and Rome, as well as various religious texts such as the Bible, are filled with stories about romantic love, as are stories of preindustrial societies such as the Ojibway Indians of North America and the San hunting-gathering society discussed in Chapter 9. Shakespeare's play *Romeo and Juliet* underscores the conflict between romantic love and the familistic and practical considerations of marriage in Western Europe during the Renaissance. However, anthropologist Charles Lindholm, who has done extensive cross-cultural research on this topic, suggests that even though romantic love may have existed in many known cultures, it didn't in many others, and that the correlation between romantic love and the reproduction of children is very weak. Lindholm asserts that societies that have arranged marriages for economic and political benefit tend to have far higher birth rates than those who do not (2001). Lindholm traces the existence of the courtly ideals and poetic expressions of romantic love to the Islamic world in the medieval period, where it eventually percolated into Renaissance European culture (2001).

Yet, both of these anthropological models of romantic love, the universal versus the particularistic form, concur that the ideals of romantic love did become more widespread in Europe, resulting in the diffusion of this form of marriage throughout Western culture. The ideals within the biblical tradition of Jewish *nomos* and expressed later in the Christian concept of *agape* and its devaluation of sexuality had some cultural effects on the concept of romantic love in marriage (Lindholm 2005; De-Munck 2005; Singer 1987). Eventually, the Roman Catholic church in AD 1439 defined marriage as based on the choice of the individuals and decreed that is was a seventh sacrament that was spiritually based (Stone 2000).

Of course, many people within the upper classes persisted in arranged marriages (as described in the novels of the British author Jane Austen). The royal families of Europe arranged the marriages of their children for political alliances, as well as for economic consolidation of property rights. Cousin marriage, as discussed for many earlier forms of societies described in previous chapters, was maintained throughout many European upper classes. Many nineteenth-century Victorians such as Charles Darwin, as well as the famous wealthy banking Rothchild family of Europe and many other families of the upper classes, married their cousins on a regular basis, just as the people of the Old Testament and early Christian and Roman era did in earlier agricultural societies. As mentioned earlier in the textbook, this "inbreeding" does not necessarily lead to harmful genetic results (Conniff 2003). (And, as we will see in later chapters, cousin marriage is still a major way in which marriage is arranged in many non-Western societies throughout the world.) However, the cultural tradition of free marital choice based on romantic love, especially among the upwardly mobile middle and lower-middle classes in Europe following the Renaissance and later Industrial Revolution, began to spread throughout the region of Europe and into Western culture, where it exists today in the United States and other regions of the world influenced by Western culture and Christianity. As many sociologists, anthropologists, and historians of Europe suggest, as industrialization and modernization proceeded to break down agricultural-structured property arrangements, extended family and kinship relationships, development of smaller family size, and geographical mobility, which tended to foster more individualism and personal autonomy, choice and new forms of self-cultivation romantic love became the mainstay of European societies (Giddens 1992; Stone 1992, 2000).

Prior to the industrialization of Europe years ago, however, many families still persisted in trying to have their children married within the same class, ethnic, and religious category, and children were often married through the intervention of parents, who arranged their relationships. Romantic love may have existed in preindustrial societies (and in many cases it was the basis for extramarital relationships), but it did not usually become the primary basis of marriage until after the Industrial Revolution. As cultural values became more individualistic, along with the rise of new groups of middle-class families, many couples began to choose their own spouses. As the extended family declined in significance, important decisions such as selection of a marriage partner increasingly were made by individuals rather than by families.

Although individuals select their own marriage partners in most industrialized societies, the parents within these societies often attempt to enhance marital choices in certain categories. For example, parents of the upper and upper-middle class often choose certain colleges and universities for their children so that they will meet suitable marriage partners. Many parents sponsor social activities for their children to meet potential marriage partners of their own socioeconomic, ethnic, and religious affiliations. In some areas, such as the Southern region of the United States and Quebec, cousin marriage was still practiced up until recently to promote the consolidation of property rights and transmit wealth within the families. Nineteen U.S. states permit first-cousin marriage (Conniff 2003; Molloy 1990). In fact, dating as an institution was very unusual as it was found in U.S. society compared even to Europe, England, or Japan. In 1948, British anthropologist Geoffrey Gorer found it surprising that dating in the United States was a way in which males and females met one another (1948).

Thus, to some extent, even in industrialized societies, individual choice of marriage partners is circumscribed by parental guidance and other cultural norms. However, many people in an industrialized society such as the United States find that because of the breakdown in family and community ties, individuals find it more difficult to meet prospective spouses. Many individuals are from homes where their parents have been divorced at least once, and consequently this reduces the possibility of meeting someone through their family. For that reason, there has been an increase in dating and matchmaking and computer dating services in postindustrialized societies such as the United States. Thousands of these dating and matchmaking services, along with Internet Web sites aimed at helping singles find a spouse, have developed within the past decade.

One exception needs to be noted with respect to the relationships between industrialization and commercialization and individualized decision making in the selection of marriage partners. Courtly love, closely resembling romantic love, was discussed in some of the classical literature such as Lady Murasaki's *Tale of Genji* in the Japanese court of the tenth century. In Japanese society, the most typical, traditional form of marriage was arranged through a go-between, a *nakoda*, who set up a meeting for a couple to get to know each other (Hendry 1987). The *nakoda* would establish an alliance between two extended households. This pattern is known as the *samurai* form of marriage because the warrior-scholars practiced it during the Tokugawa period.

With industrialization in Japanese society, romantic love has had an effect on the selection of marriage partners, and currently many Japanese individuals choose their own mates. But anthropologist Joy Hendry (1987) notes that "love marriages" are still suspect and go against the serious practical concerns of marital ties and the traditional obligations felt by people toward their parents. In many cases, *nakoda* are still used to arrange marriages in this highly modern society. Currently, there is a cultural struggle between generations of the young versus the old over what type of marriage and family relationships ought to be maintained in Japanese society (McCreery and McCreery 2005).

Approximately one-third of the marriages in Japan are the result of arranged marriages. A couple of marriageable age is brought together in a formal meeting called an *omiai*, arranged by the *nakoda*. "Love marriages" based on romantic love, called *renai kekkon*, may result in marriage, but in most cases parents still have veto power over who their children marry (Kerbo and McKinstry 1998). Marriage in Japan is still very much a family consideration, rather than just an individual's own choice or decision. Yet, some of the younger generation in Japan are beginning to opt for "romantic love" and personal choice for their marital partners. And one of the signs of this new trend in marriage is that these young Japanese, especially among the middle and upper classes will have a "Christian-style" wedding, rather than a typical Japanese wedding ceremony, some of them going to Hawaii for their ceremonies.

Divorce   All but a few industrialized societies have legalized divorce, and obtaining a divorce has become easier. In general, little social stigma is associated with divorce in industrialized societies (Quale 1988). Divorce rates tend to be higher in industrial societies than in preindustrial societies. Although historians and anthropologists find that marriage and divorce were very unstable even in medieval Europe, most marriages dissolved because of high death rates (Stone 2000). Beginning in the fourth century, the Roman Catholic Church in Europe banned divorce. By the sixth century, the Christian church in medieval Europe maintained that celibacy was the highest spiritual state for people, based on the Christian teachings of Paul (Ephesians 5:22-33), which eventually resulted in the banning of marriage

for Roman Catholic priests in the eleventh century (Stone 2000; Herlihy 1971). Anthropologists such as Jack Goody attribute these changes in divorce and marriage to the Church's opposition to the breakup of property of heirs that might have been appropriated by the Church (1983).

Among the many factors that contribute to high divorce rates in industrialized societies is the dissatisfaction that some people experience in their marital relationships. People who contract a marital bond primarily on the ideals and expectations of romantic love may experience a conflict between those ideals and the actualities of marital life. Women who are more financially independent in industrialized societies are much less likely to remain in a bad marriage. In preindustrial societies, in which marriages were actually alliances between corporate kin groups, individuals typically did not have the freedom to dissolve the marital bond. As individualistic decision making increased with the emergence of industrialization, however, partners in an unsatisfying relationship were more willing to consider divorce.

Divorce rates of most Western industrialized societies have ballooned during the last century. For example, the U.S. rate increased tenfold between 1890 and 1970 (Macionis 2001). The same pattern is evident in Russia, where traditional taboos regarding divorce have been replaced by more tolerant attitudes (Kerblay 1983).

In Japan, however, the divorce rate has decreased since industrialization (Befu 1971). In contrast to most agricultural societies, prior to the Meiji period Japan had a fairly high divorce rate. This was not due to conflicts between husband and wife; instead, divorce resulted because elders in the husband's family rejected a young bride because she did not conform easily enough to family norms, because she did not bring enough of a dowry, or for other reasons. The traditional postmarital rule of residence was patrilocal, with the wife moving in with the husband's father's household (Goode 1982). With industrialization and the breakdown of these traditional patterns, the divorce rate began to fall. More recently, however, the divorce rate has begun to increase in Japan, as industrialization creates the tensions experienced in all industrial societies. Yet the divorce rate in Japan is still only one-fifth of that of the United States (Kerbo and McKinstry 1998; Hendry 1998). To some extent, the traditional norms and expectations regarding the female gender role in Japanese society have undoubtedly had an influence on this lower divorce rate. Traditionally, Japanese women are not supposed to threaten the primacy of the husband's role as head of the family. The Japanese woman is supposed to dedicate herself to the husband and children. Work outside of the home should be undertaken only to boost family income when it is necessary, and upon having children, the Japanese woman is expected to be a full-time homemaker (Kerbo and McKinstry 1998). Consequently, many fewer Japanese women have the financial capability to sustain themselves outside of a marriage. Currently, this issue of gender and individual choice is being contested by many young people in Japan (McCreery 2001; McCreery and McCreery 2006).

Gender

Industrialization has had a profound impact on gender relationships, particularly in England, Europe, and North America. The transition from an agricultural economy to an industrial wage economy drew many women from the domestic realm into the workplace. Women have thus become more economically self-sufficient and less dependent on men for support.

Gender and the Division of Labor Although women in Western industrial societies have entered the work force in considerable numbers in the last several decades, most women work in a small number of occupations within the service economy, especially in underpaid clerical positions. In addition, women in industrial societies perform the majority of domestic tasks, such as household chores and child care, which are still considered by many the primary responsibility of women. Male occupations and the husband's income are usually considered the primary source of family income. Consequently, women in these societies have a dual burden of combining their domestic role with employment outside the home (Bernard 1981, 1987; Bannister 1991). A similar pattern is also seen in Japanese society (McCreery and McCreery 2006).

Female Status in Industrial Societies To some degree, industrialization undermined the traditional form of patriarchy. In most preindustrial societies, males held considerable authority and control over females. This authority diminished in industrial societies as women gained more independence and gender relations became more egalitarian. As we have seen, however, women are still restricted in the workplace and have a dual burden of combining outside work and domestic chores. This indicates that the cultural legacy of patriarchy still persists in most industrial societies.

As their economic role has changed, women have attempted to gain equal economic and political rights. The call for gender equality began with women from upper- and middle-class families. Unlike working-class women, these early women's

Women are joining the work force in industrial societies in increasing numbers.

rights advocates were financially secure and had much leisure time to devote to political activism. They eventually secured the right to vote in the United States and in other industrialized nations. In addition, with increasing educational levels and economic opportunities, more women entered the work force. For example, by the middle of the twentieth century, nearly 40 percent of all adult females in the United States were in the work force; by 1990 that number was almost 60 percent, as illustrated in Figure 13.2.

Feminism During the 1960s, a combination of economic and social forces fueled the feminist movement in many industrialized societies. During the 1950s many U.S. women began to question their role as solitary homemakers, especially after they participated heavily within the work force during the World War II years. They were not happy with their domestic roles as housewives serving their husbands whom they were dependent upon economically and wanted more direct participation in the outside world. **Feminism** is the belief that women are equal to men and should have

equal rights and opportunities. The contemporary feminist movement has helped many women discover that they have been denied equal rights and dignity. This movement has a much broader base of support than the early women's rights movement. Among its supporters are career women, high school and college students, homemakers, senior citizens, and even many men.

Feminists have secured some concrete gains and helped change certain attitudes in the United States. For example, in a landmark legal decision in 1972, the American Telephone and Telegraph Company (AT&T), the world's largest employer of women, was forced to pay $23 million in immediate pay increases and $15 million in back pay to employees who had suffered sex discrimination. In addition, women have been admitted to many formerly all-male institutions such as the U.S. Military Academy at West Point.

Despite these gains, many female workers continue to be segregated into low-paying service occupations. To resolve this and other problems, the feminist movement supported the Equal Rights Amendment (ERA) to the U.S. Constitution to

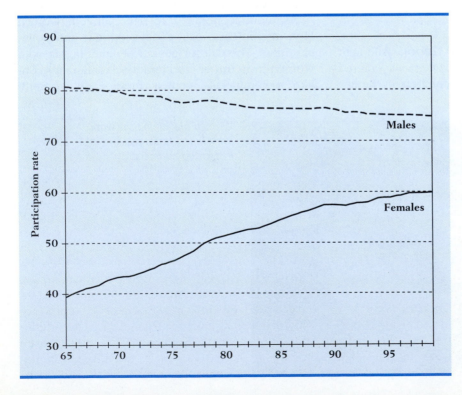

FIGURE 13.2 Trends in female and male labor force participation rates, 1965–1999. What does this say about the effects of industrialization on traditional gender roles? *Source*: Adapted from Francine D. Blau, Marianne A. Ferber, and Anne E. Winkler, *The Economics of Women, Men, and Work*, 4th ed. (Upper Saddle River, NJ: Prentice Hall, 2002), p. 86.

prohibit discrimination because of gender. Although the ERA was supported by almost three-fourths of American adults and passed by Congress in 1972, it failed to win ratification by the states in time. Apparently, the idea of full equality and equivalent pay for equivalent work has not received the full endorsement of U.S. society. Even in an advanced industrial society, the cultural legacy of patriarchy remains a persistent force.

In Japan the cultural legacy of patriarchy has retained its grip on the role of women. In the Meiji Civil Code, in newly industrializing Japan, the laws promulgated in 1898 granted very few rights for women (McCreery and McCreery 2005). Article 5 in the Police Security Regulations of 1900 explicitly forbade women from joining political organizations or even attending meetings at which political speeches were given. These laws would remain in force until after World War II.

After the U.S. occupation following World War II, women's suffrage was approved. Article 14 of the Japanese Constitution proclaimed in 1946 bans discrimination on the basis of race, creed, sex, social status, or family origin. Article 24 explicitly requires the consent of both parties to marriage. The revised Civil Code issued in 1947 abolishes the traditional *ie* corporate family system.

The next major change in Japanese women's legal status came in 1985, with the passage of the Equal Opportunities Employment Law. But legal status and social acceptance are two different things, especially when laws like this one contain no penalties for violation.

However, during the 1970s wives and mothers who moved to the suburbs were the daughters of women accustomed to being fully in charge of their homes. Just as in the United States and Europe, more and more women were entering the workforce. As elsewhere in the industrial world, the cost of educating the children was rising. Some women always had to work, simply to make ends meet. Now more looked for work to keep up with the neighbors or to be sure that their families could afford the new consumer goods that everyone wanted. Many young women typically took jobs that lasted only until they married. Then, returning to the labor force after their children started school, they could find only low-paying, part-time work. They could supplement their household's incomes but rarely earned enough to be financially independent.

Women were, however, becoming more highly educated. In 1955, only 5 percent of women received postsecondary education, and more than half of those went only to junior college. In contrast, 15 percent of men received postsecondary education, and 13.1 percent went on to four-year universities. In 1970, 6.5 percent of women and 27.3 percent of men went on to university. The ratio was similar, still three to one men over women, but this was just the beginning. As of 2002, 48.5 percent of Japanese women received some form of postsecondary education, compared to 48.8 percent of men; 33.8 percent of women attended university. Higher education combined with still limited opportunities was a recipe for dissatisfaction—and shop until you drop provided at best temporary relief (McCreery and McCreery 2006).

Yet, even when women are in the work force in Japanese society, they tend to have a second-class status when compared to men. Many college-educated women in offices are expected to wear uniforms and to serve tea and coffee to the men, and they are treated as if they are office servants (Hendry 1987; Kerbo and McKinstry 1998). They are expected to defer to men in the office and present themselves as infantile, which is interpreted as cute and polite. Most men in Japan perform almost no domestic chores and expect to be waited on by their wives. Despite this tradition of patriarchy in Japan, the Japanese woman has a powerful position within the domestic household. She manages the household budget, takes charge of the children's education, and makes long-term financial investments for the family. Thus, the outside-of-the-home and the inside-of-the-home roles for women in Japan are still strongly influenced by patriarchal traditions. There are some women active in a growing feminist movement in Japan that wants to transform gender roles, but traditional cultural expectations based on patriarchy are resistant to change (McCreery and McCreery 2006). In both the Western societies and Japan, women are marrying at a much older age than in the past. New reproductive technologies introduced into industrial and postindustrial societies to reproduce children, such as artificial insemination (AI) and in vitro fertilization (IVF), along with perhaps even cloning in some societies in the future, will undoubtedly influence the moral, legal, and social

Critical Perspectives

POSTMODERNISM AND FEMINIST ANTHROPOLOGY

POSTMODERNISM AND ANTHROPOLOGY

In this chapter, we are examining the development of industrial societies and the studies of these societies by anthropologists. We referred to the process of *modernization*, the socioeconomic, political, and religious consequences of the technological and scientific changes brought about by the Industrial Revolution. Many anthropologists, social scientists, historians, artists, and humanities scholars use the term "modernity" to refer to the changes in philosophy, literature, art, religious beliefs, and other forms of culture during the Industrial Revolution and the Enlightenment period (1600–1800s). In the discussion of the current technological and economic trends in this chapter, we used the term "postindustrial" societies to refer to the ongoing transformation in the advanced industrial societies today. This change involves the broad transition from a heavy industrialized technology and economy to a service, high-tech, information-based economy. As discussed earlier, this transition to a postindustrial society is apparent within North America, Europe, Japan, and elsewhere in the advanced industrial countries. Along with the emergence of the postindustrial transformation, new theoretical and intellectual developments have occurred within anthropology, sometimes referred to as postmodern and feminist anthropology.

Postmodern anthropologists have challenged some of the basic ethnographic methodologies and scientific assumptions within modernist anthropology. This theoretical development includes historians and anthropologists such as James Clifford, George Marcus, and Michael Fischer. The postmodernists suggest that traditional ethnographic research is based on a number of unsound assumptions. One such assumption is that the ethnographer is a detached, scientifically objective observer who is not influenced by the premises and biases of her or his own society. Clifford suggests that earlier ethnographers employed a method of themselves as the "scientific participant-observer" (1983). In early ethnographies there was no use of the pronoun "I" and everything was written as the documentation of an "objective scientist." It was as if he were some sort of computing machine without feelings, biases, or emotions, who was simply recording everything about native life.

Another type of inquiry criticized by the postmodernists is the interpretive model used by symbolic anthropologists such as Clifford Geertz, as discussed in Chapter 6. In contrast to the "objective" model, the interpretive model focuses on the understanding of symbols from the point of view of the members of the society. It assumes that the people in a particular society have a better understanding than others of their own concepts, and the interpretive anthropologist must try to reconstruct these understandings so that others can also understand the meanings of these symbols.

Postmodernists critique this type of interpretive anthropology because it is also written as if the ethnographer disappears from the setting through empathy with the subjects. In other words, the people themselves are not described as offering their own interpretations, but instead the ethnologist is looking over their shoulders and reading the cultural meanings and texts of their society and interpreting them.

One of the basic reasons for the postmodernist critiques is that the situation for ethnographic studies has changed substantially. Until recently, most subjects of ethnographic studies were illiterate peoples adjusting to the impact of the West. But as more people throughout the world become educated and familiar with the field of anthropology, Western ethnographers can no longer claim to be the sole authorities regarding anthropological knowledge. Many people in Latin America, Africa, the Middle East, and Asia can and do speak and write about their own cultures (some have even become anthropologists), and they are disseminating knowledge about their own societies. The world is no longer dependent on Western anthropologists to gather ethnographic data. Indigenous people are beginning to represent themselves and their societies to the world.

Postmodernists have recommended that ethnographers today adopt a different way of researching and writing. Instead of trying to distance themselves from their subjects, ethnographers should present themselves in dialogue with their subjects. Clifford (1983) argues that an ethnography should consist of many voices from the native population, rather than just a dialogue between the ethnographer and one of his or her informants.

Reaction to this postmodernist critique has varied within the discipline. On the one hand, some ethnographers have charged the postmodernists with characterizing traditional ethnographic methodologies unjustly. Many ethnographers, they contend, were engaged in a form of dialogue with their informants and other members of the societies being studied.

On the other hand, the postmodernist debate has stirred many anthropologists to rethink their roles. Currently, more ethnographers are writing about their actual interactions and relationships with the people they study. Ethnographers must take account of their own political position within the society under investigation. This type of data and personal reflection method is no longer pushed into the back-

ground, but instead is presented as a vital ingredient of the ethnography. In the 1980s, a number of ethnographies appeared that reflected the postmodernist emphasis on interaction between ethnographers and their subjects. Some of these new ethnographies are based on the life histories of people within the studied population.

If we look back over years of ethnographic research, we find many accounts in which anthropologists were scrupulous in their representation of people in other societies. To this extent, the postmodernist critics have exaggerated the past mistakes of ethnographers. However, the postmodernists have alerted ethnographers to some unexamined assumptions concerning their work. Today, most anthropologists do not claim a completely "objective" viewpoint. Anthropologists generally want to maintain empathy with the people they study, yet they usually attempt some critical detachment as well. Otherwise, they could easily become merely the voices and spokespersons of specific political interests and leaders in a community (Errington and Gewertz 1987).

Collaborative fieldwork, with teams of ethnographers and informants working together to understand a society, is most likely the future direction for ethnographic study. The image of a solitary ethnographer such as Margaret Mead isolated on a Pacific island is outmoded (Salzman 1989). Collaborative research will lead to

more systematic data collection and will offer opportunities to examine hypotheses of both ethnographers and subjects from a variety of perspectives.

FEMINIST ANTHROPOLOGY

Another important development that occurred within anthropological theory and is related to postmodernism was the emergence of a feminist orientation. After the beginning of the twentieth century, a number of women pioneers such as Ruth Benedict, Margaret Mead, Elsie Crews Parsons, Eleanor Leacock, and Phyllis Kaberry began to have a definite impact on the field of anthropology. Margaret Mead popularized the findings of anthropology by writing a monthly article in *Redbook* magazine, which circulated widely among women in the United States. Mead was also the first to focus on gender roles within different societies and question a rigid biological determinist view of male and female roles.

With the development of the feminist movement in U.S. society in the 1960s and 1970s and the transition to a postindustrial society, many women anthropologists initiated a feminist perspective. This feminist perspective challenged the tendency to concentrate on the male role and underestimate the position of women within different societies. Before the 1970s, most anthropologists were male, and for the most part, women were neglected in ethnographic research. As more women became involved in anthropology, they questioned the traditional emphasis on the male position and the invisibility of women in ethnographies. These feminist anthropologists emphasized that gender roles had to be taken into account in ethnographic research (Mascia-Lees and Black 2000). They also challenged essentialist or stereotypical portrayals of women. As we will see in later chapters, these feminist anthropologists have produced enormous insights regarding the role of women in societies throughout the world.

Feminist anthropologists have directed their criticisms at a variety of targets that had become prevalent in the discipline. For example, they questioned the underlying assumptions made by the sociobiologists and evolutionary psychologists regarding male and female behavioral tendencies (see Chapter 4). The feminist anthropologists argued that the view of men as sexually promiscuous, and females as sexually conservative and desiring monogamy as a reproductive strategy was an overgeneralization and essentialist stereotype. They critiqued the view that males and females were radically different based on biological traits such as hormonal differences. In addition, they directed their criticisms at the physical anthropologists who argued that females had become dependent on males for food and other resources, whereas males were developing tools and other strategies for hunting purposes. They suggested that the female role in human evolution had been overlooked. And feminist anthropologists criticized ethnographic descriptions that presented males as the more active, aggressive agent within the family, and the female as passive and inactive in behavior. These type of descriptions appeared in the ethnographies of the functionalists during the 1930s and 1940s (Mascia-Lees and Black 2000). Thus, feminist anthropologists provided new insightful hypotheses and created a more general awareness of gender and women's issues within the discipline.

A classical combination of both postmodernist and feminist anthropology is illustrated by the late Marjorie Shostak following two periods of fieldwork among the Ju/'hoansi San, hunters and gatherers of the Kalahari Desert in southwest Africa discussed in Chapter 9. Marjorie Shostak completed a life history, *The Life and Words of Nisa, A !Kung Woman* (1981). Shostak interviewed numerous Ju/'hoansi San women to gain a sense of their lives. She focused on the life history of Nisa, who discussed her family, her sex life, marriage, pregnancies, her experiences with men, and growing older. Shostak cautioned that Nisa does not represent a "typical" Ju/'hoansi San female because her life experiences are unique (as are all individuals in any society). In addition, Shostak exercised extreme care in discussing with Nisa the material that would go into the book to ensure a faithful representation of Nisa's life.

CRITICISMS OF FEMINIST ANTHROPOLOGY

Although feminist anthropology has contributed substantially to the discipline in providing a critical awareness for male anthropologists, some anthropologists argue that this perspective has become too extreme and exaggerated. For example, some feminist anthropologists have put forth the view that biological factors have absolutely nothing to do with male and female differences. An enormous amount of data from various scientifically evaluated fields has demonstrated that both nature and nurture are important in shaping gender and male and female differences. Thus, the view that nature doesn't have anything to do with gender seems to be too extreme.

In addition, some feminist anthropologists have argued that all of the scientific hypotheses and most of science is based on a Western cultural framework and an *androcentric*, or male-centered, perspective. Consequently, male anthropologists cannot do research on women in other societies because of their androcentric biases. Therefore, only women can conduct research on women and gender issues. These views also appear to be extreme. At present, most male anthropologists have been attuned to the feminist critique of anthropology and have adjusted to a more sensitive understanding of gender and women's issues. Many male anthropologists today consider themselves to be feminist anthropologists.

Also, as we have emphasized in this textbook, scientifically based hypotheses are tested by many individuals in both Western and non-Western societies, and as more women come into the field of anthropology, they will become actively involved in testing these hypotheses. Thus, science and scientific hypotheses are not just products of a Western cultural framework and an androcentric perspective. The scientific method used correctly and precisely will weed out any erroneous biases or data and will result in a more comprehensive and refined understanding of the social and cultural world.

POINTS TO PONDER

1. In what ways does postmodernism anthropology differ from its earlier modern version?

2. What are the strengths and weaknesses of postmodern anthropology?

status of gender, marriage, and other issues of males and females in these advanced postindustrial societies.

Age

Another social consequence of industrialization is the loss experienced by the elderly of traditional status and authority. This trend reflects the changes in the family structure and the nature of cultural knowledge in industrial and postindustrial societies. As the nuclear family replaced the extended family, older people no longer lived with their adult children. Pension plans and government support programs such as Social Security replaced the family as the source of economic support for the elderly. At the same time, exchanges of resources between elders and offspring became less important in industrial societies (Halperin 1987). Thus, elderly family members lost a major source of economic power.

The traditional role of the elderly in retaining and disseminating useful knowledge has also diminished. Sociologist Donald O. Cowgill (1986) hypothesizes that as the rate of technological change accelerates in industrial societies, knowledge quickly becomes obsolete, which has an effect on the status of elderly people. Industrialization promotes expanding profits through new products and innovative services, all of which favor the young, who, through formal education and training, have greater access to technological knowledge. In addition, the amount of cultural

and technical information has increased to the point where the elderly can no longer store all of it. Instead, libraries, databases, and formalized educational institutions have become the storehouses of cultural knowledge.

The result of these changes, according to Cowgill, has been the rapid disengagement of the elderly from their roles in industrial societies. Although many elderly people remain active and productive, they no longer possess the economic, political, and social status they did in preindustrial societies. In some cases, the elderly are forced to retire from their jobs in industrial societies to make way for the younger generation. For example, in industrial Japan, the elderly are forced to retire at the age of 55 and often have difficulties adjusting to their senior years.

The status and roles of the elderly have changed much more dramatically in the West than in Japan and the former Soviet Union, where the elderly retain a great deal of authority and prestige in the family (Palmore 1975; Kerblay 1983). In Japanese society, the tradition of family obligations influenced by Confucian values and ethos serves to foster the veneration of the elderly. In addition, about three-fourths of the elderly reside with their children, which encourages a greater sense of responsibility on the part of children toward their parents. In 2002, official estimates put Japan's total population at 127,435,000. Of that total 23,628,000 (18.5 percent) were age 65 or older. Only 18,102,000 (14.2 percent) were 14 or younger. In 2001, life expectancy for men had risen to 78.07 years. Life expectancy for women was 84.83 years (McCreery and McCreery 2006).

Theorists such as Cowgill suggest that because Japan and the former Soviet Union industrialized much later than Western societies, there has been less time to transform family structures and the status of the elderly. This view is supported by a comparison between the most modern industrialized urban sectors of these societies and the rural regions. For example, in the more rural regions in Russia and, up until recently, in Japan, the extended family or *ie* was still the norm, and the elderly remained influential and esteemed. Thus, the high status of the aged in Japan and Russia may represent delayed responses to industrialization (Cowgill 1986). However, presently, Japan is undergoing a rapid transformation in these patterns, and as in the United States and Western Europe, older people are becoming much more independent and are enjoying their privacy and lack of dependence on their natal families (McCreery and McCreery 2006).

Social Stratification

In earlier chapters we discussed the type of social stratification that existed in preindustrial societies. Bands and tribes were largely egalitarian, whereas chiefdoms and agricultural states had increased social inequality based on ascribed statuses. Chiefdoms and agricultural states are classified as **closed societies** because they offer little, if any, opportunity for social mobility. In contrast, industrial states are classified as **open societies** in which social status can be achieved through individual efforts. The achievement of social status is related to the complex division of labor, which is based on specialized occupational differences. Occupation becomes the most important determinant of status in industrial states. Societal rewards such as income, political power, and prestige all depend on a person's occupation.

This is not to say that industrial states are egalitarian. Rather, like some agricultural states, they have distinctive classes that consist of somewhat equivalent social statuses. The gaps among these classes in terms of wealth, power, and status are actually greater in industrial than in preindustrial

societies. Thus, although people in industrial states have the opportunity to move into a different class from that into which they were born, the degree of stratification in these societies is much more extreme than it is in preindustrial societies. Let's examine the types of stratification systems found in some industrial states.

The British Class System

Some industrial states continue to reflect their agricultural past. Great Britain, for example, is made up of a class system that retains some of its feudal-like social patterns. It has a symbolic monarchy and nobility based on ascribed statuses passed down from generation to generation. The monarchy and nobility have titles such as prince, princess, knight, peer, and earl. These individuals have to be addressed with the appropriate form: sir, lord, lady. The British political system reflects its feudal past

Some European societies have remnants of earlier feudal kingdoms.

in the structure of the House of Lords, in which membership is traditionally inherited through family. This contrasts with the House of Commons, to which individuals are freely elected. Although the monarchy and the House of Lords have relatively little power today, they play an important symbolic role in British politics.

Class divisions in modern Britain are similar to those in many other European societies. They include a small upper class that maintains its position through inheritance laws and the education of children in elite private schools; a larger middle class that includes physicians, attorneys, businesspeople, and other occupations in the service sector; and a large working class employed in the primary and secondary sectors of the economy. Yet social mobility in Great Britain is open, and people can move from one class to another.

The degree of social mobility in Great Britain, as well as in other industrial states, is to some extent a result of recent changes in the industrial economy. With advanced industrialization, an increasing percentage of jobs are found in the tertiary (service) sector, whereas the primary and secondary sectors have declined. Therefore, the number of white-collar workers has grown, and the number of blue-collar workers has decreased. Consequently, many of the sons and daughters of blue-collar workers have a higher social status than that of their parents. For example, in Great Britain approximately 40 percent of the sons of manual workers have moved into the middle class since the 1950s (Robertson 1990; Macionis 2004). Sociologists refer to this as *structural mobility*, a type of social mobility resulting from the restructuring of the economy, producing new occupational opportunities. Technological innovations, economic booms or busts, wars, and increasing jobs in the service-sector, white-collar occupations, and other events can affect this mobility from low to middle or upper class.

Class in the United States

Most research demonstrates that the rate of social mobility in the United States is about the same as in other industrial states (Macionis 2004). Although the United States differs from Great Britain in that it has never had an official class system with a titled aristocracy, it is not a classless society. The class structure of the United States consists of five basic categories based on equivalent social statuses, which are largely determined by occupation, income, and education (see Table 13.2). Although these class boundaries are very "fuzzy" and are not rigid, they continue to have an influence on whether an individual can achieve social mobility.

One of the principal cultural ideals of the United States is that any person can move up the social ladder through effort and motivation. For this reason, upper-class and upper-middle-class Americans tend to believe that economic and social inequalities arise primarily from differences in individual abilities and work habits. They believe that equal opportunities are available to any individual. These cultural beliefs therefore help justify social inequity.

In fact, many factors besides individual efforts—such as family background, wealth, property, and assets and the state of the national and world economy—affect a person's location on the socioeconomic ladder. In addition, people's ethnic and racial backgrounds can inhibit or enhance their chances of social mobility. African Americans, Native Americans, and Hispanics historically have lower rates of mobility than do Asian Americans and white, middle-class Americans.

Class in Japan and the Former Soviet Union

Most research indicates that, despite the cultural emphasis on group harmony, class divisions and conflicts exist in Japan. Sociologist Rob Steven (1983) has identified five major classes in Japanese society: the bourgeoisie or capitalist class (the owners of the major industries), the petty bourgeoisie (small-business owners), the middle class (professional and other service workers), the peasantry (rural farmers), and the working class. The primary means of social mobility in Japanese society is the educational system, which is highly regimented and rigorous from the elementary years through high school. Higher education is limited to those students who excel on various achievement exams, a system that to some extent reflects class background. As in other industrial societies, middle- and upper-class students have better opportunities. The rate of social mobility in Japan is similar to that of

Table 13.2	The American Class System in the Twenty-First Century: A Composite Estimate					
Class and Percentage of Total Population	Income	Property	Occupation	Education	Personal and Family Life	Education of Children
Upper class (1–3%)	Very high income, most of it from wealth	Great wealth old wealth, control over investment	Managers, professionals, high civil and military officials	Liberal arts education at elite schools Graduate training	Stable family life Autonomous personality	College education by right for both sexes Educational system biased in their favor
Upper-middle class (10–15%)	High income	Accumulation of property through savings	Lowest unemployment		Better physical and mental health and health care	
Lower-middle class (30–35%)	Modest income	Few assets Some savings	Small-business people and farmers, lower professionals, semiprofessionals, sales and clerical workers	Some college High school Some high school	Longer life expectancy Unstable family life	Greater chance of college than working-class children Educational system biased against them Tendency toward vocational programs
Working class (40–45%)	Low income	Few to no assets No savings No assets	Skilled labor Unskilled labor	Grade school	One-parent homes Conformist personality	
Lower class (20–25%)	Poverty income	No savings	Highest unemployment Surplus labor	Illiteracy, especially functional illiteracy	Poorer physical and mental health Lower life expectancy	Little interest in education, high dropout rates

Source: From *Social Stratification: The Interplay of Class, Race, and Gender*, 2nd ed., by Daniel W. Rossides, © 1997. Adapted by permission of Pearson Education, Inc., Upper Saddle River, NJ.

other industrial states (Lipset and Bendix 1967). However, the most current anthropological research demonstrates that a rigid class structure does not dominate Japanese society and that most people believe that through education and their own personal efforts, they can rise to more economically and socially viable positions. Some individuals from lower-class categories, just as in the United States, have risen to the top as celebrities, artists, CEOs, and other positions. Thus, the ideals of moving ahead in an increasing affluent society such as Japan tends to promote more optimism about their prospects (McCreery and McCreery 2005).

Ever since the Russian Revolution in 1917, the former Soviet Union claimed to be a classless society, because its system was not based on the private ownership of the means of production. In fact, however, it had a stratified class system based on occupation. Occupations were hierarchically ranked into four major status groups, based on income, power, and prestige. The highest-ranking statuses consisted of upper-level government officials, Politburo members who were recruited from the Communist Party. The second tier consisted of professional workers such as engineers, professors, physicians, and scientists, as well as lower-level government workers. The third tier was made up of the manual workers in the industrial economy, and the bottom rung was composed of the rural peasantry (Kerblay 1983; Dunn and Dunn 1988). Most sociologists agree that this hierarchy of statuses reflects a class-based society.

Ethnic and Racial Stratification

In addition to social stratification based on occupation, many industrial states have a system of stratification based on ethnic or racial descent. For example, in the United States, various ethnic and racial groups such as African Americans, Native American Indians, and Hispanics have traditionally occupied a subordinate status and have experienced a more restricted type of social mobility. In contrast, most Western European countries traditionally have been culturally homogeneous, without many minority ethnic groups.

Recently, however, this situation has begun to change, as many formerly colonized peoples, such as Indians, Pakistanis, and Africans, have moved to Great Britain, and other non-Western peoples have migrated to other European nations. This has led to patterns of ethnic and racial stratification and discrimination in these countries.

In the former Soviet Union, many ethnic minorities resided in Estonia, Lithuania, the Ukraine, and Turko-Mongol areas such as Azerbaijan and Uzbekistan. These ethnic minorities lived outside the central Soviet territory, the heartland of the dominant Russian majority. Historically, the Soviet state had attempted to assimilate these national minorities by making the Russian language a compulsory subject in the educational system (Eickelman 1993; Maybury-Lewis 1997; Scupin 2003). Although the Soviet state prided itself on its principles of equality and autonomy applied to its national minorities, the outbreak of ethnic unrest and rebellion in these non-Russian territories in the mid-1990s demonstrated that these populations viewed themselves as victimized by the dominant ethnic Russian populace. Thus, ethnic stratification has been a component of industrial Soviet society.

Japan appears to have even more ethnic homogeneity. The Japanese make up 99.4 percent of the population of 126 million people, with only 0.6 percent of the population being ethnic minorities (mostly Korean). Although the Japanese, like all other peoples, are the outcome of a long evolutionary history of mixture with different groups, this racialized notion of ethnic identity remains as a myth of cultural identity for the Japanese (Diamond 1998; Yoshino 1992, 1998). Cultural anthropologists have noted that this view of themselves as a "unique" race has created some distinctive patterns of ethnic stratification. For example, the small minority of Japanese of Korean ancestry have experienced widespread discrimination, even though they have adopted Japanese language, most of the norms, and cultural values. In addition, a native-born Japanese population known as the eta, or *burakumin*, consisting of about 3 million people, also occupies a lower status. Despite the fact that the *burakumin* are physically indistinguishable from most other Japanese, they reside in separated ghetto areas in Japan. They are descendants of peoples who worked in the leather-tanning industries, traditionally considered low-status professions. Most of the *burakumin* still work primarily in the shoe shops and other leather-related industries. Marriages between *burakumin* and other Japanese are still restricted, and other patterns of ethnic discrimination against this group continue (Befu 1971; Hendry 1987; Ohnuki-Tierney 1998; Scupin 2003). This ethnic discrimination has resulted in poverty, lower education attainment, delinquency, and other social problems for the *burakumin*, just as it has for some ethnic minorities in the United States. As indicated in Chapter 7 in our discussion of IQ and race, the *burakumin* also score lower on IQ tests in Japan. As was emphasized in that discussion, because these people are not biologically or racially different from other Japanese people, this fact indicates that ethnic discrimination, poverty, and related environmental conditions are more responsible for differences in intelligence than any purported biological differences.

Political Organization

As European and American societies began to industrialize, the nature of their political organization was transformed. Members of the middle class grew economically powerful and were drawn to the idea of popular sovereignty—that is, that the people, rather than the rulers, were the ultimate source of political authority. In addition, because the middle classes (particularly the upper-middle class) were the primary beneficiaries of industrial capitalism, they favored a type of government that would allow them economic freedom to pursue profits without state interference. The feudal aristocratic patterns were thus eventually replaced with representative, constitutional governments. The overriding ideal in these democratic states is freedom or personal liberty, which includes freedom of expression, the right to vote, and the right to be represented in the government. Representation is based on the election of political leaders selected from various political parties that engage in competition for offices.

Although representative governments emerged in earlier centuries, their political ideals were not immediately realized. For example, in the United States, political rights, including the right to vote, were not extended to women and other minorities until the twentieth century.

Another aspect of political change was the growth of **nationalism**, a strong sense of loyalty to the nation-state based on shared language, values, and culture. Before the development of nationalism, the primary focus of loyalty was to the local community, religion, and the family (Anderson 1983; Scupin 2003). For example, in agricultural states, peasants rarely identified with the interests of the

ruling elites. In industrial states, however, with the increase in literacy and the development of a print technology, nationalism became a unifying force. Print technology was used to create what political scientist Benedict Anderson (1983) refers to as "imagined communities," an allegiance to a nation-state that is often far removed from everyday family or local concerns. As a literate populace began to read about their history and culture in their own language, they embarked on a new self-identification, and eventually people began to express pride and loyalty to these newly defined countries.

Anderson, though, is not suggesting that nationalism is just "invented," but holds that people who begin to define themselves as members of a nation will never know most of their fellow members, meet them, or even hear of them (1983). He notes that the fact that people are willing to give up their lives for their nation or country means that nationalism has a powerful influence on people's emotions and sentiments. This loyalty to a nation is a by-product of literacy and the proliferation of the media in promoting specific ideas regarding one's nation.

Michael Herzfeld, an anthropologist who has written extensively about nationalism, notes that nationalism parallels religious cosmologies in that it creates distinctive differences between the believers and nonbelievers, insiders and outsiders,

This Nazi rally demonstrates an extreme form of nationalism in German society in the 1940s.

and it reaffirms that the world is meaningful and sacred to people (1992). Herzfeld did ethnographic research in Greece, and in his book *Ours Once More: Folklore, Ideology, and the Making of Modern Greece* (1986), he focused on how Greek nationalism was created and managed by state authorities. One of the themes in his book is how nineteenth- and twentieth-century Greek intellectuals drew on folklore from rural areas to present an image of modern Greece as a continuation of their traditional classical past. The Greek state has drawn on a classical past that has been imagined as the root of all Western civilization to produce a contemporary source of nationalism for its citizens. This classical image of Greece as the mythical foundations of Western society and democratic institutions was recently emphasized in the Olympics in 2004 in Athens, Greece. A variety of symbols and motifs from ancient Greek culture and myth were projected internationally to promote the unique national identity, culture, and foundations of Western civilization of the Greek nation. Herzfeld's historical and cultural treatment indicates that the bureaucrats and intellectuals selected certain images and neglected other aspects of the past to develop this sense of nationalism for Greek citizens. For example, they selectively underplayed the role of the Ottoman empire and the Turkish influence on Greek society for centuries. The Turks were considered outsiders and not an integral part of Greek national culture. The manufacture of nationalism by state authorities and intellectuals who romanticized the classical past and rural villages produced a culture of loyalty and sacredness for Greek national culture. Many other industrialized societies, such as England, Japan, or Russia, could be used to illustrate this same pattern and the production of nationalism, a contemporary trait of modern nation-states.

Political Organization in Socialist States

The former Soviet Union was the first nation to declare that it had a socialist government that would be dominated by the working class—the proletariat—rather than the upper or middle classes. According to Marxist theory, this socialist government was to be only a transitional stage of state development, to be followed by a true form of communism in which the state would wither away. In Marx's view, in the communist stage there would be no need for the state, or government, because everyone's needs would be completely taken care of through people who would be free to produce and create for the community.

In the ensuing years, the ideals of the socialist state ruled by the proletariat and the movement toward an egalitarian communism were not realized in the Soviet Union. Instead, the Communist Party of the Soviet Union, with about 18 million members out of a total population of about 300 million, dominated the government, selecting the bureaucratic elite (the *apparatchiki*) of about 1 million to rule over the society. The former Soviet Union became a totalitarian state that controlled the economy, the political process, the media, the educational system, and other social institutions. During certain periods of extreme repression, as under Joseph Stalin in the 1930s, millions of people were killed or exiled to forced labor camps. Citizens were prohibited from organizing politically, and official opposition to state policies was not tolerated. This form of totalitarian government also existed in the socialist countries of Eastern Europe that were dominated by the Soviet Union.

Industrialism and State Bureaucracy

One similarity among the governments of the West, Japan, and the Soviet Union is the degree to which the state has become a highly developed bureaucracy. It appears that when an industrial economy becomes highly specialized and complex, a strong, centralized government develops to help coordinate and integrate the society's complicated political and economic affairs. Of course, as previously discussed, in socialist societies such as the Soviet Union, this growth and centralization of the state is more extreme.

Law

Legal institutions are more formalized in industrial states. In general, the more complex the society, the more specialized the legal system (Schwartz and Miller 1975). As discussed in Chapter 12, legal

Anthropologists at Work

The Japanese Corporation: An Anthropological Contribution from Harumi Befu

Harumi Befu.

During the past several decades, Japan became one of the world's major economic powers. During the 1970s and 1980s many social scientists investigated the organization and management techniques of Japanese corporations to determine how the Japanese economy has grown so rapidly. At that time, many Western economists, businesspeople, and others were involved in perceiving the Japanese economy as overtaking the West through their *samurai* business managers with their laptop computers, who were waging an economic war against the United States and the West. A number of popular films in the United States, such as *Black Rain* and *Rising Sun* and others, presented the Japanese as out-maneuvering and illegally trying to subvert the United States and flooding the U.S. market with cheap consumer goods and automobiles and buying up American assets. A whole series of books by American authors Chalmers Johnson and James Fallows and many others wrote about the major threat of the Japanese economy to the United States and the West. The Harvard sociologist and specialist on the Japanese economy, Ernst Vogel, wrote a book called *Japan as Number One*, illustrating its rapid economic growth and success in the global economy.

One of the major conclusions of most of these studies on the corporations was that Japanese

corporations are run much differently from corporations in Western capitalist countries. According to these studies, Japanese corporations emphasize traditional values such as group harmony, or *wa*, and collective rather than individual performance (Ouichi 1981; Lincoln and McBride 1987). For example, rather than hiring managers based on their individual performance as indicated by grades in college, Japanese corporations recruit managers as groups from different universities. Japanese firms are more interested in how groups and teams of managers work together than they are in each person's individual effort or performance. Managers are hired, trained, and promoted as groups by the corporation, based on their ability to cooperate in *teams*. In fact, the major influence on this tradition of teamwork was an American manager, W. Edwards Deming, who was sent to advise Japanese engineers and managers during the military occupation and taught the Japanese the team-management control quality methods that were effectively used to produce consumer goods, automobiles, and electronic consumer goods. The military leader General MacArthur convinced the Japanese to begin producing automobiles for export to the West and elsewhere to build up their industrial economy. In some respects, this policy reflected the Cold War aim of build-

ing a capitalist society in the midst of Asia that could become a bulwark to the spread of Communist ideology from other areas such as the Soviet Union or China. Also, these U.S. social science studies emphasized that in contrast to Western countries, which emphasize individualism and independence, the Japanese stress mutual dependence and teamwork (see Chapter 4).

In these studies, the social scientists emphasized that to ensure this collective performance, large Japanese corporations offer lifetime employment and a concern for their employees' general welfare. Employees are rarely fired or laid off. Corporations provide recreational facilities, parties, child care and other family-related services, and other benefits to enhance corporate loyalty. Corporate decision making is also based on collective principles. Typically, several younger managers are responsible for talking to sixty or seventy people who will be affected by a decision. Proposals for a new plan or policy are discussed and then redrafted until a consensus is achieved. A decision requiring one or two phone calls to a division manager in a U.S. company may take two or three weeks in a Japanese corporation. Once a decision is reached, however, everyone involved becomes committed to the plan.

Japanese anthropologist Chia Nakane (1970) believed that this collective orientation results from the hierarchical cultural nature of Japanese social organization. Nakane viewed Japanese society as consisting of hierarchically organized groups with paternalistic leaders at the top who serve group needs. She believed that the underlying psychological process supporting this group orientation is *amae*, an emotional dependence that develops between a child and his or her mother. Through enculturation, *amae* becomes the basis of a mutual dependence that develops between superiors and subordinates throughout society. This dependence is reinforced by resources given by the superior to the subordinate and expectations of loyalty of the subordinate to the superior. Nakane suggested that this Japanese manner of organization and structure produced a much different form of society and management style than the West. This type of view is still presented in a literature known as *Nihonjinron*, "discourses on Japaneseness," which emphasizes the cultural and sometimes even the "racial" uniqueness of the Japanese people.

Ruth Benedict, the American anthropologist, was hired by the U.S. government as an anthropologist to study the Japanese culture in order to find out why Japanese military people would be so willing to sacrifice their lives in suicide raids in the *kamikaze* attacks on

U.S. warships. She begins her book *The Chrysanthemum and the Sword* with the words "The Japanese were the most alien enemy that the United States had ever fought in an all-out struggle" (1948). Benedict's research project was not to produce propaganda, it was employed to offer insights to soldiers fighting a new kind of war. She and her colleagues in the Office of Strategic Planning had to discover not only the aims and motives of Japanese leaders, but "what their government could count on from the people . . . habits of thought and emotion and the patterns into which these habits fell."

Why was it that Japanese soldiers would go on fighting to the death, even in situations where they could not win? And then, when captured, why did these fight-to-the-death warriors become model prisoners, meekly doing whatever they were told and not trying to escape as POWs from Europe or America would? And why was the Emperor never included in criticisms of their government, their officers, and their comrades? The issues Benedict faced were deadly serious (McCreery and McCreery 2006).

Unfortunately, she writes, a field trip was out of the question. She "could not go to Japan and live in their homes and watch the strains and stresses of daily life." She wasn't able "to watch them in the complicated business of arriving at a decision" or to observe how they brought up their children. She would have to make do

with what she could learn at a distance, by reading books, watching movies, and interviewing Japanese Americans interned during the war.

Not surprisingly, the Japan that Benedict describes is very much the one that Nakane had described as group-oriented and devoted to the Emperor and the natural social hierarchy in Japanese society and devoted to "unique" Japanese cultural values and race.

Every greeting and bow to one another is precisely calibrated to the status of the person receiving the greeting. To Americans who prize equality and freedom, these customs may seem oppressive. Why, then, did Japanese accept the burdens they seemed to impose? To Benedict the answer was a value the Japanese call *on*, a word for which the closest English translation is "debt."

From a Japanese perspective, any favor imposed a debt. The debt was a burden because it had to be repaid. Depending on the nature of the debt, moreover, repayment might be impossible. Repayment took one of two forms: *gimu* or *giri*. *Gimu* was owed to the Emperor and to parents. In both these cases the debt was infinite. No repayment could ever be more than partial. *Giri* was a debt with limits, but one that must be repaid, measure for measure, in precisely the right form.

Here, then, according to Benedict, were the "core" values and answer to why Japanese soldiers would fight to the death, regard themselves as dead to Japanese society if captured, and criticize their colleagues but not the Emperor. The *gimu* owed to the Emperor meant that nothing short of death could repay the debt owed. Criticism could be leveled at officers and comrades who failed in the *giri* owed to each other. The Emperor, to whom *gimu* was owed, was forever beyond criticism. *Giri* "within the circle of *on*" was *giri* owed to others. But Japanese also owed *giri* to themselves. "*Giri* to one's name" involved a highly developed sense of personal honor and quick and furious anger at any sign of disrespect. Thus, otherwise passive prisoners would explode if their captors made fun of them.

Stanford anthropologist Harumi Befu (1980) has questioned some aspect of this group model of unique social structure of Japanese society. Befu has a unique background and perspective from which to view this issue. He was born in the United States in 1930 but moved to Japan when he was six years old to receive his primary and secondary education. He returned to the United States in 1947 to carry out his undergraduate and graduate studies in anthropology. He subsequently remained in the United States and specialized in the ethnological study of Japanese society.

Befu criticized the group model of Japanese society for its tendency to overlook social conflict, individual competition, self-interest, and exploitation. Regarding the purported internal harmony of Japanese groups and society, Befu believed that many proponents of the group model have lost sight of various aspects of Japanese society. Befu believed that many of these theorists failed to distinguish between the *real* and *ideal* norms of Japanese society. Although a president of a corporation may refer to his or her company as a harmonious, happy family at an induction ceremony for new recruits, he or she acts differently at a collective bargaining session in dealing with union demands.

Befu averred that not only Western scholars but many of the Japanese themselves have accepted this group-model concept as an integral aspect of their cultural identity and as an aspect of the *Nihonjihron* "Japanese discourse on their cultural and racial uniqueness" (1992). He argued that the group model is not really a social model for Japanese society as much as a cultural model or belief system. He suggested that the group model as a social model is too simplistic to explain comprehensively a complex, postindustrial society such as Japan. Befu did not reject the group model entirely, however. Rather, he contended that the group model as well as a model based on individualism could be applied to both Japanese and Western institutions and bureaucracies. For example, at various times in both Japanese and Western corporations, individuals are in competition and conflict with one another over wealth, power, and status, while simultaneously working on group projects that will benefit the corporation as a whole. Individual competition and conflict may take a different form in Japan than it does in Western countries; nevertheless, Befu emphasized that it does exist in both regions. To that extent, Befu suggested that Japanese corporations and social life may not be as unique as either the Japanese or Westerners think they are. This is an important contribution to understanding the extreme positions that can be taken by some anthropologists in portraying others as exotic and alien in different societies.

institutions became formalized in some of the intensive agricultural states with the emergence of codified written law, records of cases and precedents, courts and government officials such as judges, procedures for deciding cases, and a police force to enforce legal decisions. These innovations in legal systems have been expanded in modern industrial societies.

In industrial states, laws become more complex and bureaucratically formalized with the development of national and local statutes, private and public codes, the differentiation between criminal and civil laws, and more specialized law-enforcement agencies. With the development of centralized national governments, a hierarchy of legal codes was formulated that ranged from national constitutions to regional and local codes. One of the most distinctive features of law in industrial societies is the proliferation of public and procedural law, referred to as administrative law (Vago 1995).

Administrative law reflects the emerging bureaucratic rules and technical requirements in the various legal institutions and agencies in industrial states. Courts in modern industrial states play an important role not only in adjudication but also in mediation and other methods of conflict resolution. In addition, the legal system is the most important means of inducing social change in complex industrial societies. For example, legislation was used to gain civil rights for ethnic minorities such as African Americans in the United States.

Japanese Law

The unique configuration of Japanese values and norms, in comparison with Western or Soviet society, has produced a different form of legal system in Japan. The Confucian ethos and traditional Japanese norms emphasizing group harmony have deeply influenced legal processes and institutions. The Japanese generally adopt extra-judicial, informal means of resolving disputes and prefer legal compromises as opposed to assigning moral blame or deciding on the rightness or wrongness of an action. When a dispute arises, a mediator is usually employed to bring about a reconciliation. The Japanese prefer the mediator to a lawyer, who is less likely to know the parties or to have a personal relationship with them. In this sense, the Japanese mediation system resembles those of small-scale tribal societies (Hendry 1987).

In Japanese society, there tends to be no legal or societal pressure for absolute justice. The proper, moral action is to accept blame for a wrongdoing and resign oneself to the consequences. Conflict resolution outside the court system and codified law tends to be the rule with respect to civil law. Obviously, one of the differences between Japan and the United States is the overwhelming cultural homogeneity of Japan. In contrast, the United States is a highly heterogeneous society with many different ethnic groups and cultural backgrounds. The relative homogeneity of Japanese society facilitates resolving conflicts through informal means rather than through the legal system, as in the United States. However, a recent study indicates that Japan's rate of litigation is beginning to increase (Vago 1995).

Warfare and Industrial Technology

We noted in Chapter 12 that warfare increased with the territorial expansion of agricultural empires such as China, Rome, the Aztec, and India. To some extent, this increase in warfare was linked to technological developments such as the invention of iron weapons. In addition, the nature of warfare began to change with the development of centralized state systems that competed with rival territories. These general tendencies were accelerated with the evolution of industrial states.

Industrial states began to develop military technologies that enabled them to carry on fierce nationalistic wars in distant regions. One of the prime motivations for these wars was to establish economic and political hegemony over foreign peoples. The industrial nation-states became much more involved in economic rivalry over profits, markets, and natural resources in other territories. Most historians conclude that these imperialist rivalries were the principal reasons for World War I.

World War I marked a watershed in the evolution of military warfare. It was a global war in which nation-states mobilized a high proportion of their male populations and reoriented their economic systems toward military production and support. The numbers of combatants and noncombatants killed far outnumbered those of any previous war in any type of society.

The combination of technological advances and centralized military organizations dramatically changed the nature of warfare. Tanks, airplanes, and other modern weapons enabled industrial states to wage tremendously destructive global warfare, as witnessed by World War II. This expanding military technology was inextricably linked to industrial technology. The rise of industries such as airlines, automobiles, petroleum and plastics, and electronics and computers were all related to the development of war technology. And,

Pablo Picasso, "Guernica" 1937, Oil on Canvas, 11'5 ½ × 25' 5 ¾. Museo Nacional Centro de Arte Reina Sofia/©2002 Estate of Pablo Picasso/Artists Rights Society (ARS), New York. This painting by Picasso symbolizes the destructiveness of industrial warfare.

of course, the atomic era began in 1945 when the United States dropped atomic bombs on Hiroshima and Nagasaki.

Religion

Ever since the Renaissance and Enlightenment period, Western industrial states have experienced extensive **secularization**, the historical decline in the influence of religion in society. Scientists such as Galileo and Charles Darwin developed ideas that challenged theological doctrines. European secular philosophies such as the Renaissance political writer Nicolo Machiavelli and other Enlightenment philosophers such as Thomas Hobbes, John Locke, and Jean Jacques Rousseau, and Voltaire increasingly proposed naturalistic (nonsupernatural), scientific explanations of both the natural and social worlds. Secularization has influenced all industrialized states. For example, most people in these societies do not perceive illness as the result of supernatural forces; rather, they rely on physicians trained in scientific medical practices to diagnose and cure diseases. However, secularization has developed much deeper roots in European culture

than in the United States. One of the major reasons for the difference is that European society had deadly genocidal religious wars for generations that political leaders and intellectuals wanted to escape from. In contrast, in U.S. society that had religious freedom and not much religious warfare, this extreme secular trend was not as apparent, and most people in the United States still participate in religious activity much more than Europeans do. Yet, there are differences among various class and education groups in both Europe and the United States.

Despite the increase of secularization in the West, religion has not completely disappeared from industrial states. For example, the United States has experienced a great deal of secularization, and yet it remains one of the most religious societies in the world. Polls indicate that almost 88 percent of all Americans profess a belief in some sort of divine power. Nearly two-thirds of Americans are affiliated with a religious organization, and many of them identify with a particular religion (National Opinion Research Center 1999). Most sociologists who have studied the question of how religious Americans are have concluded that this question is extremely complex because it relates

Critical Perspectives

GRADUATION: A RITE OF PASSAGE IN U.S. SOCIETY

As the United States continues to change from an industrial to a postindustrial society, more people are attending college to gain the skills and knowledge necessary to prepare them for careers. Consequently, one rite of passage that people increasingly look forward to is graduation from college. This rite of passage is similar to those in many other societies. Following an intensive four or five years of study, examinations, and research papers, students face the climactic rite of passage known as the commencement ceremony.

The commencement ceremony dates back to the twelfth century at the University of Bologna in what is now Italy. Shortly thereafter, it spread to other European universities. The first U.S. graduates went through their commencement in 1642 at Harvard University. These first commencement ceremonies lasted several days and were accompanied by entertainment, wrestling matches, banquets, and dances.

The academic costumes worn by graduates come directly from the late Middle Ages and the Renaissance. The black gowns and square caps, called "mortarboards," were donned to celebrate the change in status. A precise ritual dictates that the tassel that hangs off the cap should be moved from the right side to the left side when the degree is conferred.

Like rituals of passage in other societies, graduation from college represents a transition in status. In Latin, *gradus* means a step, and *degradus* means a rung on a ladder. From the first we get the word graduation; from the second, degree. Both words are connected to a stage in life, the end of one period of life and the beginning of another. To graduate means to change by degrees.

Typically, the college graduate moves from the status of a receiver to that of a giver. Up to the point of graduation, many students are subsidized and nurtured by society and especially by parents. After graduation, a person becomes a giver in all sorts of ways. A degree qualifies graduates to get jobs and to contribute to the workplace. In addition, degree holders will begin to subsidize others through taxes. Many will marry and accept such responsibilities as raising children and paying mortgages. This movement from receiver to giver represents a fundamental life-cycle transition for many U.S. students.

POINTS TO PONDER

1. As you move toward your degree in college, do you believe that what you are learning has any relationship to what you will need after your change in status?

2. In what ways would you change the educational process so that it would help you to develop your potential?

3. Do you think the grading system used by most colleges and universities is a fair means of assessing your acquisition of knowledge and skills?

4. What would you suggest as a better means of evaluating students?

5. What kinds of expectations do you have about your change in status after you receive your degree?

---

to ethnic, political, and social-class issues. Many Americans claim religious affiliation in relationship to their communal or ethnic identity; others may belong to religious organizations to gain a sense of identity and belonging or as a source of social prestige. Whatever the reasons, secularization has not substantially eroded religious beliefs and institutions in the United States.

Religion in Socialist States

In the former Soviet Union, secularization had been an aspect of the ideological apparatus of the state. According to Marxist views, religion is a set of beliefs and institutions used by the upper classes to control and regulate the lower classes. The ultimate aim of socialist societies is to eradicate religion, thereby removing a major obstacle to equality. For this reason, the former Soviet Union and socialist Eastern European nations repressed religious organizations and officially endorsed atheism.

Despite these policies, however, in the former Soviet Union 15 percent of the urban population and 30 percent of the rural population practiced religion. There were about 40 million Russian Orthodox Catholics, 600,000 Protestants, and up to 45 million Muslims in a country that has proclaimed itself as atheistic for five decades (Kerblay 1983; Eickelman 1993). Thus, religious beliefs appear to have been a continuing source of inspiration and spiritual comfort for many citizens of the former Soviet state.

Religion in Japan

Japan has also experienced a great deal of secularization as it has industrialized. Traditional Japanese religion was an amalgamation of beliefs based on an indigenous animistic form of worship referred to as Shintoism, combined with Confucianism, Taoism, and Buddhism, which spread from China. Most Japanese and Western observers agree that secularization has diminished the influence of these traditional faiths. Although the majority of Japanese still turn to Shinto shrines and Buddhist ceremonies for life-cycle rituals or personal crises, and the temples teem with people during the various holidays, most modern Japanese confess that they are not deeply religious (Befu 1971; Hendry 1987; McCreery and McCreery 2006).

Most anthropologists concur, however, that religious beliefs and practices are so thoroughly culturally embedded in Japanese culture that religion cannot easily be separated from the national identity and way of life. For example, many Japanese refer to *nihondo* (the Japanese way) as the basis of their national, ethnic, and cultural identity. *Nihondo* refers to Japanese cultural beliefs and practices, including traditional religious concepts. Thus, it appears that religion is intimately bound up with Japanese identity.

In Chapter 16 on contemporary global trends, we again turn to what anthropologists are learning about globalization and its influence on these industrial and postindustrial societies. They are in the midst of dynamic economic, social, political, and religious change that will be addressed in that chapter.

SUMMARY

The changes associated with the Industrial Revolution dramatically transformed the technologies, economies, social structures, political systems, and religions of various nations. The center of the first Industrial Revolution was in Europe. However, when taking a global perspective, anthropologists agree that this Industrial Revolution could not have occurred without the substantial influence of many other non-Western regions of the world.

These changes brought about by the Industrial Revolution are referred to collectively as modernization. The use of industrial technology required increasing amounts of fossil fuels and other nonrenewable energy sources. In contrast to preindustrial societies, industrial societies are high-energy consumers. These societies also experienced decreasing fertility and mortality rates. This pattern is known as demographic transition. With the expansion of the factory system, people increasingly came to reside in dense urban areas.

The technological and economic changes of industrial societies led to a new, complex division of labor. Industrial economies consist of the primary, secondary, and tertiary sectors, with jobs increasingly located in the tertiary sector, consisting of white-collar, service industries. Industrialization also stimulated new exchange patterns, resulting in the development of the market economy. Both capitalist and socialist systems developed in industrial societies.

Industrial expansion transformed the social structure. Occupation replaced kinship as the most important determiner of status, and the nuclear family largely replaced the extended family. Marriage and divorce increasingly reflected personal choice rather than family arrangements. Gender relationships became more egalitarian, and a majority of women entered the workforce. Still, the legacy of patriarchy and male domination continued to influence female status and the division of labor.

The status of the elderly declined in most industrial societies as a result of rapid technological change and new methods of acquiring and storing knowledge. Social stratification increased as class systems based on wealth and occupation emerged. Class systems developed in both capitalist and socialist societies. In addition, ethnicity and race influenced the patterns of stratification.

New forms of political systems, including democratic and totalitarian governments, took root in industrial societies. In both democratic-capitalist and totalitarian-socialist societies, state bureaucracies grew in size and complexity. New, complex forms of legal processes and court systems emerged. Finally, scientific and educational developments influenced religious traditions in industrial states. Secularization has affected all of these societies, yet religion has not disappeared, and it remains an important component of all industrial societies.

QUESTIONS TO THINK ABOUT

1. Characterize the types of changes that led to the Industrial Revolution.

2. Compare high and low energy-using technologies.

3. What form does the division of labor take in industrial states? Where do you think the United States falls in this scheme?

4. Compare the principal tenets of capitalism and socialism. Would it be possible to create a functional economy that combined these two systems?

5. What is meant by the terms market economy and capitalism? What are the principal advantages and disadvantages of these systems for individual participants?

6. Using a specific example, describe what is meant by a multinational corporation. What are the processes by which this multinational corporation can affect the processes of both individual countries and the global economy?

7. How has industrialization affected the family, kinship, marriage, and divorce?

8. What is the difference between a closed society and an open society? Is the United States a closed or open society? What about Japan, the former Soviet Union, and Great Britain?

9. What are some of the characteristics of Japanese industrial corporations?

10. Define the term *feminism*. What are the goals of feminists in industrialized states? Do you agree with these goals? Why or why not?

11. What are the processes whereby industrialization affects the status of elderly individuals? How can we explain the higher status of the aged in societies like Japan and Russia?

12. How do political systems differ in industrial societies compared to preindustrial societies?

13. In your experience, has secularization had an impact on your religious beliefs and practices?

KEY TERMS

capitalism

closed societies

demographic transition

feminism

industrialization

industrial society

market economy

mercantilism

modernization

monopoly capitalism

multinational corporations

nationalism

nation-states

oligopoly

open societies

primary sector

secondary sector

secularization

socialism

tertiary sector

Chapter 14

Globalization in Latin America, Africa, and the Caribbean

CHAPTER QUESTIONS

■ What were the early phases of Western colonialism, as for Latin America, Africa, and the Caribbean?

■ What were the demographic, economic, political, and religious changes associated with globalization in Latin America, Africa, and the Caribbean?

■ Why did independence, nationalist, and revolutionary movements develop in Latin America, Africa, and the Caribbean?

■ How are the Latin American, African, and Caribbean countries situated in the global economy today?

■ What have anthropologists learned about the peasantry in Latin America, Africa, and the Caribbean countries?

■ What are the characteristics of family and gender relationships in Latin America, Africa, and the Caribbean countries?

■ How has urbanization influenced Latin America, Africa, and the Caribbean countries?

Most anthropologists have focused on non-Western countries for their ethnographic research. To understand how globalization processes have influenced local conditions and cultures, they have had to adopt a broad global perspective in their research. The non-Western countries of Latin America, the Caribbean, and Africa comprise a complex of diversified regions and cultures that cannot be characterized easily. The various countries in these regions are located in different types of environmental zones, ranging from highland mountain areas to lowland river valleys to small island regions to complex urban centers. Each country is made up of various ethnic groups in different proportions. As a result of globalization, all these countries are at different stages of political and economic development. In Chapters 9–11 we discussed various band, tribal, and chiefdom societies (that are very diverse) that exist in these different regions and how globalization has had an impact on their development. This chapter begins with an overview of the spread of globalization and colonialism in Latin America, Africa, and the Caribbean. We then discuss some consequences of globalization processes on these regions. Finally, we discuss various ethnographic studies that have illuminated the effects of globalization on various institutions in these various countries.

One of the points that we want to stress is that globalization is always a painful process for any society to experience. When Europe, the United States, and Japan went through industrialization, as discussed in Chapter 13, it brought dislocation and disruption to families through rapid urbanization and other changes. People were torn away from their traditional communities of support, and ethnic and religious communities no longer provided the source of security they once did. Extensive migration, urban congestion, increases in deviance and crime, political corruption, population growth, pollution, and other social problems accompanied industrialization in these so-called First World countries.

But the countries that we discuss in this chapter and the next are facing these globalization processes in a much different way from the First World industrialized countries. The industrialized countries, such as Europe or the United States, had *centuries* to adjust to these processes, whereas other areas of the world have been experiencing aspects of globalization for a short period of time. Although these processes began during the time of colonization for most of these countries, it is only within the past few decades that globalization has penetrated deeply within the fabric of these societies.

Globalization and Colonialism in Latin America, Africa, and the Caribbean

Latin America

Following Columbus's explorations in the 1400s, Spanish and Portuguese conquistadores led expeditions to the Americas. Recall that this was the period of *mercantilism* (see Chapters 6 and 13), when European states were competing to accumulate wealth to build their national treasuries. The Portuguese and Spanish were the first Europeans to engage in this mercantilist competition. Columbus believed that he had reached islands off Asia, and the Spanish and Portuguese were anxious to acquire access to this new trade route, in part to cut off the Muslim monopoly of trade in the Mediterranean and Asia. Thus, the primary objectives of the conquistadores were to find wealth and conquer the Americas.

The indigenous societies of Latin America consisted of three major types of sociocultural systems: small-scale hunting-gathering bands; horticulturalist tribes, who lived in permanent or semipermanent villages and supplemented their diet by hunting, fishing, and gathering; and chiefdoms and agricultural empires, such as the Aztec and Inca, with great complex achievements in technology, architecture, economic organization, and statecraft.

In 1494, the Spanish and Portuguese governments agreed to the Treaty of Tordesillas, which divided the world into two major mercantilist spheres of influence. As a result, in the Americas the Portuguese took control of what is now Brazil, and the Spanish gained access to most of the remainder of Latin America.

Cortés and the Aztec Empire   The first major collision between the Spanish and the indigenous peoples occurred in 1519, when Hernando Cortés confronted the Aztec Empire in Mexico. After landing at Veracruz, Cortés encouraged many native groups who had been conquered and subjugated by the Aztecs to revolt against the Aztecs and their ruler, Montezuma. Besieged by these rebellious peoples and the superior weaponry of the Spaniards—especially guns and cannons—the Aztec state quickly crumbled. In 1521, Cortés and his Native American allies captured Tenochtitlan, establishing Spanish domination over the entire empire.

The Spanish then went on to conquer Mesoamerica, including Mexico, Honduras, and Guatemala, and areas in southeastern and southwestern North America. Similar conquests occurred in various regions of South America, such as Francisco Pizarro's conquest of the Incas. The Spanish ransacked these civilizations, taking the gold, silver, precious stones, and other valuables these people had accumulated. After this first phase of conquest and occupation, the Spanish began to exploit this

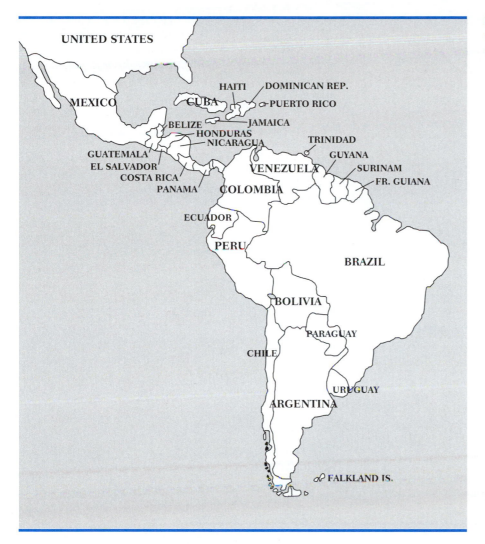

FIGURE 14.1 A map of contemporary Latin America and the Caribbean.

wealth for the benefit of their home country. They developed systems of mining, commercial agriculture, livestock raising, and trading. These new forms of economic organization drastically transformed the sociocultural systems of the Americas.

The region of Brazil in South America contained no productive agricultural states such as those of the Aztecs or Incas, and the native population consisted of only about *one* million people. Therefore, instead of searching for wealth in gold, silver, and other precious goods, the Portuguese turned immediately to developing commercial agriculture and introduced sugar plantations. The plantation system initially relied on local labor, but because there were few natives in this area, the Portuguese also imported African slaves.

Africa

European expansion into Africa began with the Portuguese, who came seeking gold; their explorers reached the West African coast in the second half of the fifteenth century. Although they did not find in Africa the vast amounts of gold that the Americas had yielded, they discovered another source of wealth: slaves.

Slave Trade In earlier chapters, we noted that slavery was an accepted institution in some chiefdoms and agricultural states around the world. Slavery existed throughout much of the ancient agricultural world, including Egypt, Greece, Rome, the Middle East, and parts of Africa. Until the twentieth century, various Middle Eastern empires maintained

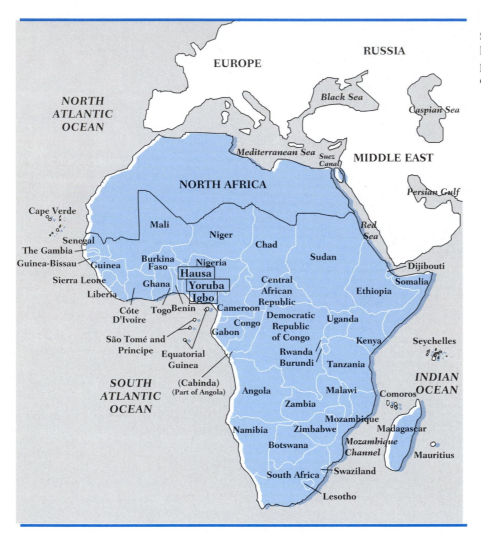

FIGURE 14.2 A map of Sub-Saharan Africa, highlighting some of the peoples discussed in the chapter.

an extensive slave trade based on African labor (Hourani 1991). In Africa, agricultural states such as the Asante kingdom kept war captives and criminals as slaves. This slavery, however, was much different from that of later Western societies (Davidson 1961; Goody 1980). In Chapter 12 we discussed the "open" forms of slavery associated with societies with abundant land and low populations. In Africa, this open system included slaves who were attached to extended families and became part of the domestic social unit. They could own property and marry, and they were protected from mutilation and murder by formalized norms or legal institutions.

The Portuguese initiated the major European slave trade around 1440. They took slaves from coastal areas of West Africa to Portugal and to some islands in the Mediterranean. African slaves became the major source of labor for the expanding plantation systems in North and South America. Portugal, Holland, and, by the 1700s, England and France became the dominant slave-trading nations.

Unlike the open forms of slavery found in Africa, these Western countries classified slaves as property, with no personal rights, who could never be incorporated into the owner's domestic family or social system. These countries traded goods and weapons with certain African groups, who, in turn, supplied the Europeans with slaves. Sometimes African leaders simply relied on the local institutions of slavery to sell their own slaves to the Europeans. In many cases, however, coastal Africans raided inland villages for slaves. These practices had emerged in the earlier slave trade with the Islamic empires to the north.

Millions of slaves were taken from Africa and transported to Latin America and the Caribbean. The Atlantic slave trade declined in the early nineteenth century, when antislavery movements in Britain and France led to the prohibition of slave trading. British ships patrolled the coasts of Africa to capture slave traders, although many ships eluded this blockade. Slave trade to the United States ended in 1808, but the complete abolition of the slave trade was not possible until countries such as Brazil and the United States abandoned their plantation systems. The United States made slavery illegal in 1865, and Brazil did so in 1888 (Davis 1984, 1996). The devastating effects of the slave trade, however, continue to plague Africa to the present.

Colonization in Africa Europeans generally did not venture into the interior of Africa for colonization during the mercantilist phase of AD 1500 and 1600. The threat of malaria and military resistance kept them in the coastal regions. During the late nineteenth century, however, European nations began to compete vigorously for African territories. To serve their needs for raw materials and overseas markets, the British, French, Dutch, Belgians, and Germans partitioned different areas of Africa into colonies, as reflected in the boundaries of present-day countries.

In West Africa, the difficult climate and the presence of diseases such as malaria discouraged large-scale European settlement. The British, French, and Germans, however, established commercial enterprises to control the production and exportation of products such as palm oil (used in soap making) and cocoa (Wolf 1997, 2001).

In central Africa, King Leopold of Belgium incorporated the 900,000 acres of the Congo as a private preserve. He controlled the basic economic assets of the region through stock ownership in companies that were allowed to develop the rubber and ivory trade. In doing so, the king used brutal methods of forced labor that caused the population to decline by one-half (from 20 million to 10 million) during his reign, from 1885 to 1908 (Miller 1988).

In East Africa during the 1880s, the Germans and the British competed for various territories to develop plantations and other enterprises. This rivalry eventually resulted in treaties that gave the British the colony of Kenya and the Germans a large territory known as Tanganyika. British and German settlers flocked to these countries and took possession of lands from the native peoples.

The colonization of southern Africa began in the late seventeenth century, when Dutch explorers built a refueling station for their ships at Cape Town. From that site, Dutch settlers, first called "Boers" and later "Afrikaners," penetrated into the region. The Boers displaced, and often enslaved, the native peoples, including foragers such as the Ju/'hoansi San and tribal peoples such as the Hottentots. They eventually adopted a racially based, hierarchical system in which the Boers held the highest ranks, followed by the coloreds (people of mixed parentage), the Bantu-speaking agriculturalists, and people like the Ju/'hoansi and Hottentots. Each group was segregated from the others and treated differently. The Boers eventually decimated most of the Hottentots through genocidal policies.

As the Dutch were settling these lands, the British were also penetrating into southern Africa. They incorporated several kingdoms, which they transformed into native reservations under British control. Fearful of British expansion, the Boers migrated north into lands that had long been inhabited by the Bantu-speaking Zulus. This migration became known as the "Great Trek." Although the Zulus fought bitterly against this encroachment, they were defeated in 1838 by the superior military technology of the Boers (Service 1977).

As the Boers moved north, they established the republics of Natal, the Orange Free State, and the Transvaal. In the meantime, gold and diamonds had been discovered in these areas, leading to intense competition between the British and the Boers. In the Boer War of 1899–1902, the British defeated the Boers and annexed all their republics. In 1910, the British established the Union of South Africa.

The Caribbean

The Caribbean islands consist of four distinct geographical regions: the first contains the Bahamas, nearest to the coast of North America; the second, called the Greater Antilles, consists of Cuba and Hispaniola (Haiti and the Dominican Republic), Jamaica, the Cayman Islands, Puerto Rico, and the Virgin

Islands; the third, the Lesser Antilles, includes Antigua, Barbuda, Dominica, St. Lucia, St. Vincent, the Grenadines, Grenada, and St. Christopher-Nevis (St. Kitts); the fourth, off the coast of South America, includes Trinidad, Tobago, Barbados, Aruba, Cuacao, and Bonaire. Some of the islands, such as Cuba, Haiti, and Puerto Rico, came under Spanish rule by 1500. Others were divided up by other European powers, such as the British, French, and Dutch.

Unlike the mainland regions, these islands did not have large, complex agricultural states with accumulated treasures. Therefore, the colonial powers introduced commercialized agriculture, usually in the form of sugar plantations, an agricultural system that had been developing in the Mediterranean region (Mintz 1985; Kephart 2003). As these sugar plantations were developed, large numbers of African slaves were imported by the Europeans to labor on these plantations. When the African slave trade began to decline, the British replaced slave labor with East Indian workers on some of the islands. Thus, the islands of the Caribbean are an extremely diverse region with Hispanic, French, Dutch, African, and East Indian cultural influences.

An example of the strong traditional African influence is evident in Haiti, Jamaica, and other islands. For example, Carriacou, a small island located in the eastern Caribbean between Grenada and St. Vincent, provides an example of the retention and reformulation of African beliefs and practices in the context of New World slavery. Most residents of Carriacou are descendants of African slaves brought to the island in the seventeenth and eighteenth centuries, first by French and later by British planters. After emancipation in the 1830s, most of the European planters left; the former slaves developed a relatively egalitarian society based on subsistence activities such as farming and fishing, supplemented by market activity and also by migration to places offering opportunities for wage labor. This relative isolation allowed Carriacou people to maintain their connections to their African past in ways not available to former slaves in other places. For example, Carriacouans continue to trace their descent from particular African ethnic groups, some of which are Igbo, Yoruba, Mandingo, Congo, and Kromanti (Asante). Along with this knowledge, talented musicians keep alive the traditional drumming patterns associated with each group, and these have been combined over the years with new songs in Creole French and Creole English.

The songs and drumming patterns are the central feature of the ritual known as the Big Drum or Nation Dance, which is held to celebrate special occasions such as the launching of a boat, a marriage, the placing of a permanent tombstone, or a bountiful harvest. A Big Drum ceremony may also be held to honor a request for food from the ancestors; such requests come to the living through dreams and are considered very important.

The Big Drum ceremony usually takes place at night in the yard of the ceremony's sponsor. An important feature of the ceremony, in addition to the drumming and singing, is food, which is prepared in sufficient quantity to be shared with all who attend the ceremony. Some of the food is set aside for the ancestors; this food, called the *saraka* or "parents' plate," is placed on a table inside the house and watched over by an elder woman called a *gangan*. This woman has "special sight" and can tell when the ancestors have come and eaten their fill; the *saraka* is then distributed among the children at the ceremony.

The ceremony, including the drumming and the sharing of food, might be considered an example of egalitarian redistribution similar to that which takes place in some tribal societies (see Chapter 10), because it serves to reinforce the Carriacouan values of egalitarianism and sharing (Hill 1977; McDaniel 1998; Kephart 2003).

On another island in Martinique, as elsewhere in the Caribbean, three centuries of people living on cane plantations resulted in the weaving of a rich fabric of cultural materials—folklore, ideas about value and tastes, the Creole language, and so on. Today, Martinicans from all walks of life recognize the central role of the plantation in the cultural makeup of the island.

Consequences of Globalization and Colonialism

Demographic Change

The immediate impact of the West on Mesoamerica, South America, Africa, and the Caribbean was disastrous for local populations. In Mesoamerica,

South America, and the Caribbean, the native population began to decline drastically. One of the major reasons for this decline was the introduction of diseases—smallpox, typhoid fever, measles, influenza, the mumps—to which the Indians had no resistance, because they had never been exposed to them before. In Brazil and the Caribbean, the importation of African slaves led to the introduction of diseases such as malaria and yellow fever. Although the numbers vary, archaeologists estimate that at least 25 million people lived in Mesoamerica when the Europeans arrived; by 1650, only 1.5 million remained (Wolf 1997).

Rapid depopulation was also due to the stresses induced by the new forms of labor to which these peoples were subjected. Large-scale slave raiding decimated native populations. The rigorous forms of enforced labor—including slavery—in mining, plantations, and livestock raising created serious health problems and caused numerous deaths. In addition, the collapse of the indigenous patterns of intensive agriculture brought about famines and food shortages. All these factors increased the social and biological stresses that aided the spread of disease in these populations (Wolf 1997).

The demographic consequences of the slave trade in Africa were also immense. Historians estimate that as many as 40 million Africans were captured from the interior between 1440 and 1870 (Davis 1984, 1996; Miller 1988). During this period, about 30 million Africans perished on their march from the inland regions or during the voyage to the New World. Approximately 12 million Africans were imported forcibly to the Americas. Many of them were in their prime reproductive years, which, in conjunction with the wars between the coastal and interior regions, may account for the slow growth of Africa's population during this period (Wolf 1997).

In the long run, however, Western expansion and colonialism in non-Western countries brought unprecedented demographic growth to the populations of these agricultural states. For example, the population of Mexico tripled in the nineteenth century from 2.5 million to 9 million, and Cuba's population increased from 550,000 to 5.8 million in 1953. Apparently, as Europeans began to change the indigenous population from traditional subsistence peasant farming to the production of cash crops, fertility rates began to rise in the traditional villages. There were labor shortages in the villages, and peasants responded by having larger extended families to try to maintain their subsistence peasant farming (Robbins 1999). And, generally, fertility rates remain high in most of the countries of Latin America, Africa, and the Caribbean.

Eventually, new medical and sanitation practices introduced by modernization led to a tremendous reduction in death rates through the control of smallpox, plague, yellow fever, and malaria. Meanwhile, birth rates remained high. The combination of reduced death rates and high birth rates led to dramatic population increases. In Chapter 16 we discuss some of the global effects of these population trends.

Economic Change

The economic changes that occurred with globalization in Latin America, Africa, and the Caribbean countries wrought a dramatic transformation in these societies. In Latin America, the Spanish developed large-scale mining operations that used forced labor. In addition to gold, the Spanish discovered vast supplies of silver in Mexico and Bolivia. The American mines eventually became the major source of bullion accumulated by mercantile Spain. For example, of the 7 million pounds of silver extracted from these mines, the Spanish Crown collected 40 percent.

New patterns of economic organization in Latin America and the Caribbean were introduced after the Iberian (Portuguese and Spanish) conquest. In the Spanish areas, the Crown rewarded the conquistadores with the *encomienda*, or grants of Indian land, tribute, and labor, which, because it was based on forced labor, reduced the Indians to dependents.

Eventually, the *encomienda* system was superseded by the hacienda (in Brazil, *fazenda*), or large-scale plantation. Established during the colonial period, *haciendas* and *fazendas* remained the major economic institutions in Latin America until the mid-twentieth century. The owners, called *hacendados* or *fazendieros*, acquired status, wealth, and power by owning the land and subjugating the tenants, or peons, who were tied to the haciendas through indebtedness and lived in shacks. In certain respects, the *haciendas* and *fazendas* were similar to the feudalistic manors of European societies described in Chapter 12.

Although the *haciendas* and *fazendas* were self-sufficient economic units providing the essential resources for the owners and tenants, they were not efficient (Wolf 1969, 1997). The *hacendados* tended to be preoccupied with their social prestige and comfortable lifestyle and did not attempt to produce cash crops for the world market or use their land productively. This pattern of inefficient, localized production and marketing of the haciendas is still visible in much of Latin America.

After three centuries of Iberian rule, much of Latin America consisted of these inefficient haciendas, economically deprived Indian communities with limited land, and a native population that was undernourished, maltreated, overworked, and reduced to bondage. An enormous social gap developed between the Indian peons and a class of individuals who identified with Iberian political and economic interests.

In Africa during the first phase of colonialism, the different European powers attempted to make their colonies economically self-sufficient. African labor was recruited for work on the commercialized plantations and in the gold and diamond mines. Native workers received substandard wages and were forced to pay head taxes to the colonial regimes. Head taxes were assessed for each individual and had to be paid in cash. By requiring cash payments, the colonial governments forced villagers to abandon subsistence agriculture and become wage laborers. In eastern and southern Africa, many choice agricultural lands were taken from the native peoples and given to British and Dutch settlers. As the demand for exports from Africa began to increase in the world-market system, the colonial powers began to develop transportation and communication systems linking coastal cities with inland regions. The purpose of these systems was to secure supplies of natural resources and human labor.

A major consequence of these colonial processes was the complete disruption of the indigenous production and exchange systems. Africans were drawn into the wage economy. Monetary systems based on European coinage were introduced, displacing former systems of exchange. The price of African labor and goods came to be determined by the world market. Global economic conditions began to shape the sociocultural systems and strategies of native peoples throughout Africa.

One major consequence of Western colonialism was the integration of many agricultural village communities into wider regional and global economic patterns. Although the precolonial traditional villages were probably never entirely self-sufficient and were tied to regional and national trading networks through Western colonialism, the village peasantry was no longer isolated from cities, and the global market determined the prices for agricultural goods. The transformation of agricultural economies triggered dramatic changes in traditional peasant rural communities. Because few peasants had enough capital to own and manage land, much of the land fell into the hands of colonial settlers, large landowners, and moneylenders. In many cases, these changes encouraged absentee land ownership and temporary tenancy. Long-term care of the land by the peasantry was sacrificed for

A Yoruban African man and family members.

An Indian peasant woman in Peru.

immediate profits. Land, labor, and capital were thus disconnected from the village kinship structures of reciprocity and redistribution, or what has been referred to as the *moral economy* (see Chapter 12). Peasants were incorporated into the global capitalist cash economy.

Religious Change

Numerous religious changes occurred with globalization. The Roman Catholic Church played a major role in Latin American society during the colonial period. Initially, the conquistadores were not sure whether the native peoples were fully human; that is, they were not certain that the natives had souls. After the Spanish authorities, backed by the Pope, ruled that the Indians did indeed have souls and could be saved, various missionaries began to convert the Indians to Catholicism. The missionaries established the pueblos and villages where the Indians were relocated and attempted to protect the Indians from the major abuses of colonialism, but they were too few and too spread out to do so.

In general, the Indians of Latin America readily accepted Catholicism. The indigenous religions of Mesoamerica, for example, were able to absorb foreign deities without giving up their own (Berdan 1982). Many local religious conceptions were

Candy skulls, called calaveras, *are given to family and friends to celebrate the Day of the Dead in Mexico.*

Anthropologists at Work

Kristin Norget: Research in Mexico

Kristin Norget.

Kristin Norget's involvement with anthropology was never a single, conscious choice but rather a result of a series of decisions concerning how she preferred to live her life and what was meaningful to her. When she was a child growing up in the prairie city of Winnipeg, in central Canada, the subject of anthropology was embodied by the big, thick book that sat on the living room table, filled with photos of apes and of archaeologists unearthing treasures from ruins in far-off places. It was not something to which she could relate readily. However, she always had the urge to travel, to see the possibility for ways of viewing and being in the world that were different from her immediate world of experience.

Her first "fieldwork" was during her last year of high school, when she spent two weeks in Jamaica doing research on Rastafarianism for a paper in a course on comparative politics. This experience, though brief, left a strong impact and inspired her to seek ways to find the same kind of connection with, and understanding about, people and culture not accessible through books and formal education alone.

Norget's first direct contact with anthropology as a more encompassing body of ideas about humanity and culture came in her first year at the University of Victoria, when anthropology was just one of several courses that she took as part of a general arts program that included languages, art history, philosophy, and English literature. In a course on cultural anthropology, she was intrigued by what anthropology offered for an immersion in themes that had always captivated her interest: art, symbolism, religion, and other creative domains of culture; people's ways of making sense of their worlds; and their innovation and richness of spirit in situations of material impoverishment. After completing her undergraduate degree in anthropology, she moved to England to begin her graduate studies at Cambridge University. There she was exposed to the classical works of British social anthro-

pology and experienced the culture shock that came from living within a particularly privileged and rare slice of English society. Although her time in Cambridge was overwhelming in some respects, it was also highly stimulating and enriching.

Norget chose as the focus of her master's research the Mexican festival of the Day of the Dead, a topic she saw could encompass her real interests in anthropology related to religion, ritual, art, and the expressive realms of culture. She had already visited Mexico as a tourist and had been fascinated by its history, art, and literature and moved by the warmth and generosity of the Mexicans she had met. Her master's thesis was the first stage of her exploration of the Day of the Dead (the Mexican commemoration of the Catholic festival All Souls' and All Saints' Days), which later evolved

somewhat analogous to Catholic beliefs. A process of religious **syncretism** developed, in which indigenous beliefs and practices blend with those of Christianity. For example, the central theological tenet of Christianity, that Jesus sacrificed his life for the salvation of humanity, was acceptable to people whose religious traditions formerly included human sacrifices for the salvation of Mesoamerican peoples (see Chapter 12). The Indians were also attracted to the elaborate rituals and colorful practices associated with the Virgin Mary and the saints. Catholic beliefs and practices were assimilated into traditional indigenous cosmologies to become powerful symbolic images and rituals.

One well-known tradition that has endured in Mexico, representing a combination of pre-Hispanic and Spanish Catholic religious beliefs and practices, is the *Día de los Muertos* (the Day of the Dead). The into a doctoral research project. She was already familiar with the Day of the Dead from museum exhibitions she had attended in England and Mexico and from the colorful popular art and iconography inspired by the festival that she had come across during her travels. Much of what she had previously seen and read about the Day of the Dead struck her as offering a rather one-dimensional, romanticized portrayal of the festival as simply a folkloric tradition with strong roots in pre-Hispanic religiosity and in a supposed quintessentially "Mexican" obsession with death. She wanted to explore the significance of the festival in a more contemporary framework, as well as to learn more about the ritualization of death in Mexico.

She chose as her fieldsite the southern Mexican city of Oaxaca, located in one of the poorest and most indigenous regions of the country. The urban milieu of Oaxaca enabled her to examine the Day of the Dead in a dynamic setting in which traditional life-ways came into direct interaction with tourism, commercialization, and other influences. Norget situated her investigation of the Day of the Dead in the context of Oaxacan urban popular culture, popular Catholicism, and other rituals concerned with death. During her fieldwork, she immersed herself in the local community of the neighborhood in which she lived, especially in the religious dimension of people's everyday lives, taking part in Bible discussion groups, masses, and other church activities, but especially in funerals and other death-related rituals. She discovered that death in Oaxaca is the inspiration for an elaborate series of ritual events and cultural discourses concerned with the reinvigoration of traditional ideas of collectivism and community in a rapidly changing and unstable social context in which such norms and values are being severely eroded. Her research deepened her fascination with the very practical way in which people use ritual as an arena for the imaginative and creative reconstruction of their social world.

Since completing her doctorate in 1993, Norget has been teaching anthropology at McGill University in Montreal. Although she finds teaching very rewarding, she is most content when she is in Mexico, immersed in research, writing, and spending time with the wide community of friends she has amassed there over the past ten years. In 1995, she was able to extend her interests in popular religiosity and Catholicism into a new research project investigating the relation between liberation theology and indigenous movements in southern Mexico. Through her work on this project, she finds an avenue for her continuing fascination with the ways that people use religion as a powerful means for articulating and actualizing their desires for a transformation of their social environment. It has also brought her into a practical involvement with the human rights struggle in Mexico as well as in Montreal, where she is an active member of various local Mexican human rights and refugee rights organizations. Norget has published articles based on her research in various international journals and is currently in the final stages of writing a book on death and its ritualization in Oaxacan popular culture.

Día de los Muertos takes place on November 2, the day after All Saints' Day (*Todos Santos*). This is the time when the souls of the dead return to earth to visit their living relatives. *Día de los Muertos* is a time when families get together for feasting. They construct altars to the dead and offer food and drink and prayers to the souls of their dead relatives. The altars usually have a photo of the dead person, along with an image of Jesus or the Virgin Mary. For those who died as children, there may be toys or sugar treats made in the shape of animals on the altar. Mexicans prepare for this day many months ahead of time. They prepare candy skulls, *calaveras*, which are given out to everyone in the family and friends. A substantial expense goes into preparing the foods, chocolate sauces (mole), and drinks, along with flowers, candles, and incense for the festivities. Food, drinks, and gifts of the *calaveras* are exchanged to

A Voodoo altar and celebration in Haiti.

symbolize strong linkages among family members, both living and dead. It is the most important ritual in Mexico exemplifying the crucial links between the past pre-Hispanic symbolic culture and the present. The *Día de los Muertos* represents the persistence of cultural traditions despite the globalizing processes and religious traditions that came with European colonialism (Norget 1996, 2000; Garciagodoy 1998).

Despite the official position of the Catholic Church in Latin America and the Caribbean, indigenous religious traditions have survived for centuries, partly because Catholicism had evolved over a long period in Europe, during which it absorbed a number of indigenous "pagan" traditions. Thus, Catholicism was predisposed to accommodate the indigenous religious traditions in the Americas (Ingham 1986).

In addition, the slaves that were imported from Africa to Latin America and the Caribbean brought traditional religious ideas and practices that were also absorbed into Catholicism. In Brazil these religious traditions are referred to as *Umbanda* and *Macumba*; in northeast Brazil, these traditions are known as *Candomble*. Catholic traditions are mixed with African beliefs and practices. In Cuba these syncretic traditions are called *Santeria* (Bowen 2005).

On the island of Haiti many of the people believe in the tradition known as *Vodoun*. *Vodoun* is a similar combination of African and a blend of other traditions. *Vodounists* believe that they communicate directly with spirits. *Vodoun* traditions have evolved into a code of ethics, education, and a system of politics that are evident throughout Haitian society. Secret *vodoun* based on highly complex spiritual cosmologies and communities control much of everyday life in Haiti. These secret societies trace their origins to escaped slaves that organized revolts against the French colonizers. They meet at night and use traditional African drumming and celebrations. The *vodounists'* complex belief system involves practices of priests or priestesses that can do harm to people. One practice is known as *zombification*. Using the poison of a puffer fish, they can cause an individual to appear to die and then recover several days later. The victims of the poisoning remain conscious but are not able to speak or move. Zombification and the threat of zombification were used by the secret societies to police the Haitian rural communities and maintain order (Metraux et al. 1989; Davis 1997). All these syncretic traditions combining traditional African religions and Catholicism are sometimes called spiritism and are evident in many parts of Latin America and the Caribbean.

With European colonization in Africa came missionaries who established schools to spread Christianity. As in Latin America, many of the missionaries in Africa were paternalistic toward the native peoples and tried to protect them from the worst abuses of colonialism. Mission schools served as both hospitals and education centers. Many people sent their children to the Christian schools because this education offered opportunities for better jobs and higher social status, and many people educated in the mission schools became part of the elite.

At the same time, however, the missionaries attempted to repress traditional religious beliefs and practices. The missionaries believed that to be "saved," the Africans had to abandon their customary practices and embrace the Christian faith. To some extent, the ethnocentrism and sometimes racism of the missionaries in Africa had tragic consequences for many native peoples. Through the educational system, Africans were taught that their traditional culture was shameful, something to be despised. In many cases, this led to a loss of ethnic and cultural identity and sometimes induced feelings of self-hatred.

As various Christian denominations missionized throughout Africa, a number of syncretistic movements began to emerge among the indigenous peoples. They became known as Independent African Church denominations referred to as "Zionist," "Spiritual," or "Prophet." The leaders of these churches are often called prophets and are known for their charismatic powers of healing. Facing the crisis created by colonialism and the loss of their traditional culture, many indigenous Africans turned to these traditions for relief. In some cases, these syncretic traditions combining traditional spiritual beliefs and Christianity have played a pivotal role in political movements throughout Africa (Comaroff 1985).

Political Changes: Independence and Nationalist Movements

One important consequence of globalization and colonialism in various Latin American, African, and Caribbean areas was the development of political movements that emphasized independence and nationalistic ideas. Some of the indigenous peoples became educated under the colonial regime and began to assert their independence. After approximately three hundred years of European domination, the various regions of Latin America and the

Caribbean began to demand their political autonomy from the colonial regimes. An educated descendant of the ancient Incans, Tupac Amaru, led a rebellion in Peru against the Spanish rulers. Simón Bolívar (1783–1830), a national hero among both Venezuelans and Colombians, led a broad-based independence/nationalist movement. In the French colony of Saint Domingue (modern-day Haiti), a major slave uprising by educated slaves influenced by the ideas that motivated the French revolution overthrew the French regime and beat back Napoleon's armies and became a warning for all the various colonial regimes in the region (Mintz 1985).

During the decades following World War II, European colonial rule ended in Africa; by the 1970s, no fewer than thirty-one former colonies had won their independence. The first country to do so, the West African nation of Ghana, became independent of Britain in 1957. Kwame Nkrumah, a charismatic leader who mobilized workers, youths, professionals, and farmers to speed up the pace of decolonization, led the Ghanian independence movement. Ghana's success intensified independence movements elsewhere. By the early 1960s, all of the West African countries, including the French colonies of Niger, Mali, Senegal, and Dahomey, had gained their independence, making a fairly smooth transition to independent political control.

In the Congo region, however, because of the Belgians' rigid exploitative political and economic policies, the independence movement was much more difficult. Belgian colonial policies had brutalized the native population, and the inadequate educational system had failed to produce an elite, affording Africans in the Belgian colonies little opportunity to gain political training for self-rule or nation building. When Belgium finally granted independence to the Congo in 1960, it was due more to international pressure than to nationalist movements.

In East Africa, the large numbers of white settlers vigorously resisted nationalist movements. In Kenya, for example, hostility between the majority Kikuyu tribe and white settlers who had appropriated much of the best farmland contributed to the Mau Mau uprisings, which resulted in thousands of deaths and the imprisonment of thousands of Kikuyu in detention camps. Jomo Kenyatta, a British-educated leader trained as an anthropologist and who had completed an anthropological study of the Kikuyu, led Kenya to independence in 1963 with his call for *Uruhu* ("freedom" in Swahili). In the colony of Tanganyika, nationalist leader Julius Nyerere organized a mass political party insisting on self-rule. Tanganyika achieved independence in 1961 and in 1964 merged with Zanzibar to form the nation of Tanzania.

In South Africa, colonization and independence eventually produced a system of racial stratification known as **apartheid**, in which different populations were assigned different statuses with varying social and political rights based on racial criteria. Dutch settlers, or Afrikaners, inaugurated the apartheid system when they came to power after World War II, and apartheid was the official policy of South Africa until recently.

Apartheid was based on white supremacy and assumed that the culture and values of nonwhite Africans rendered them incapable of social, political, and economic equality with whites. The government enforced this system through legal policies designed to bring about strict segregation among populations that were classified into different "races." The population was stratified into a hierarchy with whites, who number about 4.5 million, at the top. Approximately 60 percent of the whites are Afrikaners, and the rest are English-speaking. An intermediate category consists of coloreds—the 2.6 million people of mixed European and African ancestry—and Asians, primarily immigrants from India and Malaysia, who number about 800,000.

At the bottom of the hierarchy were the approximately 21 million black South Africans, who were divided into four major ethnic groupings: the Nguni, which includes the Xhosa, the Zulu, the Swazi, and the Ndebele; the Sotho; the Venda; and the Tsonga (Crapanzano 1986). Important cultural and linguistic differences exist among these groups.

The policies of *apartheid* affected every aspect of life in South Africa. Blacks were segregated socially and forced into lower-paying—and frequently hazardous—occupations. They could not vote or take part in strikes, and until recently they had to carry passes and observe curfews. In 1963, the South African government created a series of black states called Bantustan homelands, to which millions of black South Africans were forcibly removed.

Opposition to *apartheid* led to the emergence of various resistance and liberation movements, including the major resistance group, the African National Congress (ANC), formed in 1912. Although the ANC began as a moderate political organization calling for a unified South Africa representing all races in the government, it turned to armed struggle in response to ruthless suppression by the government. Many people were killed, and resistance leaders such as Nelson Mandela were imprisoned for many years.

Forced by international pressures, the government implemented some reforms in the 1980s and early 1990s, abolishing laws that had once confined blacks to the rural homelands, forbade them to join legal trade unions, reserved skilled jobs for whites, and prohibited interracial marriages. Black nationalist groups and the religious clergy, led by Archbishop Desmond Tutu, negotiated with the government for other political reforms.

In April 1994, all South Africans participated in a national election for the first time, electing Nelson Mandela's African National Congress (ANC) with a solid majority. Mandela, who became president, agreed to share power with whites during a five-year transitional period and tried to implement an economic blueprint for South Africa that included providing new homes, electrification projects, free and mandatory education, and millions of new jobs. In June 1999, South Africa's parliament chose Thabo Mbeki as the nation's second freely elected president. Mbeki, also a member of the ANC, is striving to carry out some of Nelson Mandela's

Nelson Mandela, the first black elected president of South Africa.

programs to develop a multiracial and multicultural democratic society (Clarke-Ekong 2003).

Explaining Revolution

In some of the countries of Latin America, Africa, and the Caribbean, revolutionary movements emerged as a response to the consequences of globalization and colonialism. Anthropologists have been examining the causes of revolution in Latin America and other non-Western countries. A **revolution** is a dramatic, fundamental change in a society's political economy brought about by the overthrow of the government and the restructuring of the economy. The classical understanding of revolution is derived from the writings of Karl Marx, who explained revolutions as the product of the struggle between the propertied and nonpropertied classes. For example, Marx predicted that the discontented proletariat would rise up against their bourgeois masters and overthrow capitalism (see Chapter 3). The revolutions in most non-Western countries, however, have not followed the Marxist model. Most countries in Latin America, Africa, or the Caribbean did not have a substantial proletariat and bourgeoisie. Rather, their revolutions were identified with the peasants.

Social scientists have found, however, that the poorest peasants did not organize and participate in peasant revolutions. People living in extreme poverty were too preoccupied with everyday subsistence to become politically active. Severe poverty tends to generate feelings of fatalism and political apathy. Consequently, anthropologists and other social scientists turned from the traditional Marxist model to find alternative models to explain revolutions. These models involve the concepts of rising expectations and relative deprivation.

The term **rising expectations** refers to how a particular group experiences improvements in economic and political conditions. Often these improvements stimulate the desire for even more improvements. For example, revolutions sometimes occur in the midst of political and economic reform. Groups that experience improvements brought about by their governments may become politically active and protest for even broader changes. **Relative deprivation** refers to a group's awareness that it lacks economic opportunities and political rights in comparison with other groups in a society.

Even though a particular group may have experienced improved economic and political conditions, it still perceives it is suffering from injustice and inequality compared with other groups. The combination of rising expectations and relative deprivation helps explain revolutionary movements in areas such as Latin America, Africa, and the Caribbean.

Although the first independence movements in Latin America brought about certain reforms, some groups were affected by rising expectations and relative deprivation. The emerging middle class, which consisted of intellectuals and businesspeople, as well as some peasants who were benefiting from the introduction of the global economy, began to organize against the *hacendados* and the governing elite. For example, the Indians and peasants played a vital role in the Mexican Revolution of 1910–1920. At that time, *one* percent of the Mexican population owned 85 percent of the land, whereas 95 percent owned no land at all (Wolf 1969; Chirot 1986). Peasant leaders such as Emiliano Zapata, who called for the redistribution of land, carried out guerrilla campaigns against the *hacendados*. Although the revolution did not establish an egalitarian state, it did bring about the redistribution of land to many of the Indian communities.

In Latin American and Caribbean countries where power remained in the hands of the elites, revolutionary movements continued to develop throughout the twentieth century. From the Cuban Revolution of the 1950s through the Nicaraguan Revolution of the 1980s, peasants joined with other dissatisfied elements in overthrowing elite families. Countries such as El Salvador continue to experience peasant revolutions. The hacienda system produced tenant farmers, sharecroppers, and day laborers on large estates, a situation that will inevitably make peasant guerrillas a continuing presence in some Latin American nations.

Uneven Development in Latin America, Africa, and the Caribbean

Throughout the twentieth century, the countries of Latin America, Africa, and the Caribbean have increasingly been incorporated into the global economy. These countries, however, differ in the degree of integration into this global economy. Some nations are peripheral agricultural states that produce a few cash crops for the international market. Others, such as Mexico, Venezuela, Brazil, and Nigeria, have a significant industrial sector and are clearly semiperipheral. In some regions, small-scale industrialists produce manufactured goods alongside the crops and cattle of the plantations. In many cases, however, these industrialists have to depend on Europe and North America for their machinery. They also discover that the internal market for their products is extremely limited because their own societies lack a consuming middle class.

Peripheral Societies

Anthropologists find that many countries in Latin America, Africa, and the Caribbean remain peripheral societies. The core societies developed these countries as export platforms, that is, nations whose economies concentrate almost exclusively on the export of raw materials and agricultural goods to the core nations. Through economic aid and military assistance, core countries such as the United States supported elite families and local sponsors of capitalist developments in these peripheral countries. The elites minimized restrictions on foreign investments and encouraged the production of cash crops for the export economy. The entire economy in these peripheral societies was reorganized to produce profits and commodities for the core societies.

A Case Study: The United Fruit Company An example of the development of a peripheral country by a multinational corporation involves the U.S.–based United Fruit Company in Central America. United Fruit obtained rights to thousands of acres of empty tropical lowlands in Central America for banana plantations. It enlisted local Indians, *mestizos*, and blacks from the Caribbean islands to work the plantations. Anthropologist Philippe Bourgois (1989a) studied one of the plantations operated by United Fruit, which expanded in 1987 to become the multinational Chiquita Brands. He investigated the archival records of United Fruit to determine how the North Americans managed the plantations.

Focusing on the Bocas Del Toro plantation, Bourgois observed the interactions among the vari-

ous ethnic groups on the plantation. He discovered that the North Americans used race and ethnicity as a form of manipulation. He described the relationship between management and labor as based on a hierarchy in which each of the four ethnic groups—blacks, *mestizos*, Indians, and white North Americans—worked at different tasks. Indian workers were used to spread corrosive fertilizers and dangerous pesticides. The management rationale for this practice was that "the Indian skin is thicker, and they don't get sick." Indians were not paid a full wage because, according to superiors, "the Indian has low physiological needs. . . . The Indian only thinks of food; he has no other aspirations. He works to eat" (1989a, x).

Blacks worked in the maintenance department's repair shops and electrical division because, Bourgois was told, they are "crafty and don't like to sweat." The *mestizo* immigrants from Nicaragua were worked as hard as the Indians because they "are tough, have leathery skin [*cueron*], and aren't afraid of sweating under the hot sun" (1989a, xi). The white North Americans were the top management because "they are the smartest race on earth." Management used these stereotypes to classify the multiethnic workers, thereby segregating each ethnic group in a separate occupation and preventing the workers from uniting to organize labor unions. Bourgois found that racism, ethnicity, inequality, exploitation, and class conflict were all interrelated in a continuing process in the day-to-day realities of a banana-plantation economy.

Semiperipheral Societies

A number of countries in Latin America and Africa, because of their valuable strategic resources, have emerged as semiperipheral societies. Two examples of peripheral societies that have become semiperipheral are Mexico and Nigeria.

Mexico Following a political revolution, Mexico gradually achieved stability under the control of a single political party, the Party of the Institutionalized Revolution (PRI). One-party rule, however, fostered corruption and inefficiency, resulting in personal enrichment for political officials. The government nationalized the key industries, including the important oil industry, which had been developed by foreign multinational corporations. Despite political authoritarianism and corruption, the Mexican economy continued to grow with gradual industrialization.

During the 1970s, as the industrial world experienced major oil shortages, the Mexican government implemented a policy of economic growth through expanded oil exports. International lending agencies and financial institutions in the core countries offered low-interest loans to stimulate industrial investment in Mexico. As a result, Mexico initially experienced an impressive growth rate of 8 percent annually and moved from a peripheral to a semiperipheral nation.

This progress was short-lived, however. Surpluses on the petroleum market in the early 1980s led to falling prices for Mexican oil. Suddenly Mexico faced difficulties in paying the interest on the loans that came due. The government had to borrow more money, at higher interest rates, to cover its international debt, which exceeded $100 billion. This excessive debt began to undermine government-sponsored development projects. Foreign banks and lending organizations such as the International Monetary Fund (IMF) demanded that the government limit its subsidies for social services, food, gasoline, and electricity. These policies led to inflation and a new austerity that adversely affected the standard of living of the poor and the middle classes of Mexico.

Another development influencing Mexico's economic status is the expansion of U.S. multinational corporations into Mexico. Since the 1980s, thousands of U.S. companies have established plants inside Mexico to take advantage of the low wage rates, lax environmental standards, and favorable tax rates there. These plants, known as *maquiladoras*, have drawn hundreds of thousands of peasants and workers, primarily women from rural communities, to expanding cities such as Juarez, a border city (Shirk and Mitchell 1989; Cravey 1998; Tiano 1994; Prieto 1997; Strada 2003). This was partially a result of the legislation known as NAFTA (North American Free Trade Agreement) that linked the economy among the United States, Canada, and Mexico to form a free trade zone and stimulate economic growth throughout the region. Among the companies that have established plants in Mexico are Fisher-Price, Ford, Emerson Electric, Zenith, Sara Lee, and General Electric.

Faced with mounting debts and unemployment, the Mexican government did everything possible to attract multinational corporations. This was also seen as a solution to the problem of the migration of Mexican workers to the United States as illegal aliens. Up until recently, the *maquiladoras* employed approximately 500,000 people and accounted for 17 percent of the Mexican economy. Although many *maquiladora* workers appeared satisfied with their jobs, the *maquiladoras* have created a number of problems for Mexico. Because they pay such low wages, they did not transform workers into consumers, which restricted their consumer and economic expansion. Other problems include occupational health hazards, the taxing of sewer systems and water supplies, and high turnover rates among workers. Currently, many of the multinationals based in Mexico are moving their companies to China, where low wages and attractive opportunities exist for corporations to lower their labor costs further and increase and maximize their profits. This globalization process has been identified by ethnographers, journalists, and other economists who do research in the area (Friedman 2005; Heyman 1999; Smart and Smart 2003).

Nigeria Under British rule, Nigeria developed an export economy centered on palm oil and peanut oil, lumber, cocoa, and metal ores. As in Mexico, after independence, a new commodity was discovered that had major consequences for Nigerian society—petroleum. The discovery of oil appeared to be an economic windfall for Nigeria, and the government saw it as the foundation for rapid economic growth. Many Africans from other nations immigrated to Nigeria in search of opportunity.

By the 1980s, more than 90 percent of Nigeria's revenues came from the sale of petroleum. These monies were used to fuel ambitious economic development schemes. Unfortunately, the Nigerian economy fell into disarray when oil prices dropped during the first half of the 1980s. In spite of tremendous economic expansion during the 1970s, unemployment rose, and the Nigerian government expelled virtually all non-Nigerian workers and their families, forcing millions of Africans to return to their former homelands, where the local economies could not absorb them.

By the late 1980s, cocoa was the only important Nigerian agricultural export. Oil production and the vast wealth that it represented for Nigeria had actually contributed to the decline of agriculture because the government invested heavily in the petroleum industry, neglecting the agricultural sector (Rossides 1990a). Consequently, Nigeria now depends on core countries for imported foods. In addition, much of its oil wealth was spent on imported goods such as automobiles, motorcycles, and televisions, which fueled inflation and did not benefit an underdeveloped industrial sector. Today, the industrial sector accounts for only about 10 percent of Nigeria's economic production. In 1995, Nigeria's annual per capita income was $970, one of the highest figures of any African country but far below that of many other semiperipheral societies (Ramsay 2001).

South Africa: An Economy in Transition

The country of South Africa, as described before, is going through a painful transition following the abolishment of *apartheid* and the development of a democratic society in which every citizen has equality in voting rights. However, the legacy of apartheid is still apparent, with inequalities among the various groups that were classified as races within South Africa. The official black unemployment rate is more than six times that of the white minority population. More than 50 percent of the black population under 30 are unemployed (Gay 2001). Black education, housing, and other material conditions are far behind the white population in South Africa. With the rise of the ANC and the election of Nelson Mandela and Thabo Mbeki as presidents, a new direction is being forged in stimulating the South African economy.

The ANC is trying to develop opportunities to close the gap between the black and white populations in education, health, and economic prospects. The South African economy was in recession prior to the abolishment of apartheid due to the international economic boycott and withdrawal of investments from its major corporations, which imposed a burden on the new leaders in their attempt to develop economic opportunities. The white population still holds the dominant positions within the South African economy, but a number of government policies are being enacted to further the education of black entrepreneurs so they can develop greater incentives for participation in economic ventures. The government is also publicizing its stability in order to attract foreign investment and venture capital into South Africa.

High crime rates, high unemployment rates, and the low educational levels of the black population continue to be the most pressing problems for maintaining stability and economic growth in South Africa. The ANC government can take pride in accelerating the rate of education among the black population. It knows that more educated and literate South Africans means more trained, skilled workers to take advantage of and create new economic opportunities for its future.

Ethnographic Studies in Latin America, Africa, and the Caribbean

As Latin American, African, and Caribbean countries were drawn increasingly into global economy, the status and lifestyles of the group called the peasantry were transformed. Anthropologists have been studying this transformation of the peasantry for many decades. For example, cultural anthropologists such as Robert Redfield (1930), Villa Rojas (Redfield and Villa Rojas 1934), Oscar Lewis (1951), and Victor Goldkind (1965) have been studying peasant communities in Latin America and the Caribbean since the 1920s.

A problem in generalizing about behavior in rural communities of non-Western countries is the tremendous variation from one community to another, although as these countries became integrated into the global economy, the peasantry became more heterogeneous. This variation is due to the different historical processes that have influenced these communities. For example, research by Eric Wolf (1955b, 1959) led to some important insights regarding the different types of peasant communities in some regions of Latin America and Asia. Wolf distinguished between *closed peasant communities* and *open peasant communities*. The **closed peasant community** is made up of peasants who lived in the highland regions of Mexico and Guatemala or in more isolated areas. In these communities, a person had ascribed economic and social status, and there was a great deal of internal solidarity and homogeneity. The peasants produced primarily for subsistence rather than for the world market. Many closed peasant communities in Central America, such as Chan Kom, consisted of Indian refugees who attempted to isolate themselves from the disruptive effects of Spanish colonial policies. They held their land in common, but much of this land was marginal.

An **open peasant community** consisted primarily of peasants who were directly drawn into the world market. These communities were located in the lowland areas of Latin America and Indonesia. Land was owned individually rather than held in common. The open peasant community evolved in response to the intrusion of colonialism, which engendered the development of plantations and the production of commodities for the core societies. In open communities, some peasants sold as much as 90 to 100 percent of their produce to outside markets, which enabled them to achieve some economic stability; however, they were subject to the fluctuations in the global economy.

Most recently, because of the global consequences of NAFTA discussed earlier and legislated in 1994, peasant lives are being transformed. Responding to the demands of NAFTA, the Mexican government has been trying to reform the agricultural system. Mexico is flooded with imported crops such as corn from the United States. The small land-holding peasants cannot compete with the prices of U.S.–produced corn. In addition, the peasants who produce sugar cane cannot export to the United States, because of a clause in the NAFTA agreement that protects the U.S. sugar industry. And the less costly U.S.–produced fructose corn syrup for soda preferred by the soft-drink industry in Mexico is also affecting the sugar cane producers.

Anthropologist James McDonald has been studying small farmers in different areas of Mexico to investigate the consequences of NAFTA and globalization (1997, 1999, 2001). Since the 1990s, after years of neglect, the Mexican government, influenced by the NAFTA agreement, has been attempting to privatize and introduce the "free market"

into the agricultural economy. Small farmers were encouraged to reorganize and form larger producer groups to take advantage of the newer, high-tech agricultural methods and make their farms more competitive, productive, and efficient. McDonald focused on a study of dairy farmers in Guanajuato and Michoacan, Mexico, who managed cows in the production of milk.

In Guanajuato, the size of the dairy ranches ranged from under 20 cows to larger ranches with as many as 200 head. Guanajuato has been successful in integrating its dairy farmers into the global economy. This region is close to the U.S. border and has a more open political system, and its economy is also dependent on remittances from migrants to the United States.

In Michoacan, the dairy farms were smaller, with only 20 head of cattle. Following NAFTA, large private commercial dairies supported by state and federal governments reorganized these dairy farmers and gave them limited training to enhance productivity and efficiency. The result of these new organizations was to create alliances between private businesspeople and politicians, who began to displace the older rural elites. These new elites concentrated their wealth and authority and dictated the policies and economic conditions for the rural farmers. In some cases, even when these new entrepreneurs had failing businesses, they managed to maintain their rewards and privileges. Politicians benefited from these arrangements and supported policies and legislation that profited the entrepreneurs. McDonald concludes that with further privatization and the new free-market policies in Mexico, extensive economic inequalities, political corruption, and continuing dislocations of the small independent farmer were bound to occur.

Like McDonald, most modern ethnographers doing research do not reside in just one location within a rural community, as ethnographers did in the past. Instead they tend to follow their subjects, like Wood Warner, who does ethnographic research on the economic changes for the Zapotecan textile weavers who travel from Oaxaca, Mexico, to the border cities of the United States and Mexico to sell their wares (2000). This multisited ethnographic research is a growing trend for anthropologists today who are examining the new changes in globalization influencing these different regions of the world. Circulations of consumer goods and services, migration, and new forms of monetary exchange are rapidly having an impact on Latin American lives.

African Peasants: A Unique Phenomenon?

Anthropologists David Brokensha and Charles Erasmus (1969) maintained that Africans were not typical peasants because of the distinctive nature of precolonial African states. They suggested that most precolonial states had very limited control over their populations and that Africans were able to retain control over their land and their economic production. Other anthropologists suggested that sub-Saharan Africans could not be characterized as peasants because in many cases they were still horticulturalists (Goldschmidt and Kunkel 1971).

Anthropologists Godfrey Wilson and Max Gluckman of the Rhodes-Livingstone Institute in southern Africa have engaged in detailed studies of African society. They distinguished six types of regions based on an array of factors, such as degree of urbanization and industrialization, relative importance of subsistence and cash cropping, and nature of the work force. They also examined such related phenomena as rural-to-urban migration, depopulation, unionization, and prevailing political issues. These and other studies helped produce an improved understanding of how the global economy directly affected the African people (Vincent 1990).

Most anthropologists now agree that the general term *peasants* does not apply to the diverse conditions found in the African agricultural or rural countryside. In some regions there were rural peoples who could be designated "peasants," whereas in other regions the term was not applicable. The historical experience of Africa was much different from that of medieval Europe, Latin America, or Asia. Environmental, economic, and political circumstances varied from region to region, involving different types of societal adaptations. In addition, the presence of so many colonial powers in Africa created greater diversity than was the case in Latin America, which was colonized almost exclusively by the Spanish and Portuguese. Thus, the current political economy of Africa is more heterogeneous than that of many other regions.

Social Structure in Latin America, Africa, and the Caribbean

Ethnographic studies have illuminated aspects of the social structure, including family and gender relations, of various countries of Latin America, Africa, and the Caribbean. As in most rural agricultural societies, the traditional family unit was an extended family that provided aid for people living in marginal subsistence conditions. But with the growth of industry and wage labor and the redistribution of land from communities to individuals, many large extended families were forced to break up. Thus, the typical family in many urban areas today is the nuclear family. Ethnographers, however, have found some unique features of kinship and social structure in these countries.

Latin American Social Relationships

Many traditional peasant communities maintain **fictive kinship ties**—that is, *extrafamilial* social ties that provide mutual-aid work groups for the planting and harvesting of crops and for other economic and political activities. George Foster described one type of fictive kinship tie in Mexican peasant communities that is known as the **dyadic contract**, a reciprocal exchange arrangement between two individuals (a dyad). According to Foster (1967), to compensate for the lack of voluntary organizations or corporate groups beyond the nuclear family in these communities, males and females established dyadic contracts to exchange labor, goods, and other needed services. These extra-kin social ties help sustain peasants who are vulnerable to the new demands of the unpredictable global market economy. Dyadic contracts can be established with people of equal or superior status or with supernatural beings such as Jesus, the Virgin Mary, and the saints. People develop dyadic contracts with these supernatural sources in hopes of inducing specific spiritual and material benefits. They care for the shrines of Jesus, the Virgin Mary, and the saints to demonstrate their loyalty and obedience.

Dyadic contracts between individuals of equal status are based on generalized reciprocal exchanges: continuing exchanges that are not short term but rather bind two people in cooperative relationships for many years. This is an attempt to develop the older forms of the moral economy that existed prior to globalization.

The dyadic contracts between people of unequal status, known as **patron-client ties**, are informal contracts between peasant villagers and nonvillagers (including supernatural beings). The patron is an individual who combines status, power, influence, and authority over the client. Patrons include politicians, government employees, town or city friends, and local priests.

One type of dyadic contract found in Latin America is known as the *compadrazgo*, associated with the rite of passage of baptism and Catholicism. Cultural anthropologists have investigated *compadrazgo* relationships extensively (Redfield 1930; Wolf and Mintz 1950; Foster 1967). This institution, brought to the Americas with Catholicism, has become an integral aspect of Latin American social relationships. During the colonial period, the *hacendado* often served as godparent to the children of peons. The result was a network of patron-client ties involving mutual obligations and responsibilities. The godparent had to furnish aid in times of distress such as illness or famine. In return, the peon had to be absolutely loyal and obedient to the *hacendado*.

The *compadrazgo* system eventually spread throughout peasant and urban areas. Every individual has a *padrino* (godfather) and *madrina* (godmother) who are sponsors at baptismal rituals. The sponsors become the coparents (*compadres*, *comadres*) of the child (Davila 1971; Romanucci-Ross 1973). The most important social relationship is the one between the *compadres* and the parents, who ideally will assist one another in any way possible. The *compadrazgo* is a remarkably flexible extra-kin relationship that sometimes reaches across class lines to help peasants cope with the tensions and anxieties of globalization and modern life in Latin America.

Machismo Gender relationships in Latin America have been strongly influenced by the Spanish and Portuguese colonial experience. The basic traditional values affecting gender relations are known as machismo, the explicit code for the behavior of Latin American males. As a part of this code, the "true man" (*macho*) is supposed to be courageous,

sexually virile, aggressive, and superior to women. A woman, in contrast, is supposed to be passive, sexually conservative and faithful, obedient, and completely devoted to her mate. These ideals and values have affected gender relations throughout Latin America.

Yet many cultural anthropologists who have done research in Latin American peasant communities have observed that the actual behaviors of males and females do not conform completely to the ideals of *machismo*. Lewis (1951) observed that in Tepotztlan males were not the dominant authoritarian figures in the family that they wanted to be, and wives were not completely submissive. Instead, in many families he found conflict between the spouses over authority. Most families tended to follow a middle course. The wife did little to challenge the authority of her husband, and the husband was not too overbearing toward his wife. May Diaz (1966) also showed that the ideals of *machismo* conflict with the actual behavioral realities of gender relations in Mexico. She observed in her study of Tonala, a small town near Guadalajara, that females often effectively opposed male domination within the family and the community.

African Social Relationships

Because many African societies are composed of horticulturalist or pastoralist peoples in transition to different forms of peasantry, their social organization largely centers on lineages and extended families. But as in other regions of the world, as globalization, industrialization, and the commercialization of agriculture develop, social organization inevitably changes.

Some cultural anthropologists have challenged basic concepts regarding the African family. For example, Niara Sudarkasa (1989), an anthropologist who did ethnographic research on the Yoruba and other West African groups, has challenged anthropologists such as George Murdock, who believe that all families worldwide can be reduced to the nuclear family (see Chapter 8). Murdock (1949) had argued that the extended family, or polygamous African family, really consists of multiple nuclear families with a common husband and father.

Sudarkasa saw this hypothesis as a distortion of the basic elements of the African family. She argued that the male-female dyad and offspring do not perform the basic functions of the family in African society. That is, the nuclear family is not the unit of economic production or consumption, not the unit of socialization, and not the unit providing emotional support. A typical African family such as that of the Yoruba consists of a group of brothers, their wives, their adult sons and grandsons, and their wives, and any unmarried children. Marriages usually are polygynous, and the husband has a room separate from his wives. Every wife has a separate domain, with her own cooking utensils and other furnishings. Cowives depend on the senior wife to be a companion and confidante. Sudarkasa concluded that the nuclear family is not the basic "building block" of the African family. She further maintained that Western cultural anthropologists misunderstand and distort the practice of polygyny in African society. She noted that most of the anthropological literature emphasizes the negative characteristics of polygyny, such as rivalry and discord among cowives. Her research demonstrated that cowives develop important emotional and social bonds with one another that create a nurturing environment for both cowives and children.

Although not all anthropologists have accepted Sudarkasa's views, most concur that there are many variations of the African family, depending on sociocultural conditions. In the urban areas of Africa, the extended family and polygyny are declining in influence. Several factors are responsible for these changes. As employment opportunities develop outside agriculture, prompting migration from rural to urban areas, extended family ties break down. Wage employment in mines and industrial firms tends to disrupt extended families that are tied to agricultural land. In addition, African governments often promote "modern" family and marriage practices to alter traditional ways of behavior, which they perceive as impeding economic development. To some extent, the elites of these societies accept Western conceptions of the family, romantic love, and monogamy.

Gender in Africa   Most African societies tend to be patriarchal, placing women in a subordinate status. In 1988, for example, women provided approximately 60 to 80 percent of the household food needs in many parts of Africa (Smith-Ivan 1988). They often worked ten to twelve hours a day, and in many instances their workload increased

after colonization and independence. As colonial regimes forced males to migrate to mines for employment, women were forced to assume the major subsistence roles for the family. Because their husbands' wages were meager, women had to grow and collect food for their families. In most cases, the lack of formal education prevented females from entering the wage-labor economy, so they were unable to buy property and send their children to school.

Despite providing much of the agricultural labor and household food needs, women in rural Africa tend to be the poorest people on the world's poorest continent. The European colonial powers often allocated land to males, but African women were given rights to land only through their relationship to males (Henn 1984; Tandon 1988). This tended to decrease the status of females in African society. Males were considered the head of the household and earned income, whereas females were viewed as the providers of the family's social needs (such as child care) and the producers of the future labor force. Following independence, males were given access to credit, training, and new skills to improve agricultural production. Because females did not have collateral through land ownership, they were denied the credit and training needed for commercialized agriculture.

The globalization of the economy and rural villages has also influenced the emergence of the major AIDs crisis in Africa. For example, one factor that influences the spread of this deadly disease is African males migrate from their rural communities long distances for job opportunities in different locations through trucking jobs outside of their regions. These men have contact with women prostitutes, who are also drawn into these jobs to support new lifestyles and support their families. The males return to their communities infected with the HIV virus and infect their wives, resulting in more medical and fatal problems for women that are widespread throughout Africa. The cost of medical drugs to contain this heterosexual spread of HIV is demanding in these developing rural communities (Robbins 2002).

Urban Women   African women in the urban regions often receive a formal education and tend to have more independence than do rural women. In West Africa, where females have traditionally

African women have had difficult problems in both rural and urban areas.

been employed in urban markets, some educated women have become prominent self-employed entrepreneurs. In general, however, even highly educated women are confined to the service sector of the urban economy, working in clerical or secretarial occupations (Robertson 1984; Smith-Ivan 1988, Friedberg 2001). Urban women without formal education who lack the support of extended families and village communities are especially vulnerable to exploitation and alienation. Without extended family ties to assist in child care, women often are restricted to unskilled, low-wage occupations, such as making clothing, that require them to remain at home.

Because South Africa was largely a settler colony and possesses a strong economy, the role of women there is somewhat different from that in other parts of Africa. Some African women are employed as domestics in white homes or as clerical and textile workers in the industrial sector. Despite their valuable contribution to these sectors of the economy, however, they earn 20 percent less than the minimum wage (Smith-Ivan 1988).

One positive development in many African countries is the increasing attention given to women. The pivotal role of women in agriculture and the urban areas is increasingly being recognized and supported by various governments. Prenatal and health care for mothers and babies have improved. New cooperatives for women in rural agriculture and improvements for women working in factories have been established by government policies. Women are also beginning to play a more important role in politics. Yet these advances could be subject to economic declines and political instability (Ramsey 2001). Thus, the role of women in both rural and urban Africa depends on the adjustment to the new demands and opportunities of globalization.

Patterns of Ethnicity in Latin America, Africa, and the Caribbean

As a result of European conquest and colonization, the ethnicity of Latin America, Africa, and the Caribbean became increasingly diverse and heterogeneous.

Ethnicity in Latin America

In Latin America, a small minority of Spanish and Portuguese rulers, never exceeding more than 5 percent of the total population, dominated the native population. Following the conquest, people born in Spain and Portugal went to Latin America to improve their social status. The Europeans eventually intermarried or had illicit relationships with native Indian women. The offspring of these interrelationships were called *mestizos*, a new social class in Latin America. After three centuries, the *mestizo* population grew to become the majority in Latin America, representing approximately 60 percent of the population. In addition, in Brazil and the Caribbean, the intermarriages of Africans and Europeans produced a group known as *mulattos*.

Gradually, in certain regions of Latin America and the Caribbean the new populations of *mestizos* and *mulattos* began to outnumber the indigenous peoples. The relative populations of these different groups vary from region to region. For example, only about 10 percent of the Mexican population speaks an Indian language, as opposed to about 50 percent in Guatemala, which is more geographically isolated. Brazil's population is about 11 percent black and 33 percent mulatto. Other areas in Bolivia, Peru, and Ecuador that are farther from the commercial coastal regions are primarily *mestizo* and Indian; only 10 percent of their populations are European or white. In contrast, in the coastal areas of Argentina and Uruguay, the European component of the population is more prominent. These communities of Latin America contain other ethnic minorities that are not highly visible among the other dominant groups. For example, ethnographers Ronald B. Loewe and Helene Hoffmann had been doing research on a Jewish community in Venta Prieto, Mexico, and the relationship between their old community and the Jewish community of Mexico City (2002). The relationship between these two communities has not been very successful over the years, resulting in some interethnic tensions and discrimination, which is being reduced through more contact and interaction. In addition, Protestantism is growing rapidly in various regions of Latin America and is usually tied to new forms of social and economic mobility (Provinzano 2000). Thus, depicting Latin America as a Roman Catholic country and an ethnically homogeneous culture is much too simplistic.

In countries such as Mexico and Guatemala, the Indian population as a minority has faced obstacles in attaining economic and political opportunities. Ethnographers have found that one of the only routes to upward social and economic mobility for the Indian population was **assimilation**, the adoption of the culture and language of the dominant group in society (Nash 1989). Some Indians did assimilate by adopting the Spanish language, clothing, and culture of the dominant majority and thereby becoming *ladino*. The ethnic distinction between a *ladino* and Indian was based on a cultural boundary. However, many Indians have tried to maintain their ethnic distinctiveness and have recently been involved in asserting their Indian ethnic identity in an attempt to attain economic and political rights.

For example, in the rain forest of southern Mexico, especially in the province of Chiapas, the Mayan Indians have been mobilized politically into what is referred to as the Zapatista movement. In 1994 after the NAFTA agreement was signed with the United States, Mexico, and Canada, the Zapatista movement, named after Emiliano Zapata (the famous Mexican revolutionary of 1910), began using armed guerilla warfare tactics against Mexican government forces to attain political and economic rights or autonomy from the government. In this area, the Mayan Indian population is dominated economically and politically by a wealthy group of landowners and ranchers. Traditionally, the Mayan Indians had a certain amount of communal land, or *ejidos*, that they could share. In the 1980s, in order to encourage private enterprise and capitalism in agriculture, the Mexican government declared that *ejido* land could be sold. The Maya lost their communal land, which they had been using for their basic subsistence. In addition, the Maya viewed NAFTA as a threat to their local corn economy, because the Mexican and North American economy would flood the market with cheap corn production. For these various reasons, the Zapatistas, led by a mysterious charismatic leader known as Sub-Comandante Marcos, declared war on the Mexican government. This movement has drawn on their traditional ethnic roots as a means of mobilizing a political struggle against a dominant majority in the midst of globalization (Nash 1997). A Mayan woman leader, Major Ana Maria, led an assault on the capital of San Cristobal de la Casas. The Mexican government and military responded with 15,000 troops to mercilessly hunt down the Zapatistas in the rain forest. However, many citizens of Mexico began to express sympathy with the Zapatistas. So, the Mexican government called off their troops.

Although most of the violence erupted during the early phase of this Zapatista movement, the ethnic resistance of these Mayan people persists to create tensions between them and the Mexican government. The Zapatista movement was not based on traditional Marxist or Maoist revolutionary ideology but instead was based on a desire to get land back that was taken from them by the government. Subcomandante Marcos, an educated man, not indigenous to the area, used the Internet and global media to spread highly poetic and literary riddles and narratives to convince the international community that the Maya were not out to grab power, but rather to gain their rights back from the Mexican government. Although this was a local indigenous ethnic political movement, it had a global impact around the world as protestors against some of the negative aspects of globalization wore signs that said "We are all Zapatistas" in Seattle, Prague, Quebec, and in the city of Cancun, Mexico. Indigenous movements can be transformed by global developments, but they can also result in new forms of globalization through the international media available today.

Ethnicity in Africa

In Africa, as another example, the term *tribe* has negative connotations and is seldom used. Consequently, peoples of different language groupings and culture refer to themselves as ethnic groups. Anthropologist Herbert Lewis (1992) has estimated that there are no fewer than 1,000 distinct ethnic groups among the more than fifty countries in Africa. As independence movements spread, many people hoped that the new African nations would develop as plural societies in which diverse ethnic groups would share power and tolerate cultural differences. These plural societies, however, generally have not developed. Anthropologists find that political parties are linked with specific ethnic groups. As one ethnic group assumes power, it usually forms a one-party state and establishes a military government that dominates other groups. This has become one of the major problems in African society.

One country that has been the subject of much ethnological research on ethnic relationships is Nigeria. The resolution of ethnic problems in Nigeria may provide a model for other African

countries. Nigeria is the most populous nation of Africa, with about 98 million people, consisting of many different ethnic groups. Approximately 300 different languages are recognized by the Nigerian government. The three major ethnic divisions, which make up two-thirds of the Nigerian population, are the Yoruba, the Hausa, and the Igbo (Ibo).

More than 12 million Yoruba live in the southwest region of Nigeria and across its borders in neighboring Benin. The Yoruba were the most highly organized precolonial urban people in West Africa. The majority of the Yoruba were subsistence peasant farmers. The men traditionally supplemented their diet through hunting and fishing.

British colonialism changed the political economy of Nigeria. Aside from commercialized agriculture that emphasized cocoa production, railways, automobiles, new manufactured goods, Christian churches and schools, and industry entered Yoruban society. One-fifth of the people live in the urban areas of Nigeria such as Lagos and Ibadan. Wage employment and industrialization are rapidly transforming the society of the Yoruba, creating new class structures and integrating the traditional kingdom into the Nigerian nation and the global economy.

To the north of the Yoruba live the Hausa, who number about 20 million. Like the Yoruba, the Hausa had developed large, urban areas with extensive trade routes. Hausa cities had elaborate markets that offered different types of foodstuffs and crafts produced by peasants and craftspeople. British anthropologist M. G. Smith (1965) conducted extensive ethnographic and historical research on Hausa society.

The Hausa made their home in a savanna where the peasants cultivated various crops and maintained cattle for trade and consumption. Hausa craftspeople smelted iron and crafted iron tools for farming, sewing, leather work, and hunting. As with the Yoruba, most Hausa peasants were engaged in subsistence agriculture, but cash crops such as cotton and peanuts were introduced by the British and changed the nature of economic production and consumption.

The third major ethnic group in Nigeria is the Igbo people of the southeastern region. Igbo anthropologist Victor Uchendu (1965) completed a major ethnographic study of the Igbo. His descriptions of Igbo society are extremely insightful

Famines and Food Problems in Africa

Although Africa has the land and resources to produce more food than its current population requires, many African countries face famine conditions. A famine is starvation that is epidemic in scale and causes death from starvation-related diseases. Agencies of the United Nations estimate that more than 14 million people continually face starvation in Africa. In the 1980s, widespread famines occurred in twenty-two African nations. Ethiopia confronted famines in 1984 and 1989. In 1992, six countries were suffering from severe famine, including Somalia and the Sudan. Despite international relief and tens of millions of dollars of food aid, African agricultural production has been stifled.

A number of anthropologists have been researching famines to provide a knowledge base for countries that face these conditions. One area that has been investigated concerns the causes of famine conditions (Shipton 1990). Researchers have found that many factors are responsible for the widespread famines in Africa. Climatic conditions, particularly droughts, decimate crops and diminish the fertility of the land. In some cases, political instability and civil war prevent food from reaching hungry people. For example, the Sudan has been destabilized by a civil war between the Muslim north and the Christian south. Both sides use food as a weapon, withholding needed grains to weaken the opposition. Similar conditions exist in Somalia, where rival tribes compete for political power by using food. In addition, in impoverished regions such as the Sudan, Somalia, and Ethiopia, poor transportation and communication facilities inhibit the shipment and distribution of food. Despite the work of international relief agencies, food frequently does not reach the famine-stricken population.

In addition, the colonial heritage of these nations contributes to the abysmal state of agricultural production. In substituting export crops for subsistence agriculture, the colonial powers promoted the growing of a single crop. This practice resulted in the loss of cultivable land, which, combined with population growth, led to problems in food production. In addition, the decrease in the availability of land resulted in fewer economic opportunities in rural regions and increased migration to overcrowded cities.

The growth of a single crop also led to widespread environmental deterioration, including soil erosion, desertification, and deforestation. This agricultural pattern depletes the soil, turning grazing land into desert. Since the late 1970s, the Sahara Desert has been expanding southward at a rate of about 12 miles per year. The country of Ethiopia loses about a billion tons of topsoil annually as a result of intensive cultivation for cash crops. The use of firewood for fuel in Africa has resulted in severe deforestation. All these developments have impeded food production.

As African countries became integrated into the world economy,

---

because he blends an anthropological focus with an insider's perspective.

Most of the Igbo were primarily root-crop subsistence farmers who grew yams, cassava, and taro. Unlike some of the other West African peoples in the area, both Igbo males and females were engaged in agricultural production. Like most other traditional West African societies, the Igbo used some of their agricultural production for exchanges within the villages and trade outside the region. Women dominated trade in the rural village markets, whereas men dominated trade with other regions.

Uchendu described the traditional political system of the Igbo as unique. Igbo villages were essentially autonomous. At the village level, a form of direct democracy operated in which all adult males participated in decision making. Leadership food problems were intensified by declining commodity prices. Western industrial nations with large-scale mechanized agriculture have produced huge surpluses of wheat, corn, rice, and soybeans. Large multinational companies based in Minneapolis and Chicago have been able to dominate the world grain trade. These companies are able to lower the prices of these grains, which has driven thousands of African farmers out of business. In many cases, government officials living in African cities support low prices for food to gain political loyalty from urban residents. Yet falling prices lower the export earnings of African states, which were already confronted with rising interest rates and debts to core nations. These developments negated government plans to increase food production. As a result, food imports have increased throughout Africa. For example, wheat imports rose by 250 percent from 1969 to 1982, just before the widespread Ethiopian famine (Connell 1987).

To resolve this food crisis, some Africans have called for increased regional trade within Africa and less reliance on the world market and global economy (Okigbo 1988). Both anthropological researchers and Africans have called for production of underutilized African food plants that would broaden their food base. They suggest growing a variety of different plant species to improve the productive capacity of the land. In addition, anthropologists suggest restoring some traditional, small-scale subsistence production to provide a more balanced system of agriculture. This would involve providing credit and education to peasant farmers. Moreover, African governments must devote greater resources to research on land use and technology.

Western and African anthropologists, in cooperation with other specialists, have been working to resolve these problems. For example, in 1984, the American Anthropological Association set up a Task Force on African Famine, which included anthropologists with fieldwork experience in Africa, specialists in food security, and members of private voluntary organizations such as Oxfam, which deal with famine.

Solomon Katz, the editor of the important reference work *The Encyclopedia of Food and Culture* (2003) has contributed to the discussion of famine problems in Africa and elsewhere (2004). Katz was a member of the Task Force on the African Famine in the 1980s. This anthropologically based task force offered a novel approach to famine issues by concentrating on local cultural knowledge and agricultural problems rather than taking a top-down macroeconomic globalization approach. The task force emphasized that the local farmers must contribute to an effective solution to these famine problems rather than an international organization that does not understand the local cultural issues and contexts. Anthropologists have a great deal of knowledge that is needed by agencies dealing with famine and food supply. The ethnographic data on local conditions in different communities are extremely valuable in famine relief and development planning to prevent future famines in Africa.

was exercised by male and female officeholders who had developed power and influence gradually. Executive, legislative, and judicial functions were divided among leaders, lineages, and age-grade associations.

After Nigeria became independent in 1960, it was confronted with the types of ethnic problems that beset many other African nations. The British had drawn political boundaries without respect to the traditional territorial areas of indigenous kingdoms or ethnic groups. For example, the Yoruba live in both Benin and Nigeria, and the Hausa reside in both Niger and Nigeria. Consequently, when Nigeria achieved independence, the presence of various ethnic groups inhibited the political unification of the new nation. Most of the Hausa, Igbo, and Yoruban peoples identified with their own ethnic groups and territories.

Cultural anthropologist Abner Cohen, who examined the role of ethnicity and political conflict in Nigeria, focused on Hausa traders in the Yoruban city of Ibadan. Cohen (1969, 1974) described how ethnic distinctions between the Hausa and Yoruba became the basis of political and economic competition. Cohen used the term *retribalization* to refer to the Hausa strategy of using ethnic affiliations as an informal network for economic and political purposes. These networks were in turn used to extend and coordinate Hausa cattle-trading activities in Ibadan. Cohen's ethnographic research in Ibadan has become a model for analyzing ethnic trends in urban areas throughout the world. Cohen demonstrated how ethnic processes and the meaningful cultural symbols used by ethnic groups can mobilize political and economic behavior. These cultural symbols aided ethnic groups in Nigeria in their struggle to attain a decent livelihood and political power in the urban communities. This process, however, generated tensions among the various ethnic groups.

Nigeria's multicultural society was racked by interethnic, religious, and political competition and conflict. In the mid-1960s, these conflicts erupted into civil war. Because the Igbo people had had no historical experience with a centralized state, they resented the imposition of political authority over them. This led to conflict among the Igbo, the Yoruba, and the Hausa. Following the collapse of a civilian government in the 1960s, the Igbo were attacked and massacred in northern Nigeria. The Igbo fled as refugees from the north and called for secession from Nigeria. In 1967, under Igbo leadership, eastern Nigeria seceded and proclaimed itself the independent Republic of Biafra. The result was a civil war in which non-African powers assisted both sides. After three years of bitter fighting and a loss of about 2 million people, Biafra was defeated, and the Igbo were reincorporated into Nigeria.

Under a series of military-dominated regimes, Nigeria has succeeded in healing the worst wounds of its civil war. One strategy was to incorporate all ethnic and religious groups into the military leadership. In addition, the country was carved into nineteen states, the boundaries cutting through the territories of the Yoruba, Hausa, and Igbo. This encouraged the development of multiethnic coalitions and a federalist political system (Ramsay 2001). Nigerians hope that when ethnic

and religious factions develop new social ties based on education, class backgrounds, and new forms of nationalism, older forms of association will weaken. Currently, however, ethnic loyalties and identities appear to be very powerful bases for social and political life in Africa. This has produced the potential for political disintegration in many African states (Lewis 1992). Nation-building projects that unify different ethnic groups remain the most formidable challenge facing Nigeria and other African countries.

More recently, another African country has faced severe ethnic violence resulting in genocide. Rwanda has experienced Africa's worst attempted genocide in modern times and is still recovering from the shock. Even where mass murder appears aimed at a specific ethnic community, questions still arise as to the meaning of ethnicity where the groups in conflict share the same language, the same national territory, and the same customs and for centuries have lived more or less peacefully side by side. The country has been beset by ethnic tension associated with the traditionally unequal relationship between the dominant Tutsi minority and the majority Hutus. Mass conflict began when Belgian colonial rulers gave the Tutsi a monopoly of state power (Middleton 2000). As we have seen elsewhere in the world, using ethnicity as a political weapon is a product of modern politics that often reflects a real or imagined inequity of resource distribution and allocation (Bowen 2001; Falola 2000; Middleton 2000).

Before the modern era some Africans did consider themselves Hutu or Tutsi, Nuer or Zande, but these labels were not the characteristic of everyday identity. A woman living in Central Africa drew her identity from where she was born, from her lineage and in-laws, and from her wealth. Tribal or ethnic identity was rarely important in everyday life and could change as people moved over vast areas in pursuit of trade or new lands. Conflicts were more often within tribal categories than between them, as people fought over sources of water, farmland, or grazing rights.

In Rwanda and Burundi, German and Belgian colonizers admired the taller people called Tutsis, who formed a small minority in both colonies. The Belgians gave the Tutsis, the minority group, privileged access to education and jobs and even instituted a minimum height requirement for entrance to college. To enable colonial officials to distinguish Tutsi from non-Tutsi, everyone was required to carry identity cards with tribal labels. Fortunately, people cannot be forced "racially" into the neat compartments that this requirement suggests. Many Hutus are tall and many Tutsis are short; furthermore, many Hutus and Tutsis had intermarried to such an extent that they were not easily distinguished physically (nor are they today). They spoke the same language and carried out the same religious practices. In most regions of the colonies the categories became economic labels: poor Tutsis became Hutus, and economically successful Hutus became Tutsis. Where the labels Hutu and Tutsi had not been much used, patrilineal descent groups with lots of cattle were simply labeled Tutsi; and as poorer lineages, Hutu. Colonial discrimination against Hutus created what had never existed before: a sense of collective Hutu identity, a Hutu cause. In the late 1950s Hutus began to rebel against Tutsi rule (encouraged by Europeans on their way out) and then created an independent, Hutu-dominated state in Rwanda; this state then gave rise to Tutsi resentments and to the creation of a Tutsi rebel army, the Rwandan Patriotic Front.

In Rwanda, the continuing slaughter stemmed from efforts by the dictator-president Juvenal Habyarimana to wipe out his political opposition, Hutu as well as Tutsi. In 1990–1991 Habyarimana began to assemble armed gangs into a militia called Interahamwe. The militia carried out its first massacre of a village in March 1992, and in 1993 they began systematically to kill Hutu moderates and Tutsis (Bowen 2000; Lemarchand 1999).

Paul Kagame, the current president of Rwanda, grew up in Uganda, where his parents fled to escape Hutu violence. He has attempted to play down any ethnic agenda in Rwanda, presenting himself as a Rwandan and not a Tutsi. Like other African countries, Rwanda is attempting to forge a national identity that will supersede any ethnic identity (Clark-Ekong 2003). Anthropologist Jennie Burnet has been doing current ethnographic work on women and other communities in Rwanda to gain an understanding of the traumatic consequences of the genocide and ethnic tensions within this African country (2004a, 2004b). It is hoped that her ethnographic work will help provide insight into the dilemmas so that these women and other ethnic groups will resolve their ethnic tensions in the future.

Ethnicity in the Caribbean

Ethnicity in the Caribbean is a complex, diverse mixture of imported African slaves, East Indian laborers, and various Europeans. One conventional ethnic classification is based on skin color, especially the distinction between black and brown. Beginning with the illicit offspring of European whites and slave women, a category of mulattoes began to gain certain advantages. At present, "brown" in many Caribbean islands such as Jamaica is synonymous with middle class, and these people are associated with the professional occupations (Eriksen 1993; Yelvington 2001; Kephart 2003).

A squatter settlement in Santo Domingo, the Dominican Republic. Wealth and poverty coexist throughout the Caribbean.

After the arrival of East Indians in the Caribbean, new ethnic relations began to develop. In contrast to the blacks, East Indians were free to develop their own ethnic communities. Thus, in the Caribbean, the East Indian descendants are divided among different linguistic and cultural groups. There are Hindu and Muslim ethnic communities, as well as Tamil and other language communities. Many of the Indians have used these ethnic ties to form effective career networks to enhance their professional careers. In response to the large Indian communities in islands such as Trinidad, the black community began to strengthen its own ethnic identity. The blacks began to develop stereotypes, such as the "backwardness" of the Indian communities and the "progressive" Europeanized black communities. Many of the black, brown, and Indian communities have been revitalizing their own ethnic identity in the context of globalization within the Caribbean region.

Patterns of Urban Anthropology

Urban anthropologists who have done research in the globalizing and transnational changes occurring in Latin America, Africa, and the Caribbean have helped improve our understanding of issues such as poverty and rural-to-urban migration (Smart and Smart 2003; Hannerz 1992). These topics are of vital interest to government officials and urban planners, economists and development technicians, and other international agencies. Population growth and urbanization in non-Western underdeveloped nations have posed global problems that urgently need to be resolved. Urban anthropologists working in these regions are providing data that can be used to help resolve these global problems.

The mass movement of people from rural areas to the cities is a major trend in these regions. Between 1950 and 1980, the proportion of the population living in urban areas increased from 41 to 65 percent. Cities such as Mexico City, Rio de Janeiro (Brazil), Buenos Aires (Argentina), San Juan (Puerto Rico), and Lagos (Nigeria) are among the largest metropolitan areas in the world. For example, it is predicted that by 2015, the population of Mexico City will exceed 20 million (World Almanac 2003). The rate of population growth and urbanization in these societies is much higher than in the postindustrial societies discussed in Chapter 13. It is projected that if growth rates remain the same, the metropolitan area of Mexico City will have more than 28 million inhabitants.

Much of this urban growth is due to internal migration. Migrants are pushed away from the countryside by population growth, poverty, lack of opportunity, and the absence of land reform. They are pulled to the city by the prospects of regular employment, education and medical care for their children, and the excitement of urban life. Rapid urbanization has led to the development of illegal squatter settlements, or high-density shantytowns, in and outside urban areas. Shantytowns provide homes for the impoverished and unskilled migrants. Anthropologists have found that in some of these settlements, some people are optimistic about finding work and improving their living conditions. In the shantytowns, the new migrants take advantage of city services such as running water, transportation, and electricity. However, in the worst slums in non-Western cities, many of these new migrants are so poor that they are forced to live in the streets.

Some anthropologists have focused their research on the poverty conditions of many of the non-Western urban centers. One well-known pioneer is Oscar Lewis, who studied families of slum dwellers in Mexico City (1961) and San Juan and New York (1966). From these studies and from other evidence collected by urban anthropologists, Lewis concluded that the cultural values of the slum dwellers inhibited them from pursuing economic opportunities. He referred to these values as the **culture of poverty**.

Lewis described the people who maintained this culture of poverty as having a sense of fatalism, apathy, and hopelessness with respect to aspirations for economic or social mobility. They tended to be suspicious and fearful, disdained authority, and did not plan for the future. Alcoholism, violence, and unstable marriages were common. According to Lewis, these values were passed on to children through the enculturation process. Thus, poverty and hopelessness were perpetuated from generation to generation.

To be fair, Lewis stressed that the culture of poverty was a result of the lack of economic opportunities in the slum neighborhoods. Moreover, he carefully noted that these attitudes affected only about 20 percent of the people living in these areas. Nevertheless, many critics have charged that Lewis's hypothesis is an example of blaming the victim; that is, it attributes poverty to the negative attitudes of poor people themselves rather than to the economic and social stratification of their society. Some anthropologists have challenged the assertion that these attitudes are widespread among slum residents. For example, Helen Safa (1974) conducted research on a shantytown in San Juan and did not find the hopelessness and apathy that were portrayed in Lewis's studies. Safa found that the poor in the shantytowns have values emphasizing hard work, thrift, and determination. Her data contained little to confirm Lewis's characterization of the poor as having a pathological culture.

Safa and other anthropologists emphasize that these culture-of-poverty values are not perpetuated from generation to generation as Lewis suggested. Rather, each individual develops attitudes and strategies toward achievement depending on the availability of real economic opportunities. According to Safa, a sense of achievement based on individual initiative had relatively little effect on real economic and social mobility. She observed that, because of rapid economic growth in Puerto Rico, a few privileged people were able to attain upward mobility. This limited mobility led poor people to believe that economic and social advancement was due to individual and personal initiative rather than socioeconomic factors. In fact, Safa contends, socioeconomic conditions in Puerto Rico are, to a great extent, a consequence of global economic processes beyond the control of individuals in the shantytowns.

Other anthropologists are investigating the patterns of rural-to-urban migrations in non-Western countries. For example, during the 1970s, a comprehensive study of highland Guatemalan Mayan Indians of San Pedro La Laguna by anthropologists William Demarest and Benjamin Paul (1981) found a significant pattern of rural-to-urban mobility among Indian males. Although the Indians were extremely resourceful in gaining employment in urban areas such as Guatemala City, the low wages did not allow them to support families. Consequently, many of them resettled in San Pedro, where they looked for wives.

As we have seen, globalization has proceeded rapidly throughout the regions of Latin America, the Caribbean, and Africa. Walmart, McDonalds, and other multinational media and developments are growing everywhere throughout these regions. Some of these developments have created rapid, unequal social and economic developments in various regions of these countries, as discussed before. As the people are adjusting to these new processes, including population growth, urbanization, industrial and rural agricultural developments, and attending social structural, political, religious, and ethnic change and tensions, in the short term it has created new problems and new challenges for them. We return to discuss some of the contemporary global trends that are influencing societies throughout the world in Chapter 16. As mentioned at the beginning of this chapter, these societies are coping with these new developments in a much more concentrated time period than the Western, industrial, European-influenced societies of the global economy. It is hoped that anthropologists can help these societies provide solutions to overcome some of their difficulties, a topic addressed in our last chapter.

SUMMARY

Globalization has had a major effect on the countries of Latin America and the Caribbean, Africa, the Middle East, and Asia. These countries were either directly or indirectly affected by Western colonialism. Demographically, diseases or slavery devastated the countries of Latin America, the Caribbean, and Africa. In the long run, all these countries were affected by declining death rates brought about by Western colonialism, but populations began to increase rapidly because of high birth rates.

Economically, these societies were drawn into the global economy and were transformed by producing commodities that were demanded by the wealthier core societies. Patterns of land ownership were reordered, and many peasants were producing for economic elites. Religious changes occurred in all these countries because of Western expansion and missionary influence.

Western colonialism eventually gave way to political movements based on nationalist, independence, and, sometimes, revolutionary tendencies. These movements represented anticolonial sentiments and resulted in many new countries around the world.

These countries were absorbed into the global economy at different levels depending on the resources that were available in their regions. Some countries remain poor and underdeveloped because their economies are heavily dependent on the wealthy core countries. Other countries, including Mexico and Nigeria, had oil resources that could be used to help develop their economies. Despite oil resources, these non-Western countries still find themselves with various obstacles to developing their economies.

Ethnographers have conducted research on the peasantry, social structures, family life, and gender and ethnic issues and tensions within these countries. Each region has unique structures based on its cultural beliefs and practices. The peasantry differs in various countries, based on the people's traditional relations and new global relationships to the world market. Family structures and gender relations are illuminated by cultural anthropologists as they study patterns that develop in relationship to the emergence of new urban areas and the changing rural areas.

Cultural anthropologists are also studying the overall patterns and consequences of urbanization in these societies, including the issues of poverty and rural-to-urban migration. They find that people throughout these countries, despite their hardships, continue to adapt their traditional social and cultural mechanisms to help them adjust to the effects of globalization.

QUESTIONS TO THINK ABOUT

1. Compare and contrast the effects of colonialism on Latin America, Africa, and the Caribbean.

2. How did globalization impinge on the traditional economies of Latin America, Africa, and Caribbean countries?

3. What were some of the religious changes that came with Western expansion into Latin America, Africa, and the Caribbean?

4. Compare the independence movements in Latin America and Africa.

5. What are some of the differences between the peripheral and semiperipheral countries in Latin America, Africa, and the Caribbean?

6. What do you think will enable the peripheral and semiperipheral countries in Latin America, Africa, and the Caribbean to sustain their economies in the future?

7. How is the peasantry different in various Latin American, African, and Caribbean countries?

8. Compare and contrast the social structure of Latin America with that of Africa.

9. How have family and gender patterns in Latin America, Africa, and the Caribbean been influenced by globalization?

10. What are the effects of urbanization in Latin America, Africa, and the Caribbean?

KEY TERMS

apartheid	dyadic contract	relative deprivation
assimilation	fictive kinship ties	revolution
closed peasant community	open peasant community	rising expectations
culture of poverty	patron-client ties	syncretism

Chapter 15

Globalization in the Middle East and Asia

CHAPTER QUESTIONS

- What insights have been contributed by anthropologists to understanding the Middle East and Asia since the 9/11/01 tragedy in the United States?

- What were the most important consequences of colonialism in the Middle East and Asia?

- What creates uneven development in the Middle East and Asia?

- What are the basic features of the family and gender relations in the Middle East and Asia?

- What are some of the factors that influence ethnic tensions in the Middle East and Asia?

- What are some of the links between globalization and Islamic movements?

Anthropology in the Middle East and Asia Following 9/11/01

Following the tragic events of 9/11/01 and the destruction of human lives with the suicidal attack on the World Trade Center, there have been an enormous number of books written about the Islamic world, the Middle East, and Asia. Many of these books have been written by religious studies specialists who study the religious texts of Islam, Buddhism, Hinduism and then interpret the culture, values, and behavior of these Asians and Middle Eastern peoples as "radically different" than peoples in Western society. Other writers are political scientists who interview the political elites in these regions; they also tend to portray these societies as not having the same kinds of democratic or other institutions that the Western societies or cultures have and predicted a "clash of civilizations," and following 9/11/01 these views have become more dominant in the Western media and in government circles (Huntington 1996).

Anthropologists have been doing ethnographic research in these areas of the Middle East and Asia for decades. Some of the earlier ethnographic research drew on simplistic understandings of "culture" as discussed in Chapter 3 on culture. One assumption put forth by these earlier anthropologists was that a "culture" or "civilization" could be summed up within a portrait based on sometimes superficial understandings of how a "culture" (values, beliefs, world views, norms, behavior) was *shared similarly by everyone* within the society in the same manner. For example, Israeli anthropologist Raphael Patai, who was fluent in Arabic, wrote a book called *The Arab Mind* in the 1950s based on a simplified view of culture and language, along with some brief observations that became extremely influential during that time period, to discuss the millions of people within the Arab world, who supposedly shared the same culture. Patai's book is recently being used by the U.S. military to train U.S. soldiers engaged in Iraq to understand Arab culture and behavior (Starrett 2004).

Earlier, we discussed how contemporary anthropologists have refined this understanding of "culture" or "civilization" to emphasize how varied the values, beliefs, world views, norms, and behavior are among men, women, young, and old and how the culture is constantly in dynamic interaction with historical, economic, political, ethnic, and religious developments. Especially with recent globalization trends in different regions of the world that are experiencing much more contact with the outside world through print, the Internet, television, films, fax, e-mail and other global media, the "culture" of these groups is in a continuing dynamic interaction with these other factors stemming from new recent trends. Anthropologists who do ethnographic research in these regions today find that there is a tremendous variety of different political and religious beliefs within any of the Middle Eastern or Asian cultures. These anthropologists reside among the people in these areas for an extensive period and interview not just the political elites, but peasants, farm workers, urban working-class people, religious clerics of many different traditions, and others. We find that the simplistic portraits of "Islamic culture," "Jewish culture," "Buddhist or Hindu culture," or "Middle Eastern or Asian civilizations" that are written about by many of these specialists or writers are too static, with "stereotypical" images that do not do justice to the tremendous variety of values, beliefs, norms, institutions, behaviors or "culture" of the billions of people in these regions.

Following the 9/11/01 tragedy, many anthropologists are consulting and advising Western governments and also work with the people in the Middle East and Asia to help provide more insight into these regions that are changing very rapidly. In this way, anthropologists hope to improve intercultural and interfaith dialogue on these issues to help reduce tensions and violence within and between these various societies in the Middle East and Asia (Scupin 2002; Geertz 2003a, 2003b).

Globalization in the Middle East and Asia

As in Latin America, Africa, and the Caribbean, the process of globalization has been going on in the Middle East and Asia since the exploration of these regions by Europeans. The Middle East and Asia are vast heterogeneous regions with different ethnic groups and cultures that have had contact with each other through trade and exploration since the first millennium. For the purposes of this chapter, the Middle East includes the area of both North Africa and Southwest Asia (Figure 15.1). Many of the countries of these regions were influenced by the development of Islamic culture and the Arabic language. Traditionally, this area was referred to as the "Near East" to distinguish it from the "Far East." At other times, it has been mistakenly labeled the "Arab world." The term Arab refers to people who speak the Arabic language; included within this category of Arabic-speaking regions are the countries of Jordan, Syria, Iraq, Saudi Arabia, Yemen, Oman, and the Persian Gulf states such as Kuwait and the United Arab Emirates. The Middle Eastern region, however, also contains non-Arabic-speaking countries such as Israel, Turkey, and Iran. Thus, the Middle East as described in this chapter comprises peoples with different histories, languages, ethnicities, and religions.

Asia is also a culturally diverse continent with a wide variety of sociocultural systems. This chapter focuses on three regions: South Asia, East Asia, and Southeast Asia (Figure 15.2). These regions contain most of the world's population, more than 3 billion people. Different forms of societies have developed in these regions, ranging from hunter-gatherer and horticultural societies of the tropical rain forests, to the pastoral nomads of northern China, to the advanced industrial society of Japan. (We have

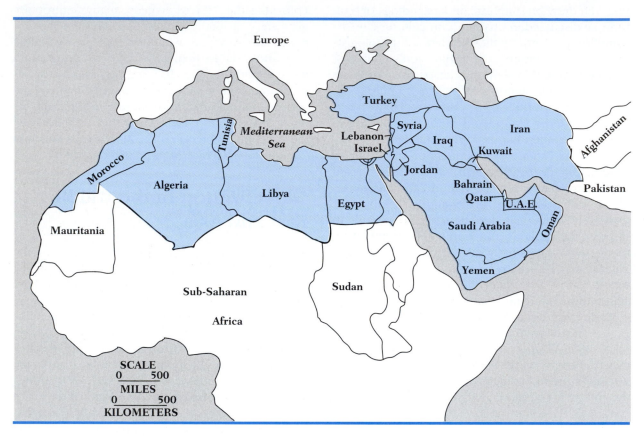

FIGURE 15.1   The Middle East.
Source: Adapted from *The Middle East and Central Asia: An Anthropological Approach*, 4th ed., by Dale F. Eickelman. © 1998.
Reprinted by permission of Prentice Hall, Upper Saddle River, NJ.

already discussed Japanese society in Chapter 13 on industrial societies.) This chapter focuses primarily on the agricultural or rural societies in Asia that have been transformed by globalization processes. This chapter discusses the findings of anthropologists who use a global perspective that reflects the ongoing changes and transitions in the societies of the Middle East and Asia.

Early Colonialism and Globalization in the Middle East and Asia

The Middle East

Aside from the Portuguese, most Europeans did not have much direct contact with the Middle East until the 1800s. As European countries industrialized,

however, they came to view the Middle East as an area ripe for imperial control. In the European view, the Middle East could supply raw materials and serve as markets for manufactured goods. Napoleon Bonaparte led an expedition to Egypt in 1798, bringing it under French rule for a brief period. He planned to incorporate Egypt as a colony that would complement French economic interests. Because of British rivalry following the Napoleonic Wars, the French had to evacuate Egypt; nevertheless, Europeans gradually attained more influence in the region.

Although the British did not directly colonize Egypt until 1882, various European advisers influenced Egyptian rulers to develop specific products for the world market. Egyptian rulers and the upper classes cooperated with Western interests in these activities to induce economic growth. Factories were built for processing sugar, and cotton became

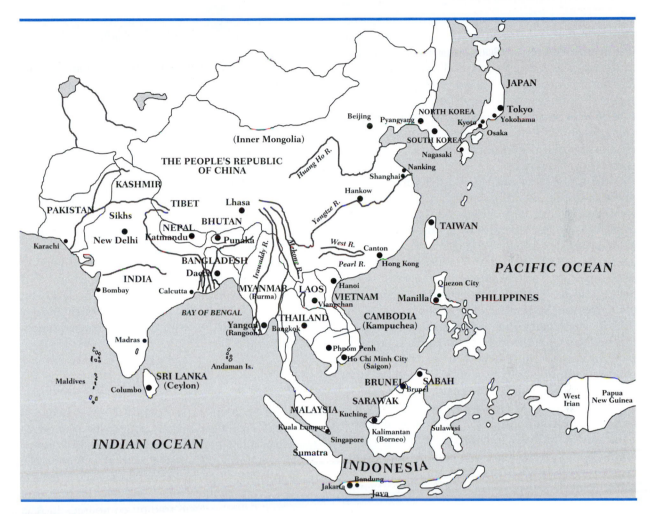

FIGURE 15.2   A map of contemporary Asia.

the most important agricultural commodity in the country. The most important development project that affected ties between the Middle East and the West was the Suez Canal, which connects the Mediterranean Sea with the Gulf of Suez. Completed in 1869, the Suez Canal was financed through capital supplied by French and British interests. The canal shortened the distance between East and West, thereby drawing the Middle East into the orbit of the core nations.

To offset British expansion in the Middle East, the French began to build a North African empire, taking control of Algeria, Tunisia, and Morocco. Morocco was considered the most "perfect" French colony, in which, through indirect rule, the French

devised a "scientific colony" that required only a small number of French officials to supervise a vast territory. Thus, the French ruled through urban elites, rural leaders, and Moroccan religious officials. They developed large commercial enterprises such as railroads and mining, as well as various agricultural operations. These commercial enterprises enabled the colony to pay for itself, a definite asset for the French.

European expansion in the Middle East continued throughout the nineteenth and early twentieth centuries. Although not directly colonized, Turkey, which was then the center of the Ottoman Empire, came under the economic control of Western interests. To reduce the disparity in economic development between their country and Europe, Turkish rulers gave concessions to French and British interests to develop industries and services in Turkey. These enterprises produced cheap goods that undermined native Turkish businesses. By the end of the nineteenth century, Turkey had become a peripheral society, exporting raw materials, providing cheap labor, and depending on core societies for manufactured goods. This led to the end of the Ottoman Empire.

Although not as industrialized as many other European countries, Russia began to expand toward the Middle East during the mid-1800s and eventually assumed control over various regions of central Asia, absorbing the Muslim populations of Samarkand, Tashkent, and Turkestan. To secure access to the warm waters of the Persian Gulf, Russia also moved into Iran (formerly Persia), taking control of the northern half of the country. The British, who maintained control of commerce in the Persian Gulf through their naval fleet, were thus threatened by this Russian expansion. As a countermeasure, they moved into southern Iran and funneled capital into the region by developing a tobacco monopoly and financing other economic projects. Eventually, in 1907, the British and Russians agreed to divide Iran into three spheres, with northern and central Iran, including Tehran, in the Russian sphere; southeastern Iran in the British sphere; and an area between in the neutral zone. The Iranians were neither consulted nor informed about the terms of this agreement (Keddie 1981).

Another area that was contested between the Russians and the British was Afghanistan. Geographically, Afghanistan is situated between the Middle East and South Asia. It is a country made up of various ethnic groups who were Muslims involved in agricultural practices and also nomadic pastoralism in the rugged mountains and deep valleys, deserts, and arid plateaus. Afghanistan was a remnant of one of the major Muslim empires founded in the seventeenth century.

In the nineteenth century, the Russians tried to colonize Afghanistan by completing a railway to the Afghan border, and the British countered by building a railway from their colonized portion of South Asia northward. This "Great Game" played out between the British and Russians left Afghanistan as a buffer state between these colonial powers. Various Afghan leaders had to negotiate between these

powers and give concessions to these powers to maintain their independence (Sidky and Akers 2005).

Following World War I, the European powers divided the Middle East into different spheres of influence. In addition to their North African empire, the French gained the countries of Lebanon and Syria as direct colonies. Other areas such as Turkey and the Arabian peninsula remained politically independent but became peripheral states.

The British took Egypt, Iraq, and Palestine as direct colonies. The British also allowed European Jews to immigrate to Palestine. Because Jewish communities had faced discrimination and persecution for centuries in European society, Jewish leaders in Europe called for the resettlement of Jews in their original homeland in Palestine. This movement, known as Zionism, influenced British policy, which led to the immigration of thousands of Jews to Palestine, with dramatic consequences for the Middle East.

Asia

Intensive economic and political contact between Asia and the West began during the period of European mercantilism. The first phase of Western expansion into Asia began with the Portuguese trade in India, China, and Southeast Asia. The next phase involved the Dutch, French, and British, who established private trading companies in Asia to secure access to exportable goods.

India, Burma, and Malaysia   Western nations resorted to direct colonization in Asia following the Industrial Revolution. For example, Britain colonized India, gaining control over the production of export cash crops such as jute, oil seeds, cotton, and wheat. Because India did not have a strong centralized state, it could not resist British colonization. The opening of the Suez Canal facilitated Britain's management of its Asian colonies, and by 1900, the British had established direct economic and political control over 300 million South Asians (Hardgrove 2005).

From their base in India, the British initiated a series of wars to incorporate Burma as a direct colony. Eventually, the British expanded their colonial domination southward to the region of Malaysia. To satisfy industrial societies' increasing demand for commodities such as tin (for the canning industry) and rubber, the British developed mining and plantations in both Burma and Malaysia. In addition, as the demand for rice grew in the world market, the British commercialized rice production for export.

China The industrial nations also attempted to carve out colonies in China. Although that country had been open to European trade ever since the Portuguese established ports in Macao in the sixteenth century, China successfully resisted direct colonization by the West for several reasons. First, it was farther from the West than were other Asian countries. Second, China had a highly centralized state empire in which mandarin officials controlled local regions and thus was a more formidable empire than were other Asian countries. Third, the Chinese government was not impressed with Western goods and technology. Chinese officials had been familiar with Western products from the time of Marco Polo in the fifteenth century and forbade the importation of Western commodities.

Despite this resistance, the British eventually gained access to China through the introduction of opium. Attempts by the Chinese government to prohibit the illegal smuggling of this drug into the country led to the Opium Wars of 1839–1842 between Great Britain and China. Britain defeated China, subsequently acquiring Hong Kong as a colony and securing other business concessions. Eventually, international settlements were established in cities such as Shanghai, which became sovereign city-states outside the Chinese government's control (DeVoe 2006).

The Dutch Empire The Dutch expanded into the East Indies, eventually incorporating the region—now known as Indonesia—into their colonial empire. By the nineteenth century, the Dutch had developed what they referred to as the Kultur-System, which lasted until 1917. Through this system, Indonesian peasants were allowed to grow only certain cash crops, such as sugar, coffee, tobacco, and indigo, for the world market. These crops were developed at the expense of subsistence crops such as rice. The policy of coerced labor and exploitation of the peasantry held back the economic development of the Indonesian islands (Geertz 1963a; Hefner 2001; Lukens-Bull 2005).

French Indo-China French imperial rivalry with Britain had direct consequences for Southeast Asia. By 1893, the French had conquered and established direct colonial rule over Cambodia, Vietnam, and Laos—a region that became known as Indochina. In northern Vietnam, French settlers directed the production of coal, zinc, and tin; in the southern areas near the Mekong River, they developed the land to produce rubber and rice exports (Scupin 2005).

Thailand: An Independent Country One country in Southeast Asia that did not become directly colonized was Thailand. The Thai monarchy, which had some experience with Western interests, developed economic and political strategies to play European rivals against one another while adopting Western innovations. European business interests were allowed to aid in the development of some goods, but not to exercise direct political control. To some extent, this suited the geopolitical strategies of both the British and the French, who preferred Thailand as a buffer state between their colonial domains (Slagter and Kerbo 2000; Scupin 2006).

The Philippines The Philippines were directly colonized first by Spain, then by the United States. Spain took control of most of the Philippine Islands during the sixteenth century. As in Latin America, the Spanish established pueblos (towns) in which colonial officials directed Filipino peasant labor and collected tribute. Eventually, *encomiendas*—land grants to Spanish settlers—developed into *haciendas*, on which tobacco, sugar, and indigo were planted for export to the world market. Aside from these agricultural enterprises, the Spanish encouraged few commercial developments. During the Spanish-American War of 1898, the United States defeated Spanish forces in both the Philippines and the Caribbean. Many Filipinos sided with the United States in hopes of achieving independence from Spain. When the United States refused to recognize Philippine independence, numerous Filipinos redirected their resistance efforts against the United States. After a protracted war in which 600,000 Filipinos lost their lives and many more were placed in concentration camps, the Philippines were directly colonized by the United States. The United States continued to organize native Filipino labor to produce cash crops such as tobacco, sugar, and indigo as export commodities for the world market (Lukens-Bull 2006).

Consequences of Colonialism for the Middle East and Asia

Demographic Change

Western expansion and colonialism in non-Western countries brought unprecedented demographic growth to the populations of these agricultural states. As in Latin America, Africa, and the Caribbean, the development of intensive cash-crop cultivation often resulted in rapid population growth. As labor shortages developed in subsistence agriculture as a result of moving labor into cash-cropping agriculture for the European market, peasant farmers began to increase their family size (Robbins 1999). This increase in fertility led to rapid population growth in many of the Middle East and Asian societies. Eventually, Europeans introduced new medical and sanitation practices that led to a tremendous reduction in death rates through the control of smallpox, plague, yellow fever, and malaria. Meanwhile, birth rates remained high. The combination of reduced death rates and high birth rates led to dramatic population increases. For example, the population of India increased by one-third between 1881 and 1931 and then doubled between 1931 and 1971. In Chapter 16 we discuss some of the global effects of these population trends.

Unlike the situation in the West, population growth in colonized non-Western countries was not coupled with sustained and rapid industrialization. The expanding Middle Eastern and Asian populations therefore had to be absorbed by the intensification of agricultural production. For example, population growth in Indonesia under the Dutch led to what Clifford Geertz has referred to as "agricultural involution" (1963a). The commercialization of agriculture and the use of coerced labor increased production somewhat, but the rates of increase could not keep pace with population growth. Agricultural yields per day of labor actually decreased. In addition, as the population grew, land became more scarce. Thus, the system of intensified agriculture was increasingly unable to feed the growing population.

As a result of colonialism, major urban centers grew quickly in the Middle East and Asia. For example, the cities of Cairo in Egypt and Tehran in Iran began to grow at tremendous rates. In India, the British created port cities such as Calcutta, Bombay, and Madras, which became international trading and financial centers. In China, Shanghai and Nanking developed into major urban centers as a result of the expansion of Western businesses. Southeast Asian cities such as Rangoon, Bangkok, Saigon, Jakarta, Kuala Lumpur, Singapore, and Manila expanded rapidly. These cities attracted rural migrants, who crowded into squatter settlements and slums.

Economic Change

The economies of the countries of the Middle East and Asia during the nineteenth century were directed toward the production of agricultural goods such as tea, sugar, tobacco, cotton, rice, tin, and rubber for export. Prices of these goods were subject to fluctuations in the world market. Land that had been converted to growing these export crops could no longer support peasant villages. Native handicrafts declined dramatically in importance in comparison with export-oriented commodity production. In addition, as in other colonized areas of the world, imported Western manufactured goods flowed into Middle Eastern and Asian nations. Thus, these societies became more dependent on core industrial societies.

As in Latin America, Africa, and the Caribbean, one major consequence of Western colonialism was the integration of many agricultural village communities into wider regional and global economic patterns. The *precolonial* traditional villages were never entirely self-sufficient and were tied to regional and national trading networks. However, under Western colonialism, the village peasantry in the Middle East and Asia was no longer isolated from cities, and the global market determined the prices for agricultural goods. This global transformation of agricultural economies triggered dramatic changes in non-Western rural communities. Because few peasants had enough capital to own and manage land, much of the land fell into the hands of colonial settlers, large landowners, and money lenders. In many cases, these changes encouraged absentee landownership and temporary tenancy. Long-term care of the land by the peasantry was sacrificed for immediate profits. As in the case of the peasants of Latin America, Africa, and the Caribbean, land, labor, and capital were thus disconnected from the village kinship structures of reciprocity and redistribution, or what has been referred to as the moral economy (see Chapter 12). As globalization occurred, these peasants were incorporated into the global cash economy. Their lives were now dependent on the fluctuations of a global economy that determined their success or failure as farmers.

Religious Change

The major religious traditions of most of the societies in the Middle East and Asia are Islam, Hinduism, and Buddhism. The Islamic tradition dates to the life of Muhammad, who was born in AD 570 in the city of Mecca, which is now in Saudi Arabia. Muslims believe that Muhammad is the final prophet in the long line of prophets referred to in the Bible. They share with Christians and Jews the faith that Abraham was the founder and first prophet of their tradition. Unlike Christians and Jews, however, they believe that Muhammad began receiving revelations from God that culminated in the major religious text known as the Qur'an (Koran). The traditions of Islam spread widely throughout areas of the Middle East and Asia (Scupin 2000; Sidky and Akers 2005).

Two other southern Asian religions—Hinduism and Buddhism—have influenced civilizations throughout the region. Both developed in India and are associated with three major doctrines. The first doctrine is known as *samsara*, or reincarnation, which refers to how an individual's soul transmigrates and is reborn in a new organism in a new cycle of existence. The second doctrine is *karma*, the belief that an individual's destiny is affected by his or her behavior in previous lives. Hinduism emphasizes that an individual must live a dutiful and ethical life to produce good karma for future existences. The third doctrine is *moksha* in Hinduism or *nirvana* in Buddhism—spiritual enlightenment—the ultimate aim and spiritual goal for all Hindus and Buddhists. Enlightenment represents the final escape from the cycle of life, death, rebirth, and suffering into an ultimate spiritual state of existence.

The Middle East and Asia already had the highly literate religious traditions of Islam, Hinduism, and Buddhism, which meant that Western Christian missionaries had a much more difficult time trying to convert native populations in these regions. The religious traditions in these regions provided the basic spiritual cosmologies, beliefs, and meanings that satisfied the vast numbers of these people in their coping with universal needs and questions. However, in many cases, the Western missionaries in these Middle Eastern and Asian countries were instrumental in teaching some of the basic cultural values of the Western world, including political ideas regarding democratic institutions, civil liberties, and individual freedom.

Political Change: Independence and Nationalism

During the nineteenth and twentieth centuries, the extension of Western power into the Middle East and Asia elicited responses ranging from native reformist activities to nationalist independence movements. Because most people in these regions were Muslims, Hindus, or Buddhists, many of the anticolonial responses reflected a religious orientation. In response to Western colonialism, Muslim, Hindu, and Buddhist leaders called for a rethinking of their religious traditions to accommodate pressures from the West. Reformers such as Muhammad Abduh in Egypt and Rabinda Tagore in India argued that the sources of Western strength developed in part from early Middle Eastern and Asian contributions to science, medicine, and scholarship (see Chapter 13). Thus, the reformists exhorted believers to look to their own indigenous religious traditions as a source of inspiration to overcome Western economic and political domination. Reformist movements spread throughout the Muslim world and the Hindu and Buddhist areas, especially among the urban, educated classes, paving the way for later nationalist and independence movements throughout the regions (Scupin 2000; Weisgrau 2000).

Similarly, most of the anticolonial, nationalist, and independence movements that emerged in Asia were linked to local religious or political developments. They were also associated with the rise of Western-educated groups that articulated nationalist demands.

A Nationalist and Independence Movement in India

As in other colonies, the British desired an educated class of Indians to serve as government clerks and cultural intermediaries between the British and the colonized people. The British sponsored a national educational system that included universities and training colleges, which educated thousands of Indians. These educated people became part of a literate middle class, familiar with Western liberal thought regarding human rights and self-determination. A small, powerful merchant class that benefited from British economic policies also emerged.

Whereas India formerly had been fragmented into separate language groups, the colonial educational system provided the educated middle classes with a common language—English. Improved transportation and communication media such as railroads, print technology, and the telegraph accelerated the movement for national unity. In addition, the educated classes became increasingly aware of the hypocrisy of British "values" such as equality and democracy as they were exposed to racism and discrimination in the form of exclusion from British private hotels, clubs, and parks.

The majority of the Indian population, however, was not middle class but was made up of peasants who lived in rural village communities and did not speak English. Thus, the middle-class nationalist movement did not directly appeal to them. This gulf between the middle classes and the peasants was bridged by a remarkable individual, Mohandas Gandhi, later called the Mahatma, or "great soul." Although from the middle class, Gandhi fused Hindu religious sentiments with Western political thought to mobilize the peasantry against British domination. Anthropologist Richard Fox contributed an extensive analysis of Gandhi's role in the anticolonial struggle (1989). In his study, Fox emphasizes the role of an individual with charismatic abilities to bring about major social and cultural change within a society (Hardgrove 2006).

Hindu traditions provided the model for Gandhi's strategies of nonviolent resistance. He called for the peaceful boycott of British-produced goods, telling the villagers to maintain their traditional weaving industries to spin their own cloth. Through his protests and boycotts, he rallied millions of Indians

Mohandas Gandhi rallied the Indian nation toward independence from the British.

in a mass movement that eventually could not be resisted. In 1947, two years after the end of World War II, the British were forced to relinquish their empire in South Asia (Hardgrove 2005; Weiss 2005).

Revolutionary Movements in Asia

As in Latin America, Africa, and the Caribbean, a number of revolutionary movements developed in the Middle East and Asia as a result of globalization and contact with Western colonialism and power. The revolutions that developed in Asia had worldwide repercussions. In China, a grassroots revolutionary movement developed out of anti-Western, nationalistic movements. In the early twentieth century, Sun Yat-sen, a doctor educated in Hawaii and Hong Kong, championed the formation of a democratic republic in China, gaining support among the peasants by calling for the redistribution of land. The movement toward democracy failed, however. Instead, the military under Chiang

Kai-shek, who did not sympathize with peasant resistance movements or democratic reforms, assumed control of China. These developments encouraged the growth of the Chinese Communist Party under Mao Zedong. Mao's guerrillas engaged in a protracted struggle against Chiang Kai-shek's forces in the 1940s.

Mao Zedong was familiar with Karl Marx's prediction that the urban *proleteriat* or working class would direct revolutions toward socialism and communism. Mao, in contrast, believed that the peasantry could become the backbone of a communist revolution (Wolf 1969; DeVoe 2006). Through the Chinese Communist Party, Mao began to mobilize the peasantry and combine traditional notions of Confucianism with his brand of Marxism, sometimes called Maoism. Calling for the overthrow of the landlords and Western forms of capitalism that he blamed for social and economic inequality, Mao made Marxism comprehensible to Chinese peasants. By 1949, after two decades of struggle, Mao and his peasant-based armies gained control of the country, renaming it the People's Republic of China.

Vietnam experienced the most dramatic nationalist and revolutionary movement of any of the French colonies of Southeast Asia. After World War II, the French attempted to reestablish their colonial regime in Indochina. Leading the opposition was Ho Chi Minh, who like many other Vietnamese,

was frustrated by French colonialism and its negative impact on his society. Ho Chi Minh believed in the communist ideal but, like Mao Zedong, adapted Marxist ideology to the particular concerns of his nationalist struggle (Wolf 1969; Scupin 2006). His well-organized peasant army, the Vietminh, defeated the French forces at Dien Bien Phu in 1954. This defeat led to the withdrawal of the French from Vietnam.

Following Dien Bien Phu, the French and the Vietminh agreed to a temporary division of the country into North Vietnam under Ho Chi Minh and South Vietnam under Ngo Dinh Diem. The nation was to be unified through elections in 1956, but the elections were never held. As a Cold War strategy, the United States, meanwhile, committed itself to the survival of an independent, noncommunist South Vietnam, supplying Diem with massive economic, political, and military support. Diem lacked widespread support among the South Vietnamese population, however, and he brutally repressed dissent against his regime. He was overthrown in a military coup in 1963.

As communist opposition, supported by North Vietnam, escalated in the South, the United States dramatically increased its level of military involvement. By 1967, more than 500,000 U.S. troops were stationed in Vietnam. Unable to defeat the Vietnamese guerrillas, the United States entered into a long period of negotiation with the Vietnamese

Mao Zedong.

Ho Chi Minh.

communists, finally signing a peace treaty in January 1973. Two years later, North Vietnam overran the South, thereby unifying the nation (Scupin 2006).

Uneven Development in the Middle East and Asia

By redirecting economic development toward an export-oriented global economy, Western colonialism and globalization transformed many of the formerly agricultural countries into *peripheral*, dependent economies. The wealthy *core* industrial societies of the West provided economic and political support to those elites who instituted policies to promote economic growth. Many of these elites in the Middle East and Asia minimized restrictions on foreign investment and opened their borders to multinational corporations. In addition, some of these societies had vital resources that enabled them to develop a special type of relationship with the wealthy industrialized core societies. However, a number of these societies, especially in Asia, began to attempt to withdraw from globalization and capitalism and develop self-sufficient economies.

Oil and the Middle East

The discovery of vast sources of oil—60 percent of the world's known reserves—in the Middle East has revolutionized trade and politics and has brought tremendous social change to the region. Oil became the major energy source for the industrial world. Multinational corporations based in the core societies developed these resources, controlling both oil production and prices, to maintain economic growth in their home countries. As nationalist independence movements spread, however, many countries demanded control over their oil. Nations such as Libya, Iran, Saudi Arabia, Iraq, and Kuwait began to *nationalize* their oil industries, and the multinational corporations eventually lost most of their controlling interests in the region.

Political conflicts between the Arabs and Israel in the 1970s resulted in a boycott of oil to the global economy by the Islamic countries and other oil-producing countries known as OPEC. This resulted in the rapid increase of the price of oil compared to the 1950s and 1960s in the world. This rapid increase in the price of oil since the 1970s has enabled the oil-producing countries of the region to accumulate vast wealth and has fueled worldwide inflation that raised the costs of all goods and raw materials. The per capita incomes of some Middle Eastern countries with smaller populations eventually surpassed those of many *core* countries. Realizing that they were dependent on a single export commodity, however, Middle Eastern countries took certain steps to diversify their economies. Smaller countries, such as Saudi Arabia, with a population of 20 million people, and Kuwait, with only 3 million—both ruled by royal dynastic families—financed some capital-intensive industries such as cement and detergent manufacturing and food processing. In doing so, these small Arab countries ensured high incomes for most of their population, which tended to enhance their political legitimacy and stability.

Oil production in countries such as Saudi Arabia has had global consequences.

Larger oil-rich countries such as Iran and Iraq pursued rapid economic development to increase national wealth and legitimize their political regimes. Shah Muhammad Reza Pahlavi of Iran and Saddam Hussein of Iraq invited multinational corporations and consultants from core countries to help diversify their industries and develop their military technology and forces. In contrast to the smaller countries, however, Iraq and Iran, with their larger populations (18 million and 42 million, respectively), had more difficulty raising economic standards for everyone immediately.

The vast majority of the people of the Middle East, however, *do not live* in oil-rich countries. These nations include Egypt, Syria, Jordan, Lebanon, and Morocco; although they have developed some industries to diversify their economies, they remain to some extent peripheral societies dependent on the wealthier industrial core societies.

Withdrawal from the Global Economy

Some countries, by adopting a socialist form of economic system, tried to develop economically outside of the capitalist global economy. In China following his victory in 1949, Mao Zedong implemented an economic development plan modeled on that of the former Soviet Union. He collectivized agriculture by appropriating the land owned by the elite and giving it to the peasants. Mao established cooperatives in which a number of villages owned agricultural land in common, and he also sponsored the development of heavy industries to stimulate economic growth. Communist Party officials, known as cadres, managed both the agricultural cooperatives and industrial firms.

When these policies failed to generate economic growth, Mao launched a radically different effort in 1958 favoring a decentralized economy. This plan, known as the Great Leap Forward, established locally based rural and urban communes that organized the production and distribution of goods and services. Each commune, consisting of 12,000 to 60,000 people, was subdivided into brigades of 100 to 700 households, production teams of about 35 households, and work teams of 8 to 10 households. Each commune was supposed to be self-sufficient, containing a banking system, police

force, schools, day-care centers, mess halls, hospitals, and old-age centers. The communes established their own production goals and reinvested their profits in the commune.

Although some aspects of the Great Leap Forward were successful, especially those involving health care and literacy, the program failed to promote agricultural and industrial development. In fact, it was marked by famine, political corruption, and economic retardation. Mao then initiated an ideological campaign to eliminate corruption and political "deviance" while restoring revolutionary consciousness. This campaign, known as the Cultural Revolution, lasted from 1966 to 1976. Mao organized young people into groups called the Red Guards to purify China of any capitalist, traditional Confucianist, or Western tendencies. Millions of people, primarily the educated classes, were arrested and forced to work on rural communes as punishment for their deviance from the communist path. By 1976, at the time of Mao's death, the Cultural Revolution had paralyzed economic development by eliminating the most skilled and educated classes, those who could have contributed to the nation's growth (DeVoe 2006).

Vietnam also tried to withdraw from the world capitalist system, implementing a socialist government based on Marxist-Leninist principles. After the end of the Vietnam War, the government instituted a five-year plan that collectivized agriculture and relocated people from urban to rural communities. By 1978, 137 collective farms had been established; 4 million people, including half the population of Ho Chi Minh City (formerly Saigon), were resettled in what were called "new economic zones." These zones were organized to produce crops and light industry as a means of encouraging economic self-sufficiency. They were managed by Communist Party officials, many of whom had no direct experience in agriculture or industry (Scupin 2006).

By 1981, Vietnam had become one of the poorest peripheral nations in the world. While food production and labor productivity decreased, inflation and unemployment rose. Military expenditures drained the economy of needed funds for capital development. Part of the reason that Vietnam was underdeveloped was the war itself. For example, the defoliation of forests as a result of U.S. bombing and the use of Agent Orange impeded the growth of timber. At the same time, however, many of the problems were a direct result of in-flexible ideological commitments and lack of expertise on the part of Communist Party bureaucrats (Pike 1990; Scupin 2006).

Ethnographic Studies of the Societies in the Middle East and Asia

A Middle Eastern Village in Transition

Ethnographic studies of peasant villages in the Middle East have contributed to a more comprehensive understanding of the interconnections between peripheral and core nations. One early study of culture change was conducted by Hani Fakhouri (1972), who studied the Egyptian village of Kafr El-Elow, which at the time of Fakhouri's study (1966–1968) was undergoing substantial changes. About 80 percent of the Egyptian population lived in about 4,000 rural villages, many of which were being drawn into the global economy through rapid industrialization and the commercialization of agriculture.

Kafr El-Elow is located 18 miles south of Cairo. Before the 1920s, it was a relatively small farming community in which the *fellaheen* (peasants) practiced small-scale subsistence agriculture. After British colonization in the nineteenth century, the *fellaheen* began to grow cotton as an export commodity. By the 1920s, water pumps had been introduced into the village, and several industries had begun to develop. Roads were constructed, linking Kafr El-Elow with nearby industrializing communities. After the 1950s, industrialization accelerated, and subsistence farming was no longer the primary aspect of the Kafr El-Elow economy. Instead, many nearby industries related to steel, natural gas, cement, textiles, railways, aircraft, and other products drew increasing numbers of *fellaheen* into the industrial work force; however, many villagers continued cultivating their crops after factory hours and on weekends to supplement their incomes.

By the 1960s, only about 10 percent of the community was made up of peasants. Although the remaining *fellaheen* continued to plow their fields with draft animals, they also used some modern machinery such as crop sprayers and irrigation pumps. At the time of Fakhouri's study, agricultural productivity was very high, and the *fellaheen* were able to harvest three or four crops a year. Wheat and corn were cultivated for domestic consumption, primarily for making bread, and vegetables were grown for cash crops and home consumption. Cash crops became important enough that the Egyptian government built refrigerated bins to store the farmers' seeds and cuttings for replanting.

Industrialization brought to Kafr El-Elow new patterns of social mobility, an influx of migrants for

Traditional Egyptian peasants.

urban labor, and rising incomes, which created new socioeconomic classes. These new classes demanded a variety of consumer goods and services not familiar to the traditional population. Bicycles, wristwatches, radios, and electricity for households became increasingly common. Preferences for Western clothing, housing, entertainment, and other commodities contributed to the decline of traditional handicraft industries and the rise of new businesses. Six businesses existed in 1930; in 1966, Fakhouri counted 78.

Middle Eastern Family, Marriage, and Gender

An enormous amount of ethnographic research is available on family, marriage, and gender in Arab, Turkish, and Iranian societies. In all these societies, the ideal form of the family has been patrilineal, endogamous, polygynous, and patriarchal. The primary sources for the ideals of the Muslim family are Islamic religious texts, principally the Qur'an and the Sharia. Cultural anthropologists have discovered, however, that the ideals of the Muslim family do not always coincide with the realities of social life in the Middle East and North Africa.

In some parts of the Arab world, such as among the Palestinian communities, the term *hamula* is used to refer to an idealized descent group (a patrilineage or patriclan) that members view as a kinship group. The *hamula* is associated with a *patronym*, the name of a particular male who is thought to be a paternal ancestor. In rural areas, the typical *hamula* is a clan that embraces various patrilineages. The head of the clan is referred to as a sheik, a hereditary position. He resolves disputes and encourages cooperation among members of the clan. The *hamula* has always been a source of pride and loyalty in rural Arab communities.

Despite the descriptions of the *hamula* as a patrilineal descent grouping and its association with a particular patronym, cultural anthropologists find that it is frequently a loosely structured group combining patrilineal, affinal, matrilineal, and neighborhood relations (Eickelman 1998). Nevertheless, under different circumstances it may serve to coordinate economic, political, and ceremonial affairs. Research on urban and rural communities in Lebanon, Kuwait, and other Arab countries suggests that loyalty to the *hamula* remains as a component of social organization throughout the Muslim world (Al-Thakeb 1985; Eickelman 1998).

The Family   As in most other agricultural states, the extended family is the ideal in the Middle East. The traditional household espoused by Arabs, Turks, and Iranians is made up of the patriarch, his wife, one or more married sons and their families, and unmarried daughters and sons. Yet, as in the case of the *hamula*, these ideals are often not realized (Bates and Rassam 1983). Economic and demographic conditions such as landlessness, poverty, and geographical mobility frequently influence the size and dimension of the Muslim family.

As industrialization and consequent urbanization influence the Middle East, the nuclear family is becoming the normative pattern. Survey research on the Muslim family from Egypt, Syria, Libya, Jordan, Lebanon, Iraq, Bahrain, and Kuwait suggests that the nuclear family has become the predominant form in both rural and urban areas (Al-Thakeb 1981, 1985). Variability in family type is often related to socioeconomic status. The ideal of the nuclear family appears to be most prevalent among the middle and upper classes, which are most influenced by globalization. Among the lower socioeconomic classes, especially families involved in agriculture, the extended family retains its importance. Yet even when the nuclear family predominates, wider kinship relations, including the *hamula*, sometimes remain important (Al-Thakeb 1985; Eickelman 1998).

Marriage   Marriage is a fundamental obligation in the Islamic tradition. Unless financially or physically unable, every Muslim male and female is required to be married. Marriage is regarded as a sacred contract between two families that legalizes intercourse and the procreation of children. In the Islamic tradition, there are no cultural beliefs or practices such as monasticism that sanction any form of life outside of marriage.

Islamic societies are known for endorsing the marriage practices of polygyny. Polygyny is mentioned once in the Qur'an (iv:3):

Marry of the women, who seem good to you, two, three, or four, and if ye fear that ye cannot do justice [to so many] the one [only].

Although polygynous marriage is permitted and to some extent represents an ideal norm from the early religious tradition within the Qu'ran in Muslim societies, anthropologists find that most marriages are monogamous. For example, fewer than 10 percent of married Kuwaiti males and about 1 percent of married Egyptian males are involved in polygynous marriages (Al-Thakeb 1985; Eickelman 1998). In Kafr El-Elow, Fakhouri (1972) found that only a few males had multiple wives. In questioning males involved in polygynous marriages, Fakhouri noted that the major rationales for taking a second wife were either the first wife's infertility or poor health or the desire of wealthy males to demonstrate their high status.

Wealthy males in both urban and rural areas contract polygynous marriages. In the traditional pattern found in rural communities, a wealthy male from the landed elite contracts a *parallel-cousin marriage* and then takes a wife from another family (Bates and Rassam 1983). Polygyny is also found among the new elite in some of the wealthy oil-producing countries. However, economic limitations and the fact that the Islamic tradition prescribes equal justice for all wives encourage monogamous marriages among the majority of Muslims.

Arranged marriage based on parental decision making still predominates in Islamic societies. Until recently, for example, Saudi Arabian males did not even view their wives until their wedding day. Some indicators suggest, however, that a degree of individual choice in marriage may become more prevalent. Anthropological research from Kuwait in the mid-1980s indicates that an individual's freedom to select a spouse varies according to education, socioeconomic status, age, and sex (Al-Thakeb 1985). As both males and females become more educated and achieve greater economic independence from their parents, they enjoy greater freedom in mate selection, though typically in many communities, females have much less choice.

Divorce Like polygyny, divorce in traditional Islamic societies was a male prerogative. To obtain a divorce, a male does not need much justification; Islamic law specifies several means whereby a male can easily repudiate his wife. It also empowers a husband to reclaim his wife without her consent within a four-month period after the divorce. Traditionally, a Muslim wife did not have the same rights to obtain a divorce. A woman could, however, divorce her husband for reasons such as impotence, insanity, and lack of economic support; but to prove these accusations, she would need a very sympathetic judge (Esposito 1998).

Cultural anthropologists find it difficult to generalize about divorce and marriage in the Muslim world. In countries such as Egypt, Turkey, and Morocco, which have greater exposure to outside global influences, divorce laws for women have become liberalized. These countries have educated middle classes that support reform. In conjunction with these Islamic reform movements, along with the modification of divorce laws, some Muslim feminists have called for the abolition of polygyny. Certain countries—for example, Tunisia and Turkey—have prohibited this practice, and others have restricted it (Eickelman 1998).

Gender The Western image of the Arab or Muslim woman is frequently that of a female hidden behind a veil and completely dominated by the demands of a patriarchal society. Early Western scholars painted a grim and unwholesome portrait of the female in the Muslim household. Cultural anthropologists find that this image obscures the complexity of gender relations in the Middle East.

The patriarchal ideal and the status of the female in the Muslim world cannot be understood without reference to two views in the Islamic doctrine. First, according to the Islamic tradition, before the origins of Islam, females were treated negatively. For example, in the pre-Islamic period, the Bedouins regularly practiced female infanticide by burying the unwanted child in sand. The Qur'an explicitly forbids this practice. Thus, Islam was viewed as having had a progressive influence on the role of women. Second, Islam condemns all sexual immorality, prescribing severe penalties for adultery. The Qur'an enjoins both males and females to be chaste and modest.

Islamic religious texts prescribe a specific set of statuses and corresponding roles for females to play in the Muslim family as daughter, sister, wife, and mother. Each of these statuses carries certain obligations, rights, privileges, and duties. These statuses are influenced by the patriarchal ideals of the Islamic texts. One passage of the Qur'an (iv:34) is often cited when referring to the role of women: "Men are in charge of women, because

God (Allah) hath made the one of them to excel the other, and because they spend of their property (for the support of women). So good women are the obedient."

This passage provides the context for the development of various laws that have influenced the status of Muslim women. For example, traditionally a woman could inherit only a one-half share of her parents' estate, whereas her brothers inherited full shares. This law assumed that a woman is fully cared for by her family, and when she marries, her husband's family will provide for her material needs. Thus, a Muslim woman does not need the full share of inheritance.

Another traditional code in Islamic law illustrates the patriarchal attitudes toward women with respect to political and legal issues. In legal cases, a woman is granted half the legal status of a man. For example, if a crime is committed, two women as opposed to one man are needed as legal witnesses for testimony. This legal equation of "two females equals one male" reflects the traditional Islamic image of women as less experienced and less capable than men in political and legal affairs.

Ethnographic research since the 1970s has demonstrated that male-female relations in these societies are far more complex than the religious texts might imply. By focusing exclusively on Islamic texts and laws, early researchers distorted and misunderstood actual practices and relations between males and females. Moreover, before the 1970s, much of the ethnographic research in Muslim societies was done by males, resulting in a skewed understanding of the position of women, because male cultural anthropologists did not have the same access to female informants as did female cultural anthropologists. Eventually, female cultural anthropologists such as Lois Beck, Lila Abu Lughod, Soraya Altorki, and Elizabeth Fernea began to study the Muslim female world.

Female cultural anthropologists discovered that the position of Muslim women cannot be categorized uniformly. One major reason for variation is the extent to which Islamic countries have been exposed to the West. Some, like Tunisia, Egypt, and Turkey, have adopted legal reforms that have improved the status of women. For example, Egyptian women have had access to secondary education since the early 1900s and have had career opportunities in medicine, law, engineering, man-

agement, and government. The Egyptian constitution accords women full equality with men, and—ideally—prohibits sexual discrimination in career opportunities. Muslim feminist movements dedicated to improving the status of women have emerged in those countries most affected by the West.

In contrast to Egypt, religiously conservative Saudi Arabia has highly restrictive cultural norms regarding women. Saudi Arabia was not colonized and thus was more isolated, and the religious and political authorities actively opposed Western values and culture within their society. The Saudi Arabian government, which has no constitution, has interpreted Islamic law to declare that any mingling of the sexes is morally wrong. Saudi women are segregated from men; they attend separate schools and upon finishing their education can seek employment only in exclusively female institutions such as women's hospitals, schools, and banks. Saudi women are forbidden by law to drive cars, and when riding on public buses they have to sit in special closed sections. All Saudi public buildings must have separate entrances and elevators for men and women (Altorki 1986; Badran 1998).

Despite legal reforms and access to education in some Muslim societies, the notion that women are subordinate to men to some extent remains firmly entrenched. For example, in Egypt a woman trained in law cannot become a judge or hold any position with legislative authority. Also, in Egypt polygyny remains legal, and men can obtain divorces with minimal justification (Hatem 1998). In many respects, the patriarchal family remains the center of Islamic social organization. Hence, in some cases attempts to reform women's status have been perceived as heretical assaults on the Islamic family and morality. Some of the recent Islamic revival movements have reactivated conservative, patriarchal cultural norms.

The Veil and Seclusion   To many Westerners, the patriarchal order of the Islamic societies is most conspicuously symbolized by the veil and the other shapeless garments worn by Muslim women. As a female approaches puberty, she is supposed to be restricted and kept from contact with males. The veil is an outward manifestation of a long extensive historical and cultural pattern (Beck and Keddie 1978; Fernea and Fernea 1979; Hatem 1998).

The wearing of the veil and the enforced seclusion of the Muslim woman are known as **purdah**. These practices reinforce a separation between the domestic private sphere of women and the male-dominated public sphere.

Veiling and *purdah* tend to be associated with urban Muslim women. Most scholars believe that the tradition of veiling originated in urban areas among upper-class women prior to the emergence of Islamic religious developments (Beck and Keddie 1978). Traditionally, many peasant and Bedouin women in the Middle East and North Africa do not wear the veil and generally have more freedom to associate with men than do Muslim women who live in towns and cities. Many urban Muslim women report that the veil and accompanying garments offer practical protection from strangers and that when in public they would feel naked and self-conscious without these garments (Fernea and Fernea 1979; Hatem 1998).

In countries such as Egypt, Turkey, and Iran that had formerly abandoned traditional dress codes, many educated, middle-class women have opted to wear the veil and the all-enveloping garments. To some extent, this return to traditional dress reflects the revival movements now occurring throughout the Islamic world. For many Muslim women, returning to the veil is one way in which they can affirm their Islamic religious and cultural identity and make a political statement of resistance to Western power and influence.

Social Structure, Family, and Gender in India and South Asia

In the aftermath of independence and the retreat of Western colonial authority in South Asia, cultural anthropologists began to explore the various societies of the region. Much of the early ethnographic research centered on rural communities of India, with cultural anthropologists such as McKim Marriott, Oscar Lewis, Milton Singer, and Alan Beals investigating the caste system of the Indian rural communities.

Origins of the Caste System   The caste system of India was briefly introduced in Chapter 12. Most scholars associate the origins of the caste system with the Aryan peoples who settled in northern India after 1500 BC. Various social divisions in Aryan society developed into broad ideological categories known as *varnas*. At the top were the *brahmins* (priests), followed by the *kshatriyas* (warriors), the *vaisyas* (merchants), and the *sudras* (commoners). This fourfold scheme provided the ideological cultural framework for organizing thousands of diverse groups.

The functional groupings in the *varna* categories are the subcastes, or, more precisely, what Indians who speak Hindi, a language in northern India, refer to as **jatis**, of which there are several thousand, hierarchically ranked. *Jatis* are based on marital, economic, and ritual relations. Marriages are

An Afghan woman with child.

endogamous (marriage within a group) with respect to *jati*; *jatis* are thus ranked endogamous descent groups. In addition, each *jati* is a specific hereditary occupational group. A person's *jati* places him or her within a fairly rigid form of social stratification.

Early cultural anthropologists have found that *jati* relationships are intimately linked with what is known as the **jajmani economy** of rural Indian villages. The typical Indian village consists of many different castes, with one caste dominating the village both economically and politically. Traditionally, all these castes were interconnected through economic exchanges within the *jajmani* economy. The dominant caste controlled the land and exchanged land-use rights for other goods and services. For example, members of the dominant caste would have their hair cut and fingernails trimmed by a barber. Then, at harvest time, the barber would get a stipulated amount of grain from his client. In addition, the barber, carpenter, potter, and water carrier would exchange their goods and services with one another in a type of barter system. Every caste, even the lowest-ranking, had access to housing, furniture, food, credit, and other goods and services through these exchanges (Marriott and Inden 1977; Quigley 1999). Also, when the British colonized India they did an extensive census and categorized various "caste" groups according to Western categories, and sometimes these misunderstandings have persisted until the present (Dirks 2001; Scupin 2003).

More recent ethnographic studies have concluded that the *jajmani* system is collapsing because of globalization and the introduction of new consumer goods and technology into Indian villages. When people can use safety razors to shave, buy imported dishware and glasses, and use electric pumps to obtain water, many of the old occupations become superfluous. Consequently, many artisans and service workers leave their villages to market their skills elsewhere or, in many cases, to join the increasing number of unskilled migrants flooding the cities.

Although the *jajmani* system is disappearing and the Indian government abolished the most reprehensible aspects of the caste system, such as "untouchability" and discrimination, in its constitution, cultural anthropologists find that the caste system like racism still persists (Scupin 2003; Hardgrove 2006). Contemporary India has caste

hotels, banks, hospitals, and co-ops. Caste organization continues to delineate political factions in India. Most elections are decided by caste voting blocs, and politicians must therefore appeal to caste allegiances for support. Thus, caste remains one of the most divisive factors facing the democratic process in India.

Cultural anthropologists find that the caste system is reinforced to some extent by the worldview or religious beliefs of Hinduism. The doctrines of karma and reincarnation reinforce concepts of purity and pollution that correlate with caste hierarchy. An individual's karma is believed to determine his or her status and ritual state. It is believed that individuals born into low castes are inherently polluted, whereas higher-caste individuals such as brahmins are ritually pure. This state of purity or pollution is permanent.

The late French anthropologist Louis Dumont (1970) argued that, from the Hindu viewpoint, humans have to be ranked in a hierarchy; egalitarian relationships are inconceivable. Dumont asserted that in this worldview, caste relations produce interdependency and reciprocity through exchanges and ritual relationships. He concluded that the cultural understandings of caste rules and ritual purity and pollution have created a system of stratification based on widespread consensus.

In contrast, other anthropologists influenced by more materialist orientations argue that caste relationships in prevailing economic and political conditions maintain that Hindu beliefs about caste were primarily ideological justifications for a system that emerged from long-standing inequalities in which a dominant group accumulated most of the land and other resources. They deny that a consensus exists concerning the appropriateness of caste relationships, citing as evidence the situation of the *harijans* (Children of God, a name given to them by Mahatma Gandhi to help alleviate discrimination against them), or *untouchables*, at the bottom of the caste hierarchy, who daily face discrimination and exploitation. Based on their research in India, anthropologists Joan Mencher and Pauline Kolenda reported that the *harijans* resent, rather than accept, this treatment (Kolenda 1978; Mencher 1974).

Other anthropologists have refined their analyses of caste relations by combining both material and cultural variables. For example, contemporary ethnographers such as Jonathan Parry, Christopher Fuller, Gloria Raheja, and Declan Quigley have described the complex interplay of material interests and cultural meanings of exchanges among castes in the *jajmani* system. They note how upper-caste brahmins accept gifts and other material items from lower-caste members, but in this exchange they ritually absorb the sins of the donors (Parry 1980; Fuller 1989; Raheja 1988; Quigley 1999). For example, Raheja emphasizes that in these *jajmani* exchanges, the lower- and upper-caste groups become equal, and strict hierarchy is undermined. Thus, the exchanges are based on material factors and on the symbolic conceptions of Hinduism.

Family and Marriage in South Asia   The most typical form of family in South Asia is the extended family, which consists of three generations: grandparents, parents, and children. It may also include brothers and their wives and children within the same household. The extended family is the ideal norm for South Asian villages because it provides a corporate structure for landowning, labor, and other functions. Cultural anthropologists find, however, that families actually go through development cycles—an extended family at one point, a large extended family at another time, and a nuclear family at still other times. But despite modernizing influences, the cultural ideal of the joint family persists, even in most urban areas (Maloney 1974; Tyler 1986; Hardgrove 2006; Mines and Lamb 2002).

Parents arrange the marriages in South Asia. As noted, in northern India people marry outside their patrilineage and village but inside their caste grouping. A married woman must switch allegiance from her father's descent group to that of her husband. After marriage, a woman moves into her husband's joint family household and must adjust to the demands of her mother-in-law. In Pakistan and Bangladesh, parallel-cousin marriage is often preferred, and polygynous marriages, in accordance with Muslim practices, are sometimes found, however again a tremendous varied pattern actually is observed by anthropologists (Weiss 2005).

The Dowry   Another marital practice, found especially in northern India, is the dowry. The Indian bride brings to the marriage an amount of wealth that to some extent represents her share of the household inheritance. Typically, the dowry includes clothing and jewelry that the bride retains for her personal property, household furnishings, and prestige goods (Tambiah 1989). Upper-caste families try to raise a large dowry payment as a sign of their elevated status. In these cases, the dowry creates alliances between elite families.

Gender and Status in South Asia   The status of women in South Asia varies from one cultural area to another. In Pakistan and Bangladesh, which are influenced by the Islamic tradition, women are secluded according to the prescriptions of *purdah*. Until recently, Hindu women of northern India were subject to similar norms. Today, however, many do not wear the veil and accompanying clothing, thereby distinguishing themselves from Muslims. Traditionally, in both Islamic and Hindu regions, a woman was expected to obey her father, her husband, and, eventually, her sons. Women ate after the men were finished and walked several paces behind them.

Older women, particularly mothers-in-law, gained more respect and status in the family. In certain cases, older women became dominant figures in the extended family, controlling the household budget. As some urban South Asian women have become educated, they have begun to resist the patriarchal tendencies of their societies. Some have even participated in emerging feminist political activities. As industrialization and urbanization continue, an increase in feminist activity would be expected. However, because about 80 percent of the population still resides in rural communities, patriarchal tendencies remain pervasive (Hardgrove 2006; Weiss 2006).

Family and Gender in China

Ethnographic research in China was severely restricted by the Chinese Communist government. During the 1970s, the United States and China developed a more formal cooperative relationship, and China began to allow some cultural anthropologists to conduct research within its borders. In the 1970s, Norman Chance became the first American cultural anthropologist allowed to conduct fieldwork in both rural and urban communes. His detailed ethnography of Half Moon Village in Red Flag Commune, near Beijing, offers important insights into the economic, social, political, and cultural developments of that period. Half Moon Village was one sector of the Red Flag Commune, which was one of the largest communes in China when it was formed in 1958. Red Flag occupied 62 square miles and contained 85,000 inhabitants in 17,000 households, organized into production brigades and work teams. The state owned the land and the sideline industries associated with the commune. The commune workforce consisted of more than 40,000 people, most of whom did agricultural work. Many of the commune's crops were sent to Beijing markets, providing a steady income for the villagers. Approximately 15 percent of the labor force worked in the commune's industrial sector.

The Family, Marriage, and Kinship in Red Flag Commune Following the Chinese Revolution, the government initiated a campaign to eradicate the patriarchal nature of the Chinese family and clan. The Communist leadership viewed the traditional family, clan, and male dominance as remnants of precommunist "feudal" China, as well as major sources of inequality. The Chinese Communist Party passed legislation such as the marriage laws of 1950 to destroy the traditional clan and extended-family ties and create more equal relationships between males and females. The marriage laws required

free choice in marriage by both partners, guaranteed monogamy, and established a woman's right to work and obtain a divorce without losing her children (DeVoe 2006; Brownell and Wasserstrom 2002).

Norman Chance's (1984) research indicated, however, that despite government attempts to alter family and kinship relations, Half Moon Village residents sought to maintain strong kinship ties for economic security. Chance discovered that many decisions concerning access to various jobs in the commune were based on kinship relationships. To ensure kinship ties, families maneuvered around government officials and decisions. In addition, younger family members looked to their elders for knowledge and advice. Chance found that within the family, harmonious relationships were emphasized according to the centuries-old Confucianist traditions.

The role and the status of women have been strongly influenced by the ideals of the Chinese Communist Party leadership. Based on his study of Half Moon Village, Chance (1984) concluded that the status of women had improved under the communist regime and that, in general, the new marriage laws had disrupted the Confucian pattern of rigid patriarchy. Young girls were no longer married off or sold. Women were no longer confined

A sign advertising the importance of the one-child policy and family planning in the People's Republic of China.

Anthropologists at Work

Susan Brownell.

Susan Brownell: Ethnography in China

Susan Brownell traces her interest in China back to the stories told by her grandmother. Her grandmother's father, Earl Leroy Brewer, was governor of Mississippi, a civil rights proponent and lawyer for the Mississippi Chinese Association in the 1910s and 1920s. Brownell's love of anthropology began as an undergraduate at the University of Virginia, where she took Victor Turner's famous seminar, in which the participants reenacted different rituals from around the world. She wrote her first paper on sports for Turner's seminar in 1981, and his ideas continued to inspire her over the years. She was also a nationally ranked track-and-field athlete (in the pentathlon and heptathlon) from 1978 to 1990. She was a six-time collegiate All-American while at Virginia and competed in the 1980 and 1984 U.S. Olympic Trials. In 1980 she also worked for six weeks as a stunt double for the feature film *Personal Best*, which depicted four years in the life of a young pentathlete played by Mariel Hemingway.

After starting the Ph.D. program at the University of California, Santa Barbara, she decided to try to combine her various interests in a dissertation on Chinese sports. While at Beijing University in 1985–1986 for a year of Chinese language studies, she joined the track team. She was chosen to represent Beijing in the 1986 Chinese National College Games, where she won a gold medal and set a national record in the heptathlon, earning fame throughout China as the American girl who won glory for Beijing University. She returned to China to study sport theory at the Beijing University of Physical Education (1987–1988). She was awarded her Ph.D. in 1990. After teaching at Middlebury College, the University of Washington, and Yale University, she joined the Department of Anthropology at the University of Missouri, St. Louis, in the fall of 1994, was promoted to associate professor in 1998, and became department chair in 2003. Brownell and Jeffrey N. Wasserstrom edited a volume entitled *Chinese Femininities, Chinese Masculinities: A Reader* (University of California Press 2002). Since 1995, Brownell has conducted fieldwork on cosmetic surgery, fashion models, and upscale fitness clubs as a way of gauging how concepts of beauty, health, and fitness are changing under the growth of global consumerism in China. Her research on cosmetic surgery included a history of ideas about the "oriental eye" in the nineteenth-century Western anthropology of race and the legacy of Western racism in contemporary cosmetic eyelid surgery in China.

Brownell drew on her direct experience of Chinese athletics in *Training the Body for China: Sports in the Moral Order of the People's Republic* (University of Chicago Press 1995), an insightful look at the culture of sports and the body in China. This was the first book on Chinese sports based on fieldwork in China by a Westerner. Brownell is an internationally recognized expert on Chinese sports and has acted as a consultant and expert on the topic for different media, including *Sports Illustrated, The Los Angeles Times, The Atlanta Journal and Constitution, The Asian Wall Street Journal, The Sports Factor* on Australian Broadcasting Corporation Radio, *The Ultimate Athlete* on The Discovery Channel, the "Taboo" Series on National Geographic Television, the NBC Sports Olympic Unit, China Central Television, National Public Radio, and many others.

She has participated in national and international conferences bringing together officials of the International Olympic Committee, the International Olympic Academy, the U.S. Olympic Committee, the Atlanta Committee for the Olympic Games, the Amateur Athletic Foundation, sports journalists, sports scholars, and others. On these occasions, she has spoken on topics such as women in Chinese sports, doping in Chinese sports, sports television broadcasting in China, and Eurocentrism in the Olympic Movement.

In 2000, Brownell was appointed by the International Olympic Committee (IOC) to the seven-member Research Council of the Olympic Studies Centre in Lausanne, Switzerland. She also actively argued on behalf of Beijing's bid to host the 2008 Olympics, which succeeded when the IOC awarded the games to Beijing in July 2001. Dr. Brownell argues the process of organizing the Olympics will intensify China's engagement in the global community. The global media attention will benefit China by creating greater openness to the outside world, and it will interject more diversity into Western-dominated global culture by directing world attention toward Chinese culture. One of Brownell's goals has been to promote a deeper understanding of China through its sports, which moves beyond the stereotype of the "Big Red Machine" with a centralized doping system. She has attempted to nudge members of the Olympic Movement and the press toward comprehending that Chinese sports people are "like us" in the problems they face due to sexism, commercialization, the complexities of international telecasting, and drug use; but that they are "unlike us" in the cultural background they bring to sports, which includes different sentiments about gender, nationalism, "fair play," and—more generally—the meaning of sports.

to the home; rather, they were encouraged to work along with the men in agriculture and industry.

Chance noted some other changes in the status of women. He regularly observed young men taking care of their children and doing tasks such as cooking, chores that were previously performed only by women. In addition, women had assumed decision-making roles in certain areas, especially in respect to family planning—a high priority for the Chinese government after 1976. After China adopted the well-known one-child policy, the Communist Party paid bonuses to families that had only one child (see Chapter 17). Families had to return the bonus to the government if they had a second child. Women were responsible for administering and monitoring this policy.

Despite these changes, however, Chance found that some remnants of the older patriarchal norms were still evident. For example, peasant women engaged in agricultural labor were unable to develop skills that would lead to better job opportunities in the factories and other sideline occupations of the commune. In contrast to men, women were restricted to unskilled jobs. In addition, women did not hold administrative positions on commune committees.

Chance also found that women's role in the family did not change dramatically. Typically, patrilocal residence rules prevailed at Half Moon Village. Chance noted that this often led to conflicts between the mother-in-law and daughter-in-law in the modern Chinese family, just as it had for centuries in the traditional Chinese family. In addition, despite the passage of the marriage laws, matchmaking and arranged marriages remained the norm, and villagers strongly disapproved of divorce. Couples still preferred male over female children to perpetuate family interests. Party officials frequently postponed efforts to alter these patriarchal patterns because such changes might cause stress and conflicts in the family unit.

Following globalization trends and the decline and collapse of rigid Maoist policies in the People's Republic of China since the 1980s, ethnographic research has found an enormous change has influenced family and gender issues in this society (DeVoe 2006; Brownell and Wasserstrom 2002). Marriage rules are tending to become more flexible based on individual choice rather than family arrangements and women are becoming more independent and educated as they encounter the global economy, new technologies introduced by outsourcing (see Chapter 6), and the new global media, including the Internet, that is influencing cultural and social change (Appadurai 1996; Scupin 2006). We return to this topic when we discuss the contemporary global trends throughout the world in Chapter 16.

Ethnic Tensions in the Middle East and Asia

Ethnic tensions have divided many Middle Eastern and Asian countries. Anthropologist Dale Eickelman notes how difficult it is to maintain a rigid primordialist perspective on ethnicity when viewing the population known as the Kurds (1995). Kurdish ethnic identity is constructed and shifted to adjust to many different circumstances and conditions. The Kurdish minority crosses several international borders. About 20 percent live in Turkey (about 10 million), several million live in Iran and Iraq, and others live in Syria. Their Kurdish identity is constructed and treated differently within these various countries of the Middle East. In general, the Kurds view themselves as an oppressed ethnic minority in all the countries in which they live and have faced considerable persecution and discrimination by all of these countries. They have struggled within all these different countries to form an autonomous country called Kurdistan, but thus far they have not succeeded. Following the U.S. invasion of Iraq in 2003, the Kurds found themselves released from the oppression and repression of severe persecution and genocidal policies directed at them by Saddam Hussein; however, currently they face hostility from the other Arab Sunni and Shia ethnic sectors of Iraqi society. These ethnic tensions may either exacerbate civil unity and stability of government in Iraq or may engender more conflict (Beeman 2004).

Cultural anthropologists have studied the ethnic problems that confront some Asians. One such problem involves the Sikhs, a population of about 18 million who live in the Punjab region bordering India and Pakistan. The Sikh religion developed in the fifteenth century as a syncretic blend of Hindu and Islamic beliefs. Sikhism is a mystical religious tradition centered on venerated leaders who founded a military fraternity that offered protection from both Muslims and Hindus. The Sikhs pride themselves on their warrior spirit. Every male carries the name Singh, which translates as "lion." The Sikhs have built a major house of worship—the golden Temple of Amritsar in the Punjab.

Anthropologist Richard Fox (1985) conducted ethnographic research among the Sikhs in 1980–1981. Using historical material and ethnographic data, he

Many Sikhs in India would like to have their own country.

focused on the development of Sikh ethnic and religious identity as a response to external pressures. The Sikhs, who had freed themselves from Muslim and Hindu domination, were confronted with colonialism and the capitalist world system that penetrated the Punjab. The British viewed the Sikhs as an important military shield that could be used for extending their control over India. They therefore treated the Sikhs as a separate race, which reinforced Sikh separateness from Muslims, Hindus, and other groups.

Eventually, the Sikhs recognized that the incorporation of their territory into the British empire would reduce their political and economic autonomy. They therefore initiated reform movements that sought to unify urban workers and rural peasants. These movements led to violent resistance against the British and, following India's national independence in 1947, to secessionist movements against the Indian government.

In 1984, a group of militant, armed Sikhs occupied the golden Temple of Amritsar, demanding political autonomy from India. The government responded by sending military troops into the

Punjab, some of whom entered the temple. This violation of their sacred temple outraged many Sikhs. Later in 1984, as resistance to Hindu domination grew, a Sikh militant assassinated Prime Minister Indira Gandhi. Conflict between Sikhs and Hindus will probably remain a problem in the twenty-first century.

Another South Asian country facing severe ethnic problems is Sri Lanka. Prior to independence from the British in 1948, this island country was called Ceylon. Under colonialism, Tamil-speaking Hindus were imported from southern India to work on rubber plantations. (Although Tamil-speaking Hindus were already in residence in Sri Lanka, British policies increased their population.) The indigenous population of Sri Lanka are Sinhalese-speaking Buddhists. By 1980, the Tamil Hindus made up 18 percent of the population and constituted a majority in northern Sri Lanka. They considered themselves victims of discrimination by the Sinhalese (Scupin 2003).

Tamil militants formed an organized paramilitary group, the Tamil Tigers, who called for the liberation of northern Sri Lanka as an independent Tamil state. Violence broke out between Tamils and Sinhalese in the north. The Sinhalese army responded with an invasion and indiscriminate killings in the Tamil communities. The Tamils responded in kind. In 1987, India sent soldiers to quell the violence. Pressured by the Sri Lankan government, India withdrew in 1989. Meanwhile, the violence continues. As anthropologist Stanley Tambiah notes, the ethnic fratricide that is ongoing in Sri Lanka is exacerbated by the continuing delivery of strategic arms from the industrialized world into the hands of these various ethnic groups (Tambiah 1991; Scupin 2003).

Another example of ethnic and political tensions in Asia has emerged since the 1950s between the Maoist government of the People's Republic and China and the region once known as Tibet. Tibet was a traditional region in the eastern Himalayan mountains that had tributary and political relationships with the government of China for many centuries. In Tibet the indigenous people maintained a different religious tradition of Buddhism, language, and culture than the Han majority culture in most of China. Traditionally, Tibet was ruled by the highest-ranking Tibetan Buddhist

monks, known as the Dali Lama, and one of five males became a Buddhist monk in the region. Following the establishment of the People's Republic of China, the Maoist government sent their military into Tibet to absorb this region into the PRC in the 1950s. In 1959, the Dali Lama, the fourteenth sacred ruling monk fled Tibet with thousands of his followers to the area of Dharmsala, in north India, as political and religious refugees to escape the PRC and the Maoist regime. After the absorption into the PRC in the 1950s the Maoist Red Guards were sent to destroy Buddhist temples, burn the religious texts, and purge the "backward feudal theocratic regime and superstitious religious culture" of the region. The PRC government recruited many Han people into Tibet (under the PRC the area of Tibet is known as Xizang) to foster the cultural assimilation of this region into the mainstream culture of the Han. Many Tibetans resisted this domination by the Han and were supported by the Dali Lama's worldwide campaign to help restore Tibetan culture, ethnicity, and religion. Over the years, recognizing the political difficulties in resisting the PRC on developing independence, the Dali Lama has campaigned for only some cultural and religious autonomy for this region. A number of anthropologists, including Melvin Goldstein, Marcia Calkowski, and others, have been doing ethnographic work in this region for many years and have been consulting with the governments there and elsewhere on the ethnic, religious, and political tensions between the Tibetans and the PRC (Maybury-Lewis 2002).

As is obvious, in the Middle East and Asia many different ethnic and cultural traditions are colliding with the process of globalization. The process of globalization is disrupting the traditional values and practices within the region, and in some cases, the overall reaction to this rapid process of change is to revert to a nostalgic past in which the traditional rural communities maintain the moral economy, the extended family, and other communal practices. This reaction to the process of rapid globalizing has at times led to tensions among political, religious, and ethnic groups throughout these regions. Continuing ethnographic research is needed within these regions to help people understand each others' traditions as one possible major step in helping to reduce these tensions.

Islamic Revitalization

One pervasive trend throughout the Muslim world since the 1970s has been Islamic fundamentalism. Contemporary fundamentalist movements have their roots in earlier reformist movements that sought to combine Islam with Western values as a means of coping with colonialism and industrialism. In countries such as Egypt, however, fundamentalist groups such as the Muslim Brotherhood rejected reform in favor of the total elimination of secular Western influences (Scupin 2000; Sidky and Akers 2005; Starrett 2004). These movements encouraged the reestablishment of an Islamic society based on the Qur'an and Sharia (Islamic law). Some groups sought to bring about these changes peacefully, whereas others believed that an Islamic state could be established only through violent revolution.

Ethnographic studies have contributed to a better understanding of the sources of Islamic revival movements. One critical factor was the 1967 Arab-Israeli War, which resulted in the crushing defeat of the Arab states and the loss of Arab territories to Israel. This event symbolized the economic and political weakness of the Islamic nations and inspired many Muslims to turn to their faith as a source of communal bonds and political strength.

Another significant factor was the oil boom. Many fundamentalists believed that by bestowing rich oil reserves on these societies, Allah was shifting power from the materialist and secular civilizations of the West to the Islamic world (Esposito 1998). The oil revenues of countries such as Libya, Iran, Saudi Arabia, and Kuwait have been used to support fundamentalist movements throughout the Muslim world.

Islamic Revolution in Iran

Islamic revivalistic movements in the Middle East surprised many Western social scientists. They assumed that with modernization and globalization these societies would become increasingly secularized and that the role of religion in economic, social, and political affairs would be reduced. Instead, most Muslim countries experienced Islamic movements that were linked to national, political, and economic issues.

One of the regions of the Middle East most affected by Islamic fundamentalist tendencies has been Iran. Through ethnographic, historical, and comparative research, anthropologists Mary Hegland, Michael Fischer, William Beeman, Henry Munson, and others have contributed to an understanding of the Islamic revival in Iran. They cite a number of factors that converged to produce this revival.

Iran is predominantly a Shi'a Islamic society. After the death of the prophet Muhammad, the Islamic community was divided into the Sunni versus the Shi'a sect. In the sixteenth century, Shah Ismail of the Safavid dynasty proclaimed Shi'ism as the official religion of Iran. From that time, many Shi'a migrated to Iran for protection from the dominant Sunni rulers elsewhere. Traditional Shi'a theology does not distinguish between religion and politics; instead, based on the doctrine of the imamate, the Shi'a maintain that their religious leaders have both theological and political authority. Consequently, Shi'a religious leaders constantly emphasize that Islamic beliefs and doctrine show no separation between religion and politics.

During the nineteenth century, the Iranian rulers, or shahs, offered a large number of concessions to British and Russian bankers and private companies and also attempted to modernize Iran's military and educational system along Western lines. These policies generated internal opposition. The newly educated classes, who had acquired Western ideals of democracy and representative government, opposed the shahs' absolute power. The clergy opposed secularization and Western education, which interfered with traditional education, which they controlled.

In 1925, the Pahlavi dynasty came to power in Iran. Reza Shah Pahlavi viewed the Shi'a religious leaders as obstacles to his plans for rapid modernization. He attempted to reduce their power by appropriating their lands, thus depriving them of income. Reza Shah decreed that secular laws would replace the Sharia and that women would no longer have to wear the veil.

During World War II, Muhammad Reza Pahlavi, supported by Russian and Western interests, replaced his father as ruler. The new shah continued the modernization and secularization policies of his father. By the 1960s, he had centralized all political authority in his hands. Many Western multinational corporations were attracted to Iran because of its

Ayatollah Khomeini.

vast oil reserves and growing gross national product. By the 1970s, about forty-three thousand Americans were living in Iran. The Iranian economy became increasingly dependent on Western imported goods, while internally, aside from oil production, few native industries were developed.

In 1963, the shah announced the White Revolution, which included the commercialization of agriculture through land reforms and the expansion of capitalism. It also included public ownership of companies and voting rights for women. The land reforms disrupted the traditional peasant economy, creating a class of landless peasants. These peasants flocked to Iranian cities in search of scarce opportunities. The White Revolution further mobilized the opposition of the religious clergy, who saw the plight of the peasants. The shah was perceived as a puppet of the United States (the Great Satan) and Western imperialism. One of the major critics was the Ayatollah Khomeini, who was arrested and exiled in 1963.

The shah's policies alienated many other sectors of Iranian society. To buttress his power, the shah—along with his secret police, the SAVAK—brutally crushed any opposition to his regime. The Westernized middle classes, the university students,

the merchants in the bazaars, and the urban poor began to sympathize with any opposition to the shah's regime. These groups allied themselves with the Muslim clergy and needed the clergy's call for an Islamic revolution. For fifteen years, Khomeini continued to attack the shah in pamphlets and taped sermons smuggled into Iran.

Although united in their opposition to the shah, various segments of Iranian society viewed the Islamic revolution in different terms. The rural migrants who flooded into the Iranian cities steadfastly supported the Islamic clergy. The Westernized middle class viewed the Islamic revolution in terms of its own democratic aspirations, believing that the religious leaders would play a secondary role in the actual administration of the Iranian state. Many university students had been influenced by the writings of Ali Shariati, who interpreted Shi'a Islam as a form of liberation theology that would free their society from foreign domination. These elements in Iranian society formed a coalition that encouraged the social and political revolution led by Khomeini and the religious clerics. A cycle of demonstrations, violent protests, and religious fervor led to the downfall of the shah, and in 1979, Khomeini returned to Iran to lead the revolution.

Ever since the overthrow of the shah, the religious clerics have assumed nearly all of the important political positions. Khomeini announced the establishment of the Islamic Republic of Iran, a theocratic state ruled by the Shi'a clergy, who used the mosques as the basic building blocks of political power. All Iranians were forced to register at a mosque, which functioned as an amalgam of government office, place of worship, and local police force. A systematic campaign was waged to purge Iranian society of its Western influences. Alcohol, gambling, prostitution, and pornography were strictly forbidden; women were required to wear head scarves, and those who refused were sent to "reeducation centers." The Shi'a regime believed it had a religious duty to export its revolution to other areas of the Islamic world.

Since the Islamic revolution, most ethnographic research has been forbidden in Iran, so collecting data on recent trends has been difficult. From press reports, it is clear that the revolution has radically changed the nature of Iranian society. The revolution was not only political but also a total social and cultural transformation. Iran is, however, racked with internal conflicts among different classes, religious factions, and political groups. Economic problems exacerbated by the reduction in oil prices and a ten-year war against Iraq led to infighting among radical militants, conservative fundamentalists, and moderates.

In May 1997, Mohammad Khatami, a moderate Muslim cleric, won Iran's presidential election in a landslide victory over more conservative candidates. Khatami attracted a broad coalition of centrists, women, youth of both genders, and middle-class intellectuals to his cause. He is believed to be a direct descendant of the Prophet Muhammad, which helped him consolidate support. Although Khatami's victory did not result in immediate changes in the country's Islamic fundamentalist path, he has tried to restrain the more conservative faction of the clergy that ruled the country since 1979.

Five years later, in 2001, Khatami again won a national election for president. The reform movement within Iran is trying to overcome the more conservative factions associated with the Islamic revolution. Although the conservative political factions have retained the controlling political force in Iran, Khatami and the reformists have inspired many of the young people, especially women, democratic media, and other elements. Increases in education and the transnational flow of information, people, and cultures accompanying globalization have fostered the development of a more democratically oriented populace. These changes have resulted in a loosening of the grip of the conservative Islamic clergy in Iran.

Although Khatami has not been able to produce a new version of a reformed society in Iran, free speech and new forms of Islamic interpretation have challenged the conservative clergy. One leading ayatollah, Hussein Ali Montazeri, has been openly questioning the legitimacy of Iran's clerical rule. However, many of the conservative clerics who rule Iran are resisting any attempt at reform of women's roles or any democratic tendencies. Thus, as in many Islamic countries today, in Iran, there is a severe political struggle between those who are more moderate and democratic in their orientation against those that are more conservative, fundamentalist, and anti-Western (Antoun 2001; Scupin 2003). Recently, under the control of the conservative fundamentalist clergy, high unemployment rates, double-digit inflation, government control of

industry, and the attempts to block any free trade and multinational enterprises in Iran have created enormous economic problems for the country. During the last election in 2004 in Iran, the moderate Islamic reformers boycotted the elections because of the conservative opposition to criticisms and a free press. This enabled the conservative clergy to develop more control of the political economy in Iran (Fathi 2004). Only time will tell whether Iran will be able to overcome factionalism and resolve its political and economic problems; however these conflicts and developments may usher in more troubling concerns regarding the proliferation of nuclear weapons in the region.

Islamic Revitalization in Afghanistan

Another region in which Islamic revitalization is playing a profound role is in Afghanistan. Afghanistan has had a very troubled history. As we have seen, the British and Russians tried to colonize the area during the nineteenth century in the so-called "Great Game" between these powers. During the nineteenth century, with British support, Afghan leaders such as Abdul Rahman attempted to modernize and unify its many ethnic groups by building roads and pacifying fractious tribes throughout the country. During the 1920s and 1930s, with increased education, many Afghan intellectuals were exposed to ideas based on constitutional democracy and nationalism. Some of these leaders tried to institute democratic processes; however, economic development programs were failing. Consequently, class-based Marxist movements began to emerge in Afghanistan, with the support of the Soviet Union. In 1973, a pro-Soviet Marxist leader staged a military coup and proclaimed himself president of the Republic of Afghanistan. Five years later, another military coup installed a communist government with the patronage of the Soviet Union.

The communist leadership and the Soviet Union underestimated the strength of the Islamic traditions and multiethnic assertiveness of Afghanistan. The ethnic groups of Afghanistan include the Pashtuns (the largest group comprises about 47 percent of the population), Tajiks, Uzbeks, Turkmen, Kirghiz, Hazara, Baluchis, and others. The Sunni Muslim constitute about 88 percent of the population, and the Shi'a comprise about 12 percent (Dupree 1980; Shahrani and Canfield 1984; Sidky and Aker 2006). These ethnic and religious coalitions began to resist the Soviet Union and the Marxist communist government. A nationwide Islamic struggle was

launched, referred to as a *jihad*, or "holy struggle," by a group of "holy warriors" called the ***Mujahidin*** (Edwards 2001).

The former Soviet Union invaded Afghanistan in 1979 to repress this Islamic resistance led by the

Anthropologists at Work

David Edwards: Ethnography in Afghanistan

David Edwards became interested in Afghanistan before he ever thought about anthropology. As a child growing up in the Midwest, he was captivated by stories of travel, especially those his grandmother would tell him. Edwards's grandmother was widowed at a relatively young age and thereafter set off to see as much of the world as she could, often aboard inexpensive freighters that took on a half-dozen or so paying passengers. One of the stories she told her grandson was about watching camel caravans unloading their wares in the central bazaar in Kabul, Afghanistan. The story caught his imagination, and he was determined to make his way to Central Asia, which he managed to do right after graduating from Princeton University in 1975.

After spending two years teaching English in Afghanistan, Edwards went back to the United States with the idea of going to graduate school in a field that would allow him to delve more fully into Afghan culture. Never having taken an anthropology course as an undergraduate, he stumbled upon this field as the right one for his interests when he read a book by Clifford Geertz.

The book's blend of elegant writing and insightful cultural analysis captured for him a sense of what he hoped to accomplish in his own research and writing, and he began graduate school in that discipline in the fall of 1977.

While he initially hoped and expected to return to Afghanistan to conduct fieldwork in a small mountain village, Edwards had to change course after the Marxist revolution, which happened toward the end of his first year of graduate school. Thereafter, Edwards redirected his research primarily toward studies of refugees and guerrilla movements, which became the focus of his fieldwork, the first stint of which took place in and around Peshawar, Pakistan, between 1982 and 1984. Peshawar is right across the border from Afghanistan and was the headquarters for most of the Islamic political parties that worked to dislodge the Marxist regime in Afghanistan from power. Edwards's research dealt mostly with the internal dynamics of these parties and their conduct of the war inside Afghanistan but also included an extended study of a camp of some 30,000 Afghan refugees located on the outskirts of Peshawar.

David Edwards.

Subsequent fieldtrips in 1986 and 1995 have taken him back to Pakistan and Afghanistan and have allowed him to follow Afghan political developments, including the takeover by the Taliban militia.

The publications that resulted from his field research have focused mostly on the evolution of Islamic political authority in Afghanistan and the social transformations brought about by the Islamic political parties in their quest for power. These publications include *Heroes of the Age: Moral Fault Lines on the Afghan Frontier* (1996) and *Before Taliban: Genealogies of the Afghan Jihad* (2002), both published by the University of California Press. Edwards is presently editing a film shot in Kabul and directing a project to train Afghan university students to conduct oral historical research. In between sabbatical leaves and research trips to Afghanistan, Edwards teaches anthropology at Williams College in Williamstown, Massachusetts.

exiled *Mujahidin* parties based in Iran and Pakistan. Cold War politics began to influence this struggle against the Russians, with many Western governments offering financial and military assistance to the *Mujahidin*. Many Afghans were driven out of their country into neighboring Pakistan. However, with increasing internal weaknesses within the USSR and the fierce resistance of the *Mujahidin*, the Soviets withdrew from Afghanistan in 1989.

Following the withdrawal of the Soviet Union, ethnic differences and varying Islamic traditions and movements presented obstacles to the unification of the Afghans. Local Islamic and ethnic factions that had developed during the Soviet occupation began to fight for power, resulting in years of warfare in Afghanistan during the 1980s and 1990s. The Western governments that patronized the *Mujahidin* during the Cold War withdrew support, fearing an Islamic revolution similar to the Iranian one. Consequently, the factional fighting among ethnic and religious groups resulted in political disorder and chaos in Afghanistan.

One Islamic faction that emerged in Afghanistan in 1994 was known as the Taliban. Anthropologists have described the social and religious background of the Taliban (Edwards 1998; Sidky and Akers 2006). The majority of Taliban the are Afghan religious students recruited from Islamic religious schools in Pakistan. (The term *Taliban* refers to religious students.) The Taliban served as a militia that scored a series of victories over other ethnic and religious factions and consolidated control over most of the regions in Afghanistan.

The Taliban received a lot of international attention because of their stringent Islamic guidelines and norms. Men were forbidden to trim their beards. Afghan women were strictly secluded from any contact with men, were not allowed to work outside of the home, and had to wear the traditional covering known as the *burqa*. Ethnographers emphasize that many of the Taliban were socialized and trained in Pakistan, outside the confines of traditional ethnic and tribal affinities within Afghanistan. Therefore, young men from different backgrounds were able to unify an Islamic revitalization movement based on a sense of frustration over twenty years of conflict, factionalism, and political disorder. The Taliban received support from many Afghans despite their attempt to impose a purified Islamic culture on the country.

However, the Taliban received support from terrorist organizations such as Al Qaeda, which was headed by Osama Bin Laden, the Saudi multimillionaire who directed terrorist activities against the United States. In 2001 following the September 11 attack on the World Trade Center and Pentagon, the United States military began a campaign to subvert the political control of the Taliban and root out Al Qaeda and other terrorists in Afghanistan. Most of the international community supported this effort to dethrone the Taliban and provide a more effective and humane political order in Afghanistan (Sidky and Akers 2006). However, even today, the Taliban has much support from different sectors of the rural and urban communities in Afghanistan who want more political order and stability within their regions.

The elections in Afghanistan in November 2004 resulted in a government led by Hamed Karzai. Karzai is a Pashtun leader who was active against the Communist regime in the 1980s and early

The Taliban asserted political control in Afghanistan beginning in 1994.

1990s. Although Karzai was initially supportive of the Taliban, he realized that they were working on the behalf of the interests of the Pakistani and Arab radical Islamic fundamentalists. His father was murdered by the Taliban in 1999. He had become an important figure and was selected as a provisional leader of Afghanistan by the Afghan leaders. Eventually, Karzai directed an opposition movement against the Taliban that was supported by the United States, Britain, and international organizations (Canfield 2004). His election is viewed as a means of providing political stability and a democratic-based government that will assist in promoting order throughout the region.

Islam Interpreted   One conclusion resulting from the many ethnographic studies of Islam in the Middle East and Asia is that this religious tradition, like all religious traditions, can have different interpretations depending on the context. The Islamic religion can be combined with diverse types of political activity. It can provide ideological support for revolutionary change, as the case of Iran suggests, or it can help sustain a specific socioeconomic and political order, as in contemporary Saudi Arabia, where some two thousand princes control the entire political economy and resources. Thus, political and religious leaders can use Islam to advance social justice, justify political oppression, or further the goals of one particular political group. Anthropologists find that a one-dimensional understanding of Islamic culture or civilization based on a simplistic stereotype or image of a static culture or civilization does not help explain the rapid cultural changes and movements emerging in these Middle Eastern and Asian regions of the world. The Islamic religious tradition is not monolithic and has many different forms in different societies. Anthropologists are studying these trends all over the Islamic world.

For example, cognitive anthropologist Scott Atran, who did extensive research in the Middle East, has been analyzing the recent phenomena of suicide bombing in the Middle East (2003). Most explanations of these terrorist and violent expressions of groups like Al Qaeda and the so-called Islamic culture rely on simplistic accounts of cultural norms, "evil" religious beliefs that reflect traditions in the Qu'ran regarding the sacredness of martyrdom, or poor education or socioeconomic conditions. Atran's analysis is based on a comprehensive holistic account that draws on a multiplicity of factors, including the manipulation of kinship and group loyalty among young people, who are viewed as expendable by their political elites, as well as global economic, political, and military strategies perceived and interpreted as hostile to their religious and political interests. Atran calls on governments to fund more anthropological research on these topics to comprehend and understand these developments, as an addition to a global war on terrorism against these violent and terrorist developments. Many

A Palestinian suicide bomber poses prior to a mission.

other anthropologists doing research in the Islamic world, such as Robert Hefner, Daniel Varisco, Steve Caton, Clifford Geertz, Henry Munson, Mary Hegland, Lois Beck, Dale Eickelman, and others, have developed more nuanced understandings of the emergence of Islamic militancy and the struggle against it by many Muslims in these societies that cannot be summed up with a simplistic "clash of civilizations" (Geertz 2003). We return to this topic once again in Chapter 16.

SUMMARY

As in Latin America, Africa, and the Caribbean, globalization has had dramatic consequences for the countries in the Middle East and Asia. These countries were either directly or indirectly affected by Western colonialism. Demographically, in the long run, all these countries experienced declining death rates brought about by Western colonialism, and populations began to increase rapidly because of economic circumstances and the maintenance of high birth rates.

Economically, these societies were drawn into the global economy and were transformed by producing commodities that were demanded by the wealthier core societies. Patterns of landownership were reordered, and many peasants were producing for economic elites. Religious changes occurred; however, since most of the population in the Middle East and Asia were committed to the traditions of Islam, Hinduism, or Buddhism, Christianity did not make significant inroads into these colonized areas.

Western colonialism eventually gave way to political movements based on nationalist, independence, and sometimes revolutionary tendencies. These movements represented anticolonial sentiments and resulted in many new countries in the Middle East and Asia. Some leaders in the Middle East, such as Gamal Nasser in Egypt, tried to develop a Pan-Arabic movement directed against Western colonialism. Countries such as India were led by charismatic leaders such as Mahatma Gandhi, who mobilized millions of people to develop a national identity and notions of self-determination. In China and Vietnam, revolutionary leaders such as Mao Zedong and Ho Chi Minh organized millions of peasants to bring about new social and political orders based on Marxist ideals mixed with indigenous cultural ideals.

These countries were absorbed into the global economy at different levels, depending on the resources that were available in their regions. Some countries remain poor and underdeveloped because their economies are heavily dependent on the wealthy core countries. In the Middle East, some countries have tremendous oil resources that could be used to help develop their economies. Despite oil resources, these Middle Eastern countries still find themselves dependent on the wealthy core industrialized nations. Many of the countries in both the Middle East and Asia face internal population problems and underdeveloped economic systems that tend to make them marginal to the global economy. Countries such as China, Burma, and Vietnam tried to withdraw from the global economy through a commitment to a socialist program.

Ethnographers have conducted research on the peasantry, social structures, family life, and gender in these countries. The peasantry is rapidly changing in the Middle East and Asia, as globalization introduces the cash economy, new consumer goods, and other changes. The peasantry differs in various countries based on the people's traditional relations and new global relationships to the world market. Family structures and gender relations are illuminated by ethnographers as they study patterns that develop in relationship to the emergence of new urban areas and the changing rural areas. Each region has unique structures based on its cultural beliefs and practices.

In the Middle East, the Islamic tradition and Arab cultural practices influence the patterns of family life and gender. However, ethnographers find a great deal of variation within these Islamic societies based on the contact these societies have had with Western countries. In addition, there are some basic misconceptions and stereotypes of the Islamic family, marriage, and gender practices that have been debunked through systematic ethnographic research.

Ethnographers in Asia have focused on some of the traditional practices regarding family and gender that have remained despite globalization and revolutionary movements in countries such as China. However, globalization is having a transformative effect on all of these institutions throughout Asia.

One of the consequences of globalization is the resurgence of Islamic movements in countries such as Iran and Afghanistan. Ethnographers have brought their analytical skills to try to comprehend and explain Islamic revitalization movements in these countries of the Middle East and Asia. This has become more important following the tragedy of 9/11/01.

QUESTIONS TO THINK ABOUT

1. Compare and contrast the Western impact on India and on China.

2. How did demographic change occur as a result of globalization in the Middle East and Asia?

3. How did globalization impinge on the traditional economies of the Middle East and Asia?

4. How did religion change as a result of colonialism and Western influence in the Middle East and Asia?

5. Compare the independence movements in India with the revolutionary movement in China.

6. What are some of the differences between the oil-producing countries of the Middle East and non–oil producers?

7. How has the peasantry changed as a result of globalization in the Middle East and Asian countries?

8. What are some of the stereotypes of family, marriage, and gender patterns in the Middle Eastern Islamic countries?

9. Discuss some of the problems of ethnicity in the Middle East and Asia that have been influenced by globalization.

10. What are some of the factors discovered by ethnographers that have influenced the Islamic revitalization movement in the Middle East?

KEY TERMS

hamula

jajmani economy

jatis

jihad

Mujahidin

purdah

Chapter 16

Contemporary Global Trends

CHAPTER OUTLINE

CHAPTER QUESTIONS

- What are some of the environmental trends that are a consequence of globalization?

- How do demographic trends differ in various societies?

- What are the results of globalization on technology and energy use?

- How does the logic-of-growth model compare with the sustainability model?

- What are some of the economic consequences of globalization?

- What are some of the political, ethnic, and religious tendencies resulting from globalization?

As we have seen throughout this text, especially in Chapter 6, global interdependence, or what we have called *globalization*, has become an undeniable fact in the contemporary world. This process began after the Neolithic revolution, when small-scale societies were either absorbed into larger states or became dependent on those states. Ever since the Industrial Revolution, the trend toward global interdependence has escalated, especially through the process of European colonialism. As the world shrinks and industrial societies continue to expand, interconnections are developing among different societies, creating a global village. The global village has been described as a world in which all regions are in contact with one another through the mass media, instantaneous communication, and highly integrated economic and political networks. This chapter reviews some of the recent trends associated with the development of this global village.

Environmental Trends

As we saw in earlier chapters, hunting-gathering, horticulturalist, pastoralist, and intensive agriculture societies survived by extracting natural resources from a particular biome or environment. In these societies, people were directly linked with nature and the environment, and they lived in relative harmony with the natural environment. This is not to suggest that humans in preindustrial societies did not harm their environments in any manner. Slash-and-burn horticulture, intensive agriculture, pastoralism, and sometimes even foraging caused some environmental damage. Overgrazing, soil erosion, and the depletion of certain species have always been part of humankind's evolutionary development. For example, birds and various species of animals were driven to extinction by the peoples in some of the Pacific islands and in prehistoric America (Diamond 1997).

With the development of globalization, however, the negative consequences for the environment have multiplied rapidly. Ironically, many people in industrial societies came to believe that they had gained mastery over the natural environment and were therefore free from its constraints. But in recent decades, people have become more aware that they are as dependent on the natural environment as were preindustrial peoples. It has become evident that the pollution created by global industrialization is threatening the ecological balance of the planet and the health of plant and animal species, including the human species.

Mechanized Agriculture and Pollution

One major source of pollution is commercialized, mechanized agriculture, known as **agribusiness**. Mechanized agriculture, or agribusiness, depends on the use of fossil fuels, chemical fertilizers, large tracts of land, and toxic poisons such as herbicides and pesticides to increase agricultural yields. This form of agriculture is not only prevalent in the industrialized world, it is also becoming common in developing countries. For example, some farmers in societies such as Mexico, India, and Indonesia have adopted mechanized agriculture. The spread of mechanized agriculture has been labeled the **Green Revolution** (Schusky 1990). Through biotechnological research, sometimes known as genetic engineering, and other methods, scientists have produced hybrid species of wheat and rice seeds that generate higher agricultural yields. To take advantage of these yields, however, farmers must use expensive, capital-intensive technology for irrigation and cultivation; nonrenewable fossil fuels such as gasoline and oil; synthetic chemical fertilizers; and toxic weed killers, or herbicides, and pesticides.

The use of capital-intensive agriculture, however, can have negative consequences for the global environment. One of the most tragic cases resulting from the Green Revolution occurred in 1984 in Bhopal, India, where toxic fumes leaking from a chemical-fertilizer plant killed or injured thousands of people. Many of the consequences of mechanized agriculture, however, are much less dramatic (and therefore less publicized), although perhaps just as dangerous. For example, research has shown that much of the food produced in both industrialized and developing countries contains traces of pesticides and other poisons. Even when governments ban the use of chemicals, the residues may remain in the food chain for many years. Because many new synthetic chemicals are being produced for agribusiness every year, the danger to the environment continues to increase.

New emerging developments in genetic engineering of various animals and plants have also been of concern to environmentalists and anthropologists. Ecological anthropologist Glen Stone has been following the spread of genetically modified (GM) crops and related biotechnology in various areas of the world (2001, 2004). Stone studies the GM crops as well as other biotechnological strategies such as "tissue culture" or other new approaches experimented with in various regions. He finds that many scientists, agricultural specialists, and economists oppose or are proponents of these GM crops in different regions of India, Africa, and elsewhere. Stone, who is based in the St. Louis region at Washington University, has been following the proposals of Monsanto based in St. Louis, who are the global leaders in promoting biotechnology and GM products to replace current practices. It targets practices such as plowing, weeding, and seed-saving for traditional crop replacement in Africa and elsewhere. For example, Monsanto suggests that traditional indigenous African hoe cultivation should be replaced by "sustainable" biotechnology. In other words, Monsanto promotes this technology as a means of increasing crop growth and modernizing agriculture everywhere. Some of the skeptics of GM for small-scale farmers have been accused of advocating a museumlike preservation of indigenous practices.

One of the problems identified by Stone in the adoption of these new GM biotechnology agricultural practices is what is referred to as "deskilling." In other words, the small farmers are replaced by machines and more high-tech agricultural developments. Farmers in the more industrialized and postindustrial countries may have access to education and information through government agencies and other institutions that may be lacking in some of the more rural peripheral countries of the world. Stone has been consulting with many other anthropologists and corporations such as Monsanto on the impact of these new biotechnologies and GM foods for agricultural developments in many regions in the world.

A new fifteen-year ethnographic study called *Slaughterhouse Blues: The Meat and Poultry Industry in North America* by Donald D. Stull and Michael J. Broadway describes the impact of corporate farming and the industrialized agribusiness in the United States and Canada (2004). These anthropologists collected a wide array of both quantitative and qualitative data on slaughterhouse employees, union offices, community leaders, and other people near these industries. The study demonstrates that the corporate meat industry from farm to factory has become increasingly centralized and integrated. Consumer demand for cheap, convenient foodstuffs results in the agribusiness corporate officers promoting cheap labor and minimal environmental and social costs, resulting in negative consequences for workers, the environment, and communities near these industries. Clean air and water are sacrificed as beef operations, hog farms, and chicken facilities influence the rural areas in North America. The dangerous work conditions and other negative consequences of these industries are often hidden costs that do not show up in the grocery stores where North American consumers shop. The anthropologists focus on the price of "progress" that influences the environments and communities in North America as a consequence of these new industrial agribusiness trends.

Air Pollution

Air pollution, especially from the emissions of motor vehicles, power generators, and waste incinerators, continues to be a major problem for industrializing societies. As less-developed countries industrialize, the degree of global air pollution steadily multiplies. It appears that atmospheric pollution is depleting the earth's ozone layer, which absorbs 99 percent of the ultraviolet radiation from the sun. These pollutants could irreversibly alter the earth's ability to support life. Satellite data show that during the period from 1978 to 1984, the ozone layer eroded at an average annual rate of 0.5 percent. In addition,

Globalization creates dense traffic and air pollution problems in major cities such as Bangkok.

acid rain produced by the burning of fossil fuels such as coal and gasoline has become a global problem, spreading across national boundaries and wreaking havoc on forests, lakes, and various species of aquatic life.

Scientific data suggest that the increased levels of carbon dioxide produced primarily by the burning of fossil fuels and tropical rain forests, methane, and nitrous oxide will create a **greenhouse effect**, or global warming. According to this hypothesis, after solar rays reach the earth's surface, the carbon dioxide (CO_2) in the atmosphere traps the heat and prevents it from radiating back into space. This process could eventually melt the polar ice caps, which would raise sea levels, flood major coastal cities, create violent weather patterns, and turn the tropics into deserts. An enormous amount of scientific data has accumulated that confirms the greenhouse effect hypothesis and global warming. Emissions of these greenhouse gases are likely to increase in the future. Predictions based on present-day estimates suggest that CO_2 emissions from industrialized countries will reach levels of 50 to 70 percent above 1990 levels by 2020.

Sufficient quantities of air pollutants such as NOx (oxides of nitrogen), SOx (oxides of sulfur), and carbon monoxide (CO) can harm human health in pulmonary functions, asthma, allergens, and eye damage problems in the short term and cancer, neurological, reproductive, respiratory, and psychological disorder problems in the long term. Anthropologists who follow the studies of these air pollutants coupled with increased lead in blood levels, noise from manufacturing in urban areas, and new psychosocial stresses recognize that urban living is having an influence on health conditions throughout the world (Schell and Denham 2003).

However, as more countries such as China begin to emit more greenhouse gases, global warming and other pollution problems could proceed more quickly. Air pollution is a major concern for developing countries such as China, Mexico, and other areas of the world. Sixteen of the world's most air polluted cities are in China. They are facing an ecological and health crisis as a result of the industrial pollution created by rapid globalization. In China, 300,000 people a year face respiratory illnesses as a result of this pollution. China accounts for 13 percent of the CO_2 emissions today. At this

level, it is becoming the world's second largest emitter of CO_2 after the United States, which generates 23 percent (Wang 1999; Xu X, Ding H, Wang X 2000). Stabilizing atmospheric concentrations of greenhouse gases will require reversing current emission trends. In addition, anthropologists find that economic and social inequality that results from globalization has resulted in more health problems for peoples without basic resources (Nyugen and Peschard 2003).

Population Trends

As discussed in Chapter 13, with industrialization, new demographic trends have arisen. A recent model used to measure population trends is based on the **demographic-transition theory**, which assumes a close connection between fertility and mortality rates and socioeconomic development (Figure 16.1). According to the demographic-transition model, societies pass through three major phases of population change. During Phase 1, a high fertility rate is counterbalanced by a high mortality rate, resulting in minimal population growth. Phase 1 describes preindustrial societies. At first, societies used various methods of population regulation, such as self-induced abortions, postpartum abstinence, infanticide, or migration to limit population growth. As preindustrial societies developed intensive agriculture, population began to increase, but

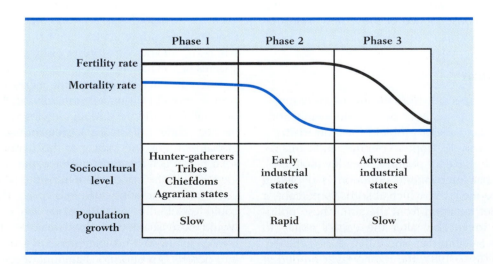

	Phase 1	Phase 2	Phase 3
Fertility rate Mortality rate			
Sociocultural level	Hunter-gatherers Tribes Chiefdoms Agrarian states	Early industrial states	Advanced industrial states
Population growth	Slow	Rapid	Slow

FIGURE 16.1 The demographic-transition model.

disease, famine, and natural disasters kept mortality rates fairly high, thus limiting growth.

In Phase 2, population tends to increase rapidly because of continued high fertility rates coupled with lower mortality rates. Mortality rates decline because of increases in the food supply, the development of scientifically based medical practices, and improved public sanitation and health care. Improvements in nutrition and health care enable people to control certain diseases, thus diminishing infant mortality rates and increasing life expectancy. Consequently, during Phase 2, population growth is dramatic. Growth of this magnitude was associated with the early phases of industrialization in Western Europe and North America, but it is also visible in many Third World societies that are now in the early stages of industrialization.

Phase 3 of the demographic-transition model represents the stage in which fertility rates begin to fall along with mortality rates. According to the model, as industrialization proceeds, family planning is introduced, and traditional institutions and religious beliefs supporting high birth rates are undermined. Values stressing individualism and upward mobility lead couples to reduce the size of their families. Phase 3 describes the stage of advanced industrial societies such as Western Europe, the United States, and Japan. Other trends, such as geographic mobility and the increased expense of rearing children, also affect reproductive decisions in industrial societies. Hence, in advanced industrial societies, as the birth rate, or fertility rate, falls, population growth begins to decline.

The Demographic-Transition Model Applied

The demographic-transition model seems to have some validity when applied to global population trends. World population during the Paleolithic period (Phase 1) is estimated to have been about 10 million (Hassan 1981). Following the agricultural revolution, around the year AD 1, global population was approximately 300 million. But after the early stages of industrialization (Phase 2), from 1650 to 1900, world population tripled from 510 million to 1.6 billion. By 1950, the global population had risen to 2.5 billion, and by 1970, another billion people had been added. By 1990, the world

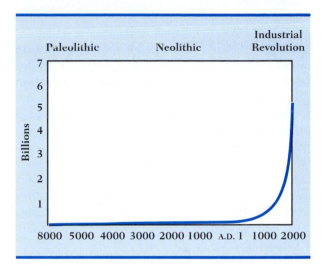

FIGURE 16.2 Global population growth. From about ten million people in the Paleolithic period, world population reached one billion by 1850. Following the Industrial Revolution and decreases in mortality rates, world population has increased to over six billion people.

population was approximately 5.4 billion, with 150 babies being born every minute (Figure 16.2). By the year 2000, world population exceeded 6 billion.

Thomas Robert Malthus (1766–1834), a British clergyman and economist, is known as the father of demography. Malthus predicted that human populations would increase at a rapid, or exponential, rate, but the production of food and other vital resources would increase at a lower rate. Thus, populations would always grow more quickly than the food supply to support them. As a result, human societies would constantly experience hunger, increases in warfare, resource scarcities, and poverty.

To measure the exponential growth rate, demographers use the concept of **doubling time**, the period it takes for a population to double. For example, a population growing at 1 percent will double in 70 years; one growing at 2 percent will take 35 years to double; and one growing at 3 percent will double in 23 years.

The industrial nations of Western Europe, the United States, and Japan have reached Phase 3 of the demographic-transition model. The U.S. population is growing at only 0.7 percent. Countries such as Germany, Hungary, Japan, and even Roman Catholic Italy actually have negative growth rates, which means that they are not replacing the number of people dying with new births. For a society to maintain a given level of population, each woman must give birth to an average of 2.1 children. At this point, the society has achieved **zero population growth (ZPG)** , meaning that the population is simply replacing itself. When the average number of births falls below 2.1, a society experiences negative growth. Thus, Japan, with an average of 1.8 births, is actually experiencing a population decline (McCreery and McCreery 2006), as is Italy, with the lowest rate of fertility in the world (1.2 births). Decreased growth rates in industrialized nations have helped lower the global growth rate from 2 to 1.7 percent.

The demographic-transition model provides a conceptual scheme for evaluating global population trends, especially for the core industrial societies, yet it must be used carefully as a hypothesis. Although the industrial societies of North America, Western Europe, and Japan have reached Phase 3, the vast majority of the world's people reside in societies that are in Phase 2, with exponential growth rates. Population growth in African countries such as Kenya is almost 4 percent (doubling every 15 years), and Mexico's growth rate is 2.6 percent (doubling every 27 years). Thus, the demographic-transition hypothesis explains population trends in industrial societies, but it may not accurately predict population growth elsewhere for Phase 3. Suggesting that all societies will follow the path of development of the advanced industrial societies is somewhat naive. As we have seen from our discussion of industrial societies in Chapter 13, it took at least 500 years of historical experience for these countries to become fully industrialized societies and reach Phase 3 of the demographic model.

Most peripheral societies maintain high birth rates related to their agricultural lifestyles. As these societies become industrialized, however, death rates tend to fall, leading to dramatic population increases. These societies have not had an extended time period to adjust to the demographic trends related to industrialization. Consequently, predicting a movement to Phase 3 is problematic. Most underdeveloped economic countries can attain population decline only through changes in technology, political economy, and social and cultural practices. Yet, new demographic studies indicate that the

population problems that were predicted in pessimistic terms in the recent past have been reevaluated. Anthropologists and demographers have discovered that as public health measures have improved with vaccinations, vitamins for pregnant women, and antibiotics, the incentives and need for large rural families and children, as was encouraged in their traditional rural communities (see Chapter 12), has been reduced. In addition, as women's living standards have improved as they move into jobs in new factories that have moved to these regions from the postindustrial world and outsourcing occupations (see Chapter 6), rates of population growth in rural areas in India, Pakistan, Africa, the Middle East, and other developing countries have decreased. Whereas the population was predicted to grow to 12 billion in 2050, those numbers have been revised to 9 billion.

The One-Child Policy in China   One developing country that has taken steps to drastically reduce its population growth is China. In the 1950s Mao Zedong perceived China's revolution as being based on peasant production and small-scale, labor-intensive technology. For this reason, he encouraged population growth among the peasantry. After Mao's death, however, a new leadership group emerged that reversed his policies regarding population growth.

In 1979, a demographic study was presented at the Second Session of the Fifth National People's Congress that indicated that if the existing average of three children per couple were maintained, China's population would reach 1.4 billion by the year 2000 and 4.3 billion by the year 2080. Alarmed by the implications of these statistics, the government introduced a one-child policy designed to achieve zero population growth (ZPG), with a target of 1.6 children per couple by the year 2000. Families that restricted their family size to one child were given free health care and free plots of land. In addition, their children would receive free education and preferential employment treatment. Families that had more than one child would be penalized through higher taxes and nonpreferential treatment. The one-child policy was enforced by neighborhood committees at the local level, and contraceptives, sterilization, and abortion services were provided free of charge. Neighborhood committees monitored every woman's reproductive cycle to determine when she was eligible to have her one child.

With some exceptions, the one-child policy has been remarkably effective. Between 1980 and 1990, the birth rate in China was reduced, and the annual growth rate fell from 2.0 percent to 1.4 percent, a record unmatched by any developing nation. This rate is similar to those of the most advanced industrial societies (Fong 2004). Incentives, propaganda campaigns, and government enforcement combined to produce a new image of the Chinese family, one that had only a single child. Billboards and TV ads throughout China showed radiant mothers nurturing their one child.

Because the one-child policy is an attempt to reverse Chinese family patterns that have existed for thousands of years, it created controversies and problems. In the agricultural areas, it generated a great deal of resentment. Many Chinese prefer sons to daughters—a long-established Confucian tradition. In some cases, couples that have a daughter may practice female infanticide so that they may have a son to assume family responsibilities. Although infanticide is a criminal offense in China, it appears to be increasing in rural areas. Moreover, anthropologist Steven Mosher (1983) reported that government officials sometimes forced women to undergo abortions to maintain the one-child policy. More recently, anthropologist Susan Greenhalgh, a Chinese population policy expert, reported that one out of every eight Chinese women married in the 1970s had suffered the trauma of a second- or third-term abortion (Evans 2000). There were many reports of full-term abortions, involuntary sterilization, forcible insertion of IUDs, the abandonment of female children, and female infanticide.

In response to some of these conflicts, the Chinese government relaxed the one-child policy in 1989. Rural families could have two children, but urban families were still restricted to one. This policy, known colloquially as "the one-son or two-child policy," placed a burden on second children who were females. Second-born daughters were subject to being placed in orphanages so that a family might have a son. China's orphanages are struggling to keep up with the number of female children. Additionally, the various minority groups have no restrictions on the number of children they can have. The minorities argued that through

the one-child policy, the majority would quickly become the dominant group in their regions. They viewed the policy as an attempt to reduce their population and pressured the government to relax restrictions on their population growth. Recently, in April 2000, the Chinese government ruled that all the children of "only children" can have two children. But the government still offers higher rewards to those couples that have only one child. Recently, demographer Vanessa Fong has investigated the unintended results of the one-child policy in China (2004). She found that many of the only children (sometimes called the "Little Emperors") are expected to be the primary providers of their elderly parents, grandparents, and parents-in-law. This results in considerable competition in the education system for these only children to aspire to elite status and gain economic opportunities to support their family networks, which sometimes results in stress because very few can obtain these elite positions. In 2004 in Beijing, there was a four-day festival for twins with 500 sets of twin children in matching clothes that were viewed by thousands of people in China. The one-child policy has produced a belief that these twins are extremely "lucky." These unintended results of the one-child policy are something that anthropologists who do ethnographic research are investigating today.

Technological Change

Ever since the Industrial Revolution, the scale of technological change has become global rather than local. Industrial technology—computers, electronics, and advances in global communications—has spread from the core nations to the developing countries. For example, as previously discussed, the Green Revolution has altered the nature of food production. Technical information on agricultural production is spread through television and satellites to villages in countries such as India and Pakistan.

Energy-Consumption Patterns

High energy consumption is not only creating environmental hazards, it has also led to increased depletion of resources. High-energy, industrialized societies such as the United States consume a major portion of the world's nonrenewable energy and resources. For example, in 1987, the United States used more than 2 billion tons of energy (the equivalent of coal), and the former Soviet Union used 1.8 billion. In contrast, Mexico used 140 million; Egypt, 33 million; Bangladesh, 6.8 million; and the Sudan, 1.5 million (*Information Please Almanac* 1991). In 1997 the United States, Russia, and China were the leading producers and consumers of energy. These three countries produced 39 percent and consumed 41 percent of world energy. In that same year, the United States, representing 5 percent of the world's population, consumed 18.6 million barrels of petroleum per day—almost 26 percent of world consumption (*Time Almanac* 2000). The U.S. Geological Survey estimates that there are about 3 trillion barrels of proven reserves of oil worldwide. The entire world should reach its peak levels of oil production in 2037, after which output is expected to fall precipitously. The 23 percent of the world's population residing in industrialized countries is consuming about 58 percent of the energy reserves that the planet is capable of producing. Yet, there is the possibility of new technologies on the horizon that may mitigate these high energy-consuming trends. Higher oil costs have resulted in more demand for automobiles that have lower energy needs for petroleum, such as the hybrid SUVs that consume less gas. These new demands may enhance our possibilities for reducing the scarcity of energy production throughout the world.

Were semiperipheral and peripheral countries, with 77 percent of the world's population, to adopt the same consumption patterns as the core nations, nonrenewable energy supplies and resources might not be sufficient to support global economic development (Schusky 1990). For example, as peripheral countries adopted mechanized farming, they increased their consumption of fossil fuels, leading to a worldwide jump in energy use. Between 1950 and 1985, the energy used to produce a ton of grain increased from 0.44 barrels of oil per ton to 1.14 barrels. By 1985, fossil-fuel energy used in farming totaled 1.7 billion barrels, about one-twelfth of the world oil output of 21 billion barrels per year (Brown 1988). These energy costs in agricultural production have continued to rise since that period.

Loss of Biodiversity

One of the major concerns regarding the consequences of globalization on the planet is the loss of biodiversity. **Biodiversity** is the genetic and biological variation within and among different species of plants and animals. Biologists are not exactly certain of how many species of plants and animals exist; new species are discovered every day. Some biologists think that there may be as many as 30 to 100 million species, or even more. Approximately 250,000 flowering plant species, 800,000 lower-plant species, and 1.5 million animal species have been identified (Raven, Berg, and Johnson 1993). About 50 percent of these species live in tropical rain forests. As humans, we are dependent on these living organisms for survival; in both preindustrial and industrial societies people rely on plant and animal species for basic foodstuffs and medicinal applications.

Many plant and animal species are threatened with extinction, causing a loss of biodiversity. Biologists estimate that at least one species becomes extinct each day. And as globalization continues, it is estimated that perhaps as many as a dozen species will be lost per day. Biologist E. O. Wilson writes in *In Search of Nature* (1996) that each year an area of rain forest half the size of Florida is cut down. If that continues, by 2020 the world will have lost forever 20 percent of its existing plant species. That is a loss of 30,000 species per year, 74 per day, 3 per hour. He goes on to say that we know almost nothing about the majority of plants and animals that the rain forest comprises. We haven't even named 90 percent of them, much less studied their properties or tapped their potential value. Wilson suggests that it is likely that a substantial portion of the planet's biodiversity will be eliminated within the next few decades. With the increase of industrialism, mechanized agriculture, and deforestation, as many as one-fourth of the world's higher-plant families may become extinct by the end of the next century.

Wilson believes that we are entering the greatest period of mass extinction in the planet's history. We have very limited knowledge of the world's plant and animal species. For example, there are approximately 250,000 different flowering plant species, but 225,000 of them have never been evaluated with respect to their agricultural, medicinal, or industrial potential (Raven, Berg, and Johnson 1993). One out of every four prescription drugs comes from flowering plants. Yet less than 1 percent has been studied for pharmacological potential. Many of these plants could be exploited as new food crops, pharmaceuticals, fibers, or petroleum substitutes. As long as biodiversity can be preserved, it represents a wealth of information and potential resources that can be extremely beneficial for humanity. In addition, with the new developments in genetic engineering, which depends on biodiversity (genetic variation), humanity may be able to find new resources that provide solutions for food and health problems.

Pessimists versus Optimists on Global Issues

Two basic perspectives—one negative, one positive—have influenced the analyses of global trends affecting the environment, population, and technology.

The Doomsday Model

The negative perspective is sometimes referred to as the Doomsday Model, or the neo-Malthusian approach. This model predicts that if current population, environmental, and technological trends continue, they will produce a series of ecological disasters that will threaten human existence. In the 1970s, a group of scientists and academics known as the Club of Rome assessed these global trends and predicted worldwide scarcities and a global economic collapse. Using elaborate computer models developed at the Massachusetts Institute of Technology, these scientists concluded that current global trends in population growth, energy-consumption patterns, and environmental pollution will exhaust the world's natural resources within the next 100 years.

The Optimists: The Logic-of-Growth Model

The Doomsday Model has been challenged by optimists such as the late economist Julian Simon (1981), who foresee a more promising future for humankind. Simon noted that health improvements, including a decrease in infant mortality and an increase in life expectancy, are a global trend. Simon also argued that pollution has abated in most societies that have experienced economic growth. Simon believed that as development and economic improvements continue in different societies, people will spend money to solve pollution problems.

Sometimes this perspective is referred to as the **logic-of-growth model**. This logic-of-growth model assumes that natural resources are infinite and that economic growth can continue indefinitely without long-term harm to the environment. For example, this model notes that Malthus had not foreseen the biotechnological revolution in agriculture that made land much more productive than was true in eighteenth-century England. Economists such as Simon believe that food-production problems in regions such as Africa can be attributed to farm collectivization, government attempts to control the prices of agricultural commodities, and other institutional problems. Simon cites statistics indicating that on a worldwide level, food prices per person are decreasing, and food production per person is increasing.

The logic-of-growth theorists cite evidence showing that the costs of energy and other natural resources have actually fallen over time because humans have found creative technological solutions for producing and extracting these resources. For example, Simon argues that the increase in the price of oil in the 1970s was purely political. The cost of producing a barrel of oil is still about 15 to 25 cents. He notes how people in the past responded to shortages of firewood used for heating by turning to coal and from coal shortages by using oil. Simon believed that this ongoing process of creative innovation will continue.

Simon and other logic-of-growth theorists further suggest that population growth is a stimulus for, rather than a deterrent to, economic progress. The title of Simon's major book is *The Ultimate Resource* (1981), which he considers to be the human mind. Productivity and solutions for economic and environmental problems come directly from the human mind. In the long run, therefore, population growth helps to raise the standard of living in society by utilizing creative ideas and technologies to extract solutions. Although Simon and other logic-of-growth theorists admit that, in the short term, population growth may inhibit economic development, they conclude that countries ought not restrict population growth forcibly and that eventually technological innovations and human creativity will solve our problems, just as they have in the past.

The Pessimists and the Optimists: An Anthropological Assessment

Most likely, both the pessimistic and the optimistic predictions regarding global problems are to some extent exaggerated. Predicting the future is risky for any social scientist, and to project complex global trends regarding population growth, environmental destruction, and technological change over many decades is highly problematic. The optimists believe that, ever since the beginnings of civilization, humanity has benefited from technological progress. A comprehensive view of the past, however, challenges this assumption. For example, we saw in Chapter 12 that the emergence of intensive agriculture—one of the major developments in human history—produced benefits for small segments of the population but adversely affected the majority of people by contributing to higher disease rates, increased inequality, and other problems. Conversely, the pessimists tend to underestimate the human capacity to devise technological solutions to global problems.

Anthropological research may help assess these global issues in a more cautious and analytic manner. With its holistic approach, anthropology has always been concerned with precisely those aspects of human interaction with the environment that are now being recognized widely by scientists studying global environmental change. The U.S. Committee on Global Change (1988) called for the development of an interdisciplinary science for understanding global change. The discipline of anthropology represents a prototype or model for the interdisciplinary science that would be needed to understand these changes (Rayner 1989). Anthropological data can help assess the causes of such phenomena as the greenhouse effect by examining land-use choices and the impacts of economic activities. Anthropology may assist in the development of policies on matters such as agriculture, biotechnology, pollution, and population growth by providing information on the links between local practices and global processes.

Ethnographic Research on the Green Revolution

An example of how ethnographic research can illuminate global problems involves studies of the Green Revolution in underdeveloped countries. Optimists such as Simon cite the Green Revolution as one of the advancements made through technology and human creativity. In their view, the Green Revolution contradicts the basic assumptions made by the neo-Malthusians that population will outgrow the finite resources (food) of a particular area of land. Use of hybrid species of high-yield wheat and rice and highly mechanized agricultural techniques has increased food production to a degree that could not have been anticipated by Malthusians of past ages.

However, many cultural anthropologists who have studied the adoption of mechanized agriculture in developing countries have found that these innovations have created unintended economic and

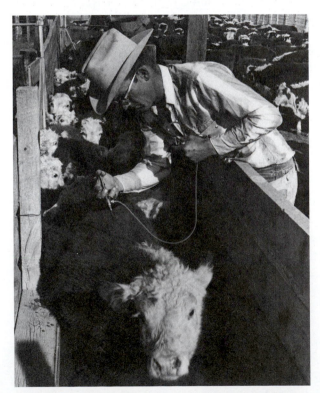

Vaccinating cattle before they are shipped to a feedlot. Industrial societies have changed the nature of agricultural production. Large corporate farming that depends on expensive energy and heavy capital investment has resulted in the decline of family farming.

social problems. In most cases, only wealthy farmers have the capital to invest in irrigation equipment, chemical fertilizers, and large tracts of land. To extend their landholdings, wealthy farmers buy out smaller farmers, creating a new class of landless peasants and a small group of wealthy farmers, which intensifies patterns of inequality and related economic and social problems (Schusky 1990).

In addition, cultural anthropologists find that in areas such as Mexico, where the Green Revolution was adopted enthusiastically, the increased agricultural yields in grains are often used to feed animals raised for human consumption. Anthropologist Billie Dewalt (1984) discovered that more than 50 percent of the annual grain production in Mexico was used to feed animals such as pigs, chickens, and cattle. His research indicates that people who can afford meat have benefited from the Green Revolution. By increasing inequalities, however, the Green Revolution has reduced the percentage of the population that can afford meat. Dewalt concluded that the commercialization and industrialization of agriculture has not only widened the gap between rich and poor in Mexico, it has led to the underutilization of food, energy, and labor, thus hindering rather than promoting agricultural development.

Case Study: The Green Revolution in Shahidpur

One ethnographic study has shown that when the Green Revolution is carried out under the right conditions, it can be successful. Cultural anthropologist Murray Leaf (1984) studied the effects of the Green Revolution in the Punjab region of northern India. Leaf conducted research in a Sikh village called Shahidpur from 1964 to 1966 and then returned in 1978. The years 1965 and 1978 mark the onset and complete adoption, respectively, of the Green Revolution in Shahidpur. Thus, Leaf was able to view the beginning and end of the process. During this period, the village switched from subsistence to mechanized agriculture.

The villagers adopted new strains of wheat, tractors, insecticides, and an irrigation technology on an experimental basis to determine whether this would increase their yields. Wealthy farmers adopted the technology readily, investing their capital in equipment and land. Poor peasants, however, also took the needed capital investment risks (with the support of government development agencies), and the risks paid off. Leaf's research demonstrates that, in contrast to modernization theory, poor peasants are not constrained by traditional cultural patterns that might inhibit rational strategies of investment and savings. When these peasants saw they would directly benefit from these investments, they were willing to accept the economic risks.

More important, the villagers were willing to acquire the knowledge and technical skills needed to manage and ensure the continuity of their agricultural production. Through a university extension center, new plant varieties and technologies were adopted on an experimental basis. The people could directly see the results of their agricultural experiments and respond appropriately to various conditions. The education was a low-cost investment with government-subsidized tuition even for the poorest families. Furthermore, the university center provided training in the maintenance and repair of farm equipment and in other nonagricultural employment fields.

Leaf suggested that a key to the success of the Green Revolution in this region (in contrast to many other rural areas) is that government officials were more interested in development than in control. Government advice was always linked to the actual reactions among the villagers. Channels of communication were always open between local and regional levels. Leaf's valuable ethnographic study has some suggestive insights for those interested in furthering the Green Revolution in the Third World. Much more ethnographic research needs to be done, however, to evaluate the successes and problems in implementing the Green Revolution.

Case Study: The Conservation of Wood in Haiti

Another area in which ethnographic research has increased our understanding of a global problem is the growing shortage of wood for fuel and construction in developing societies. This problem is most acute in regions where growing populations practice intensive agriculture. Peasant farmers spend several hours each day searching for firewood, the principal cooking fuel in poor households. This practice results in the cutting of forests, which take a long time to grow back. Deforestation has become a worldwide ecological challenge.

Anthropologist Gerald Murray (1989), who conducted research among the rural peasants in Haiti, helped design a plan to solve the problem. European powers such as the French had developed

Sugar cane cutter.

Haiti as a sugar-exporting colony. They found it profitable to cut forests to clear land for sugar cane, coffee, and indigo for European consumers. After Haiti became independent in the nineteenth century, foreign lumber companies continued to cut and export most of the nation's hardwoods. These activities, combined with population growth that created land scarcities, greatly reduced the amount of forest area. The Haitian government tried to develop a reforestation project but failed to secure the cooperation of most of the peasants. The government blamed traditional peasant attitudes and patterns of land use for the project's failure.

In contrast, Murray argued that neither traditional land-use patterns nor peasant attitudes were responsible for the failure of reforestation. He discovered that the peasants did not cooperate with the project because they did not see any immediate benefits. Most of the trees with which the peasants were familiar took many years to grow. Moreover, the peasants believed that planting trees on their small tracts of land would interfere with crop cultivation. They also feared that even if they reforested the land, the government would assume ownership of the trees and thereby deprive them of the use of the land.

Because of his study, Murray was invited to help design a reforestation plan. With assistance from other anthropologists and development specialists, he designed a program that introduced fast-growing hardwood trees as an additional cash crop for peasant farmers. The increasing demand for this type of wood for charcoal and construction made it an ideal commodity. Thousands of trees were planted all across Haiti. In addition, the plan called for the trees to be completely owned and managed by the peasantry rather than by the government. The peasants could harvest the trees whenever needed, and they knew that they would receive the direct benefits from the project. After several years, the peasants constructed their houses and sold charcoal from the new woods. Murray views this type of peasant-managed, cash-crop production as a feasible option for many undeveloped peasant communities.

A Global Solution for Global Problems

In June 1992 in Rio de Janiero, Brazil, representatives of 178 nations gathered at what was known as the Earth Summit. These representatives tried to set the stage for managing the Planet Earth through global cooperation. The issues were the environment, climate change induced by the greenhouse effect and global warming, population growth, deforestation, the loss of biodiversity, air and water pollution, and the threats of globalization throughout the world. Although the Earth Summit was successful because it received so much international attention and created worldwide awareness of global issues, the specifics of how soon problems were going to be solved, how much it would cost, and who was going to pay became extremely complicated.

A follow-up summit on climate change was held in Kyoto, Japan, in December 1997. The Kyoto Summit was organized by the Organization for Economic Co-operation and Development (OECD), which represents most industrialized countries of the world. The OECD is committed to helping its member countries move toward sustainable development for the planet's life-support system. The Kyoto Summit resulted in a protocol agreement endorsed by 110 countries to try to reduce greenhouse gases and stabilize atmospheric changes that would mitigate increasing global warming.

The Kyoto Protocol established targets and set the stage for international monitoring of greenhouse gas emissions from various countries. The Kyoto agreement set a target of overall reduction of 5.2 percent in greenhouse gases from 1990 levels by the year 2012. The European countries set a target of reducing their emissions by 8 percent; the United States by 7 percent; and Japan by 6 percent. The United Kingdom took it upon itself to set higher targets and committed itself to a 20 percent reduction of emissions by 2010. Part of the agreement encouraged the industrial countries to become partners with the developing countries to help curb greenhouse gas emissions throughout the world.

Not surprisingly, many leaders of developing countries blamed the industrialized countries for the problems. Leaders of developing countries view themselves as victims of industrialized countries. For example, the Rio Declaration was going to contain a statement of principles on deforestation that would legally prohibit developing countries from burning their tropical rain forests. The developing countries objected to this statement because it was unfairly focused on the tropical forests and included nothing regarding the deforestation of the old-growth forests in the United States, Canada, and Europe. When a compromise could not be reached, the legally binding statement was scrapped for a weaker statement with no legal implications.

In addition, the industrialized countries, including the United States, were very reluctant to participate in some issues. For example, with respect to global warming, Japan and the European community had established limits on carbon dioxide emissions. In 2001, with the election of George W. Bush as president, the U.S. administration dropped out of the Kyoto Summit agreement. The Bush administration claimed that the treaty was unacceptable because it would harm the U.S. economy. They contended that the cost of curbing greenhouse emissions from coal-burning power plants and automobiles was too great a burden on the U.S. economy and would result in the loss of jobs and profits. The U.S. administration argued that the Kyoto agreement made exceptions for countries such as China and India, who did not have to reduce their emissions, although these countries were emitting substantial amounts of greenhouse gases. Thus, the U.S. administration opted out of the agreement,

stating that it was unfair because it did not hold developing countries to the same strict emissions standards as the developed countries.

Many of the developing countries at the Rio de Janeiro summit felt that their number-one priority was economic survival rather than saving the environment. Developing countries wanted to adopt industrialization as rapidly as possible to induce economic development. Although they agreed to some of the environmental mandates of industrialized countries, they did so only by requiring the industrialized countries to contribute large sums of money toward those efforts. This resulted in various conflicts between the have and have-not countries.

The Sustainability Model

Obviously, the problems resulting from globalization are extremely complex and are not going to be resolved without some sort of global unity. Anthropological research in countries throughout the world has resulted in a perspective sometimes known as the sustainability model. The **sustainability model** suggests that societies throughout the world need environments and technologies that provide sustenance, not only for the present generation, but also for future generations. This model encourages resource management that does not degrade the environment for future generations. The sustainability model is opposed to the logic-of-growth model, which assumes that economic and technological growth will inevitably bring progress. The sustainability model is more realistic in assessing environmental and technological change and recommends policy changes to inhibit problems that are induced by globalization. Some countries are beginning to adopt this sustainability model of development by limiting their emissions, curbing population growth, and cleaning up pollution.

It must be recognized that the expansion of global multinational capitalism (see below) is not the *only source* of environmental problems in the world. As we will see, the USSR had far worse environmental pollution than the advanced capitalist industrialized societies of Europe, the United States, and elsewhere. However, anthropologists fully understand that these global problems cannot be solved by country-by-country solutions. The challenge for this generation is to provide a global, internationally based organizational context and sound scientific based research for the resolution of these problems. Neglecting these global problems is bound to result in massive difficulties for the future of humanity. Anthropological research can help in assessing these problems and thereby promote the model of sustainability.

Economic Trends

As indicated in earlier chapters, the contemporary global economy began with European expansion in the mercantilist and colonialist periods. Since World War II, this world economic system has been classified (sometimes too simplistically) into core, semiperipheral, and peripheral countries, with the United States the leading core country. Trading and financial institutions in the capitalist countries controlled the international organizations such as the World Bank and the International Monetary Fund. The industrial-socialist countries of Eastern Europe and the former Soviet Union tried not to participate directly in the capitalist world economic system and also tried to create their own client states in areas such as Cuba, Angola, and Afghanistan. By the 1980s, however, new developments in the world economy were producing a radical restructuring of the world economic system.

Multinational Corporations

One of the major factors behind the emergence of the global economic network is the multinational corporation. In Chapter 13, we discussed multinational corporations as they have evolved in both the capitalist and socialist world. In many ways, multinational corporations have opened the door for globalization by promoting the spread of technical and cultural knowledge to non-Western societies. In the modern era, multinational corporations have expanded to the point that some anthropologists consider them a new societal institution beyond the state. For example, anthropologist Alvin Wolfe (1977, 1986) discussed how multinational corporations have integrated the manufacturing processes at a supranational level. Multinational corporations have reorganized the electronics industry, garment manufacturing, and the automobile industry. Today, products might be manufactured in several different countries, and the financing

and organization of labor and also outsourcing are carried out by the multinational corporation. Wolfe suggested that this process will continue. The multinational corporations will eventually assume the management of global affairs, and the nation-state will disappear.

Jobs and Growth: A Positive Assessment   Given their power and influence, multinational corporations have become highly controversial. With their tremendous capital assets, they can radically alter a society. Some theorists believe that multinational corporations can enhance global economic development, thereby reducing poverty and hunger. As these corporations expand into Latin America, Africa, the Middle East, and Asia, they bring capital and technology and provide employment. From this vantage point, they create jobs and spur both short- and long-term economic growth.

Neocolonialism: A Negative Assessment   Dependency theorists as discussed in Chapter 6 on globalization suggest that multinational corporations have actually intensified the problems of developing countries. They contend that these corporations create benefits for a wealthy elite and a small, upwardly mobile middle class, while the vast majority of the population remains in desperate poverty. Because the multinational corporations tend to invest in capital-intensive commodities, the majority of the population does not participate in the modernization of the economy. Furthermore, the entire society becomes dependent on corporations that are based outside the region, which inhibits self-sufficiency and the development of a more diversified economy.

According to this view, multinational corporations are simply the forerunners of a new form of *neocolonialism*, aimed at supplying the industrial world with natural resources and cheap labor. Multinational corporations based in core societies encourage peripheral societies to incur loans to produce a limited number of export-oriented commodities, a process that creates a cycle of economic indebtedness and increased dependency. In contrast to the older forms of colonialism, the core countries do not incur the expenses of maintaining direct political control over these societies; rather, they keep the peripheral nations in a state of dependency and maintain indirect political control by making contributions and paying bribes to politicians. In certain cases, however, when core countries feel threatened by political developments in peripheral nations, they resort to direct military intervention.

Case Study: The Potlatch Corporation   As with other global developments, these issues can benefit from ethnographic research. In one example, anthropologist Paul Shankman (1975, 1978, 1999) researched the changes generated by a multinational corporation on the island of Western Samoa. The corporation studied by Shankman was a large wood-product firm called the Potlatch Corporation, based in the northwest coast region of the United States and named after the famed redistributional exchanges of Native Americans in that region (see Chapter 11). The Potlatch Corporation surveyed the tropical hardwood trees in a portion of Western Samoa and found a dozen species that could be used for furniture and veneers. To facilitate the leasing of large amounts of land in Western Samoa (bypassing traditional landholding arrangements), the Potlatch Corporation requested that the Samoan government set up an agency to act as a broker on behalf of the corporation. Potlatch eventually won a number of concessions from the Samoan parliament.

Although Potlatch claimed to be committed to the economic development of Western Samoa, Shankman found that the monetary rewards from leasing the land did not prove as great as the people had expected. For example, Potlatch leased 28,000 acres of land for $1.40 an acre. In one project in which it leased land from a group of seven villages, the average yearly income from leasing amounted to less than $11 per person. Royalties paid on cut timber were also low, amounting to 4 cents per cubic foot, part of which was to go back to the government for reforestation.

The Potlatch Corporation did provide jobs for three hundred people in Western Samoa, making it one of the island's largest employers. Shankman discovered, however, that most of these people were formerly employed in agriculture, civil service, and light industry. Through the Potlatch projects, labor was simply shifted from other sectors of the economy to forestry. Thus, Potlatch did not really create jobs; rather, it simply shifted them to new sectors.

Shankman believed that Potlatch's leasing policies would ultimately create a scarcity of land, and more peasants would be forced to produce on marginal land. Moreover, Shankman suggested that the inflated cost of living generated by the company, through higher wage notes, in addition to the negative consequences such as erosion of the rain forest caused by rapid lumbering, may result in long-term negative costs to the people of Samoa.

Shankman also noted that the risks assumed by the people of Western Samoa were much greater than those of the multinational corporation. If Potlatch were successful, it could recoup its initial investments very quickly. Were it to lose revenue, it could simply leave the area. In contrast, the peasants did not have any capital to fall back on were they to lose their land. Moreover, they had to live permanently with the economic, social, and ecological changes brought about by Potlatch's policies. Eventually, the Potlatch Corporation pulled out of the region. As Shankman (1990, 2000) concluded: "So much for the commitment to economic development of Western Samoa."

Other anthropologists are conducting research similar to Shankman's. The consensus at this point appears to confirm his charges that the expansion of multinational corporations has created new forms of economic dependency and neocolonialism. Thus, in the short run, the global changes wrought by multinational corporations appear to have had negative consequences for developing societies. Whether this will be true over the long run remains to be seen.

In the case of the *maquiladoras* (multinational corporations that moved into the border regions of Mexico as described in Chapter 14), many of these companies have folded up production there as labor and environmental costs have risen to relocate in China and India. Mexico has lost some 500,000 manufacturing jobs to other lower wage countries in just a few years. As China and India through telecommunication and developing global media and technology can produce at lower wages, many multinationals have moved and outsourced their manufacturing to those regions (Friedman 2005). Thus, multinational corporations continue to look for means of reducing labor costs and enhance profits which at times, at least in the short term produce negative consequences for some of the developing countries of the world.

Emerging Economic Trends

Driven by new technological and scientific developments in areas such as biotechnology, telecommunications, microprocessor information systems, and other high-tech industrialization, the world economy continues to undergo rapid changes. The globalization of the world economy has produced a vast array of products and services in interlocking markets. World trade has accelerated over the last few decades, stimulating greater economic interdependency. These trends have resulted in a restructuring of the world economic system.

Changes in Socialist Countries   The globalization of the economy has had traumatic consequences for the industrial, socialist-based economies of the former Soviet Union, Eastern Europe, and other peripheral socialist economies such as China and Vietnam. These state-administered economies did not produce the extensive economic development that they had promised. Government officials in these countries promoted five-year plans for economic development, but these plans did not lead to the production of prized consumer goods or a higher standard of living.

The late anthropologist Marvin Harris (1992) advocated an approach that focused on the *infrastructural problems* in explaining the downfall of the former Soviet Union and Eastern European socialist regimes. Harris suggested that the infrastructure, which encompasses the technological, economic, demographic, and environmental activities directed at sustaining health and well-being, always has a primary, determinant role in the functioning of a sociocultural system. The serious deficiencies and weaknesses in the infrastructure of the former Soviet Union and Eastern Europe undermined the entire fabric of society. For example, the basic energy supply based on coal and oil production became stagnant, and the generating plants for electricity were antiquated, leading to periodic blackouts and frequent breakdowns.

Harris described how the agricultural and marketing system for the production and distribution of food resulted in severe shortages, delays in delivery, hoarding, and rationing. In addition, increasing problems with, and costs incurred by, industrial pollution led to the deterioration of the socialist economies. According to Harris, the infrastructural deficiencies of these socialist systems had fundamental consequences for the basic health, safety, and ultimate survival of the people in these societies. These deficiencies eventually led to the societies' systemic breakdown.

The industrial-socialist societies faced major economic crises. Repeated failures in agriculture and industry led to frustration and unrest among the populace. Global communications with other societies, particularly those with much greater access to consumer goods, caused many people in socialist states to become frustrated with the inadequacy of their systems. These people began to question the aims and policies of their leaders.

The Soviet Union: Perestroika and Glasnost   In the former Soviet Union, Communist Party leader Mikhail Gorbachev responded to the people's criticisms and the economic crisis facing the country by instituting a series of reforms and economic restructuring known as *perestroika*. In effect, this policy involved the reintegration of the former Soviet Union into the world-capitalist system. New joint ventures with capitalist firms were undertaken; McDonald's and other multinational corporations from the West and Japan were invited to participate in the Soviet economy. Soviet industrial corporations were reorganized to emphasize competition and the maximization of private profits for individual firms. Wages and salaries in Soviet industries were no longer to be controlled by the government; rather, they would reflect market conditions and individual productivity.

To carry out *perestroika*, Gorbachev had to confront the bureaucratic elite that dominated the Soviet political economy (see Chapter 13). Because these reforms directly threatened the bureaucratic control of the political economy, he faced much resistance by government officials. Some of these bureaucrats were ideologically committed to the Marxist–Leninist model of communism and did not want the Soviet Union integrated into the world-capitalist economy. Others believed that tinkering with the economy with these reforms would induce more hardship for the Soviet people. For example, after the introduction of *perestroika* and the removal of government-controlled price restraints, the costs of food and other basic commodities skyrocketed.

As a means of implementing his economic reforms, Gorbachev also called for *glasnost*, usually translated as "openness," which involved the freedom to criticize government policies and officials. Newspapers and other media were allowed to express views that were in opposition to Communist Party dictates. *Glasnost* also permitted greater political freedom of expression as well as democratic elections and a multiparty political system. The policy of *glasnost* led to mass demonstrations against the former Soviet government and eventually to criticism and the downfall of Gorbachev himself.

As a result of the severe economic difficulties and subsequent political crises in the Soviet Union, many of the non-Russian republics began to declare sovereignty and independence. Regions such as Estonia, Lithuania, the Ukraine, Kazakhstan, Uzbekistan, Turkmenistan, and Azerbaijan cut their political ties with the Soviet Union. Although Gorbachev attempted to frustrate these developments, sometimes with a show of military force, the Soviet empire began to collapse. Eventually, all of the non-Russian regions formed their own independent republics. The independent republics not only cut political ties, leaving the Russian republic by itself; they also began to restrict the export of their domestic commodities into Russia. This exacerbated the difficult economic conditions within the Russian state itself.

The successor to Mikhail Gorbachev, Boris Yeltsin, attempted to further the *perestroika* and *glasnost* policies of his predecessor. Yeltsin's primary goal was to transform the remains of the state-managed centralized economy of Russia into an economy in which managerial and consumer decisions are based on market forces and the economy is in private hands. The Yeltsin government tried to radically restructure the political economy by ending price and wage controls, reducing or eliminating subsidies to factories and farms, slashing military expenditures, introducing new taxes, and balancing the national budget.

The United States and other European economic leaders supported these policies, which became known as "shock therapy." This economic shock therapy had some positive consequences, but most economists agree that the peculiarities of the Soviet system were bound to prolong the process of economic reform. In the meantime, many Russians who were accustomed to subsidies and government benefits had to endure substantial hardships. A number of Russian bureaucrats began to use their positions to acquire economic assets through illegal maneuvers. Ponzi schemes, which used fake banks and financial institutions to gain large sums of capital

from government organizations and the general population, were prevalent during this shock therapy period. This resulted in the rise of a capitalist oligarchy or elite in the major industrial and media sectors of the economy (Titma and Tuma 2001; Chua 2003). In addition, a lack of knowledge of how capitalism, free labor, and the market economy operate has resulted in major economic declines in agriculture and industry. In 2000, Vladimir Putin, Yeltsin's prime minister, was elected president of Russia, promising to continue the economic reforms and democratization of Russian society. The question for future economic developments in Russia is whether the people can be patient enough to endure these economic difficulties and enable the economy to grow at a pace that will enhance the overall socioeconomic conditions for the majority of people. Anthropologists who are actively engaged in ethnographic research in Russia advocate more qualitative research, in addition to just quantitative statistical research that is often used as the primary method for economists to help advise and consult with the Russian government and companies to enhance more even development (Flyberg 2004).

Eastern Europe Stimulated by the policies of *perestroika* and *glasnost*, the Eastern European nations of East Germany, Poland, Czechoslovakia, Hungary, Romania, Bulgaria, and Yugoslavia began reforms of their socialist political economies. These countries had been restricted to trading primarily with the Soviet Union and among themselves. In the German Democratic Republic (East Germany), mass demonstrations and migrations of people to West Germany led to the fall of the communist government and the destruction of the Berlin Wall. Solidarity, a popular outlawed labor union led by Lech Walesa, toppled the government of Poland. Polish workers demanded economic reforms and a better standard of living than that offered by the socialist model. Democratic elections led to Walesa's becoming prime minister. Walesa subsequently visited the United States and other Western countries in search of foreign investment. Many of the Eastern European socialist-bloc societies actively sought reintegration into the world-capitalist economy as a means of stimulating both economic growth and democratic freedom.

In a book entitled *What Was Socialism and What Comes Next* (1996), anthropologist Katherine

Verdery, who did most of her ethnographic work in the East European country of Romania, summarized some of the problems and dilemmas facing this region. She writes about how a different sense of time prevailed during the socialist period in Eastern Europe, and the new forms of capitalism and its industrial work rhythms based on progress and linear models are disrupting these societies. Verdery notes that new resurgent patterns of gender inequality based on older patriarchal forms are reemerging in these postsocialist Eastern European countries. During the socialist period, gender relations were supposed to have been equalized. However, Verdery describes how the socialist government in Romania reconfigured gender roles, making women dependent on a patrilineal-paternalistic state. After the downfall of socialism, Romania, Poland, Hungary, and other postsocialist countries have been emphasizing a return to "traditional values" regarding gender, which positions the woman once again in the home and doing household chores. To some extent, this gender organization of postsocialist society defines housework as "nonwork." As these Eastern European economies become more capitalistic, women will probably be drawn into the workforce, but in the meantime, these women are returning to the older patriarchal forms of family life.

In the final chapter of her book, Verdery comments on how the transformation of Eastern European and Russian societies may take a much different path toward capitalism than the Western European or U.S. societies have taken. The privatization of property is likely to involve very different processes than in Western societies. Former socialist leaders will undoubtedly use the legal and political process to develop economic opportunities for themselves, as they transfer the state enterprises into private hands. Verdery suggests that black markets, organized crime, and the manipulation of the legal and state apparatus by former socialist bureaucrats will all have consequences for these postsocialist societies. The future of these postsocialist societies cannot be predicted based on models of how Western capitalist states developed.

China Since Mao Zedong's death, China, under leaders such as Deng Xiaoping, introduced many tenets of capitalism. Instead of relying on Communist Party cadre who wanted to instill egalitarian ideals, the new leadership sought to develop leaders with technical, agricultural, and scientific exper-

tise. They encouraged students to obtain education in the United States and other Western nations. They abolished the commune system and reorganized agricultural and industrial production based on individual profits and wages for farmers and workers. The Chinese government called for modernization in agriculture, industry, science, and defense.

Although promoting economic change, the Chinese government has not endorsed political reform. Party bureaucrats remain entrenched in power and resist all pressure to relinquish their authority. The absence of political freedom resulted in mass demonstrations by students and others in Tiannamen Square in Beijing in 1989. The Chinese government crushed this freedom movement with military force and has continued to repress any form of political dissent that threatens its authority. Whether economic development and reintegration into the world economic system can work in China without corresponding political freedom is a question that remains to be answered.

Vietnam Confronted with being one of the poorest countries in the world, the Vietnamese government in 1981 introduced a series of economic reforms called *doi moi* (Pike 1990). Some of the younger politicians in Vietnam are calling for greater participation in the world economic system, the introduction of private enterprise, and individual material benefits in the form of wages and salaries. The Vietnamese reformers face the same problem as those in China and the Soviet Union. With their memories of their colonial experience and wars against the capitalist nations, conservative bureaucrats who are committed to Marxist–Leninist ideology oppose reintegration into the world economic system. Reformers, in contrast, actively seek support from capitalist countries and the international community to pursue their economic liberalization policies and democratization. Recently, it appears that reformers are having the stronger influence regarding state policies. For example, they were instrumental in the negotiations that resulted in the United States lifting its trade embargo against Vietnam in January 1994. This shift in U.S. policy will undoubtedly lead to increasing trade and capitalist economic activity in Vietnam. Since then some progress in industrialization and agricultural development has been significant, however, many of the conservative bureaucrats have resisted these reforms, which may threaten their bureaucratic power and authority (Scupin 2005).

Changes in the Core Societies: The United States and Japan The globalization of the world economy has also had dramatic effects on the core industrial societies, such as the United States and Japan. The United States currently exports about one-fifth of its industrial production. This is double what it was exporting in the 1950s, and that proportion is rapidly increasing. About 70 percent of those exported goods compete directly with goods produced by other nations. Some U.S. states depend heavily on the international economy. For example, approximately one-half of the workers in Ohio work directly on exports such as tires and automobiles. Honda, the major automobile company in Japan, has a large plant in Marion, Ohio. Most American corporations now conduct business on a global level. Although the United States remains the world's largest economy, with a gross national product twice the size of that of its nearest competitor, it no longer dominates as it did in the past. In fact, at the beginning of the twenty-first century, the United States had one of the largest trade deficits and the largest foreign debt of any nation.

In contrast, Japan has maintained a trade surplus. During the past several decades, the United States and Japan have engaged in global economic competition. This competition needs to be considered in the context of the world economic system.

In the 1920s, in the early phases of Japanese industrialization, Japan's population began to expand. Lacking adequate natural resources such as fertile land, raw materials, and energy supplies, Japan became increasingly dependent on imported food and other raw materials. To secure a food supply to support its growing population, the Japanese began to act as an imperial power in Asia, colonizing Korea and Taiwan and expanding into China. Japanese imperialism in Asia was one of the direct causes of World War II.

During its occupation of Japan following World War I, the United States encouraged the development of corporate capitalism. The U.S. government viewed Japan as a capitalist center that could be used to forestall the spread of communism in Asia. Some of Japan's *zaibatsu*, wealthy family conglomerates, were broken up into smaller concerns. Others, such as the Mitsui and Mitsubishi families, were encouraged to invest in new equipment and technolo-gies to induce rapid capitalist growth. Large sums of U.S. capital were funneled into corporations such as Sony to stimulate corporate capitalism. These policies led to the "economic miracle" in Japan that occurred in the 1960s. By the end of that decade, Japan had become one of the world's leading exporters.

The Japanese government, however, realized that it was still dependent on energy and food from other regions of the world. The government constantly reminded its population that Japan must "develop exports or die." The government organized the Ministry of International Trade and Industry (M.I.T.I.) to mobilize industrial firms to export products such as automobiles and electronics to ensure a balance of funds to pay for its heavy imports of food and energy. The M.I.T.I. helps finance Japan's huge exporting corporations so that it can maintain a favorable balance of trade. By the late 1980s, Japan had a large trade surplus. However, it imported approximately 8 tons of fuel, food, wood, and other raw materials for every ton of goods it exported. Yet, beginning in the late 1990s the Asian fiscal and monetary crisis had major devastating consequences for the Japanese economy, which are only being corrected recently. The Japanese lost nearly half of its wealth and assets during the period of 1997 to 2001. Undertaking major reforms in their corporate style economy and banking and financial practices as well as reducing bureaucratic corruption has helped Japan recover to some degree (McCreery and McCreery 2006).

One of the results of economic globalization in Japan had an impact on ethnic change described by anthropologists. Despite official policies that restricted immigration of "foreigners" into Japan, the country has witnessed a growing number of immigrants in recent years. Since the mid-1980s Japan has faced a labor shortage, and many immigrants are coming to seek work. Many of these jobs are unskilled or low-skilled, and the Japanese government is willing to open their doors to immigrants to work in positions that most Japanese will not accept. These newcomers work in so-called 3-K jobs: work that is *kitsui* (hard), *kitanai* (dirty), or *kiken* (dangerous) (Wehrfritz and Takayama 2000). Koreans, Chinese, Indians, and smaller numbers of people from Africa and the Middle East are now immigrating to Japan for these jobs. In addition, many illegal and undocumented immigrants are flocking to Japan. Faced with new ethnic minority problems, in 1989 the Japanese government gave special residency status to *Nikkeijin*, descendants of Japanese emigrants, mostly from Brazil and Peru. By the end of 1998, some 222,000 Brazilians and 41,000 Peruvians of Japanese ancestry had established residency in Japan. The assumption of the government is that these people will be able to assimilate into Japanese society more easily than other foreigners (Potter and Knepper 1998).

Both Japan and the United States, as well as other core capitalist countries, have become postindustrial societies, with a large component of their economy devoted to the service sector (see Chapter 13). At the same time, many of the basic manufacturing plants of these industrial economies are relocating into developing countries to exploit the cheaper labor supply. Japanese multinational corporations have relocated auto factories and other industries to developing Asian countries such as Indonesia and Thailand. Ford Motor Company has relocated an engine manufacturing plant in Mexico. As the core countries have become increasingly internationalized, economic interdependency accelerates. Some theorists believe that this interdependency may become a key component in resolving conflict among nations in the global village as trade and global and media globalization continue to develop (Wright 2000; Friedman 2005).

The Semiperipheral NICs Another result of the globalization of the economy is the rise of the newly industrializing countries (NICs) from a peripheral to a semiperipheral status in the world economic system. Included here are the nations of South Korea, Hong Kong, Singapore, and Taiwan. Popularly known as the "Little Dragons of Asia," they compete with the economic might of Japan. Both Taiwan and Korea were colonies of Japan, whereas Hong Kong and Singapore were colonies of Great Britain. As with other colonized nations, they became peripheral dependencies. These countries, however, are rapidly industrializing and have broken their bonds of dependency. In some industries, such as electronics, these nations have marketed products that compete with core countries like Japan.

The success of the NICs reflects the changing division of labor in the world economic system. As the multinationals relocated some of their labor-intensive industries to low-wage regions, the NICs were able to absorb some of these jobs. Like Japan, their success is partially due to U.S. economic support. In particular, during the 1950s and 1960s, the United States viewed South Korea and Taiwan as part of the capitalist bloc in Asia. The United States invested large sums of capital and foreign aid into these countries, thereby enabling them to develop as capitalist centers. South Korea was heavily subsidized by both United States capital in industry and agriculture to enhance its rapid growth in the 1960s and 1970s (Sorenson 2006). In addition, as in Japan, the governments in these countries directed the modernization of the economy through massive investment into export industries. The NICs have changed the context of the world economy through low-cost production methods and aggressive marketing. They have created a unique niche in the world economic system by exporting products that compete directly with those produced by the core countries. In many cases, they have expanded their overseas markets through joint ventures with multinational firms based in core countries. In other cases, they have created their own multinational corporations. For example, NIC multinational corporations have become global competitors as producers of semiconductors for electronic and computer equipment. The world's largest plastic firm is Formosa Plastics, based in Taiwan. The best-selling imported car in Canada is the Pony, made by Hyundai in South Korea. However, as in Japan, these countries went through major economic declines following the Asian fiscal crisis of the late 1990s and are only recently recovering from those trends.

Political Trends

As the world economy becomes more integrated, major political changes are taking place in the global network. During the 1950s, some modernization theorists (Chapter 6) predicted that the various nations would become very similar as they were brought closer together in the global economy. People everywhere would share the same goods and services and eventually the same cultural values. This similarity would set the stage for a unified world government. Certain current trends indicate that such a movement may be taking place; for example, in 1999, fifteen European countries agreed to accept the Euro as the form of currency exchange in order to facilitate trade and to help develop a unified European economy. More countries have been added to the European Union since that time. The EU (European Union) covers some 1.2 million square miles and contains 375 million people speaking 11 different languages. It is currently the largest market in the world, and its gross domestic product (GDP) rivals that of the United States.

In addition, a unified European parliament has been established, and Europeans no longer need passports to travel among the various different countries. Some Europeans are beginning to think of themselves as "Europeans" rather than Italians, Greeks, Germans, Irish, or British. Perhaps the nation-state may be giving way to larger political organizations and processes in future political evolution. At the same time, however, other political tendencies seem to indicate movement in the *opposite direction*; in many areas the nation-state appears to be fragmenting along linguistic, ethnic, and religious lines.

In considering these global political trends, many anthropologists suggest that the nation-state is too small for the immense problems in the world political economy: capital flows, economic development, management of technology, environmental and demographic trends, production of commodities, and labor problems. Organizations such as the United Nations, International Monetary Fund, World Bank, World Trade Organization (WTO), NAFTA, the EU, and the multinational corporations appear to be in the process of displacing the nation-state in the management of the global economy. Although the United Nations has not been effective in producing an international consensus on global problems, it may become more important in the future.

At the same time, the nation-state may be too large to care for the different needs of people at the local level. Government officials representing the nation-state may not have enough contact with the populace in local areas to respond to their needs, which can range from housing and food to the opportunity to express their cultural values. One sign of the fragmentation of the nation-state into smaller components is the increase of ethnic and religious tensions at the local level (Scupin 2003).

Ethnic Trends

Ethnic unrest and tension are prevalent in today's world. Newspapers and television news are rife with stories about ethnic violence among the peoples of the former Soviet Union and Eastern Europe, Africa, Sri Lanka, India, Ireland, the Middle East, and the United States.

Anthropologists have been systematically examining ethnicity since the 1960s. As we saw in Chapters 3 and 7, an *ethnic group* is a collectivity of people who believe they share a common history and origins. Members of ethnic groups often share cultural traits such as language, religion, dress, and food. Today, as we saw in Chapters 14 and 15, the countries of Latin America, Africa, the Caribbean, the Middle East, and Asia are *plural societies* that contain many ethnic groups.

As globalization occurs, with its rapid integration of nation-states, markets, and information technology, and as the management of economic and political development goes to the World Bank, the International Monetary Fund, the EU, the United Nations, and large multinational corporations, many peoples at the local level feel threatened by these global processes. Citizens of various countries lose faith in their government's abilities to represent their interests in these pluralistic societies. These globalization processes often exacerbate ethnic tensions and conflicts.

In previous chapters, we looked at the development of ethnonationalist movements in Latin America, the Caribbean, Africa, the Middle East, and Asia. As we saw, these ethnonationalist movements, such as the Zapatista movement in southern Mexico, were to some extent a result of earlier colonial policies and new trends in globalization such as NAFTA and trade agreements between nation-states. Many ethnic groups have expressed a desire to return to a more simple way of life and traditional culture and behavior. They distrust the new global managers and nation-state bureaucrats who they perceive as not having their local interests in mind, and these ethnonationalist movements are a reaction to these globalization tendencies. Restoring ethnic autonomy is sometimes seen as a strategy to rectify the globalization process.

The revival of local ethnic tendencies and identities is developing in the West as well as in non-Western countries. Anthropologists are studying the ethnic resurgence of the Scots, why they want more independence in the United Kingdom, and why Quebec wants to separate from the rest of Canada (Handler 1988; Cohen 1996; Buchinangi 2003; Ballinger 2003). These local ethnic movements for autonomy and separatism are a response to the weakening of older nation-state loyalties, induced by globalization. As globalization is fraught with

World Migration and Refugees

It has been estimated that some 100 million people are migrating from their homelands to other countries. Of this number, about 17 million are refugees and another 20 million have fled violence, drought, and environmental destruction (DeVoe 1992). The vast majority of the migration and refugee problems involve Africa, Latin America, the Middle East, and Asia. However, during the 1990s, thousands of refugees in Europe, primarily from Bosnia and Kosovo, began a forced migration out of their homelands. Although some of the migrants and refugees came to wealthier countries in North America or Europe, the majority marked time or tried to carve out a new existence in underdeveloped regions. Approximately 87 percent of the 17 million refugees are residing in underdeveloped countries, countries that have rapidly growing populations and severe economic and environmental problems.

A number of anthropologists are actively engaged in research projects and planning activities directed at resolving some of the basic problems that confront refugee populations. An organization known as the Committee on Refugee Issues (CORI) has developed as a division of the American Anthropological Association to sponsor and encourage research

and problem-solving projects among refugee populations. Various anthropologists are studying the Southeast Asian migrants who came to the United States following the aftermath of the Vietnam War: refugees from Vietnam, Laos, and Kampuchea (Cambodia). Most of these anthropologists are actively involved in attempting to help these refugees adapt to conditions in the United States.

Anthropologist Pamela DeVoe (1992) has been doing research among Southeast Asian refugees in the St. Louis area. DeVoe has found that Southeast Asian refugees enter the work force at the unskilled and semiskilled level within the first six months of their arrival in the United States. She found that the key problem for these refugees is the lack of adequate health benefits to cover their families. DeVoe found a lack of federal planning for a comprehensive refugee health program and an inadequate, uncoordinated state network of health services for them. Consequently, these refugees, who have to cope with traumatic experiences as a result of the stresses of migration and relocation, have few opportunities for adequate health care.

After interviewing the employers of the refugees, DeVoe discovered that many of the Southeast Asian refugee workers quit their jobs suddenly, for no apparent reason. She found that absenteeism and abrupt quitting occurred frequently, indicating that these refugees were having difficulties adjusting to U.S. society. DeVoe found that in some cases the refugees did not understand

the system of health care and the benefits available to them. Hospitals treat illnesses and bill patients over time, using a sliding scale to determine how much a person has to pay for a service. Because of the lack of language skills, however, these refugees did not understand what the health care system could do for them or what it would cost, which caused delays in health care treatment. Generally, when these delays occurred, the refugees bought over-the-counter medications or used folk remedies to treat themselves. In some cases this resulted in more severe illnesses or dangerous treatments.

DeVoe found that about 40 percent of the refugees employed in metropolitan St. Louis have work-related health-insurance benefits. Generally, as for other Americans, the expense of buying private health insurance is too costly for most refugees. Thus, health insurance is the critical problem for many of the Southeast Asian refugees in the work force in the St. Louis area. DeVoe suggested that a national comprehensive health care system would eliminate many of the problems for these refugees and help them become more self-sufficient, productive members of American society.

Other anthropologists have been using their research skills and problem-solving techniques to assist migrants who have been detained in refugee camps in different parts of the world. Anthropologist Nancy Donnelly (1992) studied the Vietnamese refugees who had been confined in detention centers in Hong Kong.

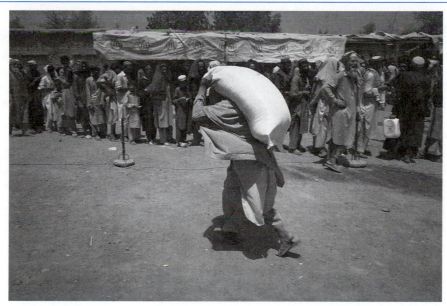

Asian refugees.

Vietnamese refugees have been coming to Hong Kong as asylum seekers since the end of the Vietnam War. Since 1979, about 180,000 men, women, and children have arrived in Hong Kong in boats. Approximately 64,000 remain in refugee-detention camps awaiting acceptance by other countries. In 1989, Hong Kong attempted to force some of the refugees to return to Vietnam, but international pressure forced Hong Kong to reverse its policy, and it has focused instead on assisting refugees to return voluntarily, if they wish to do so.

Donnelly conducted her research in 1991, visiting thirteen detention camps and agency offices that manage the camps in Hong Kong. She found that most of the camps are much like prisons and are strictly controlled by the Correctional Services Department in Hong Kong. As many as three hundred people live together in Quonset huts that are surrounded by double chain-link fences topped by barbed wire. These camps contain Vietnamese who are waiting for screening to determine their eligibility for resettlement. They have little to do most of the time. Camp life is described as rule-bound and boring, punctuated by occasional violent episodes. In general, Donnelly found that these refugees are treated as criminals. On the other hand, Donnelly found that for most of the refugees, their status in the camps was preferable to their lives in Vietnam. Everyone expressed hopes regarding freedom and a better life.

Drawing on anthropological research, Holly Ann Williams (1990) attempted to highlight general trends for family situations of people detained in refugee camps. In the initial decision-making stages of choosing to flee one's country, refugee families often face upheaval, disruption, disorientation, and possible death for friends and family members. The breakdown of customary family roles and the new, unfamiliar patterns of social organization often result in multiple stresses. In some cases, extended family units fragment into smaller nuclear units to safeguard resources and food. In other cases, when families are fleeing war conditions, males stay behind as resistance fighters. This leads to the development of many female-headed households in the refugee camps. The vast majority of the refugees in camps in Third World societies are women and children.

Once situated in the camps, scarce resources, limited food, communicable diseases, minimal health care, and overcrowding place more stress on the families. Families are crowded into living quarters with little privacy, often leading to increased marital and family conflicts, including more cases of wife and child abuse. Within the camps, refugee families experience a loss of control over their destiny; they describe camp life as a waste of time, meaningless, and pacifying.

Despite this loss of autonomy and self-determination and the consequent disintegration of the family unit, Williams reported that in many cases the individuals often try to re-create the family structure as a basis of social support. Women begin to develop the new leadership roles, economic responsibilities, and coping skills required for family maintenance in the camps. Although women experience more hardship than men in refugee camps, often being subjected to personal violence, rape, and abduction, they are sometimes able to assume leadership roles and create social support for family members.

Williams, who completed her specific research on Cambodian refugees, called on anthropologists to do more research on family dynamics in refugee camps to better understand these coping mechanisms. The United Nations High Commissioner for Refugees (UNHCR) is the organization responsible for ensuring that refugee camps maintain minimum standards of health and safety conditions. Anthropologists are engaged in studies that provide information and problem-solving strategies that can be used by various voluntary agencies and UN officials to help improve the lives of refugees confined to these camps. This has become an increasingly important project for anthropologists who can use their knowledge and research techniques in solving various global problems (Malkki 1995; Lub Kemann 2004).

anxieties and produces uncertainties in structures and institutions and as it develops in anarchic, haphazard fashion carried along by economic, technological, and cultural imperatives, the ethnic group becomes the refuge for people who feel as if they have no control over these new forces.

Religion and Secularization

Just as ethnic trends have created contradictory political trends, there are ongoing, contradictory religious trends in the context of globalization. In Chapter 13, on industrial societies and post-industrial societies, we discussed the process of *secularization*. Generally, traditional religious beliefs and rituals become separated from economic, social, and political institutions in industrial societies, and religion becomes a private affair for many people.

After the Enlightenment, social thinkers such as Auguste Comte and Karl Marx, as well as early anthropologists, predicted that as societies became increasingly industrialized and modernized, secularization would eradicate religious institutions and beliefs. Although secularization has occurred, however, religion has not disappeared in these societies. It is the case that European societies tend to be more secular than the United States. The Enlightenment philosophers and revolutionaries in France and Europe were reacting to the religious wars and conflicts in Europe throughout the medieval and Renaissance period. However, in many countries—including the United States, where there was much less religious conflict and religious freedom—there were no major violent conflicts among religious groups. Even in places such as the former Soviet Union and Poland, where government authorities prohibited religious beliefs and institutions, religion remained a vital force.

To some extent, religious institutions have survived in industrial societies because religious leaders have emphasized many of the cultural values—for example, nationalism—espoused by other institutions. In addition, the persistence of religion may also be a product of the secularization process itself. Many recent religious revivals have occurred in those societies that have been most affected by modernization. We saw this in Chapter 15 in the case of the Iranian Islamic revolution. As globalization introduces sweeping political, social, and ideological changes, many traditional beliefs and values are challenged. To cope with these destabilizing transformations, many people are reemphasizing traditional cultural values, including religion. For example, the fundamentalist movements in North America, whether Catholic, Jewish, or Protestant, can be partially understood as a reaction against secularization and modernization. For example, anthropologists Susan

Jerry Falwell has been a leader of fundamentalist Christianity in the United States.

Harding and Kathleen Stewart have been addressing the emergence of Christian fundamentalist movements that have arisen in the United States (1999). Other anthropologists have been studying Buddhist, Hindu, and Islamic fundamentalism in other parts of the world (Scupin 2000, 2003a, 2003b; Weisgrau 2000; Antoun 2000; Munson 2002).

As people recognize that globalization is not incidental to their lives but rather a recognizable transformation in their everyday circumstances, they draw on religious substance as a means of restoring power over their lives. The reconstruction and reinvigoration of their religious identity gives some people a sense of greater control in what appears to be a runaway world. Fundamentalist religious movements articulate the uncertainties and distress brought about by expanding globalization and advocate alternative ways of organizing life on a more localized level.

The Role of Anthropology

Although the political, ethnic, and religious trends discussed in this chapter are essentially global, they also obviously affect people on the local level. Not surprisingly, therefore, cultural anthropologists are actively documenting the local responses to global political and religious trends of people in the agricultural regions of Latin America, Africa, the Middle East, Asia, and nonstate societies, as well as in industrialized and postindustrialized societies. Cultural anthropologists have recorded the various dislocations of global political and religious processes in these societies and the ways in which people have attempted to cope with these global changes. The continuing agony of separatist, ethnic, and religious conflicts in Bosnia, Kosovo, Sri Lanka, and elsewhere threatens people throughout the world. In addition, many cultural anthropologists are conducting ethnographic research on recent religious trends among Christian charismatic and millenial fundamentalist movements in Latin America and elsewhere that have resulted from globalization (Robbins 2004). As we have seen in earlier chapters, anthropologists are conducting extensive ethnographic research in Africa, the Middle East, and Asia on recent religious developments.

The tragedy of 9/11/01 in the United States reflected partially the most violent disruptive expression of the reaction to global trends within the Islamic world. Of course, the causes of these violent expressions such as 9/11 or other terrorist developments throughout the world *can never be justified* by an understanding of some of the global causes and reasons for these developments. In the post September 11 United States, the terms apocalyptic and millennial are often invoked in the context of terrorist threat from the "outside." Numerous media discussions have employed these terms, already made familiar to Americans, to explain the attacks on the World Trade Center. Unfortunately, explanation too often goes no further than a facile application of long-misunderstood labels and stereotypes. Media characterizations are often too simplified in understanding these global and religious trends and conflicts. For example, Samuel Huntington, a political scientist at Harvard University, wrote an influential book *The Clash of Civilizations and the Remaking of the World Order* (1996) that continues to resonate with many people in the West and other regions of the world. Huntington argued that a unitary "Western civilization and culture" is at odds with "Islamic civilization and culture," "Hindu civilization and culture," and "Confucian civilization and culture." He envisions these primordial ethnic and regional blocs as fragmenting the world order and resulting in more conflict and instability throughout the world. Huntington's views became reinforced in many Western and American minds as well as Muslim and Asian societies as the tragedy of 9/11/01 unfolded.

However, as mentioned in Chapter 15, the anthropologists who have conducted research in the regions discussed by Huntington have produced a much different picture of ethnic relations and civilizations. Each of these regions contains tremendous internal ethnic diversity, and the voices of these many different groups are pursuing a wide range of economic-, political-, and religious-based goals and aspirations. As emphasized earlier in our discussions of culture and ethnicity (Chapters 3 and 7) these supposedly fixed "real" ethnic cultures and civilizations are in flux, producing plural, diverse, and continual dynamic change. Ethnic identities and civilizations are not static and stable. Processes of globalization and local-level political and economic processes are reproducing a constant tug of ethnic and national identity along with the weakening of those identities and commitments among many different people within societies around the world. Terrorist-minded and reform-minded peaceful groups are constantly in competition with one another in these different regions of the world. Anthropologists also find many bases for pluralistic, democratic institutions within these different areas of the world that could sustain more democratic and pluralistic tendencies (Hefner 2001; Eickelman and Piscatori 2002; Scupin 2003, 2005).

As cultural anthropologists continue to develop a more comprehensive understanding and explanation of these ethnic and global processes through intensive research, the "clash of civilization" thesis appears as a caricatured and stereotypical image that produces more distortion and simplification than what more informed on the ground ethnographic research indicates. In many societies influenced by global trends, existing institutions such as the nation-state have not been able to manage these new ethnic and religious conflicts and developments. Perhaps by understanding the specific aspirations of these different peoples through ethnographic research, national governments and the international community will be more responsive to the local and diverse needs and interests of these peoples.

As anthropologists identify the cultural variations that hamper international coordination, they may help to contribute to the reduction of ethnic and religious tensions worldwide. Anthropologist John Bennett (1987) recommended that anthropologists synthesize their local studies (the micro level) with studies of global conditions (the macro level) to identify trends that militate against international cooperation and peaceful harmony. As we will see in the following chapter, many anthropologists are trying to apply their knowledge of their ethnographic research to help improve human rights, economic and educational developments and enhance other political reforms to produce more stable and harmonious communities both locally and globally around the world.

Anthropologists should make a concerted effort to understand the underlying historical and cultural motivations that contribute to ethnic and religious conflicts. In doing so, they may aid in humankind's understanding of its existence and the need for future cooperation, interfaith dialogue, and peace within the expanding global village.

SUMMARY

Numerous global trends are altering the way of life in all societies. Environmental changes induced by globalization—new agricultural developments, the greenhouse effect, the depletion of the ozone layer, and atmospheric pollution—are creating new problems that may threaten the existence of our planet. Population growth has declined in the core countries and rose in many peripheral underdeveloped societies because of a combination of reduced mortality rates and continued high birth rates. However, with improved health conditions and new opportunities for women, it appears that the population trends are slowing globally. However, technological changes resulting from industrialism have increased the consumption of energy and other raw materials. Perhaps new forms of energy and hybrid vehicles will reduce the reliance on these scarce energies.

Global environmental, demographic, and technological changes have led to two different perspectives: one *pessimistic* and the other *optimistic*. Pessimists predict that population growth and expanded industrialism will result in global economic collapse. Optimists tend to see human creativity and technological solutions as the salvation for humanity. Both the pessimistic and optimistic views are probably exaggerated. Anthropologists are actively examining specific cases regarding the adoption of mechanized agriculture and reforestation projects to understand better these worldwide problems.

Various global economic trends have developed in recent decades. Multinational corporations are creating more economic interdependency among nations. Ethnographic research, however, indicates that the changes introduced by multinational corporations may not always generate economic development immediately in developing societies, but perhaps in the long term the results for economic growth may be positive. Other global economic trends include the reintegration of socialist societies into the world-capitalist system. Russia, Eastern Europe, China, and Vietnam are abandoning orthodox forms of socialism to join the world-market system.

The core countries such as the United States and Japan compete with one another in the global economy. This competition has resulted in the expansion of multinational corporations into various areas, leading to a new global division of labor. Countries such as South Korea and Taiwan have been moving from peripheral to semiperipheral status in the world-market system.

In contrast to global economic interdependency and modernization, political, ethnic, and religious trends often move in the opposite direction. Ethnic separatist movements often divide people, making the promotion of national goals difficult. Religious fundamentalist movements often result from the rapid modernization processes that are perceived as eroding traditional cultural and religious beliefs, sometimes resulting in terrorism that partially explains the 9/11/01 tragedy in the United States (but does not justify it in any way). Anthropological studies of these trends may help improve our understanding of both local aspirations and global processes.

QUESTIONS TO THINK ABOUT

1. In your view, what are the positive and negative consequences of globalization?

2. What is the demographic-transition theory? Do you think that this model applies to all cultures in the world?

3. Why is there concern over the loss of biodiversity?

4. What is the Doomsday Model (neo-Malthusian approach)? How does it differ from the logic-of-growth model?

5. How can an anthropologist make a difference in the changing world of today? Or is the world in need of engineers and technicians who can invent new ways of solving problems?

That is, how can the anthropological perspective be used to examine global issues such as overpopulation, deforestation, global warming, and the loss of biodiversity?

6. What types of unanticipated problems has the implementation of the Green Revolution caused in areas where it was introduced? Are there any success stories, or is the verdict all negative?

7. What is the global economy? What types of changes have occurred in the world recently that are related to the globalization of the world economy?

8. What types of contributions can anthropologists make by studying ethnic conflict and religious movements?

KEY TERMS

agribusiness	doubling time	logic-of-growth model
biodiversity	greenhouse effect	sustainability model
demographic-transition theory	Green Revolution	zero population growth (ZPG)

Chapter 17

Applied Anthropology

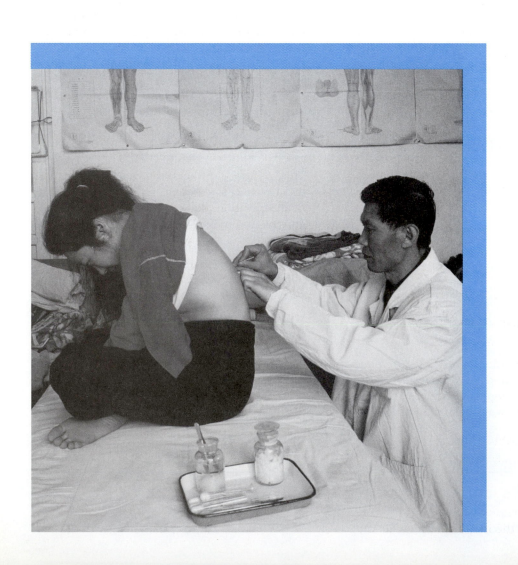

CHAPTER QUESTIONS

- What types of projects are conducted by applied anthropologists?

- What are the different roles of applied anthropologists in various projects?

- What type of research is identified with medical anthropology?

- How are archaeologists involved in applied anthropology?

- How have applied anthropologists become involved in human rights research?

As the preceding chapters illustrated, anthropologists are engaged in extensive research in the four basic subfields of the discipline: physical anthro-pology, archaeology, linguistics, and cultural anthropology. Within these fields, different specializations have emerged that allow for the in-depth gathering of data and the testing and evaluation of specific hypotheses regarding human societies and behavior. As mentioned in Chapter 1, however, one of the most important developments in the field of anthropology is **applied anthropology**, the use of data from the research in anthropology to offer practical solutions to problems faced by a society. This chapter introduces some of the issues that are relevant to applied anthropologists in solving practical problems.

The Roles of the Applied Anthropologist

The popular, if not accurate, images of anthropologists vary from the adventurous explorer seeking out lost treasure to the absentminded academic working away in the dusty halls of a university or museum. These perspectives do not provide a valid picture of the modern physical anthropologist or archaeologist. Anthropologists are increasingly engaged in a variety of activities that have direct relevance to the modern world. Rather than being confined to the halls of the university, an increasing number of anthropologists have become practitioners of anthropology. Indeed, according to a 1990 survey, 50 percent of individuals with doctorates in anthropology develop careers outside the academic area (Givens and Fillmore 1990). Similarly, a 1994 survey indicated that only 35 percent of the membership of the Society for American Archaeology, the primary national organization for archaeologists working in North America, was made up of researchers employed in academic positions, whereas approximately 8 percent were employed in museums (Zeder 1997, 47–48). Of the remainder of the membership, the largest portion, 23 percent, were employed by federal, state, or local governments, followed by 18 percent who worked in private businesses. Comparable trends can be seen in the membership of other archaeological organizations. Many physical anthropologists work with or are employed by public agencies such as the United States Agency for International Development (USAID) and the National Institutes of Health (NIH). Some also work for private firms.

Distinguishing applied anthropology from other anthropological pursuits in many respects presents a false dichotomy. Methodical and theoretical concerns are shared by all; the difference lies in perceptions of the practitioners' objectives, an arbitrary division based on the practicality of the intended outcomes. As Bronislaw Malinowski observed more than a half-century ago: "Unfortunately, there is still a strong but erroneous opinion in some circles that practical anthropology is fundamentally different from theoretical or academic anthropology. The truth is that science begins with application.... What is application in science and when does 'theory' become practical? When it first allows us a definite grip on empirical reality" (1945).

The work of many anthropologists can be seen as applied in some sense. In an overview of applied anthropology, Erve Chambers (1985) classified the different roles of applied anthropologists. Although he was primarily concerned with the applied aspects of cultural anthropology, his observations are equally relevant to the work of physical anthropologists and archaeologists. One role noted by Chambers is that of *representative*, in which the anthropologist becomes the spokesperson for the particular group being studied. Anthropologists at times have represented Native American communities in negotiations with state and federal authorities, mining companies, and development organizations. Anthropologists can also be seen as *facilitators*. In this capacity, anthropologists actively help bring about change or development in the community being researched. For example, they may take a proactive, participatory role in economic or social change to improve medical care, education, or public facilities. An alternative position is the *informant role*, in which the applied anthropologist transfers cultural knowledge obtained from anthropological research to the government or other agency that wants to promote change in a particular area. The U.S. government has employed anthropologists as on-site researchers to provide data on how local-level service clients and delivery agencies respond to government policy. Informally, many archaeologists and anthropologists become involved in local activities and educational programs that present anthropological findings to the public.

Yet another role of applied anthropologists is that of *analyst*. Rather than being just a provider of data, the practicing anthropologist sometimes becomes engaged in the actual formulation of policy. In archaeology, in particular, this has become an important area with the passage of the National Historic Preservation Act in 1966, the Native American Graves Repatriation Act of 1990, and other related legislation. These laws have afforded increased protection to some archaeological resources and mandated the consideration of archaeological resources in planning development. Archaeologists have increasingly found employment in federal, state, or local governments reviewing proposals for development and construction projects that impact cultural resources and archaeological sites. Another role Chambers identified is that of *mediator*, which involves the anthropologist as an intermediary among different interest groups that are participating in a development project. This may include private developers, government officials, and the people who will be affected by the project. As mediator, the anthropologist must try to reconcile differences among these groups, facilitating compromises that ideally will benefit all parties involved in the project. The following discussions highlight some of the applied work that physical anthropologists and archaeologists are engaged in.

The Roles of Applied Anthropologists in Planned Change

Over the years, many applied cultural anthropologists have worked in helping to improve societies through planned change. To assist governments, private developers, or other agencies, applied anthropologists are hired because of their ethnographic studies of particular societies. Government and private agencies often employ applied anthropologists to prepare **social-impact studies**, research on the possible consequences that change will have on a community. Social-impact studies involve in-depth interviews and ethnological studies in local communities to determine how various policies and developments will affect social life in those communities.

One well-known social-impact study was carried out by Thayer Scudder and Elizabeth Colson (1979; Glazier 1984) in the African country of Zambia. Scudder and Colson had conducted long-term ethnographic research for about thirty years in the Gwembe Valley in Zambia. In the mid-1950s, the Zambian government subsidized the development of a large-scale dam, which would provide for more efficient agricultural activities and electrification. Because of the location of the dam, however, the people in the Gwembe Valley would be forced to relocate. Scudder and Colson used their knowledge from their long-term research and subsequent interviews to study the potential impact of this project on the community.

From their social-impact study, Scudder and Colson concluded that the forced relocation of this rural community would create extreme stresses that would result in people clinging to familiar traditions and institutions during the period of relocation. Scudder did social-impact studies of other societies in Africa experiencing forced relocation from dams, highways, and other developments. These studies enabled Scudder and Colson to offer advice to the various African government officials, who could then assess the costs and benefits of resettling these populations and could plan their development projects, taking into consideration the impact on the people involved.

Applied anthropologists often serve as consultants to government organizations, such as the Agency for International Development (AID), that formulate policies involving foreign aid. For example, anthropologist Patrick Fleuret (1988), a full-time employee of AID, studied the problems of farmers in Uganda after the downfall of Idi Amin in 1979. Fleuret and other AID anthropologists discovered that, on the heels of the political turmoil in Uganda, many of the peasants had retreated into subsistence production rather than participate in the market economy. They also found that subsis-

Applied anthropologists often act as consultants for farmers in underdeveloped areas such as rural India.

tence production was affected by a technological problem—a scarcity of hoes for preparing the land for cultivation. In response, AID anthropologists helped design and implement a system to distribute hoes through local cooperative organizations.

This plan for the distribution of hoes reflects the development of new strategies on the part of AID and the facilitator role for applied anthropologists. Most of the development work sponsored by AID and applied anthropology in the 1950s and 1960s was aimed at large-scale development projects such as hydroelectric dams and other forms of mechanized agriculture and industrialism. Many of these large-scale projects, however, have resulted in unintended negative consequences. In the preceding chapter, we saw how the Green Revolution frequently led to increasing inequality and a mechanized agriculture system that was expensive, inefficient, and inappropriate. Often these large-scale projects were devised in terms of the modernization views proposed by economists such as Walt Rostow (see Chapter 6) and were designed to shift an underdeveloped country to industrialism very rapidly.

Most recently, AID and applied anthropologists have modified their policies on development projects in many less-developed countries. They now focus on projects that involve small-scale economic change with an emphasis on the development of appropriate technologies. Rather than relying on large-scale projects to have "trickle-down" influences on local populations, applied anthropologists have begun to focus more realistically on determining where basic needs must be fulfilled. After assessing the needs of the local population, the applied anthropologist can help facilitate change by helping people learn new skills.

One early project that placed applied anthropologists in decision-making and analytical roles was run by Allan Holmberg of Cornell University. In the 1950s and 1960s, Holmberg and Mario Vasquez, a Peruvian anthropologist, developed what is known as the Vicos Project in the Andean highlands. Vicos is the name of a *hacienda* that was leased by Cornell in 1952 as part of a program to increase education and literacy, improve sanitation and health care, and teach new agricultural methods to the Andean Indians. Prior to the Vicos Project, these Indians were peasant farmers who were not able to feed themselves. Their land on the hacienda was broken into small plots that were insufficient to raise potato crops. The Indians were indebted to the *hacendado* and were required to work on the *hacendado's* fields without pay to service their debts.

Although the applied anthropologists took on the role of a new patron to the Indians, the overall aim was to dissolve historic patterns of exploitation and to guide the Indians toward self-sufficiency (Holmberg 1962; Chambers 1985). The Indians were paid for their labor and were also introduced to new varieties of potatoes, fertilizers, and pesticides. New crops such as leafy vegetables and foods such as eggs and fruit were introduced into their diet.

Through an educational program, the Indians became acquainted with forms of representative democratic organization. Developing more independence, they eventually overturned the traditional authority structure of the hacienda. In 1962, the Indians purchased the land of the hacienda from its former owners, which gave the Indians a measure of self-sufficiency. Overall, the Vicos Project led to basic improvements in housing, nutrition, clothing, and health conditions for the Indians. It also served as a model for similar projects in other parts of the world.

Problems sometimes arise between applied anthropologists and private developers or government officials. Many developers and governments want to induce modernization and social change as rapidly as possible with capital-intensive projects, hydroelectric dams, and manufacturing facilities. In many cases, anthropologists have recommended against these innovations because of their expense and inefficient use of labor resources and the heavy cost to communities. (For example, as discussed in Chapter 16, anthropologist Billie DeWalt argued that the majority of Mexicans were not receiving benefits from the adoption of mechanized agriculture, which was being encouraged by the government.) Political officials, however, often ignore these recommendations because they are committed to programs that serve their political and personal interests. In these circumstances, applied anthropologists are often forced to take an advocacy approach, or the representative role, which means supporting the interests of the people who will be directly affected by policies and projects.

In Chapter 9, we discussed the activities of advocacy organizations such as Cultural Survival, founded by David Maybury-Lewis in 1972, which is actively engaged in trying to reduce the costs imposed by globalization on small-scale societies. Driven by trade deficits and gigantic foreign debts, many governments in developing countries want to extract as much wealth as possible from their national territories. Highway expansion, mining operations, giant hydroelectric projects, lumbering, mechanized agriculture, and other industrial developments all intrude on the traditional lifestyle and territory of small-scale societies. Applied anthropologists connected with groups such as Cultural Survival try to obtain input from the people themselves and help them represent their interests to the government or private developers.

Maybury-Lewis (1985) admits that the advocacy role in anthropology is extremely difficult, requiring great sensitivity and complex moral and political judgments. Most recently, as discussed in Chapters 9, 10, and 11, many small-scale societies and minority groups in developing countries are organizing themselves to represent their own interests. This has resulted in the diminished role of the applied anthropologist as advocate or representative. Generally, anthropologists are pleased when their role as advocates or representatives is diminished, because these roles are called for only when native people are dominated by forces from globalization that are beyond their control.

Anthropologists at Work

John McCreery: Applying Anthropology in Japan

John McCreery.

This chapter has some examples of anthropologists who work outside the academic setting. John McCreery is an anthropologist who has lived in Japan since 1980 and has developed a productive and fruitful career in the area of advertising. For a number of years, he worked as a copywriter and creative director for Hakuhodo Incorporated, Japan's second largest advertising agency. In 1984, he and his wife and business partner, Ruth McCreery, founded The Word Works, a supplier of translation, copywriting, and presentation support services to Japanese and other clients with operations in Japan. While earning his living as vice president and managing director of The Word Works, he is also a lecturer in the Graduate Program in Comparative Culture at Sophia University in Tokyo. There he teaches seminars on "The Making and Meaning of Advertising" and "Marketing in Japan." When asked, "How did an anthropologist get into advertising?" he replies, "In Taiwan I studied magicians. In Japan I joined the guild."

As an undergraduate in the honors college at Michigan State University, McCreery studied philosophy and medieval history. In the summer after his junior year, a friend recommended that he take a course in East African Ethnography taught by anthropologist Marc Swartz. The course and the thought of doing research that involved travel to exotic places were fascinating. Another friend was studying Chinese, and noting that an anthropologist should have some experience with a non-Indo-European language, McCreery decided to study Chinese as well. One thing led to another, and he wound up in graduate school at Cornell University, doing a Ph.D. in anthropology and preparing to do research in Chinese anthropology. McCreery's first field research was in Puli, a market town in central Taiwan, where he and Ruth McCreery lived and worked from September 1969 to August 1971. He returned to Taiwan in 1976–1977, the summer of 1978, and again in 1983.

At Cornell University McCreery studied with Victor Turner. In Taiwan, McCreery focused his ethnographic study on religious traditions and worked with a Taoist master, Tio Se-lian. Both Victor Turner and Tio Se-lian were teachers with a willingness to listen, a flair for the dramatic, a passion for detail, and a breadth of humanity that moved all those with whom they came in contact. They, and senior creative director Kimoto Kazuhiko, who shared these earlier mentors' traits and gave McCreery his job at Hakuhodo, are the models he tries to emulate in his work.

McCreery's essays on Chinese religion and ritual have appeared in *The Journal of Chinese Religions* and *American Ethnologist*. He is also the author of a book on Japanese consumer behavior, *Japanese Consumer Behavior: From Worker Bees to Wary Shoppers* (2000), which follows the current trends in postindustrial Japan that have resulted in new consumption preferences and behaviors for the Japanese men, women, and young people. Currently, he is involved in assessing new trends in the use of the Internet in respect to the spread of global media changes in Japan as an anthropologist. McCreery and his wife, Ruth, who run their translating business in Japan, have completed a major comprehensive chapter evaluating the prehistory, language, history, and current cultural changes in Japan based on the most state-of-the-art anthropological research in a new textbook on the *Peoples and Cultures of Asia* (Scupin 2005). McCreery maintains his contact with other anthropologists through an Internet listserve, Anthro-list, which provides lively discussions on ethnographic and theoretical issues in the field. Anthropologists from many backgrounds participate on this listserve. As a student you may want to become involved in lurking or participating on this listserve yourself.

Medical Anthropology

Another subfield of anthropology, **medical anthropology**, represents the intersection of cultural anthropology with physical anthropology. Medical anthropologists may study disease, medicine, curing, and mental illness in a cross-cultural perspective. Some focus specifically on **epidemiology**, which examines the spread and distribution of diseases and how they are influenced by cultural patterns. For example, these anthropologists may be able to determine whether coronary (heart) disease or cancer is related to particular cultural or social dietary habits, such as the consumption of foods high in sodium or saturated fats. They also study cultural perceptions of illness and their treatment. These studies can often help health providers to design more effective means for delivering health care and formulating health care policies (Schell and Denham 2003).

An illustration of medical anthropology is the work of Louis Golomb (1985), who conducted ethnographic research on curing practices in Thailand. Golomb did research on Buddhist and Muslim medical practitioners who rely on native spiritualistic beliefs to diagnose and cure diseases. These practices are based on earlier Hindu, magical, and animistic beliefs that had been syncretized with Buddhist and Muslim traditions. Practitioners draw on astrology, faith healing, massage, folk psychotherapy, exorcism, herbs, and charms and amulets to treat patients. The most traditional practitioners are curer-magicians, or shamans, who diagnose and treat every illness as an instance of spirit possession or spirit attack. Other practitioners are more skeptical of the supernatural causation of illness and diagnose health problems in reference to natural or organic causes. They frequently use herbal medicines to treat illnesses.

Golomb discovered that although Western-based scientific forms of medicine may be available, many Thais still rely on traditional practitioners. He found that even urban-educated elite, including those who had studied in the United States and other Western countries, adhered to both supernatural and scientific views. Golomb referred to this as *therapeutic pluralism.* He observed that patients do not rely on any single therapeutic approach but rather use a combination of therapies that include elements of ritual, magic, and modern scientific medications. Parasites or germs are rarely seen as the only explanations of disease; a sick person may go to a clinic to receive medication to relieve symptoms but may then seek out a traditional curer for a more complete treatment. Golomb emphasized that the multiplicity of alternative therapies encourages people to play an active role in preserving their health.

Medical anthropology plays an important role in many societies.

In Thailand, as in many other countries undergoing modernization and globalization, modern medical facilities have been established based on the scientific treatment of disease. Golomb found that personnel in these facilities are critical of traditional medical practices. Nevertheless, he discovered that although the people in the villages often respect the modern doctor's ability to diagnose diseases and prescribe medications to relieve symptoms, in most cases they don't accept the scientific explanation of the disease. In addition, villagers feel that modern medical methods are brusque and impersonal, because doctors do not offer any psychological or spiritual consolation. Doctors also do not make house calls and rarely spend much time with patients. This impersonality in the doctor–patient relationship is also due to social status differences based on wealth, education, and power. Golomb found that many public health personnel expected deference from their rural clientele. For these reasons, many people preferred to rely on traditional curers.

Through his study of traditional medical techniques and beliefs, Golomb isolated some of the strengths and weaknesses of modern medical treatment in Thailand. His work contributed to a better understanding of how to deliver health care services to rural and urban Thais. For example, the Thai Ministry of Public Health began to experiment with ways of coordinating the efforts of modern and traditional medical practitioners. Village midwives and traditional herbalists were called on to dispense modern medications and pass out information about nutrition and hygiene. Some Thai hospitals have established training sessions for traditional practitioners to learn modern medical techniques. Golomb's studies in medical anthropology offer a model for practical applications in the health field for other developing societies. This type of ethnographic study that combines globalization approaches with in-depth local cultural knowledge is an example of ongoing anthropological attempts to assist in solving practical problems for humanity.

Interventions in Substance Abuse

Another area of research and policy formulation for applied medical anthropologists is substance abuse, many of the causes of which may be explained by social and cultural factors. For example, Michael Agar (1973, 1974) did an in-depth study of heroin addicts based on the addicts' description of U.S. society and its therapeutic agencies in particular. His research involved taking on the role of a patient himself so that he could participate in some of the problems that exist between patients and staff. From that perspective he was better able to understand the "junkie" worldview.

Through his research, Agar isolated problems in the treatment of heroin addiction. He found that when the drug methadone was administered by public health officials as a substitute for heroin, many heroin addicts not in treatment became addicted to methadone, which was sold on the streets by patients. This street methadone would often be combined with wine and pills to gain a "high." In some cases, street methadone began to rival heroin as the preferred drug, being less expensive than heroin, widely available, and in a form that could be taken orally rather than injected. By providing

Some medical anthropologists study drug abuse problems.

this information, Agar helped health officials monitor their programs more effectively.

In a more recent study, Philippe Bourgois spent three and a half years investigating the use of crack cocaine in Spanish Harlem in New York City. In his award-winning ethnography, *In Search of Respect: Selling Crack in El Barrio* (1996), Bourgois noted that policymakers and drug-enforcement officials minimize the influences of poverty and low status in dealing with crack addiction. Through his investigation of cultural norms and socioeconomic conditions in Spanish Harlem, Bourgois demonstrated that crack dealers are struggling to earn money and status in the pursuit of the American dream. Despite the fact that many crack dealers have work experience, they find that many of the potential jobs in construction and factory work are reserved for non-Hispanics. In addition, unpleasant experiences in the job world lead many to perceive crack dealing as the most realistic route toward upward mobility. Most of the inner-city youths who deal crack are high school dropouts who do not regard entry-level, minimum-wage jobs as steps to better opportunities. In addition, they perceive the underground economy as an alternative to becoming subservient to the larger society. Crack dealing offers a sense of autonomy, position, and rapid short-term mobility.

Bourgois compared the use of crack to the feelings that people have in millenarian movements or other spiritual movements. As he observed:

Substance abuse in general, and crack in particular, offer the equivalent of a millenarian metamorphosis. Instantaneously, users are transformed from being unemployed, depressed high school dropouts, despised by the world—and secretly convinced that their failure is due to their own inherent stupidity, "racial laziness," and disorganization—into being a mass of heart-palpitating pleasure, followed only minutes later by a jaw-gnashing crash and wide-awake alertness that provides their life with concrete purpose: get more crack—fast! (1989b, 11)

Bourgois's depictions of the culture and economy of crack dealers and users provided useful policy suggestions. He concluded that most accounts of crack addiction deflect attention away from the economic and social conditions of the inner city, and that by focusing on the increases of violence and terror associated with crack, U.S. society is absolved from responsibility for inner-city problems. He suggested that rather than use this "blame-the-victim" approach, officials and policymakers need to revise their attitudes and help develop programs that resolve the conditions that encourage crack use.

Anthropologists at Work

An International Business Anthropologist: Amber Chand

Amber Chand is a woman of South Asian descent whose family was forced to leave the country of Uganda and relocate in England in 1973. Idi Amin had come to power through a military coup in Uganda, and all people of Asian extraction were forced out of the country as an attempt to "Africanize" the economy. The South Asian community had to relocate within three months or be executed. When this occurred in 1973, Amber was on her way to graduate school at Cambridge University. However, her father lost all his assets and property, so Amber competed for full scholarships from various universities. The University of Michigan offered her a full scholarship and she earned a master's degree in anthropology. Although her father died during that period from a heart attack, her family background in the South Asian community had instilled her with a sense of self-reliance, entrepreneurship, and

Amber Chand.

a profound global perspective and sense of social and cultural responsibility that extended beyond her own community. Initially, she drew on her anthropological experience to run a museum gift shop. Amber learned about an opportunity to import some beautiful Rajasthani paintings from India. Her friend and brother-in-law helped her cofound a multinational business called Eziba, an artisan handicrafts retail company with the explicit mission of promoting markets for entrepreneurs and artists around the world. Amber's goal was to create balanced enterprise partnerships with as many business and artists as they could.

Eziba was fostered during the rise of Internet businesses and E-commerce that has been growing, sometimes with painful costs, especially with the downfall called the Dot.com bust in the early period of 2000. However, during the heady period of E-commerce and the Internet businesses, Amber was able to recruit top CEOs from businesses such as L.L. Bean, FAO Schwarz, and Sundance Catalogs to provide a senior executive team that endorsed her global and pragmatic business orientation. Although the Internet E-commerce business side has lagged like many others after the Dot.com bust, the catalog does the major share of business, and Eziba has produced some 2.2 million catalogs to market their global venture. Amber has also opened a store within a store inside Marshall Field's department retailer. Because it was an exciting Internet start-up company, Amber was able to raise $40 million in venture capital, and Eziba has extended into 70 countries around the world and has annual sales of $10 million dollars.

Eziba has a global team traveling worldwide who must have good historical and cultural anthropological expertise as well as a business background. Amber's anthropological educational background has provided her with the global focus and cross-cultural experience to promote products that will have an authentic connection with the local consumers. For example, Amber notes that if women in Kabul, Afghanistan, are producing certain items for the global market, Eziba must understand how these women will be treated and perceived by men, because their income may outstrip the men's. Eziba promotes balanced partnerships among the various business and artisans in local areas, and Amber's goal is to pay at least 25 percent of the retail price to the producer. Sometimes she must pay more while at the same time ensuring that the company will not be overextended.

One cultural-shock problem occurred for Eziba when local artisans in Gujarat India produced and sold hundreds of beautiful Christmas tree skirts for Europe and North America with the Swastika emblazoned on them, which was associated with the Nazi regime. The Swastika is a benign religious symbol in India (and from where the Nazi derived the symbol to identify with the so-called master Aryan race connected with the Sanskrit language and religion of Hinduism). Obviously, this is the type of cross-cultural problem that can arise in a multinational business. Amber's background in anthropological training helps the company avoid these multicultural-shock problems whenever possible.

Recently, Amber went to Rwanda in Central Africa nine years after one of the worst cases of genocide and massacres in the twentieth century (see Chapter 14). She saw Hutu and Tutsi women, widows who had been traumatized by the barbarities of the genocide, weaving and producing peace baskets that have engendered some $350,000 in global trade. These peace baskets are the most significant nonagricultural export from Rwanda today. Thus, Amber and the company Eziba are not only promoting profits for their company, but also enhancing economic opportunities for people in many local regions of the world and stimulating improvements in economic and social conditions, health care, and other areas of life for many.

Based on her family and anthropological background, Amber tries to transform the language within her company away from archaic patriarchal, militaristic, and mechanistic terms. For example, instead of using the term company, she refers to Eziba as a "community." Amber found that that change in language produced a new relationship between herself and the business. She emphasizes that Eziba is not a charity and does not want Western consumers to buy the products and artwork based on their guilt expressed toward underdeveloped countries. However, Amber Chand represents an illustrative case of how anthropological knowledge can be put to use in highly practical ways in business in our rapidly changing global economy.

Applied Archaeology

One of the problems that humanity faces is how to safeguard the cultural heritage preserved in the archaeological record. Although archaeology may address questions of general interest to all of humanity, it is also important in promoting national heritage, cultural identity, and ethnic pride. Museums the world over offer displays documenting a diversity of local populations, regional histories, important events, and cultural traditions. The specialized museums focusing on particular peoples, regions, or historic periods have become increasingly important. Archaeologists must be concerned with the preservation of archaeological sites and the recovery of information from sites threatened with destruction, as well as the interpretation and presentation of their findings to the more general public.

Preservation of the past is a challenge to archaeologists, government officials, and the concerned public alike, as archaeological sites are being destroyed at an alarming rate. Archaeological materials naturally decay in the ground and sites are constantly destroyed through geological processes, erosion, and animal burrowing. Yet while natural processes contribute to the disappearance of archaeological sites, by far the greatest threat to the archaeological record is human activity. Construction projects such as dams, roads, buildings, and pipelines all disturb the ground and can destroy archaeological sites in the process. In many instances, archaeologists work only a few feet ahead of construction equipment, trying to salvage any information they can before a site disappears forever.

Some archaeological sites are intentionally destroyed by collectors searching for artifacts that have value in the antiquities market, such as arrowheads and pottery. Statues from ancient Egypt, Mayan terra cotta figurines, and Native American pottery may be worth thousands of dollars on the antiques market. To fulfill the demands, archaeological sites in many world areas are looted by pothunters, who dig to retrieve artifacts for collectors, ignoring the traces of ancient housing, burials, and cooking hearths. Removed from their context, with no record of where they came from, such artifacts are of limited value to archaeologists. The rate of destruction of North American archaeological sites is such that some researchers have estimated that 98 percent of sites predating the year 2000 will be destroyed by the middle of the twenty-first century (Herscher 1989; Knudson 1989).

The rate at which archaeological sites are being destroyed is particularly distressing because the archaeological record is an irreplaceable, nonrenewable

Table 17.1	Major Federal Legislation for the Protection of Archaeological Resources in The United States
Antiquities Act of 1906	Protects sites on federal lands
Historic Sites Act of 1935	Provides authority for designating National Historic Landmarks and for archaeological survey before destruction by development programs
National Historic Preservation Act of 1966 (amended 1976 and 1980)	Strengthens protection of sites via National Register and integrates state and local agencies into national program for site preservation
National Environmental Policy Act of 1969	Requires all federal agencies to specify impact of development programs on cultural resources
Archaeological Resources Protection Act of 1979	Provides criminal and civil penalties for looting or damaging sites on public and Native American lands
Convention on Cultural Property of 1982	Authorizes U.S. participation in 1970 UNESCO convention to prevent illegal international trade in cultural property
Cultural Property Act of 1983	Provides sanctions against U.S. import or export of illicit antiquities

Source: From *Discovering Our Past: A Brief Introduction to Archaeology* by Wendy Ashmore and Robert J. Sharer. Copyright © 1988 by Mayfield Publishing Company. Reprinted by permission of the publisher.

resource. That is, after sites are destroyed, they are gone forever, along with the unique information about the past that they contained. In many parts of the world, recognition of this fact has led to legislation aimed at protecting archaeological sites (Table 17.1). The rational for this legislation is that the past has value to the present and, hence, should be protected and interpreted for the benefit of the public.

Preserving the Past

Recognition of the value and nonrenewable nature of archaeological resources is the first step in a planning process. Archaeological resources can then be systematically identified and evaluated. Steps can be taken to preserve them by limiting development or designing projects in a way that will preserve the resource. For example, the projected path of a new road might be moved to avoid an archaeological site, or a building might be planned so that the foundations do not extend into a historic burial ground (see the photos of the African burial ground). Alternatively, if a site must be destroyed, effective planning can ensure that information about the site is recovered by archaeologists prior to its destruction.

One of the most spectacular examples of salvage archaeology arose as a result of the construction of a dam across the Nile River at Aswan, Egypt, in the 1960s. The project offered many benefits, including water for irrigation and the generation of electricity. However, the rising water behind the dam threatened thousands of archaeological sites that had lain undisturbed and safely buried by desert sand for thousands of years. The Egyptian government appealed to the international community and archaeologists from around the world to mount projects to locate and excavate the threatened sites.

Among the sites that were to be flooded by the dam was the temple of Pharaoh Rameses II at Abu Simbel, a huge monument consisting of four colossal figures carved from a cliff face on the banks of the Nile River. With help from the United Nations Educational, Scientific, and Cultural Organization (UNESCO), the Egyptian government was able to cut the monument into more than a thousand pieces, some weighing as much as 33 tons, and reassemble them above the floodwaters. Today the temple of Rameses can be seen completely restored only a few hundred feet from its original location. Numerous other archaeological sites threatened by the flooding of the Nile were partly salvaged or recorded. Unfortunately, countless other sites could not be located or even recorded before they were flooded.

The first legislation in the United States designed to protect historic sites was the Antiquities Act of 1906, which safeguarded archaeological sites on federal lands (see Table 17.1). Other, more recent legislation, such as the National Historic Preservation Act passed in 1966, has extended protection to sites threatened by projects that are funded or regulated by the government. The Federal Abandoned Shipwreck Act of 1988 gives states jurisdiction over shipwreck sights. This legislation has had a dramatic impact on the number of archaeologists in the United States and has created a new area of specialization, generally referred to as **cultural resource management** (CRM). Whereas most archaeologists had traditionally found employment teaching or working in museums, many are now working as applied archaeologists, evaluating, salvaging, and protecting archaeological resources that are threatened with destruction. Applied archaeologists conduct surveys before construction begins to determine if any sites will be affected. Government agencies such as the Forest Service have developed comprehensive programs to discover, record, protect, and interpret archaeological resources on their lands (Johnson and Schene 1987).

The restoration of Abu Simbel in Egypt. Preserving artifacts from past civilizations will present a major challenge for anthropologists in the coming decades.

Unfortunately, current legislation in the United States leaves many archaeological resources unprotected. In many countries, excavated artifacts, even those located on privately owned land, become the property of the government. This is not the case in the United States. One example of the limitations of the existing legislation is provided by the case of Slack Farm, located near Uniontown, Kentucky (Arden 1989). Archaeologists had long known that an undisturbed Native American site of the Late Mississippian period was located on the property. Dating roughly between 1450 and 1650, the site was particularly important because it was the only surviving Mississippian site from the period of first contact with Europeans. The Slack family, who had owned the land for many years, protected the site and prevented people from digging (Arden 1989). When the property was sold in 1988, however, conditions changed. Anthropologist Brian Fagan described the results:

> Ten pot hunters from Kentucky, Indiana, and Illinois paid the new owner of the land $10,000 for the right to "excavate" the site. They rented a tractor and began bulldozing their way through the village midden to reach graves. They pushed heaps of bones aside and dug through dwellings and potsherds, hearths, and stone tools associated with them. Along the way, they left detritus of their own—empty pop-top beer and soda cans—scattered on the ground alongside Late Mississippian pottery fragments. Today Slack Farm looks like a battlefield—a morass of crude shovel holes and gaping trenches. Broken human bones litter the ground, and fractured artifacts crunch underfoot. (1989, 15)

The looting at the site was eventually stopped by the Kentucky State Police, using a state law that prohibits the desecration of human graves. Archaeologists went to the site attempting to salvage what information was left, but there is no way of knowing how many artifacts were removed. The record of America's prehistoric past was irrevocably damaged.

Regrettably, the events at Slack Farm are not unique. Many states lack adequate legislation protecting archaeological sites on private land. For example, Arkansas had no laws protecting unmarked burial sites until 1991. As a result, Native American burial grounds were systematically mined for artifacts. In fact, one article written about the problem was titled "The Looting of Arkansas" (Harrington

1991). Although Arkansas now has legislation prohibiting the unauthorized excavation of burial grounds, the professional archaeologists of the Arkansas Archaeological Survey face the impossible job of trying to locate and monitor all of the state's archaeological sites. This problem is not unique. Even on federal lands, the protection of sites is dependent on a relatively small number of park rangers and personnel to police large areas. Even in national parks such as Mesa Verde or Yellowstone, archaeological sites are sometimes vandalized or looted for artifacts. Much of the success that there has been in protecting sites is largely due to the active involvement of amateur archaeologists and concerned citizens who bring archaeological remains to the attention of professionals.

The preservation of the past needs to be everyone's concern. Unfortunately, however well intended the legislation and efforts to provide protection for archaeological sites may be, they are rarely integrated into comprehensive management plans. For example, a particular county or city area might have a variety of sites and resources of historic significance identified using a variety of different criteria and presented in different lists and directories. These might include National Historic sites, designated though the National Historic Preservation office; state files of archaeological sites; data held by avocational archaeological organizations and clubs; and a variety of locations of historical importance identified by county or city historical societies. Other sites of potential historical significance might be identified though documentary research or oral traditions. Ideally all these sources of information should be integrated and used to plan development. Such comprehensive approaches to cultural resource management plans are rare rather than the norm.

Important strides have been taken in planning and coordinating efforts to identify and manage archaeological resources. Government agencies, including the National Park Service, the military, and various state agencies, have initiated plans to systematically identify and report sites on their properties. There have also been notable efforts to compile information at the county, state, and district levels. Such efforts are faced with imposing logistical concerns. For example, by the mid-1990s, more than 180,000 historic and prehistoric archaeological sites had been identified in the American southeast (including the states of Alabama, Arkansas, Florida, Georgia, Kentucky, Louisiana, Mississippi, North Carolina, South Carolina, and Tennessee). In addition, an estimated 10,000 new sites are discovered each year (Anderson and Horak 1995). A map of these resources reveals a great deal of variation in their concentration. On one hand, this diversity reflects the actual distribution of sites; on the other, it reflects the areas where archaeological research has and has not been undertaken. Incorporating the thousands of new site reports into the database requires substantial commitment of staff resources. What information should be recorded for each site? What computer resources are needed? The volume of information is difficult to process with available staff, and massive backlogs of reports waiting to be incorporated into the files often exist.

A number of archaeologists throughout the world are combining their skills to both preserve sites and the environment where those sites are located. For example, archaeologist Anabel Ford directs an important archaeological program in El Pilar, in Belize and Guatemala, where she not only does archaeological research on the Maya civilization found there, but also does extensive studies to help conserve the forest environment and the archaeological sites in the Maya forest (2004). The El Pilar site is one of the largest classical Maya civilization sites in Belize and among the major sites of Guatemala, containing 25 large plazas with pyramids, palace structures, ball courts, and significantly a causeway linking the ancient monuments across a modern political boundary. Traditionally, the El Pilar Maya had connections with the large center of Tikal, the Maya city in the heart of the Maya forest of Guatemala. Like many other archaeological sites, the El Pilar site had been looted in the years prior to the establishment of the El Pilar Archaeological Reserve for Maya Flora and Fauna. Anabel Ford rediscovered the ancient center in 1983. Since that time, El Pilar has received attention and was listed as one of the most endangered archaeological sites in the world in 1996. Straddling the Belize and Guatemalan border, El Pilar is also the site of one of the richest forest areas of biodiversity in the world and was declared a protected area in both Belize and Guatemala in 1998.

Anabel Ford recruits undergraduate and graduate students from all over the world to work with the team in archaeological field research and assist in recording data in the tropical forest that will heighten the awareness of local officials, tourism directors, and others in the region to improve conservation methods and techniques to help conserve not only the archaeological sites, but also the surrounding environment. Presently, Anabel Ford promotes the El Pilar Archaeological Reserve and her El Pilar Program is involved in creating an on-site museum to enhance this important area of cultural tourism and natural wildlife area. This preservation of the archaeological site along with the conservation of the biodiversity in the various regional environments is one of the most important areas of applied archaeology and seen as "Action Archaeology" by Anabel Ford.

Another important series of archaeological projects in the Amazon area in South America has been studying the impact of early humans on the environment that affects the plants and animals in the region as well as learning about the archaeology of the region. Archaeologists such as Thomas Neumann, Anna C. Roosevelt, Clark Erickson, and Peter Stahl and anthropological botanists such as Charles R. Clement are discovering that the early humans in this region not only had very large settlements, overturning earlier archaeological assessments that the Amazon did not support large civilizations, but are also contributing new methods and techniques that may help conserve this fragile environment (2002). The early large-scale civilizations had extensive agricultural developments that were neglected and crippled as globalization since the time of Spanish colonialism has influenced the region.

These archaeologists in the Amazon are working with soil geographers and other environmental scientists to study how the early civilizations in the region influenced the microorganisms and soil conditions that may result in more knowledge about how to restore the conditions that can sustain more productive and less costly use of the land in the future. Thus, applied archaeology can provide new knowledge that will enhance the conservation and preservation of different environments throughout the world. A broad holistic perspective involving teams of archaeologists and other scientists are needed to ensure effective site management and the compliance of developers with laws protecting archaeological sites. It also provides a holistic view of past land use that is of great use to archaeologists.

Applied Anthropology and Human Rights

Cultural Relativism and Human Rights

A recent development that has had wide-ranging consequences for applied anthropology and ethnographic research involves the ways in which anthropologists assess and respond to the values and norms of other societies. Recall our discussion of *cultural relativism*, the method used by anthropologists to understand another society through their own cultural values, beliefs, norms, and behaviors. In order to understand another society's culture and practices, the anthropologist must strive to temporarily suspend their judgment of the indigenous culture (Maybury-Lewis 2001). This difficult procedure will help the anthropologist gain insights into other cultures. Some critics have charged that anthropologists (and other people) who adopt this position cannot (or will not) make value judgments concerning values, norms, and practices of any society. If this is the case, then how can anthropol-

ogists encourage any conception of human rights that would be valid for all of humanity? Must anthropologists accept such practices as infanticide, caste and class inequalities, and female subordination out of fear of forcing their own values on other people?

Relativism Reconsidered   These criticisms have led some anthropologists to reevaluate the basic assumptions regarding cultural relativism. In his 1983 book *Culture and Morality: The Relativity of Values in Anthropology*, Elvin Hatch recounted the historical acceptance of the cultural-relativist view. As we saw in Chapter 3, this was the approach of Franz Boas, who challenged the unilineal-evolutionary models of nineteenth-century anthropologists like E. B. Tylor, with their underlying assumptions of Western cultural superiority. Boas's approach, with its emphasis on tolerance and equality, appealed to many liberal-minded Western scholars. For example, the earlier nineteenth-century ethnocentric and racist assumptions held within anthropology were used to display other people at the World's Fair in St. Louis in 1904 as barbaric, uncivilized, and savage people to the "civilized" citizens who viewed these people. For example, "pygmies" from Central Africa were given machetes to show how they "beheaded" one another in their local regions and the Igorot tribal people of the Philippines were given a dog to cook and eat daily in front of the "civilized"

Photo from the 1904 World's Fair in St. Louis showing "pygmies" beheading one another. This was never an aspect of "pygmy" culture.

citizens of the United States in order to portray them as inferior races and cultures (Brietbart 1997). Such displays of these people during that period both distorted their cultural practices and treated them in an inhumane and unethical manner by *anthropologists* of the time period, and it resulted in harmful practices toward these native peoples in different regions. Thus, the criticisms of these nineteenth-century racist and ethnocentric views and the endorsement of cultural relativism was an important human rights innovation by twentieth-century anthropologists.

However, belief in cultural relativism led to the acceptance by some early twentieth-century anthropologists of **ethical relativism**, the notion that we cannot impose the values of one society on other societies. Ethical relativists argued that because anthropologists had not discovered any universal moral values, each society's values were valid with respect to that society's circumstances and conditions. No society could claim any superior position over another regarding ethics and morality.

As many philosophers and anthropologists have noted, the argument of ethical relativism is a circular one that itself assumes a particular moral position. It is in fact a moral theory that encourages people to be tolerant toward all cultural values, norms, and practices. Hatch notes that in the history of anthropology, many who accepted the premises of ethical relativism could not maintain these assumptions in light of their data. Ethical relativists would have to tolerate practices such as homicide, child abuse, human sacrifice, torture, warfare, racial discrimination, and even genocide. In fact, even anthropologists who held the ethical-relativist position in the early period of the twentieth century condemned many cultural practices. For example, Ruth Benedict condemned the practice of the Plains Indians, who cut off the nose of an adulterous wife. Boas himself condemned racism, anti-Semitism, and other forms of bigotry. Thus, these anthropologists did not consistently adhere to the ethical-relativist paradigm.

The horrors associated with World War II eventually led most scholars to reject ethical relativism. The argument that Nazi Germany could not be condemned because of its unique moral and ethical standards appeared ludicrous to most people. In the 1950s, some anthropologists such as Robert Redfield suggested that general standards of judgment could be applied to most societies. However, these anthropologists were reluctant to impose Western standards on prestate indigenous societies. In essence, they suggested a *double standard* in which they could criticize large-scale, industrial state societies but not prestate indigenous societies.

This double standard of morality poses problems, however. Can anthropologists make value judgments about homicide, child abuse, warfare, torture, rape, and other acts of violence in a small-scale society? Why should they adopt different standards in evaluating such behaviors in prestate indigenous societies as compared with industrial societies? In both types of societies, human beings are harmed. Don't humans in all societies have equal value?

A Resolution to the Problem of Relativism   Is there a resolution to these philosophical and moral dilemmas? First, we need to distinguish between *cultural relativism* and *ethical relativism*. In other words, to understand the values, the reasoning and logic, and worldviews of another people does not mean to accept all of their practices and standards (Salmon 1997). Second, we need to realize that the culture of a society is not completely homogeneous or unified. In Chapter 3, we noted how culture was distributed differentially within any society. People do not all share the same culture within any society. For example, men and women do not share the same "culture" in a society. Ethnographic experience tells anthropologists that there are always people who may not agree with the content of the moral and ethical values of a society. Treating cultures as "uniform united wholes" is a conceptual mistake. For one thing, it ignores the *power relationships* within a society. Elites within society can maintain cultural hegemony and use harmful practices against their own members to produce conformity. In some cases, governments use the concept of relativism to justify their repressive policies and deflect criticism of these practices by the international community. In Asia, many political leaders argue that their specific culture does not correspond to the same notion of human rights as accepted in Western society. Therefore in China or Singapore, human rights may be restricted by political rulers who draw on their cultural tradition to invoke repressive and totalitarian political policies. Those who impose these harmful practices upon others may be the beneficiaries of those practices.

To get beyond the problem of ethical relativism, we ought to adopt a humanitarian standard that would be recognized by all people throughout the world. This standard would not be derived from any particular cultural values—such as the U.S. Declaration of Independence—but rather would involve the basic principle that every individual is entitled to a certain standard of "well-being." For example, no individual ought to be subjected to bodily harm through violence or starvation.

Of course, we recognize certain problems with this solution. Perhaps the key problem is that people in many societies accept—or at least appear to accept—behaviors that we would condemn as inhumane. For example, what about the Aztec practice of human sacrifice? The Aztecs firmly believed that they would be destroyed if they did not sacrifice victims to the sun deity. Would an outside group have been justified in condemning and abolishing this practice? A more recent case involves the West Irian tribe known as the Dani, who engaged in constant warfare with neighboring tribes. They believed that through revenge they had to placate the ghosts of their deceased kin killed in warfare, because unavenged ghosts bring sickness and disaster to the tribe. Another way of placating the ghosts was to bring two or three young girls related to the deceased victim to the funeral site and chop two fingers off their hands. Until recently, all Dani women lost from two to six fingers in this way (Heider 1979; Bagish 1981). Apparently these practices were accepted by many Dani males and females.

In some Islamic countries women have been accused of sexual misconduct and then executed by male members in what are called "honor killings." The practice of honor killings, which victimizes women, has been defended in some of these societies as a means to restore harmony to the society. The males argue that the shedding of blood washes away the shame of sexual dishonor. There have been a number of cases of "honor killings" among immigrant Middle Eastern families within the United States. In both Africa and the Middle East young girls are subjected to female circumcision, a polite term for the removal of the clitoris and other areas of vagina. Most human rights advocates refer to these practices as female genital mutilation/cutting (FGM

or FGC) ranging from the cutting out the clitoris to a more severe practice known as Pharoanic infibulation, which involves stitching the cut labia to cover the vagina of the woman. One of the purposes of these procedures is to reduce the pleasure related to sexual intercourse and thereby induce more fidelity from women in marriage. Chronic infections are a common result of this practice. Sexual intercourse is painful and childbirth is much more difficult for many of these women. However, the cultural ideology may maintain that an uncircumcised woman is not respectable, and few families want to risk their daughter's chances of marriage availability by not having her circumcised (Fluehr-Lobban 2003). The right of males to discipline, hit, or beat one's wife is often maintained in a male-dominated culture (Tapper 1992–1993). Other examples of these types of practices, such as headhunting, slavery, female subordination, torture, and unnecessarily dangerous child labor, also fall into this category. According to a universal humanitarian standard suggested here, all these practices could be condemned as harmful behaviors.

The Problem of Intervention

The condemnation of harmful cultural practices with reference to a universal standard is fairly easy. The abolition of such practices, however, is not. Anthropologists recommend that one should take a pragmatic approach in reducing these practices. Sometimes intervention in the cultures in which practices such as genocide are occurring would be a moral imperative. This intervention would not proceed from the standpoint of specific Western values but from the commonly recognized universal standards of humanitarianism.

Such intervention, however, must proceed cautiously and be based on a thorough knowledge of the society. Ethnographers must study the history, local conditions, social life, and various institutions to assess carefully with their empirical knowledge whether the cultural practice is shown to clearly create pain and suffering for people. For example, in Thailand, the area of ethnographic research for the author of this textbook, many young women are incorporated into the prostitution and sex tourist industry to help sustain their livelihood and increase their parent's income (Bales 1999; Barmé

2002). This prostitution and sex tourist industry must be thoroughly understood within the historical, economic, and cultural context of Thai society prior to endorsing the human rights intervention that should be invoked to abolish these practices. When these elements are present, intervention should take place in the form of a dialogue rather than preaching human rights in a monolithic manner to various people in the community. In a recent ethnographic study of the attempt to abolish female genital mutilation in the Darfur region of the Sudan, anthropologist Ellen Gruenbaum focused on seven different communities to investigate how the UN agencies, the NGOs (nongovernment organizations), and other human rights workers are influencing these practices (2004). Gruenbaum found that at times women were participating in the FGM practices such as the Pharoanic infibulation as a "perceived" means of protection against rape and illicit premarital intercourse within their communities. Rape is often used in these communities as a means of warfare. Thus, the historical and cultural context of these practices need to be investigated cautiously by anthropologists prior to advocating a rapid enforcement of human rights that may result in outright rejection of the dedicated human rights workers (Shweder 2003).

As is obvious, these suggestions are based on the highly idealistic standards of a universal humanitarianism. In many cases, intervention may not be possible, and in some cases, intervention to stamp out a particular cultural practice may cause even greater problems. In Chapters 9, 10, and 11 we saw how outside global intervention adversely affected such peoples as the Ju/'hoansi, the Mbuti, the Yanomamö and the Native Hawaiians. Communal riots, group violence, or social chaos may result from the dislocation of certain cultural practices. Thus caution, understanding, and dialogue are critical to successful intervention. We need to be sensitive to cultural differences but not allow them to produce severe harm to individuals within a society.

Universal Human Rights

Nevertheless, the espousal of universally recognized standards to eradicate harmful practices is a worthwhile, albeit, idealistic, goal. Since the time of

the Enlightenment, Western societies have prided themselves on extending human rights. Many Western theorists emphasize that human rights have spread to other parts of the world through globalization, thus providing the catalyst for social change, reform, and political liberation. At the same time, as people from other non-Western societies can testify, the West has also promoted intolerance, racism, and genocide. Western society has not always lived up to the ideals of its own tradition.

The Role of Applied Anthropology

Cultural anthropologists and applied anthropologists have a role in helping to define the universal standards for human rights in all societies. By systematically studying community standards, applied anthropologists can determine whether practices are harmful and then help provide solutions for reducing these harmful practices. This may involve consultation with local government officials and dialogue with members of the community to resolve the complex issues regarding the identified harmful

Applied anthropologists use their research to help develop human rights for women in India and in other areas of the world.

practices. The exchange of ideas across cultures through anthropological research is beginning to foster acceptance of the universal nature of some human rights regardless of cultural differences.

An illustration of this type of research and effort by applied anthropologists is the work of John Van Willigen and V. C. Channa (1991), who have done research on the harmful consequences of the dowry in India. As discussed in Chapter 15, India, like some other primarily agricultural societies, has the cultural institution known as the *dowry*, in which the bride's family gives a certain amount of cash or other goods to the groom's family upon marriage. Recently, the traditions of the dowry have led to increasing cases of what has been referred to as "dowry death" or "bride burning." Some husbands or their families have been dissatisfied with the amount of the dowry that the new wife brings into the family. Following marriage, the family of the groom begins to make additional demands for more money and goods from the wife's family. These demands result in harassment and abuse of the wife, culminating in murder. The woman is typically burned to death after being doused with kerosene, hence the use of the term *bride burning.*

Dowry deaths have increased in recent years. In 1986, 1,319 cases were reported nationally in India. There are many other cases in which the evidence is more ambiguous, however, and the deaths of these women might be reported as kitchen accidents or suicides (Van Willigen and Channa 1991). In addition, another negative result of the burdens imposed by the dowry tradition has led many pregnant women to pay for amniocentesis (a medical procedure to determine the health status of the fetus) as a means to determine the sex of the fetus. If the fetus is female, in many cases Indians have an abortion partly because of the increasing burden and expense of raising a daughter and developing a substantial dowry for marriage of the daughter. Thus, male children are preferred and female fetuses are selectively aborted.

Van Willigen, an American anthropologist, and Channa, an Indian anthropologist, studied the dowry problem together. They found that the national laws established against the institution of the dowry (the Dowry Prohibition Act of 1961, amended in 1984 and 1986) are very tough. The law makes it illegal to give or take a dowry, but the laws are ineffective in restraining the practice. In addition, a number of public-education groups have been organized in India. Using slogans such as "Say No to Dowry," they have been advertising and campaigning against the dowry practices. Yet, the problem continues to plague India.

After carefully studying the dowry practices of different regions and local areas of India, Van Willigen and Channa concluded that the increase in dowry deaths was partially the result of the rapid inflationary pressures of the Indian economy as well as the demands of a consumer-oriented economy. Consumer price increases have resulted in the increasing demands for more dowry money to buy consumer goods. It has become increasingly difficult to save resources for a substantial dowry for a daughter or sister that is satisfactory to the groom's family. Van Willigen and Channa found that aside from wealth, family "prestige" that comes with wealth expenditures is sought by the groom's family.

From the perspective of the bride's family, dowry payments provide for present consumption and future earning power for their daughter through acquiring a husband with better connections and future earning potential. In a less-developed society such as India, with extremely high unemployment and rapid inflation, the importance of investing in a husband with high future earning potential is emphasized. When asked why they give a dowry when their daughters are being married, people respond, "because we love them." The decision by the groom's family to forgo the dowry would also be very difficult.

There appears to be a very positive commitment to the institution of the dowry in India. Most people have given and received a dowry. Thus, declaring dowry a crime technically makes many people criminals. Van Willigen and Channa recommended that to be effective, the antidowry practices must be displaced by other, less problematic practices, and that the apparent causes of the practice be attacked. Women's property rights must be examined so as to increase their economic access. Traditional Hindu cultural norms regarding inheritance, which give sons the right from birth to claim the so-called ancestral properties, must be reformed. At present, male descendants inherit property, but females must pay for marriage expenses and dowry gifts. Van Willigen and Channa assert that a gender-neutral inheritance law in which women and men receive equal shares ought to be established to help reduce the discrepancy between males and females in India.

In addition, Van Willigen and Channa recommended the establishment of universal marriage registration and licenses throughout India. This may enable the government to monitor dowry abuses so that antidowry legislation could be more effective. These anthropologists conclude that a broad program to increase the social and economic status of women, along with more rigorous control of marriage registration and licensing, will be more effective in solving the dowry death problem in Indian society.

Anthropology, Human Rights, and Warfare

Another problem in relying on anthropological research for political and military policies that may endanger human rights has frequently occurred within the context of global warfare. In the early part of the twentieth century during World War I, various anthropologists served as spies and agents in different areas of the world. Later, during World War II, anthropologists were employed by the OSS (Office of Strategic Services) and encouraged to provide information regarding the German Nazi and Italian Facist regimes. During the Vietnam War a number of anthropologists were charged with actively spying and providing information on rural villages in Thailand and other Southeast Asian countries (Wakin 1992). More recently, the U.S. military, during the war on global terrorism conducted since the tragedy of 9/11, relied on antiquated ethnographic studies of Arab and Islamic societies that were based on stereotypes and perspectives on culture that have long been abandoned by current anthropologists to train their troops in the Middle East (Rudmin 2004; Starrett 2004). These older studies may have exacerbated problems that occurred in the prisons such as Abu Ghraib in Iraq and Guantanamo, Cuba, among Arabs and Muslims who were confined by the U.S. military. Thus, currently anthropologists must use their local knowledge and articulate their criticisms of antiquated ethnographic studies that may be used by their government and military and that result in harmful practices or subsequently result in more terrorism and violence, such as 9/11. This is an extremely difficult problem for many anthropologists as they conduct ethnographic research because they are at times perceived by politicians and military leaders as "ivory tower intellectuals" who do not understand military tactics and global political strategies. However, anthropologists must use their connections with the public and political officials to provide appropriate, humane, and sensitive consulting based on thorough global and local cultural knowledge to their governments and military policies to help sustain and enhance human rights and less violence, harm, and terror in the world (Scupin 2002).

One recent example of the development of consultation and advice given by anthropologists in assessing warfare issues is illustrated in the recent warfare in the Darfur region of the country of Sudan in East Africa. Anthropologist and ethicist Carolyn Fluehr-Lobban has conducted extensive ethnographic research in the Sudan for many years. This region has been wracked by an ongoing twenty-year struggle between the Islamic government based in the northern region versus the southern region. As Fluehr-Lobban indicates, most of the journalists and media outlets reporting on this war describe the war as the Arabs in the north versus the black Africans in the south (2004b). However, based on Fluehr-Lobban's extensive research in the Sudan, she notes that the Sudanese population is much more varied than what is reported by the media. The so-called Arab or Afro-Arab population of the north who dominate the country through rule consists of a variety of peoples from Southwest Asia and Europe, as well as Arab speakers. At times the word Arabic is used to identify elements of "extremism" or "terrorism" and is a simplistic portrait of people who are shaped by many different political, ethnic, and religious aspects of their identity. As a means of assessing the warfare and gaining a more accurate description of the various peoples in the region, Fluehr-Lobban, Sondra Hale, and other anthropologists have formed a Sudan Studies Association and Darfur Task Force to help provide information to the media and governments on the ethnic, religious, and political complexity of these participants in this war in the Sudan.

Anthropologists at Work

Clyde Snow: Forensic Anthropologist

Clyde Collins Snow obtained a master's degree in zoology from Texas Tech University and planned to pursue a Ph.D. in physiology, but his career plans were interrupted by military service. While stationed at Lackland Air Force Base near San Antonio, he was introduced to the field of archaeology and became fascinated with the ancient artifacts discovered in the surrounding area.

After leaving the military, Snow attended the University of Arizona, where his zoological training and archaeology interests led him to a Ph.D. in physical anthropology. He became skilled at identifying old bones and artifacts. With his doctoral degree completed, he joined the Federal Aviation Administration as a consulting forensic anthropologist, providing technical assistance in the identification of victims of aircraft accidents. Snow also lent his expertise to the design of safety equipment to prevent injuries in aircraft accidents.

As word of Snow's extraordinary skill in forensic anthropology spread, he was called to consult on and provide expert testimony in many criminal cases. His testimony was crucial at the sensational murder trial of John Wayne Gacy, accused of murdering more than thirty teenagers in the Chicago area. Snow also collaborated with experts in the reinvestigation of President John F. Kennedy's assassination. These experts built a full-scale model of Kennedy's head to determine whether Lee Harvey Oswald could have inflicted all of Kennedy's wounds. They did not uncover any scientific evidence to contradict the Warren Commission's conclusion that Oswald was the sole assassin.

Dr. Clyde Snow.

More recently, Snow and his team have been recognized for their contributions to human rights issues. Snow served as a consultant to the Argentine government's National Commission on Disappeared Persons in its efforts to determine the fate of thousands of Argentineans who were abducted and murdered by military death squads between 1976 and 1983, when the country was under the rule of a military dictatorship. As a result of his investigations, Snow was asked to testify as an expert witness in the trial of the nine junta members who ruled Argentina during the period of military repression. He also assisted people in locating their dead relatives.

Snow stresses that in his human rights investigative work he is functioning as an expert, not necessarily as an advocate. He must maintain an objective standpoint in interpreting his findings. The evidence he finds may then be presented by lawyers (as advocates) in the interests of justice. Snow's and other forensic anthropological human rights work is supported by various agencies, such as the American Association of Advanced Sciences, the Ford Foundation, the J. Roderick MacArthur Foundation, Amnesty International, Physicians for Human Rights, and Human Rights Watch (Mann and Holland 2004).

The example of applied anthropology, based on the collaboration between Western and non-Western anthropologists, government and military officials, economic consultants and advisors, and local and national government leaders to help solve a fundamental human rights issues, represents a commendable strategy for applied anthropologists in the future. It is hoped that through better cross-cultural understanding, aided by ethnographic research, and through applied anthropology, universally recognized and humanitarian standards will become widely adopted throughout the world. Many anthropologists are promoting advocacy anthropology, the use of anthropological knowledge to further human rights. Universal human rights would include the right to life and freedom from physical and psychological abuse, including torture; freedom from arbitrary arrest and imprisonment; freedom from slavery and genocide; the right to nationality; freedom of movement and departure from one's country; the right to seek asylum in other countries because of persecution in one's own country; rights to privacy, ownership of property, freedom of speech, religion, and assembly; the rights of self-determination; and the right to

adequate food, shelter, health care, and education (Sponsel 1996). Obviously, not all these rights exist in any society at present. However, most people will probably agree that these rights ought to be part of any society's obligations to its people.

As people everywhere are brought closer together with the expansion of the global village, different societies will experience greater pressures to treat one another in sensitive and humane ways. We live in a world in which our destinies are tied to one another more closely than they have ever been. Yet it is a world containing many different societies with varied norms and practices. Sometimes this leads to mutual distrust and dangerous confrontations, such as the 9/11/01 tragedy in the United States.

Anthropologists may be able to play a role in helping to bring about mutual understanding of another's right to existence. Perhaps through this understanding we may be able to develop a worldwide, pluralistic **metaculture**, a global system emphasizing fundamental human rights, with a sense of political and global responsibility. This cross-cultural understanding and mutual respect for human rights may be the most important aspect of anthropological research today.

SUMMARY

Applied anthropology is one of the specializations that has offered new opportunities for physical anthropologists, archaeologists, and ethnologists to serve as consultants to public and private agencies to help solve local and global human problems. Applied anthropologists cooperate with government officials and others in establishing economic development projects, health care systems, and substance-abuse programs. They serve in a variety of roles to help bring about solutions to human problems.

A recent development within the field of archaeology is cultural resource management, or applied archaeology. Legislation passed by state and federal authorities in the United States requires the preservation of both prehistoric and historic materials. Applied archaeologists are involved in identifying important sites that may be endangered by development. They conduct surveys and excavations to preserve data that are important to understanding the cultural heritage of the United States. Cultural resource management offers new career opportunities for archaeologists in government agencies, universities, and consulting firms.

Early cultural anthropologists who accepted the tenets of cultural relativism sometimes also embraced ethical relativism, the idea that a person could not make value judgments about other societies. Although most anthropologists reject ethical relativism, the issue of universal standards to evaluate values and harmful cultural practices is still problematic. Proposing universal standards to make value judgments and help reduce harmful cultural practices remains one of the most important tasks for applied anthropology and future ethnological research.

QUESTIONS TO THINK ABOUT

1. What is applied anthropology? Erve Chambers suggests that there are different roles that applied anthropologists play. Discuss each of these roles as they apply to present-day applied anthropological studies.

2. What is medical anthropology? What are some of the types of things that medical anthropologists do?

3. What is cultural resource management? What resources are being evaluated and preserved?

4. Examine the concepts of cultural relativism and ethical relativism. Can an anthropologist be involved in applied anthropology and adhere to either of these principles or views? Are there any problems associated with an ethical relativist perspective?

5. Is it possible to understand the values and worldview of another culture and not accept all of their practices and standards? In other words, can one be a cultural relativist and not an ethical relativist at the same time?

6. Do you think it is possible to adopt a humanitarian standard that would be accepted by everyone in the world? What might this view entail?

7. What should be the role in anthropology in respect to warfare in different regions of the world?

8. Is there such a thing as universal human rights?

KEY TERMS

applied anthropology
cultural resource management
epidemiology

ethical relativism
medical anthropology

metaculture
social-impact studies

INTERNET EXERCISES

1. Visit the website http://www.falcon-one.com/arch.html and read about the cultural landscape of the Hudson River. How have historical archaeologists "discovered" that a landscape is an artifact? What is the purpose of this type of study? Why is historical archaeology necessary, as history records events during periods covered by these studies? How does the particular study in this website relate to cultural resource management?

2. Review the World Health Organization press release at http://www.who.org/whr/1999/en/pressrelease.htm. Look at the table on life expectancies. How can the field of applied anthropology help in understanding the differences in life expectancies between countries? When looking at the table on malaria mortality rates, notice that worldwide rates have dropped dramatically whereas sub-Saharan Africa rates have not dropped much. What can applied anthropologists do to help reduce these rates?

Glossary

achieved status   A status that results at least in part from a person's specific actions.

adjudication   The settling of legal disputes through a formal, centralized authority.

age grades   Statuses defined by age, through which a person moves in the course of his or her lifetime.

age sets   Corporate groups of people who are about the same age and share specific rights, obligations, duties, and privileges in their community.

age stratification   The unequal allocation of wealth, power, and prestige among people of different ages.

agribusiness   Commercialized, mechanized agriculture.

ambilineal descent group   A corporate kinship group formed by choosing to trace relationships through either a male or a female line.

animism   The belief that the world is populated by spiritual beings such as ghosts, souls, and demons.

anthropology   The systematic study of humankind.

apartheid   A political, legal, and social system developed in South Africa in which the rights of different population groups were based on racial criteria.

applied anthropology   The use of data gathered from the other subfields of anthropology to find practical solutions to problems in a society.

archaeology   The discipline that focuses on the study of the artifacts from past societies to determine the lifestyles, history, and evolution of those societies.

artifacts   The material products of past societies.

ascribed status   A status that is attached to a person from birth; for example, sex, caste, and race.

assimilation   The adoption of the language, culture, and ethnic identity of the dominant group in a society by other groups.

authority   Power generally perceived by members of society as legitimate rather than coercive.

balanced reciprocity   A direct type of reciprocal exchange with an explicit expectation of immediate return.

band   The least complex and, most likely, oldest form of a political system.

barter   The direct exchange of one commodity for another; it does not involve the use of money.

beliefs   Specific cultural conventions concerning true or false assumptions shared by a particular group.

bilateral descent   A descent system that traces relatives through both maternal and paternal sides of the family simultaneously.

biodiversity   The genetic and biological variation within and among different species of plants and animals.

biological assimilation   The process by which formerly distinct groups merge through marriage and reproduction.

biome   An area dominated by a particular climate and distinguished by the prevalence of certain types of plants and animals.

bipedalism   The ability to walk erect on two hind legs.

brideservice   A situation in which a male resides with his wife's family for a specified amount of time.

bridewealth   Transfer of some form of wealth from the descent group of the groom to that of the bride.

capitalism   An economic system in which natural resources as well as the means of producing and distributing goods and services are privately owned.

cargo cult   Revitalization movements in Papua New Guinea that involve beliefs that Western goods are produced by supernatural forces.

carrying capacity   The upper limit of the size of a population that a specific environment can support.

caste   A social grouping into which a person is born and remains throughout his or her lifetime.

chief   A person who owns, manages, and controls the basic productive factors of the economy and has privileged access to strategic and luxury goods.

chiefdom   A political system with a formalized and centralized leadership, headed by a chief.

civilization   A form of society that has a complex government, dense urban centers, extensive food surpluses, a specialized division of labor, monumental art, and writing systems.

clan   A form of descent group in some societies whose members trace their descent to an unknown ancestor or, in some cases, to a sacred plant or animal.

closed instincts   Genetically encoded behaviors that are not open to learning.

closed peasant communities   Indian communities in highland areas of Latin America that were isolated from colonialism and the market economy.

closed society   A society in which social status is generally ascribed rather than achieved.

cognitive anthropology   The study of human psychological thought processes based on computer modeling.

colonies   Societies that are controlled politically and economically by a dominant society.

command economy   An economic system in which a political elite makes the decisions concerning production, prices, and trade.

communication   The act of transferring information.

complementary opposition   A system in which kinship groups within a segmentary lineage organization can be allies or antagonists.

composite tool   Tools made from several components, such as harpoons or spears.

consumption   The process of using natural and human-made resources within a particular economic system.

core societies   Powerful industrial nations that have exercised economic hegemony over other regions.

correlation   The simultaneous occurrence of two variables.

cosmologies   Ideas that present the universe as an orderly system, including answers to basic questions about the place of humankind.

cross-cousin marriage   A system in which a person marries the offspring of parental siblings of the opposite sex; for example, a male marries his mother's brother's daughter.

crude birth rate   The number of live births in a given year for every thousand people in a population.

crude death rate   The number of deaths in a given year for every thousand people.

cultural anthropology   The subfield of anthropology that focuses on the study of contemporary societies.

cultural assimilation   The process by which ethnic groups adopt the culture of another ethnic group.

cultural ecology   The systematic study of the relationships between the environment and society.

cultural hegemony   The control over values and norms exercised by the dominant group in a society.

cultural materialism   A research strategy that focuses on technoenvironmental and economic factors as key determinants in sociocultural evolution.

cultural relativism   The view that cultural traditions must be understood within the context of a particular society's responses to problems and opportunities.

cultural resource management   The attempt to protect and conserve artifacts and archaeological resources for the future.

cultural universals   Essential behavioral characteristics of humans found in all societies.

culture   A shared way of life that includes material products, values, beliefs, and norms that are transmitted within a particular society from generation to generation.

culture of poverty   The hypothesis that sets of values sustaining poverty are perpetuated generation after generation within a community.

culture shock   A severe psychological reaction that results from adjusting to the realities of a society radically different from one's own.

deculturation   The loss of traditional patterns of culture.

deductive method   A scientific research method that begins with a general theory, develops a specific hypothesis, and tests it.

demographic transition theory   A model used to understand population changes within a society through different stages, concluding in the decline of fertility and mortality rates in advanced industrial societies.

demography   The study of population and its relationship to society.

dependency theory   The theory that underdevelopment in Third World societies is the result of domination by capitalist, industrial societies.

dependent variable   A variable whose value changes in response to changes in the independent variable.

descent group   A corporate group identified by a person that traces his or her real or fictive kinship relationships.

dialect   Linguistic patterns involving differences in pronunciation, vocabulary, or syntax that occur within a common language family.

diffusionism   The spread of cultural traits from one society to another.

division of labor   The specialization of economic roles and activities within a society.

doubling time   The period of time required for a population to double.

dowry   Goods and wealth paid by the bride's family to the groom's family.

drives   Basic, inborn, biological urges that motivate human behavior.

dyadic contract   A reciprocal exchange arrangement between two individuals.

ecclesiastical religions   Religious traditions that develop in state societies and combine governmental and religious authority.

ecology   The study of living organisms in relationship to their environment.

economy The social relationships that organize the production, distribution, and exchange of goods and services.

egalitarian A type of social structure that emphasizes equality among different statuses.

ego Freud's term to refer to the aspect of the personality that is displayed to other individuals.

emic perspective A study of a culture from an insider's point of view.

enculturation The process of social interaction through which people learn their culture.

endogamy Marriage between two people of the same social group or category.

environmental niche A locale that contains various plants, animals, and other ecological conditions to which a species must adjust.

epidemiology The study of disease patterns in a society.

ethical relativism The belief that the values of one society should never be imposed on another society.

ethnic boundary marker The distinctions of language, clothing, or other aspects of culture that emphasize ethnicity.

ethnic group A group that shares a culture.

ethnicity Cultural differences among populations usually based on attributes such as language, religion, lifestyle, and cultural ideas about common descent or specific territory.

ethnocentrism The practice of judging another society by the values and standards of one's own.

ethnocide A process in which a dominant group or society forces other groups to abandon their traditional language and culture.

ethnogenesis The emergence of a new ethnic group.

ethnography A description of a society written by an anthropologist who conducted field research in that society.

ethnology The subfield of anthropology that focuses on the study of different contemporary cultures throughout the world.

ethnomusicology The study of the practices and culture of musical traditions of different societies.

ethnonationalist movements The process of emphasizing the cultural distinctions of a particular group for political purposes.

ethnopoetics The study of the poetry traditions and practices in different societies.

ethologist A scientist who studies the behaviors of animals in their natural setting.

etic perspective The study of a culture from an outsider's point of view.

evolution Process of change within a species over time.

evolutionary psychology The study of the mind using evolutionary findings.

exchange The transfer of natural and human-made resources from one person to another.

exogamy Marriage between people of different social groups and categories.

extended family A type of family made up of parents, children, and other kin relations residing together as a social unit.

family A social group of two or more people related by blood, marriage, or adoption who reside together for an extended period, sharing economic resources and caring for their young.

fecundity The potential number of children women are capable of bearing.

feminism The belief that women are equal to men and should have equal rights and opportunities.

fertility The number of births in a society.

feud A type of armed combat between groups in a community.

feudalism A decentralized form of political economy based on landed estates, which existed during different historical periods in agrarian societies.

fictive kinship ties Extrafamilial social ties that provide mutual-aid work groups.

First World The sector of the global economy that is composed of modern industrialized capitalist societies.

fissioning The movement of people from one group to another area when their population begins to increase and food or other resources become scarce.

folkways Norms guiding ordinary usages and conventions of everyday life.

foraging society Another classification used for a hunting-and-gathering society.

fossil The preserved remains of bones and living materials from earlier periods.

functionalism An anthropological perspective based on the assumption that society consists of institutions that serve vital purposes for people.

gender Specific behavioral traits attached to each sex by a society and defined by culture.

generalized reciprocity A type of reciprocal exchange based on the assumption that an immediate return is not expected and that the value of the exchange will balance out in the long run.

genes Discrete units of hereditary information that determine specific physical characteristics of organisms.

genetics   The study of genes, the units of heredity.

genocide   The physical extermination of a particular ethnic group in a society.

gerontocracy   Rule by elders (usually males) who control the material and reproductive resources within the community.

globalization   The worldwide impact of industrialization and its socioeconomic, political, and cultural consequences on the world.

goods   Elements of material culture produced from raw materials in the natural environment, ranging from the basic commodities for survival to luxury items.

greenhouse effect   Global warming caused by the trapping of heat from solar rays by carbon dioxide, preventing it from radiating back into space.

green revolution   The use of bioengineering and industrial technology for agricultural purposes.

hamula   Arabic term for clanlike organization.

hierarchical society   A society in which some people have greater access than others to wealth, rank, status, authority, and power.

historical linguistics   The comparison and classification of different languages to explore the historical links among them.

historical particularism   An approach to studying human societies in which each society has to be understood as a unique product of its own history.

holistic   A broad comprehensive approach to the study of humankind drawing on the four fields of anthropology, integrating both biological and cultural phenomena.

hominid   The family of primates that includes modern humans and their direct ancestors who share distinctive types of teeth, jaws, and bipedalism.

horticulture   A form of agriculture in which a limited, nonmechanized technology is utilized to cultivate plants.

hunter-gatherer society   A society that depends on hunting animals and gathering vegetation for subsistence.

hypodescent concept   A system in which children of mixed parentage acquire the social and racial status of the parent whose social and racial status is lower.

hypothesis   A testable proposition concerning the relationship among different variables within the collected data.

id   Freud's term to refer to the unconscious drives such as sex and aggression universal to all humans.

ideal culture   What people say they do or should do.

ideology   Cultural symbols and beliefs that reflect and support the interests of specific groups in a society.

imperialism   Economic and political domination and control over other societies.

incest   Sexual relations or marriage between certain relatives.

incest avoidance   Avoidance of sexual relations and marriage with members of one's own family.

incest taboo   Strong cultural norms that prohibit sexual relations or marriage with members of one's own family.

independent variable   Causal variable that produces an effect on another variable, the dependent variable.

inductive method   A method of investigation in which a scientist first makes observations and collects data and then formulates a hypothesis.

industrialization   The use of machines and other sophisticated technology to satisfy the needs of society.

industrial society   A society that uses sophisticated technology based on machinery powered by advanced fuels to produce material goods.

infanticide   Deliberate abandonment or killing of infants 1 year of age or younger.

infant mortality rate   The number of babies per thousand births in any year who die before reaching the age of 1.

instincts   Fixed, complex, genetically based, unlearned behaviors that promote the survival of a species.

intelligence   The general ability to process information and adapt to the world.

intensive agriculture   The cultivation of crops by preparing permanent fields year after year, often including the use of irrigation and fertilizers.

intensive horticulture   A method of crop production by irrigating, fertilizing, hoeing, and terracing hillsides.

jajmani   Hindi term for traditional caste-based economy in India.

jati   Hindi term for caste.

jihad   The Arabic term that refers to "struggle," against the destroyer of one's own religion and culture.

Jim Crow laws   The laws that were used to segregate African Americans from white Americans in the southern United States prior to the Civil Rights era.

kindred   Overlapping relatives from both sides of a family whom an individual recognizes as being part of his or her descent group.

kinesics   The study of body motion and gestures used in nonverbal communication.

knowledge   The storage and recall of learned information.

kula   A form of reciprocal exchange involving ceremonial items in the Trobriand islands.

language   A system of symbols with standard meanings through which members of a society communicate with one another.

levirate   The rule that a widow is expected to marry one of her deceased husband's brothers.

life expectancy The average number of years a person can expect to live.

lineages Descent groups comprised of relatives, all of whom trace their relationship through consanguineal or affinal relations to an actual, commonly known ancestor.

linguistic anthropology The branch of anthropology that focuses on the study of language.

linguistic relativism The theory that language molds habits of both cognition and perception.

linguistics The study of language.

logic-of-growth model The model and set of values that suggest that economic growth and technological developments will always represent progress for society.

mana The Polynesian term referring to supernaturally significant powers.

marginal environment An environment that is not suitable for intensive agriculture.

market economy A pattern of economic exchange based on the value of goods and services as determined by the worldwide supply and demand of these items.

marriage A social bond between two or more people sanctioned by society that involves economic cooperation and culturally approved sexual activity.

material culture Tangible products of human society.

matrilineal descent group A corporate descent group within which members calculate descent through the female line from a commonly known female ancestor.

matrilocal residence A rule of postmarital residence in which a man resides with his wife's parents.

medical anthropology The study of disease, health care systems, and theories of disease and curing in different societies.

mercantilism A system in which the government regulates the economy of a state to ensure economic growth, a positive balance of trade, and the accumulation of wealth, usually gold and silver.

middens Artifacts often found in sites of ancient dumps or trash heaps.

migration rate The rate at which people move into and out of a specific territory.

modernization Economic, social, political, and religious change that is interrelated with modern industrial and technological developments.

modernization theory A theory that the forces associated with industrialization will eventually transform all societies into modern, industrial states.

moieties Descent groups made up of clans or phratries that form two groups, dividing the entire society into equal divisions.

money A durable medium of exchange, based on a standard value, that is used to purchase goods and services.

monogamy A form of marriage that involves one spouse of each sex.

monopoly capitalism A form of capitalism dominated by oligopolies that can reduce free competition through the concentration of capital.

moral economy An economy that involves reciprocity and redistribution among close kin and other villagers in an agricultural society.

mores Stronger norms than folkways; violators are usually punished severely.

morphemes The smallest units of a language that convey meaning.

morphology The study of morphemes.

mortality The incidence of death in a society's population.

Mousterian culture The culture and artifacts associated with the Neandertal (premodern *Homo sapiens*).

muhajedin The Arabic term for "holy warrior."

multiculturalism Policies adopted by governments to be inclusive to multiple ethnic groups within a society.

multinational corporation A transnational economic organization that operates in many different regions and is not necessarily associated with any one country.

multiregional evolutionary model The hypothesis that modern *Homo sapiens* evolved from earlier archaic *Homo sapiens* in different regions of the world based on fossil evidence.

myth Assumed knowledge about the universe, the natural and supernatural worlds, and humanity's place therein.

narratives The oral or written representation of an event or story.

nationalism Strong sense of loyalty to the nation-state based on shared language, values, and culture.

nation-states Political communities that have clearly defined territorial borders with centralized authority.

natural selection A theory presented by Darwin and Wallace that nature or environmental circumstances determine which characteristics are essential for survival. Individuals with these characteristics survive and pass them on to their offspring.

negative reciprocity The opposite of reciprocity involving getting something for nothing.

net migration The total movement of a population into and out of a territory.

nonmaterial culture Intangible products of human society, including values, beliefs, and knowledge.

norms Shared rules that define how people are supposed to behave under certain circumstances.

nuclear family A family that is composed of two parents and their immediate biological offspring or adopted children.

oath The attempt to call on a supernatural source of power to sanction and bear witness to the truth or falseness of an individual's testimony.

office A formal, corporate position of authority in a group or society.

oligopoly Economic organizations that merge and dominate within an economy.

one-drop rule American social and legal custom of classifying anyone with one black ancestor, regardless of how far back, as black.

open instincts Genetically based predispositions for behavior that are subject to modification through learning.

open peasant communities Communities in which peasants are involved in producing some of their crops for the world market.

open society A society in which social status can be achieved through individual efforts.

oracle A person, sacred object, or shrine believed to have special or supernatural abilities.

paleoanthropology The study of human evolution through the analysis of fossil remains.

parallel-cousin marriage A system in which a person marries the offspring of parental siblings of the same sex; for example, a male marries his father's brother's daughter.

participant observation The method by which the ethnologist learns the culture of the group being studied by participating in the group's daily activities.

pastoralists Groups whose subsistence activities center on the care of domesticated animals.

patriarchal Male-dominated societies.

patrilineal descent group A corporate group made up of people who trace their descent through males from a common, known male ancestor.

patrilocal residence A postmarital residence rule in which a newly married couple must reside with the husband's father.

patron-client ties Informal contracts between people of unequal status.

peasants People who cultivate land in the rural areas for their basic subsistence and pay tribute to elite groups.

peripheral societies Societies that exercise little control over their own economies and are dominated by the core industrial societies.

personality Stable patterns of thought, feeling, and action associated with a specific person.

phoneme A basic unit of sound that distinguishes meaning in a language.

phones Units of sound in a language.

phonology The study of the sounds made in speech.

phratries Umbrella-like social groupings that consist of two or more clans.

plural society A society made up of different ethnic groups.

political power The ability to achieve personal ends in spite of opposition.

polyandry Marriage between a female and more than one male.

polygamy Marriage involving a spouse of one sex and two or more spouses of the opposite sex.

polygyny Marriage between one male and two or more females.

postindustrial society A society in which the tertiary or service sector of the economy predominates.

postmodernists A viewpoint that is critical of modern scientific and philosophical perspectives.

potlatch A form of redistributional exchange found among many Northwest Native American groups.

pragmatics The study of language use within a social and cultural environment.

priest A full-time, formally trained, male religious specialist.

priestess A full-time, formally trained, female religious specialist.

primary sector The sector of an industrial economy that is devoted to the extraction of natural resources.

primates A diverse order of mammals, including humans, monkeys, and apes, that share similar characteristics.

primatology The study of primates.

primogeniture An inheritance pattern in which land or other wealth is transmitted from generation to generation through the eldest male.

production The aspect of the economy that results in manufactured goods and services.

protolanguage The parent language for many ancient and modern languages.

prototype Initial classifications of the world that help the human mind organize external reality.

proxemics The study of how people in different societies perceive and use space.

psychological anthropologist An anthropologist who studies the interrelationship between the individual and culture, or enculturation.

pull factors The incentives that lead to the migration of people of one area to another.

purdah Arabic term for seclusion of women from men in public.

push factors The conditions that force people to migrate from one area to another.

qualitative data   Nonstatistical information that tends to be the most important aspect of ethnological research.

quantitative data   Data that can be expressed as numbers, including census materials, dietary information, and income and household-composition data.

racism   Beliefs and practices that advocate the superiority of certain races and the inferiority of others.

random sample   A representative sample of people of various ages or statuses in a society.

real culture   People's actual behaviors, as opposed to ideal culture.

reciprocal economic system   An exchange system based on transactional exchanges among family groups that allocate goods and services throughout the community.

reciprocity   The exchange of goods and services among people.

redistributional economic exchange   A system that involves the exchange of goods and services through a centralized organization.

regional symbiosis   The pattern in which a particular society resides in an ecological habitat divided into different resource areas that become interdependent.

relative deprivation   A group's awareness of the absence of economic opportunities and political rights for its members in contrast to those for other groups.

replacement model   The hypothesis that all modern *Homo sapiens* evolved originally in Africa about 180,000 years ago and migrated to various areas of the world replacing earlier populations based on both fossil and genetic evidence.

revitalization movement   A social movement by people faced with dramatic changes that is designed to reinstitute traditional cultural values and beliefs.

revolution   Sudden, dramatic, sweeping change that usually involves the overthrow of a government.

rising expectations   The process in which a particular group begins to experience improvements in living conditions, stimulating the desire for further improvements.

rites of legitimation   Rituals that reinforce the authority of a ruler.

rites of passage   Rituals associated with the life cycle and the movement of people between different age-status levels.

rituals   Repetitive behaviors that communicate sacred symbols to members of society.

role   A set of expected behavior patterns, obligations, and norms attached to a particular status.

Sapir–Whorf hypothesis   A hypothesis that assumes a close relationship between language and culture claiming that language defines people's experiences.

schema   The mental codification of experience that includes a particular organized way of perceiving cognitively and responding to a complex situation or set of stimuli.

scientific method   A method used to investigate the natural and social world involving critical thinking, logical reasoning, and skeptical thought.

secondary sector   The sector of an industrial economy that is devoted to processing raw materials into manufactured goods.

Second World   In the terminology of the Cold War, the industrial socialist societies in the global economy.

secularization   The decline in the influence of religion in a society.

segmentary lineage system   A type of political organization in which multiple descent groups form at different levels and serve political functions.

segregation   The institutional separation of human populations or ethnic groups from one another.

semantics   The meaning of words, phrases, and sentences.

semiperipheral societies   Societies that have some degree of industrialization and some economic autonomy in the world economy but are not as advanced as core societies.

services   Elements of nonmaterial culture derived from cultural knowledge in the form of specialized skills that benefit others, such as giving spiritual comfort or medical care.

sex   Biological and anatomical differences between males and females.

sexism   Prejudice and discrimination against people based on their sex.

shamans   Part-time religious specialists who are believed to be linked with supernatural beings and powers.

signs   Meanings that are directly associated with concrete physical phenomena.

situational learning   A type of learning in which organisms adjust their behavior in response to direct experience.

social-impact studies   Research on the possible consequences of change in a society.

socialism   An economic system in which the state owns the basic means of production.

social learning   A type of learning in which an organism observes another organism's response to a stimulus and then adds that response to its own collection of behaviors.

social stratification   Inequality of statuses in a society.

social structure   The sum of the patterns of relationships in a society.

society A group of people who reside within a specific territory and share a common culture.

socioeconomic status A particular social position determined by economic circumstances within a society.

sociolinguistics The systematic study of language use in various social settings to explore the links between language and social behavior.

sodalities Groups based on kinship, age, gender, or other principles that provide for political organization.

sorcery A conscious magical strategy, often using different objects, that is believed to bring about either harmful or beneficial results.

sororate The marriage rule requiring a widower to marry one of his deceased wife's sisters.

state A form of political system with centralized bureaucratic institutions to establish power and authority over large populations in clearly defined territories.

status A recognized social position that a person occupies in a society.

strata A group of equivalent statuses based on ranked divisions within a society.

structural linguistics An area of research that investigates the structure of language patterns as they presently exist.

subsistence patterns The means by which people obtain their food supply.

sumptuary rules Cultural norms and practices that are used to differentiate higher-status groups from lower-status groups.

superego Freud's term for the component of the personality that is formed through the individuals learning cultural norms.

sustainability model A model that emphasizes the conservation and preservation of environmental resources for future generations.

symbolic anthropology The study of culture through the interpretation of a society's symbols, values, beliefs, and ethos.

symbolic learning The ability to use and understand symbols.

symbols Arbitrary units of meaning that can stand for different concrete or abstract phenomena.

syncretism The blending of indigenous religious beliefs and practices with those introduced by outside groups.

syntax Rules for phrase and sentence construction in a language.

tabu The Polynesian term for a prohibition of specific behaviors.

technology All the human techniques and methods of reaching a specific goal in subsistence or in modifying or controlling the natural environment.

tertiary sector The sector of an industrial economy devoted to services.

theocracy A society in which people are believed to rule not because of their worldly wealth and power but because of their place in the moral and sacred order.

theories Interconnected hypotheses that offer general explanations of natural or social phenomena.

therapeutic pluralism Health care that involves the use of traditional and modern healing practices and beliefs.

Third World In the terminology of the Cold War, premodern, nonindustrialized societies in the global economy.

totem A mythical ancestor, usually a plant or animal, that symbolizes a particular group.

tribe Complex societies having decentralized political institutions that unite horticulturalist or pastoralist groups.

tribute The payment of labor, taxes, or other services from one group to another.

tributary form The type of agricultural society that uses tribute to extract labor, taxes, or other services from peasants.

ultimogeniture An inheritance system in which property and land are passed to the youngest son.

underdeveloped society A country with a low gross national product.

unilineal descent group A lineage group that traces its descent through only one side of the lineage or through only one sex.

unilineal evolution The belief, widespread during the nineteenth century, that societies were evolving in a single direction toward complexity and industrial progress.

universalistic religions Religions whose spiritual messages apply to all of humanity.

values Standards by which a society defines what is desirable and undesirable.

variable A datum that varies from case to case.

warfare Armed combat among territorial or political communities.

witchcraft The innate, unconscious psychic ability of some people that is believed to bring about harmful effects.

world-systems theory The view that core societies dominate peripheral and semiperipheral societies to create a global economic system.

worldview An integrated system of beliefs and cosmologies about natural and supernatural realities.

zero population growth The level of reproduction that maintains population at a steady state.

References

ABERLE, DAVID F. 1961. "'Arctic Hysteria' and Latah in Mongolia." In Yehudi Cohen (Ed.), *Social Structure and Personality. A Casebook.* New York: Holt, Rinehart and Winston.

———. 1966. *The Peyote Religion Among the Navajo.* New York: Wenner-Gren Foundation for Anthropological Research, Inc.

ABU-LUGHOD, LILA. 1987. *Veiled Sentiments: Honor and Poetry in a Bedouin Society.* Berkeley: University of California Press.

AGAR, MICHAEL. 1973. *Ripping and Running.* New York: Academic Press.

———. 1974. *Cognition and Ethnography.* Minneapolis: Burgess.

———. 1980. *The Professional Stranger: An Informal Introduction to Ethnography.* New York: Academic Press.

ALBA, RICHARD. 1985. *Italian Americans: Into the Twilight of Ethnicity.* Englewood Cliffs, NJ: Prentice Hall.

AL-THAKEB, FAHAD. 1981, July–December. "Size and Composition of the Arab Family: Census and Survey Data." *International Journal of Sociology of the Family* 2:171–78.

———. 1985. "The Arab Family and Modernity: Evidence from Kuwait." *Current Anthropology* 25(5):575–580.

ALVERSON, HOYT. 1994. *Semantics and Experience: Universal Metaphors of Time in English, Mandarin, Hindi, and Sesotho.* Baltimore, MD: Johns Hopkins University Press.

AMERICAN ANTHROPOLOGICAL ASSOCIATION. [1976] 1983. *Professional Ethics: Statements and Procedures of the American Anthropological Association.* Washington, DC: American Anthropological Association.

ANDERSON, BENEDICT. 1991. *Imagined Communities: Reflections on the Origin and Spread of Nationalism.* London: Verso.

ANDERSON, DAVID G., and VIRGINIA HORAK (Eds.). 1995. *Archaeological Site File Management: A Southeastern Perspective. Readings in Archaeological Resource Protection Series No. 3.* Atlanta. Interagency Archaeological Service Division.

ANDERSON, RICHARD L. 1989. *Art in Small-Scale Societies.* Upper Saddle River, NJ: Prentice Hall.

ANTOUN, RICHARD T. 2000. *Understanding Fundamentalism: Christian, Islamic, and Jewish Movements.* Walnut Creek, CA: AltaMira Press.

ANUMAN-RAJADHON, PHYA. 1961. "Thai Traditional Salutation." *Journal of the Siam Society* 49(2): 161–71.

ARDENER, EDWIN. 2004. *Social Anthropology and Language (Anthropology and Ethnography).* London: Routledge Press.

ASWAD, BARBARA. 2003. "Arab Americans." In Raymond Scupin (Ed.), *Race and Ethnicity: An Anthropological Focus on the U.S. and the World.* Upper Saddle River, NJ: Prentice Hall.

ATRAN, SCOTT. 1990. *Cognitive Foundations of Natural History.* Cambridge: Cambridge University Press.

———. 1998. "Folk Biology and the Anthropology of Science: Cognitive Universals and Cultural Particulars." *Behavioral and Brain Sciences* 21(4):547–609.

———. 2002. *In Gods We Trust: The Evolutionary Landscape of Religion.* Oxford: Oxford University Press.

———. 2003. "Genesis of Suicide Terrorism." *Science* 299 (5612):1534–1539.

ATRAN, SCOTT, DOUGLAS MEDIN, and NORBERT ROSS. 2004. "Evolution and Devolution of Knowledge: A Tale of Two Biologies" *Journal of the Royal Anthropological Institute.* 10(2): 395–420.

AUGUSTINE, SAINT. 1995. *Confessions.* Trans. G. Clark. Cambridge: Cambridge University Press.

BACHOFEN, JOHANN JAKOB. [1861] 1992. *Das Mutterecht.* In Ralph Manheim, trans., *Myth, Religion and Mother Right: Selected Writings of J.J. Bachofen.* Princeton: Princeton University Press.

BADRAN, MARGOT. 1998. "Gender, Islam and the State: Kuwaiti Women in Struggle, Pre-Invasion To Postliberation." In Yvonne Y. Haddad, and John Esposito (Eds.), *Islam, Gender, and Social Change.* Oxford: Oxford University Press.

BAGISH, HENRY H. 1981. *Confessions of a Former Cultural Relativist.* Santa Barbara, CA: Santa Barbara City College Publications.

BAILEY, R. C., G. HEAD, M. JENIKE, B. OWN, T. RECHTMAN, and E. ZECHENTER. 1989. "Hunting and Gathering in Tropical Rain Forests: Is It Possible?" *American Anthropologist* 91(1):59–82.

BAKER, LEE. D. 2004. "Franz Boas out of the Ivory Tower." *Anthropological Theory* 4:(1):29–52.

BALIKCI, ASEN. 1970. *The Netsilik Eskimo.* Garden City, NY: Natural History Press.

BAMBERGER, JOAN. 1974. "The Myth of Matriarchy: Why Men Rule in Primitive Society." In Michelle Zimbalist Rosaldo and Louise Lamphere (Eds.), *Women, Culture, and Society.* Stanford, CA: Stanford University Press.

BANKS, MARCUS. 1996. *Ethnicity: Anthropological Constructions.* London: Routledge.

BANNISTER, ROBERT C. 1991. *Jessie Bernard: The Making of a Feminist.* Bloomington: Indiana University Press.

BANTON, MICHAEL. 1998. *Racial Theories.* Cambridge: Cambridge University Press.

BARASH, DAVID P. 1987. *The Hare and the Tortoise: Culture, Biology, and Human Nature.* New York: Penguin.

BARBER, BENJAMIN R. 2001. *Jihad vs. McWorld: Terrorism's Challenge to Democracy.* New York: Ballantine Books.

BARKOW, J. H., L. COSMIDES, and J. TOOBY (Eds.). 1992. *The Adapted Mind: Evolutionary Psychology and the Generation of Culture.* New York: Oxford University Press.

BARMÈ, SCOTT. 2002. *Woman, Man, Bangkok: Love, Sex and Popular Culture in Thailand.* Lanham, MD: Rowman and Littlefield.

BARNET, A. B., and R. J. BARNET. 1998. *The Youngest Minds.* New York: Simon and Schuster.

BARNOUW, VICTOR. 1985. *Culture and Personality,* 4th ed. Homewood, IL: Dorsey Press.

BARRETT, LEONARD E. 1977. *Rastafarians: Sounds of Cultural Dissonance.* Boston: Beacon Press.

BARRETT, RICHARD A. 1984. *Culture and Conduct: An Excursion in Anthropology.* Belmont, CA: Wadsworth.

BARTH, FREDERICK. 1961. *Nomads of South Persia: The Basseri Tribe of the Khamseh Confederacy.* Boston: Little, Brown.

———. 1969. *Ethnic Groups and Boundaries.* Boston: Little, Brown.

———. 1975. *Ritual and Knowledge Among the Baktaman of New Guinea.* Oslo: Universitets Forlaget; New Haven, CT: Yale University Press.

———. 2002. "Toward a Richer Description and Analysis of Cultural Phenomena." In Richard Fox and Barbara J. King (Eds.), *Anthropology Beyond Culture.* Oxford: Berg.

BARTON, R. F. 1919. "Ifugao Law." *Publications in American Archeology and Ethnology,* Vol. 15, No. 1, pp. 92–109. Berkeley: University of California Press.

BASI, TINA. 2004. "Faces and Places: Contested Spaces and Identity Construction of Women Working in the Delhi Call Centre Industry" (Unpublished paper read at the British Association of South Asian Studies).

BATES, DANIEL G., and AMAL RASSAM. 2000. *Peoples and Cultures of the Middle East,* 2d ed. Upper Saddle River, NJ: Prentice Hall.

BEALL, C., K. SONG, R. ELSTON, and M. GOLDSTEIN. 2004. "Tibetans Show Evolution in Action." *Proceedings of the National Academy of Sciences* (forthcoming).

BECK, LOIS. 1986. *The Qashqa'i of Iran.* New Haven, CT: Yale University Press.

———. 1991. *Nomad: A Year in the Life of a Qashqa'i Tribesman in Iran.* Berkeley: University of California Press.

BECK, LOIS, and NIKKI KEDDIE (Eds.). 1978. *Women in the Muslim World.* Cambridge, MA: Harvard University Press.

BEEMAN, WILLIAM O. 1986. *Language, Status, and Power in Iran.* Bloomington: Indiana University Press.

———. 2004. "The Hawks and the Doves Are Aflutter over U.S. Iran Policy." *Los Angeles Times,* July 23.

BEFU, HARUMI. 1971. *Japan: An Anthropological Introduction.* San Francisco: Chandler.

———. 1980. "A Critique of the Group Model of Japanese Society." *Social Analysis* 5(6):205–25.

BELLAH, R., R. MADSEN, W. SULLIVAN, A. SWIDLER, and S. M. TIPTON. 1985. *Habits of the Heart: Individualism and Commitment in American Life.* New York: Harper & Row.

———. 2000. "Is There a Common American Culture?" *Journal of the American Academy of Religion* 66(3). Reprinted in Barbara Mori (Ed.). 2000. *Stand! Contending Ideas and Opinions: Race and Ethnicity.* Bellevue: Coursewise Publishing.

BENEDICT, RUTH. 1928. "Psychological Types in the Cultures of the Southwest." Reprinted in Margaret Mead (Ed.), *An Anthropologist at Work: Writings of Ruth Benedict.* Boston: Houghton Mifflin.

———. 1934. *Patterns of Culture.* Boston: Houghton Mifflin.

———. 1946. *The Chrysanthemum and the Sword.* Boston: Houghton Mifflin.

BENNETT, JOHN W. 1987. "Anthropology and the Emerging World Order: The Paradigm of Culture in an Age of Interdependence." In Kenneth Moore (Ed.), *Waymarks: The Notre Dame Inaugural Lectures in Anthropology.* Notre Dame, IN: University of Notre Dame Press.

BENNETT, LYNN. 1983. *Dangerous Wives and Sacred Sisters: Social and Symbolic Roles of High Caste Women in Nepal.* New York: Columbia University Press.

BENOKRAITIS, NIJOLE V. 2005. *Marriage and Families: Changes, Choices, and Constraints.* 5th ed. Upper Saddle River, NJ: Prentice Hall.

BENSON, JANET. 2003. "Asian Americans." In Raymond Scupin (Ed.), *Race and Ethnicity: An Anthropological Focus on the U.S. and the World.* Upper Saddle River, NJ: Prentice Hall.

BENTLEY, JEFFERY W., and GONZALO RODRIGUEZ. 2001. "Honduran Folk Entomology." *Current Anthropology* 42(2):285–300.

BERDAN, FRANCES F. 1982. *The Aztecs of Central Mexico: An Imperial Society.* New York: Holt, Rinehart and Winston.

BERGER, PETER, L., and SAMUEL P. HUNTINGTON (Eds.). *Many Globalizations: Cultural Diversity in the Contemporary World.* Oxford: Oxford University Press, 2002.

BERLIN, BRENT, and PAUL KAY. 1969. *Basic Color Terms: Their Universality and Evolution.* Berkeley: University of California Press.

BERNARD, JESSIE. 1981. *The Female World.* New York: Free Press.

BERNARD, RUSSELL H. 1992. "Preserving Language Diversity." *Human Organization* 51(1):82–89.

BERNARD, RUSSELL H., and JESÚS SALINAS PEDRAZA. 1989. *Native Ethnography: A Mexican Indian Describes His Culture.* Newbury Park, CA: Sage.

BERNARD, R. H., PERTTI PELTO, O. WERNER, J. BOSTER, K. A. ROMNEY, A. JOHNSON, C. EMBER, and A. KASAKOTT. 1986. "The Construction of Primary Data in Cultural Anthropology." *Current Anthropology* 27(4):382–96.

BERNASCONI, ROBERT (Ed.). 2001. *Race.* Maden, Mass: Blackwell Publishers, Inc.

BHAGWATI, JAGDISH. 2004. *In Defense of Globalization.* Oxford: Oxford University Press.

BICKERTON, DEREK. 1985. *Roots of Language.* Ann Arbor, MI: Karoma Publishing.

———. 1999. *Language and Human Behavior.* Seattle: University of Washington Press.

BIESELE, MEGAN. 2000. "The Ju/'hoansi San Under Two States: Impacts of the South West African Administration and the Government of the Republic of Namibia." In Peter Schweitzer, Megan Biesele, and Robert Hitchcock (Eds.), *Hunters and Gatherers in the Modern World: Conflict, Resistance, and Self Determination.* Oxford: Berghahn Books.

BIGLER, ELLEN. 2003. "Hispanic Americans/Latinos." In Raymond Scupin (Ed.), *Race and Ethnicity: An Anthropological Focus on the U.S. and the World.* Upper Saddle River, NJ: Prentice Hall.

BINFORD, LEWIS R., and SALLY BINFORD. 1966. "A Preliminary Analysis of Functional Variability in the Mousterian of Levallois Facies." *American Anthropologist* 68(2):238–95.

BIRDSELL, JOSEPH B. 1981. *Human Evolution.* 3d ed. Boston: Houghton Mifflin.

BIRDWHISTLE, RAY. 1970. *Kinesics and Context.* Philadelphia: University of Pennsylvania Press.

BISCHOF, N. 1972. "The Biological Foundations of the Incest Taboo." *Social Science Information* 2:7–36.

BLACK, EDWIN. 2004. *War against the Weak: Eugenics and America's Campaign to Create a Master Race.* New York: Thunder's Mouth Press.

BLICK, JEFFREY P. 1988. "Genocidal Warfare in Tribal Societies as a Result of European-Induced Culture Conflict." *Man* 23:654–70.

BLINDERMAN, C. 1986. *The Piltdown Inquest.* Buffalo, NY: Prometheus Books.

BLOCH, MAURICE. 1977. "The Past and the Present." *Man* 12:278–92.

———. 1983. *Marxism and Anthropology.* Oxford: Oxford University Press.

———. 1985. "From Cognition to Ideology." In R. Fardon (Ed.), *Power and Knowledge: Anthropological and Sociological Approaches.* Edinburgh: Scottish Academic Press.

BLOCH, MAURICE, and DAN SPERBER. 2002. "Kinship and Evolved Psychological Dispositions: The Mother's Brother Controversy Reconsidered." *Current Anthropology* 43(5):723–48.

BLURTON JONES, NICHOLAS. 1986. "Bushman Birth Spacing: A Test for Optimal Intervals." *Ethology and Sociobiology* 7(2):91–106.

———. 1987. "Bushman Birth Spacing: Direct Tests of Some Simple Predictions." *Ethology and Sociobiology* 8(3):183–204.

BOAS, FRANZ. 1930. *The Religion of the Kwakiutl,* Vol. 10, Part II. Contributions to Anthropology. New York: Columbia University.

———. [1940] 1966. *Race, Language, and Culture.* New York: Free Press.

BOAZ, NOEL T., and ALAN J. ALMQUIST. 1997. *Biological Anthropology: A Synthetic Approach to Human Evolution.* Upper Saddle River, NJ: Prentice Hall.

BODLEY, JOHN H. 1985. *Anthropology and Contemporary Human Problems*. 2d ed. Mountain View, CA: Mayfield.

———. 1990. *Victims of Progress*, 3d ed. Mountain View, CA: Mayfield.

BOEHM, CHRISTOPHER. 1993. "Egalitarian Behavior and Reverse Dominance Hierarchy." *Current Anthropology* 34(3):227–54.

———. 1999. *Hierarchy in the Forest: The Evolution of Egalitarian Behavior*. Cambridge, MA: Harvard University Press.

BOHANNON, PAUL, and GEORGE DALTON. 1962. *Markets in Africa*. Evanston, IL: Northwestern University Press.

BORDES, FRANÇOIS. 1968. *The Old Stone Age*. New York: McGraw-Hill.

BOROFSKY, ROBERT. 2005. *Yanomami: The Fierce Controversy and What We Can Learn From It*. Berkeley: University of California Press.

BOSERUP, ESTER. 1965. *The Conditions of Agricultural Growth: The Economics of Agrarian Change Under Population Pressure*. Chicago: Aldine.

———. 1970. *Women's Role in Economic Development*. London: Allen & Unwin.

BOSTER, JAMES. 1987. "Agreement Between Biological Classification Systems Is Not Dependent on Cultural Transmission." *American Anthropologist* 89(4):914–19.

BOURDIEU, PIERRE. 1977. *Outline of a Theory of Practice*. Cambridge: Cambridge University Press.

BOURGOIS, PHILIPPE. 1989a. "Crack in Spanish Harlem: Culture and Economy in the Inner City." *Anthropology Today* 5(4):6–11.

———. 1989b. *Ethnicity at Work: Divided Labor on a Central American Banana Plantation*. Baltimore: Johns Hopkins University Press.

———. 1996. *In Search of Respect: Selling Crack in El Barrio*. Cambridge, England: Cambridge University Press.

BOURGUIGNON, ERIKA. 1979. *Psychological Anthropology: An Introduction to Human Nature and Cultural Differences*. New York: Holt, Rinehart and Winston.

BOWEN, JOHN. 2001. "The Myth of Global Ethnic Conflict." In James E. Harf and Mark Owen Lombardi (Eds.), *Taking Sides: Clashing Views on Controversial Global Issues*. Guilford, CT: McGraw-Hill/Dushkin.

———. 2005. *Religions in Practice: An Approach to the Anthropology of Religion*. 3d ed. Boston: Pearson Education, Inc.

BOYER, PASCAL. 1994. "Cognitive Constraints on Cultural Representations: Natural Ontologies and Religious Ideas." In L. A. Hirschfeld and S. Gelman (Eds.), *Mapping the Mind: Domain-Specificity in Culture and Cognition*. New York: Cambridge University Press.

———. 1998. "Cognitive Tracks of Cultural Inheritance: How Evolved Intuitive Ontology Governs Cultural Transmission." *American Anthropologist* 100:876–889.

———. 2001. *Religion Explained: The Evolutionary Origins of Religious Thought*. New York: Basic Books.

BRAUDE, BENJAMIN. 1997. "The Sons of Noah and the Construction of Ethnic and Geographical Identities in the Medieval and Early Modern Periods." *The William and Mary Quarterly: A Magazine of Early American History and Culture* 54(1):103–142.

BREITBART, ERIC. 1997. *A World on Display: Photographs from the St. Louis World's Fair, 1904*. Albuquerque, NM: University of New Mexico Press.

BROKENSHA, DAVID, and CHARLES ERASMUS. 1969. "African 'Peasants' and Community Development." In David Brokensha and Marion Pearsall (Eds.), *The Anthropology of Development in Sub-Saharan Africa*. Society for Applied Anthropology Monograph No. 10, pp. 85–100.

BROOKE, JAMES. 1993. "Brazil's Outrage Intensifies as Toll in Massacre Hits 73." *The New York Times*, August 23, p. A6.

BROOKS, ALISON, FATIMAH L. C. JACKSON, and ROY RICHARD GRINKER. 2004. "Race and Ethnicity." In Ruth Osterweiss Selig, Marilyn R. London, and P. Ann Kaupp (Eds.), *Anthropology Explored: Revised and Expanded: The Best of Smithsonian AnthroNotes*. Washington, D.C.. Smithsonian Books.

BROWN, CECIL H. 1984. *Language and Living Things: Uniformities in Classification and Naming*. New Brunswick, NJ: Rutgers University Press.

BROWN, DONALD E. 1976. *Principles of Social Structure: Southeast Asia*. London: Duckworth Press.

———. 1991. *Human Universals*. New York: McGraw-Hill.

———. 2003. "Ethnicity and Ethnocentrism: Are They Natural?" In Raymond Scupin (Ed.), *Race and Ethnicity: An Anthropological Focus on the U.S. and the World*. Upper Saddle River, NJ: Prentice Hall.

BROWN, JUDITH K. 1970a. "Economic Organization and the Position of Women Among the Iroquois." *Ethnohistory* 17:151–67.

———. 1970b. "A Note on the Division of Labor by Sex." *American Anthropologist* 72:1073–78.

BROWN, KAREN MCCARTHY. 1992. *Mama Lola: A Voodoo Priestess in Brooklyn*. Comparative Studies in Religion and Society, No. 4. Berkeley: University of California Press.

BROWN, LESTER R. 1988. "The Vulnerability of Oil-Based Farming." *World Watch*, March/April. Reprinted in Robert Jackson (Ed.), 1990.

Global Issues 90/91. Sluice Dock, Guilford, CT: Dushkin Publishing Group.

BROWN, PENELOPE. 2002. "Language as a Model for Culture: Lessons from the Cognitive Sciences." In Richard Fox and Barbara J. King (Eds.), *Anthropology Beyond Culture*. Oxford: Berg.

BROWN, PETER, T. SUTIKNA, M. J. MORWOOD, R. P. SODJONO, E. JATMIKO, E. WAYHU SAPTOMO, and ROKUS AWE DUE. 2004. "A New Small-Bodied Hominin from the Late Pleistocene of Flores, Indonesia." *Nature* 431:1055–61.

BROWN, SUSAN LOVE. 2003. "African Americans." In Raymond Scupin (Ed.), *Race and Ethnicity: An Anthropological Focus on the U.S. and the World*. Upper Saddle River, NJ: Prentice Hall.

BRUMFIEL, ELIZABETH (Ed.). 1994. *The Economic Anthropology of the State*. Lanham, MD: University Press of America.

BURCH, ERNEST J., JR. 1970. "Marriage and Divorce Among the North Alaskan Eskimos." In Paul Bohannon (Ed.), *Divorce and After*, pp. 152–81. Garden City, NY: Doubleday.

BURNET, JENNIE, E. 2004. "Conceiving Unity: Coexistence and Reconciliation at the Microlevel in the New Rwanda." In Peter Uvin, Catherine Newbury, Alison Des Forges, and Timothy Longman (Eds.), *A River of Death: Variations, Similarities, and Consequences of the Rwanda Genocide* (forthcoming).

CALLENDER, CHARLES, and L. KOCHEMS. 1983. "The North-American Berdache." *Current Anthropology* 24:443–70.

CALLOWAY, COLIN G. 2003. *First Peoples: A Documentary Survey of American Indian History*. 2d ed. New York: Bedford Books.

CAMPBELL, ANNE, and PATRICIA C. RICE. 2004. "Why Do Anthropological Experts Disagree?" In Philip Carl Salzman and Patricia Rice (Eds.), *Thinking Anthropologically: A Practical Guide for Students*. Upper Saddle River, NJ: Prentice Hall.

CAMPBELL, BERNARD G. 1983. *Human Ecology: The Story of Our Place in Nature from Prehistory to the Present*. Chicago: Aldine.

———. 1987. *Humankind Emerging*. 5th ed. Glenview, IL: Scott, Foresman.

CANFIELD, ROBERT. 2004. "Karzai, Hamed." In Philip Mattar (Ed.), *Encyclopedia of the Modern Middle East and North Africa*. 2d ed. Chicago: Gale, MacMillan.

CARNEIRO, ROBERT. 1961. "Slash and Burn Cultivation Among the Kuikura and Its Implications for Cultural Development in the Amazon Basin." In Johannes Wilbert (Ed.), *The Evolution of Horticultural Systems in Native South America, Causes and Consequences: A Symposium. Anthropologica*, Supplement Publication No. 2, pp. 47–67.

———. 1967. "On the Relationship Between Size of Population and Complexity of Social Organization." *Southwestern Journal of Anthropology* 23:234–43.

———. 1970, August 21. "A Theory of the Origin of the 'State.'" *Science*, pp. 733–38.

———. 1988. "Indians of the Amazonian Forest." In Julie Sloan Denslow and Christine Padoch (Eds.), *People of the Tropical Rain Forests*. Berkeley: University of California Press.

CARTER, GEORGE F. 1988. "Cultural Historical Diffusion." In Peter J. Hugill and Bruce D. Dickson (Eds.), *The Transfer and Transformation of Ideas and Material Culture*. College Station: Texas A&M University Press.

CATCHPOLE, C. K., and P. J. B. SLATER. 1995. *Bird Song: Biological Themes and Variations*. Cambridge: Cambridge University.

CATON, STEVEN C. 1986. "Salam Tahiyah: Greetings from the Highlands of Yemen." *American Ethnologist* 13(2):290–308.

———. 1990. *"Peaks of Yemen I Summon": Poetry as Cultural Practice in a North Yemeni Tribe*. Berkeley: University of California Press.

———. 1999. *Lawrence of Arabia: A Film's Anthropology*. Berkeley: University of California Press.

CAVILLI-SFORZA, L., P. MENOZZI, and A. PIAZZA. 1994. *The History and Geography of Human Genes*. Princeton: Princeton University Press.

CHAGNON, NAPOLEON A. 1974. *Studying the Yanomamö*. New York: Holt, Rinehart and Winston.

———. 1997. *Yanomamö*. 5th ed. Fort Worth, TX: Harcourt Brace College Publishers.

———. 2000. "Manipulating Kinship Rules: A Form of Male Yanomamö Reproductive Competition." In Lee Cronk, Napoleon Chagnon, and William Irons (Eds.), *Adaptation and Human Behavior: An Anthropological Perspective*. New York: Aldine De Gruyter.

CHAGNON, NAPOLEON, and RAYMOND HAMES. 1979. "Protein Deficiency and Tribal Warfare in Amazonia: New Data." *Science* 20(3):910–13.

CHAGNON, NAPOLEON, and WILLIAM IRONS. 1979. *Evolutionary Biology and Human Social Behavior*. North Scituate, MA: Duxbury Press.

CHAMBERS, ERVE. 1985. *Applied Anthropology: A Practical Guide*. Englewood Cliffs, NJ: Prentice Hall.

CHANCE, NORMAN. 1984. *China's Urban Villagers: Life in a Beijing Commune*. New York: Holt, Rinehart and Winston.

CHIROT, DANIEL. 1986. *Social Change in the Modern Era*. San Diego, CA: Harcourt Brace Jovanovich.

CHOMSKY, NOAM. 1980. *Rules and Representation*. New York: Columbia University Press.

———. 1986. *Knowledge of Language: Its Nature, Origin, and Use*. New York: Praeger.

———. 1995. *The Minimalist Program*. Cambridge, MA: MIT Press.

———. 2002. *On Nature and Language*. Cambridge: Cambridge University Press. (Edited by A. Belletti and Luigi Rizzi.)

CHUA, AMY. 2003. *World on Fire: How Exporting Free Market Democracy Breeds Ethnic Hatred and Global Instability*. New York: Doubleday, a Random House book.

CLAESSON, H. J. M., P. VAN DE VELDE, and E. M. SMITH. 1985. *Development and Decline: The Evolution of Sociopolitical Organization*. South Hadley, MA: Bergin & Garvey.

CLEGG, MARGARET. 2004. "Modern Approaches to the Evolution of Speech and Language." *General Anthropology*. 10(2):8–12.

CLEGG, MARGARET, and L. C. AIELLO. 2002a. "Paying the Price of Speech? An Analysis of Mortality Statistics for Choking on Food." *American Journal of Physical Anthropology* (Supplement 30):126.

CLEGG, MARGARET, and L. C. AIELLO. 2002b. "Estimating Hyoid Bone Morphology in Earlier Hominine Species." *American Journal of Physical Anthropology* (Supplement 34).

CLEGG, MARGARET, and L. C. AIELLO. 2004. "Predicting Hominine Hyoid Bone Dimensions" *Journal of Human Evolution* (upcoming issue).

CLIFFORD, JAMES. 1983. "On Ethnographic Authority." *Representations* 1:118–146.

COHEN, ABNER. 1969. *Custom and Politics in Urban Africa*. Berkeley: University of California Press.

———. 1974. *Urban Ethnicity*. London: Tavistock.

COHEN, ANTHONY. 1996. "Personal Nationalism: A Scottish View of Some Rites, Rights, and Wrongs." *American Ethnologist* 23(4):802–15.

COHEN, MARK NATHAN. 1977. *The Food Crisis in Prehistory*. New Haven, CT: Yale University Press.

———. 1994. "Demographic Expansion: Causes and Consequences." In Tim Ingold (Ed.), *Companion Encyclopedia of Anthropology*. New York: Routledge.

COHEN, MARK NATHAN, and GEORGE J. ARMELAGOS. 1984. *Paleopathology at the Origins of Agriculture*. New York: Academic Press.

COHEN, RONALD. 1978. "Introduction." In R. Cohen and E. Service (Eds.), *Origins of the State: The Anthropology of Political Evolution*. Philadelphia: Institute for the Study of Human Issues.

COHEN, RONALD, and ELMAN SERVICE (Eds.). 1978. *Origins of the State: The Anthropology of Political Evolution*. Philadelphia: Institute for the Study of Human Issues.

COLE, DONALD POWELL. 1984. *Nomads of the Nomads: The Al-Murrah Bedouin of the Empty Quarter*. Prospect Heights, IL: Waveland Press.

COLE, MICHAEL. 1996. *Cultural Psychology: A Once and Future Discipline*. Cambridge: Harvard University Press.

COLLIER, JANE FISHBURNE. 1988. *Marriage and Inequality in Classless Societies*. Stanford, CA: Stanford University Press.

COMAROFF, JEAN. 1985. *Body of Power, Spirit of Resistance*. Chicago: University of Chicago Press.

CONNELL, DAN. 1987. "The Next African Famine." *Dollars and Sense*. Reprinted in Robert Jackson, 1990. *Global Issues 90/91*. 6th ed. Sluice Dock, Guilford, CT: Dushkin Publishing Group.

CONNIFF, RICHARD. 2003, August. "Go Ahead, Kiss Your Cousin." *Discover* 24(8):1–6.

CONVERSI, DANIELE (Ed.). 2002. *Ethnonationalism in the Contemporary World: Walker Connor and the Study of Nationalism*. London: Routledge Press.

CORNELL, STEPHAN, and DOUGLAS HARTMANN. 1998. *Ethnicity and Race: Making Identities in a Changing World*. Thousand Oaks, CA: Pine Forge Press.

COWGILL, DONALD O. 1986. *Aging Around the World*. Belmont, CA: Wadsworth.

CRAPANZANO, VINCENT. 1986. *Waiting: The Whites of South Africa*. New York: Random House.

CRAVEY, AJ. 1998. *Women and Work in Mexico's Maquiladoras*. Lanham, MD: Rowman and Littlefield.

CRONK, LEE. 1999. *That Complex Whole: Culture and the Evolution of Human Behavior*. Boulder, CO: Westview Press.

———. 2003. "Reciprocity and the Power of Giving" In James Spradley and David McCurdy (Eds.), *Conformity and Conflict: Readings in Cultural Anthropology*. Boston: Allyn and Bacon.

DAHLBERG, FRANCES (Ed.). 1981. *Woman the Gatherer*. New Haven, CT: Yale University Press.

D'ANDRADE, ROY G. 1989. "Cultural Cognition." In M. Posner, *Foundations of Cognitive Science*. Cambridge, MA: MIT Press.

———. 1995. *The Development of Cognitive Anthropology*. Cambridge: Cambridge University Press.

DARNELL, REGNA. 1998. *And Along Came Boas: Continuity and Evolution in Americanist Anthropology* (Studies in the History of Language Sciences). Amsterdam: John Benjamins Publishing Company.

DARWIN, CHARLES. 1979. *The Illustrated Origin of Species*. New York: Hill & Wang.

DAVIDSON, BASIL. 1961. *The African Slave Trade*. Boston: Atlantic; Little, Brown.

DAVILA, MARIO. 1971. "Compadrazgo: Fictive Kinship in Latin America." In Nelson Graburn (Ed.), *Readings in Kinship and Social Structure*. New York: Harper & Row.

DAVIS, DAVID BRION. 1997. "Constructing Race: A Reflection." *The William and Mary Quarterly: A Magazine of Early American History and Culture*. 54(1):7–18.

DAVIS, WADE. 1997. *The Serpent and the Rainbow*. New York: Touchstone Books.

DEACON, T. 1997. *The Symbolic Species: The Co-evolution of Language and the Brain*. New York: W.W. Norton.

DEGLER, CARL N. 1991. *In Search of Human Nature: The Decline and Revival of Darwinism in American Social Thought*. New York: Oxford University Press.

DE LA TORRE, IGNACIO. 2004. "Omo Revisited." *Current Anthropology* 45(4):439–53.

DEMBSKI, WILLIAM A. 1999. *Intelligent Design: The Bridge Between Science and Theology*. Dallas: Intervarsity Press.

D'EMILIO, JOHN. 1988. *Intimate Matters: A History of Sexuality in America*. New York: Harper & Row.

DE MUNCK, VICTOR. 1998. (Ed.) *Love and Culture*. New York: Columbia University Press.

———. 2000. *Culture, Self, and Meaning*. Prospect Heights, IL: Waveland Press.

DENOON, D., M. HUDSON, G. McCORMACK, and MORRIS SUZUKI (Eds.). 2001. *Multicultural Japan: Paleolithic to Postmodern*. Cambridge: Cambridge University Press.

DEVOE, PAMELA. 1992. "Refugee Work and Health in Mid-America." In Pamela DeVoe (Ed.), *Selected Papers on Refugee Issues*. Arlington, VA: American Anthropological Association.

———. 2006. "China." In Raymond Scupin (Ed.), *Peoples and Cultures of Asia*. Upper Saddle River, NJ: Prentice Hall.

DE WAAL, FRANZ. 2001. *The Ape and the Sushi Master: Cultural Reflections of a Primatologist*. New York: Basic Books.

DEWALT, BILLIE. 1984. "Mexico's Second Green Revolution: Food for Feed." *Mexican Studies/Estudios Mexicanos* 1:29–60.

DIAMOND, JARED. 1993. "Speaking with a Single Tongue." *Discover* (February), pp. 78–85.

———. 1997. *Guns, Germs, and Steel: The Fates of Human Societies*. New York: W. W. Norton & Co.

DIAZ, MAY N. 1966. *Tonala: Conservatism, Responsibility and Authority in a Mexican Town*. Berkeley: University of California Press.

DILLEHAY, THOMAS D. 1997. *Monte Verde: A Late Pleistocene Settlement in Chile*, Vol. 2. Washington, DC: Smithsonian Institution Press.

DIRKS, NICHOLAS B. 2001. *Castes of Mind: Colonialism and the Making of Modern India*. Princeton: Princeton University Press.

DIVALE, WILLIAM, and MARVIN HARRIS. 1976. "Population, Warfare, and the Male Supremacist Complex." *American Anthropologist* 78:521–38.

DOBKIN DE RIOS, MARLENE. 1984. *Hallucinogens: Cross-Cultural Perspectives*. Albuquerque: University of New Mexico Press.

DONNELLY, NANCY D. 1992. "The Impossible Situation of Vietnamese in Hong Kong's Detention Centers." In Pamela DeVoe (Ed.), *Selected Papers on Refugee Issues*. Arlington, VA: American Anthropological Association.

DOUGLAS, MARY. 1966. *Purity and Danger: An Analysis of the Concepts of Pollution and Taboo*. London: Routledge and Kegan Paul.

DRENNAN, ROBERT D. 1987. "Regional Demography in Chiefdoms." In Robert D. Drennan and Carlos A. Uribe (Eds.), *Chiefdoms in the Americas*. New York: University Press of America.

DRESNER, DANIEL W. 2004. "The Outsourcing Bogeyman." *Foreign Affairs* 3(3):22–35.

DRINNON, RICHARD. 1980. *Facing West: The Metaphysics of Indian-Hating and Empire Building*. Minneapolis: University of Minnesota Press.

DUMOND, DON E. 1972. "Population Growth and Political Centralization." In Brian Spooner (Ed.), *Population Growth: Anthropological Implications*. Cambridge, MA: MIT Press.

DUMONT, LOUIS. 1970. *Homo Hierarchicus: An Essay on the Caste System*, trans. Mark Sainsburg. Chicago: University of Chicago Press.

DUNN, STEPHEN P., and ETHEL DUNN. 1988. *The Peasants of Central Russia*. Prospect Heights, IL: Waveland Press.

DUPREE, LOUIS. 1980. *Afghanistan*. Princeton: Princeton University Press.

DURHAM, WILLIAM H. 1976. "Resource Competition and Human Aggression. Part I: A Review of Primitive War." *Quarterly Review of Biology* 51:385–415.

———. 2002. "Cultural Variation in Time and Space: The Case for a Population Theory of Culture." In Richard Fox and Barbara J. King (Eds.) *Anthropology Beyond Culture*. Oxford: Berg.

DYSON-HUDSON, RADA, and ERIC ALDEN SMITH. 1978. "Human Territoriality: An Ecological Reassessment." *American Anthropologist* 80(1):21–41.

EARLE, TIMOTHY. 1977. "A Reappraisal of Redistribution: Complex Hawaiian Chiefdoms." In T. Earle and J. Ericson (Eds.), *Exchange Systems in Prehistory*. New York: Academic Press.

———. 1987. "Chiefdoms in Archaeological and Ethnohistorical Perspective." *Annual Review of Anthropology* 16:299–308.

———. 1997. *How Chiefs Come to Power: The Political Economy in Prehistory*. Stanford: Stanford University Press.

EDLES, LAURA DESFOR. 2004. "Rethinking 'Race,' 'Ethnicity' and 'Culture': Is Hawai'i the 'Model Minority' State? *Ethnic and Racial Studies* 27(1):37–68.

EDWARDS, DAVID. 1998. "Learning from the Swat Pathans: Political Leadership in Afghanistan, 1978–97." *American Ethnologist* 25(4):712–28.

———. 1996. *Heroes of the Age: Moral Fault Lines on the Afghan Frontier*. Berkeley: University of California Press.

———. 2002. *Before Taliban: Genealogies of the Afghan Jihad*. Berkeley: University of California Press.

EICKELMAN, DALE F. 1976. *Moroccan Islam: Tradition and Society in a Pilgrimage Center*. Modern Middle East Series, Vol. 1. Austin and London: University of Texas Press.

———. 1982. "The Study of Islam in Local Contexts." *Contributions to Asian Studies* 17:1–16.

——— (Ed.). 1993. *Russia's Muslim Frontiers: New Directions in Cross-Cultural Analysis*. Bloomington and Indianapolis: Indiana University Press.

———. 1995. "Ethnicity." In John L. Esposito (Ed.), *The Oxford Encyclopedia of the Modern Islamic World*, Vol. I. New York: Oxford University Press.

———. 1998. *The Middle East and Central Asia: An Anthropological Approach*. Upper Saddle River, NJ: Prentice Hall.

EICKELMAN, DALE F., and JAMES PISCATORI. 2004. *Muslim Politics*. 2d ed. Princeton: Princeton University Press.

EKMAN, PAUL. 1973. "Cross-Cultural Studies of Facial Expressions." In P. Ekman (Ed.), *Darwin and Facial Expression: A Century of Research in Review*. New York: Academic Press.

EKMAN, PAUL, WALLACE V. FRIESEN, and JOHN BEAR. 1984. "The International Language of Gestures." *Psychology Today*, pp. 64–69.

ELIADE, MIRCEA. 1959. *The Sacred and the Profane: The Nature of Religion*. New York: Harper & Row.

EMBER, CAROL. 1978. "Myths About Hunter-Gatherers." *Ethnology* 17:439–48.

EMBER, CAROL R., MELVIN EMBER, and PETER N. PEREGRINE. 2002. *Physical Anthropology and Archaeology*. Upper Saddle River, NJ: Prentice Hall.

510 References

EMBER, MELVIN. 1975. "On the Origin and Extension of the Incest Taboo." *Behavior Science Research* 10:249–81.

EMBER, MELVIN, and CAROL EMBER. 1971. "The Conditions Favoring Matrilocal versus Patrilocal Residence." *American Anthropologist* 73:371–574.

———. 1979. "Male-Female Bonding: A Cross-Species Study of Mammals and Birds." *Behavior Science Research* 14:37–56.

ENDICOTT, KIRK. 1988. "The Basis of Egalitarian Social Relations Among the Batak Foragers of Malaysia." Paper read at the Eighty-Seventh Annual Meeting of the American Anthropological Association, Phoenix, AZ.

ENGELS, FREDERICK. [1884] 1972. *The Origin of the Family, Private Property, and the State*. New York: Pathfinder Press.

ENSMINGER, JEAN. (Ed.). 2002. "Experimental Economics: A Powerful New Method for Theory Testing in Anthropology." In Jean Ensminger (Ed.), *Theory in Economic Anthropology*. Walnut Creek: CA: AltaMira Press.

ERICKSON, MARK T. 1999. "Incest Avoidance: Clinical Implications of the Evolutionary Perspective." In Wenda R. Trevathan, E. O. Smith, and James J. McKenna (Eds.), *Evolutionary Medicine*. New York and Oxford: Oxford University Press.

ERIKSEN, THOMAS HYLLAND. 1993. *Ethnicity and Nationalism: Anthropological Perspectives*. London: Pluto Press.

ESPOSITO, JOHN. 1998. *Islam: The Straight Path*. 3d ed. London: Oxford University Press.

———. 2002. *Unholy War: Terror in the Name of Islam*. Oxford: Oxford University Press.

ESTIOKO-GRIFFIN, AGNES, and BION P. GRIFFIN. 1978. "Woman the Hunter: The Agta." In Frances Dahlberg (Ed.), *Woman the Gatherer*, pp. 121–52. New Haven, CT: Yale University Press.

EVANS, KARIN. 2000. "The One-Child, Maybe-One-More Policy." In Elvio Angeloni (Ed.), *Anthropology 2001/2002*. New York: McGraw-Hill, Dushkin.

EVANS-PRITCHARD, E. E. 1937. *Witchcraft, Oracles and Magic Among the Azande*. Oxford: Clarendon Press.

———. 1940. *The Nuer*. Oxford: Clarendon Press.

———. 1951. *Kinship and Marriage Among the Nuer*. Oxford: Clarendon Press.

———. 1956. *Nuer Religion*. New York: Oxford University Press.

FAGAN, BRIAN. 1984a. *The Aztecs*. New York: W. H. Freeman.

———. 1984b. *Clash of Cultures*. New York: W. H. Freeman.

———. 1988. "Black Day at Slack Farm." *Archaeology* 41(4):15–16, 73.

———. 1992. *Rape of the Nile*. Providence, RI: Moyer-Bell.

———. 1998. *From Black Land to Fifth Sun: The Science of Sacred Sites*. Cambridge, MA: Perseus Publishing.

———. 2000. *People of the Earth: An Introduction to World Prehistory*. 10th ed. New York: HarperCollins.

———. 2001. *Grahame Clark: An Intellectual Life of an Archaeologist*. Cambridge, MA: Westview.

———. 2004. *The Long Summer: How Climate Changed Civilization*. New York: Basic Books.

FAGAN, BRIAN, and CHRISTOPHER DECORSE. 2002. *In the Beginning: An Introduction to Archaeology*. 11th ed. Upper Saddle River, NJ: Prentice Hall.

FAKHOURI, HANI. 1972. *Kafr El-Elow: An Egyptian Village in Transition*. New York: Holt, Rinehart and Winston.

FARB, PETER. 1974. *Word Play: What Happens When People Talk*. New York: Knopf/Bantam.

FATHI, NAZILA. 2004. "Conservatives in Iran Battle the Spread of Foreign Investment." *New York Times International*, October 10, p. 16.

FEDARKO, KEVIN. 2004. "This Ride Is About Our Future." *Parade Magazine*, May 16:4–5.

FEDER, KENNETH L. 2002. *Frauds, Myths, and Mysteries: Science and Pseudoscience in Archaeology*. New York: McGraw-Hill.

FEDIGAN, LINDA M. 1983. "Dominance and Reproductive Success in Primates." *Yearbook of Physical Anthropology* 26:91–129.

———. 1986. "The Changing Role of Women in Models of Human Evolution." *Annual Review of Anthropology* 15:25–66.

FELL, BARRY. 1980. *Saga America*. New York: Times Mirror.

FERGUSON, R. BRIAN. 1997. "Review of War Before Civilization: The Myth of The Peaceful Savage." *American Anthropologist* 99:424–25.

FERGUSON, R. BRIAN, and NEIL L. WHITEHEAD (Eds.). 1992. *War in the Tribal Zone: Expanding States and Indigenous Warfare*. Seattle, WA: University of Washington Press.

FERNEA, ELIZABETH W., and ROBERT A. FERNEA. 1979. "A Look Behind the Veil." In *Human Nature*. Reprinted in *Anthropology 1989/90*. 1989. Sluice Dock, Guilford, CT: The Dushkin Publishing Group.

FESSLER, DANIEL M. T. 1999. "Toward an Understanding of the Universality of Second Order Emotions." In Alexander Laban Hinton (Ed.), *Biocultural Approaches to the Emotions*. Cambridge: Cambridge University Press.

FIRTH, RAYMOND. 1957. "A Note on Descent Groups in Polynesia." *Man* 57:4–8.

FISHER, HELEN E. 1992. *Anatomy of Love: The Natural History of Monogamy, Adultery, and Divorce*. New York: W. W. Norton.

FISHMAN, JOSHUA. 1980. "Social Theory and Ethnography." In Peter Sugar (Ed.), *Ethnic Diversity and Conflict in Eastern Europe*. Santa Barbara: ABC-CLIO.

FITCH, W. T. 2000. "The Phonetic Potential of Nonhuman Vocal Tracts: Comparative Cineradiographic Observations of Vocalizing Animals." *Phonetica* 57(2–4):205–18.

FITCH, W. T., and J. GIEDD. 1999. "Morphology and Development of the Human Vocal: A Study Using Magnetic Resonance Imaging." *Journal of the Acoustical Society of America* 106: (3: pt.1):1511–22.

FLEURET, PATRICK. 1988. "Farmers, Cooperatives, and Development Assistance in Uganda: An Anthropological Perspective." In David Brokensha and Peter D. Little (Eds.), *Anthropology of Development and Change in East Africa*. Boulder, CO: Westview Press.

FLINN, M. V., and B. G. ENGLAND. 1997. "Childhood Stress and Family Environment." *Current Anthropology* 36:854–66.

FLUEHR-LOBBAN, CAROLYN. 1998. "Cultural Relativism and Universal Rights." (http://www.cs.org/publications/featuredarticles/1998/fluehrlobban.htm).

———. 2000. "How Anthropology Should Respond to an Ethical Crisis." *Chronicle of Higher Education, Point of View*, October 6, 2000, B-24.

———. (Ed.). 2003. *Ethics and the Profession of Anthropology: Dialogue for Ethically Conscious Practice*. Walnut Creek, CA: AltaMira Press.

———. 2004a. "Cultural Relativism and Universal Human Rights." In Ruth Osterweiss Selig, Marilyn R. London, and P. Ann Kaupp (Eds.), *Anthropology Explored: Revised and Expanded: The Best of Smithsonian Anthronotes*. Washington, D.C.: Smithsonian Books.

———. 2004b. "Challenges of Providing Anthropological Expertise: On the 'Arab-Black Conflict' in Darfur." *Anthropology News*, October 7–8.

FOSTER, GEORGE M. 1967. *Tzintzuntzan: Mexican Peasants in a Changing World*. Boston: Little, Brown.

FOUTS, R. S. 1997. *Next of Kin: What Chimpanzees Have Taught Me about Who We Are*. New York: William Morrow and Company.

FOX, RICHARD G. 1985. *Lions of the Punjab: Culture in the Making*. Berkeley: University of California Press.

———. 1989. *Gandhian Utopia: Experiments with Culture*. Boston: Beacon Press.

FOX, RICHARD G., and BARBARA KING (Eds.). 2002. *Anthropology Beyond Culture*. Oxford: Berg.

FOX, ROBIN. 1967. *Kinship and Marriage: An Anthropological Perspective*. Baltimore: Penguin.

FRANK, ANDRE GUNNER. 1998. *Reorient: Global Economy in the Asian Age*. Berkeley: University of California Press.

FREDRICKSON, GEORGE M. 2002. *Racism: A Short History*. Princeton, NJ: Princeton University Press.

FREEMAN, DEREK. 1983. *Margaret Mead and Samoa: The Making and Unmaking of an Anthropological Myth*. Cambridge, MA: Harvard University Press.

———. 1997. *Margaret Mead and the Heretic: The Making and Unmaking of an Anthropological Myth*. New York: Penguin.

———. 1999. *The Fateful Hoaxing of Margaret Mead*. 2d ed. Boulder, CO: Westview.

FREUCHEN, PETER. 1961. *Book of the Eskimos*. Cleveland: World Publishing Co.

FREUD, SIGMUND. 1891. "Hypnosis." In S. Freud, H. Ellis, et al. (A. Roback, Ed.) (1957) *Freudiana*. (Including Unpublished Letters from Freud, Havelock Ellis, Pavlov, Bernard Shaw, Romain Rolland, et al.). Cambridge, MA: Science Art Publishers.

———. 1913. *Totem and Taboo: Some Points of Agreement Between the Mental Lives of Savages and Neurotics*, trans. James Strachey. New York: W. W. Norton.

FRIED, MORTON. 1953. *Fabric of Chinese Society: A Study of the Social Life of a Chinese County Seat*. New York: Praeger.

———. 1967. *The Evolution of Political Society: An Essay in Political Anthropology*. New York: Random House.

———. 1975. *The Notion of Tribe*. Menlo Park, CA: Cummings.

———. 1977. "First Contact and Political Theory." In Ronald K. Wetherington (Ed.), *Colloquia in Anthropology*, Vol. 1. Taos, NM: Fort Burgwin Research Center, Southern Methodist University.

———. 1978. "The State, the Chicken and the Egg: Or What Came First?" In R. Cohen and E. R. Service (Eds.), *Origins of the State: The Anthropology of Political Evolution*, pp. 35–48. Philadelphia: Institute for the Study of Human Issues.

FRIEDL, ERNESTINE. 1975. *Women and Men: An Anthropologist's View*. New York: Holt, Rinehart and Winston.

FRIEDMAN, JONATHAN. 1974. "Marxism, Structuralism, and Vulgar Materialism." *Man* 9:444–69.

———. 1992. "Narcissism, Roots, and Postmodernity: The Constitution of Selfhood in the Global Crisis." In Scott Lash and Jonathan Friedman (Eds)., *Modernity and Identity*. Oxford: Basil Blackwell.

———. 1995. *Culture Identity and Global Process*. London: Sage Publications.

———. 1998. *System, Structure, and Contradiction: the Evolution of Asiatic Social Formations*. 2d ed. Walnut Creek, CA: AltaMira Press.

——— (Ed.). 2003. *Globalization, the State, and Violence*. Walnut Creek, CA: AltaMira Press.

FRIEDMAN, THOMAS. 2006. *The World Is Flat: A Brief History of the Twenty-First Century*. New York: Farrar, Strauss and Giroux.

GANNON, J., et al. 1998. "Asymmetry of Chimpanzee Planum Temporale: Humanlike Pattern of Wernicke's Brain Language Area Homolog." *Science* 279:220–222.

GARBARINO, MERWYN. 1988. *Native American Heritage*. 2d ed. Prospect Heights, IL: Waveland Press.

GARCIAGODOY, JUANITA. 1998. *Digging the Days of the Dead: A Reading of Mexico's Dias De Muertos*. Niwot, CO: University Press of Colorado.

GARDNER, HOWARD. 1983. *Frames of Mind: The Theory of Multiple Intelligences*. New York: Basic Books.

GARDNER, PETER. 1991. "Foragers Pursuit of Individual Autonomy." *Current Anthropology* 32:543–58.

GARDNER, R. A., and B. T. GARDNER. 1969. "Teaching Sign Language to a Chimpanzee." *Science* 16:664–72.

GARN, STANLEY. 1971. *Human Races*. 3d ed. Springfield, IL: Chas. C Thomas.

GARZA, CHRISTINA ELNORA. 1991. "Studying the Natives on the Shop Floor." *Business Week*, September 30, pp. 74–78.

GAY, PHILLIP T. 2001. *Modern South Africa*. Boston: McGraw-Hill.

GEERTZ, CLIFFORD. 1960. *The Religion of Java*. Glencoe, IL: Free Press.

———. 1963a. *Agricultural Involution: The Processes of Ecological Change in Indonesia*. Berkeley and Los Angeles: University of California Press.

———. 1963b. *Peddlars and Princes: Social Change and Modernization in Two Indonesian Towns*. Chicago: University of Chicago Press.

———. 1966. "Religion as a Cultural System." In Michael Banton (Ed.), *Anthropological Approaches to the Study of Religion*. Association of Social Anthropologists Monographs, No. 3.

———. 1973. *The Interpretation of Cultures: Selected Essays by Clifford Geertz*. New York: Basic Books.

———. 1980. *Negara: The Theatre State in Nineteenth-Century Bali*. Princeton, NJ: Princeton University Press.

———. 1983. "Common Sense as a Cultural System." In Clifford Geertz (Ed.), *Local Knowledge: Further Essays in Interpretive Anthropology*. New York: Basic Books.

———. 2000. *Available Light: Anthropological Reflections on Philosophical Topics*. Princeton, NJ: Princeton University Press.

GELLNER, DAVID. 2004. *The Anthropology of Buddhism and Hinduism: Weberian Themes*. Oxford: Oxford University Press.

GELLNER, ERNEST. 1983. *Nations and Nationalism*. Oxford: Oxford University Press.

——— (Ed.). [1977] 1988. *State and Society in Soviet Thought*. Oxford: Basil Blackwell.

GELMAN, S. A. and J. P. BYRNES (Ed.). *Perspectives on Language and Thought: Interrelations in Development*. New York: Cambridge University Press.

GEWERTZ, DEBORAH. 1981. "A Historical Reconsideration of Female Dominance Among the Chambri of Papua New Guinea." *American Ethnologist* 8(1):94–106.

GIBBS, JAMES L. 1965. "The Kpelle of Liberia." In James L. Gibbs (Ed.), *Peoples of Africa*. New York: Holt, Rinehart and Winston.

GIL-WHITE, FRANCISCO. 2001. "Are Ethnic Groups Biological 'Species' to the Human Brain?" *Current Anthropology* 42(4):515–54.

GIMBUTAS, MARIJA. 1982. "Old Europe in The Fifth MILLENIUM B.C.: The European Situation on The Arrival of Indo-Europeans." In Edgar C Polome (Ed.), *The Indo-Europeans in the Fourth and Third Millennia*. New York: Karoma Press.

———. 1991. *The Civilization of the Goddess: The World of Old Europe*. San Francisco: HarperCollins.

GISHLIK, ALAN D. 2004. "Darwin's Finches: The Story of Darwin's Finches." In *Icons of Evolution? Why Much of What Jonathan Wells Writes about Evolution Is Wrong*. Washington, DC: National Center for Science Education.

GLADKIH, M. I., N. KORNEITZ, and O. SEFFER. 1984. "Mammoth-Bone Dwelling on the Russian Plain." *Scientific American* 251(5):164–75.

GLASCOCK, ANTHONY P. 1981. "Social Assets or Social Burden: Treatment of the Aged in Nonindustrial Societies." In C. L. Fry (Ed.), *Dimensions: Aging, Culture and Health*. New York: Praeger.

GLAZIER, JACK. 2003. "Jewish Americans." In Raymond Scupin (Ed.), *Race and Ethnicity: An Anthropological Focus on the U.S. and the World*. Upper Saddle River, NJ: Prentice Hall.

512 References

GLEASON, PHILIP. 1980. "American Identity and Americanization." In Stephan Thernstrom (Ed.), *Harvard Encyclopedia of American Ethnic Groups*, pp. 31–59. Cambridge, MA: Harvard University Press.

GLUCKMAN, MAX. 1953. "Bridewealth and the Stability of Marriage." *Man* 53:141–42.

GMELCH, GEORGE, and G. ZENNER (Eds.). 2002. *Urban Life: Readings in Urban Anthropology*. Prospect Heights: IL: Waveland Press.

GOBINEAU, JOSEPH-ARTHUR. [1966] 1854. *Essays on the Inequality of Human Races*. Adrian Collins, trans. Los Angeles: Noontide Press.

GODARD, VICTORIA, JOSEPH LLOBERA, and CHRIS SHORE (Eds.). 1994. *The Anthropology of Europe: Identities and Boundaries in Conflict*. Oxford: Berg Press.

GOLDBERG, STEVE. 1993. *Why Men Rule: A Theory of Male Dominance*. London: Open Court.

GOLDKIND, VICTOR. 1965. "Social Stratification in a Peasant Community: Redfield's Chan Kom Reinterpreted." *American Anthropologist* 67:863–84.

GOLDMAN, IRVING. 1970. *Ancient Polynesian Society*. Chicago: University of Chicago Press.

GOLDSCHMIDT, WALTER. 1986. *The Sebei: A Study in Adaptation*. New York: Holt, Rinehart and Winston.

———. 1989. "Inducement to Military Participation in Tribal Societies." In Paul R. Turner, et al. (Eds.), *The Anthropology of War and Peace: Perspectives on the Nuclear Age*, pp. 15–29. Granby, MA: Bergin & Garvey.

GOLDSCHMIDT, WALTER, and EVELYN J. KUNKEL. 1971. "The Structure of the Peasant Family." *American Anthropologist* 73:1058–76.

GOLOMB, LOUIS. 1985. *An Anthropology of Curing in Multiethnic Thailand*. Urbana: University of Illinois Press.

GOODALE, JANE. 1971. *Tiwi Wives: A Study of the Women of Melville Island, North Australia*. Seattle: University of Washington Press.

GOODALL, JANE. 1986. *The Chimpanzees of Gombe*. Cambridge, MA: Harvard University Press.

GOODE, WILLIAM J. 1963. *World Revolution and Family Patterns*. New York: Free Press.

———. 1982. *The Family*. 2d ed. Englewood Cliffs, NJ: Prentice Hall.

GOODENOUGH, WARD H. 1955. "A Problem in Malayo-Polynesian Social Organization." *American Anthropologist* 57:71–83.

———. 1956. "Residence Rules." *Southwestern Journal of Anthropology* 12:22–37.

GOODLUCK, HELEN. 1991. *Language Acquisition: A Linguistic Introduction*. Oxford: Blackwell.

GOODY, JACK. 1971. *Technology, Tradition, and the State in Africa*. London: Oxford University Press.

———. 1976. *Production and Reproduction: A Comparative Study of the Domestic Domain*. Cambridge: Cambridge University Press.

———. 1980. "Slavery in Time and Space." In James L. Watson (Ed.), *Asian and African Systems of Slavery*, pp. 17–42. Berkeley and Los Angeles: University of California Press.

———. 1987. *The Interface Between the Written and the Oral*. Cambridge: Cambridge University Press.

———. 1996. *The East in the West*. Cambridge: Cambridge University Press.

GOODY, JACK, and STANLEY J. TAMBIAH. 1973. *Bridewealth and Dowry*. Cambridge: Cambridge University Press.

GOODYEAR, ALBERT C. 1999. "Results of the 1999 Allendale Paleoindian Expedition." *Legacy* 4(1–3):8–13.

GOPNIK, ALISON, ANDREW N. MELTZOFF, and PATRICIA KUHL. 2001. *The Scientist in the Crib: What Early Learning Tells Us about the Mind*. New York: HarperCollins.

GORDON, ALISON. 2004. "Ape-ing Language: Communicating with Our Closest Relatives." In *Anthropology Explored: The Best of Smithsonian Anthronotes*. Washington, DC: Smithsonian Books.

GOSSETT, THOMAS F. 1963. *Race, The History of an Idea in America*. Dallas: Southern Methodist University Press.

GOUGH, KATHLEEN. 1975. "The Origin of the Family." In Rayna Reiter (Ed.), *Towards an Anthropology of Women*. New York: Monthly Review.

GOULD, S. J. 1977. *Ever Since Darwin*. New York: W. W. Norton.

———. 1985. *The Flamingo's Smile*. New York: W. W. Norton.

———. 1987. "Bushes All the Way Down." *Natural History* 87(6):12–19.

GRANT, P. R. 1999. *Ecology and Evolution of Darwin's Finches*. Princeton, NJ: Princeton University Press.

GREENBERG, JOSEPH H. 1986. "The Settlement of the Americas." *Current Anthropology* 27:477–97.

GREENBERG, JOSEPH H., KEITH DENNING, and Suzanne Kemmer (Eds.). 1990. *On Language: Selected Writings of Joseph H. Greenberg*. Palo Alto, CA: Stanford University Press.

GREENE, VICTOR. 1980. "Poles." In Stephan Thernstrom (Ed.), *Harvard Encyclopedia of American Ethnic Groups*, pp. 787–803. Cambridge, MA: Harvard University Press.

GRIFFIN, DONALD. 1985. *Animal Thinking*. Cambridge, MA: Harvard University Press.

GRUENBAUM, ELLEN. 2004. "Humanitarian Aid to Women and the Children of Darfur." *Anthropology News,* October: 8–11.

GUHA, ASHOK S. 1981. *An Evolutionary View of Economic Growth*. Oxford: Clarendon Press.

HAAS, JONATHAN. 1982. *The Evolution of the Prehistoric State*. New York: Columbia University Press.

HAILE-SELASSIE, Y. 2001. "Late Miocene Hominids from the Middle Awash, Ethiopia." *Nature* 412:178–81.

HALL, EDWARD T. 1969. *The Hidden Dimension*. New York: Anchor Press.

———. 1981. *The Silent Language*. New York: Anchor Press.

HALPERIN, RHODA. 1987. "Age in Cross-Cultural Perspective: An Evolutionary Approach." In Philip Silverman (Ed.), *The Elderly as Modern Pioneers*. Bloomington: Indiana University Press.

HALVERSON, JOHN. 1987. "Art for Art's Sake in the Paleolithic." *Current Anthropology* 28:63–89.

HAMES, RAYMOND B. 1979a. "A Comparison of the Efficiencies of the Shotgun and the Bow in Neotropical Forest Hunting." *Human Ecology* 7(3):219–52.

———. 1979b. "Relatedness and Interaction Among the Ye'Kwana: A Preliminary Analysis." In N. Chagnon and W. Irons (Eds.), *Evolutionary Biology and Human Social Behavior: An Anthropological Perspective*, pp. 238–51. North Scituate, MA: Duxbury Press.

HAMMEL, E. A., and NANCY HOWELL. 1987. "Research in Population and Culture: An Evolutionary Framework." *Current Anthropology* 28(2):141–60.

HANDLER, RICHARD. 1988. *Nationalism and the Politics of Culture in Quebec*. Madison, WI: Wisconsin University Press.

HANNERZ, ULF. 1992. *Cultural Complexity: Studies in the Social Organization of Meaning*. New York: Columbia University Press.

HARDEN, BLAINE. 2001. "The Dirt in the New Machine." *The New York Times Magazine*, August 12, pp. 35–39.

HARNER, MICHAEL J. 1972. *The Jivaro: People of the Sacred Waterfalls*. Garden City, NY: Natural History Press.

HARRINGTON, SPENCER P. M. 1991a. "The Looting of Arkansas." *Archaeology* 44(3):22–30.

HARRIS, MARVIN. 1964. *Patterns of Race in the Americas*. New York: Norton Press.

———. 1977. *Cannibals and Kings: The Origins of Cultures*. New York: Random House.

———. 1979. *Cultural Materialism: The Struggle for a Science of Culture*. New York: Random House.

———. 1985. *The Sacred Cow and the Abominable Pig: Riddles of Food and Culture*. New York: Simon & Schuster.

————. 1988. *Culture, People, Nature: An Introduction to General Anthropology,* 5th ed. New York: Harper & Row.

————. 1992. "Distinguished Lecture: Anthropology and the Theoretical and Paradigmatic Significance of the Collapse of Society and East European Communism." *American Anthropology* 94(2):295–305.

————. 1999. *Theories of Culture in Postmodern Times.* Walnut Creek, CA: AltaMira Press.

HARRIS, MARVIN, and ERIC ROSS. 1987. *Death, Sex, and Fertility: Population Regulation in Preindustrial and Developing Societies.* New York: Columbia University Press.

HARRISON, D. F. N. 1995. *The Anatomy and Physiology of the Mammalian Larynx.* Cambridge: Cambridge University Press.

HART C. W. M., ARNOLD PILLING, and JANE GOODALE. 1989. *The Tiwi of North Australia.* 3d ed. New York: Holt, Rinehart and Winston.

HARVEY, DAVID. 1990. *The Conditions of Postmodernity.* Cambridge, MA: Blackwell Publishers.

HASSAN, FEKRI A. 1981. *Demographic Archaeology.* New York: Academic Press.

HATCH, ELVIN. 1973. *Theories of Man and Culture.* New York: Columbia University Press.

————. 1983. *Culture and Morality: The Relativity of Values in Anthropology.* New York: Columbia University Press.

HAWKES, KRISTEN. 2004. "The Grandmother Effect." *Nature* 428:128–29.

HAWKES, K., K. HILL, and J. F. O'CONNELL. 1982. "Why Hunters Gather: Optimal Foraging and the Ache of Eastern Paraguay." *American Ethnologist,* 9:379–98.

HEFNER, ROBERT W. 1983. "The Culture Problem in Human Ecology: A Review Article." *Comparative Studies in Society and History* 25(3):547–56.

———— (Ed.). 1998. *Democratic Civility: the History and Cross-Cultural Possibility of a Modern Political Ideal.* New Brunswick, NJ: Transaction.

————. 2000. *Civil Islam: Muslims and Democratization in Indonesia.* Princeton, NJ: Princeton University Press.

HEIDER, KARL. 1979. *Grand Valley Dani: Peaceful Warriors.* New York: Holt, Rinehart and Winston.

————. 1991. *Landscapes of Emotion: Mapping Three Cultures of Emotion in Indonesia.* Cambridge: Cambridge University Press.

HEITZMAN, JAMES. 2004. *Network City: Planning the Information Society in Bangalore.* New Delhi: Oxford University Press.

HENDRY, JOY. 1987. *Understanding Japanese Society.* London: Croom Helm.

————. 1992. "Introduction and Individuality: Entry into a Social World." In Roger Goodman and Kirsten Refsing (Eds.), *Ideology and Practice in Modern Japan.* London: Routledge Press.

HENN, JEANNE K. 1984. "Women in the Rural Economy: Past, Present, and Future." In Margaret Jean Hay and Sharon Stichter (Eds.), *African Women South of the Sahara,* pp. 1–19. London: Longman.

HERDT, GILBERT. 1987. *The Sambia: Ritual and Custom in New Guinea.* New York: Holt, Rinehart and Winston.

HERDT, GILBERT, and ROBERT J. STOLLER. 1990. *Intimate Communications: Erotica and the Study of Culture.* New York: Columbia University Press.

HERRNSTEIN, RICHARD J., and CHARLES MURRAY. 1994. *The Bell Curve: Intelligence and Class Structure in American Life.* New York: Free Press.

HERSCHER, ELLEN. 1989. "A Future in Ruins." *Archaeology* 42(1):67–70.

HERZFELD, MICHAEL. 1986. *Ours Once More: Folklore, Ideology, and the Making of Modern Greece.* New York: Pella Publishing Co.

————. 1992. *The Social Production of Indifference: Exploring the Symbolic Roots of Western Bureaucracy.* Chicago: University of Chicago Press.

————. 2001. *Anthropology: Theoretical Practice in Culture and Society.* Malden, MA: Blackwell Publishers Inc.

HICKERSON, NANCY PARROTT. 1980. *Linguistic Anthropology.* New York: Harper & Row.

HIJAB, NADIA. 1998. *"Islam, Social Change, and the Reality of Arab Women's Lives.* In Yvonne Haddad and John Esposito (Eds.), *Islam, Gender, and Social Change.* Oxford: Oxford University Press.

HILL, D. 1977. *The Impact of Migration on the Metropolitan and Folk Society of Carriacou, Grenada.* New York: American Museum of Natural History.

HILL, K., H. KAPLAN, K. HAWKES, and A. M. HURTADO. 1985. "Men's Time Allocation to Subsistence Work Among the Ache of Eastern Paraguay." *Human Ecology* 13:29–47.

HILL-BURNETT, JAQUETTA. 1978. "Developing Anthropological Knowledge Through Application." In E. Eddy and W. Partridge (Eds.), *Applied Anthropology in America.* New York: Columbia University Press.

HINDE, ROBERT A., and JOAN STEVENSON-HINDE. 1987. *Instinct and Intelligence.* 3d ed. Burlington, NC: Scientific Publications Department, Carolina Biological Supply Company.

HINTON, ALEXANDER LABAN (Ed.). 1999. *Biocultural Approaches to the Emotions.* Cambridge: Cambridge University Press.

HIRSCHFELD, LAWRENCE. 1986. "Kinship and Cognition: Geneology and the Meaning of Kinship Terms." *Current Anthropology* 27:217–42.

————. 1989. "Rethinking the Acquisition of Kinship Terms." *International Journal of Behavioral Development* 12: 541–68.

————. 1996. *Race in the Making: Cognition, Culture, and the Child's Construction of Human Kinds.* Cambridge, MA: MIT Press.

HITCHCOCK, ROBERT. 1988. *Monitoring Research and Development in the Remote Areas of Botswana.* Gaborone: Government Printer.

————. 2001. "'Hunting is Our Heritage': The Struggle for Hunting and Gathering Rights among the San of Southern Africa." *Parks, Property, and Power: Senri Ethnological Studies, 59.* National Museum of Ethnology, Osaka, Japan.

————. 2003a. "Land, Livestock and Leadership among the Ju/'hoansi San of North Western Botswana." *Anthropologica* 45: 89–94.

————. 2003b. "Human Rights and Indigenous Peoples in Africa and Asia." In David P. Forsythe and Patrice C. McMahon. *Human Rights and Diversity: Area Studies Revisited.* Lincoln and London: University of Nebraska Press.

————. 2004a. "Sharing the Land: Kalahari San Property Rights and Resource Management." In Thomas Widlock and Wolde Gossa Tadesse (Eds.), *Property and Equality, Vol. 2: Encapsulation, Commercialization, Discrimination,* pp. 191–207. New York: Berghahn Books.

————. 2004b. "Human Rights and Anthropological Activism among the San." In Carole Nagengast and Carlos G. Velez-Ibanez (Eds.), *Human Rights: The Scholar as Activist.* Oklahoma City: Society for Applied Anthropology.

HITCHCOCK, ROBERT K., JOHN E. YELLEN, DIANE J. GELBURD, ALAN J. OSBORN, and ARON L. CROWELL. 1996. "Subsistence Hunting and Resource Management among the Ju/'hoansi of Northwestern Botswana." *African Study Monographs* 17(4):153–208.

HOBBES, THOMAS. [1651] 1958. *Leviathan.* New York: Liberal Arts Press.

HOCKETT, CHARLES F., and R. ASCHER. 1964. "The Human Revolution." *Current Anthropology* 5:135–68.

HOEBEL, E. ADAMSON. [1954] 1968. *The Law of Primitive Man.* New York: Atheneum.

HOLDEN, CONSTANCE. 2000. "Selective Power of UV." *Science,* 289:1461.

HOSTETLER, JOHN A. 1980. *Amish Society.* 3d ed. Baltimore, MD: Johns Hopkins University.

HOURANI, ALBERT. 1991. *A History of the Arab Peoples.* Cambridge: Cambridge University Press.

HOWELL, NANCY. 1976. "The Population of the Dobe Area !Kung." In Richard B. Lee and Irven

DeVore (Eds.), *Kalahari Hunter-Gatherers*. Cambridge, MA: Harvard University Press.

———. 1979. *Demography of the Dobe !Kung*. New York: Academic Press.

HOWELLS, W. W. 1976. "Explaining Modern Man: Evolutionists versus Migrationists." *Journal of Human Evolution* 5:477–96.

HSU, FRANCIS. 1948. *Under the Ancestor's Shadow: Chinese Culture and Personality*. New York: Columbia University Press.

———. 1981. *Americans and Chinese: Passage to Differences*. 3d ed. Honolulu: University of Hawaii Press.

HUNTINGTON, SAMUEL P. 1996. *The Clash of Civilizations and the Remaking of the World Order*. New York: Simon & Schuster.

HUTCHINSON, SHARON. 1996. *Nuer Dilemmas: Coping with Money, War, and the State*. Berkeley: University of California Press.

INDEN, RONALD D. 2000. *Imagining India*. Bloomington: Indiana University Press.

INGHAM, JOHN. M. 1986. *Mary, Michael, and Lucifer: Folk Catholicism in Central Mexico*. Austin: University of Texas Press.

Information Please Almanac. 1991. "Energy, Petroleum, and Coal, by Country," pp. 146–47. Boston: Houghton Mifflin.

JABLONSKI, NINA. 2004. "The Evolution of Human Skin and Skin Color." *Annual Review of Anthropology* 33:585–623.

JABLONSKI, NINA G., and LESLIE AIELLO. 1998. *The Origin and Diversification of Language*. Berkeley: University of California Press.

JABLONSKI, NINA, and GEORGE CHAPLIN. 2000. "The Evolution of Skin Color." *Journal of Human Evolution* 39(1):57–106.

JACKSON, PETER. 1995. *Dear Uncle Go: Male Homosexuality in Thailand*. Bangkok: Bua Luang Books.

JACOBSON, MATTHEW FRYE. 1998. *Whiteness of Different Color: European Immigrants and the Alchemy of Race*. Cambridge, MA: Harvard University Press.

JANKOWIAK, WILLIAM R., and EDWARD F. FISCHER. 1992. "A Cross-Cultural Perspective on Romantic Love." *Ethnology* 3(2):149–55.

JOCHIM, MICHAEL. 1998. *A Hunter-Gatherer Landscape*. New York: Plenum.

JOHANSON, DONALD, and MAITLAND EDEY. 1981. *Lucy: The Beginnings of Humankind*. New York: Simon & Schuster.

JOHANSON, DONALD C., and JAMES SHREEVE. 1989. *Lucy's Child: The Discovery of a Human Ancestor*. New York: Avon Books.

JOHNSON, ALLEN W. 1975. "Time Allocation in a Machiguenga Community." *Ethnology* 14:301–10.

JOHNSON, ALLEN, and TIMOTHY EARLE. 2000. *The Evolution of Human Societies: From Foraging Group to Agrarian State*. 2d ed. Stanford, CA: Stanford University Press.

JONES, DOUG. 2000. "Group Nepotism and Human Kinship." *Current Anthropology* 41(5):779–809.

———. 2003. "Kinship and Deep History: Exploring Connections between Culture Areas, Genes, and Language." *American Anthropologist* 105(3):501–14.

———. 2004. "The Universal Psychology of Kinship: Evidence from Language." *Trends in Cognitive Sciences* 8(5): 211–15.

KAEPPLER, ADRIENNE L. 1980. "Polynesian Music and Dance." In Elizabeth May (Ed.), *Musics of Many Cultures*. Berkeley: University of California Press.

KAMIN, LEON. 1974. *The Science and Politics of I.Q.* New York: Wiley.

KATZ, SOLOMON (Ed.). 2003. *The Encyclopedia of Food and Culture*. New York: Charles Scribner's Sons.

KEDDIE, NIKKI R. 1981. *Roots of Revolution: An Interpretive History of Modern Iran*. New Haven, CT: Yale University Press.

KEELEY, LAWRENCE H. 1996. *War before Civilization*. New York: Oxford University Press.

KEESING, ROGER M. 1975. *Kin Groups and Social Structure*. New York: Holt, Rinehart and Winston.

———. 1981. *Cultural Anthropology: A Contemporary Perspective*. New York: Holt, Rinehart and Winston.

KEHOE, ALICE BECK. 1989. *The Ghost Dance: Ethnohistory and Revitalization*. New York: Holt, Rinehart and Winston.

———. 1995. *North American Indians: A Comprehensive Account*. 2d ed. Upper Saddle River, NJ: Prentice Hall.

KELLMAN, SHELLY. 1982. "The Yanomamös: Portrait of a People in Crisis." *New Age Journal*, May. Reprinted in *Anthropology 88/89*. 1988. Sluice Dock, Guilford, CT: Dushkin Publishing Group.

KELLY, RAYMOND C. 2003. *Warless Societies and the Origin of War*. Ann Arbor: The University of Michigan Press.

KELLY, ROBERT L. 1995. *The Foraging Spectrum: Diversity in Hunter-Gatherer Lifeways*. Washington, DC: Smithsonian Institution Press.

KEPHART, RONALD. 2003. "Latin America and the Caribbean." In Raymond Scupin (Ed.), *Race and Ethnicity: An Anthropological Focus on the United States and the World*. Upper Saddle River, NJ: Prentice Hall.

KEPHART, WILLIAM M., and WILLIAM ZELLNER. 1994. *Extraordinary Groups: The Sociology of Unconventional Life Styles*. 4th ed. New York: St. Martin's Press.

KERBLAY, BASILE. 1983. *Modern Soviet Society*. New York: Pantheon.

KERBO, HAROLD R., and JOHN A. MCKINSTRY. 1998. *Modern Japan*. New York: McGraw-Hill.

KEYES, CHARLES F. 1995. *The Golden Peninsula: Culture and Adaptation in Mainland Southeast Asia*. Honolulu: University of Hawaii Press.

———. 2002. "Weber and Anthropology." *Annual Review of Anthropology* 31:233–55.

KIERNAN, BEN. 1988. "Orphans of Genocide: The Cham Muslims of Kampuchea under Pol Pot." *Bulletin of Concerned Asian Scholars* 20(4):2–33.

KIRCH, PATRICK V. 1984. *The Evolution of the Polynesian Chiefdoms*. Cambridge: Cambridge University Press.

KIRCHOFF, PAUL. 1955. "The Principles of Clanship in Human Society." *Davidson Anthropological Journal* 1:1. Reprinted in Morton H. Fried (Ed.), 1958. *Readings in Anthropology*, 2 vols. New York: Thomas Y. Crowell.

KITCHER, PHILLIP. 1982. *Abusing Science: The Case Against Creationism*. Cambridge, MA: MIT Press.

KITTLES, RICK A., and KENNETH M. WEISS. 2003. "Race, Ancestry, and Genes: Implications for Defining Disease Risk." *Annual Review of Genomics and Human Genetics* 4:33–67.

KLEIN, LAURA. 1980. "Contending with Colonization: Tlingit Men and Women in Charge." In Mona Etienne and Eleanor Leacock (Eds.), *Women and Colonization*. New York: Praeger.

KLEINFELD, JUDITH. 1975. "Positive Stereotyping: The Cultural Relativism in the Classroom." *Human Organization* 34(3):269–74.

KLUCKHORN, CLYDE. 1967. *Navajo Witchcraft*. Boston: Beacon Press.

KNAUFT, BRUCE. 1985. *Good Company and Violence: Sorcery and Social Action in Lowland New Guinea Society*. Berkeley: University of California Press.

———. 1988. "Reply to Betzig, Laura. On Reconsidering Violence in Simple Human Societies." *Current Anthropology* 29(4):629–33.

———. 1993. *South Coast New Guinea Cultures: History, Comparison, Dialectic*. Cambridge: Cambridge University Press.

———. 1996. *Genealogies for the Present in Cultural Anthropology*. London and New York: Routledge Press.

———. 1999. *From Primitive to Postcolonial in Melanesia and Anthropology*. Ann Arbor: University of Michigan Press.

——— (Ed.). 2002. *Critically Modern: Alternatives, Alterities, Anthropologies*. Bloomington: Indiana University Press.

KOBAYASHI-HILLARY, MARK. 2004. *Outsourcing to India: the Offshore Advantage.* Berlin: Springer Verlag.

KONDO, DORINNE. 1990. *Crafting Selves: Power, Gender, and Discourses of Identity in a Japanese Workplace.* Chicago: University of Chicago Press.

KONNER, MELVIN. 2002. *The Tangled Wing: Biological Constraints on the Human Spirit.* 2d ed. New York: Holt, Rinehart and Winston.

KORBIN, JILL E. 2003. "Children, Childhoods, and Violence." *Annual Review of Anthropology* 32:431–46.

KROMKOWSKI, JOHN A. *Race and Ethnicity 04/05.* 14th ed. *Annual Editions. "2000 Census Ethnicity Data."* Guilford, CT: McGraw-Hill.

KUHL, P. K., and P. IVERSON. 1995. "Linguistic experience and the 'perceptual magnet effect'." In W. Strange (Ed.), *Speech Perception and Linguistic Experience: Issues in Cross-Language Research.* Timonium, MD: York Press.

KUHL, P. K., and A. N. MELTZOFF. 1996. "Infant vocalizations in response to speech: Vocal imitation and developmental change." *Journal of the Acoustical Society of America.* 100:2425–38.

KUHL, STANLEY. 2002. *The Nazi Connection: Eugenics, American Racism, and German National Socialism.* Oxford: Oxford University Press.

KUPER, ADAM. 1988. *The Invention of Primitive Society.* London: Routledge Press.

———. 1999. *Culture: An Anthropological Account.* Cambridge, MA: Harvard University Press.

KUPER, LEO, and M. G. SMITH. 1969. *Pluralism in Africa.* Berkeley and Los Angeles: University of California Press.

KURIN, RICHARD. 1980. "Doctor, Lawyer, Indian Chief." *Natural History* 89(11):6–24.

KURTZ, DONALD V. 1982. "The Virgin of Guadalupe and the Politics of Becoming Human." *Journal of Anthropological Research* 38:194–210.

LAITMAN, JEFFREY T. 1984. "The Anatomy of Human Speech." *Natural History* 93(8):20–27.

LAKOFF, GEORGE. 1987. *Women, Fire, and Dangerous Things.* Chicago: University of Chicago Press.

LAKOFF, GEORGE, and MARK JOHNSON. 2000. *Philosophy in the Flesh: The Embodied Mind and Its Challenge to Western Thought.* New York: Basic Books.

LAMPHERE, LOUISE. 1997. "The Domestic Sphere of Women and the Public World of Men: The Strengths and Limitations of an Anthropological Dichotomy." In C. Brettel and C. Sargent (Eds.), *Gender in Cross-Cultural Perspective.* 2d ed. Upper Saddle River, NJ: Prentice Hall.

LANDES, DAVID S. 1998. *The Wealth and Poverty of Nations. Why Some Are so Rich and Some so Poor.* New York: W.W. Norton & Company.

LAUGHLIN, ROBERT M. 2004. "Linguistic Survival Among the Maya." In Ruth Osterweiss Selig, Marilyn R. London, and P. Ann Kaupp (Eds.), *Anthropology Explored: Revised and Expanded: The Best of Smithsonian Anthronotes.* Washington, DC: Smithsonian Books.

LAWRENCE, PETER. 1964. *Road Belong Cargo: A Study of the Cargo Movement in the Southern Madang District, New Guinea.* Manchester: Manchester University Press.

LEACH, EDMUND. [1953] 1954. "Bridewealth and the Stability of Marriage." *Man* 53:179–80; *Man* 54:173.

———. 1966. "Ritualization in Man in Relation to Conceptual and Social Development." *Philosophical Transactions of the Royal Society of London,* Series B 251(772):403–8.

———. 1988. "Noah's Second Son." *Anthropology Today* 4(4):2–5.

LEAF, MURRAY J. 1984. *Song of Hope: The Green Revolution in a Punjab Village.* New Brunswick, NJ: Rutgers University Press.

LEAKEY, MEAVE G., et al. 1995. "New Four-Million-Year-Old Hominid Species from Kanapoi and Allia Bay, Kenya." *Nature* 376:565–71.

———. 2001. "New Hominid Genus from Eastern Africa Shows Diverse Middle Pliocene Lineages." *Nature* 410:433 40.

LEAP, WILLIAM. 1988. "Indian Language Renewal." *Human Organization* 47(4):283–91.

LEBLANC, STEVEN A. with KATHERINE E. REGISTER. 2003. *Constant Battles: The Myth of the Peaceful, Noble Savage.* New York: St. Martin's Press.

LECHNER, FRANK L. and JOHN BOLI (Eds.). 2000. *The Globalization Reader.* Malden, MA: Blackwell Publishers, Inc.

LEE, RICHARD B. 1968. "What Do Hunters Do for a Living, Or How to Make Out on Scarce Resources." In R. B. Lee and Irven DeVore (Eds.), *Man the Hunter,* pp. 30–43. Chicago: Aldine.

———. 1969. "Kung Bushman Subsistence: An Input-Output Analysis." In A. P. Vayda (Ed.), *Environment and Cultural Behavior: Ecological Studies in Cultural Anthropology.* Garden City, NY: Natural History Press.

———. 1972a. "The Intensification of Social Life Among the !Kung Bushmen." In Brian Spooner (Ed.), *Population Growth: Anthropological Implications,* pp. 343–50. Cambridge, MA: MIT Press.

———. 1972b. "Population Growth and the Beginning of Sedentary Life Among the !Kung Bushmen." In Brian Spooner (Ed.), *Population Growth: Anthropological Implications,* pp. 330–42. Cambridge, MA: MIT Press.

———. 1979. *The !Kung San: Men, Women, and Work in a Foraging Society.* Cambridge: Cambridge University Press.

———. 1981. "Politics, Sexual and Nonsexual in an Egalitarian Society: The !Kung San." In Gerald Berreman (Ed.), *Social Inequality: Comparative and Developmental Approaches,* pp. 83–101. New York: Academic Press.

———. 1993. *The Dobe Ju/'hoansi.* Fort Worth, TX: Harcourt Brace College Publishers.

———. 2003. *The Dobe Ju/hoansi.* 3d ed. Toronto and South Melbourne: Thomson Learning.

LEE, RICHARD B., and IRVEN DEVORE (Eds.). 1968. *Man the Hunter.* Chicago: Aldine.

LEONARD, KAREN ISAKSEN. 1997. *The South Asian Americans.* Westport, CT: Greenwood Press.

LEPOWSKY, MARIA. 1993. *Fruit of the Motherland: Gender in an Egalitarian Society.* New York: Columbia University Press.

LEVINE, NANCY. 1988. *The Dynamics of Polyandry.* Chicago: University of Chicago Press.

LEVI-STRAUSS, CLAUDE. 1944. "The Social and Psychological Aspects of Chieftainship in a Primitive Tribe: The Nambikuara of Northwestern Matto Grosso." *Transactions of the New York Academy of Sciences* 7:16–32.

———. 1966. *The Savage Mind,* trans. George Weidenfeld and Nicholson, Ltd. Chicago: University of Chicago Press.

———. 1969. *The Elementary Structures of Kinship,* rev. ed., trans. J. H. Bell. Boston: Beacon Press.

LEWELLEN, TED C. 1983. *Political Anthropology: An Introduction.* South Hadley, MA: Bergin & Garvey.

———. 2002. *The Anthropology of Globalization: Cultural Anthropology Enters the 21st Century.* Westport, CT: Bergin & Garvey.

LEWIN, TAMAR. 1986. "Profile of an Anthropologist Casting an Anthropological Eye on American Consumers." *The New York Times,* May 11.

LEWIS, HERBERT. 1992. "Ethnic Loyalties Are on the Rise Globally." *Christian Science Monitor,* December 28. Reprinted in Jeffress Ramsay (Ed.), 1993. *Africa.* 5th ed. Guilford, CT.: Dushkin Publishing Group.

LEWIS, OSCAR. 1951. *Life in a Mexican Village: Tepotzlan Restudied.* Urbana: University of Illinois Press.

———. 1961. *The Children of Sanchez: Autobiography of a Mexican Family.* New York: Random House.

———. 1966. *La Vida: A Puerto Rican Family in the Culture of Poverty—San Juan and New York.* New York: Random House.

LIEBERMAN, LEONARD. 2001. "How Caucasoids Got Such Big Crania and Why They Shrank: From Morton to Rushton." *Current Anthropology* 42:69–95.

———. 2003. "A History of 'Scientific' Racialism." In Raymond Scupin (Ed.), *Race and Ethnicity: An Anthropological Focus on the U.S. and the World.* Upper Saddle River, NJ: Prentice Hall.

LIEBERMAN, PHILIP. 1984. *The Biology and Evolution of Language.* Cambridge, MA: Harvard University Press.

———. 1991. *Uniquely Human: The Evolution of Speech, Thought, and Selfless Behavior.* Cambridge: Harvard University Press.

LIEBERMAN, PHILIP, and R. C. MCCARTHY. 1999. "The Ontogeny of Cranial Base Angulation in Humans and Chimpanzees and Its Implications for Reconstruction Pharyngeal Dimensions. *Journal of Human Evolution* 36(5):487–517.

LINCOLN, JAMES R., and KERRY MCBRIDE. 1987. "Japanese Industrial Organization in Comparative Perspective." *Annual Review of Sociology* 13:289–312.

LINDENBAUM, SHIRLEY. 1972. "Sorcerers, Ghosts, and Polluting Women: An Analysis of Religious Belief and Population Control." *Ethnology* 2(3):241–53.

LINDHOLM, CHARLES. 1986. "Kinship Structure and Political Authority: The Middle East and Central Asia." *Comparative Study of Society and History* 28(2):334–55.

———. 1995. "Love as an Experience of Transcendence." In W. Jankowiak (Ed.), *Romantic Love: A Universal Experience?* New York: Columbia University Press.

———. 1996. *The Islamic Middle East: An Historical Anthropology.* Oxford: Blackwell Publishers.

———. 1998. "The Future of Love." In V. De Munck (Ed.), *Romantic Love and Sexual Behavior: Perspectives from the Social Sciences.* Westport, CT: Praeger Press.

———. 2001. *Culture Identity: The History, Theory, and Practice of Psychological Anthropology.* Boston: McGraw-Hill.

LINDHOLM, CHARLES, and CHERRY LINDHOLM. 1980. "What Price Freedom?" *Science Digest,* November-December, pp. 50–55.

LINTON, RALPH. 1936. *The Study of Man.* New York: Appleton-Century-Crofts.

———. 1942. "Age and Sex Categories." *American Sociological Review* 7:589–603.

LIPSET, SEYMOUR MARTIN, and REINHARD BENDIX. 1967. *Social Mobility in Industrial Society.* Berkeley: University of California Press.

LOCKWOOD, VICTORIA S. 2003. *Globalization and Culture Change in the Pacific.* Upper Saddle River, NJ: Prentice Hall.

LOEWE, RONALD. B., and HELENE HOFFMAN. 2002. "Building the New Zion: Unfinished Conversations Between the Jews of Venta Prieta, Mexico, and Their Neighbors to the North." *American Anthropologist* 104(4):1135–47.

LORENZ, KONRAD. 1966. *On Aggression.* New York: Harcourt, Brace & World.

LOWENSTEIN, TOM. 1993. *Ancient Land, Sacred Whale: the Inuit Hunt and Its Rituals.* New York: Farrar, Strauss and Giroux.

LUBKEMANN, STEPHEN C. 2004. "Refugees: Worldwide Displacement and International Response." In Ruth Osterweiss Selig, Marilyn R. London, and P. Ann Kaupp (Eds.), *Anthropology Explored: Revised and Expanded: The Best of Smithsonian Anthronotes.* Washington, DC: Smithsonian Books.

LUCERO, LISA J. 2003. "The Politics of Ritual: The Emergence of Classic Maya Rulers with CA Comment." *Current Anthropology* 44(4):523–58.

LUCY, JOHN. 1992. *Grammatical Categories and Cognition: A Case Study of the Linguistic Relativity Hypothesis.* Cambridge: Cambridge University Press.

LUKENS-BULL, RONALD A. 2003. "Ronald McDonald as a Javanese Saint and an Indonesian Freedom Fighter: Reflections on the Global and the Local." *Crossroads: An Interdisciplinary Journal of Southeast Asian Studies* 17(1):108–28.

LUTZ, CATHERINE. 1988. *Unnatural Emotions: Everyday Sentiments on a Micronesian Atoll and Their Challenge to Western Theory.* Chicago: University of Chicago Press.

MACDONALD, SHARON (Ed.). 1993: *Inside European Identities. Ethnography in Western Europe.* Oxford: Berg Press.

MACEACHERN, SCOTT. 2003. "Race." In Raymond Scupin (Ed.), *Race and Ethnicity: An Anthropological Focus on the U.S. and the World.* Upper Saddle River, NJ: Prentice Hall.

MACIONIS, JOHN. 2004a. *Cities and Urban Life.* 3d ed. Upper Saddle River, NJ: Prentice Hall.

———. 2004b. *Society: The Basics.* 7th ed. Upper Saddle River, NJ: Prentice Hall.

MAJERUS, M. E. N. 1998. *Melanism: Evolution in Action.* Oxford: Oxford University Press.

MALINOWSKI, BRONISLAW. [1922] 1961. *Argonauts of the Western Pacific.* New York: Dutton.

———. 1927. *Sex and Repression in Savage Society.* New York: Meridian Books.

———. 1945. Foreward in P. Kaberry (Ed.), *The Dynamics of Culture Change: An Inquiry into Race Relations in Africa.* New Haven, CT: Yale University Press.

Malkki, Liisa. 1995. "Refugees and Exile: From 'Refugee Studies' to the National Order of Things." *Annual Review of Anthropology* 24:495–523.

MALONEY, CLARENCE. 1974. *Peoples of South Asia.* New York: Holt, Rinehart and Winston.

MALOTKI, EKKEHART. 1983. *Hopi Time: A Linguistic Analysis of the Temporal Concepts in the Hopi Language.* Berlin: Mouton.

MANN, ROBERT W., and THOMAS D. HOLLAND. 2004. "America's MIAs: Forensic Anthropology in Action." In Ruth Osterweiss Selig, Marilyn R. London, and P. Ann Kaupp (Eds.), *Anthropology Explored: Revised and Expanded: The Best of Smithsonian Anthronotes.* Washington, DC: Smithsonian Books.

MAQUET, JACQUES. 1972. *Civilizations of Black Africa.* London: Oxford University Press.

MARANO, LOU. 1982. "Windigo Psychosis: The Anatomy of an Emic-Etic Confusion." *Current Anthropology* 23:385–412.

MARSELLA, ANTHONY J. 1979. "Cross-Cultural Studies of Mental Disorders." In Anthony J. Marsella, Ronald G. Tharp, and Thomas J. Cibrowski (Eds.), *Perspectives on Cross-Cultural Psychology.* New York: Academic Press.

MARSHALL, YVONNE. 1998. "By Way of Introduction from the Pacific Northwest Coast." *World Archaeology* 29(3):311–16.

MARTIN, KAY, and BARBARA VOORHIES. 1975. *Female of the Species.* New York: Columbia University Press.

MARX, KARL. [1859] 1959. *A Contribution of the Critique of Political Economy.* New York: International Publishers.

MASCIA-LEES, FRANCES, and NANCY JOHNSON BLACK. 2000. *Gender and Anthropology.* Prospect Heights, IL: Waveland Press.

MAUSS, MARCEL. 1985. "A Category of the Human Mind: The Notion of Person; the Notion of Self," trans. W. D. Halls. In Michael Carrithers, Steven Collins, and Steven Lukes (Eds.), *The Category of the Person: Anthropology, Philosophy, History.* Cambridge: Cambridge University Press.

MAY, DARLENE. 1980. "Women in Islam: Yesterday and Today." In Cyriac Pullapilly (Ed.), *Islam in the Contemporary World.* Notre Dame, IN: Cross Roads Books.

MAYBURY-LEWIS, DAVID. 1985. "A Special Sort of Pleading: Anthropology at the Service of Ethnic Groups." In R. Paine (Ed.), *Advocacy and Anthropology.* St. John's, Newfoundland: Institute of Social and Economic Research, Memorial University of Newfoundland.

———. 2002. *Indigenous Peoples, Ethnic Groups, and the State.* 2d ed. Boston: Pearson Education, Allyn & Bacon.

———. 1998. "Cultural Survival, Ethics and Political Expediency: The Anthropology of Group Rights." (http://www.cs.org/publications/featuredarticles/1998/mayburylewis.htm).

MCALLESTER, DAVID P. 1983. "North American Native Music." In Elizabeth May (Ed.), *Music of Many Cultures: An Introduction*. Berkeley: University of California Press.

———. 1984. "North America/Native America." In Jeff Todd Titon (Ed.), *Worlds of Music: An Introduction to the Music of the World's Peoples*. New York: Schirmer Books.

McCLELLAND, DAVID. 1973. "Business Drive and National Achievement." In A. Etzioni and E. Etzioni-Halevy (Eds.), *Social Change*. New York: Basic Books.

McCREERY, JOHN. 2000. *Japanese Consumer Behavior: From Worker Bees to Wary Shoppers*. Honolulu: University of Hawaii Press.

McCREERY, JOHN, and RUTH McCREERY. 2006. "Japan." In Raymond Scupin (Ed.), *Peoples and Cultures of Asia*. Upper Saddle River, NJ: Prentice Hall.

McDANIEL, L. 1998. *The Big Drum Ritual of Carriacou: Praise Songs in Memory of Flight*. Gainesville: University Press of Florida.

McDONALD, JAMES H. 1997. "Privatizing the Private Family Farmer: NAFTA and the Transformation of the Mexican Dairy Sector." *Human Organization* 56(1):321–32.

———. 1999. "The Neoliberal Project and Governmentality in Rural Mexico: Emergent Farmer Organization in the Michoacan Highlands." *Human Organization* 58(3):274–84.

———. 2001. "Reconfiguring the Countryside: Power, Control, and the (Re)Organization of Farmers in West Mexico." *Human Organization* 60(3):247–58.

McINTOSH, SUSAN. 1999. *Beyond Chiefdoms: Pathways to Complexity in Africa*. Cambridge: Cambridge University Press.

McINTOSH, S. K., and R. J. McINTOSH. 1993. "Current Directions in West African Prehistory." *Annual Review of Anthropology* 12:215–58.

McKENNA, JAMES, SARAH MOSKO, and CHRIS RICHARD. 1999. "Breastfeeding and Mother-Infant Cosleeping in Relation to SIDS Prevention." In Wenda R. Trevathan, E. O. Smith, and James J. McKenna (Eds.), *Evolutionary Medicine*. New York and Oxford: Oxford University Press.

MEAD, MARGARET. 1928. *Coming of Age in Samoa*. New York: Morrow.

———. 1935. *Sex and Temperament in Three Primitive Societies*. New York: Mentor.

MEGGITT, MERVYN. 1977. *Blood Is Their Argument: Warfare Among the Mae Enga Tribesmen of the New Guinea Highlands*. Palo Alto, CA: Mayfield.

MENCHER, JOAN P. 1965. "The Nayars of South Malabar." In M. F. Nimkorr (Ed.), *Comparative Family Systems*, pp. 162–91. Boston: Houghton Mifflin.

———. 1974. "The Caste System Upside Down: Or the Not-So-Mysterious East." *Current Anthropology* 15:469–94.

MENON, SHANTI. 1996. "Male Authority and Female Autonomy: A Study of the Nayars in South India." In M. J. Maynes, A. Waltner, B. Stroland, and U. Strasser (Eds.), *Gender, Kinship, Power: A Comparative Interdisciplinary History*. New York: Routledge.

MENSAH, ATTA ANNAM. 1983. "Music South of the Sahara." In Elizabeth May (Ed.), *Music of Many Cultures: An Introduction*. Berkeley: University of California Press.

MERRILL, WILLIAM L. 2004. "Identity in Colonial Northern Mexico." In Ruth Osterweiss Selig, Marilyn R. London, and P. Ann Kaupp (Eds.), *Anthropology Explored: Revised and Expanded: The Best of Smithsonian Anthronotes*. Washington, DC: Smithsonian Books.

MESKELL, LYNN. 1995. "Goddesses, Gimbutas and 'New Age Archaeology,'" *Antiquity* (March).

MESSENGER, JOHN. 1971. "Sex and Repression in an Irish Folk Community." In Donald S. Marshall and Robert C. Suggs (Eds.), *Human Sexual Behavior: Variations in the Ethnographic Spectrum*. New York: Basic Books.

METRAUX, AFRED, HUGO CHARTERIS, and SIDNEY MINTZ. 1989. *Voodoo in Haiti*. New York: Schocken Books.

MIDDLETON, JOHN. 1960. *Lugbara Religion*. London: Oxford University Press.

———. 1978. *Peoples of Africa*. New York: Arco.

——— (Ed.). 2000. *Encyclopedia of Africa: South of the Sahara*, Vol. 2. New York: Simon and Schuster/MacMillan.

MILLER, JOSEPH. 1988. *Way of Death: Merchant Capitalism and the Angolan Slave Trade 1730–1830*. Madison: University of Madison Press.

MOLLOY, MAUREEN. 1990. "Considered Affinity: Kinship, Marriage and Social Class in New France." *Social Science History* 14(1):2–26.

MOLNAR, STEPHEN. 1997. *Human Variation: Races, Types, and Ethnic Groups*. 4th ed. Upper Saddle River, NJ: Prentice Hall.

MONAGHAN, L., L. HINTON, and R. KEPHART. 1997. "Cant Teach a Dog to Be a Cat?: A Dialogue on Ebonics." *Anthropology Newsletter* 38(3):1, 8, 9.

MONTAGU, ASHLEY (Ed.). 1968. *Man and Aggression*. London: Oxford University Press.

———. 1997. *Man's Most Dangerous Myth: The Fallacy of Race*. 6th ed. Walnut Creek, CA: AltaMira Press.

MORAN, EMILIO F. 1982. *Human Adaptability: An Introduction to Ecological Anthropology*. Boulder, CO: Westview Press.

MORGAN, LEWIS HENRY. [1877] 1964. *Ancient Society*. Cambridge, MA: Harvard University Press.

MOSHER, STEVEN W. 1983. *The Broken Earth: The Rural Chinese*. Glencoe, IL: Free Press.

MUKERJEE, MADHUSREE. 1999. "Out of Africa, Into Asia." *Scientific American* 280(1):24.

MUMFORD, LEWIS. 1961. *The City in History: Its Origins, Its Transformations, and Its Prospects*. New York: Harcourt, Brace & World.

MURDOCK, GEORGE. 1945. "The Common Denominator of Cultures." In Ralph Linton (Ed.), *The Science of Man in the World Crisis*, pp. 123–42. New York: Columbia University Press.

———. 1949. *Social Structure*. New York: Macmillan.

———. 1959. "Cross-Language Parallels in Parental Kin Terms." *Anthropological Linguistics*. 1:1–5.

———. 1967. "Ethnographic Atlas: A Summary." *Ethnology* 6:109–236.

———. 1968. "The Current Status of the World's Hunting and Gathering Peoples." In Richard Lee and Irven DeVore (Eds.), *Man the Hunter*, pp. 13–20. Chicago: Aldine.

———. 1981a. *Atlas of World Cultures*. Pittsburgh: University of Pittsburgh Press.

———. 1981b. *Ethnographic Atlas*. Pittsburgh: University of Pittsburgh Press.

MURPHY, R. F., and L. KASDAN. 1959. "The Structure of Parallel Cousin Marriage." *American Anthropologist* 61:17–29.

MURRAY, GERALD F. 1989. "The Domestication of Wood in Haiti: A Case Study in Applied Evolution." *Anthropological Praxis*. Reprinted in Aaron Podelfsky and Peter J. Brown (Eds.), 1994. *Applying Anthropology: An Introductory Reader*. Mountain View, CA: Mayfield.

MURRAY, R. D., and SMITH, E. O. 1983. "The Role of Dominance and Intrafamilial Bonding in the Avoidance of Close Inbreeding." *Journal of Human Evolution* 12:481–86.

MYERS, DAVID G. 1998. *Psychology*. 5th ed. New York: Worth Publishers.

———. 2002. *Intuition: Its Powers and Perils*. New Haven: Yale University Press.

NAKANE, CHIA. 1970. *Japanese Society*. Rutland, VT: Charles Tuttle.

NANDA, SERENA. 1990. *Neither Man nor Woman: The Hijras of India*. Belmont, CA: Wadsworth.

———. 2000. *Gender Diversity: Crosscultural Variations*. Prospect Heights, IL: Waveland Press.

NASH, JUNE. 1997. "The Fiesta of the Word: The Zapatista Uprising and Radical Democracy in Mexico." *American Anthropologist* 99(2):261–74.

NASH, MANNING. 1989. *The Cauldron of Ethnicity in the Modern World*. Chicago: University of Chicago Press.

NATIONAL OPINION RESEARCH CENTER. 1999. *General Social Surveys, 1972–1999: Cumulative Codebook*. Chicago: University of Chicago.

NEALE, WALTER. 1976. *Monies in Societies*. San Francisco: Chandler.

NEEDHAM, RODNEY. 1967. "Percussion and Transition." *Man* 2:606–14.

NGUYEN, VINH-KIM, and KARINE PESCHARD. 2003. "Anthropology, Inequality, and Disease: A Review." *Annual Review of Anthropology* 32:447–74.

NORGET, KRISTIN. 1996. "Beauty and the Feast: Aesthetics and the Performance of Meaning in the Day of the Dead, Oaxaca, Mexico." *Journal of Latin American Lore* 19:53–64.

OBEYESKERE, GANANATH. 1992. *Apotheosis of Captain Cook: European Mythmaking in the Pacific*. Princeton, NJ: Princeton University Press.

OHNUKI-TIERNEY, EMIKO. 1998. "A Conceptual Model for the Historical Relationship Between the Self and the Internal and External Others: The Agrarian Japanese, the Ainu, and the Special Status People." In Dru Gladney (Ed.), *Making Majorities: Constituting the Nation in Japan, Korea, China, Malaysia, Fiji, Turkey, and the United States*. Stanford: Stanford University Press.

———. 1999. "We Eat Each Other's Food to Nourish Our Body: The Global and Local as Mutually Constituent Forces." In Raymond Grew (Ed.), *Food in Global History*. Boulder, CO: Westview Press.

OKIGBO, BEDE N. 1988. "Food: Finding Solutions to the Crisis." *Africa Report*, September–October.

OLIVER, DOUGLAS. 1955. *A Solomon Island Society: Kinship and Leadership Among the Siuai of Bougainville*. Cambridge, MA: Harvard University Press.

———. 1974. *Ancient Tahitian Society*, 3 vols. Honolulu: University of Hawaii Press.

OLMOS, M. F. 1997. *Sacred Possessions: Vodou, Santeria, Obeah, and the Caribbean*. New Brunswick, NJ: Rutgers University Press.

O'MEARA, TIM J. 1990. *Samoan Planters: Tradition and Economic Development in Polynesia*. New York: Holt, Rinehart and Winston.

———. 2004. Personal comments on Samoa and Mead.

OMOHUNDRO, JOHN. 1998. *Careers in Anthropology*. Mountain View, CA: Mayfield.

ORTNER, SHERRY. 1974. "Is Female to Male as Nature Is to Culture?" In Michelle Zimbalist Rosaldo and Louise Lamphere (Eds.), *Woman, Culture, and Society*, pp. 67–87. Stanford, CA: Stanford University Press.

———. 1996. *Making Gender: The Politics and Erotics of Culture*. Boston: Beacon Press.

———. 2001. *Life and Death on Mt. Everest: Sherpas and Himalayan Mountaineering*. Princeton: Princeton University Press.

OSWALT, WENDELL H. 1972. *Other Peoples, Other Customs: World Ethnography and Its History*. New York: Holt, Rinehart and Winston.

———. 1976. *An Anthropological Analysis of Food-Getting Technology*. New York: John Wiley.

———. 1999. *Eskimos and Explorers*. 2d ed. Lincoln: University of Nebraska Press.

OTTENBERG, PHOEBE. 1965. "The Afikpo Ibo of Eastern Nigeria." In James L. Gibbs (Ed.), *Peoples of Africa*. New York: Holt, Rinehart and Winston.

OTTERBEIN, KEITH. 1970. *The Evolution of War*. New Haven, CT: HRAF Press.

———. 1974. "The Anthropology of War." In John Honigmann (Ed.), *Handbook of Social and Cultural Anthropology*. Chicago: Rand McNally.

———. 1994. *Feuding and Warfare: Selected Works of Keith F. Otterbein*. Langhorne, PA: Gordon and Breach.

———. 1999. "Historical Essay: A History of the Research on Warfare in Anthropology." *American Anthropologist* 101(4):794–805.

———. 2000. "The Doves Have Been Heard From, Where Are the Hawks?" *American Anthropologist* 102(4):841–44.

OUICHI, WILLIAM G. 1981. *Theory Z: How American Business Can Meet the Japanese Challenge*. New York: Avon Books.

PALAKORNKUL, ANGKAB. 1972. *A Sociolinguistic Study of Pronominial Strategy in Spoken Bangkok Thai*. Doctoral Dissertation, University of Texas, Austin.

PALMORE, ERDMAN BALLAGH. 1975. *The Honorable Elders: A Cross-Cultural Analysis of Aging in Japan*. Durham, NC: Duke University Press.

PARRINDER, GEOFFREY. 1983. *World Religions: From Ancient History to the Present*. New York: Hamlyn Publishing Group.

PARRY, JONATHAN. 1980. "Ghosts, Greed and Sin: The Occupational Identity of the Benares Funeral Priests." *Man* 21:453–73.

PASTERNAK, BURTON. 1976. *Introduction to Kinship and Social Organization*. Englewood Cliffs, NJ: Prentice Hall.

PATTERSON, FRANCINE, and DONALD COHN. 1978. "Conversations with a Gorilla." *National Geographic* 154:454–62.

PATTERSON, FRANCINE, and EUGENE LINDEN. 1981. *The Education of Koko*. New York: Holt, Rinehart and Winston.

PATTERSON, MARY. 2000. "Sorcery and Witchcraft." In Raymond Scupin (Ed.), *Religion and Culture: An Anthropological Focus*. Upper Saddle River, NJ: Prentice Hall.

PAUL, ROBERT A. 1989. "Psychoanalytic Anthropology." *Annual Review of Anthropology* 18:177–202.

———. 1996. *Moses and Civilization: The Meaning Behind Freud's Myth*. New Haven: Yale University Press.

PEACOCK, JAMES. 1986. *The Anthropological Lens: Harsh Light, Soft Focus*. Cambridge: Cambridge University Press.

PENNOCK, ROBERT T. 2003. "Creationism and Intelligent Design." *Annual Review of Genomics and Human Genetics* 4:143–63.

PICKETT, J. M. 1999. *Acoustics of Speech Communication: the Fundamentals, Speech Perception Theory, and Technology*. Boston MA: Allyn and Bacon.

PIDDOCKE, STUART. 1965. "The Potlatch System of the Southern Kwakiutl: A New Perspective." *Southwestern Journal of Anthropology* 21:244–64.

PIERPONT, CLAUDIA ROTH. 2004. "The Measure of America: How a Rebel Anthropologist Waged a War on Racism." *The New Yorker*, March 8:48–63.

PIETERSE, JAN NEDERVEEN. 2002. *Globalization & Culture: Global Melange*. Lanham, MD: Rowman and Littlefield Publishers, Inc.

PIKE, DOUGLAS. 1990. "Change and Continuity in Vietnam." *Current History* 89(545):117–34.

PINKER, STEVEN. 1994. *The Language Instinct: How the Mind Creates Language*. New York: HarperCollins.

POPULATION REFERENCE BUREAU. 1986. *Population Data Sheet*. Washington, DC: Population Reference Bureau.

———. 1991. *World Population Data Sheet*. Washington, DC: Population Reference Bureau.

POSPISIL, LEONARD. 1963. *The Kapauku Papuans of West New Guinea*. New York: Holt, Rinehart and Winston.

———. 1967. "The Attributes of Law." In Paul Bohannon (Ed.), *Law and Warfare: Studies in the Anthropology of Conflict*. Garden City, NY: Natural History Press.

POWDERMAKER, HORTENSE. 1966. *Stranger and Friend: The Way of an Anthropologist*. New York: W. W. Norton.

PRICE, DAVID. 2001. "'The Shameful Business': Leslie Spier On the Censure of Franz Boas" *HAN* Vol. 27(2):9–12.

———. 2002. "Interlopers and Invited Guests: On Anthropology's Witting and Unwitting Links to Intelligence Agencies." *Anthropology Today* 18(6):16–21.

———. 2004. *Threatening Anthropology: McCarthyism and the FBI's Investigation of American Anthropologists*. Durham, NC: Duke University Press.

PRIETO, N. I. 1997. *Beautiful Flowers of the Maquiladora: Life Histories of Women Workers in Tijuana*. Austin: University of Texas Press.

PUSEY, ANNE. 2004. "Inbreeding Avoidance in Primates." In Arthur Wolf and William Durham, *Inbreeding, Incest, and the Incest Taboo.* Stanford: Stanford University Press.

QUALE, ROBIN G. 1988. *A History of Marriage Systems.* New York: Greenwood Press.

QUIGLEY, DECLAN. 1999. *The Interpretation of Caste.* Oxford: Oxford University Press.

QUINN, NAOMI, and DOROTHY HOLLAND. 1987. "Culture and Cognition." In D. Holland and N. Quinn (Eds.), *Cultural Models in Language and Thought.* Cambridge: Cambridge University Press.

RADCLIFFE-BROWN, A. R. [1922] 1964. *The Andaman Islanders.* New York: Free Press.

RAHEJA, GLORIA. 1988. *The Poison in the Gift: Ritual, Prestation, and the Dominant Caste in a North Indian Village.* Chicago: University of Chicago Press.

RAMSAY, JEFFRESS F. (Ed.). 2001. *Africa.* 9th ed. Guilford, CT: McGraw-Hill/Dushkin Publishing Group.

RAPPAPORT, ROY. 1979. *Ecology, Meaning, and Religion.* Richmond, VA: North Atlantic Books.

———. 1984. *Pigs for the Ancestors: Ritual in the Ecology of a New Guinea People.* New Haven, CT: Yale University Press.

RAVEN, PETER H., LINDA R. BERG, and GEORGE B. JOHNSON. 1993. *Environment.* Fort Worth, TX: Saunders College Publishing.

RAYNER, STEVE. 1989. "Fiddling While the Globe Warms." *Anthropology Today* 5(6):1–2.

REDFIELD, ROBERT. 1930. *Tepotzlan: A Mexican Village: A Study of Folk Life.* Chicago: University of Chicago Press.

REDFIELD, ROBERT, and ALFONSO VILLA ROJAS. 1934. *Chan Kom, A Maya Village.* Washington, DC: Carnegie Institute.

REICH, ROBERT B. 2003. "High-Tech Jobs Are Going Abroad! But 'That's Okay." *The Washington Post, Sunday Outlook* section. March 11th.

RELETHFORD, JOHN H. 1997. *The Human Species: An Introduction to Biological Anthropology.* 3d ed. Mountain View, CA: Mayfield.

RENFREW, COLIN. 1989. *Archaeology and Language: The Puzzle of Indo-European Origins.* Cambridge: Cambridge University Press.

RICKFORD, JOHN R. 1997. "Suite for Ebony and Phonics." *Discovery* 18(2):82–87.

RIDLEY, MATT. 1996. *The Origins of Virtue: Human Instincts and the Evolution of Cooperation.* New York: Viking Press.

RINER, REED. 1981. "The Supranational Network of Boards of Directors." *Current Anthropology* 22(2):167–72.

RIVERS, W. H. O. [1906] 1967. *Todas.* London: Macmillan.

ROBARCHEK, C. A., and C. J. ROBARCHEK. 1998. *Wuorani: The Contexts of Violence and War.* Fort Worth: Harcourt Brace.

ROBBINS, RICHARD H. 2001. *Global Problems and the Culture of Capitalism.* 2d ed. Boston: Allyn and Bacon.

———. 2004. *Global Problems and the Culture of Capitalism: With Talking Points on Global Issues.* Boston: Allyn and Bacon.

ROBERSON, DEBI, IAN DAVIES, and JULES DAVIDOFF. 2000. "Colour Categories Are Not Universal: Replications and New Evidence from Stone Age Culture." *Journal of Experimental Psychology* 129(3):369–98.

ROBERTS, JOHN M. 1967. "Oaths, Autonomic Ordeals, and Power." In Clellan S. Ford (Ed.), *Cross-Cultural Approaches: Readings in Comparative Research.* New Haven, CT: HRAF Press.

ROBERTSON, CLAIRE C. 1984. "Women in the Urban Economy." In Margaret Jean Hay and Sharon Stichter (Eds.), *African Women South of the Sahara.* London: Longman.

ROMANUCCI-ROSS, LOLA. 1973. *Conflict, Violence and Morality in a Mexican Village.* Palo Alto, CA: National Press Books.

ROSCOE, PAUL B. 1993. "The Brokers of the Lord: The Ministrations of a Christian Faith in the Sepik Basin of Papua New Guinea." In V. Lockwood, T. Harding, and B. Wallace (Eds.), *Contemporary Pacific Societies: Studies in Development and Change.* Upper Saddle River, NJ: Prentice Hall.

———. 1994. "Amity and Aggression: A Symbolic Theory of Incest." *Man* 28:1–28.

ROSMAN, ABRAHAM, and PAULA G. RUBEL. 1986. *Feasting with Mine Enemy: Rank and Exchange Among Northwest Coast Societies.* Prospect Heights, IL: Waveland Press.

ROSSIDES, DANIEL W. 1990a. *Comparative Societies: Social Types and Their Interrelations.* Upper Saddle River, NJ: Prentice Hall.

———. 1990b. *Social Stratification: The American Class System in Comparative Perspective.* Upper Saddle River, NJ: Prentice Hall.

ROSTOW, WALTER W. 1978. *The World Economy: History and Prospect.* Austin: University of Texas Press.

ROTHENBERG, JEROME. 1985. *Technicians of the Sacred: A Range of Poetries from Africa, Asia, Europe, and Oceania.* Berkeley: University of California Press.

ROUSSEAU, JEAN JACQUES. [1762] 1973. *The Social Contract.* London: Dent.

ROWLEY-CONWY, PETER. 1993. "Was There a Neanderthal Religion?" In G. Burenhult (Ed.), *The First Humans: Human Origins and History to 10,000 B.C.,* p. 70. New York: HarperCollins.

RUSELL, D. E. H. 1986. *The Secret Trauma: Incest in the Lives of Girls and Women.* New York: Basic Books.

SAFA, HELEN I. 1974. *The Urban Poor of Puerto Rico: A Study in Development and Inequality.* New York: Holt, Rinehart and Winston.

SAHLINS, MARSHALL. 1958. *Social Stratification in Polynesia.* Monograph of the American Ethnological Society. Seattle: University of Washington Press.

———. 1965. "On the Sociology of Primitive Exchange." In M. Banton (Ed.), *The Relevance of Models for Social Anthropology,* pp. 139–227. London: Tavistock.

———. 1968b. *Tribesmen.* Englewood Cliffs, NJ: Prentice Hall.

———. 1972. *Stone Age Economics.* Chicago: Aldine.

———. 1976. *The Use and Abuse of Biology: An Anthropological Critique of Sociobiology.* Ann Arbor: University of Michigan Press.

———. 1985. *Islands of History.* Chicago: University of Chicago Press.

———. 1995. *How 'Natives' Think, About Captain Cook, For Example.* Chicago: University of Chicago Press.

SALISBURY, R. F. 1962. *From Stone to Steel: Economic Consequences of a Technological Change in New Guinea.* Cambridge: Cambridge University Press.

SALMON, MERRILEE H. 1997. "Ethical Considerations in Anthropology and Archaeology, or Relativism and Justice for All." *Journal of Anthropological Research* 53:47–63.

SALZMAN, PHILIP. 1989. "The Lone Stranger and the Solitary Quest." *Anthropology Newsletter* 30(5):16, 44.

———. 2000. "Hierarchical Image and Reality: The Construction of a Tribal Chiefship." *Comparative Study of Society and History* 42(1):49–66.

———. 2004. *Pastoralists: Equality, Hierarchy, and the State.* Boulder: Westview Press.

SANDERSON, STEPHEN. 1999. *Social Transformations: A General Theory of Historical Development.* Expanded edition. Lanham, MD: Rowman and Littlefield.

SARICH, V. M., and FRANK MEILE. 2004. *Race: The Reality of Human Differences.* Boulder, CO: Westview Press.

SAVAGE-RUMBAUGH, SUE E. 1986. *Ape Language from Conditioned Response to Symbol.* New York: Columbia University Press.

SCARR, S., and R. A. WEINBERG. 1978. "Attitudes, Interests, and IQ." *Human Nature* 1(4):29–36.

SCHAFFT, GRETCHEN. 1999. "Professional Denial." *Anthropology Newsletter* 40(1):56–54 (January).

SCHALLER, GEORGE. 1976. *The Mountain Gorilla—Ecology and Behavior.* Chicago: University of Chicago Press.

SCHELL, LAWRENCE M., and MELINDA DENHAM. 2003. "Environmental Pollution in Urban Environments and Human Biology." *Annual Review of Anthropology* 32:111–34.

SCHEPARTZ, L. A. 1993. "Language and Modern Human Origins." *Yearbook of Physical Anthropology* 36:1–126.

SCHIEFFELIN, BAMBI B. 1990. *The Give and Take of Everyday Life: Language Socialization of Kaluli Children.* New York: Cambridge University Press.

SCHIEFFELIN, BAMBI, and ELINOR OCHS (Eds.). 1987. *Language Socialization Across Cultures.* Studies in the Social and Cultural Foundations of Languages, No 3. Cambridge: Cambridge University Press.

SCHILDKROUT, ENID, and ADRIENNE L. KAEPPLER. 2004. "From Tattoo to Piercing: Body Art as Visual Language." "In Ruth Osterweiss Selig, Marilyn R. London, and P. Ann Kaupp (Eds.), *Anthropology Explored: Revised and Expanded: The Best of Smithsonian Anthronotes.* Washington, DC: Smithsonian Books.

SCHLEGEL, ALICE, and ROHN ELOUL. 1988. "Marriage Transactions: Labor, Property, and Status." *American Anthropologist* 90(2):291–309.

SCHNEIDER, DAVID. 1953. "A Note on Bridewealth and the Stability of Marriage." *Man* 53:55–57.

SCHUSKY, ERNEST L. 1990. *Culture and Agriculture.* New York: Bergin and Garvey.

SCHWARTZ, RICHARD, and JAMES C. MILLER. 1975. "Legal Evolution and Societal Complexity." In Ronald L. Akers and James C. Miller (Eds.), *Law and Control in Society.* Englewood Cliffs, NJ: Prentice Hall.

SCOTT, EUGENIE C. 2004. *Evolution vs. Creationism: An Introduction.* Westport, CT: Greenwood Press.

SCOTT, JAMES. 1976. *The Moral Economy of the Peasant: Rebellion and Subsistence in Southeast Asia.* New Haven: Yale University Press.

SCUDDER, THAYER, and ELIZABETH COLSON. 1979. "Long-Term Research in Gwembe Valley, Zambia." In G. Foster (Ed.), *Long Term Field Research in Social Anthropology.* New York: Academic Press.

SCUPIN, RAYMOND. 1988. "Language, Hierarchy and Hegemony: Thai Muslim Discourse Strategies." *Language Sciences* 10(2):331–51.

———— (Ed.). 2000. *Religion and Culture: An Anthropological Focus.* Upper Saddle River, NJ: Prentice Hall.

———— (Ed.). 2003a. *Race and Ethnicity: An Anthropological Focus on the U.S. and the World.* Upper Saddle River, NJ: Prentice Hall.

————. 2003b. "The Anthropology of Islam as Applied Anthropology." *Reviews in Anthropology* 32:141–58.

———— (Ed.). 2006. *Peoples and Cultures of Asia.* Upper Saddle River, NJ: Prentice Hall.

SENGHAS, KITA S., and A. OZYUREK. A. 2004. "Children Creating Core Properties of Language: Evidence from an Emerging Sign Language in Nicaragua." *Science* 305(5691):1779–95.

SERVICE, ELMAN. 1960. "The Law of Evolutionary Potential." In Marshall D. Sahlins and Elman R. Service (Eds.), *Evolution and Culture,* pp. 93–122. Ann Arbor: University of Michigan Press.

————. [1962] 1971. *Primitive Social Organization: An Evolutionary Perspective.* New York: Random House.

————. 1975. *Origins of the State and Civilization: The Process of Cultural Evolution.* New York: W. W. Norton.

————. 1978a. "Classical and Modern Theories of the Origin of Government." In Ronald Cohen and E. R. Service (Eds.), *Origins of the State: The Anthropology of Political Evolution.* Philadelphia: Institute for Study of Human Issues.

————. 1978b. *Profiles in Ethnology.* New York: Harper & Row.

————. 1979. *The Hunters.* 2d ed. Englewood Cliffs, NJ: Prentice Hall.

SHAHRANI, M. NAZIF. 1981. "Growing in Respect: Aging Among the Kirghiz of Afghanistan." In P. Amoss and S. Harrell (Eds.), *Other Ways of Growing Old: Anthropologist Perspectives.* Stanford, CA: Stanford University Press.

SHAHRANI, M. NAZIF, and ROBERT CANFIELD (Eds.). 1984. *Revolutions and Rebellions in Afghanistan: Anthropological Perspectives.* Berkeley: University of California Press.

SHANKMAN, PAUL. 1975. "A Forestry Scheme in Samoa." *Natural History* 84(8):60–69.

————. 1978. "Notes on a Corporate 'Potlatch': The Lumber Industry in Samoa." In A. Idris-Soven, E. Idris-Soven, and M. K. Vaugh (Eds.), *The World as a Company Town: Multinational Corporations and Social Change.* The Hague: Mouton World Anthropology Series.

————. 1998. "Margaret Mead, Derek Freeman, and the Issue of Evolution." *Skeptical Inquirer* 22(6):35–39.

————. 1999. "Development, Sustainability, and the Deforestation of Samoa." *Pacific Studies* 22(3/4):167–88.

————. 2001. "Requiem for a Controversy: Whatever Happened to Margaret Mead?" *Skeptic* 9:48–53.

SHANNON, THOMAS RICHARD. 1988. *An Introduction to the World-System Perspective.* Boulder, CO: Westview Press.

SHEPHER, JOSEPH. 1983. *Incest: A Biosocial View.* New York: Academic Press.

SHIMIZU, AKITOSHI. 1987. "*Ie* and *Dozuku:* Family and Descent in Japan." *Current Anthropology* 28(4):S85–S90.

SHIPTON, PARKER. 1990. "African Famines and Food Security: Anthropological Perspectives." *Annual Review of Anthropology* 19:353–94.

SHIRK, MARTHA, and MITCHELL O'DELL JR. 1989. "One Company Evolving in Two Lands." *St. Louis Post-Dispatch*, June 25.

SHOSTAK, MARJORIE. 1981. *Nisa: The Life and Words of a !Kung Woman.* New York: Vintage Books, Random House.

SHWEDER, RICHARD. 1991. *Thinking Through Cultures: Expeditions in Cultural Psychology.* Cambridge, MA: Harvard University Press.

————. 2003. *Why Do Men Barbeque?: Recipes for Cultural Psychology.* Cambridge, MA: Harvard University Press.

SIDKY, H. 2004. *Perspectives on Culture: A Critical Introduction to Theory in Cultural Anthropology.* Upper Saddle River, NJ: Prentice Hall.

SIDKY, H., and DEBORAH AKERS. 2006. "Afghanistan." In Raymond Scupin (Ed.), *Peoples and Cultures of Asia.* Upper Saddle River, NJ: Prentice Hall.

SILLITOE, PAUL. 2001. "Pig Men and Women, Big Men and Women: Gender and Production in the New Guinea Highlands." *Ethnology* 40(3):171–93.

SILVERMAN, PHILIP, and ROBERT J. MAXWELL. 1983. "The Role and Treatment of the Elderly in 95 Societies." In Jay Sokolovsky (Ed.), *Growing Old in Different Cultures,* pp. 43–55. Belmont, CA: Wadsworth.

SIMMONS, LEO. 1945. *The Role of the Aged in Primitive Society.* London: Oxford University Press.

SIMON, JULIAN L. 1981. *The Ultimate Resource.* Princeton, NJ: Princeton University Press.

SIMPSON, J. A., and E. S. C. WIENER. 1989. "Ethnic." *Oxford English Dictionary.* 2d ed. Vol. 5. Oxford: Clarendon Press.

SLAGTER, ROBERT, and HAROLD R. KERBO. 2000. *Modern Thailand.* Boston: McGraw-Hill.

SMALL, MEREDITH. 1995. *What's Love Got to Do with It? The Evolution of Human Mating.* New York: Anchor Books.

————. 1998. *Our Babies: Ourselves.* New York: Anchor Books.

————. 2001. *Kids: How Biology and Culture Shape the Way We Raise Our Children.* New York: Doubleday.

SMART, ALAN, and JOSEPHINE SMART. 2003. "Urbanization and the Global Perspective." *Annual Reviews of Anthropology* 32(1):263–85.

SMITH, ADAM. [1776] 1937. *An Inquiry into the Nature and Causes of the Wealth of Nations*. New York: The Modern Library.

SMITH, ANTHONY. 1986. *The Ethnic Origins of Nations*. Oxford: Blackwell.

SMITH, HUSTON. 1970. *The Religions of Man*. New York: Harper & Row.

———. 1991. *The World Religions: Our Great Wisdom Traditions*. San Francisco: Harper.

SMITH, MARGO L. 1986. "Culture in International Business: Selecting Employees for Expatriate Assignments." In Hendrick Serrie (Ed.), *Anthropology and International Business*. Williamsburg, VA: Department of Anthropology, William and Mary University.

SMITH, M. G. 1965. "The Hausa of Northern Nigeria." In James L. Gibbs, Jr. (Ed.), *Peoples of Africa*. New York: Holt, Rinehart and Winston.

SMITH, NEIL. 1999. *Chomsky: Ideas and Ideals*. Cambridge: Cambridge University Press.

SMITH-IVAN, EDDA. 1988. "Introduction." In Edda Smith-Ivan, Nidhi Tandon, and Jane Connors (Eds.), *Women in Sub-Saharan Africa*, Report No. 7. London: Minority Rights Group.

SOUTHALL, AIDAN. 1956. *Alur Society: A Study in Processes and Types of Domination*. Cambridge: Heffer.

SOUTH ASIA ONLINE BRIEFING PROGRAM. 2000. June/August. Accessed at http://www.thp.org/sac/unit4/cycle.htm.

SOWELL, THOMAS. 1994. *Race and Culture*. New York: Basic Books.

———. 1995. "Ethnicity and IQ." In Steven Fraser (Ed.), *The Bell Curve Wars: Race, Intelligence and the Future of America*. New York: Basic Books.

SPERBER, DAN. 1996. *Explaining Culture: A Naturalistic Approach*. Oxford: Blackwell Publishers.

SPIRO, MELFORD. 1952. "Ghosts, Ifaluk, and Teleological Functionalism." *American Anthropologist* 54:497–503.

———. 1971. *Buddhism and Society: A Great Tradition and Its Burmese Vicissitudes*. Berkeley: University of California Press.

———. 1982. *Oedipus in the Trobriands*. Chicago: University of Chicago Press.

SPONSEL, LESLIE. 1996. "Human Rights and Advocacy Anthropology." In M. Ember and D. Levinson (Eds.), *Encyclopedia of Cultural Anthropology*, Vol. 2. New York: Henry Holt and Company.

———. 1998. "Yanomamin: An Arena of Conflict and Aggression in the Amazon." *Aggressive Behavior* 24:97–122.

STACK, CAROL B. 1975. *All Our Kin: Strategies for Survival in a Black Community*. New York: Harper & Row.

STANNER, W. E. H. 1979. "The Dreaming." In W. A. Lessa and E. Z. Vogt (Eds.), *Reader in Comparative Religion*, 4th ed., pp. 513–23. New York: Harper & Row.

STARRETT, GREGORY. 2004. "Culture Never Dies: Anthropology at Abu Ghraib." *Anthropology News*, September: 10–11.

STEINMETZ, PAUL. 1980. *Pipe, Bible and Peyote Among the Oglala Lakota*. Stockholm: Almquist and Wiksell International.

STEVEN, ROB. 1983. *Classes in Contemporary Japan*. Cambridge: Cambridge University Press.

STEWARD, JULIAN H. 1955. *Theory of Culture Change: The Methodology of Multilinear Evolution*. Urbana: University of Illinois Press.

STEWART, KATHLEEN, and SUSAN HARDING. 1999. "Bad Endings: American Apocalypsis." *Annual Review of Anthropology* 28:285–310.

STONE, LINDA. 2000. *Kinship and Gender: An Introduction*. Boulder: Westview Press.

——— (Ed.). 2001. *New Directions in Anthropological Kinship*. Lanham, MD: Rowman and Littlefield Publishers, Inc.

STRAUSS, CLAUDIA. 1992. "Models and Motives." In R. D'Andrade and C. Strauss (Eds.), *Human Motives and Cultural Models*. Cambridge: Cambridge University Press.

STRIFFLER, STEVE. 2002. "Notes and Documents: Inside a Poultry Processing Plant: An Ethnographic Portrait." *Labor History* 43(3):305–13.

STRINGER, C. B. 1993. *In Search of the Neanderthals: Solving the Puzzle of Human Origins*. London: Thames and Hudson.

STULL, DONALD D., and MICHAEL J. BROADWAY. 2004. *Slaughterhouse Blues: The Meat and Poultry Industry in North America*. Belmont, CA: Wadsworth/Thompson.

STUTLEY, MARGARET. 2003. *Shamanism: An Introduction*. London: Routledge.

SUDARKASA, NIARA. 1989. "African and Afro-American Family Structure." In Johnetta Cole (Ed.), *Anthropology for the Nineties: Introductory Readings*, pp. 132–60. New York: Free Press.

SUTTON, MARK. Q. 2004. *An Introduction to Native North America*. 2d ed. Boston: Pearson Education and Allyn and Bacon.

SWADESH, MORRIS. 1964. "Linguistics as an Instrument of Prehistory." In Dell H. Hymes (Ed.), *Language and Society*. New York: Harper & Row.

SWEET, LOUISE. 1965. "Camel Raiding of North Arabian Bedouin: A Mechanism of Ecological Adaptation." *American Anthropologist* 67:1132–50.

SYMONS, DONALD. 1979. *The Evolution of Human Sexuality*. Oxford: Oxford University Press.

TAINTER, JOSEPH A. 1990. *The Collapse of Complex Societies*. Cambridge: Cambridge University Press.

TAKAKI, RONALD. 1990a. *Iron Cage: Race and Culture in 19th Century America*. New York: Oxford University Press.

———. 1990b. *Strangers from a Different Shore: A History of Asian Americans*. New York: Penguin.

TALMON, YONINA. 1964. "Mate Selection in Collective Settlements." *American Sociological Review* 29:491–508.

TAMBIAH, STANLEY J. 1976. *World Conqueror and World Renouncer: A Study of Buddhism and Polity in Thailand against a Historical Background*. Cambridge: Cambridge University Press.

———. 1989. "Bridewealth and Dowry Revisited: The Position of Women in Sub-Saharan Africa and North India." *Current Anthropology* 30(4):413–35.

———. 1991. *Sri Lanka: Ethnic Fratricide and the Dismantling of Democracy*. Chicago: University of Chicago Press.

———. 1996. *Leveling Crowds: Ethnonationalist Conflicts and Collective Violence in South Asia*. Berkeley: University of California Press.

TANDON, NIDHI. 1988. "Women in Rural Areas." In Edda Smith-Ivan, Nidhi Tandon, and Jane Connors (Eds.), *Women in Sub-Saharan Africa*, Report No. 77. London: Minority Rights Group.

TAPPER, RICHARD, and NANCY TAPPER. 1992, 1993. "Marriage, Honor, and Responsibility: Islamic and Local Models in the Mediterranean and Middle East." *Cambridge Anthropology* 16(2).

TAX, SOL. 1953. *Penny Capitalism: A Guatemalan Indian Economy*. Smithsonian Institution, Institute of Social Anthropology, Publication No. 16. Washington, DC: U.S. Government Printing Office.

TEMPLETON, ALAN R. 1998. "Human Races: A Genetic and Evolutionary Perspective." *American Anthropologist* 100(3):632–50.

TERRACE, HERBERT S. 1986. *Nim: A Chimpanzee Who Learned Sign Language*. New York: Columbia University Press.

TESTART, ALAIN. 1988. "Some Major Problems in the Social Anthropology of Hunter-Gatherers," trans. Roy Willis. *Current Anthropology* 29(1):1–31.

THOMAS, E. M. 1958. *The Harmless People*. New York: Random House.

THOMASON, SARAH G., and TERRENCE KAUFMAN. 1988. *Language Contact, Creolization, and Genetic Linguistics*. Berkeley: University of California Press.

THOMSON, DAVID S. 2003. "The Sapir-Whorf Hypothesis: Worlds Shaped by Words." In

Spradley, James and David McCurdy (Eds.), *Conformity and Conflict: Readings in Cultural Anthropology.* Boston: Allyn and Bacon.

TIANO, S. 1994. *Patriarchy on the Line: Labor, Gender, and Ideology in the Mexican Maquila Industry.* Philadelphia, PA: Temple University Press.

TIBI, BASSAM. 1990. *Islam and the Cultural Accommodation of Social Change.* Trans. Clare Kojzl. Boulder: Westview Press.

TIERNEY, PATRICK. 2000. *Darkness in El Dorado: How Scientists and Journalists Devastated the Amazon.* New York: W. W. Norton.

TIME ALMANAC. 2000. Boston: Information Please.

TITMA, MIKK, and NANCY BRANDON TUMA. 2001. *Modern Russia.* Boston: McGraw-Hill.

TOMASELLO, M., and J. CALL. 1997. *Primate Cognition.* New York: Oxford University Press.

TRINKAUS, ERIK, and PAT SHIPMAN. 1994. *The Neandertals.* New York: Random House.

TROUILLOT, MICHEL-ROLPH. Adieu, "Culture: A New Duty Arises." In Richard Fox, and Barbara J. King (Eds.), *Anthropology Beyond Culture.* Oxford: Berg.

TSHOMBE, RICHARD KEY. 2001. "The Case of the Okapi Faunal Reserve in the Northeastern Democratic Republic of Congo." *People and Natural Resources: Changes in Times of Crisis.* Okapi Faunal Reserve Zoning Program. (http://www.cerc.Columbia.edu/elf/ELF2001CS/ TshombeCS).

TURNBULL, COLIN. 1963. *The Forest People: A Study of the Pygmies of the Congo.* New York: Simon & Schuster.

———. 1983. *The Mbuti Pygmies: Change and Adaptation.* New York: Holt, Rinehart and Winston.

TURNER, VICTOR. 1957. *Schism and Continuity in an African Society: A Study of Ndembu Village Life.* Manchester: Manchester University Press.

———. 1967. *The Forest of Symbols: Aspects of Ndembu Ritual.* Ithaca, NY: Cornell University Press.

———. 1974. *Dramas, Fields, and Metaphors: Symbolic Action in Human Society.* Ithaca, NY: Cornell University Press.

TURTON, ANDREW. 1980. "Thai Institutions of Slavery." In James L. Watson (Ed.), *Asian and African Systems of Slavery,* pp. 251–92. Berkeley: University of California Press.

TYLER, STEPHEN A. 1986. *India: An Anthropological Perspective.* Prospect Heights, IL: Waveland Press.

TYLOR, EDWARD B. 1871. *Primitive Culture.* London: J. Murray.

———. 1889. "On a Method of Investigating the Development of Institutions, Applied to Laws of Marriage and Descent." *Journal of the Royal Anthropological Institute* 18:245–72.

UCHENDU, VICTOR C. 1965. *The Igbo of Southeast Nigeria.* New York: Holt, Rinehart and Winston.

U.S. CENSUS BUREAU. 2000. *Statistical Abstracts of the United States,* 2000.

U.S. COMMITTEE ON GLOBAL CHANGE. 1988. *Toward an Understanding of Global Change.* Washington, DC: National Academy Press.

VAGO, STEVEN. 1995. *Law and Society.* 2d ed. Upper Saddle River, NJ: Prentice Hall.

VALERI, VALERIO. 1985. *Kingship and Sacrifice: Ritual and Society in Ancient Hawaii,* trans. Paula Wissing. Chicago: University of Chicago Press.

VAN DEN BERGHE, PIERRE. 1979. *Human Family Systems: An Evolutionary View.* New York: Elsevier Science Publishing Co.

———. 1980. "Incest and Exogamy: A Sociobiological Reconsideration." *Ethology and Sociobiology* 1:151–62.

———. 1981. *The Ethnic Phenomenon.* New York: Elsevier Science Publishing Co.

VAN DEN BERGHE, PIERRE, and DAVID BARASH. 1977. "Inclusive Fitness Theory and the Human Family." *American Anthropologist* 79:809–23.

VAN ESTERIK, PENNY (Ed.). 1996. *Women of Southeast Asia.* DeKalb, IL: Northern Illinois University.

VAN GENNEP, ARNOLD. 1960. *The Rites of Passage.* Chicago: University of Chicago Press.

VAN WILLIGEN, JOHN, and V. C. CHANNA. 1991. "Law, Custom, and Crimes Against Women: The Problem of Dowry Death in India." *Human Organization* 50(4):369–77.

VAYDA, ANDREW P. 1961. "Expansion and Warfare Among Swidden Agriculturalists." *American Anthropologist* 63:346–58.

VERDERY, KATHERINE. 1996. *What Was Socialism, and What Comes Next?* Princeton: Princeton University Press.

VON HUMBOLDT, W. [1836] 1972. *Linguistic Variability and Intellectual Development,* trans. C. G. Buck and F. Raven. Philadelphia: University of Pennsylvania Press.

VYGOTSKY, L. S. 1986. *Thought and Language.* Trans. A Kozulin. Cambridge, MA: MIT Press.

WAFER, JIM. 1991. *The Taste of Blood: Spirit Possession in Brazilian Candomble.* Contemporary Ethnography Series. Philadelphia: University of Pennsylvania Press.

WAKIN, ERIC. 1992. *Anthropology Goes to War: Professional Ethics and Counterinsurgency in Thailand.* Center for Southeast Asian Studies: University of Wisconsin—Madison.

WALKER, ANTHONY. 1986. *The Toda of South India: A New Look.* Delhi: Hindustan Publishing Company.

WALLACE, ANTHONY K. C. 1972. "Mental Illness, Biology, and Culture." In Francis Hsu (Ed.), *Psychological Anthropology.* Cambridge, MA: Schenkman.

WALLERSTEIN, IMMANUEL. 1974. *The Modern World-System: Capitalist Agriculture and the Origins of the European World-Economy in the Sixteenth Century.* New York: Academic Press.

———. 1979. *The Capitalist World-Economy.* New York: Cambridge University Press.

———. 1980. *The Modern World-System: II. Mercantilism and the Consolidation of the European World-Economy, 1600–1750.* New York: Academic Press.

———. 1986. *Africa and the Modern World.* Trenton, NJ: Africa World Press.

WANG, CHENG GANG. 1999. "China's Environment in the Balance." In Susan Ogden (Ed.), *China,* 9th ed. Guilford, CT: McGraw-Hill/Dushkin.

WARD, MARTHA. 2003. *World Full of Women.* 3d ed. Boston: Allyn and Bacon.

WARNER, W. 2000. "Flexible Production, Households, and Fieldwork: Multisited Zapotec Weavers in the Era of Late Capitalism." *Ethnology* 39(2):133–49.

WATSON, JAMES L. 1980. "Slavery as an Institution, Open and Closed Systems." In James L. Watson (Ed.), *Asian and African Systems of Slavery.* Berkeley: University of California Press.

——— (Ed.). 2004. *Golden Arches East: McDonald's in East Asia.* 2d ed. Palo Alto: Stanford University Press.

WATSON, PATTY JO. 1984. *Archaeological Explanation: The Scientific Method in Archaeology.* New York: Columbia University Press.

WATSON, PATTY JO, STEVEN A. LEBLANC, and CHARLES L. REDMAN. 1971. *Explanation in Archaeology: An Explicitly Scientific Approach.* New York: Columbia University Press.

WAX, ROSALIE. 1971. *Doing Fieldwork: Warnings and Advice.* Chicago: University of Chicago Press.

WEATHERFORD, JACK. 1988. *Indian Givers: How the Indians of the Americas Transformed the World.* New York: Crown.

———. 2003. "Cocaine and the Economic Deterioration of Bolivia." In James Spradley and David McCurdy (Eds.), *Conformity and Conflict: Readings in Cultural Anthropology.* Boston: Allyn and Bacon.

WEINER, ANNETTE B. 1976. *Women of Value, Men of Renown.* Austin: University of Texas Press.

———. 1987. *The Trobrianders of Papua New Guinea.* New York: Holt, Rinehart and Winston.

WEINER, J. 1994. *The Beak of the Finch.* New York: Knopf.

WEITZ, ERIC D. 2003. *A Century of Genocide: Utopias of Race and Nation.* Princeton: Princeton University Press.

WEST, FRED. 1975. *The Way of Language: An Introduction.* New York: Harcourt Brace Jovanovich.

WHITE, DOUGLAS. 1988. "Rethinking Polygyny: Co-Wives, Codes, and Cultural Systems." *Current Anthropology* 29(4):529–53.

WHITE, LESLIE. [1949] 1971. "The Symbol: The Origin and Basis of Human Behavior." In Leslie White (Ed.), *The Science of Culture: A Study of Man and Civilization.* New York: Farrar, Straus & Giroux.

———. 1959. *The Evolution of Culture.* New York: McGraw-Hill.

WHITE, T. D., G. SUWA, and B. ASFAW. 1994. "*Australopithecus ramidus,* a New Species of Early Hominid from Aramis, Ethiopia." *Nature* 37:306–12.

WHORF, BENJAMIN. 1956. *Language, Thought, and Reality: The Selected Writings of Benjamin Lee Whorf.* Cambridge, MA: MIT Press.

WIKAN, UNNI. 1991. *Behind the Veil in Arabia: Women in Oman.* Chicago: University of Chicago Press.

WILK, RICHARD R. 1995. "Consumer Goods as Dialogue about Development: Colonial Time and Television Time in Belize." In J. Friedman (Ed.), *Consumption and Identity,* Chur, Switzerland: Harwood Academic, pp. 97–118.

———. 1996. *Economies and Cultures: Foundations of Economic Anthropology.* Boulder, CO: Westview Press.

WILLIAMS, HOLLY ANN. 1990. "Families in Refugee Camps." *Human Organization* 49(2):100–9.

WILLIAMS, ROBIN M., JR. 1970. *American Society: A Sociological Interpretation.* 3d ed. New York: Knopf.

WILSON, E. O. 1975. *Sociobiology: The New Synthesis.* Cambridge, MA: Harvard University Press.

———. 1978. *On Human Nature.* Cambridge, MA: Harvard University Press.

——— (Ed.). 1988. *Biodiversity.* Washington, DC: Smithsonian Institution, National Academy of Sciences.

——— (Ed.). 1989. *Biodiversity.* Washington, DC: National Academy Press.

———. 1992. *The Diversity of Life.* Cambridge, MA: Harvard University Press.

WILSON, E. O., and LAURA SIMONDS SOUTHWORTH. 1996. *In Search of Nature.* New York: Island Press.

WILSON, MICHAEL L., MARC D. HAUSER, and RICHARD WRANGHAM. 2001. "Does Participation in Intergroup Conflict Depend on Numerical Assessment, Range Location, or Rank for Wild Chimpanzees? *Animal Behavior* 61:1203–16.

WILSON, MICHAEL L., and RICHARD WRANGHAM. 2003. "Intergroup Relations in Chimpanzees." *Annual Review of Anthropology* 32:363–92.

WILSON, MONICA. 1951. *Good Company: A Study of Nyakyusa Age-Villages.* Boston: Beacon Press.

WINZELER, ROBERT L. 1996. "Sexual Status in Southeast Asia: Comparative Perspectives on Women, Agriculture and Political Organization." In Penny Van Esterik (Ed.), *Women of Southeast Asia.* Occasional Paper No. 17. DeKalb, IL: Northern Illinois University, Center for Southeast Asian Studies.

WOLF, ARTHUR. 1970. "Childhood Association and Sexual Attraction: A Further Test of the Westermarck Hypothesis." *American Anthropologist* 72:503–15.

———. 2004. "Introduction." In Arthur Wolf and William Durham. *Inbreeding, Incest, and the Incest Taboo.* Stanford: Stanford University Press.

WOLF, ARTHUR, and WILLIAM DURHAM. 2004. *Inbreeding, Incest, and the Incest Taboo.* Stanford: Stanford University Press.

WOLF, ERIC R. 1955a. "Closed Corporate Communities in Mesoamerica and Java." *Southwestern Journal of Anthropology* 13(1):1–18.

———. 1955b. "Types of Latin American Peasantry: A Preliminary Discussion." *American Anthropologist* 57(3), Part 1:452–71.

———. 1958. "The Virgin of Guadalupe: A Mexican National Symbol." *Journal of American Folklore* 71:34–39.

———. 1959. *Sons of the Shaking Earth.* Chicago: University of Chicago Press.

———. 1964. *Anthropology.* Englewood Cliffs, NJ: Prentice Hall.

———. 1966. *Peasants.* Englewood Cliffs, NJ: Prentice Hall.

———. 1969. *Peasant Wars of the Twentieth Century.* New York: Harper & Row.

———. 1987. "Cycles of Violence: The Anthropology of War and Peace." In Kenneth Moore (Ed.), *Waymarks: The Notre Dame Inaugural Lectures in Anthropology,* pp. 127–51. Notre Dame, IN: University of Notre Dame Press.

———. [1982] 1997. *Europe and the People Without History.* Berkeley: University of California Press.

———. 1999. *Envisioning Power: Ideologies of Domination and Crisis.* Berkeley: University of California Press.

———. 2001. *Pathways of Power: Building an Anthropology of the Modern World.* Berkeley: University of California Press.

WOLF, E. R., and S. MINTZ. 1950. "An Analysis of Ritual Coparenthood (*Compadrazgo*)." *Southwestern Journal of Anthropology* 6. Reprinted in Jack A. Potter, May Diaz, and George Foster (Eds.), 1967 *Peasant Society: A Reader,* pp. 174–99. Boston: Little, Brown.

WOLFE, ALVIN. 1977. "The Supranational Organization of Production: An Evolutionary Perspective." *Current Anthropology* 18:615–35.

———. 1986. "The Multinational Corporation as a Form of Sociocultural Integration Above the Level of the State." In Hendrick Serrie (Ed.), *Anthropology and International Business,* Publication No. 28. Williamsburg, VA: Studies in Third World Societies.

WOODBURN, JAMES. 1982. "Egalitarian Societies." *Man* 17:431–51.

WORLD ALMANAC AND BOOK OF FACTS. 2001. New York: Scripps Howard Company.

WORSLEY, PETER. 1957. *The Trumpet Shall Sound.* New York: Schocken.

———. 1984. *The Three Worlds: Culture and World Development.* Chicago. University of Chicago Press.

XU Z., L. JING, D. YU, X. XU. 2000. "Air pollution and daily mortality in Shenyang, China." *Architecture and Environmental Health* 55:115–20.

YANGISAKO, SYLVIA J., and JANE F. COLLIER. 1990. "The Mode of Reproduction in Anthropology." In Deborah Rhode (Ed.), *Theoretical Perspectives on Sexual Difference.* New Haven: Yale University Press.

YELVINGTON, KEVIN. 2001. "The Anthropology of Afro-Latin America: Diasporic Dimensions." *Annual Review of Anthropology* 30:227–60.

YENGOYAN, ARAM A. 1986. "Theory in Anthropology: On the Demise of the Concept of Culture." *Comparative Studies in Society and History* 28(2):357–74.

YORBURG, BETTY. 2002. *Family Realities: A Global View.* Upper Saddle River, NJ: Prentice Hall.

ZEDER, MELINDA A. 1997. *The American Archaeologist: A Profile.* Walnut Creek, CA: AltaMira Press.

Photo Credits

Index